THE ROUGH GUIDE TO

Sweden

written and researched by

James Proctor and Neil Roland

ROUGH GUIDES

roughguides.com

Contents

Introduction to
Sweden

The mere mention of Sweden conjures up resonant images: snow-capped peaks, reindeer wandering in deep green forests and the 24-hour daylight of the midnight sun. But beyond the household names of ABBA, IKEA and Volvo, Sweden is relatively unknown. The largest of the Scandinavian countries, with an area twice that of Britain (and roughly that of California), but a population of barely nine million, Sweden has space for everyone: the countryside boasts pine, spruce and birch forest as far as the eye can see and crystal-clear lakes perfect for a summer afternoon dip – not to mention possibly the purest air you'll ever breathe. The country's south and west coasts, meanwhile, feature some of the most exquisite beaches in Europe – without the crowds.

In general Sweden is a carefree place where life is relaxed. Indeed, the Swedes' **liberal** and open attitude to virtually every aspect of life is certainly one of their most enviable qualities; people are generally left to do their own thing, providing it doesn't impinge on the rights and freedoms of others. In Sweden, rights go hand in hand with duties, and there's a strong sense of civic obligation (count how few times you see people dropping litter, for example), which in turn makes for a well-rounded and stable society. Many of the cornerstones of the Swedish welfare state, such as tremendously generous benefits and health-care perks, which Swedes still hold dear today, were laid down during forty years of unbroken rule by the Social Democrats.

Yet, over the years, foreigners have somehow confused the open Swedish attitude to society, including nudity and sexuality, with sex. Contrary to popular belief, Sweden isn't populated solely with people waiting for any opportunity to tear off their clothes and make passionate love under the midnight sun. It is, though, a country founded on honesty and straight talking – two of Sweden's most refreshing qualities.

ABOVE AERIAL VIEW OF STOCKHOLM

FACT FILE

- Sweden is the **third largest country** in western Europe – behind only France and Spain – stretching 1600km from north to south. If the country were pivoted around on its southernmost point, the top of the country would reach as far south as Naples in Italy.

- There is no translation for the Swedish word **lagom**, one of the most commonly used terms in the language. Roughly speaking, it means "just the right amount, not too much but not too little", a concept that is the very essence of Swedishness.

- More than half of Sweden's land surface is covered with **forest** – mostly coniferous – punctuated by an astonishing **100,000 lakes**.

- Sweden is home to the world's first and largest **hotel** made entirely of ice and snow. *Icehotel* is built in December using blocks of ice cut from the local Torne River. The hotel melts back into the river in May.

- In northern Sweden frozen lakes and rivers are used by drivers looking for a shortcut to their destination. The national road agency marks out **"ice roads"** and decides when the ice is thick enough to support a vehicle.

Where to go

Sweden is principally a land of forests and lakes. Its towns and cities are small by European standards and are mostly located in the southern third of the country, where the majority of Swedes live. Of its cities, serenely beautiful **Stockholm** is supreme. Sitting elegantly on fourteen different islands, where the waters of **Lake Mälaren** meet the Baltic Sea, the city boasts some fantastic architecture, fine museums and by far the best culture and nightlife in the country. The 24,000 islands which comprise the Stockholm **archipelago** are a perfect antidote to the urban bustle, offering endless opportunities to explore unspoilt island villages and to go swimming. On the west coast, **Gothenburg**, the country's second city, is also one of Sweden's most appealing destinations. Gothenburgers have a reputation for being among the friendliest people in Sweden,

MIDSUMMER MAYHEM

An atmosphere akin to Mediterranean *joie de vivre* takes over Sweden during the **midsummer solstice** (the weekend closest to June 24), when maypoles are erected as giant fertility symbols in gardens and parks across the country. Midsummer is not a time for staying in towns – everyone heads to the countryside and coasts, with Dalarna, the island of Öland and the shores of the Bohuslän coast being just a few of the most popular spots. Aided in no small part by copious quantities of **alcohol**, the population's national characteristics of reserve and restraint dissolve over midsummer weekend. Long trestle tables draped in white cloths and sagging under the weight of multiple varieties of herring, potatoes with dill and gallons of *akvavit* are set up outside, and parties go on through the light night with dancing to the strains of accordions and fiddles.

and the city's network of canals and spacious avenues is reminiscent of Amsterdam, whose architects designed it.

The south is the most cosmopolitan part of the country, owing to the proximity of Denmark and the rest of the European continent, and home to the glorious ancient university seat of **Lund**, while nearby **Malmö**, Sweden's third city, heaves with youthful nightlife around its medieval core.

Inland, southern Sweden boasts some handsome lakes, the two largest of which, **Vänern** and **Vättern**, provide splendid backdrops to some beautiful towns, not least the evocative former royal seat and the monastic centre of **Vadstena**, and **Karlstad**, the sunshine capital of Värmland, a rugged province ideal for river-rafting trips. To the east of the mainland lies **Gotland**, justifiably raved about as a haven for summer revelry, especially within the medieval walls of its unspoilt Hanseatic city, **Visby**.

Central and northern Sweden represent the most quintessentially "Swedish-looking" part of the country. In the centre lies **Dalarna**, an area of rolling hills and villages that's home to **Lake Siljan**, one of Sweden's most beautiful lakes. North of here lies some of the country's most enchanting scenery, home to bears, wolves and reindeer. To the east, the shoreline of the **Bothnian coast** contains the north's biggest cities: **Sundsvall**, **Umeå** and **Luleå** are all enjoyable, lively places in which to break your journey north.

The far north, inside the **Arctic Circle**, is the home of the **Sámi** – Sweden's indigenous people. Known as **Swedish Lapland**, it is also the land of reindeer, elk and bears, of swiftly flowing rivers and coniferous forest, all traversed by endless hiking routes. Sweden's northernmost town, **Kiruna** makes an excellent base for exploring the region's **national parks** and the world-famous **Icehotel** in nearby Jukkasjärvi. Swedish Lapland is also where you will experience the **midnight sun**: in high summer the sun never sets, whilst in midwinter the opposite is true, though you may be lucky enough to see the sky lit up by the multicoloured patterns of the **northern lights**, or aurora borealis.

NORTHERN LIGHTS

Also known by their Latin name, *aurora borealis*, the **northern lights** are visible all across northern Sweden during the dark months of winter. These spectacular displays of green-blue shimmering arcs and waves of light are caused by solar wind, or streams of particles charged by the sun, hitting the atmosphere. The colours are the characteristic hues of different elements when they hit the plasma shield that protects the Earth: blue is nitrogen and yellow-green oxygen. Although the mechanisms which produce the aurora are not completely understood, the displays are generally more impressive the closer you get to the poles – low temperatures are also rumoured to produce some of the most dramatic performances. **Gällivare** and **Kiruna**, both well inside the Arctic Circle, are arguably the best places in Sweden to catch a glimpse of the aurora, particularly during the coldest winter months from December to February. Although displays can range from just a few minutes to several hours, the night sky must be clear of cloud to see the northern lights from Earth.

Author picks

James Proctor has visited every corner of Sweden – from the sandy beaches of Skåne to the mountains of Swedish Lapland – to bring you some unique travel experiences. These are some of his own, personal favourites.

Classic journey Walking part of the Kungsleden trail (p.343) is a great way to see the wilds of Swedish Lapland, whilst for the less adventurous the views unfolding from the train window on the Inlandsbanan (p.291) are equally compelling.

Best beaches Sjaustrehammaren beach on the east coast of Gotland (p.238) is the perfect place for an overall tan, though the turquoise waters of Sandhammaren beach in Skåne (p.186) are equally sublime.

Back to nature Be it hiking, river-rafting or wild lake swimming, the unspoilt countryside of the province of Värmland (p.138) is readily accessible and yours to call your own.

Winter wonderland It's hard to beat the sheer range of activities on offer at *Icehotel* in Jukkasjärvi (p.341) for a chance to explore the snowy north of Sweden.

Island idyll Both the Stockholm and Gothenburg archipelagos (pp.78 & 128) are perfect for spending long, lazy summer days messing about in boats and swimming.

Amazing views Mountain scenery to blow your mind from the top of Åreskutan (p.308) and Nuolja in Abisko (p.345) or coastal vistas from the top of Högbonden (p.260).

Favourite place For its combination of handsome towns and villages, gloriously sandy beaches and rolling countryside studded with medieval churches, Gotland (p.229) is Sweden at its most alluring.

Our author recommendations don't end here. We've flagged up our favourite places – a perfectly sited hotel, an atmospheric café, a special restaurant – throughout the guide, highlighted with the ★ symbol.

FROM TOP VISBY, GOTLAND; STEAMER IN THE STOCKHOLM ARCHIPELAGO; ABISKO NATIONAL PARK, LAPLAND >

When to go

In general, **May to September** is the best time to visit Sweden – north or south. **Summer** weather in Sweden is similar to that in southern Britain, though there are more hours of sunshine and less rain. By the end of August, the leaves in northern Sweden start to change colour and night frosts are not uncommon; the first snows fall in September. In Stockholm, snow can fall in October but doesn't generally settle; by November, though, the ground is usually covered in a blanket of snow, which will last until the following March or even April, when there can still be snow showers. **Winters** in the south of Sweden are often mild whilst in the north you're likely to encounter snow until well into May and temperatures can fall to -30C. For more information and a temperature chart, see pp.34–35.

THE WINTER SWEDE AND THE SUMMER SWEDE

Unsurprisingly, the long, dark winters have a tangible effect on the **Swedish psyche**. During the winter months, you'll find that people are generally quieter and more withdrawn, and protect themselves from the rigours of the cold and dark by deliberately socializing indoors, often choosing to light **candles** throughout the home to create a sense of cosiness. You'll even see candles burning in public buildings and shops to brighten up the gloomiest time of year. It's during winter that Seasonal Affective Disorder, or **S.A.D.**, causes widespread depression, affecting roughly one in five people. Although you're unlikely to suffer during a short visit in winter, you're likely to encounter gloomy faces and a general sense of inertia throughout the winter months. S.A.D. is caused by a lack of daylight which leads to an increase in the production of the sleep-related hormone, melatonin, secreted from a gland in the brain.

Naturally people do all they can to alleviate the effects of winter; for example, during the period of 24-hour darkness in northern Sweden, the **Winter Swede** creates a semblance of day and night by switching on bright lights during what would be daytime, and using low-lighting during the evening hours. Once spring arrives, there's a notable bounce in people's step, and the **Summer Swede** prepares to emerge from months of enforced hibernation – you'll see people sitting in lines on park benches in the sunshine, faces tilted to the sky, making the most of the return of the sun. **Festivals** and **revelries** are thick on the ground in spring and summer, and outdoor life is lived to the full, including picnics under the midnight sun, beach parties lasting late into the night and an exodus to the countryside as people take up residence in their forest or lakeside log cabins to enjoy the brief yet intense summer months.

RIGHT FROM TOP DOGSLED RUNNING ON SNOW, LAPLAND; SAUNA, JOKKMOKK >

25

things not to miss

It's not possible to see everything Sweden has to offer in one trip, and we don't suggest you try. What follows is a selective taste of the country's highlights, from snowmobiling to sampling a smorgasbord; you can browse through to find the very best things to see and experience. All highlights have a page reference to take you straight to the guide, where you can find out more.

1

1 SNOWMOBILING
Page 342
Snowmobiling across Lapland is an exhilarating way to see Sweden in winter.

2 RIVER-RAFTING, VÄRMLAND
Page 143
Build your own raft and glide down the graceful Klarälven River, taking in some of Sweden's scenery.

3 LUND DOMKYRKAN
Page 166
This twelfth-century cathedral, with an amazing astronomical clock, is the finest Romanesque building in northern Europe.

4 SWIMMING IN A LAKE
Page 34
Amongst Sweden's 100,000 lakes, you're bound to find one you can call your own.

5 MIDNIGHT SUN
Page 329
From late May to mid-July the sun never sets in northern Sweden.

6 GOTLAND BEACHES
Page 238
Stretches of white sandy beaches and clear, warm waters are perfect places to relax and play in the summer sun.

7 BIRKA
Page 86
Get to grips with Sweden's stirring Viking past on this Stockholm island.

8 SMORGASBORD
Page 31
Eat until you drop: the smorgasbord is a perfect way to sample Sweden's excellent cuisine.

9 SÁMI CULTURE, LAPLAND
Page 330
Sights such as Jokkmokk market and Fatmomakke village in Lapland are monuments to the thriving culture of Sweden's indigenous population.

10 GOTHENBURG'S KONSTMUSEUM
Page 114
The Fürstenberg Galleries boast some of Sweden's finest late-nineteenth-century paintings, and *Poseidon* stands guard outside.

POLCIRKELN

Napapiiri

Arctic Circle

Cercle Polaire

Polarkreis

17 VASA SHIP, STOCKHOLM
Page 60
After lying in mud for centuries at the bottom of Stockholm harbour, the mighty *Vasa* warship has now been restored to her former glory.

18 CROSSING THE ARCTIC CIRCLE
Page 329
Don't leave Sweden without crossing the Arctic Circle, 66° 33′ north.

19 HERRING
Page 30
The quintessential Swedish dish best enjoyed with a cold beer or a shot of *akvavit*.

20 BOHUSLÄN COAST
Page 130
Sweden's most enchanting stretch of coastline with smooth rocky outcrops perfect for sunbathing.

21 RENAISSANCE BUILDINGS, KALMAR

Page 198

Perfectly preserved architecture in Sweden's most beautiful town square.

22 JOKKMOKK WINTER MARKET

Page 330

The Jokkmokk winter market sells everything from bearskins to candlesticks.

23 EUROPE'S LAST WILDERNESS

Page 310

Wild, rugged and remote, Sweden's far north is about as far from civilization as you can get.

24 ORSA GRÖNKLITT BJÖRNPARK

Page 292

Europe's biggest bear park is the perfect place to see Sweden's greatest predator in its natural habitat.

25 A SAUNA AND A SPLASH

Page 34

The perfect end to a long day, a Swedish sauna traditionally finishes with a roll in the snow or a plunge into cold water.

Itineraries

Sweden is a vast country, and you can't cover all of it in a single trip. Our Grand Tour concentrates on Sweden's main sights, while our other suggested routes focus on two fascinating regions, one in the south, one in the north. Each itinerary will take a packed two weeks to cover; with only a week to spare you can cover part of one, and get a flavour of the whole country or one of the regions that make Sweden special.

GRAND TOUR OF SWEDEN

Two weeks in Sweden and no idea where to start? Our Grand Tour puts you on the right track.

❶ **Stockholm** The vibrant heart of Sweden is one of Europe's saner capitals, with everything from style-conscious bars and restaurants to world-class museums and galleries. **See p.40**

❷ **Lund** Awash with students and bikes, likeable Lund boasts the country's greatest cathedral set amid its compact, cobbled centre. **See p.166**

❸ **Malmö** Sweden's gateway to Europe, Malmö is linked by frequent trains to the Danish capital, Copenhagen, and is accordingly cosmopolitan. **See p.171**

❹ **Gothenburg** Sweden's second city and Scandinavia's biggest port, handsome Gothenburg looks like Amsterdam with its canals and gabled houses. **See p.104**

❺ **Dalarna** The Swedes think of Dalarna as the most Swedish part of Sweden – all rolling hills, flower meadows and log cabins. **See p.282**

❻ **Östersund** Charming lakeside town in the centre of the country which makes a perfect break on the long journey north. **See p.303**

❼ **Jokkmokk** Tucked just inside the Arctic Circle, Jokkmokk has a strong Sámi identity and is a good place to learn more about the country's indigenous population. **See p.328**

❽ **Luleå** The most attractive of Sweden's northern cities, Luleå provides ready access to the fascinating UNESCO-listed church town at Gammelstad. **See p.271**

❾ **Sundsvall** Grandiose stone architecture immediately sets Sundsvall apart from its neighbours. The biggest city in the north, it has plenty of good restaurants and bars to sample, too. **See p.252**

THE BEST OF THE NORTH

❶ **Östersund** Go hunting for Sweden's answer to the Loch Ness monster on Lake Storsjön, which provides a magnificent backdrop to this laidback town. **See p.303**

❷ **Vildmarksvägen** For a taste of wild Sweden, take this switchback route through some of central Sweden's most remote and haunting landscapes. **See p.316**

❸ **Vilhelmina** A handy stop on the way north; make sure you book into one of the sturdy wooden cottages of the church town for an

ABOVE PEDESTRIAN PIER, MALMÖ; VILLAGE IN DALARNA

atmospheric night's accommodation.
See p.319

❹ Arvidsjaur Take a trip on a steam train or visit the traditional Sámi dwellings of the Lappstaden right in the town centre. **See p.325**

❺ Jokkmokk In addition to a great *Sámi* museum, there's also a delightful alpine flower garden. **See p.328**

❻ Abisko The starting point for the 500km Kungsleden hiking trail as well as the best place in Sweden to see the northern lights. **See p.343**

❼ Kiruna Gateway to the famous *Icehotel* in nearby Jukkasjärvi; get here before the whole town sinks into the ground. **See p.337**

❽ Luleå Visit the UNESCO-listed church town at nearby Gammelstad or ride the boat out into the stunning archipelago. **See p.271**

❾ High Coast The most beautiful stretch of the northern Swedish coast lies north of Härnösand and is best seen from the ferries which serve the offshore islands. **See p.259**

SOUTHERN SWEDEN

❶ Malmö The perfect gateway to southern Sweden, Malmö enjoys some of the country's warmest weather and features a string of city beaches ideal for topping up your tan.
See p.171

❷ Lund Enjoy the atmosphere in southern Sweden's most attractive city, renowned for its great bars and restaurants which cater to the huge student population. **See p.166**

❸ Kalmar One of southern Sweden's most underrated destinations, Kalmar is home to the fascinating Kronan exhibition. **See p.198**

❹ Gotland *The* Swedish destination, Gotland's charms are legendary: cobbled medieval streets and alleyways, superb sandy beaches and a party atmosphere that lasts all summer long.
See p.229

❺ Karlstad Busy and fun city set on the shores of Sweden's biggest lake – take a tour of the city by boat or enjoy the beaches. **See p.138**

❻ Vadstena With its moated castle and stunning abbey, historically significant Vadstena

is Sweden at its most grand and imposing.
See p.218

❼ Gothenburg The Gothenburgers are said to be the friendliest people in the whole of Sweden – pull up a chair in one of the city's many great cafés and strike up a conversation.
See p.104

❽ Varberg People have been coming to Varberg to take the waters for generations – join them and leave your clothes behind. **See p.148**

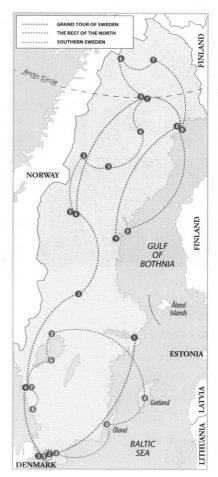

- - - - - - - - - GRAND TOUR OF SWEDEN
- - - - - - - - - THE BEST OF THE NORTH
- - - - - - - - - SOUTHERN SWEDEN

FINLAND

Arctic Circle

NORWAY

GULF OF BOTHNIA

FINLAND

Åland Islands

ESTONIA

Gotland

LATVIA

Öland

BALTIC SEA

LITHUANIA

DENMARK

CROWDS IN STOCKHOLM CELEBRATING SWEDISH NATIONAL DAY

Basics

Getting there

Given the extremely long distances and journey times involved in reaching Sweden overland, flying will not only save you considerable amounts of time but money too. The main gateways are Stockholm and Gothenburg, as well as Copenhagen in neighbouring Denmark, just a twenty-minute train ride from Malmö.

Air fares are generally cheaper when booked as far in advance as possible. Midweek travel is less expensive than weekend departures.

Flights from North America

Three airlines operate **from the US** to Sweden: SAS (Scandinavian Airlines; Ⓦ scandinavian.net) from Newark and Chicago, Continental from Newark and Delta (Ⓦ delta.com) from JFK. Less expensive tickets can sometimes be found on European airlines routing via their home hub, for example British Airways (Ⓦ ba.com) via London or Icelandair (Ⓦ icelandair.net) via Keflavík, the latter very often being a source of reasonable fares to Sweden. From **New York**, a return ticket midweek **fare** to Stockholm (8hr) will cost around US$900 in high season, US$740 in low season. From **Chicago** (9hr), prices are roughly US$150 more than from New York; from the **West Coast** (journey time at least 12hr), you'll pay around US$200–300 more.

There are no direct flights **from Canada**, so the best way of reaching Sweden is from **Toronto** via Helsinki with Finnair (Ⓦ finnair.com; summer only). Several other airlines also operate flights from Toronto and Vancouver to European cities, with connections on to Stockholm. **Fares** from Toronto (journey time 9–13hr depending on connections) are Can$1150–1350 in high season, Can$950–1150 in low season. From Vancouver (13–18hr), they're around Can$500 higher.

Flights from the UK and Ireland

Flights for Stockholm, Gothenburg and Copenhagen leave from several **UK airports**; in winter there are also direct flights from London Heathrow to Kiruna (available only through Discover the World; see p.26). **Flying to Sweden** with Ryanair (Ⓦ ryanair.com) is usually the cheapest way of getting there. Single fares can be a low as £10, though in peak season a return price of £70–100 is more realistic, depending on how early the booking

is made. The other main **airline** serving Sweden is SAS (Ⓦ scandinavian.net), whose return tickets start around £130. The Scandinavian low-cost operator, Norwegian (Ⓦ norwegian.com), is also an option; its fares are generally midway between those of Ryanair and SAS. For southern Sweden, try easyJet (Ⓦ easyJet.com) who operate into Copenhagen. **From Ireland**, there are services from Dublin only, and fares are roughly the same as from the UK.

Flights from Australia, New Zealand and South Africa

There are no direct flights to Sweden **from Australia, New Zealand or South Africa** and by far the cheapest option is to find a discounted air fare to London and arrange a flight to Sweden from there. All air fares to London from Australian east coast gateways are similarly priced, with the cheapest deals via Asia and Helsinki starting around $1850. From Perth or Darwin, flights are around $100 less. **From New Zealand** reckon on NZ$2500 as a starting point from Auckland, NZ$250 more from Wellington. **From South Africa**, count on around ZAR6000 for the cheapest return from Cape Town.

By train

Getting to Sweden **by train** is much more expensive. There are no through tickets and the total of all the tickets you'll need is likely to cost around £300–400. Hence, it's worth buying a rail pass instead; a global **InterRail** pass (from £238) or Eurail pass (from US$625) are the best options. **From London**, trains to Sweden go via Brussels, Cologne, Hamburg and Copenhagen. A typical

---

A BETTER KIND OF TRAVEL

At Rough Guides we are passionately committed to travel. We feel that travelling is the best way to understand the world we live in and the people we share it with – plus tourism has brought a great deal of benefit to developing economies around the world over the last few decades. But the growth in tourism has also damaged some places irreparably, and climate change is exacerbated by most forms of transport, especially flying. All Rough Guides' trips are carbon-offset, and every year we donate money to a variety of charities devoted to combating the effects of climate change.

journey will involve changing trains four or five times and takes around 24 hours.

RAIL CONTACTS

Rail Europe UK ☎ 0844 848 4064, US ☎ 1 800 622 8600, Canada ☎ 1 800 361 7245; ⓦ raileurope.co.uk.

Swedish Railways (SJ) ☎ 0046 771 75 75 75, ⓦ sj.se. The general agent for Swedish rail tickets.

Package holidays

Don't be put off by the idea of an inclusive **package**, as it can sometimes be the cheapest way of doing things, and a much easier way of reaching remote areas of northern Sweden in winter. City breaks are invariably less expensive than if you arrange the same trip independently. There are also an increasing number of operators (see below) offering **special-interest holidays** to Sweden, particularly Arctic expeditions.

SPECIALIST OPERATORS

Abercrombie & Kent US ☎ 1 800 554 7016, ⓦ abercrombiekent .com. Top-end tours of Scandinavia by land and sea.

Bentours International Australia ☎ 1800 221712, ⓦ bentours .com.au. The leading Australian specialist to Sweden offering air, ferry and rail tickets and a host of (often upmarket) escorted and independent tours throughout Scandinavia.

Contiki Tours US ☎ 1 888 CONTIKI, ⓦ contiki.com. Budget tours of Scandinavia for 18- to 35-year-olds.

Discover the World UK ☎ 01737 214250, ⓦ discover-the-world .co.uk. This long-established, professional and upmarket company knows the country like the back of its hand. It is the only company selling a direct flight from London Heathrow to Kiruna and the world's largest tour operator to *Icehotel* in Jukkasjärvi.

Nordic Experience UK ☎ 01206 708888, ⓦ nordicexperience .co.uk/sweden. Mid-priced holidays to various regions of Sweden, including Lapland and *Icehotel*, and trips out to lakes and mountains.

Scanam World Tours US ☎ 1 800 545 2204, ⓦ scanamtours.com. Specializes in mid-range Scandinavian tours and cruises for groups and individuals. Also offers cheap weekend breaks.

Scantours US ☎ 1 800 223 7226, ⓦ scantours.com. Major Scandinavian holiday specialists offering upmarket vacation packages and customized itineraries, including cruises and city sightseeing tours.

Taber Holidays UK ☎ 01274 875199, ⓦ taberhols.co.uk. A wide range of Swedish holidays from this Yorkshire-based tour operator – everything from tours in the Stockholm archipelago to trips on the Inlandsbanan.

Getting around

The public transport system in Sweden is one of Europe's most efficient. There's

a comprehensive train network in the south of the country; in the north travelling by train isn't quite so easy, as many loss-making branch lines have been closed. However, it's still possible to reach the main towns in the north by train, and where train services no longer exist, buses generally cover the same routes.

Look out for city and regional **discount cards**, which often give free use of local transport, free museum entry and other discounts.

By train

Other than flying, **train** travel is the quickest and easiest way of covering Sweden's vast expanses. The service is generally excellent and prices are not that high. At holiday times (see p.38) and between mid-June and mid-August, trains are often heavily booked; it's worth making reservations (often compulsory) as far in advance as you can. The national train operator is SJ (☎ 0771 75 75 75, ⓦ sj.se) which runs an extensive network across the whole of Sweden. For train and connecting bus information visit ⓦ resrobot.se. Many station names in Sweden carry the letter C after the name of the city, for example: Stockholm C; this is a "railspeak" abbreviation of Central.

Tickets

Individual train tickets are rarely cost-effective and visitors doing a lot of touring by train may be better off buying a **train pass** such as InterRail. A one-country InterRail pass for Sweden allows up to eight days' travel in one month and starts at £161. Full details can be found at ⓦ interrailnet.com. If you do need to buy an individual ticket, it's worth knowing that the sooner you buy it the cheaper it will be. The cheapest tickets, limited in number, cost 99kr on most SJ routes (145kr on X2000 trains) and are available up to ninety days before departure. **Reserved seats** on Swedish trains are not marked, so although it may appear that a seat is free it may not be so.

The Inlandsbanan

If you're in Sweden for any length of time, travelling at least part of the summer-only **Inlandsbanan** (Inland Railway; ☎ 0771 53 53 53, ⓦ grandnordic .se), which runs through central and northern Sweden, is a must. The route takes in some of the country's most unspoilt terrain – kilometre after kilometre of forests, and several lakes (the train

SWEDISH RAIL NETWORK

usually stops at one or two of them for passengers to take a quick dip), and offers a chance to see real off-the-beaten-track Sweden. For more information, see p.291. The length of the operating season varies from year to year; check the website for the latest details.

By bus

Although bus travel is a little less expensive than going by train, **long-distance buses** are generally less frequent, and so much slower that they aren't a good choice for long journeys. Most long-distance buses are operated by one of two companies, Swebus (**☎**0771 218 218, **W**swebus.se) and GoByBus (**☎**0771 15 15 15, **W**gobybus.se). Departures on Friday and Sunday cost more than on other days; a standard single ticket from Stockholm to Gothenburg, for example, costs from 349kr.

Regional buses are particularly important in the north, where they carry mail to isolated areas. Several companies operate daily services, and their fares are broadly similar to one another's (usually 250–350kr for a 1–2hr journey). Major routes are listed in the "Destinations" sections within each chapter, and you can pick up a comprehensive timetable at any bus terminal.

By plane

The main players on the Swedish **domestic airline** market are: SAS (**W**sas.se), Skyways (**W**skyways.se), Norwegian (**W**norwegian.se) and Nextjet (**W**nextjet.se). When booked well in advance, one-way fares on most routes begin around 450kr.

By ferries and boats

In a country with such an extensive coastline and many lakes, it's only natural that domestic ferry services in Sweden are many and varied. The main route is between Visby, on the Baltic island of Gotland, and Nynäshamn, on the mainland near Stockholm and Oskarshamn. High-speed catamarans as well as regular ferries operate on both routes. Departures are very popular in summer and you should try to book ahead.

Many of the various archipelagos off the coast – particularly the Stockholm archipelago with its 24,000 islands – have ferry services which link up the main islands in the group; see p.84 for more details. There's also an extensive archipelago off Luleå which is worth visiting; for details on boat services see p.277.

By car

As far as road conditions go, **driving** in Sweden is a dream. Traffic jams are rare (in fact in the north of the country yours will often be the only car on the road), roads are well maintained and motorways, where they exist, are toll-free. The only real **hazards** are reindeer (in the north), elk and deer, which wander onto the road without warning. It's difficult enough to see them at dusk, and when it's completely dark all you'll see is two red eyes as the animal leaps out in front of your car. If you hit an elk or deer, not only will you know about it (they're as big as a horse), you're bound by law to report it to the police.

To drive in Sweden you'll need your own full licence; an international driving licence isn't required. In general, **speed limits** are 110kph on motorways, 90kph or 100kph on main roads, 50kph in built-up areas, and 70kph elsewhere if unsigned; for cars towing caravans, the limit is 80kph. Fines for speeding are levied on the spot. You must drive with your headlights on 24 hours a day. Studded tyres for driving on snow and ice are allowed between October 1 and April 30, longer if there's still snow on the ground; when in use they must be fitted to all wheels.

Be attentive when it comes to **parking**. Under Swedish law you can't park within 10m of a road junction, be it a tiny residential cul-de-sac or a major intersection. Parking is also prohibited within 10m of a pedestrian crossing, and in bus lanes and loading zones. In city centres, parking isn't permitted on one night each week to allow for cleaning (see the rectangular yellow signs with days and times in Swedish, below the "no stopping" sign on every street). In winter the same applies to allow for snow clearance.

Swedish **drink-driving laws** are among the strictest in Europe, and random breath tests are commonplace. Basically, you can't have even one beer and still be under the limit; the blood alcohol level is 0.2 percent. If you're found to be over the limit you'll lose the right to drive in Sweden, face a fine (often) and a prison sentence (not infrequently).

The cost of **petrol** (*bensin*) is in line with the European average (about 15kr per litre). At filling stations, you either pay at the pump with a credit card or inside at the till – choose the pumps marked "Kassa" for this.

CAR RENTAL AGENCIES

Avis **W** avis.com
Europcar **W** europcar.com
Hertz **W** hertz.com
SIXT **W** sixt.com

Cycling

Some parts of the country were made for **cycling**: Stockholm, the southern provinces and Gotland in particular are ideal for a leisurely bike ride. Many towns are best explored by bike, and tourist offices, campsites and youth hostels often rent them out from around 150kr a day. There are a lot of cycle paths in towns, which are often shared with pedestrians.

Accommodation

Finding somewhere cheap to stay in Sweden isn't difficult. There's an extensive network of youth hostels (of an exceptionally high standard) and campsites, while hotels and guesthouses are common in towns and cities. Self-catering accommodation is generally restricted to youth hostels and campsites, where cabins are often equipped with kitchens.

Accommodation prices in Sweden vary according to the day of the week or the season. Pricing falls into two main categories: the higher price is charged for stays from Sunday to Thursday outside of the summer peak (generally mid-June to mid-Aug); the lower rate is charged on Fridays and Saturdays. This lower rate is also applied every day during the summer peak. Remember though that this rule does not apply across the board and there are some places that actually charge higher prices in summer in line with most other countries; this is usually the case with hotels on the west coast. When we give two prices in the guide, these reflect the difference in price according to season or day, with the high-season and weekend rate generally given first. Single rooms, where available, usually cost between sixty and eighty percent of the price.

Youth hostels

Youth hostels in Sweden (*vandrarhem*) turn up in the unlikeliest of places. There are over three hundred of them dotted across the country, in converted lighthouses, old castles and prisons, historic country manors, schoolrooms and even on boats. Quite simply, they offer some of the best accommodation in the country. Forget any preconceptions about youth hostelling: in Sweden, large dormitories are few, and rooms usually sleep four to six people.

The majority of hostels are run by STF (**Svenska Turistföreningen**; ☏ 08 463 22 70, ⓦ svenskaturist foreningen.se). Apart from the STF hostels there are

a number of independently run hostels, usually charging similar prices; we've mentioned the most useful in the text, and tourist offices will have details of any other local independent hostels.

Fell stations and cabins

Fell stations (*fjällstationer*) provide top-notch, hostel-like accommodation along mountain hiking routes; prices vary and are given in the guide. They're usually better equipped than the average youth hostel: rooms are private rather than dorms, and each fell station has a sauna, a shop and a kitchen.

Mountain cabins (*fjällstugor*), of which there are around ninety, are often no more than simple huts out in the wilds and are wonderful for getting away from it all. Run by the STF, they generally are often located at convenient intervals along popular walking routes. Both fell stations and mountain cabins allow you to use a sleeping bag without a sheet underneath.

Hotels and guesthouses

Hotels and **guesthouses** (usually family-run bed and breakfast establishments) needn't be expensive, and although there's little chance of finding any kind of room for under 550kr a night, you can often find good-value hotel rooms in summer, especially between mid-June and mid-August, when business people who would otherwise fill the hotels during the week are on holiday. The only parts of the country where summer discounts don't apply are in some of the popular holiday destinations in southern Sweden such as Gotland, where prices can actually go up in summer. Nearly all hotels include a huge self-service buffet breakfast in the price, which will keep you going for much of the day.

Campsites, cabins and self-catering

Practically every town or village has at least one **campsite**, and they are generally of a high standard. To pitch a tent at any of them you'll need the Camping Card Scandinavia, which costs 140kr and is issued at the first site you visit; contact the Swedish Camping Site Owners' Association (ⓦ camping.se). It costs 140–200kr for two people to pitch a tent at an official campsite and most sites are open from June to August. For details on camping rough, see p.33.

Many campsites also boast **cabins**, each of which is usually equipped with bunk beds, a kitchen and utensils, but not sheets. Self-catering in cabins is a good way to keep costs down. Cabins start around 500kr per night for a two-bed number. As usual, it's wise to ring ahead to secure one. Sweden also has a whole series of cabins for rent in spots other than campsites, often in picturesque locations such as in the middle of the forest, by a lakeshore or on the coast. For information and to make a booking, contact the local tourist office.

Food and drink

There's no escaping the fact that eating and drinking is going to take up a large slice of your budget in Sweden – though no more so than in any other northern European country. Note that although tipping in Swedish restaurants is not expected, it is customary to round the bill up to the nearest 20kr or so.

Swedish food – based largely on fish, meat and potatoes, and very varied in preparation – is always tasty and well presented and, at its best, is delicious. Unusual specialities generally come from the north of the country and include reindeer, elk meat and wild berries, while herring and salmon come in so many different guises that fish fiends will always be content. Vegetarians too should have no problems, with plenty of non-meat options available, especially in the bigger towns; elsewhere the choice may be limited to pizzas and salads. Alcoholic drinks are available in most establishments, with lager-type beers and imported wines providing no surprises; the local spirit *akvavit*, however, is worth trying at least once. It comes in dozens of weird and wonderful flavours, from lemon to cumin-and-dill.

Eating well and **eating cheaply** needn't be mutually exclusive aims in Sweden. The best strategy is to fuel up on breakfast and lunch, both of which offer good-value options. A good way to keep costs down when eating out is to resist the temptation to order a starter – throughout Sweden portions are generous and most main dishes are large enough to fill even the emptiest stomach. **Breakfast** is often included in the cost of a night's accommodation, and most restaurants have **lunchtime specials** (*dagens rätt*) that time and again are the best-value meals you'll find.

Food

Sweden's various **salmon** dishes are among the very best the cuisine has to offer – they're divine

either warm or cold, and a mainstay of any Swedish *smorgasbord* worth its salt. **Herring** is mostly served marinated, but don't let that put you off as it tastes surprisingly good. **Sauces** feature prominently in Swedish cooking, often flavoured with dill or parsley; alternatively there are many delicious creamy concoctions too.

Wild berries appear in many dishes, especially the lingonberry, which is something like a cranberry, and makes a good accompaniment to Swedish meatballs, a combination praised by many a Swede as a delicacy of the country. You'll also be able to taste orange-coloured sweet cloudberries, which grow in the marshes of Lapland and are delicious with ice cream.

Breakfast

Breakfast (*frukost*) is almost invariably a help-yourself buffet in the best Swedish tradition; you can go up to the serving table as many times as you like and eat until you're fit to explode. Youth hostels charge around 50kr for breakfast; if you stay in a hotel, it'll be included in the price of your accommodation.

Coffee is something the Swedes excel at, and is always freshly brewed, strong and delicious. A coffee costs around 25kr and the price will often buy you more than one cup. For coffee, head for the local *konditori*, a coffee and cake shop of the first order.

Snacks and light meals

For **snacks** and **light meals** you're really looking at the delights dished up by the *gatukök* (street kitchen) or *korvstånd* (sausage stall). A **gatukök** is often no more than a hole in the wall – generally conspicuous by the snaking queue and gaggle of teenagers it attracts – serving sausages, burgers, chips, soft drinks and sometimes pizza slices or chicken pieces. Chips with a sausage or burger generally comes to around 75kr. The **korvstånd** usually limits itself to sausages (hotdogs are usually around 25kr), though some have chips and burgers as well.

Self-catering

For the cheapest eating it's hard to beat the supermarkets and market stalls. Of the supermarket chains, ICA and Coop have the biggest range of produce but most supermarkets in Sweden are small local affairs selling just the basics and a few other bits and pieces. Alternatively, head for the indoor or outdoor markets, which often have fresher produce than the supermarkets, and at lower prices.

Fish is always excellent value, especially salmon. Pork and beef aren't too bad either, but chicken is slightly more expensive. Sweden is a country rich in **cheeses**, all of which are reasonably good value and make great sandwich fillers; the range runs from stronger ripened cheeses such as Västerbotten and Svecia to milder types like Grevé and Herrgårdsost. Prästost, a medium-strong cheese akin to a mature Cheddar, is also a particular favourite here.

Restaurants

Swedes eat their main meal of the day at lunchtime; do likewise and you'll save lots of cash. You don't have to restrict yourself to eating out at lunchtime; many restaurants also offer special deals in the evening, and even if they don't you're bound to find something on their menu that will fit your pocket. Remember that Swedish portions are generous and that, accordingly, you may not have room for a starter as well.

An evening meal in a mid-range restaurant will cost you 150–250kr without alcohol. A three-course meal naturally costs more; expect to pay something in the region of 400–600kr, and add around 65kr for a strong beer, or 250kr for an average bottle of wine. Dishes usually have some sort of salad accompaniment and come with bread. Bear in mind that Swedes eat early; lunch will be served from 11am, dinner from 6pm. It's always a good idea to **book a table** to avoid disappointment, particularly during the summer months of June to August when tables can be at a premium. **Smoking** is not allowed in restaurant or pubs.

At lunchtime, go for the **dagens rätt** or set dish of the day, which generally costs between 70kr and 95kr and is one way to sample Swedish *husmanskost* (home cooking). You'll also find various pizza and pasta dishes on offer in Italian restaurants, and basic meals in Thai and Chinese restaurants (sometimes a buffet-type spread). Most cafés also offer some sort of *dagens rätt* but their standard of cooking is often not as good as in restaurants.

While you're in Sweden you should sample a **smörgåsbord**, available in the larger restaurants and in hotels for around 350kr – expensive, but good for a blowout. If you're a traditionalist you should start with *akvavit*, drink beer throughout and finish with coffee. Coffee will be included in the price, but alcohol won't.

Drinks

Drinking in Sweden can be expensive, but there are ways of softening the blow. Either forgo bars and buy your booze in the state-run liquor shops, the **Systembolaget**, or seek out the happy hours

(usually called After Work i many pubs and bars. The tin usually set to coincide with so keep your eyes peeled f windows or on the pavem outdoors is frowned upon a to take alcohol onto a train own consumption (drinking alcohol purchased on trains or pavement cafés is permitted).

The Systembolaget

In any Swedish town or city, the **Systembolaget** is the only shop that sells wine, strong beer and spirits. It's run by the state, is only open office hours (generally Mon–Wed & Fri 10am–6pm, Thurs till 7pm, Sat 10am–2pm) and until quite recently kept all its alcohol on display in locked glass cabinets – this is still the case in many smaller stores. Debate over the future of the system rumbles on and Sweden is coming under increasing pressure from the European Commission to liberalize the sale of alcohol and open up the market to free competition.

What to drink

Beer is the most common alcoholic drink in Sweden, although it can be expensive. Whether you buy beer in a café, restaurant or a bar, it'll cost roughly the same, on average 45–65kr for half a litre of lager-type brew.

Unless you specify otherwise, the beer you get in a bar will be *starköl* (also referred to as *storstark*), with an alcohol content of 5.6 percent by volume. Low-alcohol beers are available for sale in supermarkets. **Wine** in restaurants is pricey; a bottle will set you back something like 300kr, and a glass around 65kr. It's also worth trying the **akvavit** or schnapps, which is made from potatoes, served ice-cold in tiny shots and washed down with beer. If you're in Sweden at Christmas, don't go home without having sampled **glögg**: mulled red wine with cloves, cinnamon, sugar and more than a shot of *akvavit*.

Where to drink

You'll find pubs and bars in all towns and some villages. In Stockholm and the larger cities the trend is towards British- and Irish-style pubs, although the atmosphere inside never quite lives up to the original. Elsewhere – particularly in the north of the country – you'll come across more down-to-earth drinking dens. Drink is no cheaper here, and the clientele is predominantly male and usually drunk.

In the summer, **café-bars** spill out onto the pavement, which is a more suitable environment for children and handy if all you want is a coffee.

...can't find a bar in an out-of-the-way ...ead for the local hotel – but be prepared to ...or the privilege. Bar **opening hours** are elastic, ...nd drinking-up time is generally some time after midnight. **Smoking** is banned in all of Sweden's restaurants, bars, cafés and nightclubs.

The media

Stockholm is the centre of the Swedish media world. All national radio and television stations are broadcast from the capital, and the country's four main daily newspapers are also based there. However, every region or city also has its own newspaper, for example Göteborgs-posten in Gothenburg or Norrbottens tidning in Lapland. In remote parts of the country, particularly in the north, these local media really come into their own; in winter, people depend on them for accurate and up-to-date information on everything from local political machinations to snow depths in the vicinity.

Newspapers

Assuming you don't read Swedish, you can keep in touch with world events by buying **English-language newspapers** in the major towns and cities, sometimes on the day of issue, more usually the day after. Municipal libraries across the country often have good selections of foreign broadsheets but they can sometimes be a little out of date. The main Swedish papers are *Dagens Nyheter* and *Svenska Dagbladet* and the tabloids, *Expressen* and *Aftonbladet*. You may also come across *Metro*, a free newspaper available at train and tube stations, which has lots of "what's on" information; its listings are in Swedish only, but will be comprehensible enough if you don't speak the language.

TV and radio

Swedish TV won't take up much space on your postcards home. There are two state channels, SVT1 and SVT2, operated by Sveriges Television (SVT), worth watching if only for the wooden in-vision continuity announcers. TV3 is a pretty dire cable station, and Sweden's only terrestrial commercial station is the somewhat downmarket TV4. TV5 is a cheesy cable channel available in most hotels that seems to show nothing but a string of American sitcoms. On all the channels, foreign programmes are in their original language, which makes for easy viewing; SVT1 and SVT2 show a lot of excellent BBC documentaries and comedy programmes.

On the **radio**, you'll find pop and rock music on P3 and classical music on P2 – all operated by state broadcaster, Sveriges Radio (Swedish Radio; W sr.se for frequencies). You'll also find **news in English** courtesy of Radio Sweden (Swedish Radio's international arm; W radiosweden.org) broadcast nationally on P2, weekdays at 3pm. Its English-language current affairs programmes about Sweden can be heard weekdays in Stockholm on 89.6MHz FM, too, and are also available as podcasts.

Festivals

Swedish festivals are for the most part organized around the seasons. Most celebrations are lively events, as Swedes are great party people – once the beer begins to flow. The highlight of the year is the Midsummer festival, when the whole country gets involved, and wild parties last well into the early hours. The date of Midsummer's Day varies from year to year but is the Saturday closest to the actual summer solstice.

MAJOR FESTIVALS AND EVENTS

Valborgsmässoafton (April 30). Walpurgis Night. One of the most important festivals in Sweden, heralding the beginning of spring with bonfires and songs.

Labour Day (May 1). A none-too-thrilling marching day for the workers' parties.

Swedish National Day (June 6). In existence since 1983, though a bit of a damp squib even though it's now a public holiday; worthy speeches are delivered in the evening and the king often puts in an appearance at Skansen in Stockholm.

Midsummer (the Fri & Sat between June 20–26). The biggest and best celebration anywhere in Sweden, with festivities centred around the maypole, an old fertility symbol, which is erected at popular gatherings across the country. The maypole is raised in June because it's often still snowing in northern Sweden in May. There's much dancing and drinking into the night – and severe hangovers the next morning.

Crayfish parties (throughout Aug). Held in the August moonlight across the country to say a wistful farewell to the short Swedish summer. Competitions are often held to establish the season's best and tastiest crayfish.

Surströmming (late Aug). In coastal areas of northern Sweden, particularly along the High Coast, parties are held at which people eat *surströmming* (see p.263), a foul-smelling fermented Baltic herring which is something of an acquired taste – though a quintessentially Swedish experience.

Nobel Prize Day (Dec 10). Official ceremonies are held in Stockholm as the winners of the annual Nobel prizes are awarded. Although this is not a public festival, it is a key date in the Swedish calendar.

St Lucia's Day (Dec 13). Led by a girl with a crown of candles, this is a procession of children who sing songs as they bring light into the darkest month. For many Swedes, this is a welcome highlight during the ever-shortening days of December and a chance to look forward to Christmas and the longer nights of January and onwards.

Sports and outdoor activities

Sweden is a wonderful place if you love the great outdoors, with fantastic hiking, fishing and, of course, winter-sports opportunities. Best of all you won't find the countryside overcrowded – there's plenty of space to get away from it all, especially in the north. You'll also find Swedish lakes and beaches refreshingly relaxed and always clean.

Skiing and winter pursuits

During the winter months, **skiing** – a sport which began in Scandinavia – is incredibly popular, and in the north of Sweden people even ski to work. The most popular ski resorts are Åre, Idre, Sälen and Riksgränsen; these and many others are packed out during the snow season when prices hit the roof. If you do intend to come to ski, it is essential to book accommodation well in advance or take a package holiday.

In northern Sweden you can ski from the end of October well into April, and at Riksgränsen in Lappland you can ski under the midnight sun from late May to the end of June when the snow finally melts. Riksgränsen is also the place to head for if you're into **snowboarding**. Kiruna is a good bet as a base for other winter pursuits, whether you fancy **dog sledding**, snowmobile riding, a night in the world's biggest igloo (*Icehotel* at Jukkasjärvi, see p.341), or **ice fishing**. Bear in mind, though, that the area around Kiruna is one of the coldest in the country, and temperatures in the surrounding mountains can sink to -50°C during a really cold snap.

Hiking

Sweden's Right of Public Access, *Allemansrätten*, means you can **walk** freely right across the entire country (see box below). A network of more than forty long-distance footpaths covers the whole of Sweden, with overnight accommodation available in mountain stations and huts. The most popular route is the **Kungsleden**, the King's Route, which can get rather busy in July at times, but is still enjoyable. The path stretches for 460km between Abisko and Hemavan, passing through some spectacular landscape in the wild and isolated northwest of the country; the trail also takes in Sweden's highest mountain, Kebnekaise (2102m).

Canoeing and rafting

There are almost one hundred thousand lakes and thousands of kilometres of rivers and canals in Sweden. Needless to say, on summer afternoons taking to a **canoe** is a popular pastime; a good area for this is the Stockholm archipelago (see p.78). Another excellent alternative is to get hold of a **raft** and glide down the Klarälven River in

---

THE COUNTRYSIDE – SOME GROUND RULES

In Sweden you're entitled by law to walk, jog, camp, cycle, ride or ski on other people's land, provided you don't cause damage to crops, forest plantations or fences; this is the centuries-old **Allemansrätten** or Everyman's Right. It also allows you to pick wild berries, mushrooms and wild flowers (except protected species), fish and swim, where there are no nearby houses. But this right brings with it certain obligations: you shouldn't get close to houses or walk across gardens or on land under seed or crops; pitch a tent on land used for farming; camp close to houses without asking permission; cut down trees or bushes; or break branches or strip the bark off trees. Nor are you allowed to drive off-road (look out for signs saying "*Ej motorfordon*", no motor vehicles, or "*Enskild väg*", private road); light a fire if there's a risk of it spreading; or disturb wildlife.

It's common sense to be wary of frightening reindeer herds in the north of Sweden; if they scatter it can mean several extra days' hard work for the herders. Also avoid tramping over the lichen – the staple diet of reindeer – covering stretches of moorland. As you might expect, any kind of hunting is forbidden without a permit. National parks have special regulations which are posted on huts and at entrances.

Värmland (see p.143); one of the companies offering these tours even allows you to build your own raft before departure.

Saunas and swimming in lakes

Most public swimming pools and hotels, even in the smallest towns, will have a **sauna**. They're generally electric and extra steam is created by tossing water onto the hot elements. The temperature inside ranges from 70°C to 120°C. Traditional wood-burning saunas are often found in the countryside and give off a wonderful smell. Public saunas are always single-sex and nude; you'll often see signs forbidding the wearing of swimming costumes, as these would collect your sweat and allow it to soak into the wooden benches. It's common practice to take a cold shower afterwards or, in winter, roll in the snow to cool off. Otherwise in the countryside, people often take a dip in a nearby lake. As Sweden boasts around 100,000 **lakes** and one of the lowest population densities in Europe, you needn't worry about stripping off for a spot of skinny-dipping.

Fishing

Sweden is an ideal country for **anglers**. Salmon are regularly caught from opposite the Parliament building right in the centre of Stockholm, because the water is so clean and fishing there is free. Fishing is also free along the coastline and in the larger lakes, including Vänern, Vättern (particularly good for salmon and char) and Mälaren. In the north of the country, Tärnaby (see p.321) offers top-class mountain fishing for char and trout; and nearby Sorsele (see p.323) is good for fly-fishing for trout, char and grayling. For salmon fishing, the river running up through the Torne Valley (see p.348) is one of the best places. In most areas you need a permit for freshwater fishing, so ask at local tourist offices.

Culture and etiquette

In many ways, Sweden is a model country: society is liberal, people are prosperous and the social and economic position of women is one of the most advanced in the world. As a result, most visitors find Sweden an easy country to visit.

Swedes, in general, are an efficient nation – planning meticulously and booking ahead to ensure they get what they want, when they want. Accordingly, spontaneity and flexibility are not high on the agenda in Sweden, which can sometimes create a mistaken impression of rudeness to the outsider. Honesty and straight-talking are two highly cherished sides of the Swedish character; a promise in Sweden is just that. Haggling over prices is not the done thing. On meeting, friends of both sexes usually hug, rather than kiss, each other. In more formal situations, people shake hands whilst saying their name.

In line with the liberal reputation Sweden gained during the 1970s as a result of countless soft porn films, nudity is widely accepted. In changing rooms, people are uninhibited about their bodies and don't feel the need to cover up with a towel. Nude lake swimming and sunbathing are common practice across the country. If other people are around, show them consideration, but you're unlikely to meet opposition.

Travel essentials

Admission charges

Entry into museums is often free. However, where this is not the case expect to pay around 50kr for admission. In winter, there is often a compulsory charge to check your coat when entering a bar or restaurant; this is usually around 30kr.

Climate

Summer **weather** in Sweden is similar to that in southern Britain, though there are more hours of sunshine; the average temperature in Stockholm, for example, is the same as that in London. By the end of August, though, northernmost Sweden is usually experiencing its first frosts. Snow can fall anytime from around September onwards and in the Stockholm area there is usually – though not always – snow cover from early December to late March. Winters in the far south of the country are mild and often snow-free. **Daylight** is just as important as temperatures in Sweden. In December, it doesn't get light in Stockholm until around 9.30am and it's dark by around 3pm. North of the Arctic Circle there's 24-hour darkness from mid-December to mid-January, and the merest glow of light at noon during the months immediately either side. Conversely, at the height of summer there's no part of Sweden which is dark for any length of time; in

AVERAGE DAILY TEMPERATURES (°C) AND PRECIPITATION (MM)

	Jan	March	May	June	July	Aug	Oct	Dec
Jokkmokk								
°C	-17	-8	6	12	14	12	1	-14
mm	30	24	35	48	78	74	41	32
Umeå								
°C	-9	-4	7	13	15	14	4	-7
mm	49	41	41	44	53	78	65	56
Östersund								
°C	-7	-4	7	12	13	12	4	-6
mm	27	23	35	57	76	60	37	31
Stockholm								
°C	-3	0	11	16	17	16	8	-1
mm	39	26	30	45	72	66	50	46
Gothenburg								
°C	-2	1	11	15	16	16	9	0
mm	62	50	51	61	68	77	84	75
Visby								
°C	-1	0	10	14	16	16	8	1
mm	48	32	29	31	50	50	50	51
Lund								
°C	-1	2	11	15	17	17	9	1
mm	54	44	43	54	66	63	60	65

the far north there's 24-hour daylight and midnight sun from the end of May until the end of June, and April and July are very light months.

Costs

Although often considered the most expensive country in Europe, Sweden is in fact cheaper than all the other Nordic countries and no more expensive than, say, France or Germany. If you don't mind having your main meal of the day at lunchtime – like the Swedes – or having picnics under the midnight sun with goodies bought from the supermarket, travelling by the efficient public transport system and going easy on the nightlife, you'll find Sweden isn't the financial drain you might expect.

You'll find you can exist – camping, self-catering, hitching, no drinking – on a fairly low budget (around £35/US$50/€40 a day), though it will be a pretty miserable experience and only sustainable for a limited period of time. Stay in hostels, eat the *dagens rätt* at lunchtime, get out and see the sights and drink the odd beer or two and you'll be looking at doubling your expenditure. Once you start having restaurant meals with wine, taking a few taxis, enjoying coffees and cakes and staying in hotel accommodation, you'll probably spend considerably more (£100–150/US$150–200/€120–170 a day).

Crime and personal safety

Sweden is in general a **safe** country to visit, and this extends to women travelling alone. However, it would be foolish to assume that Stockholm and the bigger cities are free of petty crime, fuelled as elsewhere by a growing number of drug addicts and alcoholics after easy money. Keep tabs on your cash and passport (and don't leave anything valuable in your car when you park it) and you should have little reason to visit the police. If you do, you'll find them courteous, concerned and, perhaps most importantly, usually able to speak English.

As for offences *you* might commit, a big no-no is drinking alcohol in public places (which includes trains). Being drunk in the streets can get you arrested, and drunk driving is treated especially rigorously (see p.28). Drugs offences, too, meet with the same harsh attitude that prevails throughout the majority of Europe.

Although **racism** is not a major problem in Sweden, it would be wrong to say it doesn't exist. It stems mainly from a small but vocal neo-Nazi movement, VAM (their full name translates as "White Aryan Resistance"), who occasionally daub slogans like *"Behålla Sverige Svenskt"* (Keep Sweden Swedish) on walls in towns and cities and on the Stockholm metro. Although there have been several racist murders and many attacks on dark-skinned foreigners over the past couple of years, it's still the exception rather than the rule. Keep your eyes and ears open and avoid trouble, especially on Friday and Saturday nights when drink can fuel these prejudices.

Electricity

The supply is 220V, although appliances requiring 240V will work perfectly well. Plugs have two round pins. Remember that if you're staying in a cottage out in the wilds, electricity may not be available.

Entry requirements

European Union, American, Canadian, Australian and New Zealand citizens need only a valid **passport** to enter Sweden, and can stay for up to three months. Once the three months are up, EU nationals can apply for a **resident's permit** (*uppehållstillstånd*) to cover longer visits. For further information on where to obtain the permits, contact the Swedish embassy in your home country.

SWEDISH EMBASSIES ABROAD

Australia 5 Turrana St, Yarralumla, ACT 2600 Canberra ☎ 02 6270 2700, Ⓦ swedenabroad.com.
Canada 377 Dalhousie St, Ottawa, ON K1N 9N8 ☎ 613 244 8220, Ⓦ swedenabroad.com.
Republic of Ireland 13–17 Dawson St, Dublin 2 ☎ 01 671 5822, Ⓦ swedenabroad.com.
South Africa I Parioli Complex, 1166 Park St, Pretoria ☎ 012 426 64 00, Ⓦ swedenabroad.com.
UK 11 Montagu Place, London W1H 2AL ☎ 020 7917 6400, Ⓦ swedenabroad.com.
US 2900 K St NW, Washington, DC 20007 ☎ 202 467 2600, Ⓦ swedenabroad.com.

Gay and lesbian travellers

Swedish attitudes to **gay men** and **lesbians** are remarkably liberal – on a legal level at least – when compared to most other Western countries, with both the government and the law proudly geared towards the promotion of gay rights and equality (the official age of sexual consent is 15 whether you are gay or straight).

In 1995, Sweden introduced its registered-partnership law, despite unanimous opposition in parliament from the right-wing Moderates and Christian Democrats. Ten years on, in July 2005, the Swedish parliament granted lesbians the right to artificial insemination.

Paradoxically, the acceptance of gays and lesbians in society as a whole can at best be described as sporadic, and in fact homosexuality was regarded as a psychological disease in Sweden until 1979. Outside the cities, and particularly in the north of the country where the lumberjack mentality rules supreme, there can still be widespread embarrassment and unease whenever the subject is mentioned in public.

There are very few gay bars and clubs in Sweden though gay community life in general is supported by the state-sponsored Riksförbundet för Sexuellt Likaberättigande, or RFSL (National Association for Sexual Equality; Sveavägen 59, Stockholm; ☎ 08 501 62 900, Ⓦ rfsl.se), founded in 1950 as one of the first gay rights organizations in the world. The website Ⓦ qx.se has useful information about gay and lesbian happenings in Sweden, and listings of bars and discos where they do exist.

Health

EU nationals can take advantage of Sweden's **health services** under the same terms as residents of the country. For this you'll need a European Health Insurance Card, available in the UK through post offices and Department for Work and Pensions offices. Citizens of non-EU countries will be charged for all medical services, although US visitors will find that medical treatment is far less expensive than they are accustomed to at home. Even so it is advisable to take out travel insurance (see opposite). Note that you need a doctor's prescription even to get minor painkillers in Sweden, so bring your own supplies.

There's no **local doctor** system in Sweden. Instead, go to the nearest hospital with your passport (and Health Insurance Card, if applicable) and they'll treat you; the casualty department is called *Akutmottagning* or *Vårdcentral*. The fee for staying in hospital overnight depends on the care you need.

For **dental treatment**, foreign citizens generally have to pay in full for treatment. You can spot a dental surgery by looking out for the sign "Tandläkare" or "Folktandvården". An emergency dental service is available in most major towns and cities out of hours – look in the windows of the local pharmacy for contact telephone numbers.

Mosquitoes and ticks

Mosquitoes are common throughout Sweden and it's sensible to protect yourself against bites. Although Swedish mosquitoes don't carry diseases, they can torment your every waking moment from the end of June, when the warmer weather causes them to hatch, until around mid-August. They are found in their densest concentrations in the north of the country, where there's swampy ground, and are most active early in the morning and in the late afternoon/early evening; the best way to protect yourself is to wear thick clothing (though not dark colours, which attract them) and apply mosquito **repellent** to any exposed skin. When camping, make a smoky fire of (damp) peat if feasible, as mosquitoes don't like smoke. Don't scratch mosquito bites (*myggbett*); treat them instead with Salubrin or Alsolsprit creams, or something similar, available from local chemists.

Ticks (*fästingar*) are fast becoming a big problem in Sweden due to a succession of milder winters. The country has one of the highest rates of tickborne encephalitis in Europe, a disease which causes fever and nausea, and in a third of cases spreads to the brain; it causes lasting damage in forty percent of people infected. A third of all ticks also carry the bacteria which cause Lyme disease, an illness which can lead to inflammation of the brain and nerves. The insects, which burrow painlessly into the skin, are prevalent predominantly on the east coast and islands and are active from March to November. Their preferred habitat is warm, slightly moist undergrowth, bushes and meadows with long grass. In addition to vaccination, sprays, roll-ons and creams are available in local pharmacies; eating large amounts of garlic is also effective in keeping ticks away.

Insurance

Even though EU health-care rights apply in Sweden, you'd do well to take out an insurance policy before travelling to cover against theft, loss and illness or injury. Before paying for a new policy, however, it's worth checking whether you are already covered: some all-risks home insurance policies may cover your possessions when overseas, and many private medical schemes include cover when abroad.

Internet

Internet cafés are surprisingly thin on the ground in Sweden, and only really exist in the larger cities. However, there are sometimes terminals operated by the internet provider, Sidewalk Express, in train stations, Pressbyrån newsagents and 7-Eleven food stores; access is from 19kr per hour. As an alternative, try the local tourist office or **library**.

Kids

Sweden is an exemplary country when it comes to **travelling with children**. Most hotels and youth hostels have family rooms and both men's and women's toilets – including those on trains – usually offer baby-changing areas. Always ask for children's discounts, as many activities, particularly during the summer months, are geared towards families.

Laundry

Sweden has very few public laundries. Your only option to wash your clothes on the road is at youth hostels where there is generally a laundry on site for guest use.

Living in Sweden

The Swedish Institute (☎08 453 7800, ⊛si.se) has a whole host of information about various work and study programmes across Sweden and sometimes organizes Swedish language courses abroad.

ROUGH GUIDES TRAVEL INSURANCE

Rough Guides has teamed up with WorldNomads.com to offer great travel insurance deals. Policies are available to residents of over 150 countries, with cover for a wide range of adventure sports, 24-hour emergency assistance, high levels of medical and evacuation cover and a stream of travel safety information. Roughguides.com users can take advantage of their policies online 24/7, from anywhere in the world – even if you're already travelling. And since plans often change when you're on the road, you can extend your policy and even claim online. Roughguides.com users who buy travel insurance with WorldNomads.com can also leave a positive footprint and donate to a community development project. For more information go to ⊛roughguides.com/shop.

Mail

The Swedish **post office** is a thing of the past. Postal services are instead to be found in local supermarkets and filling stations; look for the blue postal sign outside (a yellow horn and crown on a blue background) which are open longer hours than the traditional post office used to be. You can buy **stamps** (*frimärken*) at most newspaper kiosks, tobacconists, hotels, bookshops and stationers' shops, as well as at supermarkets and petrol stations. Note that **Swedish addresses** are always written with the number after the street name. In multi-floor buildings, the ground floor is always counted as the first floor.

Maps

The most useful map of **Stockholm** can only be bought in the city itself: the Stockholm Map (Stockholmskartan) is available from any office of the local transport authority, Storstockholms Lokaltrafik. This map has the advantage of showing all bus and metro routes in the capital, and includes a street index. For maps of the whole country, go for Hallwag's Sverige/Sweden (1:8,000,000). There are also regional maps produced by Kartförlaget (1:250,00 and 1:400,000), which are excellent.

If you're staying in one area for a long time, or are **hiking** or walking, you'll probably need something more detailed still, with a minimum scale of 1:400,000 – though preferably much larger for serious trekking. The Fjällkartan series covering the northwestern mountains are good; these maps, produced by Lantmäteriverket, at a scale of 1:100,000, are unfortunately rather expensive, both in Sweden and abroad.

Money

The Swedish **currency** is the *krona* (kr; plural *kronor*). It comes in coins of 1kr, 5kr and 10kr, and notes of 20kr, 50kr, 100kr, 500kr and 1000kr. There's no limit on the amount of Swedish and foreign currency you can take into Sweden. At the time of going to print, the exchange rate was around 10.50kr to £1, 6.5kr to US$1 and 9kr to €1.

The cheapest and easiest way of accessing money whilst you're in Sweden is from ATMs with your **debit card**. There will be a flat transaction fee for withdrawals, which is usually quite small, but no interest payments.

Credit cards are a good backup source of funds, and can be used either in ATMs or over the counter. Mastercard, Visa, American Express and Diners Card are accepted everywhere for goods or cash.

Traveller's cheques are a safe and simple way of carrying your money, although there can be a hefty commission when you come to change them. Some places charge per cheque, others per transaction, so it's common sense to take large denominations with you, or to try to change as much as you feel you can handle in one go.

Banks (Mon–Wed & Fri 9.30am–3pm, Thurs 9.30am–4/5.30pm; in some cities, banks may stay open to 5.30pm every weekday) have standard exchange rates but commissions can vary enormously. The best place to change money is at the yellow **Forex** offices (@forex.se), which offer more *kronor* for your currency though also charge commission. You'll find Forex branches in Sweden's main cities as well as at major airports.

Opening hours and public holidays

Shop **opening hours** are generally from 9.30am to 6pm on weekdays and 9.30am to 4pm on Saturdays. In larger towns, department stores remain open until 7pm or longer on weekdays, and some are also open on Sundays between noon and 4pm. Museums and galleries operate various opening hours, but are generally closed on Mondays outside the summer months. Banks, offices and shops are closed on public holidays (see below). They usually also close or have reduced opening hours on the eve of the holiday.

PUBLIC HOLIDAYS IN SWEDEN	
New Year's Day	January 1
Epiphany	January 6
Good Friday	March/April
Easter Sunday	March/April
Easter Monday	March/April
Labour Day	May 1
Ascension Day	Fortieth day after Easter Sunday
Whit Sunday	Seventh Sunday after Easter
National Day	June 6
Midsummer's Eve	Always on a Friday
Midsummer's Day	Saturday closest to the summer solstice
All Saints' Day	Closest Saturday to November 1
Christmas Eve	December 24
Christmas Day	December 25
Boxing Day	December 26
New Year's Eve	December 31

Phones

In the land of Ericsson, **mobile phones** work virtually everywhere and almost every Swede has at least one. Consequently, public payphones have all but disappeared. Mobile coverage in the south of the country is virtually a hundred percent. In the north there is good coverage along the main roads and the coast, and even the most remote village in Norrland has some kind of network coverage; with international roaming this means you can use your phone virtually wherever you happen to be. In order to avoid roaming charges, you can buy a Swedish SIM card from any newsagent (*pressbyrån*) for around 150kr (ask for a *startpaket*).

Shopping

Stockholm is undoubtedly the best place in Sweden to shop – it not only has the biggest selection of stores in the country but, thanks to competion, prices tend to be a little lower than elsewhere. **Glassware** is generally a good buy and Swedish glass producers are renowned for their innovation and creative designs; in Stockholm try the Åhléns and NK department stores which keep a wide range of glass products. Other items to look out for are locally produced **handicrafts** which can range from handwoven table runners to wrought-iron candlesticks. Most towns have a handicraft store selling "hantverk". For English-language **books** try the Akademibokhandeln chain found in major towns across the country, or, better, in Stockholm, the Swedish Institute, Slottsbacken 10, which has an unsurpassed stock of English-language books on Sweden and Sweden-related gifts and souvenirs.

Time

Sweden conforms to **Central European Time** (CET), which is always one hour ahead of Britain and Ireland. For most of the year Sweden is six hours ahead of New York, nine hours behind Sydney and eleven hours behind Auckland. Clocks go forward by one hour in late March and back one hour in late October (on the same days as in Britain and Ireland).

Tipping

Leaving tips is not common practice in Sweden. In the big cities, however, it is usual to round up a restaurant bill to the nearest sensible denomination, ie 277kr becomes 300kr, but there is no tradition of routinely tipping by ten to fifteen percent as in some countries.

Tourist information

All towns – and some villages – have a **tourist office** from where you can pick up free town plans and information, brochures, timetables and other literature. Most offices have internet access. During the summer they're open until late evening; out of season it's more usual for them to keep shop hours, and in the winter they're normally closed at weekends. You'll find full details of individual offices throughout the guide.

Sweden's official website for tourism and travel information, ⓦ visitsweden.com, is extremely comprehensive and worth a browse before leaving home.

Travellers with disabilities

Sweden is, in many ways, a model of awareness in terms of **disabled travel**, with assistance forthcoming from virtually all Swedes, if needed. Wheelchair access is usually available on trains (InterCity trains have wide aisles and large toilets, and often have special carriages with hydraulic lifts), and there are lifts down to the platforms at almost every Stockholm metro station. In every part of the country there'll be some taxis in the form of minivans specially converted for disabled use.

Accommodation suitable for people with disabilities is often available: most hotels have specially adapted rooms, while some chalet villages have cabins with wheelchair access. Any building with three or more storeys must, by law, have a lift installed, while all public buildings are legally required to be accessible to people with disabilities and have automatic doors. For more information, contact De Handikappades Riksförbund, (ⓣ 08 685 80 00, ⓦ dhr.se).

MAKING INTERNATIONAL CALLS TO AND FROM SWEDEN

To **call Sweden from abroad**, dial your country's international access code followed by 46 for Sweden, then dial the area code (without its first 0) and the number.

To **call abroad from Sweden**, dial 00 followed by the required country code then the area code (without its first 0) and the number.

Stockholm

THE DJURGÅRDEN FERRY CRUISING PAST BUILDINGS IN GAMLA STAN

1

Stockholm

"It is not a city at all. It is ridiculous to think of itself as a city. It is simply a rather large village, set in the middle of some forest and some lakes. You wonder what it thinks it is doing there, looking so important."

Ingmar Bergman

Without a shadow of a doubt, Stockholm is one of the most beautiful cities in Europe. Built on no fewer than fourteen islands, where the fresh water of Lake Mälaren meets the brackish Baltic Sea, clean air and open space are in plentiful supply here. One-third of the area within the city limits is made up of water, while another third comprises parks and woodlands. As a result, the capital is one of Europe's saner cities and a delightful place in which to spend time.

Broad boulevards lined with elegant buildings are reflected in the deep blue water, and rows of painted wooden houseboats bob gently alongside the cobbled waterfront. Yet Stockholm is also a hi-tech metropolis, with futuristic skyscrapers and a bustling commercial heart.

For most visitors, the first stop is the Old Town, **Gamla Stan**, a medieval jumble of cobbled streets and narrow alleyways huddled together on a triangular-shaped island. Today the area is an atmospheric mixture of buildings surrounded on all sides by a latticework of medieval lanes and alleyways. Close by is the tiny island of **Skeppsholmen**; conveniently, the island is also the site of the two most central youth hostels (see p.67). To the north of the Old Town, the district of **Norrmalm** swaps tradition for a thoroughly contemporary feel: this is downtown Stockholm where you'll find shopping malls, huge department stores and conspicuous, showy wealth. Central Station and the lively **central park**, Kungsträdgården, are located here too. Most of Stockholm's **museums and galleries** are spread across this area and two others: to the east, the more residential **Östermalm**, with its mix of grand avenues and smart houses; and to the southeast, the green park island of **Djurgården**. Here the extraordinary seventeenth-century warship, **Vasa**, rescued and preserved after sinking in Stockholm harbour, and **Skansen**, the oldest and best of Europe's open-air museums, both receive loud and deserved acclaim. The island of **Södermalm** was traditionally the working-class area of Stockholm, whose grids of streets lined with lofty stone buildings create an altogether more homely ambience than the grand and formal buildings of the city centre. It's here, in a fashionable area known as **SoFo** (south of Folkungagatan) that you'll find some of the city's most enjoyable bars and restaurants. Crossing the narrow neighbouring island of Långholmen, known for its popular beaches, you'll reach **Kungsholmen,** an island that's fast becoming a rival to its southern neighbour for trendy restaurants and drinking establishments.

Brief history

Swedish stateman **Birger Jarl** founded Stockholm in 1255 in an attempt to secure the burgeoning city of Sigtuna from maritime attack. However, it was vibrant trade

Highlights

❶ **Gamla Stan** Wander through the narrow streets and alleyways of the Old Town for a taste of medieval Stockholm. **See p.46**

❷ **Djurgårdsfärjan** Ride the ferry across Stockholm harbour for some of the best views of the city. **See p.56.**

❸ **Djurgården** Take a stroll through leafy parkland right in the city centre and enjoy some great waterside views. **See p.58**

❹ **Vasamuséet** Fascinating seventeenth-century warship raised from Stockholm harbour

and painstakingly restored to her former glory. **See p.60**

❺ **Fotografiska Muséet** Sample work by some of the world's leading photographers at this new museum which is taking the capital by storm. **See p.63**

❻ **Swimming in Lake Mälaren** Taking a dip in the refreshing waters of Lake Mälaren is a favourite summer activity for Stockholmers – join them. **See p.74**

HIGHLIGHTS ARE MARKED ON THE MAP ON PP.44–45

1

GREATER STOCKHOLM

● CAFÉS & RESTAURANTS
Blå Porten	12
Chakula	11
Ciao Ciao Grande	7
Göken	11
Il Conte	8
La Famiglia	6
Lao Wai	1
Mamas & Tapas	10
Peppar	2
Salt	9
Samuraj	5
Saturnus	3
Supper	4

■ BARS, CLUBS & LIVE-MUSIC VENUES
Cirkus	4
Crazy Daizy	3
Storstad	1
Tranan	2

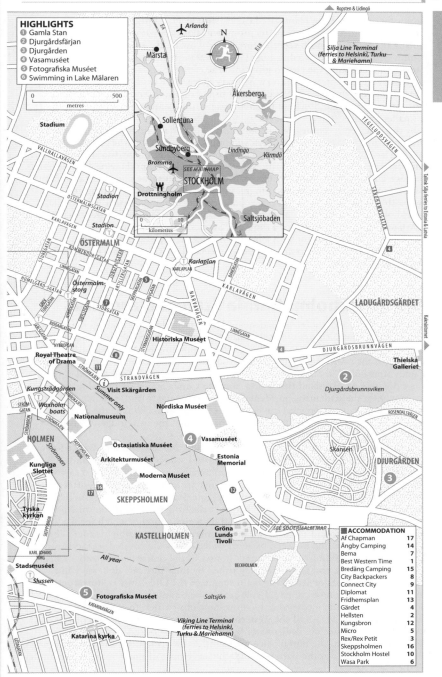

Ropsten & Lidingö

HIGHLIGHTS
① Gamla Stan
② Djurgårdsfärjan
③ Djurgården
④ Vasamuséet
⑤ Fotografiska Muséet
⑥ Swimming in Lake Mälaren

0 ─────── 500
metres

Arlanda
N
Märsta
Åkersberga
Sollentuna
Sundbyberg
Lindingö   Värmdö
Bromma
SEE MAIN MAP
STOCKHOLM
Drottningholm
Saltsjöbaden

0 ─────── 10
kilometres

Silja Line Terminal
(ferries to Helsinki, Turku
& Mariehamn)

Tallink Silja ferries to Estonia & Latvia

Kaknästornet

Stadium
VALLHALLAVÄGEN
Stadion
OSTERMALMSGATAN
KARLAVÄGEN
Stadion
ÖSTERMALM
KOMMENDÖRSGATAN
Karlaplan
KARLAPLAN
Östermalm-
storg
KARLAVÄGEN
LADUGÅRDSGÄRDET
STORGATAN
RIDDARGATAN
NYBROPLAN
Historiska Muséet
LINNÉGATAN
Royal Theatre
of Drama
DJURGÅRDSBRUNNSVÄGEN
Thielska
Galleriet
STRANDVÄGEN
Summer only
Visit Skärgården
Kungsträdgården
Waxholm
boats
Nordiska Muséet
Djurgårdsbrunnsviken
ROSENDALSVÄGEN
Nationalmuseum
HOLMEN
Östasiatiska Muséet
Vasamuséet
Skänsén
DJURGÅRDEN
Arkitekturmuséet
Estonia
Memorial
Kungliga
Slottet
Moderna Muséet
SKEPPSHOLMEN
Tyska
kyrkan
KASTELLHOLMEN
Gröna
Lunds
Tivoli
SEE SÖDERMALM MAP
All year
BECKHOLMEN
Stadsmuséet
Slussen
Fotografiska Muséet
Saltsjön
KATARINAVÄGEN
Viking Line Terminal
(ferries to Helsinki,
Turku & Mariehamn)
Katarina kyrka

ACCOMMODATION	
Af Chapman	17
Ängby Camping	14
Bema	7
Best Western Time	1
Bredäng Camping	15
City Backpackers	8
Connect City	9
Diplomat	11
Fridhemsplan	13
Gärdet	4
Hellsten	2
Kungsbron	12
Micro	5
Rex/Rex Petit	3
Skeppsholmen	16
Stockholm Hostel	10
Wasa Park	6

1

with other towns of the Hanseatic League, such as Hamburg, that helped give Stockholm, rather than Sigtuna, its prominent position within the Swedish realm during the fourteen and fifteenth centuries. Following the breakup of the Kalmar Union with Denmark, Swedish king Gustav Vasa established royal power in Stockholm, enabling the city to grow into the capital of one of Europe's major powers by the seventeenth century. Military defeat by Russia in the Great Northern War (1700–21) put paid to Swedish territorial expansion in northern and eastern Europe, and, instead, Stockholm developed politically and culturally at the centre of a smaller Swedish state.

By the nineteenth century, Stockholm was still essentially rural with country lanes, great orchards, grazing cows and even windmills in the centre of the city; the downside was the lack of pavements (until the 1840s) or piped water supply (until 1858), and the presence of open sewers, squalid streets and crowded slums. Having escaped bomb damage during World War II thanks to Swedish neutrality, the mid-twentieth century ushered in a huge **modernization** programme as part of the Social Democratic out-with-the-old-and-in-with-the-new policy: Sweden, and particularly the capital, Stockholm, was to become a place fit for working people to live. Old areas were torn down as "a thousand homes for a thousand Swedes" – as the project had it – were constructed. Today, Stockholm is a bright and elegant place, and with its great expanses of open water right in the centre, it offers a spectacular city panorama unparalleled anywhere in Europe.

Old Stockholm: Gamla Stan and around

Three islands – Riddarholmen, Staden and Helgeandsholmen – make up the **oldest part of Stockholm**, a cluster of seventeenth- and eighteenth-century buildings backed by hairline medieval alleys. It was on these three adjoining polyps of land that Birger Jarl erected the town's first fortifications. Rumours abound as to the derivation of the name "Stockholm", though it's now widely believed to mean "island cleared of trees", since the trees on the island that is now home to Gamla Stan were probably felled to make way for the settlement. Incidentally, the words *holm* (island) and *stock* (log) are still in common use today. You can experience a taste of Stockholm's medieval past at the excellent **Medeltidsmuseum**, at the northern end of the two bridges – Norrbron and Riksbron – which lead across to Gamla Stan.

Although strictly speaking only the largest island, Staden, contains **Gamla Stan**, this name is usually attached to the buildings and streets of all three islands. Once Stockholm's working centre, nowadays Gamla Stan is primarily a tourist city with many an eminently strollable area, in particular around the **Kungliga Slottet** (royal palace), **Riksdagshuset** (parliament building) and **Storkyrkan** (cathedral). The central spider's web of streets – best approached over the bridges of Norrbron or Riksbron – is a sprawl of monumental buildings and high airy churches which form a protective girdle around the narrow lanes. Some of the impossibly slender alleys lead to steep steps ascending between battered walls, others are covered passageways linking leaning buildings. The tall, dark houses in the centre were mostly owned by wealthy merchants, and are still distinguished by their intricate doorways and portals bearing coats of arms. The main square of the Old Town is **Stortorget**, an impressive collection of tall pastel-coloured stone buildings with curling gables which saw one of the medieval city's most ferocious battles, the "Stockholm Bloodbath" (see p.357). Off the western shore of Gamla Stan, the tiny islet of **Riddarholmen** houses not only one of Stockholm's most beautiful churches, **Riddarholmskyrkan**, the burial place for countless Swedish kings and queens over the centuries, but also the Baroque **Riddarhuset** (House of the Nobility), a reminder of the glory days of the Swedish aristocracy.

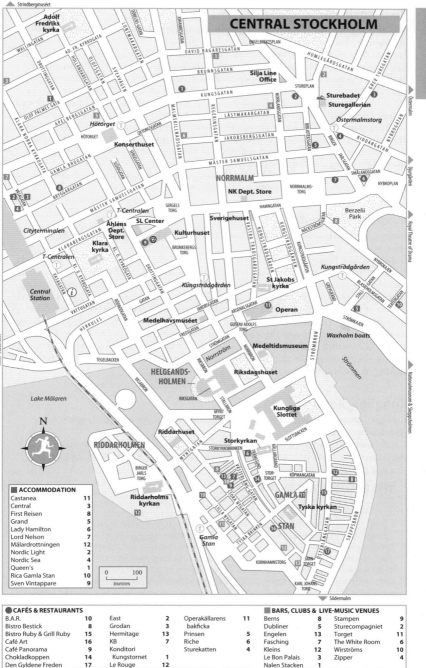

CENTRAL STOCKHOLM

ACCOMMODATION

Castanea	11
Central	3
First Reisen	8
Grand	5
Lady Hamilton	6
Lord Nelson	7
Mälardrottningen	12
Nordic Light	2
Nordic Sea	4
Queen's	1
Rica Gamla Stan	10
Sven Vintappare	9

CAFÉS & RESTAURANTS

B.A.R.	10	East	2	Operakällarens	11
Bistro Bestick	8	Grodan	3	bakficka	
Bistro Ruby & Grill Ruby	15	Hermitage	13	Prinsen	5
Café Art	16	KB	7	Riche	6
Café Panorama	9	Konditori		Sturekatten	4
Chokladkoppen	14	Kungstornet	1		
Den Gyldene Freden	17	Le Rouge	12		

BARS, CLUBS & LIVE-MUSIC VENUES

Berns	8	Stampen	9
Dubliner	5	Sturecompagniet	2
Engelen	13	Torget	11
Fasching	7	The White Room	6
Kleins	12	Wirströms	10
Le Bon Palais	3	Zipper	4
Nalen Stacken	1		

1

Riksdagshuset

Parliament building • Riksgatan 1 • Mid-June to late Aug guided tours in English Mon–Fri noon, 1, 2 & 3pm; late-Aug to mid-June Sat & Sun 1.30pm • Free • Gamla Stan T-bana

Perched on Helgeandsholmen, a small oval-shaped island wedged between Norrmalm to the north and Gamla Stan to the south, **Riksdagshuset,** the Swedish Parliament building, is where Sweden's famous welfare state was shaped and formed during the postwar years of the 1940s and 1950s. The building was completely restored in the 1970s, just seventy years after it was built, and the original, columned facade (viewed to best effect from Norrbron) is rarely used as an entrance today; the main entrance is on Riksgatan, the short street between the bridges of Riksbron and Stallbron. It's the glassy bulge at the back (which you see when coming into Stockholm from the south by train) that is the hub of most activity, and where you're shown round on **guided tours**. This being Sweden, the seating for the 349 members is in healthy, non-adversarial rows, grouped by constituency and not by party, and it is has even been known for politicians to breastfeed their children in the chamber.

Medeltidsmuseum

Museum of Medieval Stockholm • Strömparterren • Daily noon–5pm, Wed until 7pm • Free • Ⓦ medeltidsmuseet.stockholm.se • T-Centralen T-bana

In front of the Riksdag, accessed by a set of steps leading down from Norrbron, is the **Medeltidsmuseum**, where medieval ruins, tunnels and parts of Stockholm's city walls dating from the 1530s, discovered during excavations under the parliament building, have been incorporated into a walk-through underground exhibition. Reconstructed houses of timber and brick, complete with wax models peering out of the windows, help give a realistic idea of what life was like in sixteenth-century Stockholm. However, it's the extensive remains of the *Riddarholm* ship, 20m in length and dating from the early 1520s, which really draws the eye. Built in overlapping clinker-style, common during Viking times, the ship had been equipped with canons and lead shot before sinking in the Riddarholm canal in the 1520s.

Kungliga Slottet

Royal Palace • Slottsbacken • The Apartments, Treasury and Museum Tre Kronor offer a combined entry ticket costing 150kr • Ⓦ royalcourt.se • Gamla Stan T-bana

Cross Norrbron or Riksbron from the Riksdagshuset and up rears the most distinctive monumental building in Stockholm, **Kungliga Slottet** – a low, square,

---

THE ESTONIA FERRY DISASTER

The sinking of the *Estonia* ferry in September 1994 was Sweden's worst ever maritime disaster; 852 people lost their lives when the vessel went down in the Baltic Sea en route to Stockholm.

Following the disaster, an official three-nation investigation involving Sweden, Finland and Estonia concluded, to great derision from the relatives of those who died on the ferry, that poor design by the original German shipbuilders of the huge hinges which held the bow door in place was to blame for the accident. The shipyard immediately refuted the claim and said that fault lay squarely with the ferry operator, Estline, for shoddy maintenance of the vessel. Following the publication of the official accident report, a number of conspiracy theories have surfaced, most alarmingly suggesting that the Russian mafia had weapons on board, exploding a bomb on the car deck once it became clear that Swedish customs had been tipped off about their illicit cargo and imminent arrival in Stockholm. The wreck of the **Estonia** now lies on the sea bed southwest of the Finnish Åland islands, covered in a protective layer of concrete to prevent plundering. There's a memorial to those who died in the disaster near the Vasamuséet in Djurgården (see p.60).

1

yellowy-brown construction, with two arms that stretch down towards the water. Stockholm's old Tre Kronor (Three Crowns) castle burnt down at the beginning of King Karl XII's reign (1697–1718), leaving his architect, Tessin the Younger (see p.369), a free hand to design a simple and beautiful Baroque structure in its stead. Finished in 1754, the palace is a striking achievement: uniform and sombre outside, but with a magnificent Rococo interior that's a swirl of staterooms and museums. Its sheer size is quite overwhelming and it's worth focusing your explorations on one or two sections of the palace.

Palace Apartments and Treasury
Mid-May to Sept daily 10am–5pm; Oct to mid-May Tues–Sun noon–4pm • 100kr, Treasury 90kr

The rooms of state used for royal receptions are known as the **Palace Apartments**. They hold a relentlessly linear collection of furniture and tapestries, all too sumptuous to take in and inspirational only in terms of their colossal size. The **Treasury**, on the other hand, is certainly worth a visit for its ranks of jewel-studded crowns. The oldest one was made in 1650 for Karl X, while the two smaller ones belonged to princesses Sofia (1771) and Eugène (1860).

Armoury
Slottsbacken 3 • June–Aug daily 10am–6pm; Sept–May Tues–Sun 11am–5pm, Thurs until 8pm • 80kr • ⓦ livrustkammaren.se

The **Armoury** is not so much about weapons as ceremony – with suits of armour, costumes and horse-drawn carriages from the sixteenth century onwards. Also on display is the stuffed horse of King Gustav II Adolf, who died in the Battle of Lützen in 1632, and the king's blood- and mud-spattered garments, retrieved after the enemy had stripped him on the battlefield.

Museum Tre Kronor
Slottskajen • Mid-May to mid-Sept daily 10am–5pm; mid-Sept to mid-May Tues–Sun noon–4pm • 100kr • Gamla Stan T-bana

If you're a real palace junkie, check out the **Museum Tre Kronor** at Slottskajen in front of the Kungliga Slottet where you'll find part of the original Tre Kronor castle, its ruins underneath the present building.

Myntkabinett
Royal Coin Cabinet • Slottsbacken 6 • Daily 10am–4pm • 70kr, free on Mon • ⓦ myntkabinettet.se • Gamla Stan T-bana

A veritable stash of coins, banknotes and medals from across the centuries, as well as a number of silver hoards from Viking days, the **Myntkabinett** boasts over 600,000 items in its collection and is worth a quick look if money is your thing. The most engaging exhibition is the section devoted to Sweden's own coins, from the very first ones minted under King Olof Skötkonung to those of today.

Storkyrkan
Trångsund 1 • July–Aug Mon–Sat 9am–6pm, Sun 9am–4pm; Sept–May daily 9am–4pm • 40kr • Gamla Stan T-bana

South of Kungliga Slottet, the streets suddenly narrow and darken and you're into Gamla Stan proper. The highest point of the old part of Stockholm is crowned by **Storkyrkan**, built in 1279, and almost the first building you'll stumble upon. Pedantically speaking, Stockholm has no cathedral, but this rectangular brick church is now accepted as such, and the monarchs of Sweden married and were crowned here. Storkyrkan gained its present shape at the end of the fifteenth century following a series of earlier alterations and additions, but was given a Baroque remodelling in the 1730s to better fit in with the new palace taking shape next door. The interior is marvellous: twentieth-century restoration has removed the white plaster from its

1

red-brick columns, giving a warm colouring to the rest of the building. Much is made of the fifteenth-century Gothic sculpture of St George and the Dragon (see p.357), certainly an animated piece but easily overshadowed by the royal pews – more like golden billowing thrones – and the monumental black-and-silver altarpiece. Fans of organ music will enjoy the recitals that often take place on Thursdays at 8pm (50kr).

Stortorget

Stortorget, Gamla Stan's main square, one block south of Storkyrkan along either Trångsund or Källargränd, is a handsome and elegantly proportioned space crowded with eighteenth-century buildings. In 1520, Christian II used the square as an execution site during the "Stockholm Bloodbath" (see p.357), dispatching his opposition en masse with bloody finality. Now, as then, the streets **Västerlånggatan**, **Österlånggatan**, **Stora Nygatan** and **Lilla Nygatan** run the length of the Old Town, although today their time-worn buildings harbour a succession of art-and-craft shops and restaurants. Happily, the consumerism here is largely unobtrusive, and in summer buskers and evening strollers clog the narrow alleyways, making it an entertaining place to wander or to stop for a bite to eat. There are few real targets, though at some stage you'll probably pass **Köpmantorget** square (off Österlånggatan), where there's a replica of the George and Dragon statue inside the Storkyrkan. Take every opportunity, too, to wander up side streets, where you'll find fading coats of arms, covered alleys and worn cobbles at every turn.

Tyska kyrkan

German Church • On Kindstugatan, just off Västerlånggatan • May–Aug Mon–Sat 11am–5pm, Sun 12.30–5pm; Sept–April Sat & Sun noon–4pm • Free • Gamla Stan T-bana

Once belonging to Stockholm's medieval German merchants, **Tyska kyrkan** served as the meeting place of the Guild of St Gertrude. A copper-roofed red-brick building atop a rise, it was enlarged in the seventeenth century when Baroque decorators got hold of it: the result, a richly fashioned interior with the pulpit dominating the nave, is outstanding. The royal gallery in one corner – designed by Tessin the Elder – adds to the overall elegance of this church, one of Stockholm's most impressive.

Riddarhuset

House of the Nobility • Riddarhustorget 10 • Mon–Fri 11.30am–12.30pm • 50kr • ⓦ riddarhuset.se • Gamla Stan T-bana

From Storkyrkan, it's a five-minute stroll west along Storkyrkobrinken to the handsome, seventeenth-century Baroque **Riddarhuset**. Its Great Hall was used by the Swedish aristocracy for two hundred years for parliamentary debate until a law was passed in 1865 to create Sweden's current two-chamber parliament. The nobility's coats of arms – around two and a half thousand of them – are splattered across the walls. Take a peek at the Chancery downstairs, which stores heraldic bone china by the shelf-load and has racks full of fancy signet rings – essential accessories for the eighteenth-century noble-about-town.

Riddarholmen and Riddarholmskyrkan

Birger Jarls torg 3 • Mid-May to Sept daily 10am–5pm • 30kr • Gamla Stan T-bana

Riddarhuset shouldn't really be seen in isolation. It's only a matter of seconds to cross the bridge onto **Riddarholmen**, and thus to **Riddarholmskyrkan.** Originally a Franciscan monastery, the church has been the burial place of Swedish royalty for over six centuries. Since Magnus Ladulås was sealed up here in 1290, his successors have rallied round to create a Swedish royal pantheon. Amongst others, you'll find the tombs of Gustav II Adolf (in the green marble sarcophagus), Karl XII, Gustav III and Karl Johan XIV, plus other innumerable and unmemorable descendants. Walk around the back of the church for stunning views of Stadshuset and Lake Mälaren. In winter, the lake often freezes from here right up to the Västerbron bridge, a couple of kilometres further west, and people skate and take their dogs for walks along the ice.

1

Skeppsholmen

A 10min walk from Stortorget: cross Strömbron, turn right and cross Skeppsholmsbron; you can also take a ferry from Nybroplan (see p.56) or bus #65 from Central Station

Off Gamla Stan's eastern reaches lies the island of **Skeppsholmen**, home to two of Stockholm's best youth hostels. However, it's the eclectic clutch of **museums**, the first of which, the Nationalmuseum, is actually just before Skeppsholmsbron, that draw most people here.

Nationalmuseum

National Art Museum • Södra Blasieholmshamnen 2 • June–Aug Tues 11am–8pm, Wed–Sun 11am–5pm; Sept–May Wed & Fri–Sun 11am–5pm, Tues & Thurs until 8pm • 100kr • ⓦ nationalmuseum.se • Expected to close during 2012 for renovation work • Kungsträdgården T-bana

As you approach Skeppsholmsbron on the way to Skeppsholmen, you'll pass the striking waterfront **Nationalmuseum**, which contains an impressive collection of Swedish and European fine and applied arts from the late medieval period to the present day, contained on three floors.

Changing exhibitions of prints and drawings take up the **ground floor** as well as several permanent frescoes by Swedish painter Carl Larsson which adorn the six wall panels of the museum's lower staircase. There is also a museum shop and a decent café, plus lockers to leave your bags in on the ground floor.

First floor

The Nationalmuseum's **first floor** is devoted to applied art, and those with a penchant for royal curiosities will be pleased to find beds slept in by kings, cabinets leaned on by queens and plates eaten off by nobles, mainly from the centuries when Sweden was a great power. There's modern work alongside the ageing tapestries and furniture, including Art Nouveau coffeepots and vases, and a collection of simply and elegantly designed wooden chairs.

Second floor

It's the **second floor** that's most engaging – there's a plethora of European and Mediterranean sculpture, along with some mesmerizing sixteenth- and seventeenth-century Russian icons. The **paintings** on this floor include works by El Greco, Canaletto, Gainsborough, Gauguin, Rembrandt and Renoir. Something of a coup for the museum is Rembrandt's *Conspiracy of Claudius Civilis*, one of his largest monumental paintings. Depicting a scene from Tacitus' *History*, this bold work shows a gathering of well-armed chieftains. There are also some fine works by Swedish artists from the sixteenth to early twentieth centuries – most notably paintings by the nineteenth-century masters Anders Zorn and Carl Larsson. Another, by Carl Gustav Pilo, a late eighteenth-century painter, depicts the coronation of Gustav III in Gamla Stan's Storkyrkan; it's worth noting that the white plaster depicted on the columns in the painting has today been removed to expose the underlying red brick.

1

Moderna Muséet

Modern Art Museum • Exercisplan 2 • Tues 10am–8pm, Wed–Sun 10am–6pm • 100kr; 140kr with Arkitekturmuséet • ⓦ modernamuseet .se • Kungsträdgården T-bana

On Skeppsholmen itself, Stockholm's **Moderna Muséet** is one of the better modern art collections in Europe, with a comprehensive selection of work by some of the twentieth century's leading artists divided into three periods: 1900–39, 1940–69 and 1970 to the present day. Take a look at Dali's monumental *Enigma of William Tell*, showing the artist at his most conventionally unconventional, and Matisse's striking *Apollo*. Look out also for Picasso's *Guitar Player* and *Spring*, plus a whole host of Warhol, Lichtenstein, Kandinsky, Miró, Magritte and Rauschenberg.

Arkitekturmuséet

Architecture Museum • Exercisplan 4 • Tues 10am–8pm, Wed–Sun 10am–6pm • 60kr; 140kr with Moderna Muséet • ⓦ arkitekturmuseet .se • Kungsträdgården T-bana

Next door to the **Moderna Muséet** is the **Arkitekturmuséet**, serving up a taste of Swedish architecture through the ages in one of the most inspired buildings in the city – there are lots of glass walls and bright, airy exhibition space. The permanent exhibition, Architecture in Sweden – Function, Design and Aesthetic through the Ages, outlines some of the core themes of pan-Swedish architectural styles, and is housed alongside a number of temporary displays on construction styles.

Östasiatiska Muséet

Museum of Far Eastern Antiquities • Skeppsholmen 41 • Tues 11am–8pm, Wed–Sun 11am–5pm • 60kr • ⓦ ostasiatiska.se • Kungsträdgården T-bana

A steep climb up the northern tip of Skeppsholmen brings you to the **Östasiatiska Muséet**. A visit here is half a day well spent: you'll be rewarded by an array of objects displaying incredible craftsmanship, including many from China, the favourite hunting ground of Swedish archeologists. The two main exhibitions, "The Middle Kingdom" and "China before China", tackle 5000 years of imperial Chinese history through a series of engaging artefacts, including just about anything you care to mention in porcelain. There are fifth-century Chinese tomb figurines, intricate ceramics from the seventh century onwards and fine Chinese paintings on paper and silk. Alongside these, take a look at the astounding assembly of sixth-century Buddhas, Indian watercolours, gleaming bronze Krishna figures and a magnificent set of samurai armour, a gift from the Japanese crown prince in the 1920s.

The city centre: Norrmalm

Immediately to the north of Gamla Stan is the commercial heart of modern Stockholm, **Norrmalm**, a compact area full of shops and offices, restaurants, bars and cinemas, always bustling with people and street life – unfortunately, it also has a high count of ugly modern buildings.

Gustav Adolfs torg

Down on the waterfront, beside Norrbron, is **Gustav Adolfs torg**, more a traffic island than a square these days. A statue of King Gustav II Adolf marks the centre of the square, between the Opera and the Foreign Ministry opposite. Look out, too, for fishermen pulling salmon out of **Strömmen**, the fast-flowing stretch of water that winds its way through the centre of the city. Since the seventeenth century, Stockholmers have had the right to fish this outlet from Lake Mälaren to the Baltic; landing a catch here isn't as difficult as it looks, and there's usually a group of hopefuls on one of the bridges beside the square.

Kungliga Operan
Royal Opera House • Gustav Adolfs torg 2 • Ⓦ operan.se • T-Centralen T-bana

The nineteenth-century **Kungliga Operan** is the proudest, most notable – and ugliest – building on Gustav Adolfs torg. It was here, in an earlier opera house on the same site, that King Gustav III was shot at a masked ball in 1792 by one Captain Ankarström. The story is recorded in Verdi's opera *Un ballo in maschera*, and you'll find Gustav's ball costume, as well as the assassin's pistols and mask, displayed in the Palace Armoury in Gamla Stan (see p.49). The opera's famous restaurant, *Operakällaren* which faces the water, is ruinously expensive, its trendy café, *Bakfickan* (see p.70), less so.

Medelhavsmuséet
Museum of Mediterranean and Near Eastern Antiquities • Fredsgatan 2 • Tues–Thurs noon–8pm, Fri–Sun noon–5pm • 80kr • wmedelhavsmuseet.se • T-Centralen T-bana

Just off Gustav Adolfs torg, and surrounded by several government ministries, the **Medelhavsmuséet** contains an enormous display on Egypt, including several whopping great mummies; the most attractive pieces, though, are the bronze weapons, tools and domestic objects from the time before the pharaohs. The Cyprus collections are also huge, the largest such assemblage outside the island itself, depicting the island civilization over a period of six thousand years. A couple of rooms examine Islamic culture through pottery, glass and metalwork, as well as decorative elements from architecture, Arabic calligraphy and Persian miniature painting.

St Jakobs kyrka
Västra Trädgårdsgatan 2 • Tues–Thurs noon–4pm, Fri noon–6pm, Sat & Sun 2–6pm • Kungsträdgården T-bana

Though located in a prime position opposite the Royal Opera House, **St Jakobs kyrka** is often overlooked by visitors to the city. It stands on the site of an earlier chapel of St James (Jakob in Swedish) and was completed some 52 years after the death of its founder, Johan III. Although the church's doors are impressive – check out the south door with its statues of Moses and St James on either side – it's the great, golden pulpit that draws most attention. The date of the building's completion (1642) is stamped high up on the ceiling in gold relief. Organ recitals are occasionally held here, usually on Fridays at 5pm (free).

Kungsträdgården
Isbanan: Nov to early March Mon, Wed & Fri 8.30am–6pm, Tues & Thurs 8.30am–8pm, Sat & Sun 10am–6pm • Skate rental 50kr/hr

One block east of St Jakobs kyrka and the Royal Opera House, Norrmalm's eastern boundary is marked by **Kungsträdgården**, the most fashionable and central of the city's numerous parks, reaching northwards from the water as far as Hamngatan. The mouthful of a name literally means "the king's gardens", though if you're expecting perfectly designed flowerbeds and rose gardens you'll be disappointed – it's a pedestrianized paved square, albeit in the form of an elongated rectangle, with a couple of lines of elm and cherry trees, and its days as a royal kitchen garden are long gone. Today the area is Stockholm's main meeting place, especially in summer, when there's almost always something going on – free music, live theatre and other performances take place on the central open-air stage. There are also several popular **cafés**: the outdoors one off Strömgatan at Kungsträdgården's southern edge is popular in spring as a place for winter-weary Stockholmers to lap up the sunshine. In winter, the park is as busy as in summer: the **Isbanan**, an open-air ice rink at the Hamngatan end of the park, rents out skates.

1

North of the park, Hamngatan runs east to **Birger Jarlsgatan**, the main thoroughfare that divides Norrmalm from Östermalm.

Sergels torg to Hötorget

At the western end of Hamngatan, past the enormous NK department store, lies **Sergels torg**, the ugliest square in modern Stockholm. It's an open-air meeting area and venue for impromptu music performances or demonstrations.

Kulturhuset

Sergels torg 3 • June–Aug Tues–Fri 11am–6pm, Sat & Sun 11am–4pm; Sept–May Tues–Fri 11am–7pm, Sat & Sun 11am–5pm; **café** Tues–Fri 11am–8pm, Sat 11am–6pm, Sun 11am–5pm • Free, but fees for exhibitions • T-Centralen T-bana

Sergel torg's events are centred around **Kulturhuset**, whose windows overlook the milling concrete square below. Inside this building, devoted to contemporary Swedish culture, are temporary art-and-craft exhibitions and a great design store. As you come in, check with the information desk for details of poetry readings, concerts and theatre performances. Before leaving, make sure you head up to the top floor and the *Panorama* **café** (see p.70), where you can indulge in delicious apple pie and custard, and take in the best **views** of central Stockholm.

Drottninggatan

A short walk along Klarabergsgatan, west of Kulturhuset, brings you to the **Centralstationen** and **Cityterminalen**, the main hub of Stockholm's transport. The area around here is given over to unabashed consumerism, but there's little to get excited about in the streets surrounding the main drag, **Drottninggatan**, just run-of-the-mill shops selling clothing and twee gifts, punctuated by a *McDonald's* and the odd sausage stand.

Klara kyrka

Klara Östra Kyrkogatan 7 • Mon–Fri & Sun 10am–5pm, Sat 5–7.30pm • T-Centralen T-bana

The area around Drottninggatan has one highlight in the **Klara kyrka**, just to the south of Klarabergsgatan. Hemmed in on all sides, with only the spires visible from the streets around, the church is particularly delicate, with a light and flowery eighteenth-century painted interior and an impressive golden pulpit. Out in the churchyard, a memorial stone commemorates the eighteenth-century Swedish poet Carl Michael Bellman, whose popular, lengthy ballads are said to have been composed extempore; his unmarked grave is somewhere in the churchyard.

Hötorget

Hötorget T-bana

Stockholm's main market square is the cobbled **Hötorget**, where you'll find a daily open-air fruit, vegetable and flower market (roughly 9am–5pm), as well as the wonderful **Hötorgshallen**, an indoor market boasting a tantalizing array of Middle Eastern sights and smells (Mon–Thurs 10am–6pm, Fri 10am–6.30pm, Sat 10am–4pm; June & July Sat till 3pm). The tall building across the square, PUB, is a former department store where **Greta Garbo** once worked (see box below). Hötorget is also

---

GRETA GARBO IN STOCKHOLM

Greta Garbo (1905–90) began her working life in Hötorget in Stockholm. She toiled as a sales assistant in the hat section of the PUB department store on the square before hitting the big time, acting in no fewer than 27 films. She spent most of her life in the United States, dying in New York in 1990, and it wasn't until 1999 that her ashes were returned to Stockholm after a long legal battle. Garbo is buried in the Skogskyrkogården cemetery in Enskede in the south of Stockholm (take the T-bana green line to the station called Skogskyrkogården to visit).

THE ASSASSINATIONS OF OLOF PALME AND ANNA LINDH

Adolf Fredriks kyrka is of immense significance to modern Swedes, as it is the final resting place of **Olof Palme**; a simple headstone and flowers mark his grave. The then prime minister of Sweden was gunned down in front of his wife on February 28 1986, while they were on the way home from the Riviera cinema on Sveavägen. As with most Nordic leaders, Palme's fame was his security, and he had no bodyguards with him when he died. A simple **plaque** on the pavement, often respectfully bedecked with flowers, now marks the spot, near the junction with Olof Palmes Gatan, where the prime minister was shot; the assassin escaped up a nearby flight of steps.

Sweden's biggest-ever murder enquiry was launched, and as the years went by, so the allegations of police cover-ups and bungling grew. When **Christer Pettersson**, a smalltime criminal, was convicted for the murder in July 1989, most Swedes thought that was the end of the story, but his release just five months later for lack of evidence only served to reopen the bitter debate, with consequent recriminations and resignations within a much-derided police force.

Palme's death sent shockwaves through a society unused to political extremism of any kind, and has sadly led to a radical rethink of the open-government policy Sweden had pursued for decades. Although government ministers now rarely go unescorted, Sweden was rocked by the news in September 2003 that a second leading politician had been murdered on home soil; Foreign Minister **Anna Lindh** was fatally stabbed in a Stockholm department store by a man with mental illness who was later arrested and imprisoned (see p.366).

home to Stockholm's biggest cinema complex, Filmstaden Sergel; to the east, **Kungsgatan**, running across to Stureplan and Birger Jarlsgatan, has most of the rest of the city's cinemas (see p.74), interspersed with agreeable little cafés and bars.

North of Hötorget

From Hötorget, the city's two main streets, **Drottninggatan** and **Sveavägen** – the latter with some excellent restaurants and bars – run parallel to the north as far as Odengatan and the Stadsbiblioteket (City Library), set in a little park.

Adolf Fredriks kyrka

Holländargatan 14 • Mon 1–7pm, Tues–Sun 10am–4pm • Hötorget T-bana.

In secluded gardens on Sveavägen, not far north of Hötorget, sits eighteenth-century **Adolf Fredriks kyrka**, its churchyard popular with lunching office workers. Although the church has a noteworthy past – the French philosopher Descartes was buried in the church's cemetery for eleven years before his body was taken back to France in 1661 – it would have remained unremarkable were it not for one of the most tragic, and still unexplained, events in modern Swedish history: the murder of the former prime minister **Olof Palme** in 1986 (see box above).

Strindbergsmuséet

Strindberg Museum • Drottninggatan 85 • Tues–Sun noon–4pm, July & Aug from 10am • 50kr • ⓦ strindbergsmuseet.se • Rådmansgatan T-bana

At the northern end of Drottninggatan, you'll come to the intriguing **Strindbergsmuséet** in the "Blue Tower", the last building in which the writer August Strindberg lived in Stockholm between 1908 and 1912. The house is so carefully preserved that you must put plastic bags over your shoes on entering to protect the floors and furnishings. The study is a dark and gloomy place just as Strindberg left it on his death; he always wrote with the Venetian blinds and heavy curtains closed against the sunlight. Upstairs, his library is a musty room with all the books firmly behind glass, which is a great shame as Strindberg was far from a passive reader. He underlined heavily and criticized in the margins as he read, though rather less eruditely than you'd expect – "Lies!", "Crap!", "Idiot!" and "Bloody hell!" tended to be his favourite comments.

1

Kungsholmen

To the west of the city centre, **Kungsholmen** has a very different feel, with wider, residential streets, larger parks, select shops and Stockholm's Stadshuset. Whereas Norrmalm is easy to get to on foot, Kungsholmen is best reached by T-bana (either Rådhuset or Fridhemsplan T-bana stations). Venture further into Kungsholmen and you'll discover a rash of great new bars and restaurants (see p.69), and an excellent **beach** at Smedsudden (bus #4 to Västerbroplan, then a 5min walk). There's also the popular park, **Rålambshovsparken**; head through it to get to Smeduddsbadet, where you can swim in Lake Mälaren and enjoy fantastic views of the Stadhuset and the Old Town.

Stadshuset

City Hall • Hantverkargatan 1 • Daily: June–Aug guided tours every 30min 9.30am–4pm; Sept–May hourly 10am–3pm • April–Oct 90kr, Nov–March 60kr • **Tower** Daily: May & Sept 9am–4pm; June–Aug 9am–5pm • 40kr • ⓦ stockholm.se/cityhall • T-Centralen T-bana

Finished in 1923, **Stadshuset** is one of the landmarks of modern Stockholm and one of the first buildings you'll see when approaching the city from the south by train. Its simple if somewhat drab exterior brickwork is no preparation for the intriguing detail inside. If you're a visiting head of state you'll be escorted from your boat up the elegant waterside steps; for lesser mortals, the only way to view the innards is on one of the guided tours, which reveal the kitschy Viking-style legislative chamber and impressively echoing Golden Hall. Whilst here, it's worth climbing the steps to the top of the **tower** for a wonderful aerial view of the city centre and Lake Mälaren. The Stadshuset is also the departure point for **ferries** to Drottningholm, Birka, Mariefred and Gripsholm, Sigtuna and Uppsala.

Östermalm

East of Birger Jarlsgatan, the streets become noticeably broader and grander, forming a uniform grid as far as Karlaplan. **Östermalm** was one of the last areas of central Stockholm to be developed; the impressive residences here are as likely to be consulates and embassies as fashionable homes.

Nybroplan

Djurgården ferry: daily 7.30am–1am; every 15min • 40kr one-way • Östermalmstorg T-bana

The first place to head for in Östermalm is **Nybroplan**, a square at the water's edge, a ten-minute walk just east along Hamngatan from Sergels torg and marked by the white-stone **Kungliga Dramatiska Teatern**, Stockholm's showpiece Royal Dramatic Theatre, and more commonly known as Dramaten. The curved harbour in front is the departure point for all kinds of archipelago **ferries** and tours (see p.84), including a summertime (June–Aug) ferry operated by Strömma Kanalbolaget that makes the short journey to Djurgården via Skeppsholmen.

Östermalmstorg

Östermalmshallen: Nybrogatan 31 • Mon–Thurs 9.30am–6pm, Fri 9.30am–7pm, Sat 9.30am–4pm • Östermalmstorg T-bana

From the theatre continue up the hill of Sibyllegatan and you'll reach **Östermalmstorg**, an elegant square that's home to the somewhat ritzy **Östermalmshallen**, a wonderful indoor food market. Although it looks very similar to Norrmalm's Hötorgshallen, the items here are more akin to what you might find in a smart delicatessen, along with various oddities including reindeer hearts and the wicked-smelling *surströmming* (fermented Baltic herring). Wander round at lunchtime and you'll spot well-heeled ladies and gents sipping Chardonnay and munching on shrimp sandwiches.

Historiska Muséet

Museum of National Antiquities • Narvavägen 13–17 • May–Sept daily 10am–5pm; Oct–April Tues–Sun 11am–5pm, Thurs until 8pm • 70kr • ⓦ historiska.se • From Norrmalm, hop on bus #56, which runs there from Central Station via Stureplan and Linnégatan

As you wend your way around Östermalm's well-to-do streets, sooner or later you're bound to end up at the circular **Karlaplan**, a handy T-bana and bus interchange full of media types coming off shift from the Swedish Radio and Television buildings at the eastern end of Karlavägen. From here, it's a short walk down Narvavägen – or you can jump on a #44 bus – to the **Historiska Muséet**, the most wide-ranging historical display in Stockholm, covering a period of ten thousand years from the Stone Age to the Middle Ages with extensive displays of battles, beliefs and trading patterns. In particular, the exhibition of medieval church art, containing a breathtaking array of ornately decorated triptychs from across the country, is sure to impress.

The Viking Age

The section devoted to Sweden's **Viking** past is particularly engaging and informative in its efforts to portray Scandinavia's former inhabitants not as warriors but as farmers and tradesmen. Exhibits feature a magnificent 2.5m-high "picture stone" from Gotland showing the entry of Viking warriors into Valhalla plus Sweden's best-preserved Viking-age boat, dated at around 1000 years old, which was discovered near Uppsala alongside a decapitated stallion and a greyhound, which were to accompany the body found in the boat into the afterlife. There's a lifelike model of the village of Birka (see p.86), too, complete with an animated film showing daily life.

The Gold Room

It's the **Gold Room**, in the basement, with a magnificent 52kg of gold and 200kg of silver including several fifth-century gold collars and other fine pieces of jewellery, that really steals the show. One of the collars is thought to have been worn by a king in the province of Västergötland and features seven rings superimposed on each other, all magnificiently adorned with soldered figures.

Millesgården

Carl Milles Väg 2 • Mid-May to Sept daily 11am–5pm; Oct to mid-May Tues–Sun 11am–5pm • 95kr • ⓦ millesgarden.se • Take the T-bana to Ropsten, then the Lidingöbanan train over the bridge to Torsvikstorg, and walk down Herserudsvägen

Northeast of the city centre, Lidingö is a commuter island close to the ferry terminals serving Finland, Estonia and Latvia. The residential district of Stockholm's well-to-do, the island is home to the startling **Millesgården**, the outdoor sculpture collection of **Carl Milles** (1875–1955), one of Sweden's greatest sculptors and art collectors.

Phalanxes of gods, angels and beasts sit on terraces carved into the island's steep cliffs, many of the animated, classical figures also perching precariously on soaring pillars, which overlook the distant harbour. A huge *Poseidon* rears over the army of sculptures, the most remarkable of which, *God's Hand*, has a small boy delicately balancing on the outstretched finger of a monumental hand. Those who've been elsewhere in Sweden may find much of the collection familiar, as it includes copies and casts of originals adorning countless provincial towns. If this collection inspires, it's worth tracking down three other pieces by Milles in the capital – his statue of Gustav Vasa in the Nordiska Muséet on Djurgården (see p.58); the Orpheus Fountain in Norrmalm's Hötorget; and, out at Nacka Strand (Waxholm boat from Strömkajen), the magnificent *Gud på*

1

Himmelsbågen, a claw-shaped vertical piece of steel topped with the figure of a boy, forming a stunning entrance marker to Stockholm harbour.

Djurgården

You can walk here through the centre along Strandvägen, but it's quite a hike – around 30min from Sergels torg to the Djurgårdsbron bridge across to the island. Using public transport, take bus #44 from Karlaplan; from Norrmalm, bus #69, the Djurgården tram or the ferry from Nybroplan (Jun–Aug only; see p.56); or from Gamla Stan, the ferry from Skeppsbron (all year; see p.65)

East of Gamla Stan and south of Östermalm, occupying a forested island in Stockholm harbour, **Djurgården** (pronounced "Yoor-gorden") is Stockholm's most enjoyable city park. This finger-shaped island stretches over 3km in length from Djurgårdsbron bridge in the west (linking it to Strandvägen in Östermalm) to Blockhusudden point in the east. Royal hunting grounds throughout the sixteenth to eighteenth centuries, Djurgården is a perfect place to escape the bustle of the capital amongst the groves of pines and spruce, and is also home to some of Stockholm's finest **museums**. A full day is just about enough to see everything.

Nordiska Muséet

Nordic Museum • Djurgårdsvägen 6 • June–Aug daily 10am–5pm; Sept–May Mon–Fri 10am–4pm, Wed until 8pm, Sat & Sun 11am–5pm • 80kr • ⓦ nordiskamuseet.se

The palatial **Nordiska Muséet**, just over Djurgårdsbron from Strandvägen, provides a good grounding to what has made the Swedish nation tick over generations. The displays of trends and traditions are a valiant attempt to represent the last five hundred years of Swedish cultural history and folk art in an accessible fashion, with household furniture, items of clothing and other bits and bobs for perusal. On the ground floor of the cathedral-like interior, you can't fail to spot Carl Milles's phenomenal oak statue of Gustav Vasa (1496–1560), the sixteenth-century king who drove out the Danes (see p.357).

Skansen

Djurgårdsslätten 49–51 • Daily: May & Sept 10am–8pm; June–Sept 10am–10pm; Oct–April 10am–3pm • 70–130kr depending on time of year • ⓦ skansen.se

It's **Skansen**, a ten-minute walk south along Djurgårdsvägen from the Nordiska Muséet, that most people come to Djurgården for: a vast open-air museum with 150 reconstructed buildings, from a whole town square to windmills, farms and manor houses, laid out on a region-by-region basis. Each section boasts its own daily activities – including traditional handicrafts, games and displays – that anyone can join in. Best of the buildings are the warm and functional *Sámi* dwellings, and the craftsmen's workshops in the old-town quarter. You can also potter around a **zoo** (containing Nordic animals such as brown bears, elk and reindeer, as well as non-native species like monkeys), and an **aquarium** with poisonous snakes and turtles. Partly because of the attention paid to accuracy, and partly due to the admirable lack of commercialization, Skansen manages to avoid the tackiness associated with similar ventures in other countries. Even the snack bars dole out traditional foods and in winter serve up great bowls of warming soup.

Gröna Lunds Tivoli

Lilla Allmänna Gränd 9, immediately opposite Skansen's main gates and at the end of the #44 bus route • Daily: late April to Sept noon–10pm • 90kr; an optional all-day åkband pass costs 299kr for unlimited rides (219kr after 7pm) or alternatively you can pay per ride • ⓦ gronalund.com

Though Stockholm's main fairground is not a patch on its more famous namesake in Copenhagen, **Gröna Lunds Tivoli** is decidedly cleaner and less seedy. The talk of the

FROM TOP A SWING RIDE AT GRÖNA LUNDS TIVOLI(P.58); AERIAL VIEW OVER STOCKHOLM (P.40); RIDDARHUSET (P.50) >

1

place is still the ominous Fritt Fall, a hair-raising vertical drop of around 80m in a matter of seconds, and the Fritt Fall Tilt, which involves being catapulted face-first towards the ground from on high – do lunch later. At night the emphasis shifts as the park becomes the stomping ground for hundreds of Stockholm's teenagers.

Vasamuséet

Vasa Museum • Galärvarvsvägen 14 • June–Aug daily 8.30am–6pm; Sept–May Tues–Sun 10am–5pm, Wed until 8pm • 110kr • Ⓦ vasamuseet.se

Housed in an oddly shaped building close to Nordiska Muséet, **Vasamuséet** is without question head and shoulders above Stockholm's other museums. It contains the perfectly preserved seventeenth-century warship, the *Vasa*, which was built on the orders of King Gustav II Adolf, but sank in Stockholm harbour on her maiden voyage in 1628. A victim of engineering miscalculation, the *Vasa*'s hull was too narrow to withstand even the slightest swell which, when coupled with top-heavy rigging, made her a maritime disaster waiting to happen. On August 10 she went down with all hands barely a few hundred metres from her moorings. Preserved in mud for over three hundred years, the ship was raised along with twelve thousand objects in 1961, and now forms the centrepiece of the museum.

Adjacent to the Vasamuséet, three 2.5m-high granite walls now stand in the form of a triangle as a **memorial** to those who died in the *Estonia* ferry distaster in 1994 (see box, p.48); the inscription reads simply "their names and their fate, we shall never forget".

The museum

The museum itself is built over part of the old naval dockyard. Impressive though the building is, nothing prepares you for the sheer size of the **ship**: 62m long, the main mast originally 50m above the keel, it sits virtually complete in a cradle of supporting mechanical tackle. Surrounding walkways bring you nose-to-nose with cannon hatches and restored decorative relief, the gilded wooden sculptures on the soaring prow designed to intimidate the enemy and proclaim Swedish might. Carved into the ship's stern, the resplendent figures of two naked cherubs complete with podgy stomachs and rosy cheeks, proudly bearing the Swedish crown between them, are truly remarkable for their fine detail and garish colours. Adjacent **exhibition halls** and presentations on several levels take care of all the retrieved items, which give an invaluable insight into life on board – everything from combs to wooden barrels for preserving food supplies. There are reconstructions of life on board, detailed models of the *Vasa*, displays relating to contemporary social and political life, and a fascinating film of the rescue operation; between June and August there are also hourly English-language guided tours, which run less frequently at other times of the year.

Thielska Galleriet

Thiel Gallery • Sjötullsbacken 6–8 • Daily noon–4pm • 80kr • Ⓦ thielska-galleriet.se • Bus #69 from Norrmalm

At the far eastern end of Djurgården, known as Blockhusudden, the **Thielska Galleriet** is one of Stockholm's major treasures, a fine example of both Swedish architecture and Nordic art. The house was built by Ferdinand Boberg at the turn of the twentieth century for banker and art connoisseur Ernest Thiel, and turned into an art gallery after he sold it to the state in 1924. Thiel knew many contemporary Nordic artists personally and gathered an impressive collection of paintings over the years, many of which are on show today. There are works by Carl Larsson, Anders Zorn – most notably his portraits and female nudes – Edvard Munch, Bruno Liljefors and August Strindberg, whose paintings of wild Swedish landscapes are displayed. The museum enjoys a dramatic setting at the very tip of Djurgården; indeed the views out over Stockholm harbour and across to the district of Nacka on the southern shore warrant a trip out here.

Södermalm

On foot from Gamla Stan, head south along any of the parallel streets towards Kornhamnstorg or Järntorget squares, and continue past the Slussen T-bana station where Götgatan, Södermalm's main north–south thoroughfare, begins. By public transport, take bus #2 from Norrmalm, #3 from Kungsholmen or #53 from Central Station; get off either service at Folkungagatan; alternatively ride the T-bana to Medborgarplatsen or Mariatorget

Whatever you do in Stockholm, don't miss the delights of the city's southern island, **Södermalm**, whose craggy cliffs, turrets and towers rise high above the clogged traffic interchange at Slussen. The perched buildings are vaguely forbidding, but venture beyond the main roads skirting the island and a lively and surprisingly green area unfolds, one that is at heart emphatically working class. After dark, you'll probably end up in one of Söder's bars or restaurants (see p.71) in the hip area known as **So-Fo**; this is the handful of streets lined with cafés and restaurants which lie "**so**uth of **Fo**lkungagatan" (hence the name), predominantly Åsögatan, Bondegatan and Skånegatan. It's best to get your bearings on Södermalm during the day, though, as its grids of streets can become confusing in the dark.

Stadsmuséet

Stockholm City Museum • Södermalmstorg • Tues–Sun 11am–5pm, Thurs until 8pm • Free • Ⓦ stadsmuseum.stockholm.se • Slussen T-bana

In Södermalmstorg, right by the Slussen T-bana station, is the rewarding **Stadsmuséet**. The Baroque building, designed by Tessin the Elder and finished by his son in 1685, was once the town hall for this part of Stockholm; now it houses collections relating to the city's history as a seaport and industrial centre. However, the most engaging offerings are actually outside the museum: walking tours of Södermalm in the footsteps of Lisbet Salander and Mikael Blomkvist, the main characters of the Stieg Larsson *Millenium* novels, plus a chance to rediscover 1970s Stockholm with a walking tour devoted to key sites in ABBA's musical history.

SWEDEN'S FAB FOUR: ABBA

Overturning odds of 20–1, Anni-Frid Lyngstad, Benny Andersson, Björn Ulvæus and Agnetha Fältskog first came to the world's attention as they stormed to victory in April 1974 at the Eurovision Song Contest with *Waterloo*. **ABBA** went on to become the biggest-selling group in the world, topping the charts for a decade with hits like *Dancing Queen* (performed to celebrate the marriage of Swedish King Carl Gustaf to German commoner Silvia Sommerlath in 1976), *Mamma Mia* and *Money Money Money*, and became second only to Volvo as Sweden's biggest export earner. The winning combination led to a string of number-one hits and even a film, *ABBA – The Movie,* released to popular acclaim in 1978.

However, the relentless workload of recording and touring took its toll; frictions within the group surfaced and the two couples – Agnetha and Björn, and Anni-Frid and Benny – divorced and ABBA called it a day in 1983. News of the split was broken by the Swedish newspaper, *Dagens Nyheter* – Agnetha had casually dropped the bombshell into a conversation and to this day carries the blame for the break-up. Having withdrawn from public life, she now lives as a virtual recluse on the island of Ekerö in Lake Mälaren. Anni-Frid, on the other hand, married a German prince, lives in Switzerland and spends her time championing environmental causes. After a spell in Henley-on-Thames, near London, during the 1980s, Björn is now back in Stockholm where he partly owns the domestic airline, Nextjet, and writes and produces music with Benny, who's now opened his own hotel on Södermalm, *Rival* (see p.67). Together they've worked on a string of musicals including *Chess* and *Mamma Mia*, which uses 27 ABBA songs to tell the tale of the relationship between a mother and her daughter.

1

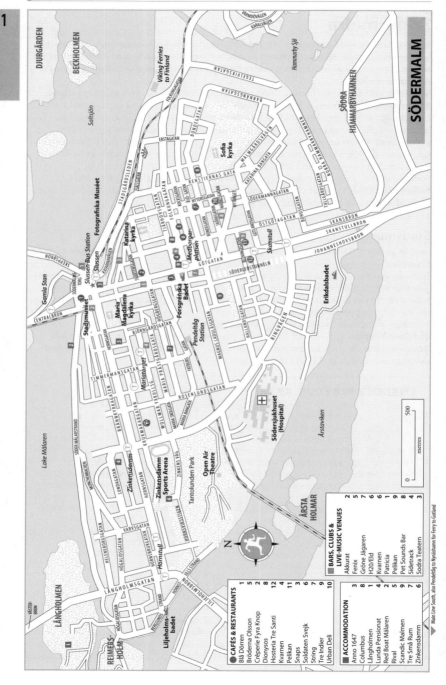

SÖDERMALM

DJURGÅRDEN

BECKHOLMEN

Saltsjön

VÄRMDÖVÄGEN
KANALVÄGEN

Viking Ferries
to Finland

Hammarby Sjö

SÖDRA
HAMMARBYHAMNEN

Gamla Stan

Lake Mälaren

LÅNGHOLMEN

REIMERS-
HOLME

ÅRSTA
HOLMAR

Årstaviken

Södersjukhuset
(Hospital)

Liljeholms-
badet

Open Air
Theatre

Tantolunden Park

Zinkensdamm
Sports Arena

Sofia
kyrka

Katarina
kyrka

Maria
Magdalena
kyrka

Stadsmuseet

Fotografiska Muséet

Slussen Bus Station

Medborgar-
platsen

Forsgrenska
Badet

Pendeltåg
Station

Eriksdalsbadet

Skanstull

Stadsgårdsleden

N

0   500   metres

● CAFÉS & RESTAURANTS
Blå Dörren   1
Bröderna Olsson   5
Créperie Fyra Knop   2
Dionysos   8
Hosteria Tre Santi   12
Kvarnen   4
Pelikan   11
Snaps   3
Soldaten Svejk   6
String   7
Tre Indier   9
Urban Deli   10

■ ACCOMMODATION
Anno 1647   3
Columbus   8
Långholmen   1
Lunda Pensionat   4
Red Boat Mälaren   2
Rival   5
Scandic Malmen   9
Tre Små Rum   7
Zinkensdamm   6

■ BARS, CLUBS &
LIVE-MUSIC VENUES
Akkurat   2
Fenix   5
Gröne Jägaren   7
H2O/Eld   6
Kvarnen   1
Patricia   9
Pelikan   8
Pet Sounds Bar   4
Sidetrack   4
Sodra Teatern   3

Main Line South, also Pendeltåg to Nynäshamn for ferry to Gotland

Fotografiska Muséet

Photographical Museum • Stora Tullhuset, Stadsgårdshamnen 22 • Daily 10am–9pm • 110kr • ⓦ fotografiska.eu • Slussen T-bana

A mere five minutes' walk from Slussen along Stadsgårdsleden towards the Viking Line ferry terminal, Stockholm's latest attraction, the **Fotografiska Muséet**, is housed inside one of the city's former red-brick customs warehouses. Spread across three floors of airy exhibition space, the museum showcases the work of world-renowned photographers both in print and on film. Exhibitions change frequently though there's every chance that one of the big names will be on display when you visit: recent displays have included Robert Mapplethorpe, France's Sarah Moon and Scottish photographer Albert Watson, whose work featured on over two hundred magazine covers, including *Vogue*. For unsurpassed views of the Stockholm waterfront, head up to the museum's top-floor **café** where the vistas are as breathtaking as the photographic work downstairs.

Katarina kyrka

Högbergsgatan 13 • Mon–Fri 11am–5pm, Sat & Sun 10am–5pm; Oct–March closed Mon • Medborgarplatsen T-bana

The Renaissance-style **Katarina kyrka** stands on the site where the victims of the so-called "Stockholm Bloodbath" (see p.357) – the betrayed nobility of Sweden who had opposed King Christian II's Danish invasion – were buried in 1520. They were burned as heretics outside the city walls, and it proved a vicious and effective coup, Christian disposing of the opposition in one fell swoop. In 1723, a devastating fire tore through the church, reducing it to ruins, an event that was repeated in 1990 when the building fell victim to another tragic blaze. Painstaking rebuilding work was finally completed five years later when the building reopened.

Mariatorget

Södermalm's main square, **Mariatorget**, is a pleasant leafy space surrounded by grand Art Nouveau buildings on all sides. This is one of the most desirable places for Stockholmers to live, close to the stylish bars and restaurants that are the favourite haunts of Stockholm's young and terminally hip, in particular Benny Andersson's *Rival* hotel and bar (see p.67).

Långholmen

Get to Långholmen by taking the T-bana to Hornstull and then following signs to the youth hostel, or on bus #4, which crosses Västerbron on its way from Södermalm, Kungsholmen, Norrmalm and Östermalm – incidentally, this bus ride is an excellent way of seeing a lot of the city for very little cost

True to its name, which means "long island", **Långholmen** is a skinny sliver of land that lies off the northwestern tip of Södermalm, crossed by the mighty Västerbron bridge linking Södermalm with Kungsholmen. There are a couple of popular **beaches** here (see box, p.74). Leafy and peaceful, Långholmen is a delightful place to take a walk; on the way you'll also get some stunning views of the city towards Stadhuset and Gamla Stan.

ARRIVAL AND DEPARTURE   **STOCKHOLM**

BY PLANE

Arlanda airport Most flights to Stockholm arrive at Arlanda airport (ⓣ 08 797 60 00, ⓦ arlanda.se/en), 45km north of Stockholm. Trains operate all day long every 15min from the two dedicated Arlanda Express stations beneath the airport (Arlanda Norra for Terminal 5, Arlanda Södra for the other terminals), the trip to Central Station in Stockholm taking just 20min (260kr one-way; ⓦ arlandaexpress.com).

The main company operating buses into Stockholm is Flygbussarna, who run all day to Stockholm's long-distance bus station, Cityterminalen, every 10–15min (40min; 119kr single; ⓦ flygbussarna.se). Taxis from the airport into town (30–40min) cost around 520kr. If you pick up a rental car and drive into central Stockholm you will be subject to a congestion charge; cameras register vehicles automatically and your credit card will be debited accordingly.

1

Bromma airport Some domestic flights and all flights with Brussels Airlines arrive at the more central Bromma airport, which is connected to Cityterminalen by Flygbussarna – buses run two to three times per hour (20min; 79kr single).

Ryanair airports Most of Ryanair's Stockholm flights arrive at Skavsta airport, 100km south of the capital close to the town of Nyköping, whilst others come in to Västerås, 100km west of Stockholm; Skavsta and Västerås buses operate in connection with flight arrival and departure times (both routes 1hr 20min; 139kr one-way).

BY TRAIN

By train, you'll arrive at Stockholm Central Station (the station is also known as Stockholm C, which is an abbreviation of "Central" in railspeak throughout Sweden), a cavernous structure on Vasagatan in the city centre. All branches of the Tunnelbana ("T-bana"), Stockholm's efficient metro system, meet at T-Centralen, the T-bana station directly below the main station.

Destinations Copenhagen (6 daily; 5hr); Gällivare (1 daily; 15hr); Gävle (hourly; 1hr 20min); Gothenburg (hourly; 3hr by X2000, 5hr by InterCity); Karlstad (9 daily; 2hr 30min); Kiruna (1 daily; 16hr); Läggesta (for Mariefred; hourly; 35min); Luleå (2 daily; 13hr 30min); Malmö (hourly; 4hr 20min); Mora (4 daily; 3hr 30min); Narvik (1 daily; 19hr); Nyköping (8 daily; 1hr); Oslo (2 daily; 6hr); Östersund (4 daily; 6hr 30min); Sundsvall (9 daily; 3hr 20min); Umeå (2 daily; 9hr 30min); Uppsala (every 20min; 40min); Västerås (hourly; 1hr).

BY BUS

By bus, your arrival point will be the huge glass structure known as Cityterminalen (☎08 762 59 97), a high-tech terminal adjacent to Central Station which handles all bus services. You can get to the northern end of Central Station's main hall using a series of escalators and walkways.

Destinations Gävle (1 daily; 4hr 30min); Gothenburg (10 daily; 7hr); Helsingborg (2 daily; 8hr 30min); Jönköping (2 daily; 5hr); Kalmar (2 daily; 6hr); Malmö (2 daily; 10hr); Norrköping (hourly; 1hr 20min); Östersund (1 daily; 8hr 30min); Umeå (1 daily; 9hr 20min).

GETTING AROUND

At first, Stockholm can be a confusing place, winding and twisting its way across islands, over water and through parkland. To get your bearings, the best bet is to walk: it takes about half an hour to cross central Stockholm on foot, from west to east or north to south. Sooner or later though, you'll probably want to use some form of transport. While routes are easy enough to master, it's best to avoid paying per trip on the city's transport system which can prove very expensive, and make use instead of the passes and discount cards available (see box below).

TRAVELCARDS

Buying a travelcard, available from Pressbyrå newsagents, SL-Centers and the ticket machines at T-bana stations, will save you time and money. First, buy SL's Access card (20kr), a smartcard onto which you load the travelcard you want: for example, 24hr (115kr), 72hr (215kr) or seven days (300kr); you are then entitled to unlimited travel by bus and T-bana plus the ferries to Djurgården.

BY BUS AND TRAIN

Storstockholms Lokaltrafik (SL; ⓦsl.se) operates a comprehensive system of buses and underground trains, which extends well out of the city centre. Its main information office is the SL-Center on the lower level of Stockholm C close to the entrance to the T-bana (Mon–Sat 6.30am–11.15pm, Sun 7am–11.15pm). It stocks timetables for the city's bus and T-bana systems and archipelago boats. Up-to-date information on the public transport system in English can also be obtained by phoning ☎08 600 10 00. Note that you can no longer purchase tickets with cash on the city's buses; buy a travelcard instead (see opposite).

THE TUNNELBANA

The quickest and most useful form of transport is the Tunnelbana (T-bana; ⓦsl.se), Stockholm's metro system, which comprises three main lines (red, green and blue). Station entrances are marked with a blue letter "T" on a white background. From Sunday to Thursday trains operate from around 5am until around midnight, but on Fridays and Saturdays – as well as the evening before a public holiday – there are services all through the night (roughly every 30–40min).

THE STOCKHOLM CARD

If you're planning to visit several museums, the best pass to have is the **Stockholm Card**, which gives unlimited travel on the T-bana, city buses and the Djurgården ferry, as well as free entry to around eighty museums and attractions. Cards are valid for 24, 48, 72 or 120 hours (425,550,650 and 895kr respectively) and are available from the tourist office or at ⓦvisitstockholm.com.

1

CANOEING IN STOCKHOLM

One of the most fun ways to see Stockholm is from the water. The best place in town to **rent boats** is *Djurgårdsbrons Sjöcafé*, at Galärvarvsvägen 2 (☎08 660 57 57), by the bridge across to Djurgården. It costs 400kr to rent a canoe for 24 hours, or 125kr/hr; kayaks cost 110kr/hr or 400kr/24hr. For canoes in the archipelago, try Skärgårdens Kanotcenter at Vegabacken 22 on Vaxholm (☎08 541 377 90, ⊛kanotcenter.com); take bus #670 from Tekniska Högskolan in Stockholm. Alternatively, ask locally on the other islands – corner shops often have a couple of canoes or boats for rent.

BUSES

Buses are often less direct than the metro because of the city's layout – route maps are available from the SL-Center (see opposite). Stockholm's buses are pushchair- and pram-friendly; a special area halfway down the bus is set aside for these. You can no longer buy tickets from the driver; get a travelcard instead (see opposite).

Night buses Replace the T-bana after midnight, except on Friday and Saturday (and the night before a public holiday), when it runs all night.

FERRIES AND BOATS

Ferries provide access to the sprawling archipelago, and sail from outside the *Grand Hotel* on Strömkajen (see p.66). They also link some of the central islands: Södermalm and Djurgården are connected with Nybroplan in Norrmalm (a small square behind the *Grand*) via the Vasa museum and Gröna Lund (June–Aug only); Djurgården is linked with Skeppsbron in Gamla Stan (year-round). For details of services to the archipelago, see p.84; for Birka see p.87; for Mariefred see p.88.

Boats on Lake Mälaren to Birka and Mariefred leave from outside Stadshuset on Kungsholmen.

BIKES, TAXIS AND CARS

Bike rental *Djurgårdsbrons Sjöcafé* at Galärvarvsvägen 2 (☎08 660 57 57), just over the bridge that leads to Djurgården, or from Servicedepån-Cykelstallet at Scheelegatan 15 on Kungsholmen (☎08 651 00 66, ⊛cykelstallet.se); reckon on paying 250kr/day.

Taxi ranks Several around the city (including one outside Central Station); you can also ring one of the three main operators: Taxi Stockholm (☎08 15 00 00, ⊛taxistockholm .se), Taxi Kurir (☎08 30 00 00, ⊛taxikurir.se) or Taxi 020 (☎020 20 20 20, ⊛taxi020.se). The meter will show around 45kr when you get in and will then race upwards at an alarming speed: 84kr for every 10km during the day (124kr per 10km on Fri & Sat nights and public holidays). A trip across the city centre will cost 100–200kr.

By car Be extremely careful when parking: see p.28. For car rental, see p.28 and be aware of the congestion charge in central Stockholm (see p.63).

INFORMATION

Tourist office Stockholm's tourist office (*turistbyrå*) is at Vasagatan 14, opposite Central Station (Mon–Fri 9am–7pm, Sat 10am–5pm, Sun 10am–4pm; ☎08 508 285 08, ⊛visitstockholm.com), which hands out fistfuls of free brochures, and carries the useful *What's On* (see below). You'll also be able to buy the Stockholm Card (see opposite), which can be invaluable if you're planning to visit several museums. **Listings information** *What's On*, free from the tourist office, is particularly good for all kinds of listings. It contains day-by-day information about a whole range of events

– gigs, theatre, festivals, dance – sponsored by the city, lots of which are free and based in Stockholm's many parks. There's also a free Saturday supplement to the *DN* newspaper, *På stan* – get someone to translate if your Swedish isn't up to it – that details all manner of entertainments, from the latest films to club listings; it's also available in bars and restaurants. **Gay information** A useful resource is RFSL (National Association for Sexual Equality), Sveavägen 59 ☎08 501 629 00, ⊛rfsl.se). The free newspaper, *QX* (⊛qx.se), available at gay bars and clubs, is handy for listings.

ACCOMMODATION

Stockholm has plenty of accommodation to suit every taste and pocket, from elegant upmarket hotels with waterfront views to youth hostels in unusual places – two are on boats and another is in a former prison. From mid-June to mid-August it is always a good idea to book your accommodation in advance, either directly with the hotel or hostel or through ⊛visitstockholm.com.

HOTELS AND PENSIONS

Summer in Stockholm means a buyer's market for hotel rooms as business travel declines; double rooms can cost as little as 495kr. The cheapest choices on the whole are found to the north of Cityterminalen in the streets to the west of Adolf Fredriks kyrka. Don't rule out the more expensive

1

places, however: there are some attractive weekend and summer prices that make a spot of luxury nearer the waterfront a little more affordable. All of the following establishments include breakfast in the price, unless otherwise stated.

GREATER STOCKHOLM

Bema Upplandsgatan 13 ☎ 08 23 26 75, ⓦ hotelbema .se; bus #65 from Central Station; map pp.44–45. A 10min walk from the station in a quiet residential area facing the leafy Tegnérlunden park, this small pension-style hotel has twelve en-suite rooms with beechwood furniture and modern Swedish decor. **850kr/1050kr**

Best Western Time Vanadisvägen 12 ☎ 08 545 473 00, ⓦ timehotel.se; Odenplan T-bana; map pp.44–45. Newly built hotel with around 150 contemporary, brightly decorated airy rooms featuring wooden floors and French balconies. Self-catering studios are also available. Rooms on the top floor have their own terrace. **1290kr/1850kr**

Connect City Ahlströmergatan 41 ☎ 08 441 02 20, ⓦ connecthotels.se; Fridhemsplan T-bana; map 44–45. A bright, airy and modern hotel on Kungsholmen with oak floors and fully tiled bathrooms. True, this hotel is never going to win any prizes for original design but at these prices it really doesn't matter. **760kr/1015kr**

Diplomat Strandvägen 7C ☎ 08 459 68 00, ⓦ diplomathotel.com; Östermalmstorg T-bana or bus #69; map 44–45. One of the city's top hotels, offering individually decorated rooms with wonderful views over Stockholm's inner harbour. Although the suites in this Art Nouveau town house don't come cheap, they represent much better value than the cheaper double rooms at the *Grand*. **1572kr/2422kr**

Hellsten Luntmakargatan 68 ☎ 08 661 86 00, ⓦ hellsten.se; Rådmansgatan T-bana; map 44–45. Dating from 1898, the original bourgeois family apartments in this building have been lovingly restored; some still have their tile stoves whilst others have been individually decorated with antique Asian or African furniture. **1090kr/2090kr**

Kungsbron Västra Järnvägsgatan 17 ☎ 08 654 28 00, ⓦ kungsbronhotel.se; T-Centralen T-bana; map 44–45. It's hard to get more central than this new budget design hotel right by Central Station. Rooms, both with and without windows, are on the small side, though tastefully decorated in modern Scandinavian style. **895kr**

Micro Tegnérlunden 8☎08 545 455 69, ⓦ hotelmicro .se; Rådmansgatan T-bana; map 44–45. Windowless cabin-style basement rooms with bunk beds and shared facilities, all decked out in bright marine colours, give this budget hotel a strangely maritime feel. Basic, maybe, but certainly a great money-saving option. **645kr**

Rex Luntmakargatan 73 ☎ 08 16 00 40, ⓦ rexhotel.se;

> ### TOP FIVE PLACES TO STAY
> **Af Chapman** p.67
> **Castanea** p.68
> **Rival** p.67
> **Sven Vintappare** p.67
> **Tre Små Rum** p.67

Rådmansgatan T-bana; map 44–45. The original pine floors and sweeping staircase from 1866 have been lovingly restored to create a sense of style and elegance throughout this tasteful hotel, whose rooms are topped off with granite bathrooms. **990kr/1890kr**

Rex Petit Luntmakargatan 73 ☎ 08 23 66 99, ⓦ rexpetit.se; Rådmansgatan T-bana; map 44–45. Twenty-two small (6m square) basement rooms, without windows, in the vaulted stone cellars of the *Rex* hotel. Rooms have bunk beds and most have private bathrooms. Definitely not for the claustrophobic but great prices. **695kr/1095kr**

Wasa Park St Eriksplan 1, Norrmalm ☎ 08 545 453 00, ⓦ wasaparkhotel.se; Sankt Eriksplan T-bana; map 44–45. A clean, simple budget hotel dating from the early 1900s; a bit out of the centre but cheap. Although there are no en-suite facilities, rooms are spacious and each has a TV. **850kr**

CENTRAL STOCKHOLM

Central Vasagatan 38 ☎ 08 566 208 00, ⓦ profilhotels .se; T-Centralen T-bana; map p.47. A friendly, modern and comfortable place on one of Stockholm's main streets, whose city-centre location is arguably its best feature. Rooms are a little uninspiring for the price but the location is the selling point and it's worth considering if surrounding places are full. **1395kr/2060kr**

First Reisen Skeppsbron 12 ☎ 08 22 32 60, ⓦ firsthotels.com/reisen; Gamla Stan or Slussen T-bana; map p.47. One of Stockholm's classic hotels, dating back to the eighteenth century. Rooms are decked out with handsome wood panelling and all have bathtubs (not the norm in Sweden). The more expensive options even have their own jacuzzi, saunas and balconies overlooking the waterfront. **1616kr/1886kr**

Grand Södra Blasieholmshamn 8 ☎ 08 679 35 00, ⓦ grandhotel.se; Kungsträdgården T-bana; map p.47. Set in a late nineteenth-century waterside building, this is Scandinavia's most refined hotel, providing the last word in luxury. Prices have fallen in recent years but it's only worth it if you're staying in the best rooms. **2160kr/3040kr**

Lady Hamilton Storkyrkobrinken 5 ☎ 08 506 401 00, ⓦ ladyhamiltonhotel.se; Gamla Stan T-bana; map p.47. Traditional hotel in a building dating from the 1470s, with charming rooms tastefully decorated in old-fashioned Swedish style – lots of antique furniture and folk artefacts

– though with modern touches such as bathroom underfloor heating. 1990kr/2390kr

Lord Nelson Västerlånggatan 22 ☏ 08 506 401 20, ⓦ lordnelsonhotel.se; Gamla Stan T-bana; map p.47. Sister hotel to the *Lady Hamilton*, this is the narrowest hotel in Sweden at just 5m wide and stuffed full of naval antiques and curiosities including an original letter from Nelson to Lady Hamilton. Rooms are small with ship's teak floorboards and lots of mahogany and brass. 1611kr/1790kr

Mälardrottningen Riddarholmen ☏ 08 545 187 80, ⓦ malardrottningen.se; Gamla Stan T-bana; map p.47. Moored off the island of Riddarholmen, this elegant white ship was formerly the gin palace of American millionairess Barbara Hutton. Its cabin-style rooms are a little cramped but make a fun change. 956kr/1084kr

Nordic Light Vasaplan 7 ☏ 08 505 630 00, ⓦ nordiclighthotel.com; T-Centralen T-bana; map p.47. The last word in Nordic design – standard rooms are individually decorated in shades of white and steely grey, inspired by Lapland's amazing northern lights. Painfully contemporary rather than satisfyingly comfortable. 1165kr/2270kr

Nordic Sea Vasaplan 2–4 ☏ 08 505 630 00, ⓦ nordicseahotel.com; T-Centralen T-bana; map p.47. The focus here is on bold designs and colours – maritime blues and greens predominate. Be sure to ask to see your room on check-in since some are tiny and only have views of the train station. 1250kr/2270kr

Queen's Drottninggatan 71A ☏ 08 24 94 60, ⓦ queenshotel.se; Hötorget T-bana; map p.47. Sympathetically renovated hotel with individually decorated en-suite rooms taking their decorative cue from the turn of the last century. A perfect and surprisingly quiet location for Stockholm's central shopping district. 1450kr/1550kr

Rica Gamla Stan Lilla Nygatan 25 ☏ 08 723 72 50, ⓦ rica.se; Gamla Stan T-bana; map p.47. Wonderfully situated in an elegant medieval building in Gamla Stan, with stylish yet old-fashioned rooms in 1700s Swedish design; all 51 are individually decorated with antiques, and feature paintings of Swedish royals from centuries past. 1795kr/2095kr

★ **Sven Vintappare** Sven Vintappares Gränd 3 ☏ 08 22 41 40, ⓦ hotelsvenvintappare.se; Gamla Stan T-bana; map p.47. Housed in a charming building from 1607 with just seven rooms all decorated in Swedish Gustavian style. The bathrooms are to die for, their granite floors and marble walls completing the sense of royal elegance. 1795kr

SÖDERMALM

Anno 1647 Mariagränd 3 ☏ 08 442 16 80, ⓦ anno1647 .se; Slussen T-bana; map p.62. Located in a seventeenth-century building, with pine floors and period furniture, this

hotel is an oasis of elegance and Gustavian charm and has perfect views of the colourful roofs and buildings of Gamla Stan. 2040kr

Columbus Tjärhovsgatan 11 ☏ 08 503 112 00, ⓦ columbushotell.se; Medborgarplatsen T-bana; map p.62. Although the exterior looks almost school-like, the rooms in this building dating from 1780 ooze old-fashioned charm, and high ceilings and generously sized windows create an agreeable sense of space. 1350kr/1650kr

Lunda Pensionat Lundagatan 31 ☏ 073 643 57 69, ⓦ lundapensionat.se; Zinkensdamm T-bana; map p.62. Compact rooms with shared facilities in this comfortable B&B. There's a guest kitchen, too, for self-catering. However, it's the views of Stockholm that make this place a real winner for the money. 695kr

★ **Rival** Mariatorget 3 ☏ 08 545 789 00, ⓦ rival.se; Mariatorget T-bana; map p.62. Owned by Benny Andersson of ABBA who designed the hotel in a combination of 1930s and contemporary Swedish style to recapture the former glamour of the building, which even includes a bistro and a bakery. Some rooms have balconies overlooking the square. 1595kr/2495kr

Scandic Malmen Götgatan 49–51 ☏ 08 517 347 00, ⓦ scandichotels.com/malmen; Medborgarplatsen T-bana; map p.62. Comfortable, if predictable, chain hotel rooms with wooden floors and modern Scandinavian decor, though it's the location close to So-Fo that makes this massive hotel with over 330 rooms worth considering. 1096kr/1506kr

★ **Tre Små Rum** Högbergsgatan 81 ☏ 08 641 23 71, ⓦ tresmarum.se; Mariatorget T-bana; map p.62. A clean, modern option in the heart of Södermalm; the seven simple basement rooms with shared bathrooms are very popular, so book in advance. A help-yourself breakfast from the kitchen fridge is available. 795kr

Zinkensdamm Zinkens Väg 20 ☏ 08 616 81 10, ⓦ zinkensdamm.com; Zinkensdamm T-bana; map p.62. Comfortable, well-appointed and homely hotel rooms, all en suite, with tasteful wallpaper and wooden floors located in a separate wing of the youth hostel (see p.68), right on the doorstep of Tantolunden park. 1110kr/1890kr

HOSTELS

There are no fewer than six official STF hostels in central Stockholm, two of which – *Af Chapman* and *Fridhemsplan* – are among the best in Sweden. There are also a number of independently run places, which tend to be slightly more expensive. The prices we give for STF hostels are for youth-hostel members; non-members pay 50kr more.

STF HOSTELS

★ **Af Chapman** Flaggmansvägen 8, Skeppsholmen ☏ 08 463 22 66, ⓦ stfchapman.com; Kungsträdgården

1

T-bana or bus #65 from Central Station; map pp.44–45. This smart square-rigged 1888 ship – a landmark in its own right – has views over Gamla Stan that are unsurpassed at the price. One of the best places to stay in Stockholm, though advance reservations are a must. Dorms 315kr, doubles 710kr

Fridhemsplan Sankt Eriksgatan 20 ☎08 653 88 00, ⓦfridhemsplan.se; Fridhemsplan T-bana; map pp.44–45. This vast modern hostel can take 390 people and has TVs and internet connection points in all rooms. There are no dorms here – accommodation is in two- to four-bed rooms, with hotel-quality beds in each. Beds 275kr, doubles 625kr

Gärdet Sandhamnsgatan 59A ☎08 463 22 99, ⓦstfturist.se/gardet; Karlaplan T-bana; map pp.44–45. A new and well-appointed addition to STF's Stockholm hostels in the Östermalm district. Accommodation is in one- to four-bed en-suite rooms with cooking facilities. There's free wi-fi throughout the building. Dorms 380kr, doubles 720kr

Långholmen Kronohäktet, Långholmsmuren 20 ☎08 720 85 00, ⓦlangholmen.com; Hornstull T-bana; map p.62. On the island of Långholmen, Stockholm's grandest STF hostel is set in the former prison building dating from 1724. The cells are converted into smart private and dormitory rooms, still with their original, extremely small windows. Dorms 240kr, doubles 580kr

Skeppsholmen Flaggmansvägen 8 ☎08 463 22 66, ⓦstfchapman.com; Kungsträdgården T-bana or bus #65 direct; map pp.44–45. Right in the centre and immensely popular, this former craftsman's workshop is of a similar standard to *Af Chapman*, at the foot of whose gangplank it lies; there are no kitchen or laundry facilities. Dorms 215kr, doubles 590kr

Zinkensdamm Zinkens Väg 20 ☎08 616 81 00, ⓦzinkensdamm.com; Zinkensdamm T-bana; map, p.62. A huge hostel with 490 beds in an excellent location for exploring Södermalm, though it's a 30min walk from the city centre. Kitchen and laundry facilities available (also see p.67). Dorms 235kr, doubles 600kr

INDEPENDENT HOSTELS

★ **Castanea** Kindstugatan 1 ☎08 22 35 51, ⓦcastaneahostel.com; Gamla Stan T-bana; map p.47.

It doesn't come any cheaper than this to stay in the heart of the Old Town's warren of narrow cobbled streets. Rooms are stylishly decorated in modern Scandinavian style with wooden floors. Dorms 195kr, doubles 600kr

★ **City Backpackers** Upplandsgatan 2A ☎08 20 69 20, ⓦcitybackpackers.se; T-Centralen T-bana; map pp.44–45. Friendly hostel with a hundred beds, only 5min from the Central Station. The owners and staff have travelled widely and specialize in helping backpackers get the most out of Stockholm with personal suggestions and tips. Double rooms have private facilities. Dorms 190kr, doubles 890kr

Red Boat Mälaren Södermälarstrand, Kajplats 6, Södermalm ☎08 644 43 85, ⓦtheredboat.com; Slussen T-bana; map p.62. Housed in an old Göta canal steamer, this hostel enjoys a fantastic location overlooking the Stadshuset. Cabins are compact but comfortable and clean. There are no cooking facilities on board due to the risk of fire. Double cabin 650kr

Stockholm Hostel Ahlströmergatan 15 ☎070 156 55 25, ⓦstockholmhostel.se; Fridhemsplan T-bana; map pp.44–45. Newly built, contemporary design hostel on Kungsholmen whose rooms all have private facilities and their own television. Two kitchens are available for guests' use and there's free wi-fi throughout the building. Dorms 250kr, doubles 790kr

CAMPING

With the nearest year-round sites a good half-hour out of the city centre, camping out of season in Stockholm can prove rather inconvenient, though this being Sweden, both sites listed are well equipped with modern service buildings providing showers and laundry facilities. Pitching a tent costs from 140kr per person.

Ängby Camping Blackebergsvägen 20 ☎08 37 04 20, ⓦangbycamping.se; Ängbyplan T-bana; turn left when leaving the station; map pp.44–45. West of the city on the lakeshore where there are good beaches. Open all year, but phone ahead to book Oct to April.

Bredäng Camping ☎08 97 70 71, ⓦbredangcamping .se; Bredäng T-bana; map pp.44–45. Southwest of the city with views over Lake Mälaren. Open all year though only the campsite's cabins are open between mid-Oct and mid-April. Two-person cabins 750kr

EATING

Eating out in Stockholm needn't be expensive – observe a few rules and you'll manage quite well. If money is tight, switch your main meal of the day to lunchtime, when on weekdays almost every café and restaurant offers an excellent-value set menu, known as *dagens rätt*, for 75–95kr. For evening meals, don't assume that Chinese or Italian places will be the least expensive; more often than not they're overpriced and serve food that's pretty tasteless. You're much better off seeking out one of Stockholm's many Swedish restaurants, where you're likely to find an extensive menu of traditional fare as well as some good international dishes. In fact, the culinary craze in Stockholm for French dishes with a hint of Swedish home cooking is still going strong, and can lead to some surprising and delicious combinations.

CAFÉS AND RESTAURANTS
Day or night, the main areas for decent eating are: in the city centre, the triangle marked out by Norrmalmstorg, Birger Jarlsgatan and Stureplan; in Östermalm, Grev Turegatan; and in Södermalm, the So-Fo district around Folkungagatan, Skånegatan and Bondegatan. In Kungsholmen, restaurants are more spread out, so it helps to know your destination before you set off. Several places in Gamla Stan are also worth checking out, though they tend to be a little expensive. Being organized is always the name of the game in Sweden, and to be sure of a table you should always book ahead.

GREATER STOCKHOLM
★ **Blå Porten** Djurgårdsvägen 64 ✆ 08 663 87 59; bus #44; map pp.44–45. Glorious café set in a glass-walled building overlooking a courtyard with outdoor seating around an old fountain. The open sandwiches and lunches here are Provencal-influenced and include a wide choice of quiches, pies, salads and soups, including vegetarian options. Mains around 100–150kr. Mon–Fri 11am–10pm, Sat & Sun 11am–7pm.

★ **Chakula** Pontonjärgatan 28 ✆ 08 654 90 30; Fridhemsplan T-bana; map pp.44–45. This African restaurant with its ornate wooden wall carvings is a real find: lots of cinnamon, cloves and ginger in dishes originating in Kenya, Tanzania and South Africa. Reckon on 145–260kr for a main course. Mon–Fri 11am–2pm & 5pm–midnight, Sat 5pm–midnight.

Ciao Ciao Grande Storgatan 11 ✆ 08 667 64 20; Östermalmstorg T-bana; map pp.44–45. A safe bet for dependable, tasty and relatively inexpensive Italian food, including really excellent pizzas, in the heart of pricey Östermalm. Pizzas go for 76–145kr, pasta dishes 150–200kr and meat mains weigh in around 249kr. Mon–Wed 11am–10pm, Thurs–Fri 11am–10.30pm, Sat noon–10.30pm, Sun noon–10pm.

Göken Pontonjärgatan 28 ✆ 08 654 49 28; Fridhemsplan T-bana; map pp.44–45. This small friendly place is big on pink, glitter and kitsch and is a firm favourite with Stockholm's gay crowd. An excellent choice for modern Swedish food, such as marinated rack of lamb (245kr) and pan-fried tuna (225kr). Mon–Fri 11am–2pm & 5pm till late, Sat & Sun 5pm till late.

Il Conte Grevgatan 9 ✆ 08 661 26 28; Östermalmstorg T-bana; map pp.44–45. This sophisticated Italian restaurant with linen tablecloths and subtle lighting is the best Italian in town; pasta mains, such as seafood linguine, are 155–205kr. Meat dishes like roast lamb in mustard sauce cost 225–265kr. Mon–Fri 11am–2pm & 5–11.30pm, Sat & Sun 5–11.30pm.

La Famiglia Alströmergatan 45 ✆ 08 650 63 10; Fridhemsplan T-bana; map pp.44–45. Intimate and cosy Italian with chequered tablecloths and candles; Frank

TOP FIVE PLACES TO EAT
B.A.R. p.70
Blå Porten p.69
Grodan p.70
Mamas & Tapas p.69
Sturekatten p.71

Sinatra once ate here. Portions are generous, and pasta dishes cost from 145kr, grilled meat dishes 205–245kr and a three-course set menu is 275kr. Mon–Thurs & Sun 5.30–10pm, Fri & Sat 5–11pm.

Lao Wai Luntmakargatan 74 ✆ 08 673 78 00; Rådmansgatan T-bana; map pp.44–45. Sweden's first East Asian restaurant, and still decidedly good though with barely half a dozen tables. Authentic vegetarian Sichuan Chinese and Taiwanese main courses for 175–195kr, such as soya meatballs stuffed with shiitake mushrooms, Chinese cabbage and broccoli. Mon–Fri 11am–2pm, Tues–Sat 5.30–10pm.

★ **Mamas & Tapas** Scheelegatan 3 ✆ 08 653 53 90; Rådhuset T-bana; map pp.44–45. Consistently one of Stockholm's best restaurants and the place to come for authentic and reasonably priced Spanish cuisine. Tapas from 47kr, paella 98kr and a good-value mixed meat platter including pork, steak, chorizo and vegetables for 158kr. Mon–Fri 5pm–1am, Sat 2pm–1am, Sun 2–9pm.

Peppar Torsgatan 34 ✆ 08 34 20 52; Sankt Eriksplan T-bana; map pp.44–45. Attractive Cajun restaurant, with decent-sized portions at fair prices – mains are 150–250kr. Dozens of posters pinned to the walls help create an agreeable, studenty rock-and-roll atmosphere which complements the southern American food perfectly. Mon–Sat 5pm–1am.

Salt Hantverkaregatan 34 ✆ 08 652 11 00; Rådhuset T-bana; map pp.44–45. Complete with stuffed elk's head and antlers on the wall, this is the place to come for inspired modern Swedish home cooking (145–225kr per dish), including elk burgers with chips (145kr) and the classic Biff Rydberg (180kr) with egg yolk and mustard crème. Mon–Thurs 10.30am–11pm, Fri 10.30am–midnight, Sat 3pm–midnight.

Samuraj Kommendörsgatan 40 ✆ 08 663 68 68; Karlaplan T-bana; map pp.44–45. This good and dependable Japanese place is known for its fine food and friendly staff, with mains such as grilled salmon in teriyaki sauce (168kr) at the lower end of the price range (up to around 215kr). Mon–Fri 11am–10pm, Sat & Sun 4–10pm.

Saturnus Erikbergsgatan 6; Rådmansgatan T-bana; map pp.44–45. Stockholm's answer to a French patisserie-cum-boulangerie with a subtle Parisian atmosphere, albeit at 60 degrees north. Excellent range of sandwiches for 50–150kr, salads from 138kr and the biggest and best

1

cinnamon buns in town. Mon–Fri 8am–8pm, Sat & Sun 9am–7pm.

Supper Tegnérgatan 37 ☎08 23 24 24; Rådmansgatan T-bana; map pp.44–45. Stylish and popular South American restaurant, curiously located in a windowless basement. Starters include the likes of crabcakes with lime chilli for 118kr, mains might cover, for example, pork with sweet potatoes, at 198–205kr. Mon & Tues 5pm–midnight, Wed–Sat 5pm–1am.

CENTRAL STOCKHOLM

★ **B.A.R.** Blasieholmsgatan 4A ☎08 611 53 35; Kungsträdgården T-bana; map p.47. *The* place to eat fish in Stockholm. Go up to the fish counter and choose the piece you'd like to eat (90–330kr). There are also home-made sausages and steaks on offer, plus gravad lax tartare (110kr) and seafood casserole (195kr). Mon–Fri 11.30am–2.30pm & 5pm–1am, Sat 4pm–1am, Sun 5–9pm.

Bistro Bestick Bryggargatan 8 ☎08 20 31 20; T-Centralen T-bana; map p.47. Newly opened and rather compact contemporary Swedish bistro with stark white walls and comfy sofas, serving up delicious home-cooking dishes such as Wallenbergare, meatballs and gravad lax in the range 110–245kr; home-baked sourdough bread, too. Tues–Fri 11am–10pm, Sat 5–10pm.

Bistro Ruby and Grill Ruby Österlånggatan 14 ☎08 20 57 76; Gamla Stan T-bana; map p.47. *Bistro Ruby* is a long-established French place, tastefully done up in Parisian style with red walls covered with artwork. Mains, such as steak frites or tenderloin with mustard cream, cost 175–345kr. Next door, though in the same building, is *Grill Ruby*, which serves up TexMex and American-style charcoal grills of meat and fish (179–499kr) and weekend brunches. Both daily 5pm till late, Bistro Ruby closed Sun.

★ **Café Panorama** Sergels torg 3; T-Centralen T-bana; map p.47. Top-floor café inside Kulturhuset with superb views over central Stockholm (try to get one of the window tables). Lunch is dependable and inexpensive, though it's the apple pie and vanilla sauce that's the real winner. Tues–Fri 11am–8pm, Sat 11am–6pm, Sun 11am–5pm.

Chokladkoppen Stortorget 18; Gamla Stan T-bana; map p.47. A fabulous, if rather cramped, café overlooking Gamla Stan's grand old square, specializing in white-chocolate cheesecake and blueberry pie. Also has tasty salmon quiches and light lunch dishes and is justifiable popular with the city's gay lunchgoers. Daily 9am–11pm.

Den Gyldene Freden Österlånggatan 51 ☎08 24 97 60; Gamla Stan T-bana; map p.47. Opened in 1722, Stockholm's oldest restaurant is housed in a combination of vaulted cellars and regular serving rooms whose interiors are pure eighteenth century. Traditional Swedish mains such as pike-perch for around 300kr, or better-value

home-cooking dishes, such as meatballs, from 165kr. Mon–Sat 5–11pm.

East Stureplan 13 ☎08 611 49 59; Östermalmstorg T-bana; map p.47. Trendy to a T, this is the place for top-quality cuisine from Japan, Korea, Thailand and Vietnam; try the delicious chicken soup with mushrooms, coconut, lime and galangal for 120kr. Mains are 112–229kr, though a sushi and sashimi combo costs 295kr. Mon–Fri 11.30am–3am, Sat & Sun 5pm–3am.

★ **Grodan** Grev Turegatan 16 ☎08 679 61 00; Östermalmstorg T-bana; map p.47. Choose the bistro to the right over the chi-chi restaurant to the left where Swedish home cooking meets French: fish stew with shrimps and aioli (195kr), beef steak with horseradish and fries (185kr) or potato pancake with pork and lingonberries (139kr). Mon–Wed 11.30am–midnight, Thurs & Fri 11.30am–1am, Sat noon–1am, Sun 1–10pm.

Hermitage Stora Nygatan 11 ☎08 411 95 00; Gamla Stan T-bana; map p.47. Long-established and well-respected vegetarian restaurant whose food is often quite spicy and Middle Eastern in style. Buffet lunches go for 90kr and a set dinner 100kr. Mon–Sat 11am–8pm, Sun 11am–7pm.

KB Smålandsgatan 7 ☎08 679 60 32; Östermalmstorg T-bana; map p.47. Excellent Scandinavian food with plenty of seafood in posh 1930s surroundings. Reckon on over 200–300kr for a main course such as fish stew or Norwegian cod, or why not try the assorted herring plate for 125kr. Mon–Fri 11.30am–midnight, Sat 1pm–midnight.

Konditori Kungstornet Kungsgatan 28; Hötorget T-bana; map p.47. Busy and rather small retro-style coffee house with wood panelling, dark-green sofas and an upstairs jukebox which first opened in the 1930s. Excellent cakes and pastries as well as substantial sandwiches. Mon–Fri 7am–11pm, Sat 8am–midnight, Sun 10am–10pm.

Le Rouge Österlånggatan 17 ☎08 505 244 60; Gamla Stan T-bana; map p.47. A gloriously OTT Moulin Rouge-style bistro, inspired by nineteenth-century Paris, where red is *de rigueur*: everything from the drapes to the sofas are bright red. Tuna steak is 265kr, moules frites 135kr and chicken tajine 225kr. Mon–Thurs 11.30am–2pm & 5pm–1am, Fri 11.30am–1am, Sat 5pm–1am.

Operakällarens bakficka Operahuset, Gustav Adolfs torg ☎08 676 58 09; Kungsträdgården T-bana; map p.47. A sound choice for Swedish home cooking served around the bar in this charming little place which resembles the snug of a British pub: meatballs in a cream sauce with gherkins (160kr) and mixed herring platter (150kr) are always on the menu. Mon–Fri 11.30am–11pm, Sat noon–10pm, Sun 1pm–midnight.

Prinsen Mäster Samuelsgatan 4 ☎08 611 13 31; Östermalmstorg T-bana; map p.47. A long-standing

1

haunt of artists, musicians and writers enchanted by its soft lighting, glass panelling and wall etchings. The food is top-notch Swedish home cooking, with the likes of Wallenbergare, Biff Rydberg and herring, all around 189–299kr. Mon–Fri 11.30am–11.30pm, Sat 1–11.30pm, Sun 1–10.30pm.

Riche Birger Jarlsgatan 4 ☎08 545 035 60; Östermalmstorg T-bana; map p.47. In Strindberg's day, this was Stockholm's answer to a genuine Parisian bistro. Today, *Riche* is just that: a busy French brasserie serving a range of Swedish and French dishes such as ling in mussel sauce (140kr) and roast pork with julienne vegetables (245kr). Mon 7.30am–midnight, Tues–Fri 7.30am–2am, Sat noon–2am, Sun noon–midnight.

★ **Sturekatten** Riddargatan 4; Östermalmstorg T-bana; map p.47. With antique tables and chairs seemingly lifted from grandmother's sitting room, this cosy café has tremendous cakes and pastries as well as filling sandwiches to boot, making it one of the most enjoyable cafés in Stockholm. Mon–Fri 8am–8pm, Sat 9am–5pm, Sun noon–5pm.

SÖDERMALM

Blå Dörren Södermalmstorg 6 ☎08 743 07 40; Slussen T-bana; map p.62. Unpretentious and popular beer hall-cum-restaurant with vaulted ceilings offering excellent Swedish traditional dishes (124–224kr) such as meatballs, steaks and *pytt i panna*. Great location for both Gamla Stan and Södermalm. Mon 10.30am–11pm, Tues–Thurs 10.30am–midnight, Fri 10.30am–1am, Sat 1pm–1am, Sun 1–11pm.

Bröderna Olsson Folkungagatan 84 ☎08 640 84 46; Medborgarplatsen T-bana; map p.62. A fun American-style diner where every dish is laced with garlic. Mains such as Thai-spiced garlic prawns or deep-fried garlic with halloumi cost 135–275kr. There's also an extensive choice of vodkas and *akvavits* -- and even garlic beer. Daily 5pm–1am.

★ **Crêperie Fyra Knop** Svartensgatan 4 ☎08 640 77 27; Slussen T-bana, Götgatan exit; map p.62. Excellent, affordable galettes and crêpes for 92–112kr, served in this tiny French-owned and -run restaurant which consists of one intimate little room with rough maroon walls, battered wooden chairs and tables and an ancient Stella Artois advertisement. Daily 5–11pm.

Dionysos Bondegatan 56 ☎08 641 91 13; Medborgarplatsen T-bana; map p.62. Tasteful Greek restaurant with a homely feel: it's been here since 1974 and is just as good as ever. The food is accomplished: grilled halloumi for 80kr, souvlaki for 165kr. All mains are accompanied by potato wedges. Mon–Fri 10am–midnight, Sat 11am–midnight, Sun 11am–11pm.

Hosteria Tre Santi Blekingegatan 32 ☎08 644 18 16; Skanstull T-bana; map p.62. Excellent upmarket Italian restaurant known for its generous portions. Pasta dishes cost

145–165kr, meat mains are 205–285kr, whilst fish is 185–285kr; the accompanying home-made sauces are exceptionally good. Try the tasty scampi risotto for 205kr. Mon & Tues 5–11pm, Wed–Sat 5pm–midnight, Sun 4–10pm.

Kvarnen Tjärhovsgatan 4; Medborgarplatsen T-bana; map p.62. Classic Stockholm beer hall with great Swedish home cooking: meatballs with lingonberries and gherkins and *pytt i panna* for 125–225kr. Reindeer is always on the menu, served with mushrooms and a creamy sauce for 155kr. Mon–Fri 11am–3am, Sat & Sun 5pm–3am.

★ **Pelikan** Blekingegatan 40; Skanstull T-bana; map p.62. Atmospheric beer hall (from the entrance hall turn right) with excellent traditional food, such as *pytt i panna* for 154kr or meatballs for 174kr. Left of the entrance hall is a smarter restaurant, though still based on home cooking. Mains 154–238kr. Mon–Thurs & Sun 5pm–midnight, Fri & Sat 5pm–1am.

Snaps Götgatan 48 ☎08 640 28 68; Medborgarplatsen T-bana; map p.62. Good, but reasonably priced Swedish food (mains 195–295kr) and an extensive range of schnapps (hence the Swedish name, *snaps*), set in a 300-year-old building. Very popular, especially in summer, when there's outdoor seating in the square. Mon–Wed 5pm–1am, Thurs–Sat 5pm–3am.

Soldaten Svejk Östgatagatan 35 ☎08 641 33 66; Medborgarplatsen T-bana; map p.62. Lively pub that draws in a lot of students. Simple, Eastern and Central European-inspired menu with dishes (schnitzel and various spicy sausages are always available) for 106–133kr, and a large selection of Czech beers. Mon–Thurs 5pm–midnight, Fri & Sat 5pm–1am, Sun 5–11pm.

String Nytorgsgatan 38 ☎08 714 85 14; Medborgarplatsen T-bana; map p.62. Busy, retro studeny café with brown plastic chairs and battered wooden tables. Good for a wide range of hot and cold sandwiches from 35kr and salads from 75kr. There's a breakfast buffet on Sat & Sun (10.30am–1pm) for 70kr. Mon, Tues & Thurs 9.30am–8pm, Wed 9.30am–11pm, Fri 9.30am–6pm, Sat & Sun 10.30am–6pm.

Tre Indier Åsogatan 92 ☎08 641 03 55; Medborgarplatsen T-bana; map p.62. A lively Indian restaurant that's slightly tucked away, located at the corner of the tiny street, Möregatan, and Åsögatan. There's an extensive menu and the curry dishes are genuinely tasty and well prepared. Mains go for 110–150kr. Mon–Thurs 11am–10pm, Fri 11am–11pm, Sat noon–11pm, Sun noon–10pm.

★ **Urban Deli** Nytorget 4 ☎08 599 091 80; Medborgarplatsen T-bana; map p.62. Attached to an impressively well-stocked deli, the long bar and stools and handful of tables at this chi-chi bistro are always busy: the fish stew (169kr), smoked salmon (145kr) and sausage with tarragon (195kr) are good bets. Mon–Thurs & Sun 8am–midnight, Fri & Sat 8am–1am.

1

DRINKING

As elsewhere in Sweden, the majority of Stockholmers do their drinking and eating together, and all of the places listed below also serve food – Södermalm is by far the best place to head for. The scourge of Swedish nightlife – high alcohol prices – has been neutralized in recent years due to increased competition. The tired old stories about drinking requiring a second mortgage are quite simply no longer true. Happy hours or "After work", as they're also known, at various places also throw up some bargains – watch out for signs outside bars and pubs advertising their particular times. **Gay bars** are few and far between: those that do exist are listed below.

GREATER STOCKHOLM

Storstad Odengatan 41 ☎ 08 673 38 00; Rådmansgatan T-bana; map pp.44–45. Light and airy lounge and bar with high ceilings that is a firm favourite for Stockholm's media pack and local celebrities. Packed with a credit-card-flashing crowd at weekends. Mon–Thurs 4pm–1am, Fri 4pm–3am, Sat 6pm–3am.

Tranan Karlbergsvägen 14 ☎ 08 527 281 00; Sankt Eriksplan T-bana; map pp.44–45. An atmospheric old workers' beer hall housed in a basement that's been in operation since 1929. One of Stockholm's best and most popular drinking holes with live music in the basement bar. Mon–Thurs 5pm–midnight, Fri & Sat 5pm–1am, Sun 5–11pm.

CENTRAL STOCKHOLM

Berns Berzelii Park, Nybroplan ☎ 08 566 322 22; Kungsträdgården T-bana; map p.47. One of the chicest bars in town, with decor by the British designer Sir Terence Conran. Originally made famous by writer August Strindberg, who picked up character ideas here for his novel, *The Red Room*. Mon–Wed & Sun 11.30am–1am, Thurs–Sat 11.30am–3am.

Dubliner Holländargatan 1 ☎ 08 679 77 07; Hötorget T-bana; map p.47. One of the busiest Irish pubs in town with a fantastically large selection of foreign beers on tap and by the bottle, with live music most evenings, often Irish folk. Mon–Thurs 11am–1am, Fri 11am–3am, Sat noon–3am, Sun 1–10pm.

Kleins Kornhamnstorg 51 ☎ 08 20 99 45; Gamla Stan T-bana; map p.47. One of the most popular bars in Gamla Stan, though its tiny dimensions mean it can get a bit cramped. Definitely worth a look, though be sure to keep your eye on your possessions. Mon–Fri 4pm–3am, Sat & Sun 2pm–3am.

Torget Mälartorget 13 ☎ 08 20 55 60; Gamla Stan T-bana; map p.47. This elegant place is Stockholm's main gay bar, good for a drink at any time, and always busy. The modern Swedish food here is justifiably popular, so always reserve ahead if you want to eat. Mon–Thurs 5pm–1am, Fri–Sun 4pm–1am.

Wirströms Stora Nygatan 13 ☎ 08 21 28 74; Gamla Stan T-bana; map p.47. A great favourite among Stockholm's ex-pat community who come here to talk football and sample the large selection of beers and whiskies. There are also a few bar meals such as fish and chips and burgers. Mon–Sat noon–1am, Sun 1pm–1am.

SÖDERMALM

Akkurat Hornsgatan 18 ☎ 08 644 00 15; Slussen T-bana; map p.62. This famous spot is known for its 280 different whiskies and extensive beer selection on tap and by the bottle, including an impressive array of Belgian varieties. Often has live music at weekends. Mon 11am–midnight, Tues–Fri 11am–1am, Sat 3pm–1am, Sun 6pm–1am.

Fenix Götgatan 40 ☎ 08 640 45; Slussen T-bana, Götgatan exit; map p.62. A loud and brash American-style bar that's always packed with clientele who are here for the sole purpose of drinking large quantities of beer – and practising their latest chat-up lines in English. Mon–Thurs 4pm–1am, Fri 1pm–1am, Sat & Sun noon–1am.

Gröne Jägaren Götgatan 64 ☎ 08 640 96 00; Medborgarplatsen T-bana; map p.62. An inordinately popular, and at times, rather drunken bar with some of the cheapest beer in the capital – the clientele is predominantly male and talk here is mainly of women, football and cars. Regular karaoke and pub quizzes. Mon–Fri 10.30am–1am, Sat & Sun 11am–1am.

H2O/Eld Tjärhovsgatan 4 ☎ 08 643 03 80; Medborgarplatsen T-bana; map p.62. Two basement bars underneath the *Kvarnen* beer hall. *H2O* is decorated entirely in blue and white ceramic tiles, and is a place to hang out at the bar whilst *Eld* has a resident DJ most nights of the week. Both attract Stockholm's well-dressed, well-heeled and well-tipsy. Mon–Fri 11am–3am, Sat & Sun 5pm–3am.

Kvarnen Tjärhovsgatan 4 ☎ 08 643 03 80; Medborgarplatsen T-bana; map p.62. Busy beer hall on the same site as *H2O/Eld*; this one, at ground level, is a favourite haunt of football fans supporting Hammarby, who come here to celebrate their team's every win and defeat. Mon–Fri 11am–3am, Sat & Sun 5pm–3am.

Pelikan Blekingegatan 40 ☎ 08 556 090 90; Skanstull T-bana; map p.62. Long-established beer hall is full of character – and characters – and is one of the city's most satisfying and relaxing places for an evening's drinking. It's a good place to strike up a conversation with local Swedes. Mon–Thurs 5pm–midnight, Fri & Sat 5pm–1am, Sun 5pm–midnight.

Pet Sounds Bar Skånegatan 80 ☎ 08 643 82 25; Medborgarplatsen T-bana; map p.62. One of the most popular places in So-Fo for a drink, run by the eponymous record store a few doors down; head to the basement bar where there's live music and DJs on Fri and Sat. Tues 5pm–midnight, Wed–Sat 4pm–1am, Sun 4pm–midnight.

Sidetrack Wollmar Yxkullsgatan 7 ☎ 08 641 16 88; Mariatorget T-bana; map p.62. Dark, narrow and intimate British-style basement pub popular with gay leather and denim boys. The modern Swedish food here is also worth considering, though try to reserve a table ahead. Wed–Sat 6pm–1am.

NIGHTLIFE

The club scene in Stockholm is limited. Cover charges aren't too high at around 150kr, but beer gets more expensive as the night goes on, reaching as much as 85kr a glass. In Stockholm, as in the rest of Sweden, the gay scene is small; we've listed what the city has to offer below.

GREATER STOCKHOLM

Crazy Daizy Fleminggatan 2–4 ☎ 08 508 267 18; Rådhuset T-bana; map pp.44–45. Very popular club attached to a restaurant, attracting 30- and 40-somethings with a mix of disco and Latino beats and live music. Generally, people come to eat here first and then stay on to dance. Fri & Sat 9pm–3am.

CENTRAL STOCKHOLM

Berns 2.35:1 Berzelii Park, Nybroplan ☎ 08 566 322 00; Kungsträdgården T-bana; map p.47. A Stockholm institution – head downstairs for *Berns* legendary nightclub which has long held the status as the capital's leading dance spot. It's the stunning mix of nineteenth-century Baroque, contemporary design and beautiful people that creates such a buzz. Wed & Thurs 11pm–3am, Fri & Sat 11pm–4.30am.

Le Bon Palais Barnhusgatan 12–14 ☎ 08 10 09 32; T-Centralen T-bana; map p.47. One of the city's most popular and biggest dance-restaurants with five bars and two dancefloors, close to the Central Station, attracting a crowd in the 30–50 age bracket. Fri & Sat 7.30pm–3am.

Sturecompagniet Sturegatan 4 ☎ 08 545 076 70; Östermalmstorg T-bana; map p.47. Long established as one of Stockholm's leading (and biggest) nightspots, playing house and techno, with three floors of bars; something for everybody, although it can get packed and the queues to get in are always long. Thurs–Sat 10pm–3am.

The White Room Jakobsbergsgatan 29 ☎ 08 545 076 65; T-Centralen Hötorget; map p.47. Playing a vibrant mix of 1990s music, this club right in the city centre is always packed at weekends with people reliving 1999. Be young, beautiful and trendy and let the champagne flow. Wed, Fri & Sat 11pm–5am.

Zipper Lästmakargatan 8 ☎ 08 20 62 90; Östermalmstorg T-bana; map p.47. Right in the heart of the city and undoubtedly the busiest gay club in town with three dancefloors, including one playing 1980s favourites, which is often packed to the rafters. Sat 10pm–1am.

SÖDERMALM

Patricia Stadsgårdskajen, Slussen ☎ 08 743 05 70; Slussen T-bana; map p.62. Formerly the royal yacht of Britain's late Queen Mother, today a restaurant-disco-bar with chart and 1980s music. The menu, with a huge variety of imaginative main courses (fajitas and Cajun steaks are always available) is quite simply terrific. Gay on Sun. Wed & Thurs 5pm–1am, Fri & Sat 6pm–5am, Sun 6pm–3am.

Södra Teatern Mosebacke torg 3, Södermalm ☎ 08 531 994 90; Slussen T-bana; map p.62. One of the longest-established clubs in town; every night sees a different type of club or event taking place – everything from jazz to new bands, R&B to disco. In short, if it's in Stockholm, it's here. Mon & Tues 5–11pm, Wed & Thurs 5pm–1am, Sat 10.30am–2am, Sun 10.30am–11pm.

LIVE MUSIC: ROCK, POP AND JAZZ

When there's live **rock** and **jazz** music at bars and cafés, it will mostly be provided by local bands, for which you'll pay around 120kr entrance. Most international big names make it to Stockholm, playing at a variety of seated halls and stadiums – tickets for these are, of course, much more expensive. The main **large venue** is the Stockholm Globe Arena in Johanneshov (☎ 0771 31 00 00, ⓦ globen.se; Gullmarsplan T-bana).

GREATER STOCKHOLM

Cirkus Djurgårdsslätten 43–45 ☎ 08 587 987 00, ⓦ cirkus.se; bus #44; map pp.44–45. Occasional rock, R&B performances, classical concerts and theatre take place in the original circular arena dating from 1892 that is still one of the main venues on Stockholm's cultural scene. Opening times vary according to event.

CENTRAL STOCKHOLM

Engelen Kornhamnstorg 59 ☎ 08 505 560 00, ⓦ wallmans.com; Gamla Stan T-bana; map p.47. Great place to see cover bands who perform most nights in various guises: jazz, rock or blues. *Engelen* has a large and loyal clientele, so arrive early to get in. There's also a dancefloor downstairs. Daily 4pm–3am.

1

Fasching Kungsgatan 63, Norrmalm ☎ 08 534 829 64, ⓦ fasching.se; Hötorget T-bana; map p.47. If you're after local or foreign contemporary jazz, this is the place to come. However, there's also a fair smattering of salsa and soul on offer, too. Can get quite crowded. Mon–Thurs & Sun 6pm–midnight, Fri & Sat 7pm–4am.

Nalen Stacken Regeringsgatan 74 ☎ 08 505 292 00, ⓦ nalen.com; T-Centralen T-bana; map p.47. Once *the* place to hear music in the city (even the Beatles were booked to play here), now offering rock with a smattering of jazz and swing. Opening times vary according to event.

Stampen Stora Nygatan 5 ☎ 08 20 57 93, ⓦ stampen .se; Gamla Stan T-bana; map p.47. Rowdy jazz club, which is best known for swing, dixie and trad, though there's also mainstream, blues and 1950s and 1960s rock, too. *Stampen* has been cranking out live music virtually every night for the past forty years and is still going strong. Mon, Tues & Thurs 8pm–1am, Wed 5pm–1am, Fri & Sat 8pm–2am.

SÖDERMALM

Södra Teatern Mosebacke torg 3 ☎ 08 531 994 90, ⓦ mosebacke.se; Slussen T-bana; map p.62. This is one of the best places in the capital for world music, hip-hop, rock and pop – if it's happening anywhere, it's happening here. Opening times vary according to event.

CLASSICAL MUSIC

Classical music is always easy to find in Stockholm. There's generally something on at one of the following venues: Konserthuset in Hötorget, Norrmalm (☎ 08 786 02 00, ⓦ konserthuset.se); Berwaldhallen, Strandvägen 69, Östermalm (☎ 08 784 18 00, ⓦ berwaldhallen.se); and Musikaliska Akademien, Blasieholmstorg 8, near the National Art Museum (☎ 08 407 18 00, ⓦ musakad.se). **Organ music** can be heard at Adolf Fredriks kyrka, Holländargatan 16, Norrmalm; St Jakobs kyrka in Kungsträdgården, Norrmalm; Gustav Vasa kyrka in Odenplan; and Storkyrkan in Gamla Stan – consult *What's On* (see p.65). Operan, on Gustav Adolfs torg, is Stockholm's main **opera** house (☎ 08 791 44 00, ⓦ operan.se); for less rarefied presentations, check out the programme at Dramaten, Nybroplan, Östermalm (☎ 08 667 06 80, ⓦ dramaten.se).

THEATRE AND CINEMA

Stockholm has dozens of **theatres**, but naturally most productions are in Swedish. For **English-language performances** check out Sweden's oldest English-language theatre company, Stockholm Players (ⓦ stockholmplayers .se), established in the 1920s. If you want other tickets, it's worth waiting for reduced-price standby tickets, available from the kiosk in Norrmalmstorg. **Kulturhuset** (☎ 08 508 315 08, ⓦ kulturhuset.stockholm.se) in Sergels torg has a full range of artistic and cultural events, most of them free; the information desk on the ground floor has free programmes. **Cinema-going** is an incredibly popular pastime in Stockholm. The largest venue in the city centre is Filmstaden Sergel in Hötorget (☎ 08 562 600 00, ⓦ sf.se), but there are also a good number of cinemas the entire length of Kungsgatan between Sveavägen and Birger Jarlsgatan, which are always very lively on Saturday night. Tickets cost around 150kr and films are never dubbed into Swedish.

SWIMMING IN STOCKHOLM

The water in Stockholm is clean and perfect for swimming during the long days of summer. The best **beaches** are all west of the city centre: **Långholmens strandbad** to the west of Västerbron bridge on Långholmen, rocky **Klippbadet** to the east of the bridge and across on Kungsholmen at **Smeddsudden**, with a large grassy area for sunbathing; take bus #4. Alternatively, Södermalm is the place to go for **swimming pools;** there are three in fairly close proximity: Forsgrénskabadet in Medborgarplatsen (☎ 08 508 403 15; Medborgarplatsen T-bana); Erikdalsbadet, Hammarby Slussväg 20, (☎ 08 508 402 50; Skanstull T-bana), which has an open-air pool; and the wonderful little Liljeholmsbadet, Bergsundsgatan 2, (☎ 08 668 67 80; Hornstull T-bana), a pool in a boat-like pontoon contraption that floats in Lake Mälaren and has nude swimming for women on Mondays, for men on Fridays, though it is closed mid-June to mid-August; the water here is always 30°C. For unofficial **nude** bathing, head out to one of the islands in the archipelago and find your own private spot.

The best **gay** beach is at Kärsön (Brommaplan T-bana then any bus towards Drottningholm palace). Get off at the stop over the bridge, Brostugan, and walk to the right along the water's edge.

DIRECTORY

Embassies and consulates Australia, Klarabergsviadukten 63 ☎08 613 29 00, ⓦsweden .embassy.gov.au; Canada, Klarabergsgatan 23 ☎08 453 30 00, ⓦcanadaemb.se; Ireland, Hovslagargatan 5 ☎08 545 040 40, ⓦembassyofireland.se; New Zealand, Nybrogatan 11 ☎08 459 69 40, ⓦnzembassy.com/sweden; South Africa, Fleminggatan 20, Fourth floor ☎08 24 39 50, ⓦsouthafrica.se; UK, Skarpögatan 6–8 ☎08 671 30 00, ⓦukinsweden.fco.gov.uk; US, Dag Hammarskjöldsväg 31 ☎08 783 53 00, ⓦstockholm.usembassy.gov.

Emergencies Ring ☎112 for police, ambulance or fire services.

Exchange Forex exchange offices at Central Station, Cityterminalen, Vasagatan 16, Stureplan, , Terminal 2 & 5, Arlanda airport and Skavsta airport. More information at ⓦforex.se.

Health care CityAkuten, Apelbergsgatan 48 ☎020 15 01 50 is a walk-in clinic offering on-the-spot treatment for minor ailments to anyone in Stockholm.

Internet access Sidewalk Express has dozens of internet points (19kr/hr) across Stockholm, for example, at Central Station, Cityterminalen and many 7-Eleven supermarkets. See ⓦsidewalkexpress.se for complete listings. Most hotels and youth hostels have free access for guests.

Laundry Self-service laundry at Västmannagatan 61B (Mon–Fri 8.30am–6.30pm, Sat 9.30am–3pm; ⓦtvattomaten.se).

Left luggage There are lockers at Central Station and the Cityterminalen bus station.

Lost property Klara Östra Kyrkogatan 6, ☎08 600 10 00.

Pharmacy 24hr service at Klarabergsgatan 64, ☎0771 45 04 50.

Police Kungsholmsgatan 37 ☎08 401 01 00.

Radio English-language programming from Radio Sweden can be heard in Stockholm on 89.6 FM Monday to Friday at 3pm and 8.30pm; more information at ⓦradiosweden.org.

Self-catering Try Hötorgshallen in Hötorget and the market outside for fruit and vegetables. Otherwise, head for the basement supermarket of the Åhléns department store at Sergels torg or those at Järntorget in Gamla Stan and Katarinavägen 3–7 at Slussen.

Day-trips from Stockholm

VIKING CROSS, BIRKA

Day-trips from Stockholm

Move away from Stockholm, and it's easy to appreciate its unique geographical location. Water surrounds the city and – although you can travel by train and bus – it's worth making the effort to ply the serene waters of Lake Mälaren or the Stockholm archipelago by boat. The archipelago is made up of a staggering 24,000 islands, islets and rocks, as the Swedish mainland slowly splinters into the Baltic Sea; it's a summer paradise for holidaying city dwellers.

A boat trip inland along Lake Mälaren is also a must, either to the Viking island of **Birka**, where you can see the remains of Sweden's most important medieval trading centre and a dizzying array of ancient finds, or to **Drottningholm**, the seventeenth-century royal residence situated right on the lakeside. Another easy excursion on Lake Mälaren leads to the impressive castle of **Gripsholm** at Mariefred.

Also within easy day-trip reach are the ancient Swedish capital and medieval university town of **Uppsala** and one of the country's oldest settlements, **Sigtuna**, complete with its rune stones and ruined churches.

If you've flown in with Ryanair, consider spending a day in lakeside **Västerås**, with its fascinating mix of the new and old – including a sixth-century royal burial mound, or handsome **Nyköping** on the Baltic coast which rewards visitors with its laid-back seaside atmosphere and impressive castle.

The Stockholm archipelago

If you arrived in Stockholm by plane, you'll already have had a tantalizing glimpse of the **Stockholm archipelago**. In Swedish the word for archipelago is *skärgård* – literally "garden of skerries" and a pretty accurate description: the array of hundreds upon hundreds of pine-clad islands and islets is the only one of its kind in the world. Most of the little-known islands are flat and are wonderful places for **walking**; we've picked out the most rewarding islands for strolls and hikes, and have suggested a few trails which are a good way to take in the sweeping sea vistas and unspoilt nature here. The archipelago, though, holds another secret, little known even to most Swedes – many of **ABBA**'s most famous hits were written out here, on the island of Viggsö where the famous foursome owned a couple of summer cottages (see box, p.81).

The easiest and fastest section of the archipelago to reach, and consequently the most popular with day-tripping Stockholmers, the **central archipelago** is the islands at their most stunning: hundreds of rocks, skerries, islets and islands jostle for space in the pristine waters of the Baltic, giving the impression of giant stepping-stones leading back to the mainland.

The islands in the northern stretches of the *skärgård* are far fewer in number. As a result, the appearance of the **northern archipelago** is very different: characterized by open vistas and sea swells rather than narrow sounds and passageways, the islands here

LINNÉTRÄDGÅRDEN, UPPSALA

Highlights

❶ Gällnö island, Stockholm archipelago Walk through deep green forest and swim from the shores of an island edged by purple reeds and carpets of wildflowers. **See p.81**

❷ Birka, Lake Mälaren Get to grips with Viking history in Sweden's oldest town. **See p.86**

❸ Utter Inn, Västerås A night spent underwater in this mini-oil-rig-cum-hotel in Lake Mälaren is one of Sweden's most unusual accommodation choices. **See p.92**

❹ Island beaches, Västerås The chain of islands in Lake Mälaren offer the perfect

opportunity to chill out and work on your all-over tan. **See p.93**

❺ Uppsala Potter around the beautiful Linnéträdgården and learn about the fascinating life of the world's leading botanist, Carl von Linné. **See p.93**

❻ Gamla Uppsala Royal burial mounds and a beautiful medieval church add mystery to this ancient pagan settlement. **See p.98**

❼ Nyköping Rent your own boat or take a trip out to the enchanting islands that make up the Nyköping archipelago. **See p.101**

HIGHLIGHTS ARE MARKED ON THE MAP ON P.80

are very much at the mercy of the sea and weather. Although sharing more in appearance with the denser central archipelago than its more barren northern counterpart, the **southern archipelago** is generally much quieter in terms of visitor numbers, because it's harder to reach from central Stockholm.

Vaxholm

1hr from Stockholm by boat

Just an hour from the capital, the island of **Vaxholm** is a popular weekend destination for Stockholmers. Its eponymous town has an atmospheric wooden harbour, whose imposing **fortress** (daily: June noon–4pm; July & Aug 11am–5pm; 50kr; ⓦvaxholmsfastning.se) once guarded the waterways into the city, superseding the fortifications at Riddarholmen. Having successfully staved off attacks from the Danes and the Russians in the seventeenth and eighteenth centuries, the fortress is now an unremarkable museum of military bits and

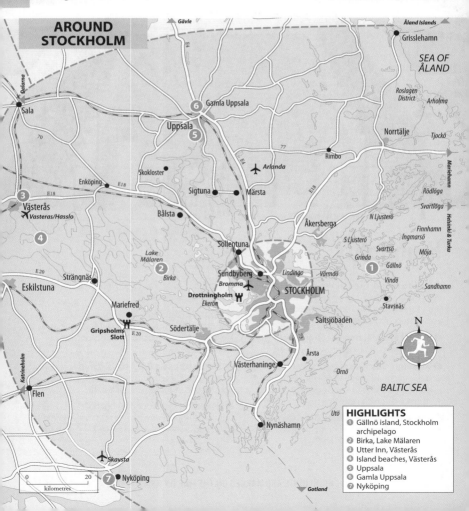

AROUND STOCKHOLM

SEA OF ÅLAND

BALTIC SEA

HIGHLIGHTS
① Gällnö island, Stockholm archipelago
② Birka, Lake Mälaren
③ Utter Inn, Västerås
④ Island beaches, Västerås
⑤ Uppsala
⑥ Gamla Uppsala
⑦ Nyköping

0   20
kilometres

pieces However, since all boats to and from Stockholm dock at Vaxholm, it's often swarming with visitors, so do yourself a favour – stay on the boat and seek out one of the archipelago's quieter islands, which are quite frankly more worthy of your attention.

Grinda

1hr 20min from Stockholm by boat

Grinda, a thickly wooded island typical of the central archipelago, with some sandy beaches. It's particularly popular with families and so can be busy, particularly at weekends. In its favour, Grinda has frequent boat connections, a pleasant **youth hostel** (see p.85), several ad hoc **campsites**, a **restaurant** and a **café** in the centre of the island. To enjoy the sunshine on summer afternoons, head for beaches on the southern side of the island, as the tall trees on the northern side block out the sun. Boats dock at two jetties at its southern (Södra Grinda) and northern ends (Norra Grinda); a walk between the two takes thirty to forty minutes.

Gällnö

1hr 30min–2hr from Stockholm by boat

A beautiful low-lying island covered with thick pine forest, **Gällnö** is the archipelago at its best. Home to just thirty people, a couple of whom farm the land near the jetty, Gällnö has been designated a nature reserve: you can spot deer in the forest or watch eider ducks diving for fish. The **youth hostel** (see p.85) is well signposted from the main village, where there's also a small **shop** selling provisions. From here, there's the choice of two **walks**: either head east through the forest for Gällnönäs, from where you can pick up boats back to Stockholm or further out into the islands, or continue past the youth hostel, following signs for Brännholmen until you arrive at a small bay popular with yachties. Look for the hut where the toilet is, as one of its walls bears a map and sign on the outside showing the path leading from here to the row-boats – these enable you to cross the narrow sound (around 15m wide) separating Gällnö from its neighbour, Karklö. When you head across, remember to leave one boat on either side of the sound (see box, p.84).

Karklö

2hr from Stockholm by boat

Karklö is one of the most unspoilt islands in the archipelago and, combined with Gällnö, makes for an excellent day-trip from Stockholm. There are no shops or roads here, only tracks which meander across the island and around farmers' fields, connecting the spot where the row-boats are moored with the main jetty on the other side, where the boats from Stockholm dock. The paths can be difficult to find at times, so it's best to ask directions in the main village, which is close to the row-boat moorings.

THANK VIGGSÖ FOR THE MUSIC

The rocky outcrop topped by dense pine forest that lies sandwiched between Grinda and much larger Värmdö to the south holds a big secret. It was here on the island of **Viggsö** that **ABBA** composed *Dancing Queen*, *Fernando* and several other chart-topping hits; shots of Viggsö were also used in *ABBA The Movie*. Agnetha and Björn bought a summer cottage here in 1971, closely followed in 1974 by Benny and Anni-Frid; the sound of piano music drifting across the treetops a sure sign that one or other couple had sailed their boat out from Stockholm to spend a few days away from the city. The two men would spend days at a time in Björn's yellow wooden outhouse hammering away at a battered upright piano and strumming an old guitar – the restorative calm of Viggsö was at the heart of much of ABBA's music-making.

2

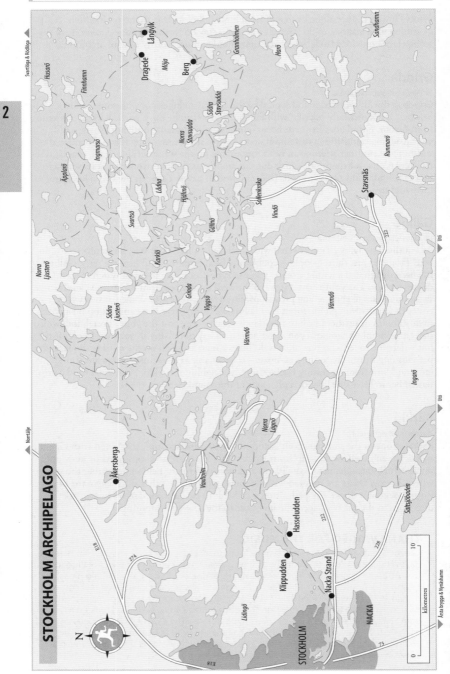

STOCKHOLM ARCHIPELAGO

Svartsö

2–3hr from Stockholm by boat

North of Gällno, **Svartsö** is busier than its neighbour, though it's never overrun with visitors and there's plenty of space to unwind and sunbathe on the rocky shores – particularly on the western edge of the island. With its fields of grazing sheep, thick virgin forest and crystal-clear lakes, Svartsö has a more pastoral feel than some of the other surrounding islands, where forest predominates, and there are also good roads which make it ideal for cycling or walking.

From the northern jetty, where most boats from Stockholm arrive, there's a pleasant walk – lasting about ninety minutes – along the road towards the two lakes in the centre of the island. Just before you arrive at the lakes, turn right into the path that follows the lakeside, passing a few houses on the way. The road then becomes a track heading into the forest. Continue past a couple of hayfields in a forest clearing, and eventually you'll glimpse the sea through the trees at the forest edge; this is an ideal place to sunbathe nude or stop for a picnic. Past a farmhouse and a couple of barns, the track eventually turns into a road again; from here it's another twenty- to thirty-minutes' walk to the village of **Alsvik**, with its post office and **shop** where you can buy snacks and refreshments – ferry connections back to the capital also depart from here.

Ingmarsö

2hr 30min–3hr from Stockholm by boat

Ingmarsö is an excellent island for walkers. Most boats dock at the northern jetty (Norra Ingmarsö), and from here you can do an enjoyable roundabout **walk** that takes you across the island and onto neighbouring Finnhamn, from where you can catch a boat back. Follow the main road away from the northern jetty, and after about fifteen minutes, turn left at the signpost marked "Båtdraget" and "Femsund". Before making this turn you may want to continue straight ahead for five minutes to the island's **supermarket** to stock up on provisions, before retracing your steps to the signpost. The road to Femsund eventually turns into a track – marked by blue dots on tree trunks – which strikes out through the forest heading for Kålmårsön. After about an hour, the path skirts a wonderfully isolated lake, where you can swim and sunbathe, before passing through more unspoilt forest and emerging at a small bay filled with yachts. Look carefully here for the continuation of the path – still marked with blue dots – which will take you to rowing-boat moorings at the narrow sound (around 20m wide) between here and Finnhamn. If you fail to locate the path, follow the coast round to the right for roughly ten to fifteen minutes while facing the yachts in the bay. It takes about two and a half hours to get to the sound from the northern jetty. Row over to Finnhamn, remembering to leave one row-boat on either side of the sound (see box, 84).

Finnhamn

The journey time back to Stockholm is around two hours

Although only a tiny island, **Finnhamn** is often busy because of its popular **youth hostel** (see p.85). To walk from the row-boat moorings to the main jetty and the youth hostel takes around forty minutes. During summer, the café by the jetty serves up simple snacks and refreshments. If the crowds are too much here, head southeast from Finnhamn's tiny main village for the adjoining islet of Lilla Jolpan, where there are some good bathing opportunities.

Svartlöga and Rödlöga

For a shorter boat journey, you can get here in 90min from Furusund, a coastal town reached from central Stockholm in about 2hr by a combination of T-bana and bus: from Danderyds sjukhus T-bana, take bus #676 to Norrtälje, and change to the #634 to Furusund

Lying far out in the Baltic towards Finland, Svartlöga and Rödlöga (4hr from Stockholm by boat) have untouched nature in plenty. **Svartlöga** is the only island in the archipelago whose forest is totally deciduous, and was one of the few to escape Russian incursions in 1719 during the Great Northern War. There are several good rocky beaches on which to relax after the long journey here. Neighbouring **Rödlöga** is a much tinier red-granite affair, with no roads – just leafy paths, overgrown hedgerows thick with wild roses and wonderful secluded beaches.

2

Sandhamn

2hr from Stockholm by boat

With its fine harbour, the island of **Sandhamn** has been a destination for seafarers since the eighteenth century and remains so today, attracting yachts of all shapes and sizes. The main village is a haven of narrow alleyways, winding streets and overgrown verandas. If you fancy staying overnight there are a couple of options (see opposite).

Utö

3hr 30min from Stockholm by boat

Far out in the southern reaches of the archipelago, **Utö** is flat and thus ideal for cycling; it's not bad for bathing and picnics either. There are excellent views from the island's windmill on Kvarnbacken hill, ten minutes' walk southwest of the jetty. There's also a youth hostel (see opposite).

ARRIVAL AND DEPARTURE   THE ARCHIPELAGO

By boat Getting to the islands is easy, with Waxholmsbolaget (☎ 08 679 58 30, ⓦ waxholmsbolaget .se) operating the majority of the passenger-only sailings into the archipelago; its boats leave daily from Strömkajen in front of the Grand Hotel and the National Museum.
Tickets Tickets are reasonable: Grinda, for example, is 90kr one-way, whereas Finnhamn, one of the furthest islands, is

130kr; pay on the boat. If you're planning to visit several islands, it might be worth buying the Båtluffarkort (Archipelago Card; 420kr, plus a 40kr refundable deposit on return of the card), which gives five days' unlimited travel on all Waxholmbolaget lines. If there's no direct boat to your destination, connections can often be made on the island of Vaxholm.

INFORMATION

Tourist office For timetables and ideas of where to go, drop into the Visit Skärgården information office (☎ 08 10 02 22, ⓦ visitskargarden.se; June–Aug Mon-Fri 9am–4.30pm, Sat &

Sun 10am–4pm; Sept–May Mon-Fri 10am-4pm) on Strandvägen at Kajplats 18, where staff can also help with accommodation and eating options.

ACCOMMODATION

There are few **hotels** in the archipelago but it does have plenty of well-equipped and comfortable **youth hostels**, all of which are open in the summer (May–Sept). It's also possible to rent **summer cottages** on the islands for 3000–6000kr

---

DON'T MISS THE BOAT

If you're waiting for the boat out in the archipelago, you must **raise the semaphore flag** on the jetty to indicate that you want to be picked up; torches are kept in the huts on the jetties for the same purpose at night.

In some parts of the archipelago, it's possible to visit a couple of islands on the same trip by taking the ferry to your first port of call, then **rowing across** to a neighbouring island, from where you return to Stockholm by the ferry again – we've detailed these options in the text. For this purpose, there'll be a row-boat either side of the water separating you from your destination. When you use the boats, you have to ensure there's always one left on either side – this entails rowing across, attaching the other boat to yours, rowing back to your starting point, where you leave one boat behind, and then rowing across one last time.

a week for four people – for more information on prices, contact the tourist office in Stockholm. For summer stays, you'll need to book well in advance – at least six months before – or you may well find that you've been pipped to the post by holidaying Swedes. It's important to remember that there are very few restaurants in the archipelago and opening times fluctuate. It's a much wiser idea to buy some provisions and go self-catering.

GRINDA

Grinda Wärdshus Södra Brygga ☎ 08 542 494 91, ⓦ grindawardshus.se. Youth hostel, hotel and cabin accommodation on the south coast, east of the southern jetty. The hostel and cabins close Nov–April but the hotel stays open all year and can be wonderfully peaceful out of season. Hostel double 600kr; hotel double with private facilities and breakfast 900kr; two-person cabin 1000kr

GÄLLNÖ

Youth hostel Gällnöby ☎ 08 571 661 17, ⓦ gallno.se. This idyllic STF hostel is surrounded by low-hanging trees and a pretty garden. The track leading to it is well signposted from the tiny main village. Open mid-May to Sept. Dorms 200kr, doubles 400kr

FINNHAMN

Youth hostel Finnhamns brygga ☎ 08 542 462 12, ⓦ finnhamn.se. Another STF gem, this one is set in a dramatically located yellow building complete with waterfront sauna, and perched on rocks looking out to sea. Open all year. Dorms 275kr, doubles 550kr

SANDHAMN

Sandhamns Värdshus Main village ☎ 08 571 530 51, ⓦ sandhamns-vardshus.se. An agreeable bed-and-breakfast establishment housed in an attractive timber building by the shore, also serving excellent seafood. Contrary to the Swedish norm, prices rise here in summer and at weekends. 1290kr/990kr

Seglarhotellet Main village ☎ 08 574 504 00, ⓦ sandhamn.com. An exclusive and rather swanky hotel, catering for wealthy yachties and serving excellent seafood; some of the rooms have desirable balconies overlooking the sea. Self-catering apartments also available. Doubles 2390kr, apartments 2590kr

UTÖ

Youth hostel Gruvbryggan, near where the ferry docks ☎ 08 504 203 00, ⓦ utovardshus.se. This comfortable hostel has three elegant wooden verandas overlooking the sea and has two self-catering kitchens on site. Open May–Sept. Dorms 350kr, doubles 700kr

Around Lake Mälaren

Freshwater **Lake Mälaren** dominates the countryside west of Stockholm, and provides the backdrop to some of the capital region's most appealing day-trip destinations. Boats sail frequently to **Drottningholm**, home to the Swedish royal family, as well as pretty **Mariefred**, an enchanting little town on the lake's southern shore with a magnificent castle. Sweden's main settlement during the ninth and tenth centuries, **Birka**, an island in Mälaren accessed by boat from Stockholm, is great for anyone interested in Sweden's stirring Viking past. The main city on the lake is **Västerås**, a modern and thoroughly enjoyable place with good sandy beaches and some impressive Viking remains, too.

Drottningholm

Palace April & Oct Sat & Sun 11am–3.30pm; May–Aug daily 11am–4.30pm; Sept daily 11am–3.30pm; Nov–March Sat & Sun noon–3.30pm • 80kr, 120kr including the Kina slott **Kina slott** May–Aug daily 11am–4.30pm; Sept noon–3.30pm; 70kr, 120kr including the Palace • ⓦ royalcourt.se

Even if your time in Stockholm is limited, try to see the architecturally harmonious royal palace of **Drottningholm**. Beautifully located on the shores of leafy **Lovön**, an island 11km west of the centre and less than an hour away, **Drottningholm** is perhaps the greatest achievement of the two architects **Tessin**, father and son. Work began in 1662 on the orders of King Karl X's widow, Eleonora, with Tessin the Elder modelling the new palace in a thoroughly French style – giving rise to the stock comparisons with Versailles. Apart from anything else, it's considerably smaller than its French contemporary, utilizing false perspective and trompe l'oeil to bolster the elegant, though rather narrow, interior. On Tessin the Elder's death in

1681, the palace was completed by his son, then already at work on Stockholm's Kungliga Slottet.

Inside, good English notes are available to help you sort out the riot of Rococo decoration in the rooms, which largely dates from the time when Drottningholm was bestowed as a wedding gift on Princess Louisa Ulrika (a sister of Frederick the Great of Prussia). No hints, however, are needed to spot the influences in the Baroque "French" and the later "English" **gardens** that back onto the palace.

Since 1981, the Swedish royal family has lived out at Drottningholm, instead of in the city centre, using it as a permanent home. This move has accelerated efforts to restore parts of the palace to their original appearance, and the monumental **grand staircase** is now once again exactly as envisaged by Tessin the Elder.

Also within the extensive palace grounds is the **Kina slott (Chinese Pavilion)**, a sort of eighteenth-century royal summerhouse. Originally built by King Adolf Fredrik as a birthday gift to Queen Louisa Ulrika in 1753, the structure is Rococo in design and, though it includes some Chinese flourishes which were the height of fashion at the time of construction, it is predominantly European in appearance.

Slottsteater

Court Theatre • May–Aug daily 11am–4.30pm; Sept noon–3pm; obligatory guided tours every hour • 90kr • ⓦ dtm.se

Within the palace grounds, the **Slottsteater** dates from 1766, but its heyday was a decade later, when Gustav III imported French plays and theatrical companies, making Drottningholm the centre of Swedish artistic life. Take the guided tour and you'll get a florid but accurate account of the theatre's decoration: money to complete the building ran out in the eighteenth century, meaning that things are not what they seem – painted papier-mâché frontages are *krona*-pinching substitutes for the real thing. The original backdrops and stage machinery are still in place though, and the tour comes complete with a display of eighteenth-century special effects including wind and thunder machines, trapdoors and simulated lighting.

ARRIVAL   DROTTNINGHOLM

By boat Boats sail from Stadshusbron on Kungsholmen to Drottningholm during the summer months (May to early Sept daily 9.30am–6pm, hourly; early Sept to late Oct Sat & Sun 2 daily; 90kr one-way, 120kr return), and take just under an hour each way.

By T-bana and bus Take the T-bana to Brommaplan and then any bus from Brommaplan bus terminal (immediately outside the T-bana station). Buses leave from the stop marked for Drottningholm. The Stockholm Card and SL travelcards are valid to Drottningholm.

Birka

The island of **Björkö** (the name means "island of birches"), in Lake Mälaren, is the site of Sweden's oldest town, **BIRKA**, which was founded around 750AD and is now a UNESCO World Heritage site. For over two centuries, Birka was the most important Viking trading centre in the northern countries, benefiting from its strategic location near the mouth of Lake Mälaren on the portage route to Russia and the Byzantine Empire. Today, a visit here is not only an opportunity to get to grips with Sweden's stirring Viking heritage, thanks to the site's excellent museum, but it's also a chance to explore the tranquil waters of Lake Mälaren – should you choose to take the boat here, which is by far the best means of getting to Birka.

Brief history

After Birka was founded in the mid-eighth century, tradesmen and merchants were quick to take advantage of the prosperous and rapidly expanding village, and the population soon grew to around one thousand. The future patron saint of Scandinavia, **Ansgar**, came here in 830 as a missionary at the instruction of the Holy Roman Emperor, Louis I, and established a church in an attempt to Christianize the heathen

Swedes. They showed little interest and the Frankish monk preached on the island for just over a year before being recalled. Birka reached its height during the tenth century before sliding into decline: falling water levels in Lake Mälaren, the superior location of the Baltic island of Gotland for handling Russian-Byzantine trade and the emergence of nearby rival Sigtuna all led to its gradual disappearance after 975.

The museum

Major excavations began on the island in 1990 and the **Birka museum** (open in connection with boat arrivals and departures) now recounts the village's history in superb detail. Exhibitions explain how, during Viking times, Björkö was actually two separate islands, with the main settlement located in the northwest corner of the northernmost island. As the land rose after the last Ice Age, the narrow channel between the two islands vanished, resulting in today's single kidney-shaped island; remains of jetties have been found where the channel would have been, as well as a rampart which acted as an outer wall for the settlement. Displays of historical artefacts as well as scale models of the harbour and craftsmen's quarters are also available for persual – the developed nature of Viking society is evident from the finds: scissors, pottery and even keys have all been excavated.

The graveyard

Among the remains of Viking-age life, the most striking is Birka's **graveyard**, which is the largest Viking-age burial ground in Scandinavia with around four hundred burial mounds, some accompanied by standing stones. Totally surrounding the site of the former village, the graveyard can be found outside the rampart by turning right from where the boat arrives.

ARRIVAL AND INFORMATION   **BIRKA**

By boat From Stockholm, Strömma Kanalbolaget sail from Stadshusbron outside Stadshuset on Kungsholmen (early May to early Sept Mon–Fri 9.30am, Sat & Sun 10am; 2hr; 310kr return including museum entry; ⓦ stromma .se/birka). Between July and mid-August Rederi Mälarstaden also operate a boat (Fri only 9.45am from Västerås; ⓦ rederimalarstaden.se; 345kr return) between Västerås and Birka; it's therefore possible to sail between Stockholm and Västerås by changing boats at Birka.
Website For complete information about Birka, check out ⓦ raa.se/birka, where you'll find full details in English about Birka's history as well as practical visitor information, including the latest ferry schedules.

Mariefred

Located on the graceful southern shores of Lake Mälaren, **MARIEFRED** is a tiny, quintessentially Swedish village about an hour west of the city, whose peaceful attractions are bolstered by one of Sweden's finest castles, **Gripsholm**, which you might recognize if you owned any ABBA albums back in the 1970s and 1980s (see p.88), and just a short walk from the centre. A couple of minutes up from the quayside and you're strolling through narrow streets where the well-kept wooden houses and little squares have scarcely changed in decades. Other than the castle, the only real sight is the **railway museum**, which offers a rare chance in Sweden to see working steam engines.

Railway Museum

Steam trains leave Mariefred roughly hourly 11am–4pm Sat & Sun May–Sept and daily 10am–4pm late June to mid-Aug • 80kr return, includes entrance to the museum • ☎ 0159 210 08, ⓦ oslj.nu
Steam-train fans will love the **Railway Museum** at the railway station in Läggesta (alight here for Mariefred), an adjoining small village five minutes' bus ride south of Mariefred – you'll probably have noticed the narrow-gauge tracks running all the way to the quayside. There's an exhibition of old rolling stock and workshops, given added interest by the fact that narrow-gauge **steam trains** still run between Mariefred and **Läggesta**, a twenty-minute ride away on the Östra Sörmlands Järnväg railway. From Läggesta, it's

possible to pick up the regular SJ train back to Stockholm; check for connections at the Mariefred tourist office. Of course, you could always come to Mariefred from Stockholm by this route too (see below).

Gripsholms slott

Mid-May to mid-Sept daily 10am–4pm; mid-Sept to Nov Sat & Sun noon–3pm • 80kr • English guided tours (mid-May to mid-Sept daily 1pm; 1hr; 20kr extra) • ⊛ royalcourt.se

Lovely though Mariefred is, it's really only a preface to seeing **Gripsholms slott**, the imposing red-brick castle built on a round island just to the south (walk up the quayside, and you'll see the path to the castle running across the grass by the water's edge). In the late fourteenth century, Bo Johnsson Grip, the Swedish high chancellor, began to build a fortified castle at Mariefred, although the present building owes more to two Gustavs – Gustav Vasa, who started rebuilding in the sixteenth century, and Gustav III, who was responsible for major restructuring a couple of centuries later. Rather than the hybrid that might be expected, the result is rather pleasing – an engaging textbook castle with turrets, great halls, corridors and battlements. There are optional English-language **guided tours**, on which the key elements of the castle's construction and history are pointed out: there's a vast portrait collection that includes recently commissioned works depicting political and cultural figures as well as assorted royalty and nobility; some fine decorative and architectural work; and, as at Drottningholm, a private theatre, built for Gustav III. It's too delicate to be used for performances these days, but in summer, plays and other events are staged out in the castle grounds; more information can be obtained from Mariefred's tourist office (see below). Even **ABBA** have put in an appearance here – in February 1974 Gripsholm was used as the cover shot for their *Waterloo* album.

ARRIVAL AND DEPARTURE   MARIEFRED

By train There's a service from Stockholm to Läggesta, from where connecting buses and, at certain times of year, steam trains (see p.87) shuttle passengers into Mariefred. Destination Stockholm (hourly; 35min).

By steamboat In summer, you can get here from Stockholm on the *S/S Mariefred*, which leaves from Klara Mälarstrand, near Stadshuset on Kungsholmen (late May to mid-June & late Aug to mid-Sept Sat & Sun 10am; mid-June to mid-Aug Tues–Sun 10am; 3hr 30min each way; 190kr one-way, 260kr return; ⊛ mariefred.info); buy your ticket on board.

INFORMATION

Tourist office Located on a houseboat down by the harbour at Hamnplanen (mid-May to mid-June & early to mid-Sept Mon–Fri 10am–4pm, Sat 9am–4pm; mid-June to late June & Aug Mon–Fri 10am–6pm, Sat & Sun 9am–4pm; July daily 9am–7pm; ☎0159 296 99, ⊛ strangnas.se).

ACCOMMODATION

Djurgårdsporten Djurgårdsgatan 2 ☎0159 124 15, ✉ djurgardsporten@live.se. Basic but centrally located youth hostel; books up early in summer so make sure you reserve well in advance. Dorms <u>200kr</u>, doubles <u>400kr</u>

Gripsholms Värdhus Kyrkogatan 1 ☎0159 347 50, ⊛ gripsholms-vardshus.se. Gloriously opulent rooms full of elegant period furniture in a beautifully restored inn (the oldest in Sweden) overlooking the castle and the lake. Supplements from 500kr per night will upgrade you to one of several luxurious suites. <u>2290kr</u>

EATING

Anna på torget Kyrkogatan 11. Head to this café in the main square for coffee and cakes and don't miss its mouthwatering tart of the month (*månadens tårta*). Also serves its own brand of hand-selected fair-trade coffee. Mon–Thurs 9am–6pm, Sat 10am–11pm, Sun 10am–6pm.

Gripsholms Slottspaviljong In the park between the castle and the town centre. There's a good selection of salmon and meat dishes at this open-air café, costing around 105–195kr, as well as light lunches and snacks. May–Aug daily 10am–9pm.

Gripsholms Värdhus Kyrkogatan 1 ☎0159 347 50. Treat yourself to lunch here and save a fortune over the regular evening prices; whenever you eat, though, the modern Swedish food is excellent (mains cost 225–315kr)

and the restaurant enjoys terrific views over to Gripsholm. Mon–Fri 11.30am–10pm, Sat noon–10pm, Sun noon–9pm.

Mariefreds Hamnkafe Hamnplanen. This simple café down by the harbour is the best place in town to enjoy freshly baked waffles and cinnamon buns with a cup of coffee. June Sat & Sun 10am–6pm, July and first 2 weeks of Aug daily 10am–6pm.

Västerås

Capital of the county of Västmanland and Sweden's sixth biggest city, **VÄSTERÅS** is an immediately likeable mix of old and new. Today, this lakeside conurbation, 100km west of Stockholm, carefully balances its dependence on ABB, the industrial technology giant, with a rich history dating back to Viking times. If you're looking for a place that's lively and cosmopolitan, yet retains cobbled squares, picturesque wooden houses and even a sixth-century royal burial mound, you won't go far wrong here. Västerås also boasts some of Lake Mälaren's best **beaches**, all a short ferry ride from the city centre.

Svartån River

From the train station, it's a short stroll up Köpmangatan to the twin cobbled squares of Bondtorget and Storatorget. The slender lane from the southwestern corner of Bondtorget leads to the narrow **Svartån river**, which runs right through the centre of the city; the bridge over the river here (known as Apotekarbron) has great views of the old wooden cottages which nestle eave-to-eave along the riverside. Although it may not appear significant (the Svartån is actually much wider further upstream), the river was a decisive factor in making Västerås the headquarters of one of the world's largest engineering companies, **Asea-Brown-Boveri** (ABB), which needed a ready source of water for production; if you arrived by train from Stockholm you'll have passed its metallurgy and distribution centres on approaching the station.

Asea Stream

In Storatorget look out for the striking sculpture of a string of cyclists, the *Asea Stream*, which is supposed to portray the original workers of ABB as they made their way to work; today the sculpture is also a reminder of the impressive fact that Västerås has over 300km of bicycle tracks and is a veritable haven for cyclists.

Domkyrkan

Västra Kyrkogatan • Mon–Fri 8am–5pm, Sat & Sun 9.30am–5pm

North of the two main squares, the brick **Domkyrkan** dates from the thirteenth century, although its two outer aisles are formed from a number of chapels built around the existing church during the following two centuries. The original tower was destroyed by fire, leaving Nicodemus Tessin the Younger (who also built the Kungliga Slottet in Stockholm, see p.48) to design the current structure in 1693. The highly ornate gilded oak triptych above the altar was made in Antwerp, and depicts the suffering and resurrection of Christ. To the right of the altar lies the tomb of Erik XIV, who died an unceremonious death imprisoned in Örbyhus castle in 1577 after eating his favourite pea soup – little did he realize it was laced with arsenic. Local rumour has it that the king's feet had to be cut off in order for his body to fit the coffin, which was built too small. Today though, his elegant, black-marble sarcophagus rests on a plinth of reddish sandstone from Öland.

Kyrkbacken

Beyond the cathedral is the most charming district of Västerås, **Kyrkbacken**, a hilly area that stretches just a few hundred metres. Here, steep cobblestone alleys wind between well-preserved old wooden houses where artisans and the petit bourgeoisie lived in the eighteenth century. Thankfully, the area was saved from the great fire of

2

1714 – which destroyed much of Västerås – and the wholesale restructuring of the 1960s. At the top end of Djäknegatan, the main street of the district, look for a narrow alley called Brunnsgränd, along which is a house bearing the sign "Mästermansgården": it was once the abode of the most hated and ostracized man in the district – the town executioner.

Stadshuset
A quick walk past the restaurants and shops of Vasagatan in the city centre will bring you to Storagatan, and eventually to the eye-catching modern **Stadshuset** in Fiskatorget – the building is a far cry from the Dominican monastery which once stood on this spot. Although home to the city's administration, the Stadshuset is best known for its 47 bells, the largest of which is known as "the Monk" and can be heard across the city at lunchtimes.

Västerås Konstmuseum and Länsmuseum
Art museum and county museum • Karlsgatan 2 • Tues, Wed & Fri 10am–5pm, Thurs 10am–8pm, Sat & Sun noon–4pm • Free • Ⓦ vasteraskonstmuseum.se; Ⓦ vastmanlandslansmuseum.se

In new premises at Karlsgatan 2, the town's compact art museum, the **Västerås Konstmuseum**, is rather disappointing. It's worth a quick look for its contemporary collections of Swedish and other Nordic art – but don't expect too much. Sharing the same building, the **Länsmuseum** unfortunately also lacks direction, containing a rag-tag collection of obscure items such as children's dolls and old typewriters, plonked in glass cabinets; you'll glean little about the province's history from this load of junk.

The Anundshög burial mound
To get here, take bus #40 from the centre of town (bus times are at Ⓦ vl.se); buy your bus ticket at the tourist office, as it's no longer possible to buy them on the bus.

Whilst in Västerås, try not to miss nearby **Anundshög**, the largest royal burial mound in Sweden, just 6km northeast of the city. Dating from the sixth century, the mound – at 60m in diameter and 14m high – is said to be the resting place of King Bröt-Anund and his stash of gold. Although unexcavated, the mound is widely thought to contain the remains of a cremation burial and a stone cist. Anundshög was also used for sessions of the local *ting*, or Viking parliament, and several other smaller burial mounds nearby suggest that the site was an important Viking meeting place over several centuries. Beside the main mound lie a large number of **standing stones** arranged end-to-end in the shape of two ships measuring 53m and 50m in diameter. The nearby **rune stone** dates from around 1000 AD though it's not thought to be connected to the burial mound. The stone's inscription, when translated, reads "Folkvid erected all these stones for his son, Hedin, brother of Anund. Vred carved the runes."

ARRIVAL AND DEPARTURE   VÄSTERÅS

By plane The airport, served by Ryanair flights from London Stansted, is just 6km east of the city, from where pre-booked shuttle taxis (☎ 018 18 50 00; Ⓦ taxivasteras. se) run to the centre (50kr).
By train The train station is on Södra Ringvägen, with a

sea of bicycles neatly standing in racks right outside.
Destinations Stockholm (hourly; 1hr); Gothenburg (6 daily; 4hr).
By bus Arriving by bus you'll be dropped at the terminal adjacent to the train station.

INFORMATION

Tourist office Kopparbergsvägen 1 (Mon–Fri 10am–6pm, Sat 10am–3pm; also July to mid-Aug Sun 10am–2pm; ☎ 021 39 01 00, Ⓦ www.vasterasmalarstaden.se).

Barely a 2min walk from the train station, with plenty of information and internet access.

CLOCKWISE FROM TOP LEFT THE UTTER INN, LAKE MÄLAREN(P.92). GÄLLNÖ, STOCKHOLM ARCHIPELAGO (P.81); TRADITIONAL WOODEN BUILDINGS, NYKÖPING (P.101); THRONE ROOM, DROTTNINGHOLM (P.85) >

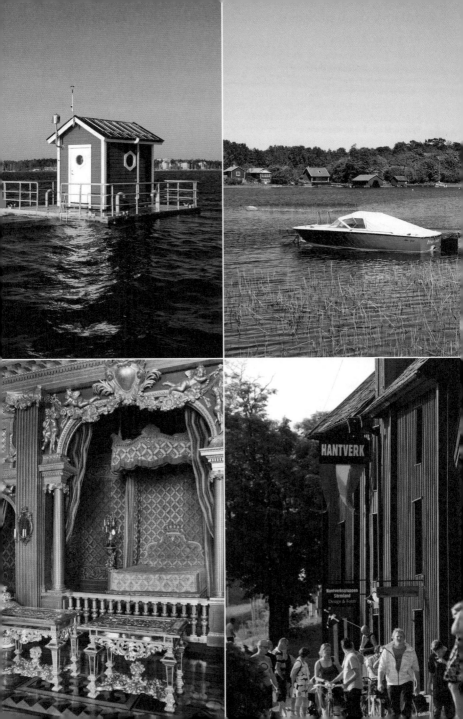

2

ACCOMMODATION

Arkad Östermalmsgatan 25 ☎021 12 04 80, ⓦhotellarkad.se. Individually designed rooms ranging from contemporary Swedish to nineteenth-century classic. Excellent sauna suite incorporating darts and pool. Some rooms include a small kitchen for self-catering which represent excellent value for money. **795kr/1250kr**

Björnö Stug- & aktivitetscenter Björnö, ☎021 261 00, ⓦbjornoab.se. Located 7km southeast of Västerås, close to the airport, this place has good-value cabins for rent and also rents kayaks and arranges fishing trips. Open all year round. Two-berth cabin **380kr**

Elite Stadshotellet Storatorget ☎021 10 28 00, ⓦwww.vasteras.elite.se. This classic Jugendstil hotel opened in 1907 and oozes old-world charm with its sweeping staircases, elaborate chandeliers and elegant rooms where contemporary and antique meet. Superb location in the main square at the heart of everything. **950kr/1350kr**

First Plaza Karlsgatan 9A ☎021 10 10 10, ⓦfirsthotels .com/plaza. Known locally as the "Skyscraper", this 25-storey glass-and-chrome structure is the last word in Scandinavian chic. Rooms are light and airy, featuring stylish, contemporary Swedish design and have panoramic views of the city and Lake Mälaren. The summer/weekend rate is particularly good value. **900kr/1400kr**

★ **Hotell Hackspett** Vasaparken ☎021 39 01 00, ⓦwww.vasterasmalarstaden.se. A fabulous one-room treehouse 13m off the ground in the largest oak tree in Vasaparken, bookable only through the tourist office. **1200kr** per person on a B&B basis or **1500kr** per person for half-board

Klipper Kungsgatan 4 ☎021 41 00 00, ⓦklipperhotel .se. This centrally located option overlooking the lazy Svartån River in the old town offers charming rooms done out in early nineteenth-century style. Make your own bed and forego breakfast to cut the low rate by 200kr. **695kr/945kr**

★ **Utter Inn** Lake Mälaren ☎021 39 01 00, ⓦwww .vasterasmalarstaden.se. A platform 1km out into Lake Mälaren, not unlike a mini oil rig, whose one and only bedroom is actually underwater. Whilst not for the claustrophobic, it's certainly memorable. Bookable only through the tourist office. **1250kr** per person on a B&B basis or **1500kr** per person for half-board

Västerås Vasagatan 22 ☎021 18 03 30, ⓦhotell vasteras.se. Modern if rather cramped rooms in this well-located hotel in town right in the city centre. A worthwhile 100kr extra gets you a superior room with a balcony overlooking one of the main shopping streets. **710kr/1095kr**

EATING AND DRINKING

Västerås has easily the best **restaurants** of any town around Lake Mälaren. You'll find all kinds of cuisine, from Thai to Greek, traditional Swedish to British-style pub food. The city also has a lively **drinking** scene, including one cocktail bar 24 floors up, from where there are unsurpassed views of the lake.

Akropolis Smedjegatan 6 ☎021 12 38 48. Dine amid Greek busts, Ionic columns and Olympic torches at this smart Greek restaurant serving Greek salad (65kr), souvlaki (149kr) and a range of grilled meat dishes (from 145kr). Mon–Thurs 11am–10pm, Fri 11am–11pm, Sat noon–11pm, Sun noon–9pm.

Bellman Storatorget 6 ☎021 41 33 55. The smartest restaurant in town with eighteenth-century furniture and linen tablecloths serving modern Swedish dishes such as elk fillet in red wine sauce with chanterelle mushrooms (245kr). Count on 139–245kr per dish. Mon–Thurs 11am–11pm, Fri 11am–1am, Sat noon–1am.

Bill o Bob Storatorget 5 ☎021 41 99 21. This pub restaurant with curious stained-glass windows covers all corners: everything from lamb steak (279kr) and grilled salmon (220kr) to egg and bacon (69kr) and *pytt i panna* (89kr). Mon & Tues 4–11pm, Wed & Thurs 4pm–midnight, Fri 4pm–2am, Sat noon–2am.

Bishops Arms Storatorget. Enjoyable British-style pub perfectly located in the main square, attached to the *Elite Stadshotellet*, with a large selection of beers and single malt whiskies. Pub food also available and there's outdoor seating in summer. Mon & Sun 5–11pm, Tues–Thurs 4pm–midnight, Fri 3pm–1am, Sat 1pm–1am.

Frank Bistro Storatorget 3 ☎021 13 65 00. Serving modern Swedish gourmet dishes, there's no set menu at this trendy little restaurant off the main square, instead, it's whatever the chefs decide to cook up – always inspired and delicious; 475kr for three courses. Tues–Sat 5pm till late.

Kalle på Spången Kungsgatan 2. Snug and cosy café with tabletop candles serving up great baguettes, pasta salads, lasagne and soup as well as cakes and a good choice of coffees. It also has a couple of outdoor tables in summer. Mon–Sat 10am–10pm, Sun 11am–10pm.

Karlsson på taket Karlsgatan 9A ☎021 10 10 98. Chi-chi café-restaurant on the 23rd floor of the *First Plaza*. Not as expensive as you might imagine and the views are fantastic. Reckon on around 225–290kr per main dish, for example corn-fed chicken with truffles or steak with morel mushrooms. Mon–Sat 5–11pm.

Limone Storagatan 4 ☎021 41 75 60. Stylish modern Italian restaurant with high-backed leather chairs and painted walls, serving top-notch pasta starters from 87kr and regular meat mains, for example, saltimbocca with

VÄSTERÅS BEACHES AND BOAT TRIPS

Boats run from Färjkajen quay in the harbour, southwest of the train station to a string of small islands in Lake Mälaren blessed with great **beaches**.

The closest is **Östra Holmen**, which is noted for its three excellent **nudist beaches** on the southern shore. It's popular with locals who come here to enjoy the wide open views of Lake Mälaren and to explore the island's undisturbed shoreline – an easy circular walk of around 2km.

Further south, much larger **Ridön** traces its history back to Viking times, and is today a peaceful haven of forest, sheltered coves ideal for **swimming**. A country lane winds across the centre of the island from west to east; there's a small **café** and wooden bell tower at the point where this lane meets the path leading up from the ferry jetty.

Two other uninhabited islands, **Almö-Lindö** and tiny **Skåpholmen** are perfect for seekers of total solitude. Almö-Lindö, which the boat reaches first, is the better bet since it's larger, has more varied terrain and some good swimming beaches – though no facilities. **Skåpholmen** is a skinny sliver of an island, again with no facilities.

Detailed **ferry times** can be found at ⓦ rederimalarstaden.se but generally boats sail several times daily between late May and early September.

Parma ham and sage for around 225kr. Mon–Fri 11am–1.30pm & 5.30–10pm, Sat 5.30–10pm.

Piazza di Spagna Vasagatan 26 ☎021 12 42 10. The best Italian in town and a very popular place for lunch. Pizzas cost 80–130kr whilst mains such as fillet of venison in cognac sauce, pepper steak or fried scampi are fairly priced at around 200kr. Mon–Tues 11am–10pm, Wed–Fri 11am–11pm, Sat 11.30am–11pm, Sun 1–10pm.

★ **Spicy Hot** Sturegatan 20A ☎021 18 17 40. A rather understated interior with simple wooden tables and chairs, but the food here is top-notch: excellent Thai curries and stir fries cost 92kr, and there's a range of vegetarian dishes. Mon–Sat 11am–10pm, Sun noon–9pm.

Tabazco Storagatan 36 ☎021 21 91 90. Locals flock to this retro lounge restaurant (with flock wallpaper wherever you look), for superb tapas (35–62kr) such as marinated lamb, calamari and tortilla. The restaurant is set back from the road in the courtyard. Tues 5–10pm, Wed & Thurs 5pm–midnight, Fri 4pm–1am, Sat 5pm–1am.

Varda Vasagatan 14 ☎021 14 81 50. Chi-chi lounge restaurant with floor-to-ceiling windows and a stylish, contemporary interior that really draws the crowds. Try the roast reindeer fried with spices (297kr) or the baked salmon with spinach (219kr). Mon & Tues 11.30am–2pm & 5–11pm, Wed & Thurs 11.30am–2pm & 5pm–midnight, Fri 11.30am–1am, Sat noon–1am, Sun 1–10pm.

Uppsala and Nyköping

Away from Lake Mälaren and the archipelago, several other destinations make ideal day-trips from Stockholm. **Uppsala**, a vibrant university city, lies 70km to the north and boasts some great museums, including the home and gardens of world-renowned botanist Carl von Linné, whilst nearby **Sigtuna**, with its rambling cobbled streets and ruined churches, is steeped in history dating back to the eleventh century. In the opposite direction, 100km southwest of the capital, historic **Nyköping** not only offers an introduction to small-town Sweden but also makes a handy stop if you're heading on from Stockholm Skavsta airport.

Uppsala and around

First impressions as the train pulls into **UPPSALA**, only an hour northeast of Stockholm, are encouraging, as the red-washed castle looms up behind the railway sidings with the cathedral dominant in the foreground. A medieval seat of religion and learning, Uppsala clings to the past through its cathedral and university, and a striking succession of related buildings in their vicinity. The city is regarded as the historical and religious centre of the country, and attracts day-trippers seeking a lively alternative to Stockholm as well as travellers looking for a worthwhile stop on the long trek north.

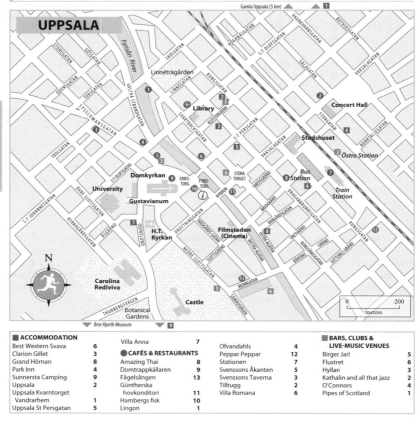

Concert Hall

Vaksala torg 1 • Mon–Fri 9am–6pm, Sat 10am–4pm • Free • Ⓦ ukk.se

From the train and bus stations, it's best to make the new **Concert Hall** your first port of call, barely a five-minute walk away on Storgatan, just the other side of the train tracks. A mammoth structure of brushed steel and glass, whose facade resembles the keys of a giant piano keyboard, it's certainly divided local opinion; many people believe it's little more than a huge carbuncle. Be that as it may, venture inside and take the escalators to the top floor for a superb **view** of the entire city. It hosts Swedish-language theatre as well as musical productions.

Domkyrkan

Domkyrkoplan 2 • Daily 8am–6pm • Free • Ⓦ uppsaladomkyrka.se

From the concert hall, Vaksalagatan leads back under the train tracks and up towards the great **Domkyrkan**, Scandinavia's largest cathedral and the centre of the medieval town. Built as a Gothic boast to the people of Trondheim in Norway that even their mighty church, the Nidarosdom, could be overshadowed, it loses out to its rival only on building materials – local brick rather than imported stone. The echoing interior remains impressive, particularly the French Gothic ambulatory, flanked by tiny chapels and bathed in a golden, decorative glow. One chapel contains a lively set of restored fourteenth-century wall paintings that recount the legend of St Erik, Sweden's patron saint: his coronation, subsequent crusade to Finland, eventual defeat and execution at the hands of the Danes. The Relics of Erik are zealously guarded in a chapel off the nave: poke around and you'll also find the tombs of the Reformation rebel Gustav Vasa and his son Johan III, and that of the botanist Linnaeus (see box, p.96), who lived in Uppsala. Time and fire have led to the rest of the cathedral being rebuilt, scrubbed and painted to the extent that it resembles a museum more than a thirteenth-century place of worship; even the characteristic twin spires are late nineteenth-century additions.

Gustavianum
Akademigatan 3 • Tues–Sun 11am–4pm • 50kr

Opposite the west end of the cathedral, the onion-domed **Gustavianum** was built in 1625 as part of the university, and is much touted by the tourist office for the masterpiece of kitsch that is the **Augsburg Art Cabinet** – a treasure chest of black oak containing all manner of knick-knacks presented to Gustav II Adolf by the Lutheran councillors of Augsburg in 1632 – and the world's first ever thermometer from 1745 owned by none other than Anders Celsius, inventor of the temperature scale. Whilst here be sure to make it up to the top floor to see the perfectly preserved **anatomical theatre** from 1660 where convicts' bodies were once carved up in the name of science, until the church stepped in to end the practice. The same building houses a couple of small collections of Egyptian, Classical and Viking antiquities.

The university
Övre Slottsgatan • Mon–Fri 8am–4pm

The current **university** building is the imposing nineteenth-century Renaissance-style edifice opposite Gustavianum. Originally a seminary, today it's used for lectures and seminars and hosts the graduation ceremonies each May. Among the more famous alumni are Carl von Linné (Linnaeus; see p.96) and Anders Celsius. No one will mind you strolling in for a quick look, but the rest of the building is not open to the public.

Carolina Rediviva
Dag Hammerskjölds väg 1 • Mid-May to Sept Mon–Thurs 9am–6.30pm, Fri until 5.30pm, Sat 10am–5pm, Sun 10am–4pm; rest of year Mon–Fri 9am–8pm, Sat 10am–5pm • Mid-May to Sept 20kr, otherwise free

From the university, Övre Slottsgatan leads south to the **Carolina Rediviva**, the university library and one of Scandinavia's largest, with around five million books. On April 30 (Valborgsmässoafton) each year the students meet here to celebrate the official first day of spring (usually in the snow), all wearing the traditional student cap that gives them the appearance of disaffected sailors. Take a look in the **manuscript room**, where there's a collection of rare letters and other paraphernalia. The beautiful sixth-century Silver Bible is on permanent display, as is Mozart's original manuscript for *The Magic Flute*.

The castle
Övre Slottsgatan • Guided tours in English mid-June to early Sept Tues–Sun 1pm & 3pm • 80kr

When compared to the glorious building of the university, the **castle** up on the hill, built by Gustav Vasa in the mid-sixteenth century, is a disappointment. Certainly significant chapters of Sweden's history were played out here over the centuries: the Uppsala Assembly of 1593, which established the supremacy of the Lutheran Church, took place in the Hall of State, where also, in 1630, the Parliament resolved to enter the Thirty Years' War. Sadly though, much of the castle was destroyed in the 1702 fire that also did away with three-quarters of the city, and only one side and two towers – the L-shape of today – remain of what was once an opulent rectangular palace. Inside, admission also includes access to the castle's art museum but, quite frankly, it won't make your postcards home.

2

CARL VON LINNÉ

Born in Småland in 1707, **Carl von Linné**, who styled himself Carolus Linnaeus, is undoubtedly Sweden's most revered scientist. His international reputation was secured by the introduction of his **binomial classification**, a two-part nomenclature that enabled plants and animals to be consistently named and categorized into families; it was Linnaeus who invented the term *homo sapiens*, for example. Only very recently has the basis of his classifications been undermined by genetic methods, resulting in the complete realignment of certain plant families.

Linnéträdgården

Linnaeus Garden • Svartbäcksgatan 27 • May–Sept Tues–Sun 11am–5pm (gates close at 8pm) • 60kr including the museum • Ⓦ linnaeus.uu.se

The beautiful **Linnéträdgården** contains around 1300 varieties of plants. These are Sweden's oldest botanical gardens, established in 1655 by Olof Rudbeck the Elder, and relaid out by Linnaeus (see box above) in 1741 with perennials and annuals either side of the central path; some of the species he introduced and classified still survive here. Incidentally, you can see the garden behind Linnaeus's head on the 100kr note.

The **museum** adjoining the garden was home to Linnaeus and his family from 1743 to 1778, and attempts to evoke his life through a partially restored library, his writing room and even the bed where he breathed his last.

Bror Hjorth museum

Norbyvägen 26 • Thurs–Sun noon–4pm, also mid-June to mid-Aug Tues & Wed noon–4pm • 40kr, free on Fri • Ⓦ brorhjorthshus.se • Buses #6 and #7 run here from Stora torget in the city centre (10min)

The first sight that greets arrivals at Uppsala train station is an erotic statue of a man with an oversized penis, the work of Uppsala-born sculptor and painter, **Bror Hjorth** (1894–1968), a former professor of drawing at the Swedish Royal Academy of Fine Arts, who's considered one of Sweden's greatest artists. A modernist with roots in folk art, his numerous public art commissions can be seen right across the country – perhaps most strikingly in the church in Jukkasjärvi in Lapland (see p.342). His former home and studio in Uppsala, west of the city centre have now been turned into a **museum** containing the largest and most representative collection of his work in the country.

Linne's Hammarby

May & Sept Fri–Sun 11am–5pm; June–Aug Tues–Sun 11am–5pm (gates always close at 8pm) • 60kr including the garden • Ⓦ hammarby.uu.se • Take bus #102 (or less frequently #186) from the bus station and get off at Hammarby vägskäl from where it's a 2km walk; bus times are at Ⓦ ul.se

In 1754, Carl von Linné (see box above) acquired a country estate at **Hammarby**, 15km southeast of Uppsala, and built a house there. Today, the beautiful homestead, complete with unique wallpaper of botanical engravings, is open to the public and makes a great day-trip. It's surrounded by lush gardens including a collection of Siberian plants and a gene bank for the fruit species of the Lake Mälaren region.

ARRIVAL AND DEPARTURE   UPPSALA

By plane Uppsala can be easily reached from Arlanda airport, Sweden's main airport; trains connect Arlanda C station with Uppsala (daily every 20min; 20min; 126kr) whilst bus #801 also runs to the city (daily every 15–30min; 40min; 78kr).

By train Uppsala's new Resecentrum, on Kungsgatan, the city's revamped bus and train interchange, is the place to catch all trains to and from the city.

Destinations Arlanda airport (every 20 min; 20min); Gällivare (1 daily; 14hr); Gävle (hourly; 40min); Kiruna (1 daily; 15hr); Luleå (2 daily; 12hr); Mora (4 daily; 2hr 50min); Narvik (1 daily; 18hr 30min); Nyköping (8 daily; 1hr 40min); Östersund (4 daily; 5hr); Stockholm (every 20min; 40min); Sundsvall (9 daily; 2hr 40min); Umeå (2 daily; 8hr 40min).

INFORMATION

Tourist office Fyris torg 8 (Mon–Fri 10am–6pm, Sat 10am–3pm; July & Aug same hours plus Sun 11am–3pm;

☎ 018 727 48 00, Ⓦ uppsala.to). Has bundles of leaflets about the city and free internet access.

ACCOMMODATION

Best Western Svava Bangårdsgatan 24 ☎018 13 00 30, ⓦhotelsvava.com. Modern hotel with all creature comforts, including specially designed rooms for people with disabilities and those with allergies. Outside the summer period, a free light evening meal is included in the room rate Mon–Thurs & Sun. 1150kr/1593kr

Clarion Gillet Dragarbrunnsgatan 23 ☎018 68 18 00, ⓦclarionhotelgillet.se. A contemporary beauty with Scandinavian designer rooms and stylish bathrooms with black-and-white tiles, all just a stone's throw from the cathedral. The pool, sauna and gym complex is the best in Uppsala. 1130kr/1430kr

★ **Grand Hörnan** Bangårdsgatan 1 ☎018 13 93 80, ⓦgrandhotellhornan.com. Dating from 1907, this wonderfully elegant place boasts rooms decorated in grand, late nineteenth-century style, many with chandeliers and drapes. Rooms vary in size but the very best are at the front, overlooking the Fyrisån River. 1295kr/1645kr

Park Inn Storgatan 30 ☎018 68 11 00, ⓦparkinn.se /hotell-uppsala. A trendy hotel next to the concert hall and the train station. Invitingly cosy designer rooms containing the latest Scandinavian chic. The larger business rooms (400kr extra) have bathtubs – quite unusual for Sweden. 920kr/1820kr

Uppsala Kungsgatan 27 ☎018 480 50 00, ⓦprofilhotels .se. Style-concious hotel close to the Linnaeus garden with Scandinavian colours and designs taking pride of place,

resulting in eye-catching natural fabrics and woods which help make this hotel one of Uppsala's best. 849kr/1650kr

Uppsala Kvarntorget Vandrarhem Kvarntorget 3 ☎018 24 20 08, ⓦuppsalavandrarhem.se. Bright, modern and sizeable STF hostel with 148 regular beds, rather than bunks, in its rooms. There are also doubles with private facilities for around 100kr more. Dorms 240kr, doubles 595kr

Uppsala St Persgatan Vandrarhem St Persgatan 16 ☎018 10 00 08, ⓦuppsalacityhostel.se. Though just a third of the size of its neighbour in Kvantorget, this STF hostel is more centrally located and consequently fills faster. Dorms and double rooms available with bunks and regular beds. Dorms 170kr; doubles 400kr

Villa Anna Odinslund 3 ☎018 580 20 00, ⓦvillaanna .se. Undoubtedly one of the best hotels in Sweden, this intimate place has just eight rooms and three suites, all individually decorated, in an elegant nineteenth-century residence close to the cathedral. The staff's attention to detail is second to none. 3000kr

CAMPING

Sunnersta Camping Mälärvägen 2, Graneberg ☎018 727 60 84. Located 7km south of the centre (take bus #20 from outside the train station), the campsite also has cabins by Lake Mälaren for rent. Open May–Aug. Tents 150kr, two-berth cabin 300kr

EATING

In keeping with its status as one of Sweden's largest cities and major university centres, Uppsala boasts an impressive range of sophisticated **restaurants**. Almost all of them are located in the grid of streets bordered by the Fyrisån River, St Olofsgatan and Bangårdsgatan, and since it can be busy in Uppsala in summer, booking a table is worthwhile.

CAFÉS AND RESTAURANTS

★ **Amazing Thai** Dragarbrunnsgatan 46 ☎018 15 30 10. This place has even won awards from the Thai government for its tasty food and is the best Thai in town: stir fries and curries from 139kr or the daily buffet (from 5pm) for a tremendously good value 159kr. Mon–Thurs 11am–10pm, Fri & Sat 11am–11pm, Sun noon–10pm.

Domtrappkällaren St Eriks Gränd 5 ☎018 13 09 55. One of the most chi-chi places in town, with an old vaulted roof and a great atmosphere. Mains such as honey-fried reindeer fillet with raspberry sauce or oven-baked halibut go for 175–325kr; excellent set lunches, too, for just 95kr. Mon–Fri 11am–11pm, Sat 5–11pm.

Fågelsången Munkgatan 3. Plying the masses with caffeine since 1954, this agreeable café is an Uppsala institution, renowned for its terrific selection of pastries and cakes as well as good-value sandwiches: a cheese and ham ciabatta costs just 40kr. Mon–Fri 7.30am–7pm, Sat & Sun 9am–6pm.

Güntherska hovkonditori Östra Ågatan 31. Gloriously old-fashioned café dating from 1870 which serves simple lunch dishes for around 80kr, and a mouthwatering selection of cakes and pastries under the mellow light of ageing chandeliers. Mon–Sat 8am–6pm, Sun 10.30am–5pm.

Hambergs fisk Fyris torg 8 ☎018 71 21 50. A smartly tiled seafood restaurant with a massive lobster hanging in the window. It serves a good selection of Mediterranean fish which is imported directly from France, as well as the usual Swedish classics like salmon. Particularly popular at lunchtime. Reckon on 170–270kr per dish. Tues–Sat 11.30am–10pm.

★ **Lingon** Svartbäcksgatan 30 ☎018 10 12 24. Upmarket Swedish home cooking served in genteel surroundings resembling an elegant country manor or alfresco at the rear. Mains are 160–235kr and feature classics such as fried meatballs, Wallenbergare and whitefish roe. Mon–Fri 11am–2.30pm & 5pm till late, Sat & Sun noon–4pm & 5pm till late.

2

Ofvandahls Sysslomangatan 3–5 ☎ 018 13 42 04. Near the old part of town, this lively café with antique furniture and fittings opened in 1878. Don't leave town without trying the famous home-made cakes (*tårtor*) which include the delicious blueberry cake and mouthwatering Black Forest gateau. Mon–Fri 7.30am–6pm, Sat 9am–5pm, Sun 11am–5pm.

Peppar Peppar Suttungs gränd 3 ☎ 018 13 13 60. This cosy red-brick building, once a tractor factory, has mutated into one of Uppsala's finest restaurants serving modern Swedish-French dishes such as leg of lamb in red wine sauce with celery purée: mains 168–288kr. Mon–Wed 5pm till late, Thurs–Sun 4pm till late.

Stationen Olof Palmes Plats 6 ☎ 018 15 35 00. Located in Uppsala's glorious old station building from 1866, this place is three things in one: a Parisian brasserie, a London pub and a Roman café, serving something for everyone. Mon & Tues 6.30am–midnight, Wed & Thurs 6.30am–1am, Fri 6.30am–2am, Sat 9am–2am, Sun 9am–midnight.

Svenssons Åkanten St Eriks torg ☎ 018 15 01 50. The wonderful riverside summer-only restaurant beside the Saluhallen market hall has great views and is a firm favourite with Uppsala folk. Lots of barbecue dishes such as chicken breast (175kr) as well as lighter salads (170kr). Mon–Fri 11.30am till late, Sat & Sun noon till late.

Svenssons Taverna Sysslomangatan 14 ☎ 018 10 09 08. This is one of Uppsala's most popular eating spots, specializing in deep-pan pizzas from 125kr. Other mains include a few Asian-inspired dishes such as Thai chowder (175kr) and Malaysian grill (165kr) as well as burgers (159kr). Daily 5pm till late.

Tilltugg Vaksalagatan 24 ☎ 018 12 97 01. A style-conscious lounge bar with light-grey leather chairs and a bar dressed in mosaic tiles. It serves a terrific range of tapas for 27–69kr, ranging from olives to garlic-and-chilli scampi. Mixed tapas plates from 99kr. Wed & Thurs 6–11pm, Fri & Sat 6pm–1am.

Villa Romana Gamla Torget 4 ☎ 018 12 50 90. A decent Italian restaurant with elegant old wallpaper and a nice wooden floor serving pasta dishes such as linguine with scallops for 159–175kr and meat and fish mains courses, including grilled sirloin in marsala, at 175–265kr. Mon–Fri 11am–11pm, Sat & Sun noon–11pm.

DRINKING AND NIGHTLIFE

By evening Uppsala's large student population makes its presence felt and more often than not the city centre is abuzz with life. The most popular places for a drink are all within easy walking distance of each other and are listed below.

BARS, CLUBS AND LIVE MUSIC

Birger Jarl Nedre Slottsgatan 3 ☎ 018 13 50 00. A fun and popular place for a drink and a favourite hangout for Uppsala's large student population. Bar snacks such as burgers and ribs are available. A good bet, too, for live music. Fri & Sat 9pm till late.

Flustret Svandammen 1 ☎ 018 10 04 44. This fancy, twin-towered, Tivoli-style building has consistently been one of the busiest drinking holes in town since the 1950s, attracting students and locals alike. A pub and nightclub rolled into one that really rocks at the weekend. Fri & Sat 5pm–3am.

★ **Hyllan** St Eriks torg ☎ 018 15 01 50, ⓦ svenssonsskrogar.se. The contemporary brick and steel surrounds of this urban loft bar would fit perfectly in New York. Located in the roof space of the Saluhallen, this is Uppsala at its most sophisticated. Times vary according to event, see website for details.

Kathalin and all that jazz Roslagsgatan 1 ☎ 018 14 06 80. Uppsala's premier spot for live jazz (Fri & Sat nights) located in the converted goods sheds known as Östra Station behind the main train station. Also serves light bar snacks. Mon–Sat 4pm till late.

O'Connors Storatorget 1 ☎ 018 14 40 10. A first-floor Irish pub in the main square with over forty different beers on tap and a staggering two hundred whiskey varieties. It's a good place to start the evening – always busy and fun. Mon–Thurs 4pm–2am, Fri & Sat 2pm–3am, Sun 2pm–1am.

Pipes of Scotland Kungsgatan 27 ☎ 018 480 50 02. Attached to the *Uppsala* hotel, this is one of the better British pubs in town. People flock here for the After Work happy hour (Mon–Fri 5–7pm) which includes a finger buffet. Mon–Thurs 5pm–midnight, Fri & Sat 4pm–1am, Sun 5–10pm.

Gamla Uppsala

Five kilometres to the north of Uppsala, three huge royal **burial mounds** dating back to the sixth century mark the original site of the town, **Gamla Uppsala**. According to legend, they are the final resting places of three ancient kings – Aun, Egil and Adlis. Though the site developed into an important trading and administrative centre, it was originally established as a pagan settlement and a place of ancient sacrificial rites by the Svear tribe. In the eleventh century, the German chronicler, Adam of Bremen, described the cult of the *æsir* (the Norse gods Odin, Thor and Freyr) practised in Uppsala: every ninth year, the deaths of nine people would be demanded at the festival of Fröblot, the victims left hanging from a nearby tree until their corpses rotted. Two centuries later, the great medieval storyteller, Snorri Sturluson of Iceland, depicted Uppsala as the true home of the Ynglinga dynasty (the original royal family in Scandinavia who also worshipped Freyr), a place where grand sacrificial festivals were held in honour of their god.

Gamla Uppsala kyrka
Daily 9am–4pm

2

The pagan temple where Uppsala's bloody sacrifices took place is now marked by the Christian **Gamla Uppsala kyrka**, which was built over pagan remains when the Swedish kings first took baptism in the new faith. Built predominantly of stone yet characterized by its rear nave wall of stepped red-brick gabling, this is one of the most breathtakingly beautiful churches in Sweden, with an understated simplicity at the very heart of its appeal. Although what survives of the church today is only a remnant of the original cathedral, the relics inside more than compensate for the downscaling. In the porch are two impressive collecting chests, one made from an oak log and fitted with iron locks, which dates from the earliest days of the church. Entering the nave, look out for the cabinet on the left containing a superb collection of church silver, including a fourteenth-century chalice and a censer from the 1200s. Nearby, in the nave wall, a stone memorial to Anders Celsius, inventor of the temperature scale that bears his name, is a worthy tribute. Outside, if you haven't yet set eyes on a genuine rune stone in Sweden, look carefully in the church walls at the back to find a perfectly preserved example from the eleventh century.

The burial mounds

Southeast of the church, the **tinghög** or parliament hill (the only burial mound not fenced in) was once the site of the local *ting* where, until the sixteenth century, a Viking parliament was held to deliberate on all matters affecting Uppsala. Immediately west of here, a path leads around the three main mounds, the first of which, **östhögen** – the east mound – dates from around 550. Following the 1846–47 excavations of Gamla Uppsala, this hill yielded the site's most astonishing artefacts: the cremated remains of a woman – possibly a priestess of the god Freyr – buried in magnificent wool, linen and silk clothing, as well as a necklace bearing a powerful image of a Valkyrie. The adjacent central mound, **mitthögen**, is thought to be around fifty years older than its neighbour but has still to be excavated. Finally, the western **västhögen** has been dated from the late sixth century, and following excavations in 1874 revealed male bone fragments and jewellery commensurate with high status.

Historical Centre

May to Aug daily 10am–4pm; Sept & Oct Mon, Wed, Sat & Sun noon–3pm • 60kr • ⓦ raa.se/gamlauppsala

The finds are proudly displayed at the entrance to the new and enjoyable **Gamla Uppsala Historical Centre**, a brave and successful attempt to portray early Swedish history in a wider non-Viking context. You can gawp at an archeologist's dream – gold fragments, ancient pieces of glass and precious ivory game pieces – as well as amble through exhibitions illustrating the origin of local myths. There's also a full account of Uppsala's golden period, which ended in the thirteenth century.

ARRIVAL AND DEPARTURE	GAMLA UPPSALA

By bus Buses #2, #110 and #115 from Vaksalagatan in Uppsala drop you at the Gamla Uppsala terminus, in reality nothing more than a bus stop next to a level crossing opposite the Historical Centre. From the bus stop cross the busy Stockholm–Uppsala mainline at the level crossing to reach the site; from the Centre paths lead to the church and burial mounds.

EATING

Odinsborg Ärnavägen 4 ☎018 32 35 25. Between the Historical Centre and the church and built in Swedish National Romantic style, this place serves a Viking spread (365kr) of chicken and ribs which you eat with your fingers – you can even dress in period costume. Lunches available, too. Mon–Fri 10am–4pm, Sat & Sun 10am–6pm.

Sigtuna

For additional ancient history, look no further than **SIGTUNA**, 40km south of Uppsala, a compact little town that dates all the way back to Viking times, with extensive ruined churches and rune stones right in the centre. Apart from its ruins, it looks like any other old Swedish town with cobbled streets and squares. Scratch the surface though, and you'll understand what made Sigtuna so important. Founded in 980 by King Erik Segersäll, Sigtuna grew from a village to become Sweden's first town. Fittingly, it contains Sweden's oldest street, Storagatan; the original, laid out during the king's reign, still lies under its modern-day counterpart. Sigtuna also boasts three intriguing **ruined churches** dating from the twelfth century. The Sigtuna district also contains more rune stones than any other area in Sweden – around 150 of them have been found to date – and several can be seen close to the ruins of the church of St Lars along Prästgatan.

St Per and St Olof

Two of Sigtuna's most impressive ruins, the churches of **St Per** and **St Olof**, lie along Storagatan itself. Much of the west and central towers of St Per's still remain from the early 1100s; experts believe it likely that the church functioned as a cathedral until the diocese was moved to nearby Uppsala (see p.93). The unusual formation of the vault in the central tower was influenced by church design then current in England and Normandy. Further east along Storagatan, St Olof's has impressively thick walls and a short nave, the latter suggesting that the church was never completed.

Mariakyrkan

Uppsalavägen 4 • Daily 9am–5pm

Close to the church ruins on Olofsgatan is the very much functioning **Mariakyrkan**, constructed of red brick during the mid-thirteenth century to serve the local Dominican monastery. Inside, the walls and ceiling are richly adorned with restored paintings from the fourteenth and fifteenth centuries.

Sigtuna museum

Storagatan 55 • Daily noon–4pm; closed Mon Sept–May • 20kr • ⓦ sigtunamuseum.se

On the main road, Storagatan, the **Sigtuna museum** includes material on Sigtuna's role as Sweden's foremost trading centre. Coins bear witness to the fact that this was the first town in the land to mint coins, in 995, plus there's booty from abroad: gold rings and even an eleventh-century clay egg, from Kiev.

ARRIVAL AND DEPARTURE   SIGTUNA

To reach Sigtuna from Uppsala or Stockholm, take the train to Märsta, from where **buses** #570 and #575 run the short distance to the town – the total journey time is around 45min. From Arlanda airport take bus #579.
Destinations Arlanda (hourly; 25min); Märsta (every 20min; 20min).

INFORMATION

Tourist office Storagatan 33 (June Mon–Fri 10am–6pm, Sat 10am–5pm, Sun 11am–5pm; July & Aug Mon–Sat 10am–6pm, Sun 11am–5pm; Sept Mon–Fri 10am–5pm, Sat & Sun 11am–4pm; Oct–May Mon–Fri 10am–4pm, Sat 11am–4pm, Sun noon–4pm; ☎08 594 806 50, ⓦsal. sigtuna.se/turism).

ACCOMMODATION

Fågelsångens vandrarhem Fågelsångsvägen 3 ☎ 0731 82 11 95, ✉ fagelsangensvandrarhem@hotmail .com. This is a delightful little youth hostel with no dorm beds and only two rooms (100kr extra for sheets), right in the town centre by the main square. Booking ahead is essential. Doubles <u>500kr</u>

Sigtuna Stadshotell Stora Nygatan 3 ☎ 08 592 501 00, ⓦ sigtunastadshotell.se. Luxurious five-star hotel stuffed full of period fittings from the early 1900s when the hotel first opened as well as contemporary Scandinavian design furniture. Useful as an alternative to more mainstream hotels at Arlanda airport, just 10km away. <u>2490kr</u>

EATING AND DRINKING

Båthuset Strandpromenaden ☎ 08 592 567 80. Set on a floating pontoon in the harbour, this little wooden restaurant dishes up delicious fish and beef mains for around 250kr; the tasty fish and seafood stew is particularly good (238kr). Tues–Sat 6–10pm.

Farbror Blå Storatorget 4 ☎ 08 592 560 50. Located next to the town hall, this place serves excellent Swedish home cooking – mains cost around 200kr. There's also a popular outdoor terrace where people gather to listen to local bands. Daily 10am till late.

La Passione Södergatan 29C ☎ 08 591 409 80. The best place for Italian food is a 10- to 15min bus ride away opposite the train station in Märsta; rack of lamb with rosemary is 189kr whilst fresh pasta dishes go for 109– 169kr. Mon 9am–2pm, Tues–Thurs 9am–10pm, Fri 9am–midnight, Sat 4pm–midnight.

Tant Bruns kaffestuga Laurentii gränd 3. This atmospheric old café specializes in home-made bread and is housed in a seventeenth-century building (the oldest wooden structure in Sigtuna) with outdoor seating in summer in a small flower garden. Mon–Fri 10am–5pm, Sat & Sun 10am–6pm.

Nyköping

If you're looking for a taste of provincial Sweden before pushing on further south or, alternatively, to Stockholm Skavsta airport, historic **NYKÖPING**, 100km southwest of Stockholm, is perfect. Indeed, since Ryanair established a base in 2003 at Skavsta (7km northwest of the town), the airport has effectively become Nyköping's lifeblood, supplying a steady flow of arriving and departing Ryanair passengers. Capital of the surrounding pastoral province of Södermanland, Nyköping's underrated charms include an excellent museum in and around the ruins of its thirteenth-century **castle**, and a thriving harbour – a regular target for the Stockholm yachting set – that bustles with life in summer.

St Nicolai kyrka

Storatorget • Mon–Fri 10am–4pm, Sat & Sun 10am–2pm (try the back door if the front one on the square is locked)

On the main square, Storatorget, opposite the tourist office, stands the vast **St Nicolai kyrka** with its white, vaulted ceiling. The building dates from around 1260, although most of what you see is the result of sixteenth-century refurbishment. The pillars here are adorned with dozens of beautiful, heavily moulded silver candle sconces. It's the Baroque pulpit, though, that's the highlight; crafted in Norrköping in 1748, it was modelled on the one in the Storkyrkan in Stockholm. Outside, standing proudly on a nearby rocky outcrop, is the red 1692 bell tower, the only wooden building not destroyed in 1719 when the town was attacked from the sea by invading Russian troops who burnt virtually the entire place to the ground.

Nyköpingshus

King's Tower: June–Aug daily 11am–5pm • Free • ⓦ sormlandsmuseum.se

From Storatorget, it's just a couple of minutes' wander south, down Slottsgatan with the river to your left, to Kungsgatan. Here you'll see the **King's Tower**, the main part of Nyköpingshus castle. A late twelfth-century defensive tower, built to protect the trading port at the estuary of the Nyköping river, it was subsequently converted into a **fortress** by King Magnus Ladulås.

In the sixteenth century, Gustav Vasa fortified the castle with gun towers; his son Karl, who became duke of Södermanland, converted the place into one of Sweden's grandest Renaissance palaces. Devastating fires here in 1665 and 1719 reduced all lesser buildings

2

THE LAST SUPPER

It was in the King's Tower in 1317 that the infamous **Nyköping Banquet** took place: one of King Magnus's three sons, Birger, invited his brothers Erik and Valdemar to celebrate Christmas at Nyköping and provided a grand banquet. Once the meal was complete, and the visiting brothers had retired to bed, Birger had them thrown in the castle's dungeon, threw the key into the river and left them to starve to death. In the nineteenth century, a key was caught by a boy fishing in the river; whether the rusting item he found, now on display in the museum, really is the one last touched by Birger, no one knows.

to ash and gutted the castle. With no money forthcoming from the national coffers, it was never rebuilt; only the King's Tower was saved from demolition and became used as a granary. Today, the riverside tower and the adjoining early eighteenth-century house built for the county governor form a **museum complex**. Wandering through the original gatehouse (*porthuset*) beneath Karl's heraldic shield, you reach the extensively restored King's Tower. On the first floor, a stylish job has been done of rebuilding the graceful archways that lead into the Guard Room. The rest of the museum is fairly uninspiring, the best exhibition being a display of medieval shoes and boots.

ARRIVAL AND DEPARTURE NYKÖPING

By plane From Skavsta airport, buses #515 and #715 run to the bus station on Västra Kvarngatan, just 500m south of the train station. It's no longer possible to buy tickets on the bus with cash so have your credit card ready.

By train The train station on Järnvägsgatan is a 10min walk west of the centre – first head south along Järnvägsgatan, then east on Repslagaregatan, then south

again on Brunnsgatan. Although it's not widely known, handy direct trains run to Nyköping from Gävle, Uppsala and Arlanda airport via Stockholm; these services are the easiest way to travel between Arlanda and Skavsta airports. Destinations Arlanda airport (8 daily; 1hr 30min); Stockholm (hourly; 1hr); Uppsala (8 daily; 2hr).

INFORMATION

Tourist office Rådhuset, Storatorget (June–Aug Mon–Fri 8am–6pm, Sat & Sun 10am–4pm; Sept–May Mon–Fri 9am–5pm; ☎ 0155 24 82 00, ✆ visitnykoping.se). This

central and enthusiastic office is housed in the former town hall building and has internet access.

ACCOMMODATION

Staying in Nyköping is remarkably good value and significantly cheaper than Stockholm. There's a good selection of budget options as well as one or two more upmarket choices, and advance booking is not needed.

Clarion Collection Kompaniet Folkungavägen 1 ☎ 0155 28 80 20, ✆ choicehotels.se. Near the harbour and overlooking the river, this huge structure of curving red brick is the most stylish and well-appointed hotel in town. The rooms are airy, neutrally decorated and have wooden floors; free evening buffet included. **990kr/1390kr**

Connect Skavsta General Schybergs väg 23, Skavsta airport ☎ 0155 22 02 20 ✆ connecthotels.se. Opposite the terminal building, this modern design hotel has both en-suite doubles and simpler "Quick Sleep" budget rooms with bunk beds and shared facilities for around 300kr less. Regular buses run into Nyköping and Stockholm from opposite the hotel. **795kr**

Forty Towers Fruängsgatan 21 ☎ 0155 21 75 80, ✆ hotelfortytowers.com. Bizarre choice of name for this cheap, basic pile, close to the town's picturesque theatre, enjoying a good central location. Newly renovated rooms

with private facilities, though still rather cramped. **895kr**

★ **Lanterna** Östra Längdgatan 8 ☎ 0155 45 50 30, ✆ hotellanterna.se. A delightful family-run hotel overlooking the harbour that's done out in cosy, country-home style with floral wallpaper, wooden flooring, draped curtains and flower vases. Rooms on the ground floor cost 100kr less. No weekend or summer reductions. **1190kr**

★ **Railway Hostel** Södra Bangårdsgatan ☎ 0155 28 29 20, ✆ railway.nu. This handy hostel is located at the train station and comprises a number of dorms sleeping a maximum of five, and double rooms. The bus to Skavsta airport leaves from right outside the hostel. Dorms **185kr**, doubles **415kr**

Scandic Nyköping City Brunnsgatan 31 ☎ 0155 29 35 00, ✆ scandichotels.se/nykopingcity. Modern, bright and airy Scandinavian design hotel in the heart of Nyköping. All 98 rooms are tastefully appointed with either

BOAT TRIPS FROM NYKÖPING

During the summer months M/S *Storsand* (late June to late Aug Mon, Tues & Wed at 11am and 3pm; 170kr return; buy tickets onboard; ⓦ trosarederi.se) sails out of the town's tiny harbour bound for the countless rocks, skerries and islands that make up the Nyköping archipelago.

LÅNGSKÄR AND ÅLÖ

After just forty minutes, the boat puts in at **Långskär**, which, as its Swedish name suggests, is a long sliver of an island and a great place to jump ashore and explore. An unspoilt haven of smooth rocks, ideal for sunbathing, and secluded bays, the island is a perfect getaway. From Långskär, it's another hour to larger, though still modestly sized **Ålö,** which supported a solitary farm for two hundred years until the 1950s. Today, it's another unspoilt island just waiting to be explored; take a picnic and wander off in search of your own "*smultronställe*" as the Swedes call it, literally "a place where the wild strawberries grow" – a place of perfect peace.

BOAT RENTAL IN NYKÖPING

A great way to explore the islands and coastline around Nyköping is to get out on the water yourself. Between May and September you can rent **canoes** from Gästhamnen Nyköping at the seaward end of the harbour (☏ 0155 21 72 30 or ☏ 070 659 21 96, ⓦ www.nykopingsgasthamn .se); ask for the harbour master.

---

wooden or carpeted floors and there's also a steam sauna and jacuzzi available to guests. **1110kr/1300kr**

CAMPING
Strandstuvikens Camping Strandstuviken ☏ 0155 978 10, ⓦ strandstuviken.se. Located in a mature pine forest 9km southeast of Nyköping on the Baltic coast. The campsite also has a number of four-berth cabins available to rent. Open May to mid-Sept. Tents **150kr**, cabins **500kr**

EATING AND DRINKING

Most of Nyköping's **eating** and **drinking** options are, unsurprisingly, at the harbour. Outside the summer season, though, the scene moves to the town centre where, curiously for a modestly sized town, there's a good range of choice to suit all pockets.

Hamnmagasinet Skeppsbron 1 ☏ 0155 26 92 92. A classy, brick-walled establishment that stands out as the leading harbourside restaurant, with a large open-air terrace. Plenty of no-nonsense grilled fish and meat dishes with home-cooking specials going for just 98kr. May–Aug: Mon & Tues 11am–midnight, Wed–Fri 11am–2pm, Sat noon–2am, Sun noon–midnight.

Hellmanska Gården Västra Trädgårdsgatan 24 ☏ 0155 21 05 25. Set in a converted warehouse from the 1700s whose lovely summer courtyard has a beautiful magnolia tree at its centre. Serves great sandwiches, fruit flans, quiches and light lunches as well as fresh bread from its own bakery. Mon–Fri 10am–6pm, Sat 10am–4pm, Sun noon–4pm.

★ **Lamduan Thai Food** Östra Storgatan 27 ☏ 0155 21 61 11. The lurid green walls and adorning pictures of Thai royals notwithstanding, the genuinely tasty food here is worth seeking out: mains are 89–109kr. The lunch buffet at 75kr is also good value. Mon–Fri 11am–9pm, Sat noon–9pm, Sun 1–9pm.

Oliver Twist Fruängsgatan 28 ☏ 0155 21 63 05. Close to the bus station, this popular wood-panelled English pub does a good range in food as well as drink: chicken breast filled with mozzarella (169kr), pepper steak (199kr) and flounder with prawn sauce (169kr) are all available. Mon–Thurs noon–11pm, Fri & Sat noon–midnight, Sun noon–10pm.

★ **Rökeriet** Östra Skeppsbron 7 ☏ 0155 21 38 38. In the red warehouse standing beside the roundabout north of the harbour, this fish smokery and fine restaurant with outside seating is a Nyköping institution and renowned for its excellent lunch menu of smoked salmon, mackerel and gravad lax for 150kr. May to Aug Mon–Fri 4pm till late, Sat & Sun noon till late.

Skafferiet Västra Storgatan 29 ☏ 0155 26 99 50. Nyköping's all-day bistro serves light meals such as ciabatta salad, escargots provencales and fish and seafood soup (89–129kr) until 5pm when they switch to a selection of meats for which you choose your own sauce (from 159kr). Mon–Fri 5–10pm, Sat noon–3pm & 6–10pm.

Voyage Brunnsgatan 31 ☏ 0155 29 35 00. Attached to the *Scandic* hotel, this wonderful 1960s retro place, decorated with black-and-white photos of jumbo jets, serves excellent modern Swedish food: steamed, cured ling with lime butter (195kr) and Sörmland venison with potato gratin (205kr). Daily 6–10pm.

Gothenburg

LILLA BOMMEN HARBOUR AT NIGHT

Gothenburg

Of all the cities in southern Sweden, the grandest is the western port of Gothenburg. Designed by the Dutch in 1621, the country's second largest city boasts splendid Neoclassical architecture, masses of sculpture-strewn parkland and a welcoming and relaxed spirit. The cityscape of broad avenues, elegant squares, trams and canals is not only one of the prettiest in Sweden, but also the backdrop to Scandinavia's biggest seaport, making the city a truly cosmopolitan destination. There is a certain resentment on the west coast that Stockholm wins out in the national glory stakes, but Gothenburg's easier-going atmosphere – and its closer proximity to western Europe – makes it first choice as a place to live for many Swedes. Talk to any Gothenburger and they will soon disparage the more frenetic lives of the "08-ers" – 08 being the telephone code for Stockholm.

At the heart of the city is the historic **old town**: this is the best place to start your sightseeing, although Gothenburg's attractions are by no means restricted to this area. Tucked between the Göta River to the north and the zigzagging Rosenlundkanalen to the south, the old town's tightly gridded streets are lined with impressive facades, interesting food markets and a couple of worthwhile museums, most notably the **Stadsmuseum** and, up by the harbour, the **Maritiman**, a repository of all things nautical. Just across the canal that skirts the southern edges of the old town is **Trädgårdsföreningen** park, in summer full of colourful flowers and picnicking city dwellers.

Heading further south into the modern centre, **Avenyn** is Gothenburg's showcase boulevard, alive with flashy restaurants and bars. However, it's the roads off Avenyn that are the area's most interesting, with alternative-style café-bars and some of Gothenburg's best museums, including the **Konstmuseum** (Art Museum) further south in **Götaplatsen**. For family entertainment day or night, the classic **Liseberg Amusement Park**, just to the southeast of the Avenyn district, has been a meeting place for Gothenburgers since the 1920s.

In Vasastan, a small district to the west of Avenyn, crammed with intricately decorated late nineteenth-century apartment buildings and peppered with appealing little cafés, you'll find the **Röhsska Museum** of applied arts. Vasastan stretches west to **Haga**, the old working-class district, now a haven for the trendy and moneyed. Haga Nygatan, the main thoroughfare, leads on to Linnégatan, the arterial road through **Linné**. Fast establishing itself as the most vibrant part of the city, it's home to the most interesting evening haunts, with new cafés, bars and restaurants opening up alongside long-established antique emporiums and sex shops. Further out, the rolling **Slottsskogsparken** park holds the **Naturhistoriska Museet** (Natural History Museum), as well as being an alluringly pretty place to sunbathe.

Brief history

Founded on its present site in the seventeenth century by Gustav II Adolf, Gothenburg was the Swedes' fifth attempt to create a centre free from Danish

The Gothenburg City Card p.119
The Gothenburg Package p.120

Self-catering p.122

UTKIKEN

Highlights

❶ **Utkiken** For breathtaking views of the city and the Göta River, make straight for the top of the Utkiken tower – and enjoy a coffee whilst up there. **See p.110**

❷ **Boat trip** Hop on a boat in Lilla Bommen harbour for the fascinating trip to Nya Älvsborg fortress across the river. **See p.110**

❸ **Stora Saluhallen** Grab lunch at KåGes, a Gothenburg institution, inside Stora Saluhallen and pick up a few picnic treats from the well-stocked market stores. **See p.113 & p.122**

❹ **Avenyn** Stroll the length of Gothenburg's main boulevard, buzzing Avenyn, and admire the city from the vantage point of Kungsplatsen. **See p.113**

❺ **Fürstenberg galleries** The highlight of the city's grand Konstmuseum, housing paintings by Sweden's finest nineteenth- and early twentieth-century artists. **See p.114**

❻ **Café life in Haga** Sip a coffee at the laidback cafés in Gothenburg's version of Greenwich Village – perfect for people-watching. **See p.116**

HIGHLIGHTS ARE MARKED ON THE MAPS ON P.109 & P.112

influence. The Danes had enjoyed control of Sweden's west coast since the Middle Ages, and extracted extortionate tolls from all vessels entering the country. Sweden's medieval centre of trade had been 40km further up the Göta River than present-day Gothenburg, but to avoid the tolls it was moved to a site north of the present location. It wasn't until Karl XI chose the island of Hisingen, today the site of the city's northern suburbs, as the location for Sweden's trading nucleus that the settlement was first called Gothenburg.

Over the ensuing centuries, the British, Dutch and German traders who settled here during left a rich architectural and cultural legacy. The city is graced with terraces of grand **merchants' houses** featuring carved stone, stucco and painted tiles. The influence of the Orient was also strong, reflecting the all-important trade links between Sweden and the Far East, and is still visible in the chinoiserie detail on many buildings. This trade was monopolized for over eighty years during the nineteenth century by the hugely successful **Swedish East India Company**, whose Gothenburg auction house, selling exotic spices, teas and fine cloths, attracted merchants from all over the world.

The old town and the harbour

The **old town** is divided in two by the **Stora Hamnkanalen**, to the north of which is the **harbour**, where the impressive shipyards make for a dramatic backdrop. The streets south of the canal stretch down to Rosenlundskanalen and the excellent Stadsmuseum. Straddling the Stora Hamnkanalen is the stately main square, **Gustav Adolfs torg**, a good starting point for sightseeing around the old town; you can easily see the whole area in a day.

Gustav Adolfs torg

At the centre of **Gustav Adolfs torg**, a copper statue of Gustav II Adolf points ostentatiously to the spot where he reputedly declared: "Here I will build my city." This isn't the original German-made statue of the city founder however: that one was kidnapped on its way to Sweden and, rather than pay the ransom demanded, the Gothenburgers commissioned a new one.

Rådhuset

To the east of Gustav Adolfs torg, with the canal behind you, stands the **Rådhuset**, which isn't a town hall as the name suggests, but has housed the criminal law courts since 1673. The dull Neoclassical facade is dramatically improved by an extension designed by the ground-breaking Functionalist architect Gunnar Asplund in 1937.

Nordstan

Norra Hamngatan • Mon–Fri 10am–8pm, Sat 10am–6pm, Sun 11am–5pm • ⓦ nordstan.se

Heading north from Gustav Adolfs torg along Östra Hamngatan, you'll pass Sweden's biggest shopping centre, the amorphous **Nordstan**. Packed with glitzy boutiques and branches of just about every Swedish chain store you choose to mention, it's Gothenburg's most ostentatious show of wealth.

Centralstation

If you have time to spare and haven't yet seen the city's impressive **Centralstation**, take a short detour along Burggrevegatan to Drottningtorget. Dating from 1856, this is the

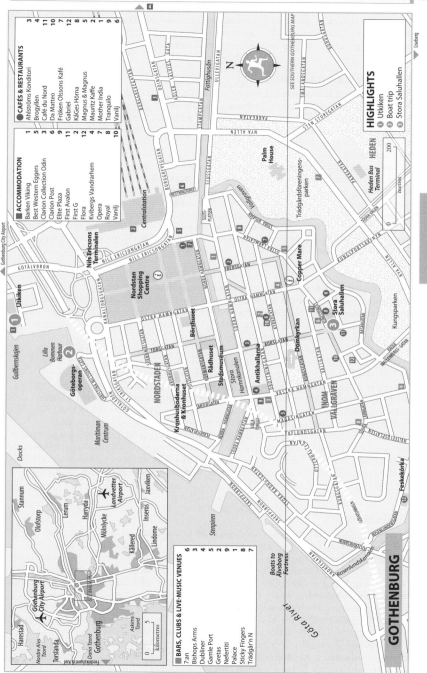

GOTHENBURG

HIGHLIGHTS

1 Utkiken
2 Boat trip
3 Stora Saluhallen

CAFÉS & RESTAURANTS

Ahlströms Konditori	3
Brogyllen	4
Café du Nord	11
Da Matteo	10
Fröken Olssons Kafé	7
Gabriel	12
KåGes Hörna	8
Magnus & Magnus	5
Mauritz Kaffe	2
Mother India	1
Tranquilo	9
Vanili	6

ACCOMMODATION

Barken Viking	3
Best Western Eggers	5
Clarion Collection Odin	4
Clarion Post	6
Elite Plaza	7
First Avalon	9
First G	11
Flora	2
Kvibergs Vandrarhem	12
Opera	8
Royal	1
Vanili	10

BARS, CLUBS & LIVE-MUSIC VENUES

7:an	6
Bishops Arms	3
Dubliner	4
Gamle Port	5
Gretas	2
Nefertiti	9
Palace	1
Sticky Fingers	8
Trädgår'n N	7

oldest train station in the country and its period facade fronts a grand and marvellously preserved interior – take a look at the wooden beam-ends in the ticket hall, each one carved in the likeness of one of the city-council members of the day.

Lilla Bommen harbour

At the riverside **Lilla Bommen harbour** Gothenburg's industrial decline is juxtaposed with its artistic regeneration to dramatic visual effect. To the west, beyond the harbour, redundant shipyard cranes loom across the sky, making a sombre background to the industrially themed bronze and pink-granite sculptures dotted along the waterfront.

Nya Älvsborg

Boat departures early May to Aug daily every 90min 9/10am–4/5pm • 30min • 160kr, includes tour

Boats leave from Lilla Bommen for the popular excursion to the island fortress of **Nya Älvsborg** built in the seventeenth century to defend the harbour and the city; the surviving buildings have been turned into a museum and café. On the half-hour guided tours of the square tower, chapel and prison cells (included in the price of the boat trip) you'll hear about violent confrontations with the Danes, and some of the methods used to keep prisoners from swimming away – check out the set of iron shackles weighing over 36kg.

Utkiken

Lookout Point • Lilla Bommen • July–Aug daily 11am–4pm; Sept–June Mon–Fri 11am–3pm • 30kr

North along the riverbank is **Utkiken**; designed by the Scottish architect Ralph Erskine (who also designed the Sydney Opera House) in the late 1980s, this 86m-high office building resembles a half-used red lipstick. Its top storey offers panoramic views of Gothenburg and the harbour, and there's a café, too.

Maritiman

Packhusplatsen 12 • April & Oct Fri–Sun 11am–4pm; May–Sept daily 11am–6pm • 90kr • ⓦ maritiman.se

Walking west along the quay, it's just a couple of minutes to **Maritiman**, the city's engaging maritime museum, which comprises nineteen boats, including the 1915 lightship, *Fladen*, a submarine and a freighter which once sailed regularly from Gothenburg across the North Sea to the east coast of England, each giving a glimpse of how seamen lived and worked on board. The most impressive ship is a monstrous naval destroyer, *Småland*, which saw active service until 1979. There's a rather good café on another of the ships, the ferry *Dan Broström*, with outdoor seating available on the upper deck.

Stadsmuseum

City Museum • Norra Hamngatan 12 • Tues & Thurs–Sun 10am–5pm, Wed 10am–8pm • 40kr • ⓦ stadsmuseum.goteborg.se

The **Stadsmuseum** is Gothenburg's biggest museum. It is located in the Ostindiska Huset, which housed the offices, goods store and auction house of the enormously influential **Swedish East India Company**. Envious of the major maritime nations, two Gothenburg-based industrialists, Colin Campbell and Niklas Sahlgren, set up the firm in the early eighteenth century. Granted the sole Swedish rights to trade with China in 1731, the company monopolized all Swedish trade with the Far East for over eighty years, on condition that the bounty – tea, silk, porcelain, spices and arrack (an East Indian schnapps used to make Swedish punch) – had to be sold and auctioned in Gothenburg. As a result, Chinese influence pervaded Gothenburg society, and wealthy financiers adorned their homes and gardens with Chinese motifs. By 1813, unrest caused by the French Revolution and competition from British and Dutch tea traders meant that profits slid, and the company lost its monopoly. The headquarters, however, remain an imposing reminder of the power and prestige the company – and Gothenburg – once had.

Elsewhere in the museum, other main exhibits focus on Gothenburg's Viking past and include the impressive remains of the *Äskekärr* longboat, a trading vessel dating from around 900 which was found 30km up the Göta River from present-day Gothenburg. There's also a breathtaking collection of medieval triptychs from churches across western Sweden, as well as a thorough account of the founding of Gothenburg in 1621 and its development through the centuries.

South of Stora Hamnkanalen: the quayside

Crossing Stora Hamnkanalen from the Stadsmuseum, you'll come to **Lilla Torget**. In itself, the square is nothing to get excited about, but, having nodded at the statue of Jonas Alströmer – the man who introduced the potato to Sweden in the eighteenth century – continue a couple of minutes' walk west to the quayside, **Stenpiren** (Stone Pier). It was from here that hundreds of emigrants said their last goodbyes before sailing off to a "New Sweden" in the United States, in 1638. The granite **Delaware Monument** marking Swedish emigration was carted off to America from Gothenburg in the early part of the nineteenth century, and it wasn't until 1938 that celebrated sculptor Carl Milles cast a replacement in bronze, which stands here looking out to sea.

Domkyrkan

Kungsgatan 37 • Mon–Fri 8am–6pm, Sat & Sun 10am–4pm

A few blocks south of the canal, and left off Västra Hamngatan, is the Neoclassical cathedral, **Domkyrkan**, built in 1815 – the two previous cathedrals were destroyed by fires in 1721 and 1802. Four giant sandstone columns stand at the portico, and inside, the altarpiece is a picture of gilded opulence. The plain white walls concentrate the eye on the unusual post-Resurrection cross – devoid of a Jesus, and with his gilded grave clothes strewn around, it summons images of an adolescent's bedroom floor. Another quirky feature is the twin glassed-in verandas that run down either side of the cathedral; looking like glamorous trams with net curtains, they were actually designed for the bishop's private conversations.

Brunnsparken

Continuing east past the cathedral and north towards Stora Hamnkanalen, the leafy square known as **Brunnsparken** soon comes into view, with Gustav Adolfs torg just across the canal. The sedate house facing the square is now a snazzy restaurant and nightclub called *Palace* (see p.124), but in 1752 the building was home to Pontus and Gothilda Fürstenberg, the city's leading arts patrons. They opened up the top floor as an art gallery and later donated their entire collection – the biggest batch of Nordic paintings in the country – to the city's **Konstmuseum**. As a tribute to the Fürstenbergs, the museum made over the top floor into an exact replica of the original gallery.

Along Rosenlundskanalen

Following the zigzagging **Rosenlundskanalen** that marks the southern perimeter of old Gothenburg – a moat during the days when the city was fortified – makes for a fine twenty-minute stroll, past pretty waterside views and a number of interesting diversions.

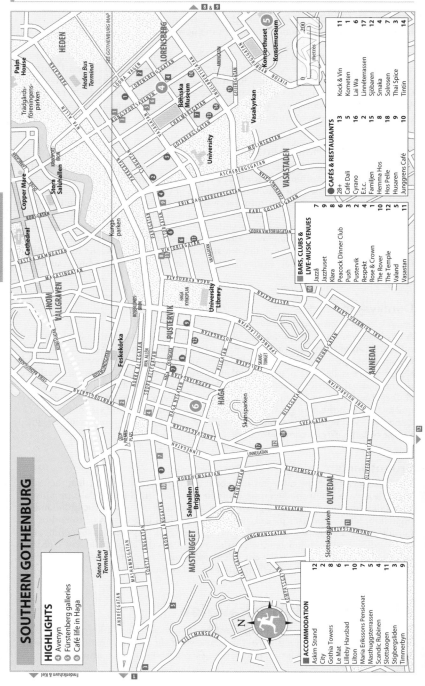

Trädgårdsföreningen park

The main entrance is just across the canal from Stora Nygatan, close to Kungsportsplatsen • Mon–Fri 7am–8pm, Sat & Sun 9am–8pm • 20kr • **Palm House** Daily 10am–6pm • July–Sept 100kr; free at other times of year

Just southeast of Brunnsparken, **Stora Nygatan** wends its way south along the canal's most scenic stretch; to one side are Neoclassical buildings all stuccoed in cinnamon and cream, and to the other is the green expanse of well-groomed **Trädgårdsföreningen** park, which contains a number of attractions. The most impressive of these is the 1878 **Palm House**; designed as a copy of London's Crystal Palace, and looking like a huge English conservatory, it contains a wealth of very un-Swedish plant life, including tropical, Mediterranean and Asian flowers.

Further on is the **Rosarium**, which, with nearly three thousand varieties of rose, provides a myriad of colours throughout the year. In summer it hosts lunchtime concerts and a special children's theatre (details are available at the tourist office).

Kungsportsplatsen and Stora Saluhallen

Market: Mon–Fri 9am–6pm, Sat 10am–3pm

Continuing west from Trädgårdsföreningen park, you'll pass **Kungsportsplatsen**, in the centre of which stands a useful landmark, a sculpture known as the "Copper Mare" – though it's immediately obvious if you look from beneath that this is no mare. A few minutes further on, and one block in from the canal at Kungstorget, stands **Stora Saluhallen**, a pretty, barrel-roofed indoor market built in the 1880s. Busy with shoppers perusing the forty-odd stalls and shops and full of atmosphere, it's a great place to wander, as is the market outside.

Feskekôrka

Fisktorget • Tues–Fri 10am–6pm, Sat 10am–3pm

Five minutes' walk west of Kungsportsplatsen is Gothenburg's oldest food market, the Neo-Gothic **Feskekôrka**, or "Fish Church", whose strong aromas may well hit you long before you reach the door. Despite its undeniably ecclesiastical appearance, the nearest this 1874 building comes to religion is the devotion shown by the fish-lovers who come to buy their dinner here. Inside, every kind of seafood, from cod to crustaceans, lies in gleaming, pungent silver, pink and black mounds, while in a gallery upstairs there's a tiny but excellent restaurant (see p.122).

Avenyn and around

Running all the way from Rosenlundskanalen southeast to Götaplatsen is the wide, cobbled length of Kungsportsavenyn. Known more simply as **Avenyn**, this "avenue" teems with life and is Gothenburg's showiest thoroughfare. The ground floor of almost every grand old nineteenth-century home has been converted into a café, bar or restaurant, which the young and beautiful inhabit whilst sipping overpriced drinks and posing at tables that, from mid-spring to September, spill out onto the street. Avenyn is arguably one of the best places in the city for people-watching, and no visit to Gothenburg is complete without a stroll down it. At the southern end of the avenue on **Götaplatsen** is the fascinating **Konstmuseum**, which contains a fine collection of international art from various periods.

Poseidon

At the top of Avenyn, **Götaplatsen** is modern Gothenburg's main square, in the centre of which stands Carl Milles's **Poseidon** – a giant, nude, bronze body-builder with a staggeringly ugly face. The size of the figure's penis caused moral outrage when the sculpture first appeared in 1931, and it was subsequently dramatically reduced to its current, rather pathetic proportions, totally out of keeping with a statue that's 7m high. Today, although from the front *Poseidon* appears to be squeezing the living daylights out of what looks like a massive fish, if you climb the steps of the **Konserthuset** (Concert Hall) to the right and view the statue sideways-on, it becomes clear that Milles won the battle over *Poseidon*'s manhood to stupendous effect, as the enormous fish appears to be the original penis.

Konstmuseum

Art Museum • Götaplatsen • Tues & Thurs 11am–6pm, Wed 11am–9pm, Fri–Sun 11am–5pm • 40kr • ⓦ konstmuseum.goteborg.se

Behind *Poseidon* stands Götaplatsen's most impressive attraction, the superb **Konstmuseum**, its massive, symmetrical facade reminiscent of the fascist architecture of 1930s Germany. This is one of the city's finest museums, and it's easy to spend half a day absorbing the diverse and extensive collections, the highlights of which are picked out below. A delightful little park, **Näckrosdammen**, lies just behind the museum; with its late-spring rhododendrons and big, duck-filled pond, it's a lovely place for a stroll.

Hasselblad Center
ⓦ hasselbladfoundation.org

On the ground floor, to the left of the ticket desk, the **Hasselblad Center** contains excellent exhibitions of contemporary photography. Displays are temporary and aim to showcase the work of internationally renowned photographers as well as those from up-and-coming Nordic artists.

European and Swedish collections

The Konstmuseum's collections of European art date from fifteenth to the seventeenth centuries and fill a total of six rooms. Pride of place is taken by Rembrandt's *Knight with Falcon*, although Rubens is also well represented with works such as *Adoration of the Magi* on display. Elsewhere, you'll find paintings by the celebrated masters of French Impressionism and artists closely linked to them: Monet, Gauguin, Renoir and Cézanne, for example. Look out, in particular, for Van Gogh's *Olive Grove, Saint Rémy* from 1899 which is widely considered to be one of the artist's most powerful works in terms of vitality and expression. Collections of Swedish art are dominated by Alexander Roslin who is represented by a portrait of French aristocrats and a group portrait of the well-to-do Grill family.

Fürstenberg Galleries

Best of all, and the main reason to visit, are the **Fürstenberg Galleries** on the top floor, which celebrate the work of some of Scandinavia's most prolific and revered early twentieth-century artists; well-known works by Carl Larsson, Anders Zorn and Carl Wilhelmson reflect the seasons and landscapes of the Nordic countries, and evoke a vivid picture of Scandinavian life at that time. Paintings to look out for include Larsson's *Lilla Suzanne*, which touchingly depicts the elated face of a baby and is one of his most realistic works; Anders Zorn's *Bathers*, flushed with a pale pink summer glow and exemplifying the painter's feeling for light and the human form; and the sensitive portraits by Ernst Josephson, most notably his full-length portrait of Carl Skånberg – easily mistaken for the young Winston Churchill. The Danish artist Peter Kroyer's marvellous *Hip Hip Hooray* again plays with light, and a couple of works by Hugo Birger also deserve your attention. One depicts the interior of the original Fürstenberg Gallery (see p.111), while his massive *Scandinavian Artists' Breakfast in Paris*, dominating an entire wall, puts some faces to the artists' names – a pamphlet in the room will help identify them. Also worth a look is an entire room of Larsson's bright, fantastical wall-sized paintings.

Liseberg and around

Southeast of Avenyn is the **Liseberg Amusement Park**, alive both during the day and at night throughout the summer. In its shadow to the south is one of Gothenburg's most engaging museums, **Universeum**, particularly fascinating for children, while the absorbing **Världskulturmuséet** is just next door.

Liseberg Amusement Park

Örgrytevägen 5 • Daily: late April–May & Sept 3pm–10pm; June 1–10pm; July & Aug 11am–11pm • Mid-June to mid-Aug 90kr, otherwise 80kr; all-day ride pass 310kr, or buy tickets as you go – a coupon costs 20kr, each attraction requires 1–4 coupons • Ⓦ liseberg.se

Just a few minutes' walk southeast from Götaplatsen, **Liseberg Amusement Park** is a riot of party lights and bubblegum-pink paintwork. Opened in 1923, this is Scandinavia's largest amusement park, and with its flowers, trees, fountains and clusters of lights, it's great fun for adults as well as children, and leagues away from the neon and plastic mini-cities that constitute so many theme parks around the world. The old and the young dance to live bands most evenings, and although louder and more youth-dominated at night (especially on Sat), it's all good-humoured. Pride of place at Liseberg goes to "Kanonen", an ambitious roller coaster which reaches its top speed just two seconds after being fired bullet-like from its start point, before plummeting 24m at a ninety-degree angle.

Christmas market

If you're around between mid-November and late December, head for the enjoyable **Christmas market**, where stalls selling handicrafts and presents are lit by around three million fairy lights. This being Sweden, the commercialism is remarkably low-key, and the pervasive smell of *glögg* (mulled wine), roasted almonds and freshly made waffles adds to the enjoyment. This is also a good place to sample the traditional Swedish *julbord*, a Christmas **smorgasbord** full of hams, cheeses and heavenly cakes (booking required for the *julbord*, ☎ 031 40 02 00).

Universeum

Södra Vägen 50 • Daily: late June to mid-Aug 9am–8pm; mid-Aug to late June 10am–6pm • Late June to mid-Aug 195kr, otherwise 160kr • Ⓦ universeum.se

Just a few steps from Liseberg, the city's science and environment museum, **Universeum**, is well worth an hour or so of your time. Designed by Gothenburg architect Gert Wingårdh, and contained within a splendidly organic building with soaring glass, wood and concrete walls, it couldn't be more in contrast to the fairy lights and pink paint of the amusement park reflected in its vast windows. Water is a major theme (the complex holds the world's largest recirculating water system, processing three million litres a day), and once inside, you can walk some 3km through various different environments – Swedish mountain streams, rainforest, open ocean complete with sharks and stingrays – all of which feel extremely authentic; expect to emerge dripping. There's also an interactive "explora zone" for kids to discover robots, models and all kinds of technological wizardry, plenty of information in English and a **café** with good-value meals and organic coffee.

Världskulturmuséet

Museum of World Culture • Södra Vägen 54 • Late June to early Aug Tues–Sun noon–5pm; early Aug to late June Tues & Fri–Sun noon–5pm, Wed & Thurs noon–9pm • Free • Ⓦ varldskulturmuseet.se

Next door to Universeum is the unusually interesting **Världskulturmuséet**. A glass and concrete colossus complete with a four-storey glass atrium, the building has been awarded one of Sweden's most prestigious architectural prizes for its innovative design. Through a series of changing exhibitions, the museum aims to reflect the depth, variety and ever-evolving nature of world culture – past displays have focused on sexuality in India, human trafficking around the world and the native people who live along the Orinoco.

Vasastan

Having explored the city centre, don't miss the opportunity to wander into the **Vasastan** district, where the streets are lined with fine nineteenth-century and National Romantic architecture, and the cafés are cheaper, more laidback and much more charismatic than those in the centre. The area also boasts Gothenburg's collection of applied arts, the **Röhsska Museum**, and several fine university buildings.

Vasagatan

Along **Vasagatan**, the main street through the district, and parallel **Engelbrektsgatan** to the south, you'll come across solid, stately and rangy buildings that epitomize Gothenburg's nineteenth-century commercial wealth and civic pride. White-stuccoed or red-and-cream brick facades are decorated with elaborate ceramic tiles, intricate stone-and-brick animal carvings, shiny metal cupolas and classical windows. With the detail spread gracefully across these six-storey terraces, the overall effect is of restrained grandeur. Many of the houses also have Continental-style wrought-iron balconies; it's easy to imagine high-society gatherings spilling out into the night on warm summer evenings. In contrast, interspersed among all this nineteenth-century swagger are some perfect examples of early twentieth-century National Romantic architecture, with rough-hewn stone and Art Nouveau swirls in plaster and brickwork; look particularly at the low-numbered buildings along Engelbrektsgatan.

Röhsska Museum

Vasagatan 37–39 · Tues noon–8pm, Wed–Fri noon–5pm, Sat & Sun 11am–5pm · 40kr · Ⓦ designmuseum.se

The excellent **Röhsska Museum** is Sweden's main museum of design, fashion and applied arts and an aesthetic Aladdin's cave, with each floor concentrating on different areas of decorative and functional art, from early-dynasty Chinese ceramics to European arts and crafts from the sixteenth and seventeenth centuries. Most arresting is the first floor, which is devoted to twentieth-century decor and features all manner of recognizable designs for domestic furniture and appliances from the 1910s to the twenty-first century – enough to send anyone over the age of 10 on a giddy nostalgia trip.

Haga

A 10min stroll west along Vasagatan; alternatively take tram #2 or #13 from Vasaplatsen to Olivedalsgatan

The city's oldest working-class suburb is **Haga**; once so run-down that demolition was on the cards, today it's one of Gothenburg's most enjoyable quarters. The transformation took place in the early 1980s, after someone saw potential in the web of artisans' homes known as "governor's houses", distinctive early nineteenth-century buildings constructed with a stone ground floor and two wooden upper storeys.

Haga Nygatan

Haga is now a miniature version of Greenwich Village, with well-off and socially aware 20- and 30-somethings hanging out in the style-conscious cafés and shops along its

CLOCKWISE FROM TOP LEFT CAFÉ LIFE, HAGA(P.116); KONSTMUSEUM (P.114); *KANELBULLAR* AND COFFEE AT HUSAREN CAFÉ (P.122); FESKEKÖRKA (P.113) >

cobbled streets. There are a couple of good cafés (see p.122) along the main thoroughfare, **Haga Nygatan**, which is really somewhere to come during the day, when there are tables out on the street and the atmosphere is friendly and villagey – if a little self-consciously fashionable. Apart from the boutiques, which sell things like Art Deco light fittings, calming crystals and nineteenth-century Swedish kitchenware, it's worth noting the intervening apartment buildings; these red-brick edifices were originally almshouses funded by the Dickson family, the city's British industrialist forefathers who played a big part in the success of the East India Company – Robert Dickson's name is still emblazoned on the facades.

Linné

To the west of Haga, the cosmopolitan district of **Linné** is named after the botanist Carl von Linné, who created the system for classifying plants used the world over (see p.96). To get here, turn south off Haga Nygatan into Landsvägsgatan, which joins up with **Linnégatan** – the main thoroughfare. In recent years, so many stylish cafés and restaurants have sprung up along the main drag that Linné is now considered Gothenburg's "second Avenyn", although without the attitude; the street is lined with Dutch-inspired nineteenth-century architecture, tall and elegant buildings interspersed with steep little side roads. However, it's the main roads leading off Linnégatan, prosaically named First Long Street (Första Långgatan), Second Long Street (Andra) and so on up to Fourth (Fjärde), that give the area its real character; the not-very-long Second and Third streets contain a mix of dark antique stores, basement cafés and sex shops.

On the left as you head up Linnégatan towards Järntorget is the forbidding building where King Oskar II had his private apartment – and his women. Directly opposite is a modern apartment block that's worth a second glance; it replaced a property whose republican owner so hated both the monarchy and the morals of the king that he had a run of colourful ceramic panels depicting the devil installed, facing the royal apartment. Sadly, the Gothenburg propensity for doing away with its own past meant the "devil building", as it was known, was recently demolished, but two of the grotesque panels have been incorporated into the new apartment block.

Slottsskogsparken

A 5min walk south from Linnégatan or take tram #13 or #2 to Linnéplatsen · **Botanical Gardens:** Daily 9am–dusk; greenhouses May–Aug daily 10am–5pm, Sept–April 10am–4pm · Gardens voluntary 20kr, greenhouses 20kr · ⓦ gotbot.se

Slottsskogsparken is a huge, tranquil expanse of parkland with farm animals and birdlife, including pink flamingoes in summer. On its south side are the impressive **Botaniska Trädgården**, a vast glasshouse akin to London's Kew Gardens, which, at almost two square kilometres, are the biggest in Europe. The gardens hold some sixteen thousand species of plants; highlights are some of Sweden's biggest orchids, the summer flower plantations and the adjoining arboretum.

ARRIVAL AND DEPARTURE   GOTHENBURG

By plane Gothenburg has two airports: Ryanair flights arrive at Gothenburg City (also known as Säve; ⓦ goteborgcityairport.se), 17km north of the city, and all other airlines use Landvetter (ⓦ swedavia.se), 25km east of the city. Both airports are connected to Nils Ericsons Terminalen by bus (from City airport after each flight arrival;

30min; 60kr; from Landvetter daily every 15–20min; 30min; 80kr).
By train All trains arrive at Centralstation, which forms one side of Drottningtorget.
Destinations Copenhagen via Kastrup airport (hourly; 4hr); Kalmar (5 daily; 4hr); Karlstad (5 daily; 2hr 50min);

Luleå (1 daily; 18hr); Malmö (hourly; 3hr); Örebro (7 daily; 2hr 45min); Stockholm (hourly; 3hr by X2000, 5hr InterCity); Oslo (3 daily; 4hr); Östersund (1 daily; 12hr); Umeå (1 daily; 13hr 30min); Västerås (7 daily; 3hr 45min).

By bus Long-distance buses use Nils Ericsons Terminalen, beside the train station, which can be reached by an undercover walkway.

Destinations Copenhagen via Kastrup airport (10 daily; 4hr); Falun (1 daily; 8hr); Karlstad (6 daily; 4hr); Malmö (16 daily; 3hr); Oslo (10 daily; 4hr); Stockholm (8 daily; 6hr).

By ferry Stena Line (☎031 704 00 00, ⊕stenaline.se) operates ferries from Fredrikshavn in Denmark, which dock just a 20min walk from the city centre, close to the Masthuggstorget tram stop on lines #3, #9 and #11; its services from Kiel in Germany put in close to the arching Älvsborgsbron bridge, a couple of kilometres west of the centre – take lines #3 or #9 into town from Jægerdorffsplatsen.

Destinations Frederikshavn (4–8 daily; 2hr by catamaran, 3hr 15min by ferry); Kiel (1 daily; 14hr).

INFORMATION

Tourist offices The one handiest for those arriving by train or bus is in Nordstan, the indoor shopping centre near Centralstation (Mon–Fri 10am–8pm, Sat 10am–6pm, Sun noon–5pm). The main office, however, is on the canal front at Kungsportsplatsen 2 (May Mon–Fri 9.30am–6pm, Sat & Sun 10am–2pm; June & mid- to late Aug daily 9.30am–6pm; July to mid-Aug daily 9.30am–8pm; Sept– April Mon–Fri 9.30am–5pm, Sat 10am–2pm; ☎031 368 42 00, ⊕goteborg.com). Both offices provide information,

a room-booking service and the useful *Göteborgsguiden* detailing events, music and nightspots in town.

Listings information Pick up the Saturday edition of the *Göteborgs-Posten* newspaper, whose weekend supplement, *Två Dagar*, has the latest listings of bars, concerts and clubs.

Gay information RFSL Stora Badhusgatan 6 ☎031 13 83 00, ⊕rfsl.se/goteborg. This friendly office has the latest information on the city's limited gay scene and will know of any special events taking place, too.

GETTING AROUND

It's easy to walk to almost anywhere of interest in Gothenburg. The streets are wide and pedestrian-friendly, and the canals and the grid system of avenues make orientation simple.

BY TRAM AND BUS

Both are operated by Västtrafik (☎0771 41 43 00, ⊕vasttrafik.se/en). A free transport map is available at both tourist offices.

By tram The most convenient form of public transport: a colour-coded system of tram lines serves the city and its outskirts – you can tell at a glance which line a tram is on, as the route colour will appear on the front. Trams run daily every few minutes from 5am to midnight, with a reduced service running after midnight on Fri and Sat nights.

By bus Gothenburg has a fairly extensive bus network, but pedestrianization in the city centre can lead to some odd and lengthy detours. You shouldn't need to use buses much in the centre, but useful routes are detailed in the text where necessary.

Tickets The best-value tickets to buy are travelpasses; these give unlimited travel for 24hr (65kr) or 72hr (130kr) on trams, buses and ferries within the city. Buy them from the

Tidpunkten travel information offices at Brunnsparken, Drottningtorget and Nils Ericsonsplatsen, or from Pressbyrån newsagents or 7-Eleven supermarkets. It is no longer possible to buy individual tickets with cash onboard buses and trams.

BY BIKE AND CAR

The city is one of the best in Europe for cycling: most main roads have cycle lanes, and motorists really do seem to give way to those on two wheels. The tourist offices can provide you with the excellent *cykelkarta*, which clearly shows all the cycle routes throughout the city, and out to the archipelago.

Bike rental You can rent a bike from Cykelkungen at Chalmersgatan 19 (☎031 18 43 00, ⊕cykelkungen.se; 150kr/day) or, alternatively, the *Slottskogens* and *Stigbergssliden* hostels (see p.121).

By taxi Taxis can be summoned by calling Taxi Göteborg on ☎031 65 00 00 or Taxi Kurir on ☎031 27 27 27; you can also pick one up at the rank at Centralstation.

THE GOTHENBURG CITY CARD

The Gothenburg City Card provides unlimited bus and tram travel within the city; free entry to all the city museums and the Liseberg Amusement Park; free boat trips to the Elfsborg fortress; and a fifty-percent reduction on day-trips to Fredrikshavn in Denmark with Stena Line. It also provides free parking in roadside spaces (but not at privately run or multistorey car parks). Buy the card from the tourist offices or online at ⊕goteborg.com (285kr for 24hr, 395kr for 48hr; 565kr for 72hr).

THE GOTHENBURG PACKAGE

Summer reductions mean that even the better hotels can prove surprisingly affordable, and most places also take part in the **Gothenburg Package**, a scheme coordinated by the tourist office. This is a real bargain as it offers daily, year-round accommodation in a double room, breakfast and a Gothenburg Pass, all from 645kr per person per night, and there's generally a fifty-percent discount for **children**. To take advantage of the Gothenburg Package, contact the tourist office (see p.119) or book online at ⓦ goteborg.com.

ACCOMMODATION

Gothenburg has plenty of good **accommodation** to choose from, with no shortage of comfortable **hostels**. You should have little trouble finding accommodation whenever you turn up, though in summer it's a good idea to book ahead if you are on a tighter budget, or if you want to stay in the most popular **hostels**. There are several **campsites**, though none is very central, the closest being just beyond Liseberg Amusement Park.

3

HOTELS AND PENSIONS
CENTRAL GOTHENBURG
Barken Viking Gullbergskajen ☎031 63 58 00, ⓦ liseberg.se; map p.109. Moored by the Opera House, this hotel on a grand, four-masted sailing ship built in Denmark in 1906 is a charismatic and comfortable choice. It features cosy rooms full of maritime furnishings and beautiful wood panelling. **1400kr**

★ **Best Western Eggers** Drottningtorget ☎031 333 44 40, ⓦ hoteleggers.se; map p.109. Dating from 1820, this place has individually furnished bedrooms and many original features including stuccoed ceilings and cut-glass chandeliers; used for secret wartime discussions between British and Nazi military negotiators, it's also said to be haunted. **1450kr/2350kr**

★ **Clarion Collection Odin** Odinsgatan 6 ☎031 745 22 00, ⓦ hotelodin.se; map p.109. Offering designer studios with kitchenettes rather than regular hotel rooms, this hotel is unique in Gothenburg. The superior rooms boast a fully fitted kitchen, dining area and work space – a real home from home near the train station. **1180kr/1480kr**

Clarion Post Drottningtorget 10 ☎031 61 90 00, ⓦ clarionpost.se; map p.109. Gothenburg's grand former central post office has been extended and converted into a stunning new design hotel, complete with a swimming pool on the top floor. Rooms contain the latest style-conscious Scandinavian fittings and furnishings. **1020kr/1680kr**

Elite Plaza Västra Hamngatan 3 ☎031 720 40 00, ⓦ elite.se; map p.109. The magnificent facade of this opulent hotel, which dates from 1889, hides a stunning blend of contemporary and classic decor, with majestic vaulted ceilings and mosaic floors complemented by striking modern paintings. Worth pushing the boat out for. **1650kr**

★ **First Avalon** Kungstorget 9 ☎031 751 02 00, ⓦ avalonhotel.se; map p.109. Gothenburg's best design hotel, stuffed full of pop art, mosaic pillars and lime-green and orange drapes – there's even a pool on the roof. Rooms, though stylish to a T, can be a little on the cramped side. **1341kr/1791kr**

First G Nils Ericsonsplatsen 4 ☎031 63 72 00, ⓦ firsthotels.se; map p.109. The last word in contemporary Nordic design, the rooms, curiously suspended over part of the railway station, are full of natural fibres and materials, and the predominantly green and brown decor creates a wonderfully calming atmosphere. **1079kr/1709kr**

★ **Flora** Grönsakstorget 2 ☎031 13 86 16, ⓦ hotelflora.se; map p.109. Stylish designer rooms with wooden floors, flat-screen TVs and the latest Scandinavian chic at this highly praised family-run hotel. The loft rooms are particularly cosy, featuring velux windows in the roof. **1355kr/1645kr**

Royal Drottninggatan 67 ☎031 700 11 70, ⓦ hotel-royal.com; map p.109. Dating from 1852 and the oldest hotel in Gothenburg, this place oozes grandeur and charm, from the Art Nouveau marble staircase to the individually decorated rooms. Service is personal and friendly. **1495kr**

★ **Vanilj** Kyrkogatan 38 ☎031 711 62 20, ⓦ hotelvanilj.se; map p.109. Housed in a former snuff factory from the 1800s, all 32 rooms in this small and friendly hotel are a delight: contemporary and elegant but with a touch of old-fashioned charm. Not surprisingly, they get snapped up fast. **995kr/1295kr**

SOUTHERN GOTHENBURG
City Lorensbergsgatan 6 ☎031 708 40 00, ⓦ cityhotelgbg.se; map p.112. Excellently located in a parallel street to Avenyn, the City's rooms are nothing special, though they are all bright and airy with high ceilings and perfectly comfortable. Share facilities and you can save a further 200–300kr. **1095kr**

Gothia Towers Mässansgata 24 ☎031 750 88 10, ⓦ gothiatowers.com; map p.112. Inside the twin mirrored towers just opposite Liseberg is a subtle, well-designed, contemporary hotel, with wonderful uninterrupted views over the city from the upper floors. A third tower is under construction and is expected to open in 2014. **1101kr/2195kr**

Le Mat Viktoriagatan 6 📞031 17 36 30, 🌐hotelvasa .se; map p.112. A newly opened eco-friendly, cooperative hotel with fifteen modern rooms sharing facilities, decorated in warm colours of aubergine and turquoise, and serving locally sourced produce for breakfast. The hotel aims to employ staff other hotels have overlooked. **770kr/880kr**

★ **Lilton** Föreningsgatan 9 📞031 82 88 08, 🌐lilton .se; map p.112. This cosy, ivy-covered place, with individually decorated rooms, is one of Gothenburg's hidden gems. It's quiet and friendly, with splendid National Romantic and Art Nouveau buildings close by, and even has its own courtyard of roses and peonies. **1295kr/1195kr**

Maria Erikssons Pensionat Chalmersgatan 27A 📞031 20 70 30, 🌐mariaspensionat.nu; map p.112. With just ten comfortable rooms decorated in modern Scandinavian style, this place is well positioned on a road running parallel with Avenyn. Rooms with shared facilities cost 100kr less. Breakfast is not included. **1000kr**

Scandic Rubinen Kungsportsavenyn 24 📞031 751 54 00, 🌐scandic.se; map p.112. It's hard to get more central than this hotel, which enjoys a perfect location on Avenyn. The good-sized rooms have wooden floors and are decorated in warm reds, oranges and maroons, whilst the public areas all bear a hint of Mexico. **1260kr/1400kr**

HOSTELS

Kvibergs Vandrarhem Lilla Regementsvägen 35 📞031 43 50 55, 🌐vandrarhem.com; tram #7 or #11 from Centralstation; map p.109. Just 10min by tram from Centralstation and offering a little taste of the countryside. No dorm beds but cosy single and double rooms which cost a little less during Sept–May. **510kr**

Masthuggsterrassen Masthuggsterrassen 10H 📞031 42 48 20, 🌐mastenvandrarhem.com; tram #3, #9 or #11 from Centralstation; map p.112. Up the steps from Masthuggstorget and a couple of minutes' walk from the terminal for the Stena Line ferry from Denmark. Has

decent-sized double rooms and an on-site kitchen for self-catering. Dorms **195kr**, doubles **500kr**

★ **Slottskogen** Vegagatan 21 📞031 42 65 20, 🌐sov .nu; from Centralstation take tram #1 or #2 to Olivedalsgatan; map p.112. Superbly appointed and well-designed hostel with 165 beds, a TV in every room and washbasin in most. On-site sauna, solarium and billiards available. Dorms **215kr**, doubles **250kr**

Stigbergsliden Stigbergsliden 10 📞031 24 16 20, 🌐hostel-gothenburg.com; map p.112. This excellent STF hostel, built in 1830 as a seamen's house, is well placed for the Linné area. All rooms have basins, and there's disabled access, laundry facilities and a pleasant back courtyard. Dorms **160kr**, doubles **420kr**

CAMPING

Two of the following campsites also provide cabins, which are worth considering, especially if there are more than two of you. Facilities are invariably squeaky clean and in good working order – there's usually a well-equipped kitchen too – but you'll have to pay extra for bedding. If you want to camp, you'll generally pay around 120kr per night for two people in July or Aug, or 60kr the rest of the year.

Askim Strand 📞031 28 62 61, 🌐liseberg.se; from Nils Ericson terminalen take bus #80 towards Snipen and alight at Askimsbadet; map p.112. Set beside sandy beaches 12km from the centre, this campsite also has comfortable two-bed cabins. Open late April to early Sept. Cabins **1295kr**

Lilleby Havsbad 📞031 56 22 40, 🌐lillebycamping.se; bus #121 from Centralstation and change to #23 towards Silvik at Torslanda torg; map p.112. About 1hr from the city centre in Torslanda, this splendid seaside location is some compensation for the trek. June–Aug only. Tents **250kr**

Timmerbyn Olbergsgatan 9 📞031 84 02 00, 🌐liseberg.se; from Centralstation take tram #5 to Welandergatan, direction Torp; map p.112. This site, 4km from the centre, close to Liseberg Amusement Park and set among forest and lakes, offers two-bed cabins. There are huge discounts outside June–Aug. Cabins **1345kr**

EATING

Gothenburg has a multitude of eating places, catering for every budget and for most tastes; among the best to try are the pan-European restaurants which draw on Swedish staples such as good breads, exceptional herring and salmon and, in summer, glorious soft fruits.

CAFÉS AND KONDITORI

During the past few years, café life has really come into its own in Gothenburg, the profusion of new places throughout the city adding to the more traditional *konditori*. Cafés also offer a wide range of light meals and are fast becoming the best places to go for good food at reasonable prices.

CENTRAL GOTHENBURG

Ahlströms Konditori Korsgatan 2 📞031 13 48 93; map p.109. Dating from 1901, this traditional café/bakery is very much of the old school, as are many of its patrons. The original features have been watered down by modernization, but it's still a great place for a coffee. Mon–Fri 7.30am–7pm, Sat 9.30am–4.30pm.

3

SELF-CATERING

Self-catering in Gothenburg will save you a considerable amount of money over eating regularly in cafés and restaurants. There are several great places to buy good, fresh food, particularly succulent, locally caught fish and seafood. Bustling, historic **Saluhallen** at Kungstorget (Mon–Fri 9am–6pm, Sat 10am–3pm) is a delightful sensory experience, with a great choice of meats, fish, fruits, vegetables and a huge range of delectable breads. For excellent fresh fish, **Feskekôrka** at Fisktorget (Tues–Fri 10am–6pm, Sat 10am–3pm; see p.113) is an absolute must. The conveniently located Coop Konsum supermarket at Kungsportsavenyn 26–28 (Mon–Sat 8am–11pm, Sun 11am–11pm) sells a wide range of fruits, fish and meats, and also has a good deli counter.

Brogyllen Västra Hamngatan 2 ☎031 13 87 13; map p.109. High ceilings and chandeliers add an old-world charm to this pleasant *konditori* which is one of the best places in town for watching the world go by – large windows look out on the canal. Mon–Thurs 7.30am–8pm, Fri 7.30am–7pm, Sat 8.30am–5pm, Sun 9.30am–5pm.

Da Matteo Södra Larmgatan 14 ☎031 774 28 81; map p.109. In the Victoriapassagen arcade, this homely café is a perfect example of Gothenburg's foray into cool little Italian-style coffee houses. There's a smart brick-walled and tiled interior, plus outdoor seating. Mon–Fri 8am–7pm, Sat 9am–5pm, Sun 10am–5pm.

Fröken Olssons Kafé Östra Larmgatan 14 ☎031 13 81 93; map p.109. Ecological coffee, lactose-free drinks, vegetarian and vegan meals are the speciality at this right-on café decked out in orange tiles. Look out also for the truly enormous cakes on silver cake trays. Mon–Fri 9am–8pm, Sat & Sun 9am–6pm.

Mauritz Kaffe Fredsgatan 2 ☎031 80 69 71; map p.109. Very small and unassuming, this place is run by the founder's great-grandson; the family have been importing coffee into Gothenburg since 1888. Come here for excellent coffee, apple, rhubarb or plum buns or home-baked rye rolls with Grevé cheese. Mon–Fri 9.30am–6pm, Sat 9.30am–3pm.

★ **Vanilj** Kyrkogatan 38 ☎031 13 40 54; map p.109. A light and airy modern café with wooden floors, serving up great *kanelbullar* (cinnamon buns) as well as a wide range of pies, salads and breads. Outdoor seating in summer in the rear courtyard. Mon–Fri 7.30am–9pm, Sat 11am–9pm, Sun noon–6pm.

SOUTHERN GOTHENBURG

Café Dali Vasagatan 42 ☎031 711 05 08; map p.112. Popular with students, and set in an orange-painted basement, this is a friendly, stylish place for sandwiches and delicious chocolate cake. A good place to get to know local students. Mon–Fri 7am–10pm, Sat & Sun 9am–10pm.

Husaren Haga Nygatan 28 ☎031 13 63 78; map p.112. *The* place to sample Sweden's famous *kanelbullar* (cinnamon buns) which are served here as big as a dinner plate, costing just 35kr. There's also a good selection of cakes, sandwiches and other light snacks. Mon–Thurs 8am–8pm, Fri 8am–7pm, Sat & Sun 8am–6pm.

Junggrens Café Avenyn 37 ☎031 16 17 51; map p.112. With chandeliers and wall paintings of old Gothenburg, this atmospheric and convivial place has been here since 1898. Hard to beat for its prime location at the top of Avenyn. Mon–Fri 8am–10pm, Sat & Sun 9am–10pm.

Tintin Engelbrektsgatan 22 ☎031 18 07 70; map p.112. One of the very few cafés in Gothenburg open around the clock, this busy place is popular with a younger crowd and dishes up mounds of food and coffee at low prices. Open 24hr.

RESTAURANTS

If you want to avoid paying over the odds, it's generally best to steer clear of Avenyn itself and to eat your main meal at lunchtime, when you can fill up on *dagens rätt* deals for 75–95kr. Some of the best deals are to be found in the Haga and Linné districts.

CENTRAL GOTHENBURG

Café du Nord Kungstorget 3 ☎031 13 37 74; map p.109. Serving the best meatballs in town: four of them with mashed potato and lingonberries costs just 80kr. Alternatively, buy them individually (12kr each) and add green salad (25kr), mash (15kr) and lingonberries (5kr). Also has tuna or Greek salads and sandwiches from 39kr. Mon–Sat 7am–9pm, Sun 11am–7pm.

Gabriel Feskekôrka fish hall, Fisktorget 4 ☎031 13 90 51; map p.109. Excellent upstairs fish restaurant serving up Swedish classics such as gravad lax with dill potatoes (155kr), open prawn sandwich with mushrooms and mashed potatoes (155kr) and a delicious fish soup à la Gabriel for 135kr. Tues–Thurs 11am–5pm, Fri 11am–6pm, Sat 11am–3pm.

KåGes Hörna Stora Saluhallen, Kungstorget ☎031 13 04 50; map p.109. An atmospheric old diner located inside the Saluhallen and accessed through the door closest to the *Avalon* hotel, serving home-cooking classics such as salmon burgers, meatballs and apple pie at fantastic prices – mains around 55kr. Mon–Fri 11am–5.30pm, Sat 11am–2.45pm.

Kometen Vasagatan 58 ☎031 13 79 88; map p.109. Handily located just off Avenyn, this place has been serving

Gothenburgers with good-quality home cooking for over 75 years and is justifiably popular: its Janssons temptation, herring and Wiener schnitzel are all excellent. Mains cost 225–335kr. Mon–Fri 11.30am–10.30pm, Sat noon–10.30pm, Sun 1–10pm.

Magnus & Magnus Magasinsgatan 8 ☎031 13 30 00; map p.109. This intimate little place oozes sophistication. Against a backdrop of velvet drapes and fresh flowers, diners are teased with a list of ingredients: cod, lamb, wild garlic, almonds, for example, and the results are mouthwatering. Two courses 395kr, three courses 495kr. Mon–Thurs 6pm till late, Fri–Sun 5pm till late.

★ **Mother India** Köpmansgatan 27 ☎031 15 47 41; map p.109. This tiny basement Indian restaurant is tucked away down a side street opposite the Nils Ericsson Terminalen and beside the *Scandic Hotel*. Authentically tasty curries (from 79kr), and a good range of vegetarian options such as paneer balti at 79kr. Mon–Fri 11am–10pm, Sat & Sun 1–10pm.

★ **Tranquilo** Kungstorget 14 ☎031 13 45 55; map p.109. Mexican food is the order of the day at this funky restaurant with live DJs playing salsa sounds at weekends. Try the leg of lamb braised in chilli and tequila served with salsa verde and tortillas (240kr). Otherwise, mains around 160kr. Mon–Thurs noon–midnight, Fri & Sat noon–3am.

SOUTHERN GOTHENBURG

28+ Götabergsgatan 28 ☎031 20 21 61; map p.112. Very fine French-style gourmet restaurant, whose name refers to the fat percentage of its renowned cheese, also sold in the shop near the entrance. Mains around 250kr such as the delicious grilled halibut with truffle purée. Mon–Sat 6pm till late.

Cyrano Prinsgatan 7 ☎031 14 31 10; map p.112. A superb Provencal-style bistro serving French classics: escargots (from 94kr), moules marseillaises (135kr) and frogs' legs in pernod (135kr). A set three-course menu costs 340kr, or there's the choice of a salad, pizza and dessert for 245kr. Mon–Fri 5–11pm, Sat 2–11pm, Sun 2–9pm.

E.t.c. Vasaplatsen 4 ☎031 13 06 02; map p.112. This cool, elegant white-painted basement is a good bet for tasty pasta (135–155kr), as well as Mediterranean meat and fish dishes such as roast lamb with grilled aubergine and peppers (235kr). Mon–Thurs 11am–midnight, Fri 11am–1am, Sat 1pm–1am, Sun 2–9.30pm.

Familjen Arkivgatan 7 ☎031 20 79 79; map p.112. A popular brasserie decked out with black-and-white photographs of Gothenburgers at play, serving locally sourced tapas such as mackerel in tomato sauce, home-made sausage and a selection of charcuterie. A three-course menu goes for 325kr. Mon–Thurs 5pm–midnight, Fri & Sat 5pm–1am.

Hemma Hos Haga Nygatan 12 ☎031 13 40 90; map p.112. Very popular though rather cramped restaurant serving Swedish tapas using ingredients from right across the country – for example, Västerbotten cheese quiche,

herring on rye bread and goats' cheese terrine, all around the 79kr mark. Mon–Thurs 11.30am–11pm, Fri & Sat noon–1am, Sun noon–11pm.

★ **Hos Pelle** Djupedalsgatan 2 ☎031 12 10 31; map p.112. This sophisticated wine bar and restaurant offers modern Swedish fare such as gravad lax, grilled steak with herb butter and fish and seafood stew (mains 125–245kr). There's also a three-course menu for 325kr. Mon 6–10pm, Tues–Thurs 6–11pm, Fri & Sat 5.30–11pm.

Kock & Vin Viktoriagatan 12 ☎031 701 79 79; map p.112. An excellent choice for modern Swedish food with a hint of the Mediterranean, served amid airy surrounds and chandeliers. Mains such as brawn of rabbit with pearl barley, cucumber and pickled turnip, are around the 275kr mark. Mon–Sat 6pm till late.

Lai Wa Storgatan 11 ☎031 711 02 39; map p.112. Established in 1975, this is the best Chinese in town with dependable mains (110kr) like beef with bamboo shoots and a good number of vegetarian dishes, including stir-fried vegetables with glass noodles in satay sauce for 110kr. Mon–Fri 3–10pm, Sat noon–10pm, Sun noon–9pm.

★ **Linnéterrassen** Linnégatan 32 ☎031 24 08 90; map p.112. Swedish home cooking served in a beautifully restored house with wall panelling and chandeliers, or on the open-air terrace. Exceptional value with mains in the range of 100–239kr, including a herring platter, fish gratin, meatballs and pan-fried pork with onions and potatoes. Mon–Fri 4pm–1am, Sat & Sun 1pm–1am.

Sjöbaren Haga Nygatan 25 ☎031 711 97 80; map p.112. Small and cosy fish and shellfish restaurant with a superb range of food. Highlights include fresh pasta with marinated shellfish (149kr) and a smoked and marinated salmon combo (145kr). Mon–Thurs 11am–11pm, Fri 11am–midnight, Sat noon–midnight, Sun 1–9pm.

★ **Smaka** Vasaplatsen 3 ☎031 13 22 47; map p.112. This elegant restaurant with a striking blue interior is *the* place to sample moderately priced traditional local fare (mains 139–225kr) such as meatballs with lingonberries or herring with boiled egg and mashed potoato. Mon–Fri 5pm–2am, Sat & Sun 5pm–3am.

Solrosen Kaponjärgatan 4A ☎031 711 66 97; map p.112. The oldest vegetarian restaurant in Gothenburg serving well-prepared veggie and vegan delights: the set dish of the day including the salad buffet costs 80kr. The salad buffet alone is an excellent-value 60kr. Mon–Thurs 11.30am–11pm, Fri 11.30am–midnight, Sat 1pm–midnight, Sun 2–8pm.

Thai Spice Andra Långgatan 8 ☎031 42 30 35; map p.112. Not only is the Thai food at this agreeable neighbourhood place genuinely tasty and spicy, the prices are also quite exceptional: any dish with chicken is just 75kr, add 10kr for beef or prawns. Mon 11am–2pm, Tues–Fri 11am–8.30pm, Sat 1–8.30pm, Sun 2–8pm.

3

DRINKING AND NIGHTLIFE

There's an excellent choice of places to **drink**, and even the hippest bars often serve food and so have a bit of a restaurant atmosphere. Although it's not uncommon for Gothenburgers to drink themselves to oblivion, the atmosphere around the bars is generally non-aggressive. Gothenburg's main **nightclubs** are mostly clustered in the city centre around Vasagatan, Avenyn and Storgatan.

BARS AND PUBS

We've listed some of the city's most popular pubs and bar-restaurants below. The bar scene along Avenyn notwithstanding, the atmosphere is generally a bit low-key in the city centre at night. Having first sampled the delights of Avenyn, head for the area around Järntorget in Haga where there are great places to drink into the early hours.

CENTRAL GOTHENBURG

7:an Kungstorget 7 ☏ 031 774 04 77; map p.109. Pronounced *shoo-ann* and meaning simply "number seven", this is one of the city's better beer halls, located close to Stora Saluhallen. The interior is dark, intimate and old-fashioned in feel – a quintessential Gothenburg experience. Mon & Tues 1pm–midnight, Wed–Fri 1pm–1am, Sat 11am–1am, Sun 1–11pm.

Bishops Arms Västra Hamngatan 3 ☏ 031 720 40 45; map p.109. Attached to the glamorous *Elite Plaza* hotel (see p.120), this pub boasts a wide range of beers. It's all faux "olde Englishe" inside, but nicely done and a cut above similarly styled places around the country. Mon 5pm–midnight, Tues–Thurs 5pm–1am, Fri & Sat 5pm–2am, Sun 5pm–11pm.

Dubliner Östra Hamngatan 50b ☏ 031 13 90 20; map p.109. For some time, Swedes have been overtaken with a nostalgia for all things old and Irish (or at least a Swedish interpretation of what's old and Irish), this being the most popular exponent. Mon–Sat 11am till late, Sun noon till late.

Gamle Port Östra Larmgatan 18 ☏ 031 711 24 30; map p.109. The city's oldest watering hole, with cosy leather chairs in the downstairs pub and live music on Fri and Sat nights, plus a loud and raucous disco upstairs playing 1980s music and techno. Daily 11am till late.

Gretas Drottninggattan 35 ☏ 031 13 69 49; map p.109. Gay bar, restaurant and nightclub all rolled into *the one and only* gay nightspot in town. Occasional drag shows and other live performances; if you're aiming to eat here be sure to book well in advance. Fri & Sat 9pm–4am.

Palace Södra Hamngatan 2 ☏ 031 80 25 21; map p.109. The rather splendid former home of the Fürstenbergs and their art gallery (see p.111) is a very popular spot, particularly on Thurs when over-27s gravitate here for a night of 1970s and 1980s hits. Mon–Wed 11.30am–11pm, Thurs & Fri 11.30am–3am, Sat noon–3am, Sun 1–6pm.

SOUTHERN GOTHENBURG

Jazzå Andra Långgatan 4B ☏ 031 14 16 90; map p.112. Busy bar attracting a young crowd with the live music on offer – usually jazz and blues. There's also a small menu and a couple of tables on the pavement outside. Mon–Thurs & Sun 5pm–1am, Fri 5pm–2am, Sat 4pm–2am.

Pustervik Järntorgsgatan 12 ☏ 031 13 06 80, ⓦ pusterviksbiljetter.com; map p.112. A popular bar and club off Järntorget where there's a good chance of live music – everything from up-and-coming new bands to big names. Check the website for the latest events and to buy tickets. Times vary.

Rose & Crown Avenyn 6 ☏ 031 10 58 27; map p.112. One of a bevy of British-oriented neighbourhood pubs that are very much in vogue with Gothenburgers; this one has plenty of British paraphernalia plus live sports matches, karaoke and a Saturday Night Fever 1970s disco. Mon–Thurs 5pm–1am, Fri & Sat noon–3am, Sun noon–10pm.

The Rover Andra Långgatan 12 ☏ 031 775 04 90; map p.112. Fun Anglo-Irish pub selling Boddingtons, with other ales, lagers and cider on tap, plus a wide range of bottled beers. Lamb, steaks and fish dishes for around 170kr. Daily 5pm till late.

The Temple Linnégatan 42 ☏ 031 311 251 60; map p.112. Skip the rather small bricked-walled interior of this Linné neighbourhood pub and opt instead for the popular outdoor terrace where local people come to eat, drink and socialize. Gets really busy on warm summer evenings. Mon–Thurs 4pm–midnight, Fri & Sat 4pm–1am, Sun 4–11pm.

CLUBS

Klara Viktoriagatan 1 ☏ 031 13 38 54; map p.112. The best of all the more alternative nightspots, this long-established and eminently likeable bar and restaurant has live music which varies each night. Restaurant and bar open daily, club only Sat 10pm–2am.

Peacock Dinner Club Avenyn 21 ☏ 031 13 88 55; map p.109. The centrepoint of this elegant dining club is an oval gold bar that's home to the DJ. Sofas are arranged around it in the shape of a peacock's tail feathers – perfect for surveying the scene. Tues & Wed 6pm–1am, Thurs 6pm–3am, Fri 5pm–4am, Sat 6pm–4am.

Push Avenyn 11 ☏ 031 701 80 94; map p.112. Open again following a thorough redesign, this is the place to come for an irresistible mix of pop, rock and party music. Fri night is busiest when the action spills out onto the outdoor terrace. Wed 10pm–3am, Fri 10am–5am, Sat 10pm–4.30am.

Respekt Järntorget 7 ☎ 031 775 18 00; map p.112. Though rather unappealing from the outside, this rambling place covers one square kilometre and boasts a number of different dancefloors with everything from disco and hip-hop to soul and R&B. Occasional live music. Opening times vary.

Trädgår'n Nya Allén 11 ☎ 031 10 20 80; map p.109. One of the city's liveliest haunts, this hip club offers five bars, a casino, a disco playing house and party favourites

and show bands. You can also eat here before heading on to the club. Fri & Sat 10pm–4am.

Valand Vasagatan 41 ☎ 031 18 30 93; map p.112. The oldest of the traditional nightclubs in town, playing the latest radio hits as well as classic rock tracks. *Valand* boasts two dancefloors as well as four bars, and is always crowded. Fri & Sat 10pm–4am.

Vasastan Viktoriagatan 2A ☎ 031 13 03 02; map p.112. A suave spot where confident 20- and 30-somethings enjoy a mellow atmosphere. It's also a popular place to eat before the club opens. Fri & Sat 6pm–3am.

ENTERTAINMENT

Gothenburg's large student community means there are plenty of local **live bands** which tend to play in a cluster of bars in the city centre. The best nights to catch a live performance are Friday and Saturday. **Classical music** concerts are held regularly in the Konserthuset, Götaplatsen (☎ 031 726 53 90, ⓦ gso.se), and occasionally at Stadsteatern, Götaplatsen (☎ 031 708 71 00, ⓦ stadsteatern.goteborg.se; programme details can be obtained from the tourist office). For **opera**, head to the renowned Göteborgsoperan at Christina Nilssons gata at the harbour (☎ 031 13 13 00, ⓦ opera.se).

JAZZ AND ROCK VENUES

Jazzhuset Erik Dahlbergsgatan 3 ☎ 031 13 35 44; map p.112. Drawing the crowds since 1977, this club not only puts on trad and Dixieland jazz, and swing, but has branched out into indie, garage rock, synth and electronica. Fri & Sat 10pm–3am.

Nefertiti Hvitfeldtsplatsen 6 ☎ 031 711 15 33, ⓦ nefertiti.se; map p.109. The premier place for jazz in Gothenburg with modern jazz, big-band and folk music as well as reggae, blues and soul. Events are advertised online. Times vary.

Sticky Fingers Kaserntorget 7 ☎ 031 701 07 17; map p.109. This rock club first opened its doors in the late 1980s

and has been supporting local talent ever since, hosting live bands several nights a week. Wed 8pm–1am, Thurs 8pm–2am, Fri & Sat 9pm–4am.

CINEMA

There are plenty of cinemas around the city, and English-language films (which make up the majority of what's shown) are always subtitled in Swedish, never dubbed. The most central complexes are Bio Palatset, Kungstorget 2 (☎ 031 774 22 90), and Filmstaden Bergakungen, at Skånegatan 16B (☎ 0771 11 12 13). For a great art-house cinema, check out Hagabio at Linnégatan 21 (☎ 031 42 88 10).

DIRECTORY

Dentist Akuttandvården, Odinsgatan 10 ☎ 031 80 78 00.
Doctor Sahlgrenska Hospital at Per Dubbsgatan (☎ 031 342 10 00). City Akuten, a private clinic, has doctors on duty 8am–6pm at Nordstadstorget 6 (☎ 031 10 10 10).
Emergency services Ambulance, police, and fire brigade are on ☎ 112.
Exchange Forex exchange offices Centralstation, Avenyn 22, Nordstan shopping centre and Kungsportsplatsen. More information at ⓦ forex.se.
Internet access Sidewalk Express have lots of internet points across Gothenburg, for example, at Centralstation and at most 7-Eleven supermarkets. See ⓦ sidewalkexpress .se for complete listings.

Laundry Betjänten HomeMaid, inside the Nordstan shopping centre (Mon–Fri noon–6pm; ☎ 031 711 61 29).
Left luggage Lockers at Centralstation.
Pharmacy Götgatan 12, in Nordstan shopping centre ☎ 0771 45 04 50. Daily 8am–10pm.
Police Spannmålsgatan 6 ☎ 031 739 20 00.
Swimming The biggest and best pool is Valhallabadet, Valhallagatan 3 (Mon 7am–8pm, Tues & Thurs 7am–7pm, Wed 6.30am–8pm, Fri 6.30am–7pm, Sat 7am–3pm, Sun 11am–3pm; ☎ 031 61 19 56), next to the Scandinavium sports complex.

3

Around Gothenburg

SMÖGEN, BOHUSLÄN COAST

Around Gothenburg

The coastline around Gothenburg is one big playground for the city's inhabitants and should be your first stop when moving on from the centre. Remarkably, the **Gothenburg archipelago**, a vast array of forested islands, rocky bluffs and skerries, scattered off the city's western shore, is still little known by visitors. Gothenburgers, however, rave about it – with good reason – and the archipelago is considerably less expensive to reach than the equivalent in Stockholm. North of Gothenburg, the rugged and picturesque **Bohuslän coast**, which runs all the way to the Norwegian border, attracts countless tourists each summer, the majority of them Scandinavian and German. The most popular spot is the island town of **Marstrand**, with its impressive fortress and richly ornamental ancient buildings, but there are several other worthwhile attractions further up the coast, not least the buzzing summer destination of **Smögen** and the nearby wildlife park, **Nordens Ark**.

Northeast of the city, the shores of beautiful **Lake Vänern** make a splendid backdrop for the journey to the lake region's main town, **Karlstad**, a thoroughly likeable place the perfect jumping-off point for **river-rafting** trips through the rural province of **Värmland**.

The Gothenburg archipelago

On a fine day, Gothenburgers make for the **coastal islands**, where bathing in the sea and sun is a real pleasure and it's hard to imagine you're so close to a city; regular boats leave for the archipelago from Saltholmen, at the end of tram lines #9 and #11.

Saltholmen

Around 5km west of the city centre is **SALTHOLMEN**, at the tip of Gothenburg's most westerly peninsula, the jumping-off point for boats to the islands. Outcrops of smooth rocks provide a multitude of hidden sun-worshipping areas, where **nude bathing** is quite the norm. The zone around to your left, on the south side of the peninsula, has become a recognized gay bathing area. Climbing to Saltholmen's highest point, the views are quite idyllic, with boats flecking the water and the offshore islands stretching out into the distance. There's a delightful little outdoor **café** at Saltholmen too.

Brännö

It's a short hop from Saltholmen to one of the archipelago's most popular destinations, **BRÄNNÖ**, a compact island measuring barely a couple of square kilometres, mainly given over to summerhouses converted from fishermen's shacks, and crowded with Gothenburgers through high season. This pastoral island is known for its strong folk-music traditions and throughout the summer months, on Thursday evenings, there's dancing and music at the jetty in Husvik at the southern end of the island; it's an easy 1km walk here from the main ferry jetty, Rödsten.

Styrsö

Located in the middle of the archipelago, **STYRSÖ** has just three hamlets (Tången, Bratten and Skäret) where most of its residents live all year. The main settlement,

Lake Vänern p.139   **Rafting on the Klarälven River** p.143
Karlstad's boat buses p.140

RAFTING ON THE KLARÄLVEN RIVER

Highlights

❶ Vrångö Chill undisturbed and work on your overall tan on this idyllic island on the furthest reaches of the Gothenburg archipelago. **See p.130**

❷ Marstrand Rub shoulders with the summer yachting crowd and watch the sun set over one of western Sweden's most attractive towns. **See p.130**

❸ Fiskebäckskil This picture-perfect fishing village on the Bohuslän coast is home to painter Carl Wilhelmson's studio. **See p.133**

❹ Karlstad This shimmering lakeside town on Lake Vänern is known for its long hours of sunshine, great beaches and laidback inhabitants. **See p.138**

❺ Mårbacka Get to know one of the Swedes' most loved writers, Nobel prize winner, Selma Lagerlöf, at her former home in central Värmland. **See p.142**

❻ Rafting on the Klarälven River, Värmland Build your own raft and glide down one of Sweden's most enchanting rivers. **See p.143**

HIGHLIGHTS ARE MARKED ON THE MAP ON P.131

Bratten, is contained in a series of narrow alleyways, clustered around the church. The main reason to come here is to visit the island's family-friendly beach, **Brattenbadet**, a five-minute walk north of the ferry jetty.

Vrångö

If you're looking for unspoilt nature aplenty, a beguiling shoreline punctuated with skerries and islets and a perfect place to get away from it all, the furthest of the main islands, candle-shaped **VRÅNGÖ**, is sure to please. Its one small village lies on the island's west coast, opposite where the ferry from Saltholmen puts in. From the jetty, turn left for the undulating walking path that leads around the island's southernmost point to the village. On the way you'll pass a perfect lagoon with a great beach and a spit of flat stone forming one side. Beyond here are countless creeks and bays where you can sunbathe naked, should you choose, undisturbed. The path continues north of the village, cutting through a nature reserve, on its way back to the ferry quay on the eastern shore.

ARRIVAL AND INFORMATION   GOTHENBURG ARCHIPELAGO

By boat Ferries run every hour or two from Saltholmen to Brännö (20min), Styrsö (30min) and Vrångö (50min); detailed timetables can be found at ⓦstyrsobolaget.se. Travel cards are valid on board the boats – simply flash your card at the card reader as you board – no extra ticket is needed, and bikes go free.

Useful websites Information for the main islands can be found at ⓦbranno.nu, ⓦstyrso.nu (in Swedish) and ⓦvrango.com.

ACCOMMODATION AND EATING

Pensionat Baggen Brännö ⓣ031 97 38 80, ⓦbrannovardshus.se. Located in the middle of the island (ask for directions), this cosy guesthouse has simple double rooms with shared facilities. <u>920kr/795kr</u>

Värdshus Brännö. Next door to the *Pensionat Baggen*, with mains at around 250kr. Open for lunch and dinner.

The Bohuslän coast

A chain of **islands** linked by a thread of bridges and short ferry crossings make up the region of **Bohuslän** where, despite the summer crowds, it's still easy enough to find a private spot to swim. Sailing is also a popular pastime among the many Swedes who have summer cottages here, and all the way along the coast you'll see yachts gliding through the water. Another feature of the Bohuslän landscape you can't fail to miss is the large number of **churches** here. The region has a long tradition of religious observance, fuelled in the early nineteenth century by the dogmatic Calvinist clergyman Henric Schartau, who believed that closed curtains were a sign of sin within – even today, many island homes still have curtainless windows. The churches, dating from the 1840s up to the early twentieth century, are mostly white, simple affairs, and look like windmills without sails. Once you've seen the inside of one you've mostly seen them all, but the few that are exquisite or unusual have been highlighted in the guide. Each church is usually open between 10am and 3pm, but the clergyman invariably lives next door and will be happy to unlock the building at other times.

Marstrand

About 50km northwest of Gothenburg, the island town of **MARSTRAND** buzzes with activity in the summer, as holiday-makers come to sail, bathe and take one of the highly entertaining historical tours around its impressive **castle**, Carlstens fästning. With ornate wooden buildings lining the bustling **harbour**, Marstrand is a delightful place to visit and, as an easy day-trip from Gothenburg, it shouldn't be missed.

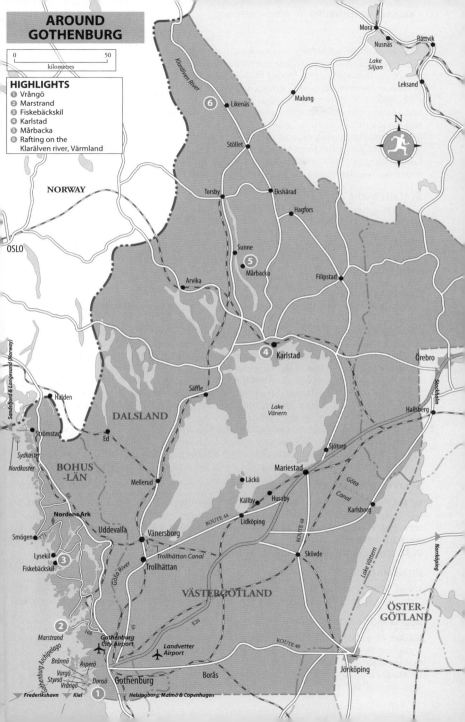

AROUND GOTHENBURG

0   50
kilometres

HIGHLIGHTS
1 Vrångö
2 Marstrand
3 Fiskebäckskil
4 Karlstad
5 Mårbacka
6 Rafting on the
    Klarälven river, Värmland

NORWAY

OSLO

N

Mora
Nusnäs
Rättvik
Lake Siljan
Leksand

Malung

6 Likenäs

Stöllet

Klarälven River

Torsby
Ekshärad

Hagfors

Sunne
5 Mårbacka

Filipstad

Arvika

Örebro

4 Karlstad

Säffle

Lake Vänern

Stockholm

Hallsberg

Halden

DALSLAND

Sandefjord & Langesund (Norway)

Strömstad

Ed

Sydkoster
Nordkoster

BOHUS
-LÄN

Mellerud

Sjötorp

Läckö

Mariestad

Göta Canal

Nordens Ark

Källby
Husaby

Karlsborg

Smögen

Uddevalla

Vänersborg

Lidköping

ROUTE 44

Lysekil
3

ROUTE 48

Fiskebäckskil

Trollhättan Canal

Trollhättan

Skövde

Lake Vättern

Norrköping

VÄSTERGÖTLAND

Göta River

ÖSTER-
GÖTLAND

Marstrand
2

Gothenburg Archipelago

Gothenburg
City Airport

Landvetter
Airport

ROUTE 40

Brännö
Asperö
Vargö
Styrsö
Vrångö
Donsö

Gothenburg
1

Borås

Jönköping

Frederikshavn Kiel

Helsingborg, Malmö & Copenhagen

Brief history

The town's colourful **history** – as so often in western Sweden – mainly revolves around fish. Founded under Norwegian rule in the thirteenth century, it achieved remarkable prosperity through herring fishing during the following century, when the ruling king, Håkon of Norway, obtained permission from the pope to allow fishing in the town even on holy days. Rich herring pickings, however, eventually led to greed and corruption, and Marstrand became known as the most immoral town in Scandinavia. The murder of a cleric in 1586 was seen as an omen: soon after, the whole town burned to the ground and the herring mysteriously disappeared from its waters, neither the fish nor Marstrand's prosperity to partially return until the 1770s. The town fell behind Gothenburg in importance, and by the 1820s, the old herring salting-houses had been converted into bathhouses as Marstrand reinvented itself as a fashionable bathing resort.

St Maria kyrka

On leaving the ferry, head up Hospitalsgatan and turn right into Kyrkogatan and after a couple of minutes, you'll arrive at a small square, surrounded by beautiful wooden houses painted in pastel hues; the locals play *boules* here beneath the shade of a huge, ancient beech tree. Across the square is the squat, white **St Maria kyrka**, whose interior is simple and unremarkable. From here, all the streets, lined with wooden villas, climb steeply to the castle.

Carlstens fästning

Kungsgatan • Daily: early to mid-June & Aug 11am–4pm; mid-June to July 11am–6pm; rest of year 11am–4pm • 75kr including guided tour • For English-language tours, book ahead on ☎ 0303 602 65 • ⓦ carlsten.se

Carlstens fästning is an imposing sweep of stone walls solidly wedged into the rough rock above. You could easily spend half a day clambering around the castle walls and down the weather-smoothed rocks to the sea, where there are always plenty of places to bathe in private. The informal **tours** take 45 minutes, and guides will explain about Carlstens' most noted prisoner-resident, **Lasse-Maja**, a thief who got rich by dressing as a woman to seduce and rob wealthy farmers. A sort of Swedish Robin Hood, Maja was known for giving his spoils to the poor. Incarcerated here for 26 years, Lasse-Maja ingratiated himself with the officers by deploying his cooking skills in a kitchen not renowned for its cuisine. His culinary expertise eventually won him a pardon: when the new king – who was reputed to hate Swedish cooking – visited, Lasse-Maja had the foresight to serve him French food. Some tours include climbing the 100m-high towers, built in 1658. The views from the top are stunning, but the steep, spiral climb is quite exhausting.

ARRIVAL AND DEPARTURE   MARSTRAND

By bus Bus #210 leaves Nils Ericson Terminalen in Gothenburg for Marstrand hourly (from early morning until late evening; 50min), terminating at the foot passenger ferry over to Marstrand.

By car Take the E6 north out of Gothenburg, and then Route 168 west, leading right to the ferry stop; cars are not permitted on Marstrand, so you must park at the ferry quay on the island of Koön and travel across to Marstrand as a foot passenger (every 15min; 5min; 20kr return).

INFORMATION

Tourist office Hamngatan 33 (early June Mon–Sat 11am–5pm, Sun noon–4pm; late June to Aug Mon–Fri 10am–6pm, Sat & Sun 11am–5pm; ☎ 0303 600 87, ⓦ marstrand.se). Close to the harbour where the ferry docks.

ACCOMMODATION

Båtellet Kungsplan 15 ☎ 0303 600 10, ✉ batellet @gmail.com. The island's hostel is set in an old bathhouse and looks out onto idyllic islands. Rooms are quite plain but the facilities are good, and include a sauna, laundry, swimming pool and restaurant. No double rooms in summer. Dorms 365kr, doubles 730kr

Grand Rådhusgatan 2 ☎ 0303 603 22, ⓦ grandmarstrand.se. Built in 1892 and the former residence of King Oscar II (who spent summers here in room 24), the *Grand* is a real classic. Expertly refurbished

with period furniture from the early 1900s, this glorious hotel more than lives up to its name. **1895kr/2195kr**
Hotel Nautic Långgatan 6 ☎0303 610 30, ⓦhotellnautic.com. Although rooms at this mid-range

hotel are rather modest in size and decor, it's the lovely setting, surrounded by water and sailing boats, which is the real attraction. Just 100kr more gets you a room with a balcony. **1400kr**

EATING AND DRINKING

★ **Bröderna Arvidssons Fisk** Hamngatan by Paradisparken ☎0303 600 40. Those in the market for cheap eats are well catered for at this very good smoked-fish stall. Serves fish and chips as well as burgers, sausages and ice cream, plus fresh fish and seafood. Mon–Thurs 10am–9pm, Fri & Sat 10am till late, Sun 10am–5pm.
Lasse-Maja Krog Hamngatan 31 ☎0303 611 22. Named after Marstrand's infamous prisoner (see opposite), this spot is very popular with locals and tourists alike for its wide-ranging meat and fish menu with main courses from 198kr, such as seafood spaghetti and pan-fried catfish. May–Sept daily noon–midnight.
Marstrands Wärdshus Hamngatan 23 ☎0303 603 69. This long-established favourite is very popular for its large,

sunny quayside terrace with basic wooden tables, where you can eat deliciously fresh seafood such as open prawn sandwiches and juicy fish dishes for 150–250kr. Easter to Sept daily noon–1am.
Societetshuset Långgatan 1 ☎0303 606 00. Three restaurants within one classic old house, all serving a good range of meat and fish dishes in an old-fashioned atmosphere, though prices are high. Reckon on 250kr upwards for a main dish. Wed–Sun 5pm till late.
Tenan Rådhusgatan 2 ☎0303 603 22. Inside the *Grand* hotel, this charming option has been serving the house speciality of garlic-fried crayfish gratin (245kr) for decades. Otherwise reckon on around 325kr per dish such as pan-fried cod and sirloin steak. Daily 6.30pm till late.

Fiskebäckskil

FISKEBÄCKSKIL, 50km north of Marstrand, is one of the most attractive villages along the entire length of the Bohuslän coast. Peppered with imposing old wooden houses perched high up on rocky rises, many with fancily carved porches and intricate glazed verandas, it also boasts several attractions that are well worth exploring.

Saltarvet

Saltängen • July & Aug Wed–Sun noon–6pm • 50kr • ☎0523 222 70, ⓦsaltarvet.se

Arriving by road from the south, you'll find the remarkably stylish **art café**, *Saltarvet* just on the right where the road enters the village at Saltängen. Its galleries display constantly changing exhibitions of contemporary Swedish artists.

Carl Wilhelmson's house

Carl Wilhelmsons väg 1 • Open one day a year; contact tourist office for exact details • 60kr

Fiskebäckskil's most famous son is the artist **Carl Wilhelmson** (1866–1928), who was born near the marina. He made his name nationally with his powerful, evocative portraits and landscapes, which beautifully reflect west-coast Swedish life at the end of the nineteenth century. In 1912, he had a strikingly elegant cottage built close to his birthplace, with splendid views over the waters towards Lysekil, its double-height windows letting the famous Nordic light flood in. Reproductions of his work line the walls (the originals are mostly in Gothenburg's Konstmuseum or the Nationalmuseum in Stockholm), the subjects often being the scenery just outside these windows. The most poignant of the prints, *On The Hill*, shows a scene from Wilhelmson's childhood. Aged 9, he had stood unnoticed behind a group of old men sitting on a rock in Fiskebäckskil, while they discussed a hurricane which had wrecked twenty ships the day before, killing his father, a sea captain. When they became aware of the boy's presence, they asked him not to say anything, and he kept the secret from his mother, who only learnt of her husband's death from the post-boat captain a month later.

The church

Fiskebäckskilsvägen • Daily 10am–9pm

Not far from Carl Wilhelmson's house, close to the marina, the **church** dates from 1772 and has an opulent yet almost domestic feel about its interior. There are chandeliers, gold-plated sconces, etched-glass mirrors with hand-carved wood frames and fresh flowers at the ends of each pew. The luxuriance of the decor is thanks to donations from Bohuslän's richest eighteenth-century landowner, Margaretha Huitfeldt, who also paid for the wrought-iron and sheet-metal spire, crowned with a gold-plated weathercock. The wooden, barrel-vaulted ceiling is worth a glance, too: it's covered in eighteenth-century murals, the oddest aspect of which is the scattering of angels' heads. Outside, in the graveyard close to the main door, is Wilhelmson's rather plain grave, his likeness carved into the granite tombstone. More unusual is the grave in the far corner, where an English officer and a German soldier, who died in the Great North Sea Battle of 1916, were buried together.

ARRIVAL AND DEPARTURE FISKEBÄCKSKIL

By bus From Marstrand, take bus #210 to Kungälvsmotet then bus #841 to Bökenäs skola, where you change again for the #845 to Fiskebäckskil – although this sounds rather complicated, it's actually quite straightforward as the buses connect with each other. The journey is generally possible several times a day but since timings change you should always check ⓦ vasttrafik.se before setting out.

By car Due to the fragmented nature of the coast, from Marstrand first head back onto the E6, from where the easiest approach is via Herrestad and Route 161 southwest via Bökenäs.

ACCOMMODATION AND EATING

Brygghuset Fiskebäckskilsvägen 28 ☎0523 222 22. Located on the marina below the church, this is the place for a really exceptional fish supper: the pan-fried redfish with scallops and mango is sensational. Mains cost 265–295kr. Daily noon till late.

Gullmarsstrand Hotel Strandvägen 2 ☎0523 66 77 88. This hotel also boasts an excellent if expensive restaurant (reckon on around 300kr for a main dish); the menu changes frequently but there's an emphasis on fresh fish and seafood such as halibut and scallops. Mon–Fri noon–2pm & 6–8.30pm, Sat 6–8.30pm.

Gullmarsstrand Strandvägen 2 ☎0523 66 77 88, ⓦ gullmarsstrand.se. Located right on the water, next to the Lysekil ferry, this fine, stylish hotel, decked out in minimalist Nordic furnishings, has plenty of light, airy rooms looking out over the sea. 1595kr/1997kr

Lysekil

The largest coastal town in this area is **LYSEKIL**, at the tip of a peninsula with the Gullmarsfjorden twisting to the east and the Skagerrak to the west. While the journey into town by Route 162 does not reveal it as immediately attractive, Lysekil does have plenty to recommend it.

Lysekils kyrka

Övre Kyrkogatan 2 • Daily: June–Aug 11am–7pm; Sept–May 11am–4pm

Walk up any set of steps from the waterfront and you'll reach the **Lysekils kyrka**, the town's most imposing landmark and visible for miles around. It's hewn from the surrounding pink granite, with beaten copper doors and windows painted by early twentieth-century artist Albert Eldh.

Havets Hus

Strandvägen 9 • Daily: Feb to mid-June & late Aug to early Nov 10am–4pm; mid-June to late Aug 10am–6pm • 95kr • ⓦ havetshus.se

From the tourist office, it's a five-minute walk through the village to **Havets Hus**, an amazing museum of marine life featuring no fewer than forty aquaria. The chief attraction, though, is an 8m-long underwater tunnel, containing 140,000 litres of saltwater and home to dozens of enormous fish, including sharks, that swim around you.

The beach and the waterfront

From Havets Hus, continue west along the shore and you'll reach the best **beach** in town, Pinnevik, in about ten minutes. From here, a walking trail heads west across to the rocky headland, Stångehuvud, made of the local pink granite, *Bohusgraniten*, where it's also possible to sunbathe and swim; maps are available at the tourist office. The villas en route to Havets Hus, with their intricately carved eaves, porticoes and windows, are worth a look, too. Lysekil was a popular bathing resort in the nineteenth century, and these ornate houses are a reminder of the time when the rich and neurotic came to take the waters. The bizarre, castellated, rough granite house on the inland side of the main road was built as home for a Herr Laurin, then Lysekil's wealthiest man; it now plays host to the offices of the local newspaper. A better-known local figure of the past is **Carl Curman**, a self-styled health guru. Of the town's ornate, mustard-and-chocolate-brown Hansel-and-Gretel houses on the waterside of the main road, his was the fanciest (a bronze bust of him stands behind it, at the water's edge). In his day in the late nineteenth century, Curman managed to convince his patients that sunbathing on the exposed rock was dangerous, as "the amount of air must be regulated", and persuaded them that it was in the interests of their health to pay to use the bathhouses, which he conveniently owned. Today, the classic old bathhouses are a popular place for segregated **nude bathing** (free).

ARRIVAL AND INFORMATION   LYSEKIL

By bus Express buses #840 and #841 come here from Gothenburg (hourly; 1hr 50min).

By ferry From Fiskebäckskil, an hourly passenger ferry runs all day (15min; 32kr) and sails to Lysekil from the end of Kaptensgatan.

By car From Fiskebäckskil drive towards Bökenäs for 10km, then take Route 161 and the regular all-day free car ferry between Finssbo and Skår (10min) across to the town.

Tourist office Södra Hamngatan 6, the main road along the waterfront (late June to early Aug Mon–Fri 11am–5pm, Sat & Sun 11am–3pm; ☎ 0523 130 50, ⓦ lysekilsturist.se).

ACCOMMODATION

★ **Havshotellet** Turistgatan 13 ☎ 0523 797 50, ⓦ strandflickorna.se. This hotel is set in an archetypal red-and-white house from 1905 with a cosy interior full of period furnishings. Also has two luxury waterfront rooms, built on stilts over the sea, which are perfect for a special occasion. **1239kr/1596kr**

Stadshotellet Kungstorget ☎ 0523 140 30, ⓦ stadshotellet-lysekil.se. An attractive place, facing the town's appealing park, this grand old double-fronted hotel dates from 1880 and is full of period charm. It also enjoys an enviable central location, just a stone's throw from the Gullmarsfjorden. **1190kr**

Strand Vandrarhem Strandvägen 1 ☎ 0523 797 51, ⓦ strandflickorna.se. A rather upmarket hostel pleasingly placed on the waterfront next to Havets Hus, whose rooms all have private facilities, free broadband access and television. Breakfast is not included and you must make up your own bed on arrival. Dorms **300kr,** doubles **850kr**

EATING

Café Kungsgatan Kungsgatan 32 ☎ 0523 160 01. Located up in the town centre, this is the best option for light meals such as quiche, potato salad with accompaniments, various other salads and a good variety of sandwiches. Also serves excellent *kanelbullar*. Mon–Fri 10.30am–6pm, Sat 10.30am–3pm.

Pråmen ☎ 0523 134 52. For a good-value fish supper and a beer, this pontoon restaurant-bar floating in Södra Hamnen, is a pleasant spot, with views back towards Fiskebäckskil and dishes around 189kr; the fish and seafood stew with parmesan and aioli is especially delicious. Daily noon till late.

Rosvik Rosviksgatan 6 ☎ 0523 100 54. Set just back from the waterfront this pleasant restaurant is run by mother and daughters and serves up a good array of frequently changing local produce with an emphasis on freshly caught fish dishes for around 200kr. Mon–Fri 11.30am till late, Sat & Sun noon till late.

Nordens Ark

Åby Säteri 5 • Daily: mid-April to mid-June & mid-Aug to Sept 10am–5pm; mid-June to mid-Aug 10am–7pm; Oct to mid–April 10am–4pm • 190kr • ⓦ nordensark.se

From Lysekil, head back along Route 162 and turn left (west) for **Nordens Ark**, a wildlife sanctuary on the Åby fjord. It's a twenty-minute drive north from Lysekil, and on the way you'll pass a couple of notable churches, in particular the one at **Brastad**, an

1870s Gothic building with an oddly haphazard appearance: every farm in the neighbourhood donated a lump of its own granite towards the construction, but none of the bits matched.

Don't be put off by the yeti-sized puffin plonked at the entrance to the sanctuary. This non-profit-making place is a wildlife sanctuary for endangered animals, where animal welfare takes priority over human voyeurism. Red pandas, lynxes, snow leopards and arctic foxes are among the rare creatures being bred and reared in a mountainous landscape of dense forest and grassy clearings that's kept as close as possible to the animals' natural habitat. The enclosures are so large, and the paths and bridges across the site so discreet, that it's a good idea to bring a pair of binoculars with you.

Smögen

Fifteen kilometres west of Nordens Ark along the coast, the old fishing village and island of **SMÖGEN** is one of the most picturesque and enjoyable destinations in the whole of Bohuslän. Today, the village is an attractive mix of shops and boutiques in old seafront wooden houses, fronted by a quay that runs for several hundred metres that's famous across Sweden and known as the **Smögenbryggan**. Smögen first hit the big time in the late 1960s as tourists began to discover its unassuming charms. Then, during the 1970s, it became the number-one summer destination for Swedish teens and 20-somethings who came here to party all night long in the countless bars that once lined the jetty. Things are quieter now and Smögen, though still busy, is once again regaining its dignity. When it comes to **beaches**, most people take the boat (every 30min; 10min; 80kr return) from the harbour to the tiny, low-lying island of **Hallö** where the smooth, flat rocks that make up the entire island, which is also a nature reserve, are perfect for sunbathing and swimming.

ARRIVAL AND INFORMATION
SMÖGEN

By bus It's a straightforward journey from Lysekil (1hr 15min) involving a change of buses (the #850 from Lysekil, then the #862 from Hallinden to Smögen).

By car From Lysekil, you'll have to return on Route 162, then take Route 171, as there is no crossing over Åbyfjorden. Smögen is linked to the mainland and its neighbour, Kungshamn, by bridge.

Tourist office Back on the mainland in Kungshamn, at Bäckevikstorget 5 opposite the bus station (late June to mid-Aug Mon–Fri 10am–6pm, Sat 10am–5pm, Sun 10am–3pm; mid-Aug to late June Mon–Wed & Fri 9am–5pm, Thurs 9am–1pm; ☎ 0523 66 55 50, ⦿ sotenasturism.se).

ACCOMMODATION

Makrillvikens Makrillgatan ☎ 0523 315 65, ⦿ makrillviken.se. For sensibly priced accommodation, this youth hostel, located in a former wooden bathhouse set amid rocky outcrops of granite, is hard to beat. It has open sea views and a sauna right on the waterfront. Another 100kr or so gets a double room with private facilities. Dorms <u>300kr</u>, doubles <u>700kr</u>

Smögens Havsbad Hotellgatan 26 ☎ 0523 66 84 50, ⦿ smogenshavsbad.se. Set in an attractive fin-de-siècle house bordered by granite boulders, this elegant hotel also boasts a spa, lounge, and a good restaurant and bar with superb sea views. <u>1490kr/2380kr</u>

EATING

Coffeeroom Sillgatan 10. By far the best café in the village just 50m from the foot of Storgatan, serving American-style eats such as breakfast pancakes, bagels, chocolate cupcakes and peanut butter sandwiches though its speciality is a great variety of milkshakes. June–Aug daily 9am–11pm.

Lagergrens Madenvägen 12. Close to *Skärets Krog*, this is a more laidback establishment, good for a drink and simpler mains like Caesar salad, chicken breast or glazed tuna; reckon on around 250kr per main dish. Mid-June to mid-Aug daily 9am till late.

Skärets Krog Madenvägen 1 ☎ 0523 323 17. Located on the water, the most popular restaurant in the village is a loud but thoroughly enjoyable place, particularly on a balmy summer evening, and is renowned for its excellent fish dishes, such as grilled saithe, which cost around 300kr. June–Aug daily 8pm–3am.

CLOCKWISE FROM TOP LEFT MARSTRAND(P.130); SELMA LAGERLÖF'S HOME, MÅRBACKA (P.142); FISKEBÄCKSKIL (P.133)
WROUGHT-IRON CROSS, EKSHÄRAD (P.143) >

Värmland

Inland from the Bohuslän coast, the landscape is dominated by the largest lake in Western Europe, **Vänern**. Sitting proudly on the lake's northern shores, the provincial capital of Värmland, **Karlstad**, makes an agreeable destination after seeing the highlights of the Swedish west coast; both Route 45 and the rail network lead here from Gothenburg. The city provides ready access to an extensive area of sweeping forests, fertile farmland and lazy rivers once used to float timber into Vänern, and now an excellent way of seeing this most peaceful part of western Sweden.

Karlstad

Resting elegantly on the northern shore of Lake Vänern, **KARLSTAD** is named after King Karl IX, who granted the place its town charter in 1584. Since then, the town has been beset by several disasters: devastating **fires** ripped through the centre in 1616 and 1729, but it was in 1865, when fire broke out in a bakery on the corner of Östra Torggatan and Drottninggatan, that Karlstad suffered its worst calamity; virtually the entire town, including the cathedral, burned to the ground – of the 241 buildings that made up the

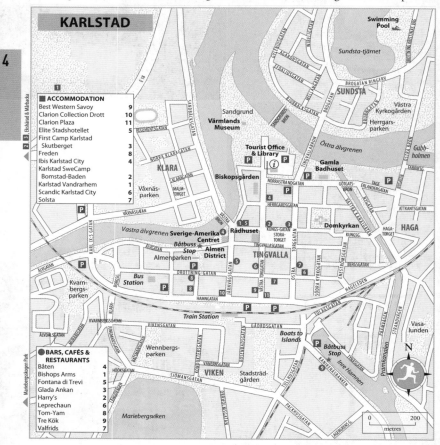

KARLSTAD

ACCOMMODATION
Best Western Savoy	9
Clarion Collection Drott	10
Clarion Plaza	11
Elite Stadshotellet	5
First Camp Karlstad Skutberget	3
Freden	8
Ibis Karlstad City	4
Karlstad SweCamp Bomstad-Baden	2
Karlstad Vandrarhem	1
Scandic Karlstad City	6
Solsta	7

BARS, CAFÉS & RESTAURANTS
Båten	4
Bishops Arms	1
Fontana di Trevi	5
Glada Ankan	3
Harry's	2
Leprechaun	6
Tom-Yam	8
Tre Kök	9
Valfrids	7

> ## LAKE VÄNERN
>
> Covering a whopping 5600 square kilometres (four times the size of Greater London), **Lake Vänern** (ⓦ vanerland.com) totally dominates the map of Sweden, stretching 140km in length from Trollhättan, northeast of Gothenburg, up to Karlstad. Travelling along the lake you could be forgiven for thinking you're on the coast: the endless vistas of water and sky really do resemble those of the sea. Indeed, such is its size that the Swedish Met Office even produces a shipping forecast for the lake.
>
> Vänern was created after the last Ice Age about ten thousand years ago. Very slowly, as the land began to rise following the retreat of the ice, islands formed in the extensive waters that once covered this part of southern Sweden; with further landrise, today's familiar pattern of forest and lake gradually took shape. Consequently, Vänern – and neighbouring Vättern – contain several species of marine life left over from the Ice Age and not normally found in freshwater lakes.

town, only seven survived. Sweden had not experienced such a catastrophe in living memory, and a national emergency fund was immediately set up to help pay for reconstruction. Building began apace, with an emphasis on wide streets and large open squares to act as firebreaks. The result is an elegant and thoroughly likeable town that's the perfect base from which to tour the surrounding country and lakeside.

Rådhuset

It's best to start your wanderings around Karlstad in the large and airy market square, Storatorget. The Neoclassical **Rådhuset**, on the square's western side, was the object of much local admiration upon its completion in 1867, just two years after the great fire; local worthies were particularly pleased with the two stone Värmland eagles that adorn the building's roof, no doubt hoping the birds would help ward off another devastating blaze.

In front of the Rådhuset, the rather austere **Peace Monument**, unveiled in 1955, commemorates the peaceful dissolution of the union between Sweden and Norway in 1905, which was negotiated in the town; when translated, the inscription reads "feuds feed folk hatred, peace promotes people's understanding".

Sverige-Amerika Centret

Sweden-America Centre • Residenstorget 1 (ring the doorbell to gain entry) • Mon–Fri 9am–4pm, Sept–May Tues to 7pm • 40kr • ⓦ swedenamerica.se

Housed on the ground floor of the elegant Residenset (provincial governor's residence), the **Sverige-Amerika Centret** charts Swedish emigration to America in general, and in particular, that of the people of Värmland. During the latter half of the nineteenth century, one third of the province's population left for a fresh start in the New World as a result of grinding poverty and poor prospects at home. In addition to the changing exhibitions, there's a research centre with documentation on all those who made the journey.

Domkyrkan

Östra Kyrkogatan 4 • Mid-June to mid-Aug Mon–Fri 9am–7pm, Sat 10am–4pm, Sun 10am–6pm; mid-Aug to mid-June Mon–Wed & Fri 9am–4pm, Thurs & Sat–Sun 9am–7pm

Across Östra Torggatan from the main square, the **Domkyrkan** was consecrated in 1730, although only its arches and walls survived the flames of 1865. Its most interesting features are the altar, made from Gotland limestone with a cross of Orrefors crystal, and the font, also crystal.

Östra bron

Continuing east along Kungsgatan and over the narrow Pråmkanalen into Hagatorget square, the road swings left and changes its name to Nygatan ahead of the longest arched **stone bridge** in Sweden, **Östra bron**. Completed in 1811, this massive construction is made up of twelve arches and spans 168m across the eastern branch of the Klarälven River. It's claimed the bridge's builder, Anders Jacobsson, threw himself off the bridge and drowned, afraid his life's achievement would collapse; his name is engraved on a memorial stone tablet in the centre of the bridge. On sunny days, the nearby wooded island of **Gubbholmen**, reached by crossing Östra bron and turning right, is a popular place for soaking up the rays and an ideal place for a picnic. Heading back towards town, turn right into Tage Erlandergatan from Östra bron, and carry on until you reach the old bathhouse, **Gamla Badhuset**, on Norra Strandgatan, which functioned as a spa and swimming baths until 1978; the building's exterior is worth a quick glance for its impressive red stonework.

Biskopsgården

At the junction of Norra Strandgatan and Västra Torggatan is the bishop's residence, **Biskopsgården**, dating from 1781 and, as such, one of the handful of buildings in Karlstad not destroyed in the great fire. A two-storey yellow wooden building with a mansard roof, it owes its survival to the massive elm trees on its south side which formed a natural firebreak, and to the sterling fire-fighting efforts of the bishop of the time, which gave rise to the local saying "the bishop swore and doused the flames whilst the governor wept and prayed". The only other houses that survived are in the Almen district of town, next to the river at Älvgatan; though their facades are all nineteenth century, their oldest parts date from the century before.

Värmlands Museum

Sandgrundsudden • Mon–Wed & Fri 10am–6pm, Thurs 10am–8pm, Sat & Sun 11am–5pm • 60kr • ⓦ varmlandsmuseum.se

From Biskopsgården, a two-minute stroll north along Västra Torggatan leads to Sandgrundsudden point and **Värmlands Museum**, a comprehensive account of the province's life and times with engaging displays devoted to the discovery of iron during the 1500s which helped to secure Värmland's economic lifeline for several centuries, particularly in the remote northern and eastern areas of the province. The museum also houses a sizeable collection of local art. Look out especially for Värmland artist **Lars Lerin**: his watercolour of the harbourside in the Faroese capital, Tórshavn, is particularly pleasing.

Mariebergsskogen

Treffenbergsvägen • Daily 7am–10pm • Free • ⓦ mariebergsskogen.se

Originally based on the Skansen open-air museum in Stockholm, **Mariebergsskogen**, 2km southwest of the centre, was established in 1920 when a number of old wooden buildings from across Värmland, including a smoking house, windmill and storehouse, were relocated here. Today, as well as the original open-air museum, the **Lillskogen** section (daily 9am–4pm; free) contains a children's animal park with rabbits, cows, pigs and goats.

Naturum Värmland

Mid-June to mid-Aug daily 11am–5pm; mid-Aug to mid-June Tues–Sun 11am–5pm • Free • Bus #3 or the båtbussen in summer

It's the **Naturum Värmland** nature centre, built right on the water's edge overlooking Mariebergsviken bay, that really makes a trip here worthwhile. The centre was designed to accentuate the closeness to nature: glass exterior walls offering cinemascope views out over the surrounding trees and the lake help create the impression that you really are out in the wilds. Aimed predominantly at children, it provides a fascinating insight

---

KARLSTAD'S BOAT BUSES

Between June and August every summer, a flotilla of gleaming, wooden boat buses – **båtbussar** – ply the waters around Karlstad and make a great way of seeing the city. Though routes vary slightly from year to year, the most popular is the hour-long trip from Residenset, just west of Storatorget, via the Pråmkanalen and the harbour area, to Mariebergsskogen (see above). Tickets cost just 23kr and can be bought on board. Timetables are at ⓦ karlstad.se.

into local flora and fauna as well as the different landscapes found in the province, from marshland to dense forest. For grown-ups, it's the excellent and informative short film (in Swedish only) about the province's wildlife that's the real highlight.

The beaches

Mid-June to mid-Aug bus #56 hourly from Storatorget

The Karlstad region is renowned throughout Sweden for its relatively long hours of sunshine, something the locals make the most of during the summer months. The **sandy beach** by the campsites at Bomstad, 7km west of the city along the E18, extends for several kilometres and is known as the Värmland Riviera. It benefits from the sheltered waters of Kattfjorden, one of Vänern's northern bays, and the shallow waters here heat up quickly during the long summer days, making swimming deliciously enjoyable. Adjoining to the east, **Skutberget** offers smooth **rocks** which gently slope down to the lake. There's also an unofficial – though popular – **nudist beach** here, at the western end of the beach by *First Camp Karlstad Skutberget*.

ARRIVAL AND DEPARTURE
KARLSTAD

By train From Gothenburg, there are two ways to reach Karlstad: regular direct services run up the western shore, covering the journey in around 3hr; alternatively, a limited service (Mon–Fri only) runs around the eastern shore via Laxå, also taking 3hr. The Värmland capital is also served by international trains between Stockholm and Oslo (it's roughly halfway between the two), as well as the more frequent services to and from Stockholm. The train station is on Hamngatan.

Destinations Gothenburg (5 daily via Trollhättan, 2hr 50min; 3 daily Mon–Fri via Laxå, 3hr 10min); Oslo (5 daily; 3hr); Stockholm (9 daily; 2hr 30min); Sunne (9 daily; 50min).

By bus The bus station is located at the western end of Drottninggatan.

Destinations Falun (1 daily; 4hr); Gothenburg (6 daily; 4hr); Oslo (8 daily; 3hr); Stockholm (10 daily; 4hr).

INFORMATION

Tourist office In the library at Västra Torggatan 26 (mid-June to mid-Aug Mon–Fri 9am–7pm, Sat 10am–6pm, Sun 10am–4pm; ☏ 054 540 24 70, ⓦ destinationkarlstad.se). A good place to pick up general information about the city as well as rafting trips on the Klarälven River (see p.143); it

also has timetables for buses throughout Värmland (also available at ⓦ värmlandstrafik.se), to help you plan trips elsewhere in the province.

Internet access There's internet access at the train station with Sidewalk Express and at the tourist office.

ACCOMMODATION

Best Western Savoy Västra Torggatan 1A ☏ 054 15 66 40, ⓦ www.savoy-karlstad.se. Modern chain hotel with comfortable rooms featuring wooden floors and light decor. What the rooms lack in character is more than compensated by the fantastic weekend and summer prices which make this central hotel a sound choice. 895kr/1295kr
Clarion Collection Drott Järnvägsgatan 1 ☏ 054 10 10 10, ⓦ drotthotel.se. Just 50m from the train station, this is a smart, elegant hotel dating from 1909 and full of old-fashioned charm, wooden floors and period furniture. The daily evening buffet is free to residents. 890kr/1190kr
Clarion Plaza Västra Torggatan 2 ☏ 054 10 02 00, ⓦ choicehotels.se. Large, modern, plush four-star hotel very much with the business traveller in mind; there's modern Nordic decor and a fantastic sauna offering panoramic views over the city. Attractive weekend and summer rates are among the best in town. 790kr/1090kr
★ **Elite Stadshotellet** Kungsgatan 22 ☏ 054 29 30 00, ⓦ www.karlstad.elite.se. Built in 1870 and

beautifully located next to the river, this is Karlstad's best hotel. Whilst the interior with its sweeping staircases and chandeliers conjures up sumptuous old-style elegance, the rooms offer modern Swedish design at its very best. 765kr/1232kr
Freden Fredsgatan 1A ☏ 054 21 65 82, ⓦ fredenhotel .com. Cheap and cheerful place close to the bus and train stations, whose rooms all share facilities, though they do have washbasins. Breakfast costs 60kr extra. Hostel-style double rooms with bunks are also available for 520kr. 580kr/680kr
Ibis Karlstad City Västra Torggatan 20 ☏ 054 17 28 30, ⓦ ibishotel.com. Good-value modern hotel in the centre of town with sixty modern, comfortable en-suite rooms, boasting a large breakfast buffet, though at an extra cost of 85kr per person. 475kr/675kr
Karlstad Vandrarhem Kasernhöjden 19 ☏ 054 56 68 40, ✉ karlstad.vandrarhem@swipnet.se; buses #1, 4 and 56. The town's elegant STF youth hostel, with top-quality beds and televisions in all rooms, is set in a grand

former military building located just 1km from the centre. Dorms <u>200kr</u>, doubles <u>560kr</u>

Scandic Karlstad City Drottninggatan 4 ❶ 054 770 55 00, ⓦ scandichotels.com. One of the most stylish hotels in town, its Nordic minimalist decor and warm wooden floors represent Swedish design at its best; superior rooms 608–620 have their own balcony and cost just 200kr extra – well worth it. <u>1020kr/1410kr</u>

Solsta Drottninggatan 13 ❶ 054 15 68 45, ⓦ solstahotell .se. A good, central budget option on the city's main shopping street with cable TV and fridge in all rooms and access to a microwave and kettle for self-catering. <u>805kr/995kr</u>

CAMPING

First Camp Karlstad Skutberget Skutberget ❶ 054 53 51 20, ⓦ firstcamp.se/karlstad; bus #56 runs from Storatorget via the bus station between mid-June and mid-Aug. A 7km drive west out of the town along the E18, located beyond IKEA, beside Lake Vänern. Also has cabins. Open all year. Tents <u>140kr</u>, cabins <u>445kr</u>

Karlstad Swecamp Bomstad-Baden Bomstad-Baden ❶ 054 53 50 68, ⓦ bomstadbaden.se; bus #56 runs from Storatorget mid-June to mid-Aug. Beautifully situated on the shore of Lake Vänern, with a wide range of cabins. Open all year. Tents <u>140kr</u>, cabins <u>440kr</u>

EATING AND NIGHTLIFE

Båten Älvgatan 4 ❶ 054 10 11 63. An upmarket fish restaurant housed on a boat moored close to the main square, serving sophisticated dishes such as cod steak with lobster terrine and zander with chive sauce (around 290kr). Tues–Thurs 5pm–midnight, Fri & Sat 5pm–1am.

Bishops Arms Kungsgatan 22. Classic British-style pub enjoying a great location overlooking the river, with outdoor seating in summer and a wide range of beers. It's also a popular spot for a bite to eat, serving pub meals such as burgers and steaks. Mon–Thurs 4pm–midnight, Fri & Sat 4pm–1am, Sun 4pm–11pm.

Fontana di Trevi Järnvägsgatan 8 ❶ 054 21 05 00. Karlstad's best Italian restaurant, with suspended brass lanterns and a beamed ceiling that create an intimate and romantic atmosphere. Pizzas cost from 87kr, while there are mains such as an excellent breast of chicken stuffed with Parma ham and mozzarella for 185kr. Mon–Thurs 11am–10pm, Fri 11am–11pm, Sat noon–11pm, Sun noon–8pm.

Glada Ankan Kungsgatan 12 ❶ 054 21 05 51. A lively first-floor restaurant with a balcony overlooking the main square, with burgers, pizzas and burritos from 139kr, chicken breast with salad for 189kr and salmon fillet at 179kr. Mon–Thurs 5pm–11pm, Fri 11am–11pm, Sat 3pm–11pm.

Harry's Kungsgatan 16 ❶ 054 10 20 20. There's a wooden Native American figure to welcome guests, half-built brick walls and chandeliers at every turn. It's one of Karlstad's most popular eating spots with cheeseburgers

(159kr), chicken risotto (189kr), smoked salmon (179kr), halibut (229kr) and steak (215kr). Mon & Tues 4–11pm, Wed & Fri 4pm–2am, Thurs 4pm–1am, Sat 2pm–2am.

Leprechaun Östra Torggatan 4. Small and dark, Karlstad's best Irish pub is a firm favourite, particularly for its Irish jam evenings and whiskey-tasting sessions which make use of the pub's impressive array of bottles. Mon & Tues 4–11pm, Wed & Thurs 4pm–midnight, Fri 3pm–1am, Sat 1pm–1am.

★ **Tom-Yam** Drottninggatan 35 ❶ 054 18 51 00. Authentic Thai food is served up here by a friendly Swedish guy and his Thai wife: red salmon curry (192kr), stir-fried chicken with roast cashews in oyster sauce (169kr) or an exceptional beef massamam curry (179kr). Tues & Thurs 4–9pm, Wed 11am–1.30pm & 4–9pm, Fri 11am–1.30pm & 4–10pm, Sat 4–10pm.

★ **Tre Kök** Gustaf Lovéns gata 9 ❶ 054 15 00 20. Located in Karlstad's inner harbour, this stylish brasserie serves some inspirational twists on home-cooking classics. Menus change frequently but at lunchtime there's always a buffet with soup, pasta and a favourite *husmanskost* dish. Mon 11.15am–2pm, Tues–Sat 11.15am–2pm & 6–10pm.

Valfrids Östra Torggatan 8 ❶ 054 18 30 40. A well-respected lounge restaurant that's big on style, with black-and-white leather chairs and floral wallpaper. Here Swedish food meets the best of Asian cuisine: pork skewer with Asian noodles, for example. Mains around 185kr. Daily 5pm–1am.

Around Karlstad: Selma Lagerlöf's house at Mårbacka

40km north of Karlstad • Mid-May to early July & mid- to late Aug daily 10am–4pm; early July to mid-Aug daily 10am–5pm • 90kr • ⓦ marbacka.com

Selma Lagerlöf (1858–1940) was the first female winner of the Nobel Prize for Literature, in 1909, and is arguably Sweden's best-known author of her generation and familiar to every Swede. Her fantastical prose was seen as a revolt against the social realism of late nineteenth-century writing; commissioned to write a geography book for Swedish children, Lagerlöf came up with *The Wonderful Adventures of Nils*, a saga of myth and legend infused with affection for the Swedish countryside, which became compulsory reading at every school in the country. Lagerlöf never married, but had a long-term relationship with another woman, though this wasn't generally acknowledged until their love letters were published some fifty years after Lagerlöf's death. The first woman to gain membership of the Swedish Literary Academy, her be-hatted features now appear on 20kr notes, which Swedes affectionately refer to as "Selmas".

Her house, complete with portico supporting a wonderfully long balcony, was completely rebuilt after Lagerlöf won the Nobel Prize. Upstairs is her **study**, much as she left it, along with a panelled library and an extensive collection of her work.

ARRIVAL AND DEPARTURE MÅRBACKA

By train and taxi From Karlstad take the train to Sunne. Sunne Taxi (☏0565 102 07), at Sunne train station, will take you the 10km to Mårbacka for around 200kr.
By train and bus Alternatively, from Sunne bus station, bus #215 runs to Mårbacka on Tues and Fri but must be pre-booked on ☏0771 32 32 00. Timetables are at ⓦvarmlandstrafik.se
By car From Karlstad take Route 62 north towards Ekshärad and then the signed left turn for Mårbacka just before the village of Ransäter.

Northern Värmland: Ekshärad

To explore northern Värmland, home to bears, wolves and lynx, pretty **EKSHÄRAD** makes a perfect base. Whilst here, check out the ornately decorated eighteenth- and nineteenth-century wrought-iron crosses in the church graveyard beside the main crossroad.

Eskhärad is a good spot for getting out onto the **Klarälven River**, a 500km-long waterway that begins over the border in Norway near Lake Femunden, entering Sweden at Långflon in the north of Värmland at slightly over half of its course. The Klarälven was one of the last Swedish rivers where timber was floated downstream to sawmills; the practice only ceased here in 1991.

ARRIVAL AND DEPARTURE EKSHÄRAD

By bus From Karlstad bus station take bus #600 and tell the driver you're going to the rafts in Gunnerud (Mon–Fri 2 daily, Sun 1 daily; 1hr 50min; ⓦvarmlandstrafik.se). From Gunnerud it's another 15min on the same bus to Ekshärad.
By car From Karlstad take Route 62 north and Gunnerud is located just after the junction with Route 246 to Hagfors.

ACCOMMODATION AND EATING

Byns Camping Ekshärad ☏0563 407 76, ⓦbynscamping.eu. British-run riverside campsite located on the other side of the river from the village centre; take the second right after the bridge. Has cabins as well as tent sites. Open late May to Aug. Tents __140kr__, cabins __275kr__
Wärdshuset Pilgrimen Klarälvsvägen 35 ☏0563 405 90, ⓦwardshusetpilgrimen.com. Accommodation at this pleasant inn is located at the rear of the main building, with dorm beds as well as simple double rooms. The restaurant (daily noon–1pm) in the main building serves a range of meat and fish dishes for around 150kr and has weekday lunch buffet. Dorms __175kr__, doubles __350kr__

RAFTING ON THE KLARÄLVEN RIVER

Between June and August, two companies operate **trips** along the river on sixteen-square-metre **timber rafts**, each of which holds two people; book ahead no matter which company you choose. Their prices are roughly the same, but with Branäs Sverigeflotten you build the raft yourself, supervised by a member of staff, using the 3m-long logs and the rope provided; no other materials are allowed. Once you're under way, you'll find the water flows at around 2km/hr, which gives you time to swim, fish and study the countryside and animals (beavers and elk are plentiful). At night, you sleep in a tent either on the raft (which is moored) or on the riverbank.

Branäs Sverigeflotten Transtrand 22, Branäs ☏0564 402 27, ⓦsverigeflotten.com. Call in advance to find out where to meet; a bus leaves the riverside Byns Camping in Ekshärad (see above) at 9.30am for the start point (either Ransby or Värnäs). 2300kr
Vildmark i Värmland Röbjörkeby 7, Torsby ☏0560 140 40, ⓦvildmark.se. Assemble on day one at Gunnerud beside Route 62 south of Ekshärad. 2260kr

The southwest

GIRL ON SANDHAMMAREN BEACH, SKÅNE

5

The southwest

The southwestern provinces of Halland, Skåne and Blekinge were on the frontiers of Swedish-Danish conflicts for more than three hundred years. In the fourteenth to seventeenth centuries, the flatlands and fishing ports south of Gothenburg were constantly traded between the two countries, and the presence of several fortresses still bears witness to the area's status as a buffer in medieval times.

Halland, a finger of land facing Denmark, has a coastline of smooth, sandy beaches and bare, granite outcrops, punctuated by a number of small, distinctive towns. The most charismatic of these is the old bathing resort of **Varberg**, dominated by its tremendous thirteenth-century fortress; also notable is the small, beautifully intact medieval core of **Falkenberg**, while the regional capital, **Halmstad**, is popular for its extensive beaches and nightlife.

Further south, in the ancient province of **Skåne**, the coastline softens into curving beaches backed by gently undulating fields. This was one of the first parts of the country to be settled, and the scene of some of the bloodiest battles during the medieval conflict with Denmark. Although Skåne was finally ceded to Sweden in the late seventeenth century, Danish influence died hard and is still evident in the thick Skåne accent – often incomprehensible to other Swedes and the butt of many a joke – and in the province's architecture. Today Skåne is known as the breadbasket of Sweden and its landscapes are those of slabs of yellow rape, crimson poppies and lush green fields contrasting with charming white churches and black windmills. In the north of the province, **Båstad** is renowned for glamorous living through its close links to the country's tennis elite. One of Sweden's best areas for **walking** and **cycling**, the **Bjäre peninsula** lies to the west of Båstad and comprises forested hill ranges, spectacular rock formations and dramatic cliffs. To the south of the town, both **Helsingborg**, with its laidback, cosmopolitan atmosphere, and bustling **Malmö**, Sweden's third city, have undergone some dramatic changes in recent years: Helsingborg's harbour has been transformed by an influx of stylish bars, while Malmö has seen the most significant development in recent Swedish history – the completion of the 16km-long **bridge** linking the city to Copenhagen, and thus Sweden to the rest of Europe via the Öresund Strait.

Just north of Malmö, the university town of **Lund**, with its wealth of classic architecture, has a distinctive bohemian atmosphere that contrasts with Malmö's more down-to-earth heritage, whilst east from Malmö, you'll encounter the pretty medieval town of **Ystad** on the south coast, and then the splendid countryside of **Österlen**, whose pastoral scenery is studded with Viking monuments, such as the "Swedish Stonehenge" at **Ales Stenar** and the southwest's most alluring beaches. Beyond here to the east, the ledge of land running to the Baltic is **Blekinge** province. Among its several small and not particularly distinguished resorts, **Karlskrona** stands out, a Baroque beauty built on a number of islands.

THE CRYPT AT LUND'S DOMKYRKAN

Highlights

❶ Varberg Fortress Stay in one of the old prison cells in the splendid youth hostel set within the fortress, which dominates the landscape of the west coast. **See p.148**

❷ Helsingborg Do as the locals do and ride the boat to-and-fro to Denmark as many times as you like and enjoy a delicious lunch or drink onboard at the same time. **See p.161**

❸ Hallands Väderö A boat trip to this unspoilt island off the Bjäre peninsula offers a chance to commune with nature – and spot seals. **See p.161**

❹ Domkyrkan, Lund Beneath the finest Romanesque cathedral in Northern Europe lies the eerie crypt where Finn the Giant is said to have been turned to stone. **See p.166**

❺ Lilla torg, Malmö This beautiful cobbled square in the city centre is a fine place to down a beer or two and rest your feet and mind. **See p.173**

❻ Sandhammaren beach, Skåne Visit the miles of seamless, fine sands beneath the hot skies of Sweden's southern coast. **See p.186**

HIGHLIGHTS ARE MARKED ON THE MAP ON P.148

5

In addition, this is one of the easiest regions of Sweden to **get around**; trains run to all the main towns and services are frequent; we've given details under each town account.

Varberg

More atmospheric than any other town in Halland, the fashionable little nineteenth-century bathing resort of **VARBERG** boasts surprisingly varied sights – its imposing fortress the most striking – a laidback atmosphere and plenty of good places to eat. The rocky coastline becomes sandier heading south, and there are plenty of opportunities for bathing and windsurfing. All of Varberg's sights are concentrated along or near the seafront, although in summer the main square, Stortorget, throngs with **markets** and pavement cafés.

The fortress

Tours: late June to mid-Aug daily 11am–4pm on the hour • 75kr

The thirteenth-century moated **fortress**, set on a rocky promontory, is Varberg's most prominent attraction. It was home to the Swedish king Magnus Eriksson, who signed

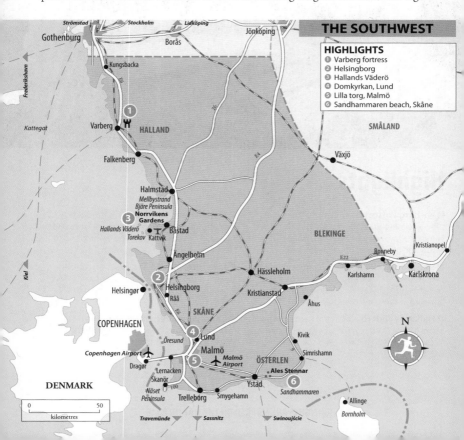

THE SOUTHWEST

HIGHLIGHTS
① Varberg fortress
② Helsingborg
③ Hallands Väderö
④ Domkyrkan, Lund
⑤ Lilla torg, Malmö
⑥ Sandhammaren beach, Skåne

important peace treaties with Denmark here in 1343, aimed at preventing further incursions into Swedish territory. The great bastions were added for protection by the Danish king Christian IV in the seventeenth century; ironically, they were completed just in time for him to see the fortress fall permanently to Sweden in 1645. The entrance is on the fortress's seaward side, either through the great archways towards the central courtyard or by a side route, the uneven stone steps which lead up to a delightful terrace **café**. **Tours** in English will take you into the dungeons and among the impressive cocoa-coloured buildings that make up the inner courtyard, and you can even stay in a private **youth hostel** in the fortress, which has been carefully preserved to retain most of its original features (see p.150).

The museum

Late June to late Aug daily 10am–6pm; late Aug to late June Mon–Fri 10am–4pm, Sat & Sun noon–4pm • 70kr • ⓦ lansmuseet.varberg.se

It's the fortress's **museum** that deserves most of your attention. The most unnerving exhibit is **the Bocksten Man**, a murder victim who was garrotted, drowned, impaled (three stakes were thrust through his body, in the belief this would stop his spirit seeking out his murderers) and thrown into a local bog around 1350, where he remained until 1936 when a farmer dug him up while planting crops. His entire garb preserved by the acidity of the bog, the Bocksten Man sports the Western world's most complete medieval costume, including a cloak, a hood, shoes and stockings. In addition to the skeleton, an unnerving Madame Tussaud-like figure with thick, ringleted blond hair now forms the centrepiece of the exhibition and provides a truly arresting idea of what the Bocksten Man really looked like. An engaging film with English subtitles runs through the carbon-14 dating procedure used to establish the man's age.

Elsewhere in the museum check out the sensitive work of Richard Bergh, Nils Kreuger and Karl Nordström, the so-called **Varberg School**. These three artists linked up in the last years of the nineteenth century and developed a plein-air style that reflected the moods and atmosphere of Halland and Varberg in particular. Night scenes of the fortress beneath the stars show the strong influence of Van Gogh; in other paintings, the misty colours create a melancholy atmosphere. Check out, too, the collection of ungainly swimming trunks and bikinis sported by bathers in Varberg down the years. Refreshingly Scandinavian, it was still common to bathe naked until the late 1910s, a practice depicted by the **Näcken** (see p.302), a nude male water sprite who features prominently in Swedish folklore.

The prison

Overlooking the sea, and painted custard and cream, the 1850 **fortress prison** seems like a soft option next to the looming fortress in whose shadow it lies. The first Swedish prison built after the American practice of having cells for individual inmates was begun, it housed lifers until 1931, when the last one ended his days here.

Kallbadhuset

Cold Bathhouse • Otto Torells gata 7 • Wed 1–8pm, Sat & Sun 9am–5pm • 65kr • ⓦ kallbadhuset.se

A couple of fine remnants from Varberg's time as a spa resort lie within a minute of the fortress. On the side of the fortress facing the town is the grand **Societetshuset**, a wedding-dress-like confection of cream-and-green carved wood, set in its own small park. This was where upper-class ladies took their repose after bathing in the splendid 1903-built **Kallbadhuset** nearby, just to the north of the fortress and overlooking the harbour. Beautifully renovated to its original splendour, this dainty bathhouse has single-sex nude bathing areas and is topped at each corner by Moorish cupolas.

5

ARRIVAL AND DEPARTURE VARBERG

By train Regular trains run up and down the coast between Gothenburg and Copenhagen, all calling at Varberg. From the train station, turn right down Vallgatan, and you'll find the town centre off to the left and the fortress to the right.

Destinations Copenhagen (hourly; 3hr); Gothenburg (hourly; 35min); Malmö (hourly; 2hr 30min).

By ferry Varberg is a handy entry point to southern Sweden: a twice-daily Stena Line ferry sails between here and Grenå in Denmark (4hr).

INFORMATION

Tourist office Västra Vallgatan 39 (April to mid-June & mid-Aug to Sept Mon–Fri 10am–6pm, Sat 10am–2pm; mid-June to mid-Aug Mon–Sat 9.30am–7pm, Sun 1–6pm; Oct–March Mon–Fri 10am–5pm; ☎ 0340 868 00, ⓦ varberg.se). This office, Just off the main square, has free town maps and internet access.

ACCOMMODATION

There's a wide variety of really good places to stay in Varberg – some of them representing excellent value. The west coast can be busy in summer so it pays to book well in advance, no matter where you choose to stay.

★ **Best Western Varberg Stadshotell** Kungsgatan 24–26 ☎ 0340 69 01 00, ⓦ www.varbergsstadshotell .com. Top-quality luxury rooms at this central hotel in the main square. However, it's the beautifully appointed Asian-style spa on the top floor with saunas and vitality pool for water massage that makes a stay here worthwhile. **1395kr/1595kr**

Clarion Collection Fregatten Hamnplan ☎ 0340 67 70 00, ⓦ cchotelfregatten.se. Varberg's twin-turreted former cold-storage warehouse has been converted into a swanky hotel overlooking the harbour with well-appointed, modern rooms. An evening buffet is included in the room rate. **1070kr/1470kr**

Gästis Borgmästaregatan 1 ☎ 0340 180 50, ⓦ hotell gastis.nu. Varberg's oldest hotel, dating from 1786, whose rooms are individually decorated and mix old and new styles. There's a well-appointed spa in the basement with a steam bath and cold plunge pool, too. **1495kr/1625kr**

Okéns Bed & Breakfast Västra Vallgatan 25 ☎ 0340 808 15, ⓦ okens.se. A good-value, family-run establishment with sixteen individually decorated, homely rooms, some with four-poster beds. After leaving Florida, the owners wanted to create a hotel with old-world charm – they have succeeded. **975kr/1025kr**

Varbergs Fästning Off Strandgatan ☎ 0340 868 28, ⓦ fastningensvandrarhem.se. Sleep in the original cells of the former fortress prison, complete with spy-hole in the door though only nos. 7, 13 & 19 have windows. Regular doubles are also available next door. Dorms **260kr**, doubles **520kr**

CAMPING

Apelviken Sanatorievägen 4 ☎ 0340 64 13 00, ⓦ apelviken.se. Varberg's main campsite enjoys a perfect location looking out over the sea and is an easy 2km walk south of the fortress along Strandpromenaden. It also has cabins for rent. Tents **140kr**, cabins **400kr**

EATING AND DRINKING

There are plenty of good places to eat in Varberg, mostly along Kungsgatan, which runs north of the main square. It's a good idea to book a table since Varberg is a popular holiday spot in summer.

Bodegan Societetsparken ☎ 0340 67 65 00. Located in the Societetshuset behind the fortress, this swinging place has live music and a bar menu of burgers (155kr), barbecued meats (from 185kr) and fajitas (235kr). Mid-June to mid-Aug daily 5pm till late.

Café Mignon Drottninggatan 23. This delightful café is located in Varberg's former pharmacy and boasts an ornately decorated glass ceiling. A good choice of sandwiches and cakes, including home-baked scones. Also serves a daily breakfast from 65kr. Mon–Thurs

---

VARBERG'S NUDIST BEACHES

In keeping with Varberg's long tradition as a bathing resort, the town has three **separate-sex nudist beaches**, barely a ten-minute walk from the town centre. Take the signed Strandpromenaden footpath along the shore to reach the first of them: **Skarpe Nord** for women only; next comes another women-only beach, the coarsely named **Kärringhålan**, or "Old Crone's Gap"; then, five minutes beyond here, **Goda Hopp** ("High Hopes") is the men's nudist beach. All beaches consist of smooth rocks rather than sand, and steps lead into the sea for easy swimming.

5

7.30am–7pm, Fri 7.30am–6pm, Sat 7am–5pm, Sun 9.30am–6pm.

★ **Grappa** Brunnsparken ☎0340 179 20. This intimate, candle-lit restaurant is the place to come for Mediterranean food in Varberg: the pork fillet with roast Italian sausage and lentils (259kr) and steak with bacon ragout and roast peppers (345kr) are both excellent. Mon–Fri 4pm till late, Sat noon till late.

Harry's Kungsgatan 18. The most popular place to drink in town with a large open-air terrace. Live music in summer and regular happy hours. There's also a choice of burgers and other light meals. Mon & Tues 4–11pm, Wed & Thurs 4pm–midnight, Fri & Sat 4pm–2am.

Restaurang Stadt Kungsgatan 24-26 ☎0340 69 01 00. Top-notch restaurant inside the *Stadshotell* with chandeliers and marble pillars: the food is equally impressive with a choice of modern Swedish classics such as Arctic char, saddle of veal and stuffed chicken breast. Mains 225–359kr. Mon–Fri 11.30am–1.30pm & 7–10pm, Sat 7–10pm.

Zorba Västra Vallgatan 37 ☎0340 52 02 99. Close to the tourist office on Varberg's main road, this Greek restaurant is worth seeking out for its delicious Hellenic specialities for around 170kr, though the interior furniture is uninspiringly flat-pack. Wed–Fri 5pm till late, Sat & Sun noon till late.

Falkenberg

It's a fifteen-minute train ride south from Varberg to the decidedly likeable medieval town of **FALKENBERG** (falcons were once used for hunting here, hence the name), with some lively museums and a gloriously long beach. It's a well-preserved little town that really comes alive in July and August, when most of the tourists arrive.

Falkenberg has a long-standing reputation as a centre for **fly-fishing** on the Ätran River. A succession of wealthy **English gentlemen** came here throughout the nineteenth century; one such devotee, London lawyer William Wilkinson, went so far as to write a book about the experience, *Days In Falkenberg* (1894). In it, he described the place where the well-to-do visitors stayed as "an ancient inn with a beautiful garden leading down to the river". This building, one of the few here to have escaped the dozen or so town fires which devastated the town over the centuries (most recently in the 1840s), now houses *Falkmanska Caféet*, the best café in town (see p.153).

These upper-class Englishmen brought considerable wealth with them, and had a tremendous influence on the town. Predictably enough, they made no attempt to adapt to local culture: Falkenbergers had to learn English, and throughout the latter half of the nineteenth century, baby boys here were named Charles instead of the Swedish Karl, while the most popular girl's name was Frances, after Wilkinson's daughter. English influence can be seen even today: near the post office there is a British telephone box donated by Oswaldtwistle in Lancashire.

St Laurentii kyrka

Storgatan 50 • Mon–Fri 10am–6pm

The **old town**, to the west of the curving river, comprises a dense network of low, wooden cottages and cobbled lanes. Nestling among them is the fine twelfth-century **St Laurentii kyrka**, its ceiling and interior walls awash with seventeenth- and eighteenth-century paintings. It's hard to believe that this gem of a church was – in the early twentieth century – variously a shooting range, a cinema and a gymnasium; indeed its secular usage saved it from demolition after the Neo-Gothic "new" church was built at

5

the end of the nineteenth century. When St Laurentii kyrka was reconsecrated in the 1920s, its sixteenth-century font and silverware were traced to, and recovered from, places all over northern Europe.

Sculptures

Falkenberg is full of quirky **sculptures** that make for amusing viewing. Right outside Falkenberg Museum you'll find a diverting piece called *Wall*, which you may not realize is a sculpture at all. Per Kirkeby, a celebrated Danish artist, built the two brick walls here for a major exhibition in 1997, to close off the wide space below the museum building down to the river. A series of entrances and window openings are designed to let shadows fall at striking angles – though predictably, the more conservative locals loathe the piece. The most fun sculpture is one taking up the whole wall at the corner of Nygatan and Torggatan in the centre: *Drömbanken*, by Walter Bengtsson, is a witty, surrealist explosion of naked women, cats, mutant elks, bare feet and beds.

Fotomuseum Olympia

Sandgatan 13A · Tues–Thurs 2–6pm, Sun 2–5pm · 40kr

Falkenberg boasts the rather unusual **Fotomuseum Olympia**, home of the town's first purpose-built cinema which opened in 1912. It has over one thousand cameras and a remarkable collection of cinematic paraphernalia, including some superb local peasant portraits taken in 1898. The oldest pictures on show are English and date back to the 1840s. There's also an impressive section on Sweden's well-loved author Selma Lagerlöf at her home in Mårbacka in Värmland (see p.142).

Carlsberg Sverige brewery

Årstadvägen 164 · 2hr tours July only Mon–Thurs 11am & 2pm · 195kr · Tours must be booked in advance by phone · ☎ 0346 72 12 53, ⓦ smakkallan.se

For a completely different experience to the other attractions in Falkenberg, head to the Carlsberg Sverige **brewery** where Sweden's popular beer, Falcon, has been brewed since 1896, and is available for sampling at the end of the tour.

ARRIVAL AND INFORMATION   FALKENBERG

By train Trains arrive at Falkenberg's new station, an inconvenient 10min bus ride from the centre; shuttle buses run regularly into town dropping at Storatorget and the bus station.

Destinations Copenhagen (hourly; 2hr 45); Gothenburg (hourly; 50min); Malmö (hourly; 2hr 15min).

Tourist office Holgersgatan 11 (June–Aug Mon–Sat 9.30am–6pm, Sun 1–6pm; Sept to mid-June Mon–Wed & Fri 10am–5pm, Thurs 10am–6pm; ☎ 0346 88 61 00, ⓦ visitfalkenberg.se). Has free internet access.

ACCOMMODATION

Like neighbouring Varberg, Falkenberg is a popular destination for holidaying Swedes so it pays to book early if you're intending to come here during the Swedish holiday season of mid-June to mid-August. At other times, there's no need to book ahead.

Falkberget Motellvägen 3 ☎ 0346 71 18 80, ⓦ falkberget.se. This is the place to come if you're looking for self-catering apartments. There are 64 of them here in various shapes and sizes, located in a great spot close to the river. **995kr**

Falkenberg Strandbad Havsbadsallén 2A ☎ 0346 71 49 00, ⓦ strandbaden.se. A newly renovated top-of-the-range luxury hotel decorated in colonial style with model

rhinos and elephants at every turn. If you want total indulgence right on the beach at reasonable prices, look no further. **1100kr**

Grand Hotellgatan 1 ☎ 0346 144 50, ⓦ grandhotelfalkenberg.se. This elegant, waterside hotel overlooks the historic Tullbron bridge and enjoys the best location in Falkenberg. The smaller standard rooms cost several hundred *kronor* less and are certainly

> **SWIMMING IN FALKENBERG**
>
> Just fifteen minutes' walk south from town, **Skrea Strand** is a fine, 2km stretch of sandy beach, perfect for swimming. At the northern end, a relaxing diversion is the large bathing and tennis complex of **Klitterbadet**, which has an indoor 50m saltwater pool plus a shallow children's pool, a vast sauna, jacuzzi and steam rooms. At the southern end of the long beach, all the way down past the busy wooden holiday cabins, lie some secluded coves; in early summer the marshy grassland here is full of wild violets and clover.

worth considering since the standard is still high. 1050kr/1350kr

Hwitan Storgatan 24 ☏0346 820 90, ⓦhwitan.se. Overlooking a picturesque open courtyard surrounded by low-built houses dating from 1703, the rooms here are cosy and intimate with period furnishings. The ageing bathrooms, though, are in need of renovation. 1095kr

Skrea Camping Sommarvägen ☏0346 171 07, ⓦskreacamping.se. A comfortable youth hostel and campsite together on the beachfront. Get here by following Strandvägen to the beach. No dorm beds. Open all year. Doubles 500kr, cabins 500kr

EATING AND DRINKING

The birthplace of Sia Glass – a popular **ice cream** made by Sweden's oldest family firm, established in 1569 – and **Falcon beer**, Falkenberg caters well to the tastebuds. Although the variety of food on offer isn't huge, the town's restaurants and bars are of a standard to make eating and drinking here a pleasant experience.

★ **Falkmanska Caféet** Storgatan 42. This welcoming café is the best in town. Housed in one of Falkenberg's oldest buildings, dating from the 1690s, it features mellow furnishings and a lovely garden. There's a wide range of sandwiches and decadent home-made cakes. Mon–Fri 8am–6pm, Sat 10am–3pm.

★ **Gustaf Bratt** Brogatan 1 ☏0346 103 31. Housed in a former grain warehouse from 1860, this popular restaurant has a good range of tasty fish and meat dishes: the fish gratin with flounder and prawns is excellent (225kr). There are pizzas, too, for 89kr. Mon–Sat 6pm till late, Sun 1–9pm.

Harry's Rådhustorget 3A. Enjoying a prime location in the main square, this was Sweden's first ever *Harry's*, the American-style bar now found across the country. It's always packed with drinkers and in summer there's outside seating, too. Mon–Thurs 5pm till late, Fri 5pm–3am, Sat noon–3am, Sun 1–9pm.

★ **Källaren Laxen** Storgatan 34 ☏0346 108 74. Modern Swedish cuisine with a hint of the Mediterranean: the chicken roulade, wrapped in bacon with thyme gravy (279kr) and the pan-fried hake with smoked crayfish (298kr) are good bets. Tues & Wed 6pm till late, Thurs & Fri 11.30am–2pm & 6pm till late, Sat noon–3pm & 6pm till late.

Laxbutiken Heberg ☏0346 511 10. Located 9km south of Falkenberg, signed at exit 49 off the E6. Fans of salmon really should make the effort to come to this salmon restaurant near the village of Heberg. It serves up an array of superb dishes (115–210kr), with salmon the main ingredient. Lunchtime herring buffet, too. Daily 10am–7pm.

Royal Thai Storgatan 25 ☏0346 805 99. A friendly place with a wide variety of good-value Southeast Asian mains: beef or chicken dishes cost 95kr; add another 10kr for prawns. The lunch buffet is good value 75kr and features several classic dishes. Mon–Fri 11.30am–2.30pm & 6pm till late.

Halmstad

The principal town in Halland, **HALMSTAD** was once a grand walled city and an important Danish stronghold. Today, although most of the original buildings have disappeared, the town makes a pleasant enough stop on the long haul south from Gothenburg, thanks to the extensive – if rather crowded – **beaches** not far away, and a range of really good places to eat.

Brief history

In 1619, the town's **castle** was used by the Danish king Christian IV to entertain his Swedish counterpart, Gustav II Adolf; records show that there were seven solid days of festivities. The bonhomie, however, didn't last much longer, and Christian was soon building great stone-and-earth fortifications around the city, all surrounded by a moat,

5

with access afforded by four stone gateways. However, it was a fire soon after, rather than the Swedes, that all but destroyed the city; the only buildings to survive were the castle and the church. Undeterred, Christian took the opportunity to create a contemporary Renaissance town with a grid of straight streets; today the main street, Storgatan, still contains a number of impressive merchants' houses from that time. After the final defeat of the Danes in 1645, Halmstad lost its military significance, and the walls were torn down. Today, just one of the great gateways, Norre Port, remains; the moat has been filled in and a road, Karl XIs vägen, runs directly above where the water would have been.

Stora torg

At the centre of the large, lively market square, **Stora torg**, is Carl Milles's *Europa and the Bull*, a fountain with mermen twisted around it, all with Milles's characteristically muscular bodies, ugly faces and oversized nipples.

St Nikolai kyrka

Kyrkogatan 4 • Daily June–Aug 8.30am–6pm; Sept–May Mon–Fri 8.30am–3pm, Sat & Sun 8.30am–6pm

Flanking one side of Stora torg is the grand **St Nikolai kyrka**. Dating from the fourteenth century, its monumental size bears witness to Halmstad's former

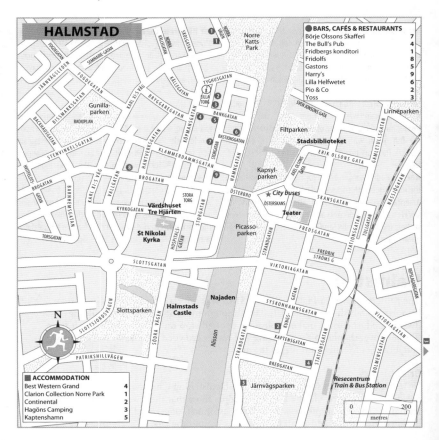

HALMSTAD

Norre
Katts
Park

Gunilla-
parken

RADIOPLAN

Filtparken

Stadsbiblioteket

Linnéparken

Kapsyl-
parken

STORA
TORG

City buses

**Värdshuset
Tre Hjärten**

**St Nikolai
Kyrka**

Picasso-
parken

Teater

Slottsparken

**Halmstads
Castle**

Najaden

Järnvägsparken

Nissan

**Resecentrum
Train & Bus Station**

0 — 200 metres

● BARS, CAFÉS & RESTAURANTS
Börje Olssons Skafferi	7
The Bull's Pub	4
Fridbergs konditori	1
Fridolfs	8
Gastons	5
Harry's	9
Lilla Helfwetet	6
Pio & Co	2
Yoss	3

■ ACCOMMODATION
Best Western Grand	4
Clarion Collection Norre Park	1
Continental	2
Hagöns Camping	3
Kaptenshamn	5

5

importance, although the only signs of the town's medieval origins that remain are the splodges of bare rock beneath the plain, brick columns.

Värdshuset Tre Hjärtan

Adjacent to the church at Kyrkogatan 7, the **Värdshuset Tre Hjärtan** (Three Hearts) restaurant is a vast, proud building with a crossbeamed ceiling; its name derives from the three hearts that make up the town's emblem, Christian IV having granted the town the right to use it in gratitude for their loyalty to Denmark. It's worth taking your coffee and cake upstairs, where the beams and ceiling are beautifully hand-painted, and photographs of nineteenth-century Halmstad adorn the walls.

Halmstad Castle and Najaden

Aschebergsvägen 1 • Early June to Aug Tues & Thurs 6–8pm, Sat 11am–3pm • Free

Not far from Österbron bridge in the town centre, **Halmstad Castle** is a striking, coral-red affair half-hidden by trees, which contains the tourist office (see p.156). Moored in front is **Najaden**, a fully rigged sailing ship built in 1897 and once used for training by the Swedish navy.

Storgatan and around

Leading north from the square, pedestrianized **Storgatan** – the main thoroughfare for restaurants and nightlife (see p.156) – is a charming street, with some creaking old houses built in the years following the 1619 fire; the great stone arch of **Norre Port** marks the street's end.

Norre Katt park

Norre Katts Gränd • Café: June–Aug daily 11am–8pm

To the right of the Norre Port arch is the splendid **Norre Katt park**, a delightful, shady place that slopes down towards the river and is dotted with mature beech, copper beech and horse-chestnut trees, with great weeping willows by the water. The town's most serene spot is at the park's centre, where there's a lily pond crossed by a bridge. A popular **café**, *Rotundan*, housed in an ornate former bandstand, overlooks the spot.

Halmstads Konstmuseum

Tollsgatan • Tues–Sun noon–4pm, Wed till 8pm • Free • Ⓦ hallmus.se

At the northernmost edge of Norre Katt park, by the river, is **Halmstads Konstmuseum**, the town's modern art museum. Inside you'll find a changing exhibition of the museum's collection of regional art by local painters such as Roj Friberg and Lotta Antonsson, plus a small section devoted to the work of the Halmstad Group (see p.157).

Hallandsgården

Galgberget • Mid-June to mid-Aug noon–6pm • Guided tours 2pm daily • Free

Beyond the Konstmuseum, up on Galgberget (Gallows Hill), is a collection of a dozen or so typically Halland buildings which were moved to the site in 1925 to form a miniature outdoor museum, **Hallandsgården**, including a windmill from Morup and a schoolhouse from Eldsberga. There are sweeping views of the Halmstad coastline and Laholmbukten bay from the top of the tower, located beside the steps up to Hallandsgården.

Martin Luthers kyrka

Östra Lyckan 5 • June–Aug daily 9am–1pm; Sept–May Mon–Fri 9am–3pm

A kilometre east of the centre on Långgatan, one of the main roads out of town, stands the gleaming 1970s **Martin Luthers kyrka** The first church in Scandinavia to be

5

assembled entirely of steel, this unique creation looks from the outside like a clumsily opened sardine can, with jagged and curled edges, and stained glass. Inside it's just as unusual: all the walls are a rust-orange version of the outer skin, and there are some striking ornaments. The building is famed for its acoustics, and holds occasional concerts (details from the tourist office).

ARRIVAL AND DEPARTURE   HALMSTAD

By train It takes under 20min to get here from Falkenberg by train, and you arrive at the new Resecentrum travel centre. To get into town from here, follow Bredgatan west to the Nissan River, then walk north along Strandgatan to the bridge across to the centre of town; it takes about 15–20min.

Destinations Copenhagen (hourly; 2hr 30min); Falkenberg (hourly; 17min); Gothenburg (hourly; 1hr 10min); Malmö (hourly; 2hr).
By bus All long-distance buses use the new Resecentrum travel centre. Town buses depart from Österskans beside the theatre.

INFORMATION

Tourist office Lilla torg at the northern end of Storgatan (May, June & mid- to late Aug Mon–Fri 9am–6pm, Sat 10am–3pm; late June to mid-Aug Mon–Fri 9am–7pm, Sat 10am–6pm, Sun 11am–6pm; Sept–April Mon–Fri 10am–5pm; ☎035 12 02 00, ⓦ destinationhalmstad.se). Has free internet access.

ACCOMMODATION

There's a good selection of good-quality accommodation available in Halmstad. However, it's worth remembering that the town centre is a fifteen- to twenty-minute walk from the travel centre, which may influence your choice.

Best Western Grand Stationsgatan 44 ☎035 280 81 00, ⓦ grandhotel.nu. Cosy, traditional and ideally located for the travel centre, this hotel dates from 1905 and is full of old-world charm. Rooms are spacious, with parquet floors and a mix of period and contemporary furnishings. <u>1095kr/1495kr</u>
Clarion Collection Norre Park Norra vägen 7 ☎035 21 85 55, ⓦ norrepark.se. Overlooking the beautiful Norre Katt park, this hotel is reached through the Norre Port arch. Rooms are elegantly decorated in turn-of-the-century style: all have high ceilings, potted plants in the window and most have wooden floors. <u>990kr/1390kr</u>
Continental Kungsgatan 5 ☎035 17 63 00, ⓦ continental-halmstad.se. Just a 2min walk from the travel centre, this elegant building was built in 1904 in the

early *Jugendstil* and National Romantic styles and has a bright, well-preserved interior and classy rooms to match. <u>1090kr/1490kr</u>
Hagöns Camping Östra Stranden ☎035 12 53 63, ⓦ hagonscamping.se. Located 3km to the east of the town centre, this pleasant campsite sits beside a sandy beach and a nature reserve and has four-berth cabins. Open late April to Aug. Tents <u>140kr</u>, cabins <u>1000kr</u>
Kaptenshamn Stuvaregatan 8 ☎035 12 04 00, ⓦ halmstadvandrarhem.se. Centrally located, this new hostel is one of the very few budget options in Halmstad. Rooms are plainly decorated and share facilities; there's also a kitchen on site for self-catering. Breakfast is an extra 70kr. Dorms <u>250kr</u>, doubles <u>500kr</u>

EATING AND DRINKING

People congregate in the trendy restaurants, bars and clubs along cobbled, pedestrianized **Storgatan**, many of which have shaded outdoor areas along the street. **Lilla torg**, just behind, also swarms with people on summer evenings.

Börje Olssons Skafferi Storgatan 23 ☎035 21 16 70. A large, airy Italian café and deli with a great quiche buffet (89kr) at lunchtimes as well as a tasty range of takeaway ciabatta sandwiches (50kr) and a good choice of speciality coffees. Mon–Fri 10am–6pm, Sat 10am–3pm.
★ **The Bull's Pub** Bankgatan 5 ☎035 14 09 21. Very popular, modern English-style bar, rather than pub, with live music and after-work specials that bring people from across town. Also serves light meals and has outdoor seating in summer. Mon–Thurs 5pm till late, Fri 11.30am–2am, Sat 12.30pm–2am, Sun 3pm till late.
Fribergs Konditori Norra vägen 9 ☎035 12 51 11.

Traditional coffee house overlooking the park with black-and-white pictures of Halmstad adorning the interior. A nice relaxed atmosphere and a good place for a coffee and slice of cake. Mon–Fri 9am–6pm, Sat & Sun 9am–4pm.
Fridolfs Brogatan 26 ☎035 21 16 66. There's a maritime feel to the interior of this cosy neighbourhood restaurant, serving a classic mix of French and Swedish: marinated lamb with garlic and herbs and veal fillet with roast peppers for example. Mains are 199–279kr. Mon–Sat 6pm till late, Sun 5pm till late.
Gastons Storgatan 31 ☎035 10 84 80. The food at this stylish bistro with Art Deco ceilings and lighting is modern

Swedish at its best: the grilled red snapper, red curry salmon and seafood pasta are all excellent. Mains cost around 155–235kr. Mon–Fri 5.30pm till late, Sat noon–3pm & 5.30–10pm.

Harry's Storgatan 22 ☎ 035 10 55 95. Massively popular pub attesting to the delight taken by some Swedes in all things American. It also does reasonably priced steaks (169kr) and burgers (149kr), as well as a couple of fish dishes (169kr). Mon 5–11pm, Tues–Thurs 5pm–1am, Fri 4pm–2am, Sat noon–2am, Sun 4–11pm.

Lilla Helfwetet Hamngatan 37 ☎ 035 21 04 20. A stylish Italian place with gloriously high ceilings located in a former turbine engine room by the river serving the likes of grilled halibut with risotto, rack of lamb with goat's cheese compote and pizzas. Mains are 185–295kr. Mon & Sat

6pm till late, Tues–Thurs 11am–4pm & 6pm till late, Fri 11am–2pm & 5pm till late.

★ **Pio & Co** Storgatan 37 ☎ 035 21 06 69. A lovely, intimate place with brick walls, where the speciality (*fiskplanka*) is fish served on wooden planks with clouds of mashed potato (239kr). The menu consists of modern Swedish dishes (188–235kr). Mon–Sat 6pm till late, Sun 5pm till late.

Yoss Storgatan 35 ☎ 035 18 76 49. This chi-chi French-Italian bistro has some of the best prices in town: mains go for 129–189kr and include oven-baked chicken in a blue cheese sauce, lamb fillet on a bed of mushrooms and swordfish provencale. Mon–Thurs 11am–2.30pm & 5.30–10pm, Fri 11am–2pm & 5.30–10.30pm, Sat noon–10.30pm.

Around Halmstad

Halmstad is perfectly placed for a quick jaunt to some of southern Sweden's most glorious **beaches** – sweeping strands of golden sand which are surprisingly busy during the short summer months – in addition to the **Mjellby Konstmuseum**, which offers art lovers a chance to appreciate the work of the well-known (in Sweden, at least) Halmstad Group.

The Mjellby Konstmuseum

Mjällby · July & Aug Tues–Sun 11am–5pm; Sept–June Tues–Sun noon–5pm · 60kr · ⓦ mjellbykonstmuseum.se · Take bus #330 and alight at the bus stop called "Mjällby"

Five kilometres north of Halmstad is the **Mjellby Konstmuseum**, containing works by the **Halmstad Group**, a body of six local artists from the 1920s who championed Cubism and Surrealism in Sweden. The group, comprising brothers Eric and Axel Olson, their cousin Waldemar Lorentzon and three others, worked together in an artistic alliance for fifty years. The group's members had studied in Berlin and Paris and were strongly influenced by Magritte and Dalí, producing work that caused considerable controversy from the 1920s to the 1940s and sometimes working collectively on projects – an almost unheard-of practice in Swedish art. A changing exhibition of their work is on display in the museum.

Halmstad's beaches

Bus #10 runs to Tylösand hourly from Österskans in the town centre

Eight kilometres west of the town centre, Halmstad's most popular **beach** is at **Tylösand**, which in July and August becomes packed with bronzing bodies, as do the surrounding bars and restaurants in the evenings. There's a smuggler's cove to wander around at **Tjuvahålan**, signposted directly off the beach, and plenty of excellent spots for bathing, including **Svärjarehålan** around the headland to the east, where a bathing beach has been adapted for the disabled. To reach less crowded areas, walk 45 minutes north from Tjuvahålan to **Frösakull** and **Ringenäs**, the latter of which is popular for windsurfing.

Östra Stranden and Hagön

Bus #63 runs to both beaches hourly from Österskan in town; get off at the stop called "Hästskon" at the corner of Sommarvägen and Ryttarevägen and walk west through the forest

The best beach to the east of town is at **Östra Stranden**, where there is also a large, well-equipped campsite. The long beach – sandy and less crowded than at Tylösand – is excellent for children as the waters are particularly shallow. A little further south is

5

Hagön, a secluded **nudist beach** where privacy is afforded by the deep hollows between the dunes, behind which is a nature reserve.

Båstad

Thirty-five kilometres south of Halmstad, a journey of around twenty minutes by train, lies **BÅSTAD** (pronounced bow-sta). The northernmost town in the ancient province of **Skåne**, its character is markedly different from other towns along the coast. Cradled by the **Bjäre peninsula** (see p.160), which bulges westwards into the Kattegat (the waters between Sweden and Danish Jutland), Båstad is Sweden's **tennis centre**, where the Swedish Open is played at the beginning of July – the centre court down by the harbour has been newly rebuilt and is truly impressive. The town also boasts an extremely beautiful setting, with forested hills on the horizon to the south.

There is a downside, though, which can blunt enthusiasm for the place. Ever since King Gustav V chose to take part in the 1930 national tennis championship and Ludvig Nobel (nephew to Alfred of the Nobel Prize) gave financial backing to the tournament, wealthy retired Stockholmers have flocked here, bringing an ostentatious smugness to the town for the annual competition held during the second week of July. The locals themselves, however, are quite down-to-earth, and most view this arrogance as a financial lifeline. Despite all this, Båstad isn't a prohibitively expensive place to stay, and makes a good base from which to explore the peninsula.

The square and Sancta Maria kyrka

Italienska vägen 2 • Church: June–Aug Mon–Fri 8am–6pm, Sat & Sun 10am–3pm; Sept–May Mon–Fri 8am–3.30pm, Sat & Sun 10am–3pm

From the train station, it's a half-hour walk eastwards up Köpmansgatan to the central old square and tourist office (see opposite). Once you get close to the centre, you'll see that the street's architecture is unusual for Sweden, and somewhat reminiscent of provincial France, with shuttered, low-rise shops and houses. In the square is the fifteenth-century **Sancta Maria kyrka**, a cool haven on a hot summer's day. The altar painting is striking, depicting Jesus on his cross with a couple of skulls and haphazardly strewn human bones on the ground beneath.

The waterfront

For a feel of old Båstad, take a stroll down the ancient cottage-flanked Agardhsgatan, off Hamngatan and parallel with the seashore. To reach the **beach** head down Tennisvägen, off Köpmansgatan, and through a glamorous residential area until you reach Strandpromenaden, where you can take a lovely evening stroll as the sun sets on the calm waters. West of here, the old 1880s bathhouses have all been converted into restaurants and bars which owe much of their popularity to their proximity to the tennis courts where the famous tournament is played. Just a few steps further lies the harbour, thick with boat masts.

Norrvikens Trädgårdar

Norrviken Gardens • June–Aug daily 10am–5pm • 60kr • ⓦ norrvikenstradgardar.net

Heading west out of Båstad along the coast road, it's just a couple of kilometres to **Norrvikens Trädgårdar**, a paradise for horticulturists and lovers of symmetry. With the sea as a backdrop, these fine gardens were designed by Rudolf Abelin at the end of the nineteenth century; he is buried in a magnificent hollow of rhododendrons near the entrance. The best walk is the "King's Ravine", ablaze in late spring and early summer

5

with fiery azaleas and more blushing rhododendrons, and leading to a fine Japanese-style garden. At the centre of the grounds there's an open-air theatre with occasional productions (details available at the tourist office in Båstad).

ARRIVAL AND DEPARTURE
BÅSTAD

By train Until the much-delayed rail tunnel through the Hallandsås ridge of hills outside Båstad is complete and the town's new train station opens, it remains a lamentably long walk of around half an hour up Köpmangatan into the town centre from the existing station.

Destinations Copenhagen (hourly; 2hr); Gothenburg (hourly; 1hr 40min); Malmö (hourly; 1hr 30min).
By bus To reach the Bjäre peninsula, you need to take a bus from the bus station off Musterivägen near the Spara supermarket.
Destination Torekov (6 daily; 30min).

INFORMATION

Tourist office Kyrkogatan 1 on the main square (mid-June to mid-Aug Mon–Fri 10am–6pm, Sat & Sun 11am–2pm; mid-Aug to mid-June Mon–Fri 10am–5pm,

Sat 11am–2pm; ☎0431 750 45, ⓦbastad.com). Has maps and information about the town and the Bjäre peninsula.

ACCOMMODATION

Accommodation in Båstad is plentiful, but to find somewhere to stay during the Swedish Open in July, you'll need to book months in advance. Unlike the rest of Sweden, prices increase dramatically during the summer as a result of the town's sporting endeavours.

Enehall Stationsterrasen 10 ☎0431 750 15, ⓦenehall.se. Rooms are located in nine different houses grouped together just a few metres from the train station. Although simply furnished, all rooms are perfectly comfortable, clean and have private facilities. **1180kr**

Falken Hamngatan 22 ☎0431 36 95 94, ⓦvillafalken.com. This most charming and charismatic B&B is wonderfully located just above the harbour in delightful gardens. A 1916-built villa, the house has been lovingly maintained and has a welcoming atmosphere. **800kr**

Hjorten Roxmansvägen 23 ☎0431 701 09, ⓦhjorten.net. This homely pension just off the main road, Köpmansgatan, dates from 1910 and is the oldest in town. It represents good value for money, though the decor is a little frilly and fussy. Open June–Aug only. **1050kr/850kr**

Pensionat Neptun Havsbadsvägen 18 ☎0431 36 91 30, ⓦpensionatneptun.se. A pleasant, traditional wooden house with two enormous verandas that's just 100m from the beach, offering amazingly good-value

accommodation in well-appointed and tastefully decorated doubles. **590kr/550kr**

Sigfridsgården Ängelholmsvägen 26 ☎0431 36 69 18, ⓦsigfridsgarden.se. Well-regarded B&B with tastefully decorated, light and airy rooms overlooking a pleasant flower garden, located roughly halfway between the train station and the main square. There's also a small café and art gallery onsite. **1090kr/860kr**

★ **Skansen** Kyrkogatan 2 ☎0431 55 81 00, ⓦhotelskansen.se. This beautifully designed hotel, set in a cream bathhouse with stylish annexe villas, includes a great health spa (included in all room rates). Rooms in the tennis pavilion annexe and the neighbouring annexe cost 100kr less. **1860kr**

CAMPING

Norrvikens Camping Kattviksvägen 347 ☎0431 36 91 70, ⓦcaravanclub.se. In a pretty spot right by the sea, this site is a couple of kilometres west of the town centre. Open late March to Sept. Tents **165kr**

EATING AND DRINKING

In Båstad, eating and drinking is as much a pastime as tennis, and most of the waterside eating establishments and hotels here have two-course dinner offers, with menus changing weekly

Fiskekajen Hamngatan 8 ☎070 336 92 69. Down at the harbour, this is the place to come to get your fishy fix – they have seemingly everything from cold-smoked salmon on rye bread (95kr) to a delicious fish and seafood stew (185kr). June–Aug daily 11am–10pm.

★ **Hamnkrogen** Strandpromenaden ☎0431 724 77. Undoubtedly the best of the waterfront seafood

places with a large wooden deck overlooking the marina. A plentiful, frequently changing choice of fish and meat specials (179–298kr). Easter to Aug daily noon till late.

★ **Pepe's Bodega** Hamngatan 6 ☎0431 36 91 69. A very popular place with Båstad's 20-somethings, serving pizzas from 185kr and tapas such as gazpacho and calamari from 32kr. The food is good and, this being Båstad, the bar

5

also stocks champagne and cocktails. Daily noon till late.

Sand Kyrkogatan 2 ☎0431 55 81 09. Attached to *Hotel Skansen* with glorious views out over the sea, this is an excellent-quality à la carte restaurant (mains from 275kr) serving up rack of lamb, steaks, turbot and corn-fed chicken. Mon–Fri 11.30am–2pm & 6pm till late, Sat noon–2.30pm & 6pm till late, Sun noon–3pm.

Sands Bakficka Hamngatan 1 ☎0431 55 81 09. A bright and breezy bistro which does a roaring trade during the summer months, dishing up open sandwiches, coffees and cakes. Really nice views out over the sea from here. June–Aug 9am–8pm, Sat & Sun 9am–10pm.

Solbackens Café & Wåffelbruk Munkgatan 10 ☎0431 702 00. This Båstad institution first opened its doors in 1907 and has been serving delicious fresh waffles and cream ever since. Seating is arranged on a series of terraces with views out over the sea. June–Aug daily 1–5pm.

The Bjäre peninsula

Jutting into the Kattegat directly west of Båstad and deserving a couple of days' exploration, the **Bjäre peninsula**'s natural beauty has a magical quality to it. Its varied scenery includes wide fertile fields where potatoes and strawberries are grown, splintered red-rock cliff formations and remote islands ringed by seals, thick with birds and historical ruins.

Kattvik and around

About 8km west of Båstad, and beyond Norrvikens Trädgårdar is **KATTVIK**. Once a village busy with stone-grinding mills, it is now largely the domain of wealthy, elderly Stockholmers, who snap up the few houses on the market as soon as they are up for sale. Kattvik achieved its moment of fame when Richard Gere chose a cottage here as a venue for a summer romance.

Kai's fish smokery

A kilometre from Kattvik off the Torekov road (follow the sign "*rökt fisk*") is **Kai's fish smokery**, an old farm where fish is smoked in little furnaces fired by sawdust from the nearby clog factory. Here you can have a taste of – and buy – the very best smoked fish in the area; as well as the usual mackerel and salmon, sample *horngädda* (garpike), a scaly fish with bright green bones, and *sjurygg* (lumpsucker), an extraordinarily ugly, seven-crested fish with oily, flavoursome flesh.

Hovs Hallar nature reserve

Heading north along the coast road or the signposted walking trail, the undulating meadows and beamed cottages you'll encounter have a rural and peculiarly English feel. To continue along the coast after taking the trail from Kattvik, follow the path for **Hovs Hallar nature reserve**, leading off at the T-junction (20min walk). Wandering across to the reserve from the car park, you can clamber down any of several paths towards the sea. The views are breathtaking – screaming gulls circling overhead and waves crashing onto the unique red-stone cliffs – though it's something of a tourist magnet during the summer.

Torekov

On the peninsula's western coast, **TOREKOV** is just 5km from Hovs Hallar nature reserve. The village is named after a little girl later known as St Thora, who, so the story goes, was drowned by her wicked stepmother; the body was washed ashore and given a Christian burial by a blind man, who then miraculously regained his sight. It's a perfect place to chill; indeed, one odd sight is the daily ritual of elderly men in dressing gowns wandering along the pier – so sought after is the property here, these old boys promenade in bathrobes to set themselves apart from the visitors.

Hallands Väderö

Boats April–Oct; departures vary by month, though there's generally a boat every 1–2hr • 100kr return • Detailed timetable at ⓦ vaderotrafiken.se

The main reason to venture to Torekov is to take one of the old fishing **boats** which regularly leave from its little harbour for the island nature reserve of **HALLANDS VÄDERÖ**. The island is a scenic mix of trees and bare rocks with isolated fishermen's cottages dotted around its edges, while the skies above are filled with countless birds – gulls, eiders, guillemots and cormorants.

Seal safaris

Late June to early Aug Thurs only 6pm • 200kr • ☎ 0431 36 34 940, ⓦ vaderotrafiken.se

One particularly beautiful spot on Hallands Väderö is at its southernmost tip, where weather-smoothed islets stand out amid the tranquil turquoise waters. If you're lucky, you may be able to make out the colony of seals living on the furthest rocks; there are organized "**seal safaris**" there.

English graveyard

On the south of Hallands Väderö is the **English graveyard**, surrounded by mossy, dry-stone walls. It holds the remains of English sailors who were killed here in 1809, when the British fleet was stationed on the island in order to bombard Copenhagen during the Napoleonic Wars. Torekov church would not allow them to be buried on its soil as the sailors' faith was, strangely, considered unknown.

GETTING AROUND THE BJÄRE PENINSULA

By bus Bus #525 runs through the centre of the peninsula from Båstad to Torekov, and stops at the small hamlets of Hov and Karup on the peninsula's southern coast en route.
By bike The well-known Skåneleden walking trail runs around the entire perimeter of the peninsula and makes for a great bicycle ride. Bike rental is available in Båstad at Sven's Cykelaffär at Tennisvägen 31 (☎ 0431 701 26; 100kr/day).

ACCOMMODATION

Delfin Bed & Breakfast Kattvik ☎ 0431 731 20, ✉ delfin.kattvik@telia.com. A friendly and peaceful B&B with just three rooms sharing facilities), this makes an idyllic base for exploring the region. Breakfast with home-baked bread is served in the garden or on the terrace. **790kr**

Hotell Hovs Hallar Hovshallavägen 160 ☎ 0431 44 83 70, whovshallar.com. Overlooking the cliffs by Hovs Hallar nature reserve, most rooms at this smart, modern hotel have their own terrace or balcony and some have sea views; nine smaller rooms cost 300kr less. **1250kr**

EATING

Värdshus Hovs Hallar Hovshallavägen 160 ☎ 0431 44 83 70. This famed restaurant serves fine à la carte meals (mains 195–265kr) and lunch specials (115kr). Particularly popular is the monthly herring table (noon–4pm; last Sun of month); reservations are recommended at all times. Mon–Fri 11.30am–2.30pm & 6–9pm, Sat & Sun 6–9pm.

Helsingborg

Long gone are the days when the locals of **HELSINGBORG** joked that the most rewarding sight here was Helsingør, the Danish town whose castle – Hamlet's celebrated Elsinore (Kronoborg castle) – is visible, just 4km across the Öresund strait. Bright and pleasing, Helsingborg has a tremendous sense of buoyancy. With its beautifully developed harbour area, an explosion of stylish bars, great cafés and restaurants among the warren of cobbled streets, plus an excellent **museum**, it is one of the best town bases Sweden has to offer.

Brief history

In the past, the links between Helsingborg and Copenhagen were less convivial than they are now. After the Danes fortified the town in the eleventh century, the Swedes

5

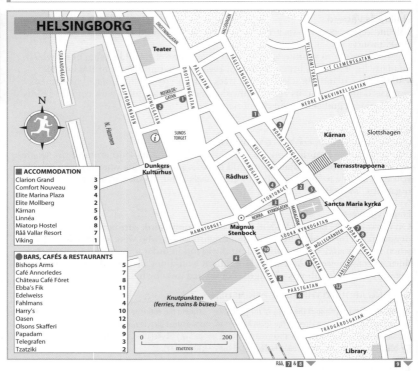

HELSINGBORG

Teater

N

ACCOMMODATION

Clarion Grand	3
Comfort Nouveau	9
Elite Marina Plaza	4
Elite Mollberg	2
Kärnan	5
Linnéa	6
Miatorp Hostel	8
Råå Vallar Resort	7
Viking	1

BARS, CAFÉS & RESTAURANTS

Bishops Arms	5
Café Annorledes	7
Château Café Fôret	8
Ebba's Fik	11
Edelweiss	1
Fahlmans	4
Harry's	10
Oasen	12
Olsons Skafferi	6
Papadam	9
Telegrafen	3
Tzatziki	2

Dunkers Kulturhus

Rådhus

Kärnan   Slottshagen

Terrasstrapporna

Sancta Maria kyrka

Magnus Stenbock

Knutpunkten
(ferries, trains & buses)

Library

0   200
metres

conquered and lost it again on six violent occasions, finally winning out in 1710 under Magnus Stenbock's leadership. By this time, the Danes had torn down much of the town and on its final recapture, the Swedes contributed to the destruction by razing most of its twelfth-century castle – except for the 5m-thick walled **keep** (*kärnan*), which still dominates the centre. By the early eighteenth century, war and epidemics had reduced the population to just seven hundred, and only with the onset of industrialization in the 1850s did Helsingborg experience a new prosperity. Shipping and the railways turned the town's fortunes round, as is evident from the formidable late nineteenth-century commercial buildings in the centre and some splendid villas to the north, overlooking the Öresund.

Rådhus

The most obvious starting point is on the waterfront, by the bronze **statue** of former Skåne governor, Magnus Stenbock, on his charger. With your back to the Öresund and Denmark, to your left is the **Rådhus**, a heavy-handed, Neo-Gothic pile, complete with turrets and conical towers. The extravagance of provincial nineteenth-century prosperity, and the architect's admiration for medieval Italy, make it worth seeing inside (ask about tours at the tourist office), in particular for the many fabulous stained-glass windows, which tell the history of the town. The ones to look out for are those in the entrance hall, depicting Queen Margareta releasing her rival, Albert of Mecklenburg, in Helsingborg in 1395, and the last window in the city-council chamber, showing Jean Baptiste Bernadotte arriving at Helsingborg in 1810, having accepted the Swedish crown. When he greeted General von Essen at the harbour, farce ensued as their

5

elaborate gold jewellery and medals became entangled in the embrace. The original wall and ceiling frescoes were deemed too costly to restore and were painted over in 1968, though have now been uncovered.

Dunkers Kulturhus

Kungsgatan 11 • Tues–Sun 10am–5pm, Thurs until 8pm • Exhibitions 70kr; otherwise free • Ⓦ dunkerskulturhus.se

Crossing over the road towards the Kattegat from the Magnus Stenbock statue, you'll see the **harbour**, divided in two by the new bridge to the pier. To the north of the bridge is the exceptional city museum, **Dunkers Kulturhus**. The white-brick building contains a first-rate museum exploring the city's history. The centre is named after Henry Dunker, a local man and pioneer of galoshes – he developed the process for keeping rubber soft in winter and non-sticky in summer and his brand, Tretorn, became a world leader until the factories closed in 1979. When he died in 1962, he left 58 million *kronor* to set up a foundation and this museum is a major recipient. If you're expecting traditional exhibitions, its dramatic special sound effects and lighting certainly come as a surprise. The history of Helsingborg, with water as the theme, from Ice Age to present day is tremendous fun, though there's no explanation in any language so it's more sensory than educational; the coverage of the town's social, economic and military history has far more explanation in English. There are also some **galleries** showing temporary art exhibitions year round. The museum contains a fine **restaurant**, overlooking the Öresund, and a bistro serving light meals.

The kärnan and around

Keep • Slottshagsgatan • Daily: April, May & Sept Tues–Fri 9am–4pm, Sat & Sun 11am–4pm; June–Aug daily 11am–7pm; Oct–March Tues–Sun 11am–3pm • 40kr

Returning to the bottom of **Stortorget** – the central "square", so elongated that it's more like a boulevard – it's a short stroll upwards to the steps leading to the remains of the medieval **castle**, dominated by the massive castellated bulk of the **kärnan**, surrounded by some fine parkland. The keep and Sancta Maria kyrka (see below) were the sole survivors of the ravages of war, but the former lost its military significance once Sweden finally won the day. It was due for demolition in the mid-nineteenth century, only surviving because seafarers found it a valuable landmark. What cannon fire failed to achieve, however, neglect and the weather succeeded in bringing about: the keep was a ruin when restoration began in 1894. It looks like a huge brick stood on end and is worth climbing today more for the views than the scant historical exhibitions within.

Sancta Maria kyrka

Mariatorget • Mon–Fri 8am–4pm, Sat & Sun 9am–4pm

From the parkland at the keep's base, it's just a few steps to a charming **rose and magnolia garden**, exuding scent and colour all summer. To the side of this, you can wander down a rhododendron-edged path, Hallbergs Trappor, to the **Sancta Maria kyrka**, which squats in its own square by a very French-looking avenue of beech trees. Resembling a basilica, and Danish Gothic in style, the church was begun in 1300 and completed a century later. Its rather plain facade belies a striking interior, with a clever contrast between the early seventeenth-century Renaissance-style ornamentation of its pulpit and gilded reredos, and the jewel-like contemporary stained-glass windows.

Norra and Södra Storgatan

Walking back to Stortorget from the church, you arrive at **Norra** and **Södra Storgatan** (the streets that meet at the foot of the stairs to the *kärnan*), which comprised Helsingborg's main thoroughfare in medieval times and so are lined with the oldest of the town's merchants' houses. As you head up Norra Storgatan, the 1681 **Henckelska**

5

house is hidden behind a plain stuccoed wall; once you have pushed your way through the trees that have grown over the entrance archway, you'll see a rambling mix of beams and windows, with a fine little topiary garden hidden beyond a passage to the right. The garden was laid out in 1766 for the future wife of King Gustav III, who was to spend one night at the beautiful eighteenth-century **Gamlegård house** opposite.

The windmill

On Södra Storgatan, take the opening to the left of the old cream brick building at no. 31, opposite the modern Maria Församling House, to find a real historical gem. After a fairly arduous climb of 92 steps, you'll find a handsome nineteenth-century **windmill**, which you're free to enter using a narrow ramp. Around the windmill are a number of exquisite farm cottages, and inside the low (120cm) doors is a treasure trove of items from eighteenth-century peasant interiors: straw beds, cradles, hand-painted grandmother clocks and the like. A further reward for your climb is the fact that one house, built in 1763 and brought to this site in 1909, serves **waffles**: it's *Möllebackens Våffelbruk* (May–Aug daily noon–8pm). Established in 1912, they still use the original recipes.

ARRIVAL AND DEPARTURE   HELSINGBORG

By train All services arrive and depart from the underground platforms of the Knutpunkten travel interchange.
Destinations Copenhagen (hourly; 1hr 10min); Gothenburg (hourly; 2hr 20min); Kristianstad (hourly; 1hr 30min); Malmö (hourly; 40min).

By ferry Scandlines (ⓦ scandlines.se) operate from the first floor of the Knutpunkten terminal all day long to and from Helsingør.
Destination Helsingør, Denmark (every 20min; 20min).

INFORMATION

Tourist office Inside Dunkers Kulturhus at Kungsgatan 11 (Mon–Fri 10am–6pm, Thurs until 8pm, Sat & Sun 10am–5pm; ☏ 042 10 43 50;

ⓦ www.helsingborgsturistbyra.skane.com).
Internet access At the tourist office and with Sidewalk Express, at the 7-Eleven, Järnvägsgatan 19.

ACCOMMODATION

Clarion Grand Stortorget 8–12 ☏ 042 38 04 00, ⓦ clarionhelsingborg.se. Built in 1926, this is one of Helsingborg's biggest and grandest hotels. The interior is a successful blend of modern and classic design with good-sized rooms in a superbly central location. **780kr/1380kr**
Comfort Nouveau Gasverksgatan 11 ☏ 042 37 19 50, wchoicehotels.no/info/SE046. This lacks the grandeur of other Stortorget hotels, but is pretty central and has all the comforts of the top hotels, including a swimming pool and a sauna. Serves exceptionally good breakfasts. **695kr/995kr**
Elite Marina Plaza Kungstorget 6 ☏ 042 19 21 00, welite.se. Right at the harbourside, next to Knutpunkten. Taking inspiration from the sun, wind and water, the rooms

at this modern and well-equipped hotel are bright, airy and contemporary in design and some have sea views. **807kr/1317kr**
Eilte Mollberg Stortorget 18 ☏ 042 37 37 00, ⓦ elite .se. Every inch a premier hotel, with a grand nineteenth-century facade, though rooms are simpler, smaller and more homely than at its sister hotel, the *Marina Plaza*. **680kr/1020kr**
Kärnan Järnvägsgatan 17 ☏ 042 12 08 20, ⓦ hotelkarnan.se. Opposite Knutpunkten, this comfortable staff-owned hotel prides itself on home-from-home rooms with modern furnishings, and the generous buffet breakfast is arguably the best in town. There's also a small library-cum-bar and sauna. **1095kr**

BACK AND FORTH TO HELSINGØR

For a taste of what the locals traditionally do for fun, buy a **foot passenger ferry** ticket to Helsingør. Scandlines' ferries run every 20min (64kr return; ⓦ scandlines.se) and hop on the boat to Denmark. Tickets are available on the first floor in the Knutpunkten terminal. Try to go on the *Aurora* or *Hamlet*, which have better restaurants and bars than the *Tycho Brahe*; you can see in the timetable which ship operates which departure. The idea is to "*tura*" as it's called in Swedish, that is to go back and forth as many times as you like on the same ticket. Good-value lunches and dinners are also served on the boats and you can also buy duty-free.

Linnéa Prästgatan 2–4 ☎ 042 37 24 00, whotell-linnea.se. Good value, central option in an elegant building from 1887, with cosy, agreeable rooms with period furnishings as well as special offers on two-night stays over a weekend. **1095kr/1195kr**

Miatorp Hostel Planteringsvägen 71 ☎ 042 13 11 30, ⓦ miatorp.nu; a 20min walk south of the centre along Södergatan, Västra Sandgatan and finally Planteringsvägen or bus #1 or #2. All rooms at this STF hostel are modern, clean and en suite. Dorms **320kr**, doubles **640kr**

★ **Viking** Fågelsångsgatan 1 ☎ 042 14 44 20, ⓦ hotellviking.se. This is the place to try first. Very

appealing, quiet old hotel with beautifully appointed period rooms in a splendid location close to some of the finest buildings in town. Room 15 has its own private jacuzzi and costs about 500kr more than a regular double. Excellent service and a cosy atmosphere. **1070kr/1278kr**

CAMPING

Råå Vallar Resort Kustgatan in the district of Råå, 2km south of town ☎ 042 18 26 00, ⓦ nordiccamping. se; take bus #1 from the town centre. This campsite is well located for Helsingborg's nudist beach, which is right next door at the foot of Högastensgatan. There's also a selection of cabins available. Tents **140kr**, cabins **790kr**

EATING AND DRINKING

The city has a good range of excellent restaurants, including a host of stylish bar-restaurants along the restored harbourfront. These places can seem samey, though, and it's the older restaurants that continue to provide the variety. During the day, there are some great cafés and *konditori*.

CAFÉS

Café Annorledes Södra Storgatan 15 ☎ 042 13 72 04. A friendly café with a genteel 1950s atmosphere known for its extremely reasonable breakfasts (53kr) featuring porridge, yoghurt, eggs and cheese. There's also a good selection of salads, quiches and cakes – the walnut one is especially good. Mon–Fri 9am–6pm, Sat 10am–4pm.

★ **Château Café Forêt** Södra Storgatan 19 ☎ 042 12 90 35. Resembling a French or Belgian modern café-bistro, this is the place to come for a taste of the Gallic continent with excellent home-made breads and freshly squeezed fruit juices. Tues–Fri 10am–6pm, Sat 11am–4pm.

★ **Ebba's Fik** Bruksgatan 20 ☎ 042 28 14. An amazing jumble of 1950s furnishings, and even a jukebox belting out the likes of Little Richard. Every detail of the era – from crockery to menu board – is here. Excellent egg and bacon fry-ups and delicious home-made Swedish beefburgers too. Mon–Fri 9am–6pm, Sat 9am–4pm.

Fahlmans Stortorget 11 ☎ 042 21 30 60. This classic bakery/café has been serving elaborate cakes and pastries since 1914 and is *the* place for decadent apple meringue pie – a meal in itself. Also try the chocolate and marzipan confections or filling sandwiches. Mon–Fri 8am–6.30pm, Sat 8.30am–4.30pm, Sun 10am–4.30pm.

BAR AND RESTAURANTS

Bishops Arms Södra Storgatan 2 ☎ 042 37 37 77. At the top end of Stortorget, this centrally located pub is a firm favourite among Helsingborgers for its relatively genuine British pub feel, and its extensive range of beers, most on tap. Mon & Tues 4pm–midnight, Wed & Thurs 4pm–1am, Fri & Sat 4pm–2am, Sun 4–10pm.

★ **Edelweiss** Drottninggatan 15 ☎ 042 21 37 37. A fun German restaurant-cum-beerhall with a tremendous selection of real German beers, as well as Wiener schnitzel

(195kr), a mammoth plate of Bavarian sausages, sauerkraut and mashed potato (149kr) and other German staples (149–199kr). Tues–Thurs 5–10pm, Fri & Sat 5pm–1am, Sun 4–10pm.

Harry's Järnvägsgatan 7 ☎ 042 13 91 91. Very popular place for a drink and rather more stylish than the usual *Harry's*, with soft leather armchairs and chandeliers throughout. There's a nightclub here on Thurs, Fri & Sat nights. Mon 11.30am–midnight, Tues & Wed 11.30am–1am, Thurs 11.30am–3pm, Fri 11.30am–4am, Sat noon–4am.

Oasen Bruksgatan 25 ☎ 042 12 80 74. This restaurant serves nothing but fondues: meat (209kr), seafood (249kr) and Mexican (229kr). Its speciality is a totally wicked Toblerone fondue (89kr) with Cointreau and brandy into which you dip marshmallows, bananas and other fruit. Tues–Thurs 6pm till late, Fri & Sat 5pm till late.

Olsons Skafferi Mariagatan 6 ☎ 042 14 07 80. With not a pizza in sight, this great Italian place located in a half-timbered building offers wonderfully prepared fish, meat and pasta dishes (149–239kr) in a relaxed atmosphere using Italian bases with Swedish overtones. Mon–Sat 11am–10.30pm.

Papadam Bruksgatan 10 ☎ 042 12 16 00. Finally, decent Indian food has made it to Helsingborg. Balti dishes are 169kr, an excellent chicken curry with spinach is 139kr, whereas lunch (served until 4pm) is an exceptionally good-value 65kr. Mon–Thurs 11am–10pm, Fri & Sat 11am–11pm, Sun 1–10pm.

Telegrafen Norra Storgatan 14 ☎ 042 18 14 50. A long-term favourite, this cosy British-style pub with wooden floors and a bar lined with tattered old books can do no wrong – Swedes seem to love the mock-Britannia. Snacks such as burgers and nachos available. Thurs–Sat 5pm till late.

5

Tzatziki Roskildegatan 2 ☎042 13 21 85. With a predictably blue-and-white colour scheme, the food here is anything but predictable – genuinely, tasty Greek specialities such as calamari, marinated chicken skewers and Greek yoghurt with honey and walnuts. There's also a large selection of meze (35–89kr). Mon–Thurs 4–10pm, Fri & Sat till 11pm.

Lund

"There is a very tangible Lund spirit – those with it have … an ironic distance to everything, including themselves and Lund, a barb to deflate pompous self-importance", wrote the Swedish essayist Jan Mårtensson. His compatriot, poet Peter Ortman, for his part once described what he termed "Lund syndrome": "a mix of paranoia, exhibitionism and megalomania". Whatever it is about the place, there is indeed a special spirit to **LUND** – a sense of tolerance (it's more relaxed than other Swedish cities), and a belief that people should be judged by what they do, not by what they have.

A few kilometres inland and 54km south of Helsingborg, Lund's reputation as a glorious old **university city** is well founded. An ocean of bikes is the first image to greet you at the train station, and like Oxford in England – with which Lund is usually aptly compared – there is a bohemian, laidback eccentricity in the air. With a twelfth-century Romanesque **cathedral**, medieval streets lined with a variety of architectural styles, and a wealth of cafés and restaurants, Lund is an enchanting little city that could well captivate you for a couple of days; it has a wide range of **museums**, a couple of them excellent, a mix of architectural grandeur, plus the buzz of student life. While Lund does lose much of its atmosphere during the summer months, some places remain open through June to August.

The Domkyrkan

Kyrkogatan 6 • Mon–Fri 8am–6pm, Sat 9.30am–5pm, Sun 9.30am–6pm • Free

The magnificent **Domkyrkan** is built of storm-cloud charcoal and white stone, giving it an imposing monochrome appearance. Before going inside, have a look round the back of the building; on the way there, you'll notice the grotesque animal and bird gargoyles over the side entrances, their features blunted by eight centuries of weathering. At the very back, the most beautiful part of the exterior, the three-storey **apse** above the crypt, is revealed, crowned with an exquisite gallery.

The interior

The majestic **interior** is surprisingly unadorned, an elegant mass of watery-grey ribbed stone arches and stone-flagged flooring. One of the world's finest masterpieces of Romanesque architecture, the cathedral was built in the twelfth century when Lund became the first independent archbishopric in Scandinavia, laying the foundation for a period of wealth and eminence that lasted until the advent of Protestantism. There are several striking features, such as the elaborately

---

LUND ORIENTATION

Lund is a wonderful town to wander around, its cobbled streets festooned with climbing roses. To help get your bearings, it's worth noting that the main thoroughfare changes its name several times. In the centre, it's called Kyrkogatan; to the north, Bredgatan (there's no need to venture further north than the pretty old brick house at no. 16); to the south, Stora Södergatan. **Lundagård** (the city's academic heart), the **Domkyrkan** and **Stortorget** are all along this route. Lund's crowning glory is its cathedral; just 100m north of Stortorget, and only a short walk east from the station, it is the obvious place to begin your exploration.

5

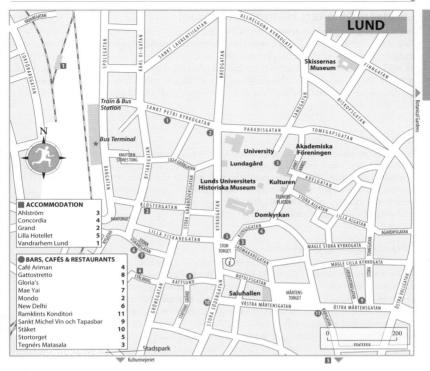

LUND

ACCOMMODATION
Ahlström	3
Concordia	4
Grand	2
Lilla Hotellet	5
Vandrarhem Lund	1

BARS, CAFÉS & RESTAURANTS
Café Ariman	4
Gattostretto	8
Gloria's	1
Mae Yai	7
Mondo	2
New Delhi	6
Ramklints Konditori	11
Sankt Michel Vin och Tapasbar	9
Stäket	10
Stortorget	5
Tegnérs Matasala	3

carved fourteenth-century choir stalls depicting Old Testament scenes, and the grotesque carvings hidden beneath the seats. The most vividly coloured feature is just to the left of the entrance, an amazing **astronomical clock** dating from the 1440s, which shows hours, days, weeks and the courses of the sun and moon in the zodiac. Each day at noon and 3pm, the clock also reveals its ecclesiastical Punch-and-Judy show, as two knights pop out and clash swords as many times as the clock strikes, followed by little mechanical doors opening to trumpet-blowing heralds and the Three Wise Men trundling slowly to the Virgin Mary.

The crypt

The dimly lit and dramatic **crypt** beneath the apse has been left almost untouched since the twelfth century, and should not be missed. Here, the thick smattering of what look like tombstones is really comprised of memorial slabs, brought down to the crypt from just above; but there is one actual tomb – that of **Birger Gunnarsson**, Lund's last archbishop. A short man from a poor family, Gunnarsson chose the principal altar-facing position for his tomb, dictating that his stone effigy above it should be tall and regal. Two **pillars** here are gripped by stone figures – one of a man, another of a woman and child. Local legend has it that Finn the Giant built the cathedral for St Lawrence; in return, unless the saint could guess his name, Finn wanted the sun, the moon or the saint's eyes. Lawrence was just preparing to end his days in blindness when he heard Finn's wife boasting to her baby, "Soon Father Finn will bring some eyes for you to play with." The relieved saint rushed to Finn declaring the name. The livid giant, his wife and child rushed to the crypt to pull down the columns, and were instantly turned to stone. Even without the fable, the column-hugging figures are fascinating to view.

5

Lunds Universitets Historiska Museum

Lund University Historical Museum • Kraftstorg 12 • Tues–Fri 11am–4pm, Sun noon–4pm • 50kr • ⓦ luhm.lu.se

Just behind the cathedral, the **Lunds Universitets Historiska Museum** is for the most part rather dull unless you have a specialist interest in ecclesiastical history. The statues from Skåne's churches, in the medieval exhibition, deserve a look though, mainly because of the way they are arranged. The crowd of Jesuses hanging on crosses have an ominous quality worthy of Hitchcock, while in the next room all the Madonnas are paired off with the baby Jesuses.

Kulturen

Tegnerplatsen • Mid-April to Sept daily 11am–5pm; Oct to mid-April Tues–Sun noon–4pm • 90kr; June–Aug 120kr • ⓦ kulturen.com

A few minutes' walk from the Lunds Universitets Historiska Museum is the town's best museum, **Kulturen**. It's easy to spend the best part of a day just wandering around this privately owned open-air museum, a virtual town of perfectly preserved cottages, farms, merchants' houses, gardens and even churches, brought from seven Swedish regions and encompassing as many centuries.

Skissernas Museum

Museum of Sketches • Finngatan 2 • Tues–Sun noon–5pm, Wed until 9pm • 50kr • ⓦ adk.lu.se

A few streets north from the cathedral, the **Skissernas Museum** houses a fascinating collection of around 25,000 preliminary sketches and original maquettes of works of art from around the world. An ever-changing selection of them is displayed; usually one room is full of work by all the major Swedish artists, while in another are sketches by international giants, such as Chagall, Matisse, Léger, Miró and Dufy; the best-known sculptural sketches here are by Picasso and Henry Moore. Outside, the sculptures on display include preliminary versions of pieces found in town squares all over Sweden, including those by Bror Marklund.

Botanical Gardens

Östra Vallgatan 20 • Daily 6am–8pm, greenhouses noon–3pm • Free

An antidote to museum fatigue, the **Botanical Gardens** are as much a venue for picnicking and chilling out as a botanical experience. The greenhouses and rock gardens are the best areas to view; the rarest sights here are the Far Eastern paper-mulberry trees and the huge tulip trees – part of the same family as magnolias – with masses of flowers in June.

ARRIVAL AND DEPARTURE
LUND

By train Trains arrive at the western edge of the centre. From the train station, the centre is a 2min walk, and everything of interest is within easy reach, with all the sights no more than 10min away.

Destinations Copenhagen (hourly; 45min); Gothenburg (hourly; 3hr); Karlskrona (hourly; 2hr 40min); Kristianstad (hourly; 45min); Malmö (very frequent; 12min); Stockholm (hourly; 4hr 10min).

INFORMATION

Tourist office Botulfsgatan 1A, just south of the Domkyrkan (Mon–Fri 10am–6pm, Sat 10am–2pm; June–Aug Sat 10am–3pm & Sun 11am–3pm; ☎ 046 35 50 40,

ⓦ lund.se/tourism). Has free internet access as well as maps and copies of the information booklet, *Lund*.

ACCOMMODATION

Although there are plenty of luxury hotels in Lund, budget choices are extremely limited and Malmö, just 12min away by

CLOCKWISE FROM TOP LEFT TURNING TORSO, MALMÖ (P.176); STANDING STONES, ALES STENAR (P.185); YSTAD (P.182); JOHANNA LARSSON IN THE FINAL OF THE 2011 SWEDISH OPEN, BÅSTAD(P.158) >

5

train, has a much greater range. Lund is, nevertheless, a popular destination, so be sure to book ahead, especially for the youth hostel and cheaper options.

Ahlström Skomakaregatan 3 ☎046 211 01 74, ⓦhotellahlstrom.se. Good-quality, very central cheapie though only two of the sixteen rooms are en suite; one room also has a kitchen (450kr extra). No breakfast room: it's served on a tray brought to the room. 650kr/850kr

Concordia Stålbrogatan 1 ☎046 13 50 50, ⓦconcordia. se. A couple of streets southwest of Stortorget, this former student hostel has been upgraded into a very homely contemporary hotel with airy, modern Swedish designer rooms – some, though, are rather cramped. There's a sauna too. 995kr/1495kr

Grand Bantorget 1 ☎046 280 61 00, ⓦgrandilund.se. This imposing nineteenth-century pink-sandstone edifice straddles an entire side of a small, stately and central square. Top of the range, comfortable and unpretentious

with period furnishings and chandeliers, this hotel oozes opulence and is perfect for a special occasion. 1214kr/1736kr

Lilla Hotellet Bankgatan 7 ☎046 32 88 88, ⓦlillahotelletilund.se. Located in no fewer than five interlinked, low-roofed Lund townhouses, painted in subtle pastel shades, from the 1850s, rooms here are cosy and nicely appointed, decorated in modern Swedish style and colours. 1050kr/1450kr

★ **Vandrarhem Lund** Vävaregatan 22 ☎046 14 28 20, ⓦtrainhostel.com. This atmospheric STF hostel is housed in the carriages of a 1940s train and accessed through the tunnel behind the train station, with bunks exactly as they would be in a train sleeping car. Bunks 200/230kr, compartment 1460kr

EATING AND DRINKING

There are plenty of charming places to eat and drink in Lund, many frequented by students helping keep prices low, especially for beer. For provisions, the Saluhallen market at Mårtenstorget (Mon–Fri 9.30am–6pm, Sat 9am–3pm), sells a range of fish, cheeses and meats, including Lund's own tasty speciality sausage, *knake*.

CAFÉS

Café Ariman Kungsgatan 2 ☎046 13 12 63. Attached to the Nordic Law Department, this classic left-wing coffee house is located in a striking red-brick building. It's frequented by wannabe writers and artists, with goatees, ponytails and blonde dreadlocks predominating. Cheap snacks, coffee and cakes. Mon 11am–midnight, Tues–Thurs 11am–1am, Fri & Sat 11am–3am, Sun 1–11pm.

Mondo Kyrkogatan 23 ☎046 14 81 58. In a quaint, half-timbered house with tiled interior walls, this pleasant little café serves bagels, baguettes, pasta salads and ciabattas. Does takeaway, too, and is a popular student haunt. Mon–Fri 8am–8pm, Sat & Sun 10am–6pm.

Ramklints Konditori Mårtenstorget 10 ☎046 211 06 44. This is a place to pop in for a takeaway sandwich or a cake rather than somewhere to sit and linger as the interior is rather plain. However, its baked goods are always fresh and tasty. Mon–Fri 7.30am–6.30pm, Sat 8am–5pm, Sun 9.30am–4.30pm.

RESTAURANTS

Gattostretto Kattesund 6A ☎046 32 07 77. Compact neighbourhood Italian which really draws the crowds: great prices such as pasta of the day (75kr), tuna salad (74kr) and ravioli with ricotta, basil and pine nuts (139kr). Mon–Sat 11am till late.

Gloria's Sankt Petri Kyrkogatan 9 ☎046 15 19 85. Serving TexMex and Cajun food, *Gloria's* sports bar is very popular, particularly when there's a match on the big screen. Try the blackened chicken with corn salsa (139kr) or

the tasty scampi platter (169kr). Mon & Tues 11.30am–11pm, Wed & Thurs 11.30am–midnight, Fri 11.30am–3am, Sat 12.30pm–3am, Sun 1–11pm.

Mae Yai Stora Fiskaregatan 15B ☎046 13 00 93. This plain and simple Thai restaurant is very popular with the town's student population for its decent and generous Asian stir-fries and curries: most dishes are 85kr, 10kr less for takeaways. Mon–Fri 11.30am–11pm, Sat noon–10pm, Sun 11am–11pm.

New Delhi Stora Fiskaregatan 15 ☎046 15 25 61. A really good Indian restaurant that's made more of an effort on interior decor than its Thai neighbour, but whose mains are slightly more expensive (from 109kr). The chicken jalfrezi (109kr) is a winner every time. Mon–Thurs 11am–10pm, Fri 11am–11pm, Sat noon–11pm, Sun 3–10pm.

Sankt Michel Vin och Tapasbar Östra Mårtensgatan 13 ☎046 14 14 30. Taking inspiration from similar restaurants in Barcelona, this is Lund's very own Spanish tapas bar with a great selection of mouthwatering morsels such as fried feta, gazpacho and calamari; 55kr each, or four for 195kr. Mon 5–10pm, Tues–Thurs 5–11pm, Fri & Sat 5pm–midnight.

Stäket Stora Södergatan 6 ☎046 211 93 67. A step-gabled vaulted house built in 1570 is the characterful setting for this fondue- (from 170kr) and meat-oriented place. A mixed grill is 195kr, grilled duck breast is 205kr, and venison steak in lingonberry sauce costs 220kr. Mon–Thurs 11am–11pm, Fri 11am–midnight, Sat noon–midnight, Sun 1–11pm.

★ **Stortorget** Stortorget 1. Housed in a National Romantic building that was formerly a bank, this trendy brasserie specializes in modern Swedish dishes, for example, pork with salsify with black-eyed peas for 164kr. Mains 154–214kr. Mon–Thurs 11.30am–11pm, Fri & Sat 11.30am–1am.

Tegnérs Matsalar Sandgatan 2 ● 046 13 13 33. Next to Akademiska Föreningen, the student union. Forget any preconceptions about student cafés being tatty, stale sandwich bars. Lunch (75kr) is self-service and you eat as much as you like from a delicious spread. Mon–Fri 11.30am–1.30pm.

Malmö

Founded in the late thirteenth century, **MALMÖ** was once Denmark's second most important city, after Copenhagen. The high density of herring in the sea off the Malmö coast – it was said that the fish could be scooped straight out with a trowel – brought ambitious German merchants flocking; their influence can be seen in the striking fourteenth-century St Petri kyrka in the city centre.

Today, with its attractive medieval centre, a myriad of cobbled and mainly pedestrianized streets, full of busy restaurants and bars, Malmö has plenty of style. Beyond its compact centre, it's endowed with the stunning and dramatic **skyscraper**, the **Turning Torso** (see p.176), a string of popular **beaches** and some interesting cultural diversions south of the centre around **Möllevångstorget square**.

Brief history

Eric of Pomerania gave Malmö its most significant medieval boost, when, in the fifteenth century, he built the castle, endowed it with its own mint and gave Malmö its own flag – the gold-and-red griffin of his own family crest. It wasn't until the Swedish king Karl X marched his armies across the frozen Öresund to within striking distance of Copenhagen in 1658 that the Danes were forced into handing back the counties of Skåne, Blekinge and Bohuslän to the Swedes. For Malmö, too far from its own (uninterested) capital, this meant a period of stagnation, cut off from nearby Copenhagen. Not until the full thrust of industrialization, triggered by the tobacco merchant Frans Suell's enlargement of the harbour in 1775 (his jaunty bronze likeness, on Norra Vallgatan opposite the train station, overlooks his handiwork), did Malmö begin its dramatic commercial recovery. In 1840, boats began regular trips to Copenhagen, and Malmö's great Kockums shipyard was opened; limestone quarrying, too, became big business here in the nineteenth century.

During the last few decades of the twentieth century, Malmö found itself facing commercial crisis after a series of economic miscalculations, which included investing heavily in the shipping industry as it went into decline in the 1970s. But recent years have witnessed a dramatic renaissance, reflected in the upbeat, thoroughly likeable atmosphere pervading the town today. Since the opening of the **Öresund bridge** linking the town to Copenhagen, the city's fortunes have been further improved, with Danes discovering what this gateway to Sweden has to offer, as opposed to the one-way traffic of Swedes to Denmark in the past.

Stortorget

The laying out of **Stortorget**, the proud main square, necessitated the tearing down of much of Malmö's medieval centre in the mid-sixteenth century. Among the elaborate sixteenth- to nineteenth-century buildings, the 1546 **Rådhus** draws the most attention. It's an impressive pageant of architectural fiddling and crowded with statuary: restoration programmes in the last century robbed the building of its original design, and the finicky exterior is now in Dutch Renaissance style. To add to the pomp, the red-and-gold flag of Skåne, of which Malmö is so proud, flaps above the roofs. The cellars, home to the *Rådhuskällaren* restaurant (see p.179), have been used as a tavern

5

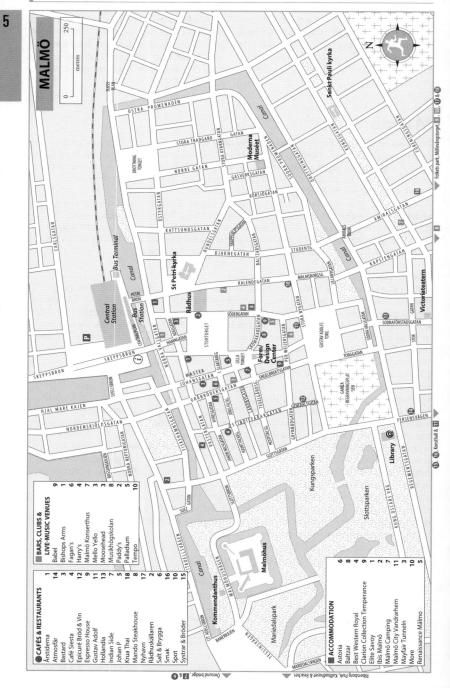

MALMÖ

0 — 250 metres

Central Station

Bus Terminal

Bus Station

St Petri kyrka

Rådhus

Moderna Museet

Sankt Pauli kyrka

Victoriateatern

Form/Design Center

Malmöhus

Kommendanthus

Mariedalspark

Kungsparken

Slottsparken

Library

Follets park, Möllevångstorget · 9 · 10 · 17 · 48 ▶

8 ▶

13 · 16, Konsthall & 11 ▶

Ribersborg Park, Kallbadhuset & beaches ▲

Öresund bridge · 7 & 6 ◀

● CAFÉS & RESTAURANTS

Årstiderna	1
Atmosfär	14
Bastard	3
Café Siesta	4
Epicure Bröd & Vin	12
Espresso House	9
Gustav Adolf	11
Hollandia	13
Indian Side	7
Johan P	5
Krua Thai	18
Mando Steakhouse	8
Nyhavn	17
Rådhuskällaren	2
Salt & Brygga	6
Smak	16
Spot	10
Systrar & Bröder	15

■ BARS, CLUBS & LIVE-MUSIC VENUES

Babel	9
Bishops Arms	1
Fagan's	6
Harry's	4
Malmö Konserthus	7
Mello Yello	3
Moosehead	8
Musikhögskolan	7
Paddy's	2
Palladium	5
Tempo	10

■ ACCOMMODATION

Astoria	6
Baltzar	8
Best Western Royal	4
Clarion Collection Temperance	9
Elite Savoy	2
Ibis Malmö	7
Malmö Camping	11
Malmö City Vandrarhem	3
Mayfair Tunneln	10
More	1
Renaissance Malmö	5

for more than four hundred years. To the south of the town hall, have a look inside **Apoteket Lejonet** (Lion Pharmacy – Swedish pharmacies are always named after creatures of strength): the outside is gargoyled and balconied, the inside a busy mix of inlaid woods, carvings and etched glass. From here, **Södergatan**, Malmö's main pedestrianized shopping street, leads down towards the canal. At the Stortorget end, there's a jaunty troupe of sculptured bronze musicians. On the opposite side of the square, the crumbling, step-gabled red-brick building was once the home of the sixteenth-century mayor and master of the Danish mint, Jörgen Kock. Danish coins were struck in Malmö on the site of the present Malmöhus castle (see p.174), until irate local Swedes stormed the building and destroyed it in 1534. The cellars of Jörgen's pretty home contain the *Årstiderna* restaurant (see p.178), the only entry point for visitors today. In the centre of the square, a statue of Karl X, high on his charger, presides over the city he liberated from centuries of Danish rule.

St Petri kyrka
Göran Olsgatan • Daily 10am–6pm

A block east of Stortorget, behind the Rådhus, the dark, forbidding exterior of the Gothic **St Petri kyrka** belies a light and airy interior. The church, which is effectively Malmö's cathedral, has its roots in the fourteenth century, and, although Baltic in inspiration, has ended up owing much to German influences, for it was beneath its unusually lofty and elegantly vaulted roof that the German community came to pray – probably for the continuation of the "sea silver", the herrings that brought them to Malmö in the first place. The ecclesiastical vandalism, brought by the Reformation, of whitewashing over medieval roof murals started early at St Petri; almost the whole interior turned white in 1553. Consequently, your eyes are drawn not to the roof but to the pulpit and a four-tiered altarpiece, both of striking workmanship and elaborate embellishment. The only part of the church left with its original artwork was a side-chapel, the **Krämare** (merchant's).

Lilla torg
Despite the size of Stortorget, it still proved too small to suffice as the town's sole main square, so in the sixteenth century **Lilla torg** was tacked onto its southwest corner, over a patch of marshland. With its half-timbered houses, flowerpots and cobbles, this is where most locals and tourists congregate. During the day, people come to take a leisurely drink in one of the many bars and wander around the summer jewellery stalls. At night, Lilla torg explodes in a frenzy of activity, the venues all merging into a mass of bodies who converge from all over the city and beyond.

Form/Design Center
Lilla torg 9 • Tues–Sat 11am–5pm, Sun noon–4pm • Free • ⓦ formdesigncenter.com

Head under the arch on Lilla torg to get to the **Form/Design Center**. Built into a seventeenth-century grain store, it concentrates on Swedish contemporary design in textiles, ceramics and furniture. It's all well presented, if a little pretentious. The courtyard entrance contains several small trendy boutiques and there's a simple café.

Moderna Muséet
Modern Museum • Gasverksgatan 22 • Tues–Sun 11am–6pm • 50kr • ⓦ modernamuseet.se

A few streets removed from the other sights of the old town, **Moderna Muséet** is well worth a visit if you're interested in contemporary art. This new museum is housed in an elaborately designed building, the Rooseum, dating from 1900 and originally the home of Malmö electricity company's steam turbines. The structure has been turned into

5

several galleries, playing host to temporary exhibitions of the museum's rich collection from 1900 onwards, as well as classics of modern art from the likes of Matisse, Picasso and Dalí.

Malmöhus and around

Malmöhusvägen 6 • Daily: June–Aug 10am–4pm; Sept–May noon–4pm • 40kr • Ⓦ malmo.se

Take any of the streets running west from Stortorget or Lilla torg and you soon come up against the edge of **Kungsparken**, within striking distance of the fifteenth-century castle of **Malmöhus**. For a more head-on approach, walk west (away from the station) up Citadellsvägen; from here the low castle, with its grassy ramparts and two circular keeps, is straight ahead over the wide moat. It's one of Sweden's least aesthetically pleasing castles, with mean windows and patched-up brickwork, but the inside is worth a peek.

After Sweden's destruction of Denmark's mint here in 1534, the Danish king Christian III built a new fortress two years later. This was only to be of unforeseen benefit to his enemies, who, once back in control of Skåne, used it to repel an attacking Danish army in 1677. For a time a prison (its most notable inmate the earl of Bothwell, Mary Queen of Scots' third husband), the castle declined in importance once back in Swedish hands, and it was used for grain storage until becoming a museum in 1937.

The museum

Once in the **museum**, pass swiftly through the natural history section, a taxidermal Noah's Ark holding no surprises; the most rewarding part of the museum is upstairs in the so-called **art museum**, part of the historical exhibition, where an ambitious series of furnished rooms covers most modern styles, from the mid-sixteenth-century Renaissance period through Baroque, Rococo, pastel-pale Gustavian and Neoclassical. A stylish interior from the *Jugendstil* (Art Nouveau) period is also impressive, while other rooms have Functionalist and post-Functionalist interiors, with some wacky colour and texture combinations. Other sections of the historical exhibition include a display of medieval skeletons from Malmö's churchyards, showing the signs of infection with contemporary diseases like leprosy and tuberculosis – less gruesome than you might imagine. It's more interesting to head into the castle itself, with its spartan but authentic interiors.

Banérskajen

A little further west, running off Malmöhusvägen, is a tiny walkway, **Banérskajen**, lined with higgledy-piggledy fishing shacks selling fresh and smoked fish – a rare little area of traditional Malmö that contrasts with the lively pace of the rest of the city.

South of the centre

Tourists are still rarely encouraged to venture further south of the city than the canal banks that enclose the old town, but those who do are rewarded with the hip multicultural district around **Möllenvångstorget** (see opposite). The buildings and areas

---

MALMÖ'S PARKS

Malmö is justifiably proud of its beautiful **parks**, a chain of which run southwards from the grounds of Malmöhus, and there's a great deal of pleasure to be had by simply strolling around these lovely green expanses, with free guided tours on their flora and royal history also available (ask at the tourist office).

Heading south from the castle, the first park you encounter is **Kungspark**, with its graceful trees and classic sculptures, bordering the canal. Just on the south side of the curving river is **Slottsparken**, with graceful, mature trees and places to picnic; further south is the largest of the parks, **Pildammsparken**, boasting several tranquil lakes.

off **Amiralsgatan**, to the southeast, give an interesting insight into Malmö's mix of cultures and its Social Democratic roots (the city has been at the forefront of left-wing politics for the last century, and was central to the creation and development of Sweden's Social Democratic Party). Around **Fersens väg**, several blocks west of Amiralsgatan, there are some charming enclaves of antique shops, cafés and quirky buildings, and the impressive Konsthall art exhibition centre.

South towards the Konsthall

Heading south from Malmöhus along Slottsgatan, first cross over Regementsgatan and then cut across three blocks east to cobbled Södra Förstadsgatan; at no. 4 is a splendid house designed in 1904, its National Romantic facade covered with flower and animal motifs. A little further along the same road at no. 18, the **Victoriateatern** is Sweden's oldest still-operating cinema, dating from 1912; it's all fine Art Nouveau swirls of dark oak and bevelled glass. Back on Fersens väg (the southward continuation of Slottsgatan after crossing Regementsgatan), you'll pass the city **theatre** on your right, with its amusing sculpture of tiers of people – the naked supporting the clothed on their shoulders.

Konsthall

Arts Centre • St Johannesgatan 7 • Daily 11am–5pm, Wed until 9pm • Free • ⓦ konsthall.malmo.se.

Arriving at St Johannesgatan, head for the single-storey glass and concrete building at no. 7: the **Konsthall**, an enormous white-painted space showing vast modern works in regular temporary exhibitions. There's lots of room to stand back and take in the visual feast.

Folkets park

From the canal, head east along Regementsgatan and turn right into Amiralsgatan, from where it's a ten-minute walk south to **Folkets park**, Sweden's oldest existing public park, which was once the pride of the community. Recently restored with an elegant new water feature at the Möllevången exit, Folkets park contains a basic amusement park, and at its centre, a ballroom named the **Moriskan**, an odd, low building with Russian-style golden domes topped with crescents. Both the park and the ballroom are now privately owned, a far cry from the original aims of the park's Social Democratic founders. Severe carved busts of these city fathers are dotted all over the park. The socialist agitator August Palm made the first of his several historic speeches here in 1881, marking the beginning of a 66-year period of unbroken Social Democratic rule in Sweden.

South to Möllevångstorget

More interesting than the giant twirling teacup fun rides in Folkets park is the multicultural character of the city south from here. Strolling from the park's southern exit down Möllevången to **Möllevångstorget**, you enter an area populated almost entirely by people of non-Swedish descent, where Arab, Asian and Balkan émigré families predominate. The vast square is a haven of exotic food stores, side by side with shops selling pure junk and more recently established Chinese restaurants and karaoke pubs. On a hot summer afternoon it's easy to forget you're in Sweden at all, the more makeshift and ramshackle atmosphere around the bright fruit and veg stands contrasting with the clean, clinical order of the average Swedish neighbourhood. It's worth taking a close look at the provocative **sculpture** at the square's centre: four naked, bronze men strain under the colossal weight of a huge chunk of rock bearing carved representations of Malmö's smoking chimneys, while two naked women press their hands into the men's backs in support. It's a poignant image, marrying toil in a city founded on limestone-quarrying with the Social Democratic vision of the working man's struggle.

5

THE ÖRESUND BRIDGE

Linking Malmö with Copenhagen in Denmark (and thus Sweden with the rest of continental Europe), the elegant **Öresund bridge** was finally completed in 1999, after a forty-year debate. From Lernacken, a few kilometres south of Malmö, the bridge runs to a 4km-long artificial island off the Danish coast, from where an immersed tunnel carries traffic and trains across to the mainland – a total distance of 16km. The bridge itself has two levels, the upper for a four-lane highway and the lower for two sets of train tracks, and comprises three sections: a central high bridge, spanning 1km, and approach bridges to either side, each over 3km long. In December 2010, **Citytunneln**, a new underground rail tunnel was opened beneath the city, speeding trains directly into the heart of Malmö from Denmark; the journey to Copenhagen is faster and more frequent as a result.

The Turning Torso

From the western side of Malmöhus, Malmö's most breathtaking sight looms on the horizon: the **Turning Torso**. An easy walk north along Mariedalsvägen, crossing the canal over Varvsbron, leads you to Västra Varvsgatan, which streaks in a straight line to the city's Västra Hamnen district, home to the **skyscraper** that bears down on you as you approach. The tallest building in Scandinavia, this sleek, twisting tower of steel curves 90° clockwise as it rises to a height of 190m above the ground. It was designed to reshape the city skyline that had been dominated for decades by the massive Kockum shipyard crane, and now houses luxury flats and penthouses.

Malmö's beaches

Ribersborg kallbadhus: Contact for opening hours • ☎ 040 26 03 66, ⓦ ribban.com • Bus #32 runs here from the centre of town

Separated from the Turning Torso by delightful **Ribersborg park**, Malmö's long stretch of sandy **beaches** stretches several kilometres to the old limestone-quarrying area of Limhamn to the southwest. Fringed by dunes and grassland, the beaches, popular with young families as the water remains shallow for several metres out to sea, are numbered according to the jetty which gives access into the water. At jetty #1, the **Ribersborgs kallbadhus** is a cold-water bathhouse offering separate-sex **nude bathing** areas and sauna whilst the last jetty, #10, denotes Malmö's popular **nudist beach**.

ARRIVAL AND DEPARTURE · MALMÖ

By train Malmö's newly rebuilt Centralstation is on two levels; all services to and from Denmark use the underground platforms.
Destinations Berlin (1 daily; 8hr 30min); Copenhagen via Kastrup airport (every 20min; 20min); Gothenburg (hourly; 3hr); Helsingborg (hourly; 40min); Karlskrona (hourly; 3hr); Lund (very frequent; 12min); Stockholm (hourly; 4hr 20min); Ystad (hourly; 50min).

By bus The main bus terminal is in the square immediately outside the train station. Since the train service is so comprehensive, though, you're unlikely to use buses much, unless heading to Skanör (6 daily; 50min). For long-distance bus information call Skånetrafiken on ☎ 0771 77 77 77.

INFORMATION

Tourist office Opposite Centralstation at Skeppsbron 2 (late June–Aug Mon–Fri 9am–7pm, Sat & Sun 9am–4pm; Sept–May Mon–Fri 9am–5pm, Sat & Sun 10am–2.30pm; ☎ 040 34 12 00, ⓦ malmotown.com). Offers a wealth of free information, including the English-language listings brochure *Malmö Guide*, and free internet access.

GETTING AROUND

By bus Although the city centre is easy to walk around, its central squares and streets all interlinked, you'll need to use the city bus service to reach some of the sights and places to stay. You cannot buy tickets on the bus so instead get a prepaid travel pass (see opposite).
By taxi Several taxi companies in Malmö operate a fixed-price system within the city and surrounding area, but you should always agree the price before you start your journey. To give a rough idea of costs, a trip across the centre costs around 150kr. Taxi 97 ☎ 040 97 97 97, Taxi Kurir ☎ 040 700 00, Taxi Skåne ☎ 040 33 03 30.

By boat Canal boat tours, known as Rundan Sightseeing,

5

THE MALMÖ CARD

The very useful **Malmökortet** (Malmö Card; available for 1 or 2 days at 170kr and 200kr respectively) entitles you to free museum entry, free parking at public car parks and unlimited bus journeys within town. It also gives various other discounts on certain sights. Pick up *The Malmö Card* leaflet from the tourist office for full details or check ⓦ malmotown.com.

make a fun way of seeing the city; they leave daily from the canal opposite the *Elite Savoy* hotel (late April to Sept daily 11am–7pm; 50min; 120kr; ⓦ rundan.se). Alternatively, pedal boats let you tour around the canal network at your own pace. They're moored at Amiralsbron (late April to Sept daily 11am–7pm; 130kr/hr; ⓦ cityboats.se).

By bike To strike out to the south of the city or further

afield, bike rental is a good idea. The best place is Fridhems Cykelaffär at Tessins väg 13 (☎ 040 26 03 35): head down Citadellsvägen past Malmöhus, take the first left, Mariedalsvägen, then right into Tessins väg. Otherwise, try Cykelkliniken, Regementsgatan 12, across the canal from Gustav Adolfs torg (☎ 040 611 66 66), where a day's rental is 120kr.

ACCOMMODATION

There are some really good and surprisingly affordable **hotels** in Malmö; the city is eager to attract tourists, and competition between the hotels can be fierce. Most hotels can be booked online at ⓦ malmo.se/hotellbokning where special deals are sometimes also available.

Astoria Gråbrödersgatan 7 ☎ 040 786 60, ⓦ hotelastoria.se. A few minutes from the train station across the canal, this is a good, comfortable hotel with wooden floors and modern Scandinavian decor, worth checking out for its weekend and summer prices. **1000kr/1395kr**

Baltzar Södergatan 20 ☎ 040 665 57 00, ⓦ baltzarhotel.se. Very central (between the two main squares), this is a swanky place done out in swags and flourishes that are more British than Swedish in design with chandeliers and handwoven carpets rather than polished wood floors throughout. **855kr/1400kr**

★ **Best Western** Royal Norra Vallgatan 94 ☎ 040 664 25 00, ⓦ www.bwhotelroyal.se. Exceptionally cosy rooms for a chain hotel (this was until recently a long-standing family-run place) whose modern interiors really are a home from home. The anonymous chain hotel feel has yet to pervade this winning little place. **895kr/1435kr**

Clarion Collection Temperance Engelbrektsgatan 16 ☎ 040 710 20, ⓦ choice.se. As you would expect from the Choice chain, rooms are first-class, modern and classically Swedish in design with polished dark wood floors, cosy furnishings and top facilities including a sauna and

solarium. Free evening buffet included. **1090kr/1590kr**

Elite Savoy Norra Vallgatan 62 ☎ 040 664 48 00, ⓦ savoy.elite.se. This is where Lenin, Bardot and Dietrich all stayed, with a brass plaque to prove it. Now part of the upmarket Elite chain, it's lost its edge but the rooms are big and very comfortable, and the extensive breakfast is an experience in itself. **850kr/1650kr**

Ibis Malmö Stadiongatan 21 ☎ 040 672 85 70, ⓦ ibishotel.com; bus #34. Although a 30–45min walk from the centre, the prices at this simple yet functional place make up for the inconvenience. Just 150kr gets you a bigger room with better facilities. **599kr/895kr**

Malmö City Vandrarhem Rönngatan 1 ☎ 040/611 62 20, ✉ malmo.city@stfturist.se. This great STF hostel, which even boasts its own roof terrace, has a variety of dorms sleeping up to six people. Sixteen rooms have en-suite facilities. Check-in is 4–7pm. Dorms **230kr**, doubles **560kr**

Mayfair Tunneln Adelgatan 4 ☎ 040 10 16 20, ⓦ themayfairhotel.se. Very central luxury place and one of the finest of Malmö's more intimate hotels. Rooms are well furnished in cherry and Gustavian pastels. A sumptuous buffet breakfast is served in the vaulted cellar restaurant. **855kr/1140kr**

SKÅNE TRAVEL PASS

An amazing money-saver if you're spending any significant time in Skåne is **Jojo Sommar** (summer travel pass). For 485kr, it allows unlimited journeys between mid-June and mid-Aug on buses and trains throughout Skåne. It comes as a smartcard which you buy at Skånetrafiken information centres throughout the province, Pressbyrån newsagents or 7-Eleven stores. Alternatively, a 24hr/72hr **travel pass** valid for the whole of Skåne at any time of year costs 195kr/395kr respectively. Buy this most easily from Skånetrafiken information centres. More information on all tickets is at ⓦ skanetrafiken.se.

5

★ **More** Amiralsgatan 12 ☎ 040 795 94, ⓦ themorehotel.com. Good-value and stylishly decorated studio rooms and small apartments for rent in a renovated and central former chocolate factory close to Konserthuset. All rooms have kitchen facilities, sitting areas and private bathroom. 975kr/1575kr

Renaissance Malmö Mäster Johansgatan 15 ☎ 040 24 85 00, ⓦ marriott.com. Built within Malmö's former Saluhallen indoor market, this is the city's most luxurious hotel with contemporary chic at every turn: soft lighting in purples and pinks, floral wall patterns and fresh flowers throughout. 973kr/1840kr

CAMPING

Malmö Camping Strandgatan 101 in Limhamn ☎ 040 15 51 65, ⓦ firstcamp.se; bus #34 from town. This vast but pleasant campsite is not far from the Öresund bridge; it's located right by the sea and has great views across to Denmark. Also has a number of cottages for rent. Open all year. Tents 140kr, cottages 700kr

EATING AND DRINKING

Between Malmö's many **eating places** you're bound to find something to whet your appetite. Over recent years the influx of immigrants (and second-generation Swedes) has created a demand for all types of cuisine, not just traditional Swedish. Most of Malmö's restaurants, brasseries and cafés are concentrated in and around its three central squares, with Lilla torg attracting the biggest crowds. For cheaper eats and a very un-Swedish atmosphere, head south of the centre to Möllenvångstorget, the heart of Malmö's immigrant community.

CAFÉS

Café Siesta Hjorttackegatan 1 ☎ 040 611 10 27. A great little café with stark white walls and leather stools serving light Scandinavian lunches such as a tasty open sandwiches with salmon, herring or prawns (55kr), Janssons frestelse (85kr) and beef with lingonberries (129kr). Mon 4–11pm, Tues–Thurs & Sun 11.30am–11pm, Fri & Sat 11.30am–12.30am.

Espresso House Skomakaregatan 2 ☎ 040 510 11 01. Close to both Stora and Lilla torg. Part of the excellent chain, this one serves great chocolate cake, muffins and ciabattas, and a delicious Chai *latte* flavoured with cloves and cardamom. Mon–Fri 7.30am–8pm, Sat 9am–7pm, Sun 10am–6pm.

Gustav Adolf Gustav Adolfs torg 43 ☎ 040 611 22 72. Long established and stylishly renovated with rough brick walls and floral wallpaper, this is still a popular spot, for coffee and cakes and its Sun brunch buffet for 159kr. Mon–Thurs & Sun 11am–11pm, Fri & Sat 11am–1am.

Hollandia Södra Förstadsgatan 8 ☎ 040 12 48 86. The oldest café in Malmö, dating from 1905, a classic *konditori* with marble busts, chandeliers and a window full of breads and pastries. The house speciality is mouthwatering chocolate cake. Mon–Fri 8am–7pm, Sat 9am–5.30pm, Sun 11am–6pm.

Systrar & Bröder Östra Rönneholmsvägen 26 ☎ 040 97 34 70. Superb breads, cakes and a full range of ciabattas plus a great-value daily breakfast buffet for just 65kr are on offer at this hip joint with leatherette bench seats and a 1960s ambience. Mon–Fri 7.30am–6pm, Sat 8am–3pm, Sun 9am–3pm.

RESTAURANTS

Årstiderna Frans Suellsgatan 3 ☎ 040 23 09 10. This fine old basement restaurant with rough brick walls and period furniture is *the* place for classic Swedish dishes. Its four-course Swedish menu with whitefish roe, herb-baked reindeer fillet, Västerbotten cheese and finally cloudberries with ice cream is 595kr. Mon–Fri 11.30am–midnight, Sat 5pm–midnight.

Atmosfär Fersens väg 4 ☎ 040 12 50 77. Stylish to a T, this chi-chi brasserie serves a blend of accomplished Swedish and Mediterranean dishes such as steak tartare with capers and Vänern fish roe with onion and crème fraîche; mains 120kr. Mon–Fri 11.30am–2pm & 5pm–1am, Sat 5pm–1am.

Bastard Mäster Johansgatan 11 4 ☎ 040 12 13 18. The place to sample modern European home cooking, as interpreted by one of Sweden's top chefs, with plenty of odd off-cuts and unusual ingredients (hence the name) such as ox heart, pig's neck and livers of various origins. Tues–Thurs 5pm–midnight, Fri & Sat 5pm–2am.

Epicuré Bröd & Vin Generalsgatan 4 ☎ 040 97 11 00. Discreetly located and wonderfully rustic Italian restaurant with mosaic-topped tables and a superb menu based on the cuisine of southern Italy which changes daily; mains 88–179kr. Rear courtyard open in summer. Mon–Sat 11.30am–10pm.

★ **Indian Side** Lilla torg 7 ☎ 040 30 77 44. Stylish Indian brasserie in a half-timbered building from around 1600 with outdoor seating, too: all the classics are here such as rogan josh and chicken tikka masala at quite respectable prices. Reckon on 150kr for a main course, 28–75kr for a starter. Mon–Fri & Sun 11.30am–10pm, Fri & Sat 11.30am–1am.

Johan P Landbygatan 5 ☎ 040 97 18 18. This place has a good reputation for totally delicious fish dishes and the selection of fresh fish is the best in the city, although it doesn't come cheap: grilled turbot is 398kr, smoked eel is 250kr and bouillebaisse is 198kr. Mon–Thurs 11.30am–10pm, Fri 11.30am–11pm, Sat noon–11pm, Sun 1–9pm.

★ **Krua Thai** Möllevångstorget 14 ☎ 040 12 22 87. In the big square south of the city centre, this informal and unlicensed restaurant serves the best Thai food in town with mains such as pad thai or massamam curry for a reasonable 89kr. Mon 11am–3pm, Tues–Fri 11am–3pm & 5–10pm, Sat 1–10pm, Sun 2–10pm.

★ **Mando Steakhouse** Skomakaregatan 4 ☎ 040 780 00. All meat at this inordinately popular steakhouse with curious copper-plated interior walls comes from local farms and is grilled over lava stones to give it a special barbecue flavour. Mains cost 99–218kr. Mon–Fri 11.30am till late, Sat noon till late.

Nyhavn Möllevångstorget 8 ☎ 040 12 88 30. A Danish restaurant run by a Danish-Turkish émigré, with old Danish newspapers adorning the walls. Chief among the offerings are *smørrebrod* with all manner of possible toppings, plus rich Danish meals, all for around 150kr. Outdoor seating available. Daily 11am–1am.

Rådhuskällaren Stortorget 1 ☎ 040 790 20. This restaurant is housed in the long vaulted cellars of the gloriously decorated town hall. The emphasis here is on traditional Swedish dishes such as venison with hash browns and mushroom gravy (235kr) and elk burger with sea buckthorn gelée and juniper sauce (189kr). Mon–Wed 5–10pm, Thurs–Sat 5–11pm.

★ **Salt & Brygga** Sundspromenaden 7 ☎ 040 611 59 40. Superb location by the water's edge in Västra Hamnen with superb views of the Öresund bridge. Everything on the menu here is organic with seasonal specialities such as a delicious nettle soup. A three-course set menu is 395kr or 450kr. Mon–Fri 11.30am–3pm & 5–9pm, Sat 12.30–9pm.

Smak St Johannesgatan 7 ☎ 040 50 50 35. Inside the Konsthall building, this relaxed café-restaurant does a good line in vegetarian, organic meat and fish dishes using locally sourced ingredients. It's also a very popular place for weekend brunch. Daily 11am–5pm.

Spot Stora Nygatan 33 ☎ 040 12 02 03. An extremely popular and chic Italian trattoria with tiled walls and floor serving good Italian fare at sensible prices: ricotta and spinach tortellini, for example, or pasta with pesto and bacon, both 119kr. Mon–Thurs 11.30am–9pm, Fri 11.30am–10pm, Sat 11am–10pm, Sun noon–6pm.

NIGHTLIFE AND ENTERTAINMENT

Gone are the days when the only entertainment in Malmö was watching rich drunks become poor drunks at the blackjack table in the Centralstation bar. Nowadays there are some decent **live-music** venues and **discos**, most of which are cheaper to get into than their other European counterparts. For **drinking**, Lilla torg is where Malmöites and tourists alike head in the evenings. The square buzzes with activity, as the smell of beer wafts between the old, beamed houses, and music and chatter fill the air. With a largely 20- and 30-something crowd, the atmosphere is like that of a summer carnival.

BARS

Bishops Arms Norra Vallgatan 62 ☎ 040 664 48 88. This is a cosy but rather staid pub with a heavy-handed insistence on looking British. However, it does have an impressive range of beers on tap. Mon & Tues 4pm–midnight, Wed–Sat 4pm–1am, Sun 4–11pm.

Fagan's Per Weijersgatan 4 ☎ 040 97 09 90. Malmö's leading Irish pub with lots of whiskeys and Irish beers available. At happy hour (Mon–Thurs 4–6pm, Fri 3–7pm) the place is absolutely packed. Thurs is quiz night; on Fri and Sat nights there's live music. Mon & Tues 4–11pm, Wed 4pm–midnight, Thurs 4pm–1am, Fri 3pm–2am, Sat 2pm–2am, Sun 3–10pm.

Harry's Södergatan 14 ☎ 040 12 34 90. People start arriving here from 3pm onwards to make the most of the happy hours that run Mon–Fri until 6pm. There's also a popular nightclub here on Fri and Sat nights. Mon 1–11pm, Tues–Thurs 1pm–midnight, Fri 1–4am, Sat noon–4am, Sun noon–5pm.

Mello Yello Lilla torg 1 ☎ 040 30 45 25. A popular haunt for the 25-plus age group. Lots of people come here to enjoy a bite to eat as well as a drink and there's a good choice of burgers and steaks. Gets lively as the night progresses. Mon–Fri 3.30pm–1am, Sat & Sun noon–1am.

Moosehead Lilla torg 1 ☎ 040 12 04 23. With rough brick walls and a gorgeous stucco cornice, this stylish bar is one of the most fun places to drink and a firm favourite with the 20-somethings– and it's known for its great burgers, too. Mon–Thurs 4pm–1am, Fri 3pm–1am, Sat noon–1am, Sun noon–11pm.

THE MALMÖ FESTIVAL

Every August Malmö plays host to the annual **Malmöfestivalen** (ⓦ malmofestivalen.se), one of the biggest in Sweden. Sprawling across the city from the parks around Malmöhus to Stortorget and Gustav Adolfs torg, the festival's grand opening, always on a Friday, is marked by a giant crayfish party in Stortorget, when thousands of people bring their own crayfish and *akvavit* to sing and dance the night away. Over the eight days, there's free music and entertainment across the city. World food is dished up from a multitude of stalls: Pakistani, Somali and Bosnian dishes alongside more traditional elk kebabs and Swedish pancakes.

5

Paddy's Kalendegatan 7 ☎ 040 786 00. This is a laid-back place for a drink right in the centre of town, known for its good Guinness. Pub quizzes on Mon, live music on Fri and Sat with soul and funk covers. Mon & Tues 4pm–midnight, Wed & Thurs 4pm–1am, Fri & Sat 4pm–2am.

Tempo Södra Skolgatan 30 ☎ 040 12 60 21. This compact little bar close to Möllevångstorget is always packed with students and would-be musicians who come here to relax and enjoy the music chosen by the resident DJ. Mon & Tues 5pm–midnight, Wed & Thurs 5pm–1am, Fri & Sat 4pm–1am.

LIVE-MUSIC VENUES

Babel Spånggatan 38 ☎ 040 10 30 20, ⓦ babelmalmo.se. *The* place to see live music in Malmö

with latest appearances advertised online. Club nights, too, are inordinately popular, especially on Wed. Times vary.

Malmö Konserthus Föreningsgatan 35 ☎ 040 34 35 00, ⓦ mso.se. Classical music performances take place here, at the home of the Malmö Symphony Orchestra. Check with the tourist office for programme details. Times vary.

Musikhögskolan Ystadvägen 25 ☎ 040 32 54 50. Classical music venue. Check with the tourist office for programme details.

Palladium Södergatan 15 ☎ 040 10 30 20, ⓦ palladium.nu. A good place to see live music and dance performances, with a variety of Scandinavian R&B and rock bands playing in the original 1920s interior. Times vary.

DIRECTORY

Doctor On call ☎ 1177.

Internet access Sidewalk Express have several internet points across Malmö, for example, at Centralstation and at the 7-Eleven supermarkets at Baltzargatan 22 and Södra

Förstadsgatan 78A. See ⓦ sidewalkexpress.se for complete listings.

Pharmacy Apoteket Gripen, Bergsgatan 48 (daily 8am–10pm).

Skanör and around

Leaving Malmö, it's barely 30km due south along the E6 and then Route 100 to Sweden's most southwesterly point and the adjoining medieval town of **SKANÖR**, site of a tremendous beach and nature reserve, plus a remarkable Viking-style settlement at nearby **Foteviken**.

Skanör was once an important commercial centre and was founded as part of the Hanseatic commercial system. In the early twentieth century, the town became a fashionable bathing resort for wealthy Malmö families. Today, Skanör's simple pleasures lie in wandering through the medieval streets and admiring the pretty half-timbered houses around the main square, Rådhustorget, and along Mellangatan.

Sankt Olofs kyrka

Kyrkogatan 5 • Mon–Fri 8am–4pm

In all probability, Skanör's church, **Sankt Olofs kyrka**, dates from the early 1200s though over the following centuries it was extended and its windows, in particular, are High Gothic. It's also one of very few churches in the south of Sweden to have a crypt. When the herring stocks in the Baltic disappeared in the sixteenth century, the town lost its importance, and so the church was never updated, making it all the more appealing today.

The beaches

There's not much to see in Skanör itself, but its **beaches** are superb: long ribbons of white sand bordering an extensive **bird and nature reserve**. North of the town centre, a 5km-long sandy strand stretches out to a point known as **Svanrevet**, where there's a well-known and popular **nudist beach;** simply take the footpath which leads north from Kyrkogatan out towards the beach. Close by is the splendid **Flommen nature reserve**, dominated by wetland meadows carpeted with blue butterfly iris, and sea-holly sprouting between the sand dunes.

A few kilometres to the south of Skanör is Sweden's oldest nature reserve, **Näbben**, one of twelve on the peninsula here. It's home to a huge population of birds – on a good day in September or October you can spot more than fifty species. You can walk southwards, towards the tip of the peninsula, passing the splendid **Ule näbbe beach** on the way, to Sweden's oldest **lighthouse**, Kolabacken, whose beam was created by burning charcoal. At the very tip is the **Måkläppen spit**, a nature reserve known as a refuge for both grey and harbour seals (closed Feb–Oct).

Foteviken Viking Museum

Museivägen 24, Höllviken • May & early Sept Tues–Fri 10am–4pm, June–Aug daily 10am–4pm • 80kr • ☎ 040 33 08 00, ⓦ foteviken.se

Barely 9km east of Skanör, the **Foteviken Viking Museum**, just outside the village of Höllviken (follow the signs), is reputedly located at a pagan sacrificial site, **Foteviken**, which was a market town and centre for herring fishing during Viking times. Today, the whole area has been transformed into a working **Viking-style village** comprising houses, workshops, a sacrificial temple and shipyard – a virtually self-sufficient settlement with an astonishing ring of authenticity. The idea was to show the way of life here in the twelfth century, but more than this, the place has become a magnet for people from all over Europe who want to live as Vikings, together with a not inconsiderable number of characters sporting wild beards and lots of beads, who firmly believe they *are* Vikings.

The village

The resulting atmosphere is that of a hippy commune in a time warp. Everyone dresses entirely in home-spun garments of loose, coarse linen, coloured with dyes made from local grasses and herbs. The villagers' simply crafted footwear is made from leather which they cure themselves, and if you wander into the **cure-houses** you'll see the pelts of locally caught mink – along with elk and wild-boar hides donated by local abattoirs. Dotted around the ever-growing village are ant-hill-like **kilns** and **clay ovens** used to bake bread and fire the bowls from which the villagers eat.

Weavers' cottage

Hidden in among the two dozen or so dwelling houses, look out for the **weavers' cottage** which contains the village's answer to the Bayeux Tapestry: a wall-hanging here depicts the Battle of Foteviken of June 4, 1134, in which King Nils of Denmark is seen trying to reconquer Skåne from the rebellious pretender Erik Emune. And it's worth heading down to the shore where longships, based on the designs of excavated wrecks, are built.

ACCOMMODATION   SKANÖR AND AROUND

Fotevikens Stugby Museivägen 24, Höllviken ☎ 040 33 08 05, ⓦ fotevikensstugby.se. The holiday village next to the Viking museum contains a number of comfortable four- and eight-bed log cabins which can be rented by the day or week, each with kitchenette and bathroom. **670kr/770kr**

Hotell Gässlingen Rådhustorget 6 ☎ 040 45 91 00, ⓦ hotel-gasslingen.com. Located a few metres from

Skanör's town hall, this is an elegant and charming place to stay with its own swimming pool and fitness centre. Perfect for a taste of luxury close to nature. **1850kr**

Spelabäcken Mellangatan 58 ☎ 040 47 53 00, ⓦ spelabacken.se. A pleasant, small hotel which boasts a sauna and solarium but is less ornate than its sister establishment, the *Gässlingen*. It has a perfect location on pretty Mellangatan right at the heart of the town. **1195kr**

EATING

Fiskrögeri Hamngatan ☎ 040 47 40 50. This simple, elegant restaurant at the harbour serves superb fish dishes, with a remarkable range of smoked and pickled fish; 102kr buys a plate of five varieties of herring. April, May & Sept Thurs & Fri 6–10pm, Sat noon–10pm, Sun noon–8pm; June–Aug Mon–Sat noon–11pm, Sun noon–10pm.

Skanörs Gästgifvaregård Mellangatan 13 ☎ 040 47 56 90. This restaurant has a reputation for well-prepared, local produce served in sizeable proportions in a historic setting including pan-fried halibut and duck breast with chanterelle mushrooms; mains are 195–275kr. Mon–Fri 11.30am–2pm & 5–10pm, Sat 1–10pm, Sun 1–8pm.

5 Ystad

An hour by local train from Malmö, the medieval market town of **YSTAD** is exquisitely well preserved and boasts a prettiness that may come as a surprise if you've arrived at the train station down by the murky docks. In the historic centre though, you can marvel at the quaint, cobbled lanes, lined with cross-timbered cottages, and the town's chocolate-box central square, oozing rural charm. With the stunningly beautiful coastal region of Österlen stretching northeast from town all the way to Kristianstad (see p.186), Ystad is a splendid place to base yourself for a day or so. It also offers the option of a quick hop to the Danish island of Bornholm (see p.184).

Stortorget

Leaving the train or bus stations or the ferry terminals, head west until you reach Hamngatan, where you take a right up the street. This brings you to the well-proportioned **Stortorget**, a grand old square around which twist picturesque streets. West of the church here is Mattorget, a small square, away from which leads Lilla Västergatan, the main street in the seventeenth and eighteenth centuries; strolling down it today, you'll see the best of the town's Lilliputian cottages.

St Maria kyrka

Stortorget • Daily 10am–4pm

In Stortorget itself, the thirteenth-century **St Maria kyrka** is a handsome centrepiece, with additions dating from nearly every century since it was built. In the 1880s, these rich decorative features were removed, as they were thought "unsightly", and only the most interesting ones were put back during a restoration programme forty years later. Inside, the Baroque early seventeenth-century pulpit is worth a look for the fearsome face carved beneath it, while opposite is the somewhat chilling medieval crucifix,

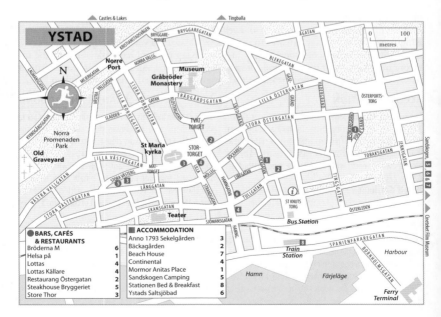

● BARS, CAFÉS & RESTAURANTS	
Bröderna M	6
Helsa på	1
Lottas	4
Lottas Källare	4
Restaurang Östergatan	2
Steakhouse Bryggeriet	5
Store Thor	3

■ ACCOMMODATION	
Anno 1793 Sekelgården	3
Bäckagården	2
Beach House	7
Continental	4
Mormor Anitas Place	1
Sandskogen Camping	5
Stationen Bed & Breakfast	8
Ystads Saltsjöbad	6

WALLANDER COUNTRY

Kurt Wallander, the anti-hero of author Henning Mankell's crime novels, is one of Sweden's best-known fictional characters. Millions of people across the world have followed Wallander's investigations as he hurries through Ystad's streets, the location for the novels and the spin-off TV series. With the tourist office's special guide in hand, fans can set off in search of some of the town's most famous fictional sites such as Wallander's apartment on Mariagatan and his favourite café, *Fridolfs*. In line with Mankell's no-nonsense approach to his fame, he specifically requested that there should not be a Wallander theme park in Ystad.

---

placed here on the orders of Karl XII to remind the preacher of Christ's suffering. The figure of Christ wears a mop of actual human hair – sacrificed by a local parishioner in the nineteenth century, in an attempt to make it look realistic. Notice also the green box pews to either side of the entrance, which were reserved for women who had not yet been received back into the church after childbirth.

Norra Promenaden

Not far from Stortorget, up Lilla or Stora Norregatan, is **Norreport**, the original northern arched entrance to the town. From here, you can stroll through **Norra Promenaden**, an avenue lined with mature horse-chestnut trees and surrounded by parkland. Here you'll find a white pavilion, built in the 1870s to house a genteel café and a dance hall with a brass band.

The monastery

June–Aug Mon–Fri 10am–5pm, Sat & Sun noon–4pm; Sept–May Tues–Fri noon–5pm, Sat & Sun noon–4pm • 30kr • Ⓦ klostret.ystad.se

Another short stroll from Stortorget, past Garvaregränd's art-and-craft workshops (one of which, Krukmakaren, is in a fantastically higgledy-piggledy house on the right), then up Klostergatan, brings you to the town's thirteenth-century **monastery**, now a simple **museum**. The collection is pretty standard local history paraphernalia, but given piquancy by its medieval surroundings. After the monks were driven out during the Reformation, the monastery declined and was used, among other things, as a hospital and a distillery, before becoming a museum in the early twentieth century. The museum has a small **café** serving coffee and cake for 30kr. Brightly painted low cottages line the streets around here; a brief stroll down the most picturesque of these, **Vädergränd**, off Lilla Östergatan, makes for a worthwhile foray. Look particularly at no. 4 – the 1727 Gamla Handtwerfargården, a grocery in a timewarp.

THE NIGHT BUGLER OF YSTAD

Staying in Ystad, you'll soon get acquainted with a tradition that harks back to the seventeenth century: from a room in St Maria church watchtower, a night watchman (*tornväktaren*) sounds a **bugle** every fifteen minutes from 9.15pm to 1am. The haunting sound isn't disturbing, though it's audible wherever you stay in the centre. The sounding through the night was to assure the town that the watchman was still awake (until the mid-nineteenth century, he was liable to be executed if he slept on duty); however, the real purpose of this activity was as a safeguard against the outbreak of **fire**. The idea was that if one of the thatched cottages went up in flames, the bugle would sound repeatedly for all to go and help extinguish the blaze. The melancholic bellowing only ceased during World War II, though then the residents complained they couldn't sleep in the unbroken silence. If you look carefully from Stortorget, you can just see the instrument appear at little openings in the tower walls each time it's played.

5

Cineteket Film Museum

Elis Nilssons väg 8, beyond the eastern end of Regementsgatan • Daily except Fri 10am–6pm • 50k, tours 75kr • ☎0411 57 70 57, ⓦ ystad.se/cineteket

In addition to a self-guided walking tour of Ystad, *Wallander* fans may wish to visit the town's new **Cineteket Film Museum** to see inside a real film studio where, amongst other productions, the BBC *Wallander* films were recorded, and to learn about film production techniques. There's also a chance to take part in a three-hour guided tour of locations used in the films.

ARRIVAL AND DEPARTURE   YSTAD

By train From the train station, cross over the tracks to the square, St Knuts torg, where buses from Lund and Kristianstad will also drop you off.
Destinations Malmö (every 30min; 50min); Copenhagen via Kastrup airport (5 daily; 1hr 20min).
By ferry The ferry terminals for the Danish island of

Bornholm and Swinoujscie in Poland are 300m southeast of the train station.
Destinations Bornholm (3–5 daily; 1hr 20min; ⓦ bornholmerfaergen.dk); Swinoujscie (2 daily; 6hr 30min–9hr; ⓦ polferries.se).

INFORMATION

Tourist office St Knuts torg (mid-June to Aug Mon–Fri 9am–7pm, Sat 10am–6pm, Sun 11am–6pm; rest of year Mon–Fri 9am–5pm; ☎0411 57 76 81, ⓦ visitosterlen.se). Has internet access and can supply copies of a 1753 map of Ystad that's still a serviceable guide to the old streets and

the *Wallander* walking guide.
Bike rental Bikes – a great way to see the surrounding cycle-friendly landscape – can be rented from Roslin Cykel, Jennygatan 11 (☎0411 123 15), just east of the bus and train terminals.

ACCOMMODATION

There are several good and reasonably priced **hotels** in town, and one at the beach. Prices are considerably less than Malmö so if money is tight, staying here and travelling up to Malmö will save lots.

★ **Anno 1793 Sekelgården** Långgatan 18 ☎0411 739 00, ⓦ sekelgarden.se. The best place to stay in town, this is a small family-run hotel in a merchant's house from 1793, with en-suite rooms in both the main house and the old tannery at the back. **995kr/1295kr**
Bäckagården Dammgatan 36 ☎0411 198 48, ⓦ www .backagarden.nu. A small-scale guesthouse with just eight rooms with private facilities in a beautiful, converted private town house just behind the tourist office and complete with a tranquil garden. Also a lovely common sitting room with open fire. **790kr**
Beach House Fritidsvägen 9 ☎0411 665 66, ⓦ beachhouseystad.se; 2km east of the town centre and reached by buses #304, #322 & #392. A great location for this gloriously rambling B&B set right on the beach at Sandskogen, originally built against coastal erosion. Breakfast is an extra 70kr. **685kr/895kr**
Continental Hamngatan 13 ☎0411 137 00, ⓦ hotelcontinental-ystad.se. Sweden's oldest hotel first opened its doors in 1829 and still has a grand lobby of marble, and crystal chandeliers, plus bright, comfortable rooms with parquet floors. The breakfast buffet is a treat. **1290kr/1490kr**
Mormor Anitas Place Stickgatan 13 ☎070 686 53 76, ⓦ mormoranitasplace.se. Rather elegant, upmarket B&B

with chandeliers and art on the walls in a charming eighteenth-century house in a quiet street in the town centre. There's a gorgeous courtyard garden, too, for guests' use, bedecked with flowers. **950kr**
Stationen Bed & Breakfast Spanienfararegatan 25 ☎070 857 79 95, ⓦ turistlogi.se. A perfect location for the train station and the ferries, this family-owned B&B is housed in Ystad's brick station building, right on the platform. It has comfortable, high-ceilinged rooms and there's a kitchen for self-catering, too. **800kr**
Ystads Saltsjöbad Saltsjöbadsvägen 6 ☎0411 136 30, ⓦ ysb.se. Renowned for its beachside position, just east of town, this large, 100-year-old spa resort hotel (with endless modern extensions) has a sauna, pool and a restaurant in the original saltwater bathing house which is located right on the beach. **1980kr**

CAMPING

Sandskogens Camping Fritidsvägen ☎0411 192 70, ⓦ sandskogenscamping.se; 2km east of the town centre and reached by buses #304, #322 & #392. Next to the *Beach House* B&B, in a beautiful location overlooking a large sandy beach that stretches for around 30km to the southeast. Also has cabins. Tents **140kr**, cabins **550kr**

EATING, DRINKING AND ENTERTAINMENT

There is a fair selection of places to eat in Ystad, with some atmospheric **cafés** and fine **restaurants**; most of the latter are on or around Stortorget. Ystad stages its annual **opera festival** through most of July. You can get information on performances and book tickets at the tourist office.

Bröderna M Hamngatan 11 ☎0411 19 99 99. This is the pizzeria which features in the *Wallander* novels, though today it's a cosy lounge bar and restaurant. Mains such as honey and chilli-marinated chicken with mango chutney are 175–199kr. Burgers and pizzas, too. Mon & Tues 11.30am–9pm, Wed & Thurs 11.30am–10pm, Fri 11.30am–11pm, Sat noon–11pm, Sun 2–9pm.

Helsa på Per Helsas Gård, Besökaregränd 3. Find the door to the courtyard and you'll discover a curiously old-fashioned yet bohemian café set in a half-timbered house with outdoor seating in summer. They bake all their own produce and the café is also licensed. Mon–Fri 11am–5pm, Sat 11am–3pm.

Lottas Stortorget 11 ☎0411 788 00. Justifiably the most popular restaurant in town, packed each evening in summer and serving beautifully presented, scrumptious fish and meat dishes such as oven-baked chicken with couscous and cod in white wine sauce for 142–226kr. Mon–Sat 5–10pm.

Lottas Källare Stortorget 11 ☎0411 788 00. In the cellars below *Lottas* restaurant, this cosy bar offers several English beers including the so-called "Manchester United".

It's a great place to come to meet local people as this is the most popular watering hole in town. Mon–Sat 5–10pm.

Restaurang Östergatan Stora Östergatan 1 ☎0411 55 55 88. The place for fine dining in Ystad, with linen tablecloths and chandeliers. This elegant restaurant serves expertly cooked French cuisine such as beef bearnaise with haricots verts and haddock poached in milk served with tangy horseradish. Mains 155–275kr. Mon–Thurs noon–10pm, Fri & Sat noon–midnight.

Steakhouse Bryggeriet Långgatan 20 ☎0411 699 99. The rough, beamed interior dominated by two copper beer casks creates a welcoming ambience at this meat-lover's treat. The well-cooked steaks and other meat mains are 159–215kr and there are even a couple of vegetarian dishes, too. Mon–Fri 11.30am–11pm, Sat noon–11pm, Sun 1–10pm.

Store Thor Stortorget 1 ☎0411 185 10. Located in the cellars of the fourteenth-century Rådhuset but has tables in the square in summer. Serves a decent herring platter for 109kr, chicken breast with vegetables for 195kr and lamb wrapped in bacon at 245kr. Mon–Fri 11.30am–2pm & 5pm–1am, Sat 5pm–1am.

The Österlen coast

The landscape of the southeastern corner of Skåne, known as **Österlen**, is like a Mondrian painting: horizons of sunburst-yellow fields of rape running to cobalt-blue summer skies, punctuated only by white cottages, fields of blood-red poppies and the odd black windmill. Along with the vivid beauty of its countryside, Österlen has a number of engaging sights, notably picture-perfect villages, plenty of smooth, sandy beaches, and the Viking ruin of **Ales Stenar**. It's not surprising the area has lured writers and artists to settle here more than anywhere else in Sweden.

Ales Stenar

From Ystad take either bus #322 or #392 to Kåseberga (20min) from where it's a signed walk of around 200m

Above the harbour of the old fishing village of Kåseberga is **Ales Stenar**, an awe-inspiring Swedish Stonehenge. Believed to have been a Viking meeting place, it consists of 56 **stones** forming a 67m-long boat-shaped edifice, prow and stern denoted by two appreciably larger **monoliths**. The site was hidden for centuries beneath shifting sands, which were cleared in 1958; even now, the bases of the stones are concealed in several metres of sand. It's difficult to imagine how these great stones, not native to the region, might have been transported here. Ales Stenar stands on a windy, flat-topped hill, which most of the tourists snapping away don't bother to climb; once at the top, though (it's a steep 10min hike), there's a majestic timelessness about the spot that more than rewards the effort.

5

Hagestad Nature Reserve and Sandhammaren beach

A signposted drive 5km east of Kåseberga and also accessible on buses #322 and #392 from Ystad

For a day in really splendid natural surroundings, it's hard to beat the **Hagestad Nature Reserve**, the best of the three reserves around the village of **Backåkra**. Thousands of pines were planted here in the eighteenth and nineteenth centuries to bind the sandy earth, and, together with oaks and birches, they make up a densely forested area; the clumps of gnarled, stunted oaks are particularly distinctive. It's especially beautiful in midsummer when orchids and heathers colour the forest floor; if you're lucky, you may also see elk, badgers and roe deer, while buzzards and golden orioles are often sighted above. The reserve is also the home of the most glorious **beach** in Skåne, known as **Sandhammaren**: walk along any path towards the sea and you'll soon reach a bright white ribbon of sand – marked "Sandhammaren" on signs – backed by steep dunes and lapped by turquoise waters.

Dag Hammarskjöld museum

Backåkravägen 73 (signposted from Backåkra) • Daily mid-June to mid-Aug noon–5pm • Free • ☎ 0411 52 60 10

In the midst of the nature reserve, uphill on heathland towards Backåkra is an old farmstead once owned by **Dag Hammarskjöld**, United Nations secretary-general in the 1950s. His love of the Skåne coast led him to buy the farm and the surrounding sixty acres in order to save it from developers. Killed in a plane crash in Zambia in 1961, Hammarskjöld willed the farm and its contents to STF, which now runs the house as a **museum**. It contains amazing pieces of art from all over the world, including an ancient Egyptian painting of the jackal-headed god Anubis, Greek bronzes from 200 BC and contemporary pieces by the Wakefield sculptor Barbara Hepworth (whose work also stands outside the UN's headquarters in New York on Hammarskjöld's instigation), Picasso and Matisse.

GETTING AROUND   THE ÖSTERLEN COAST

By public transport Getting around this part of the country by public transport needs a bit of forward planning but is perfectly feasible; timetables and journey planners are at ⓦ skanetrafiken.se.

By taxi Another option to get to Ales Stenar, for example, is to take a taxi from Ystad; for a set price of 450kr return,

including 1hr waiting time, a car will take you there and back – book on ☎ 0411 720 00 and find them at the station.

By car With your own wheels, getting around is straightforward; roads are good and with a decent map it's no problem to visit the sites by car.

ACCOMMODATION AND EATING

Löderups Strandbad Södra Strandbadsvägen 40, Löderup ☎ 0411 52 63 11, ⓦ loderupsstrandbad.com. Located just west of Backåkra, this is a beautifully situated year-round campsite, which also has a dozen regular double rooms and cabins. There's also an open-air swimming pool on site, plus a café and restaurant at nearby Gökvägen. Doubles 790kr/940kr, tents 140kr, cabins 1500kr

STF Backåkra youth hostel Östra Kustvägen, Backåkra ☎ 0411 52 60 80, ⓔ backakra.vandrarhem@ tele2.se. A well-equipped hostel in an old school house with a bus stop right outside; most rooms have bunk beds, though the doubles have regular beds. You also can rent bikes here. Open mid-June to mid-Aug. Dorms 280kr, doubles 560kr

Kristianstad

Eighty kilometres northeast of Ystad, quiet **KRISTIANSTAD** (pronounced "cri-SHAN-sta") is eastern Skåne's most substantial historic centre and a convenient gateway to Sweden's southern coast. With its beautiful little **Tivoli Park** containing a fine Art Nouveau theatre, **boat trips** into the local bird-rich wetlands and a most elegant **cathedral**, Kristianstad can easily detain you for a relaxed day-long visit.

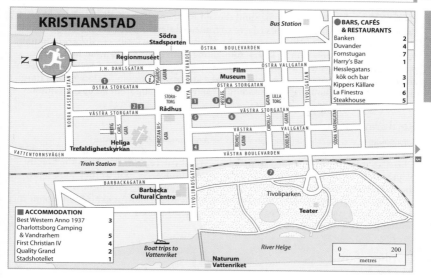

Brief history

Dating from 1614, when it was created by Christian IV, Denmark's seventeenth-century "builder-king", during Denmark's 44-year rule here, it's the earliest and most evocative of his Renaissance towns. With beautifully proportioned central squares and broad, gridded streets flanking the wide river, it was a shining example of the king's architectural preoccupations. Christian nurtured plans to make the fortified town one of Denmark's most important, and it wasn't until the mid-nineteenth century that the fortifications were finally levelled, allowing the town to spill beyond the original perimeter. The late-nineteenth century saw the creation of Parisian-style boulevards, pleasant to wander through today, though the many bland buildings erected during the 1960s and 1970s have left the town with a rather dull appearance.

Heliga Trefaldighetskyrkan

Holy Trinity church • Västra Storgatan 19 • Daily 8am–5pm

The most obvious starting point for a visit to town is the 1618 **Heliga Trefaldighetskyrkan**, right opposite the train station. It symbolizes all that was glorious about Christian IV's Renaissance ideas: the grandiose exterior has seven magnificent spiralled gables, and the building's high windows allow light to flood the white interior. Inside, the most striking features are the elaborately carved pew ends: each is over 2m tall, and no two are the same. The gilded Baroque magnificence of the 1630 organ facade is also worth a look.

Stora torg

Diagonally across from the Heliga Trefaldighetskyrkan, the main square, **Stora torg**, contains the late nineteenth-century **Rådhus**, built in imitation of Christian's Renaissance design. Inside the entrance, a bronze copy of the king's 1643 bust is something of a revelation: Christian sports a goatee beard, one earring and a single dreadlock, and exposes a nipple decorated with a flower motif, itself a source of interest for a baby elephant round the royal neck. Opposite the town hall, and in marked

5

contrast to it, the 1920s post office and the old Riksbank have an identical 1920s brick design; while the adjacent 1640s Mayor's House is different again, with a Neoclassical yellow-stuccoed facade. The square also boasts Palle Pernevi's splintered *Icarus* fountain, which depicts the unfortunate Greek soul falling from heaven into what looks like a scaffolded building site. The town's streets are peppered with modern **sculptures**; one of the best is Axel Olsson's bronze *Romeo & Julia* at Östra Storgatan 3, close to Storatorg, depicting an accordion player serenading a woman emerging from an open window.

Regionmuséet

Regional museum • June–Aug daily 11am–5pm; Sept–May Tues–Sun noon–5pm • Free • ⓦ regionmuseet.se

Behind the old bank is the **Regionmuséet**. Construction of the building was started by Christian in 1616; he intended to make it a grand palace, but, thanks to the bloody Skåne wars, work got no further than the low buildings. As soon as they were built, the stables here were turned into an arsenal containing ammunition for the pro-Danish partisans. Today, the museum is home to permanent exhibitions about the town's military and industrial past. There's also an **art gallery** showing good contemporary exhibitions.

Tivoliparken

Wander down any of the roads to the right and you'll reach **Tivoliparken**, known locally as the "English Park", with avenues of horse-chestnut and copper beech trees. In its centre is a fine Art Nouveau **theatre**, a stylish white building whose designer, Axel Anderberg, also designed the Stockholm Opera.

Vattenriket

Boat tours: May–Aug daily 9am, 2pm & 6pm • 195kr • ⓦ landskapet.se

From the lakeshore in the park, boats operated by Landskapet JO leave for three-hour tours of the nearby marshes and wetlands, a UNESCO World Heritage site known as **Vattenriket** and renowned for its rich vegetation as well as extensive bird and marine life. Departures must be booked in advance through the website. Before boarding the boats, try to check out the bird's-eye tour of Vattenriket shown in the Opteryx flight simulator inside the Vattenriket Naturum nature centre (daily 11am–5pm; free), accessed via the wooden footbridge from the southwest corner of Tivoliparken.

ARRIVAL AND INFORMATION   KRISTIANSTAD

By train All train services pull in at Kristianstad C, on Västra Boulevarden.
Destinations Copenhagen via Kastrup airport (hourly; 1hr 40min); Helsingborg (hourly; 1hr 30min); Karlskrona (hourly; 1hr 40min); Malmö (hourly; 1hr 15min).
By bus The SkåneExpressen #4 bus from Ystad (1hr 30min) stops outside the train station.

Tourist office Östra Storgatan 25, a 5min walk from the station (mid-June to mid-Aug Mon–Fri 10am–7pm, Sat 10am–3pm, Sun 10am–2pm; mid-Aug to mid-June Mon–Fri 10am–5pm, Sat 11am–3pm; ☎ 044 13 53 35, ⓦ kristianstad.se/en/tourism). Has free internet terminals.

ACCOMMODATION

There's rarely a big demand for accommodation in Kristianstad, so arriving in summer without a reservation shouldn't pose a problem. The centre is compact and most hotels are within easy reach of attractions and restaurants.

Best Western Anno 1937 Västra Storgatan 17 ☎ 044 12 61 50, ⓦ hotelanno.se. A rather cramped hotel over two storeys housed in a building dating from the turn of the last century – with annoyingly low ceilings. Rooms are comfortable, some with wooden beams, but lack any real style. **930kr/1270kr**

Charlottsborgs Camping & Vandrarhem 3km west of the town centre at Jacobs väg 34 ☎ 044 21 07 67,

ⓦcharlottsborgsvandrarhem.se; bus #2. A combined campsite and youth hostel, where campers can use all the hostel facilities including the TV and lounge room. There are cottages for two people, too. Dorms 170kr, doubles 600kr, tents 140kr, cottages 680kr

First Christian IV Västra Boulevarden 15 ⓣ044 20 38 50, ⓦfirsthotels.com. The most glamorous hotel in town, just south of Stora torg, located in a rather splendid building that was once home to a bank, retaining its original fireplaces and parquet floors; the vaults are now a wine cellar. 748kr/1298kr

Quality Grand Västra Storgatan 15 ⓣ044 28 48 00, ⓦchoicehotels.se. This modern, modest-looking place offers excellent friendly service and well-equipped en-suite rooms, with supremely comfortable beds, wooden floors and the best prices in town. Rooms are individually decorated with inspiration from Kristianstad's past. 649kr

Stadshotellet Nya Boulevarden 8 ⓣ044 10 02 55, ⓦstadshotelletkristianstad.se. The lobby is all panelled opulence in this old Freemasons' hall; the rooms, though, are a let-down with cheap, modern decor that is rather out of keeping with the rest of the building. 895kr/1095kr

EATING AND DRINKING

Eating in Kristianstad throws up several opportunities, though the prettiest café, *Fornstugan*, is only open during the short summer season. Otherwise, there's a fair range of restaurants clustered around the central square.

CAFÉS AND RESTAURANTS

Banken Östra Storgatan 27 ⓣ044 10 20 23. In the old Riksbanken building, this is one of the most popular of the town's restaurant-cum-bars. The menu features burgers (145kr), spare ribs (199kr) and chicken skewers (145kr). There's 20 percent off a range of food Wed–Fri until 7pm. Tues 5pm–midnight, Wed 5pm–2am, Thurs 5pm–1am, Fri 4pm–3am, Sat 5pm–3am.

Duvander Hesslegatan 6. A classic and central *konditori* with high ceilings and ornate cornices which has been serving cakes and meringues since 1934. It's a popular place for lunch when people come for pasta salads, sandwiches, soup and quiche. Mon–Fri 7.30am–7pm, Sat 8am–5pm, Sun 10am–5pm.

Fornstugan Tivoli Park. An atmospheric and elaborately carved Hansel-and-Gretel lodge in the middle of the park which is Kristianstad's most pleasant café; the outdoor seating area opens in fine weather, though the whole place closes if it rains. Serves waffles, coffee and cakes. May–Aug daily 11.30am–6.30pm.

Kippers Källare Östra Storgatan 9 ⓣ044 10 62 00. An atmospheric choice in a vaulted cellar dating from 1615 and once regularly frequented by Danish King Christian IV. It specializes in tapas of all varieties (35–105kr) but also has well-prepared steaks around 265kr. Tues & Thurs 6–11pm, Wed 6pm–1am, Fri & Sat 6pm–3am.

La Finestra Västra Storgatan 30 ⓣ044 20 97 20. A compact Italian place with bar stools it serves foccacia, pasta and lasagne until 6pm, then pizzas until closing time. Inordinately popular at lunchtime when takeaway (including pizza) is the best option. Tues-Fri 11am–10pm, Sat & Sun noon–10pm.

Steakhouse Nya Boulevarden 6A ⓣ044 12 00 20. This first-floor restaurant overlooking the main square specializes in all kind of barbecued meat dishes such as veal fillets, T-bone steaks and marinated pork (around 250kr). However, there's also a number of main-course salads for 99kr. Mon–Thurs 5–10.30pm, Fri & Sat 5–11pm, Sun 5–10pm.

BARS

Harry's Bar Östra Storgatan 9 ⓣ044 10 62 00. For a convivial drink, try this place (not belonging to the chain *Harry's*), popular with a 30-something crowd. There's also a variety of bar snacks including a mouthwatering fish burger with fennel coleslaw and caper sauce (155kr). Tues & Thurs 6–11pm, Wed 6pm–1am, Fri & Sat 6pm–3am.

Hesslegatans kök och bar Hesslegatan 1A ⓣ044 21 09 80. The largest selection of beers in town (around 70 or so in total from places ranging from China to Iceland) is to be found at this attractive bar, whose interior is hung with black lanterns and features motifs of horsemen with their mounts. Mon, Tues & Thurs 11.30am–2pm, Wed 11.30am–2pm & 6–10pm, Fri 11.30am–2pm & 6pm–2am, Sat 6pm–2am.

The southeast

TOWN WALL, VISBY

The southeast

Although a less obvious target than the coastal cities and resorts of the southwest, Sweden's southeast certainly repays a visit. The provinces of Sörmland, Östergötland, Småland and Blekinge boast impressive castles, ancient lakeside sites and numerous glassworks amid the forests of the so-called "Glass Kingdom", while off the east coast, Sweden's largest Baltic islands offer beautifully preserved medieval towns and fairytale landscapes. Train transport, especially between the towns close to the eastern shore of Lake Vättern and Stockholm, is good; speedy, regular services mean that you could see some places on a day-trip from Stockholm.

Blekinge is something of a poor relation to its neighbours in terms of tourism. Towns here put out an endless stream of glossy brochures touting their attractions, but in truth, even Swedes themselves admit the province remains the forgotten corner of the south; perfect if you're looking for a quiet getaway. **Småland**, in particular, encompasses a varied geography and some stridently different towns. **Kalmar** is a very likeable stop; a glorious historic fortress town, it deserves more time than its tag as a jumping-off point for the island of Öland suggests. Inland, great swathes of dense forest are rescued from monotony by the many **glass factories** that continue the county's traditional industry, famous the world over for its design and quality, though today drowning in its own marketing hyperbole. In **Växjö**, the largest town in the southeast, two superb museums deal with the art of glass-making and the history of Swedish emigration: agricultural reforms that denied peasants access to common land, combined with a series of bad harvests, led to more than a million Swedes – a sixth of the population – emigrating to America between 1860 and 1930. At the northern edge of the province and perched on the southernmost tip of Lake Vättern, **Jönköping** is known as Sweden's Jerusalem for its remarkable number of Free Churches; it's also a great base for exploring the beautiful eastern shore of Vättern.

The idyllic pastoral landscape of **Östergötland** borders the eastern shores of the lake and reaches as far east as the Baltic. One of its highlights, and popular with domestic tourists, is the small lakeside town of **Vadstena**, its medieval streets dwarfed by austere monastic edifices, a Renaissance palace and an imposing abbey, brought into being by the zealous determination of Sweden's first female saint, Birgitta. Just off the southeast coast lie Sweden's two largest islands, Öland and Gotland: adjacent slithers of land with unusually temperate climates for their latitudes. They were domestic tourist havens for years, but now an increasing number of foreigners are discovering their charms – lots of summer sun, delectable beaches and some impressive historic (and prehistoric) sights. **Öland** – the smaller island and closer to the mainland – has a mix of shady forests and flowering meadows that make it a tranquil spot for a few days' exploration. **Gotland**'s

KALMAR SLOTT

Highlights

❶ **Karlskrona** A riot of Baroque architecture and a rich naval past make this seaside town one of the most enticing in southern Sweden. **See p.194**

❷ **Kalmar Slott** Visit the exquisite interior of this sensational, twelfth-century castle that has been beautifully remodelled into a Renaissance palace. **See p.199**

❸ **Kullzénska Caféet**, **Kalmar** Tuck into scrumptious cakes amid the wonderful faded gentility of this eighteenth-century home. **See p.203**

❹ **Utvandrarnas Hus, Växjö** The exhibition of the poignant stories of millions of Swedes forced to emigrate to the United States in the nineteenth century is an essential stop on any visit to Småland. **See p.208**

❺ **Vadstena** This atmospheric town on the eastern shores of Lake Vättern is home to the massive abbey founded by Sweden's first female saint, Birgitta. **See p.218**

❻ **Visby, Gotland** Visit the remarkable walled city of the former Hanseatic League stronghold and take in the party along with the thousands of young Swedes who visit this superb Baltic island every summer. **See p.231**

❼ **Sjaustrehammaren beach, Gotland** Get back to nature on this unspoilt sandy beach near Ljugarn, backed by pine forest and open flower meadows. **See p.238**

HIGHLIGHTS ARE MARKED ON THE MAP ON P.194

well-known highlight is its Hanseatic medieval capital, **Visby**, a city pervaded by a carnival atmosphere in summer when ferry-loads of young Swedes come to sunbathe and party. The rest of the island, however, is little visited by tourists, and all the more magical for that.

Karlskrona

The only real place of interest in Belkinge is the handsome town of **KARLSKRONA**, the provincial capital, which really is something special and merits, say, a day or so of your time. Set on the largest link in a chain of breezy islands, this fine example of Baroque exuberance, founded by Karl XI in 1680, is unique in southern Sweden.

THE SOUTHEAST

HIGHLIGHTS
1 Karlskrona
2 Kalmar Slott
3 Kullzénska Caféet, Kalmar
4 Utvandrarnas Hus, Växjö
5 Vadstena
6 Visby, Gotland
7 Sjaustrehammaren beach, Gotland

Brief history

No sooner had the base for the Swedish Baltic fleet been chosen (the seas here are ice-free in winter) than architects from across the country were dispatched to draw up plans for the town's grid of wide avenues and grand buildings. These were to provide the classical purity and Baroque splendour commensurate with a town destined to become Sweden's second city. Built to accommodate the king's naval parades, Karlskrona's original layout has survived intact, a fact which has earned it a place on UNESCO's World Heritage list, despite the anonymous blocks plonked between the town's splendid churches.

Today, cadets in uniform still career around its streets, many of which are named after Swedish admirals and battleships; the town's biggest museum is, unsurprisingly, dedicated to maritime history (see p.196).

Stortorget

The centre of Karlskrona today occupies the island of **Trossö**, connected to the mainland by the main road, Österleden (the E22). Climb uphill past Hoglands Park, named after an eighteenth-century battle between the Swedish and Russian navies (Hogland is an island in the Gulf of Finland), to the main square, **Stortorget**, at the highest point and geographical centre of the island. It's a vast and beautiful space, dominated by two complementary **churches**; both were designed by Tessin the Younger and are stuccoed in burnt orange with dove-grey stone colonnades.

Trefaldighetskyrkan

Stortorget • June–Aug daily 10am–4pm; Sept–May Mon–Fri 11am–3pm, Sat 9.30am–2pm • Guided tours can be requested

The more interesting of the churches is the circular, domed **Trefaldighetskyrkan**. Built for the town's German merchant community in 1709, its most remarkable feature is its domed ceiling, painted with hundreds of rosettes. The altar is also distinctive, with golden angelic faces peering out of a gilded meringue of clouds. In the crypt are the remains of two of Karlskrona's most revered men, Count Hans Wachtmeister, responsible for much of the building of the town in the late seventeenth century; and Johan Törnström, the Admiralty sculptor, who made most of the fabulous ship figureheads on show at the Marinmuseum (see p.196).

Fredrikskyrkan

Stortorget • Mon–Fri 11am–3pm, Sat 9.30am–2pm

Fredrikskyrkan, a few steps away from Trefaldighetskyrkan, is an elegant, light-flooded church with towers, but holds fewer surprises inside. Construction began in 1720 in classic Baroque style according to plans drawn up by Nicodemus Tessin, who also designed Stockholm's cathedral and royal palace. Disaster struck just decades after completion, though, and large parts of the church were destroyed in a devastating fire which ripped through the roof section. Rebuilding began apace and today's elegant structure stood ready in 1806.

Museum Kulenovic Collection

Stortorget 5 • Mon–Sat 10am–6pm, Sun 11am–6pm • 50kr • ☎ 0455 255 73, ⊛ kulenoviccollection.se

Housed in the former water tower beside the square, the **Museum Kulenovic Collection** contains a remarkable collection of sculptures, Renaissance paintings and general objets d'art first begun by the Kulenovic family from Yugoslavia in the 1450s; the collection ended up in Karlskrona after two brothers moved here during the Tito period. The highlight is a mesmerizing painting of the Angel Gabriel by Rembrandt from 1637; a copy hangs in the Louvre in Paris whilst the original is here in Karlskrona. Check out, too, the amazing miniature bronze horses from Persia from 200 AD, plus the sculpture of the Devil with an erect penis.

Kungliga Amiralitetskyrkan

Royal Admiralty Church • Amiralitetstorget • Daily 11am–3pm

Down from Stortorget, the leafy square ahead is **Amiralitetstorget**, at its centre the huge, apricot-and-grey-painted wooden bell tower of the **Kungliga Amiralitetskyrkan**. To see the church itself, head down Vallgatan on the left of the square, passing the symmetrical austerity of the Marine Officers' School; just before you reach the harbour, the beautifully proportioned, entirely wooden building is up on the right. Sweden's biggest wooden church, it was built in 1685.

Marinmuseum

Maritime Museum • Stumholmen • June–Aug daily 10am–6pm; Sept–May Tues–Sun 11am–5pm • 90kr • ⓦ marinmuseum.se

Located on the tiny island of Stumholmen at the foot of Kyrkogatan, Karlskrona's **Marinmuseum** has a facade like a futuristic Greek temple; a portrait of Karl XI, who had the navy moved from Stockholm to Karlskrona in 1680, features in the hallway, a pet lion at his feet gazing up at the king's most unappealing, bloated face. Down a spiral staircase from here is a transparent underwater tunnel offering a view of hundreds of fish in the murky depths. The best room, though, contains the **figureheads** designed and made by the royal sculptor to the navy, Johan Törnström. King Gustav III declared that ships of the line should be named after manly virtues, and so have male figureheads, while frigates have female ones. Among the finest is one made for the ship *Försiktigheten* (*Prudence*; 1784) – a metre-long foot, perfectly proportioned and complete with toenails.

6

A BEGGAR'S TALE

Outside the entrance to Kungliga Amiralitetskyrkan, take a look at one of the city's best-known landmarks: the wooden statue of **Rosenbom**, around which hangs a sorrowful tale. Mats Rosenbom, one of the first settlers on Trossö island, lived nearby with his family and earned his keep in the shipyard. However, after a fever killed six of his children and left him and his wife too ill to work, he applied for, and was granted, a beggar's licence. One New Year's Eve, while begging at the homes of leading townspeople, he became somewhat drunk from the festive wine on offer and forgot to raise his hat to thank the wealthy German figurehead carver, Fritz Kolbe. When admonished for this, Rosenbom retorted, "If you want thanks for your crumbs to the poor, you can take my hat off yourself!" Enraged, Kolbe struck him between the eyes and sent him away, but the beggar, unable to make it home, froze stiff and died in a snowdrift by the church. Next morning, Kolbe found the beggar frozen to death and, filled with remorse, carved a figure of Rosenbom which stands at the spot where he died. It's designed so that you have to raise his hat yourself to give some money.

Blekingemuseum

Borgmästaregatan 21 • June–Aug daily 10am–6pm; Sept–May Tues–Sun 11am–5pm, Wed until 7pm • Free

The provincial collections housed within the rather dreary **Blekingemuseum** down at the harbourfront, especially when compared to Karlskrona's other treasures, are unlikely to set your pulse racing. Housed in the 1705 wooden home built for Count Wachtmeister, it's the pleasant summertime café that's infinitely more appealing than the exhibits on shipbuilding and the like.

Konsthall

Arts Centre • Borgmästaregatan 17 • Tues–Sun noon–5pm, Wed till 7pm • Free • ⓦ karlskrona.se/konsthall

Just behind the Blekingemuseum, housed in the town's striking former cinema, the new **Konsthall** is the place to look for temporary exhibitions of modern art as well as occasional dance and music productions.

ARRIVAL AND DEPARTURE
KARLSKRONA

By train The train station is 200m north of Hoglands Park. To travel to and from Kalmar by train, change at Emmaboda. Destinations Copenhagen via Kastrup airport (hourly; 3hr 30min); Emmaboda (hourly; 45min); Kristianstad (hourly; 1hr 40min); Malmö (hourly; 2hr 50min).

By ferry The Stena Line ferry to and from Gdynia (just outside Gdansk; 10hr 30min), sails once daily from Verkövägen 101, 10km from Karlskrona centre; see ⓦ stenaline.se for details of transport to the port.

INFORMATION

Tourist office Stortorget 2, just behind Frederikskyrkan (June–Aug daily 9am–8pm; Sept–May Mon–Fri 9am–6pm, Sat 10am–4pm; ☏ 0455 30 34 90, ⓦ karlskrona.se/tourism). A 10min stroll from the train station, with internet access.

ACCOMMODATION

Aston Landbrogatan 1 ☏ 0455 194 70, ⓦ hotellaston .se. This comfortable place has been redecorated using modern furniture and classic fittings and the result is simple elegance. Over the years it's been popular with ships' crews whilst their boats were being refitted – photographs of this period adorn the walls. 895kr/1195kr

Clarion Collection Carlscrona Skeppsbrokajen ☏ 0455 36 15 00, ⓦ choice.se. A great hotel close to the station in a contemporary glass-fronted building. Rooms are well appointed and decked out with specially commissioned maritime and historical wallpapers – a really nice touch. The weekend and summer prices are exceptionally good value. 770kr/1380kr

First Statt Ronnebygatan 37 ☏ 0455 555 50, ⓦ firsthotels.se. The Empire-style rooms in this 1890 building on the main shopping street are stylish in the extreme and at these prices it's hard to go wrong. Note this is cheaper than the other First hotel in town. 705kr/961kr

Scandic Karlskrona Skeppsgossegatan 2 ☏ 0455 37 20 00. Beautifully situated on the edge of Fisktorget

6

overlooking the sea, rooms at this new hotel are bright and breezy with minimal decor and lots of bright and breezy oranges and greens on the walls. **990kr/1360kr**

Siesta Borgmästaregatan 5 ☎0455 801 80, ⓦhotellsiesta.com. Just off Stortorget, this really quite agreeable little hotel has chosen a warm terracotta-red colour scheme throughout, with contemporary designs and furnishings. Smaller economy rooms cost 300kr less than the regular ones. **1150kr**

STF Vandrarhem Karlskrona Drottninggatan 39 and Bredgatan 16 ☎0455 100 20. Two central locations

– though only the Drottninggatan hostel is open all year. Bredgatan operates June–Aug only; check-in and reception is at Drottninggatan. Dorms **240kr**, en-suite doubles **580kr**

CAMPING

Dragsö Camping Dragsövägen, Dragsö island ☎0455 153 54, ⓦdragso.se; bus #7 to Saltö, the island before Dragsö, from where it's a 1km walk across the bridge. A pleasant waterside campsite that's about around 2.5km from the centre of town. Also has modern cabins for rent. Tents **140kr**, cabins **500kr**

EATING AND DRINKING

Karlskrona is surprisingly poor for good restaurants – most proper eating places are along Ronnebygatan – and, even more strangely given its location, has almost nothing in the way of decent fish places.

Café Tre G Landbrogatan 9 ☎0455 31 03 33. Opposite Hoglands Park, with black-and-white photographs hung on the walls, this stylish café does a good range of baked potatoes and pasta salads as well as cakes and sandwiches. The city's only café open on a Sunday. Mon–Fri 9am–9pm, Sat 9am–6pm, Sun 10am–6pm.

Castello Stortorget 5 3 ☎0455 255 73. Attached to the Kulenovic museum and with great views over the Baroque splendour of the main square, this is a sound choice for expertly cooked pasta dishes as well as mains (89–219kr) like chicken in basil sauce and steak in calvados. Daily 11am–6pm; closed Sun Sept–May.

Fox and Anchor Norra Smedjegatan 1 ☎0455 229 10. British-style drinking den serving 54 different types of beer and over 200 whisky varieties. There's also some decent grub: burgers, fish & chips and steaks; reckon on around 150kr for something substantial. Mon & Tues 5–11pm, Wed 5pm–midnight, Thurs 5pm–1am, Fri 4pm–1am, Sat 6pm–1am.

Lisas Sjökrog Skeppsbrokajen ☎0455 61 83 83. If you want to eat fish in Karlskrona, this is the place to come. A floating restaurant with great views of the marina serving unusual dishes like pan-fried swordfish in chilli coconut sauce as well as more mainstream choices such as plaice and zander. Mains around 200kr. Mon–Fri 11.30am–11pm, Sat noon–11pm, Sun noon–10pm.

Michelangelo Ronnebygatan 29 ☎0455 121 95. With copies of Renaissance paintings on the rough brick walls, this elegant Italian restaurant has a good choice of fine cuisine: meat and fish dishes, such as braised veal medallions with pancetta and sage, are 159–225kr. Mon–Fri 11.30am–2pm & 5–11pm, Sat 5–11pm, Sun 4–10pm.

Montmartre Ronnebygatan 18 ☎0455 31 18 33. With rough brick walls and velvet drapes, this candlelit bistro is the cosiest of all the Italian places in town: huge pizzas for 71–98kr, pasta at 82–95kr and meat mains like steak marinated in garlic at 139–219kr. Mon–Fri 4–10.30pm, Sat 1–10.30pm, Sun 1–9.30pm.

★ **Nivå** Stortorget ☎0455 103 71. Semi-circular glass-fronted steakhouse perfectly situated on the edge of the main square with great views of the Baroque splendour all around. Burgers from 145kr, steaks from 169kr, though there's also a couple of fish dishes. Mon & Tues noon–11pm, Wed, Fri & Sat noon–3am, Thurs noon–midnight.

Nya Skafferiet Rådhusgatan 9 ☎0455 171 78. A really good deli and café combined where you can buy air-dried hams, meats, cheeses for picnics as well as filled baguettes, croissants, great coffees and the best hot chocolate in town. Excellent lunch buffet, too. Mon–Fri 10am–6pm, Sat 10am–3pm.

Kalmar

Delightful, breezy **KALMAR**, set on a huddle of islands at the southeastern edge of Småland province, has treasures enough to make it one of southern Sweden's most delightful towns. Chief among its highlights are the **Länsmuseum**, home to an exhibition on the sunken warship, the *Kronan*, and an exquisite fourteenth-century **castle**, Scandinavia's finest preserved Renaissance palace. The town is also perfectly sited for reaching the Baltic island of Öland (see p.203), which is just 6km away across the connecting bridge.

KALMAR

● CAFÉS, BARS & RESTAURANTS

Athena	5
Calmar Hamnkrog	10
Hanssons krog	4
Källaren Kronan	8
Krögers	6
Kullzénska Caféet	3
Larmgatan 10	7
Ming Palace	9
Stekhuset	1
Thai Silk Palace	2

■ ACCOMMODATION

Best Western Kalmarsund	2
Calmar Stadshotell	3
Clarion Collection Packhuset	6
Frimurarehotellet	4
Slottshotellet	5
Stensö Camping	7
Svanen	1

Kalmar Slott and around

Kungsgatan 1 • May, June & Sept daily 10am–4pm; July daily 10am–6pm; Aug daily 10am–5pm; Oct Sat & Sun 11am–3.30pm; guided tours in English 11.30am, 1.30pm & 2.30pm • 80kr • ⓦ kalmarslott.kalmar.se

Beautifully set on its own island, just south of Stadsparken, is the castle, **Kalmar Slott**. Its foundations were probably laid in the twelfth century; a century later, it became the best-defended castle in Sweden under King Magnus Ladulås. Today, if the castle doesn't appear to be defending anything in particular, that's because a devastating fire in the 1640s laid waste to Gamla Stan, after which Kalmar was moved to its present site on Kvarnholmen.

Brief history

The most significant event to take place within the castle's walls was when the Danish Queen Margareta instigated the **Union of Kalmar** in 1397, which made her ruler over all Scandinavia, but given the level of hatred between the Swedes and Danes, the union didn't stand much chance of long-term success. The castle was subject to eleven **sieges** as the two rival nations took power in turn; surprisingly, it remained almost unscathed. By the time Gustav Vasa became king of Sweden in 1523, Kalmar Slott was beginning to show signs of wear and tear, and so the king set about rebuilding it, while his sons, who later became Eric XIV and Johan III, took care of decorating the interior. The result, a fine Renaissance palace, is still preserved in fantastic detail today.

6

The interior

Unlike many other southern Swedish castles, this one is straight out of a storybook, boasting turrets, ramparts, a moat and drawbridge and a dungeon. The fully furnished interior – reached by crossing an authentically reconstructed wooden **drawbridge** and going through a stone-arched tunnel beyond the grassy ramparts – is great fun for a wander. Among the many highlights are the **King's Chamber** with its coffered ceiling, the **Queen's Suite** and the **Golden Room**. The tour guides will tell you that the castle is rattling with ghosts, but for more tangible evidence of life during the Vasa period, the kitchen fireplace is good enough; it was built to accommodate the simultaneous roasting of three cows. There's a splendidly minimalist **café** just inside the walls, dominated by a wonderfully evocative oil painting of a moody chamber interior.

The King's Chamber

The **King's Chamber** (King Eric's bedroom) is the most visually exciting – the wall frieze is a riot of vividly painted animals and shows a wild boar attacking Eric and another man saving him. Eric apparently suffered from paranoia, believing his younger brother Johan wanted to kill him. To this end, he had a secret door, which you can see cut into the extravagantly inlaid wall panels, with escape routes to the roof in the event of fraternal attack. Eric's suspicions may have been justified – Johan is widely believed to have poisoned him with arsenic in 1569.

The Queen's Suite

Though originally in the King's Chamber, his oak **bed** now resides in the **Queen's Suite**, which is otherwise surprisingly void of furniture. It is the only surviving piece of furniture from the castle and was originally stolen from Denmark. It is curiously decorated with carved faces on the posts, but all their noses have been chopped off – the king believed that the nose contained the soul and didn't want the avenging souls of the rightful owners coming to haunt him.

The Golden Room

Adjoining the Queen's Suite, the **Golden Room**, with its magnificent ceiling, should have been Johan's bedroom but sibling hatred meant he didn't sleep here while Eric lived. There are a couple of huge and intriguing portraits: though Gustav Vasa was already of an advanced age when his was painted, he appears young-looking, with unseemly muscular legs. The royal artist had been ordered to seek out the soldier with the best legs and paint those, before attempting a sympathetic portrayal of Vasa's face. The portrait next to his is of Queen Margareta, her ghostly white countenance achieved in real life through the daily application of lead and arsenic. Isolated on another wall is King Eric's portrait, hung much higher up than the others: his family believed that the mental illness from which he supposedly suffered could be caught by looking into his eyes – even images of them.

Konstmuseum

Stadsparken • Tues, Thurs & Sun noon–5pm, Wed till 7pm • 50kr • ⓦ kalmarkonstmuseum.se

Having left the castle, wandering back towards the town centre along Slottsvägen will bring you to Kalmar's grotesque **Konstmuseum**, a monstrous cube of a building dressed in black wooden panels plonked unceremoniously in the middle of Stadsparken, where there's an emphasis on Abstract Expressionist work painted by Swedish artists in the 1940s and 1950s. The museum's collection contains several nineteenth- and twentieth-century Swedish nude and landscape paintings, including some fine works by Anders Zorn and Carl Larsson, though exhibitions change regularly. In addition, there are often temporary displays of contemporary art.

Gamla Stan

For a feel of Kalmar's quaint **Gamla Stan**, it's best to head into the small warren of cobbled lanes west of *Slottshotellet*, which overlooks Stadsparken and is only a minute's walk along Slottsvägen from the Konstmuseum. The old wooden cottages, painted egg-yolk yellow and wisteria blue, are at their prettiest on Gamla Kungsgatan and Västerlångatan. These little streets surround the attractive **Gamla kyrkogården** (old churchyard), whose seventeenth- and eighteenth-century gravestones have been restored.

6

Domkyrkan

Norra Långgatan 33 • Daily: June–Aug 9am–8pm; Sept–May 9am–4pm

The elegantly gridded Renaissance New Town is laid out around the grand **Domkyrkan** in Stortorget. Designed in 1660 by Nicodemus Tessin the Elder (as was the nearby Rådhus) after a visit to Rome, this vast and airy church in Italian Renaissance style is today a complete misnomer: Kalmar has no bishop and the church no dome. Inside, the altar, designed by Tessin the Younger, shimmers with gold, as do the *Faith* and *Mercy* sculptures around it. The huge *Deposition* painting above the altar depicts in unusually graphic detail Jesus being taken down from the Cross by men on ladders, his lifeless form hoisted down with ropes. The pulpit is also worth a look; its roof is a three-tiered confection crowned with a statue of Christ surrounded by gnome-like sleeping soldiers, below which angels brandish instruments of torture, while on the "most inferior" level, a quartet of women symbolize such qualities as maternal love and erudition.

The Kronan Exhibition

July–Aug daily 10am–5pm; Sept–June Mon–Fri 10am–4pm, Sat & Sun 11am–4pm • 80kr July–Aug, 60kr Sept–June • ⓦ regalskeppetkronan.se

From Stortorget, it's a few minutes' walk south down Östra Sjögatan and then left into Ölandsgatan to the **Kalmar läns muséet**, Kalmar's regional museum. The centrepiece of the museum is the awe-inspiring **Kronan exhibition**, housed in a refurbished steam mill. Built by the seventeenth-century British designer Francis Sheldon, the royal ship *Kronan* was once one of the world's three largest vessels; it had three complete decks and was twice the size of the *Vasa*, which sank off Stockholm in 1628 (see p.60).

Brief history

The *Kronan* itself went down, fully manned, in 1676, resulting in the loss of 800 of its 842 crew. Its captain, Admiral Creutz, had received a royal order to attack and recapture the Baltic island of Gotland. Pursued by the Danish, Creutz, who had remarkably little naval experience – just one week at sea – was eager to impress his king and engage in combat. To this end, he ignored pleas from his crew and ordered the *Kronan* to turn and face the enemy. A gale caused the ship to heave, and water gushed into her open gun ports, knocking over a lantern, which ignited the entire gunpowder magazine. Within seconds, an explosion ripped the mammoth vessel apart.

Salvage and reconstruction

It wasn't until 1980 that the whereabouts of the ship's remains were detected, 26m down off the coast of Öland, using super-sensitive scanning equipment. A salvage operation began, led by the great-great-great-great-grandson of the ship's captain, and 25,000 artefacts have so far been recovered. On the ground floor you come face to face with a dozen of the ship's mighty bronze cannons, richly decorated with coats of arms. However, up on the first floor, things really take off with a full and imaginative **walk-through reconstruction** of the gun decks and admiral's cabin, while the moments leading up to the disaster have been pieced together brilliantly. The ship's **treasure trove** of gold coins is also displayed, but it's the incredibly preserved **clothing** – hats, jackets, buckled leather shoes and even silk bows and cufflinks – which bring this exceptional show to life. Check out, too, the remarkable twelve pewter flasks dating from the mid-1600s which, when salvaged, still contained their original barley-based *akvavit* with an alcohol content of 41.1 percent. The wreck site, the size of half a football pitch, is still being explored and yields around one thousand items each year.

ARRIVAL AND DEPARTURE   KALMAR

By train Kalmar's train station is on Stationsgatan, at the southern end of the new town on the island of Kvarnholmen. Change at Emmaboda for trains to Kristianstad.

Destinations Copenhagen via Kastrup airport (10 daily; 3hr 45min); Emmaboda (hourly; 45min); Gothenburg (5 daily; 4hr); Malmö (10 daily; 3hr 15min); Växjo (10 daily; 1hr).

INFORMATION

Tourist office Ölandskajen 9 (Jan–April & Oct–Dec Mon–Fri 10am–5pm; May & Sept Mon–Fri 9am–5pm, Sat 10am–3pm; early June & late Aug Mon–Fri 9am–9pm, Sat 10am–4pm; mid-June to mid-Aug Mon–Fri 9am–9pm,

Sat & Sun 10am–5pm; ☎0480 41 77 00, ⓦkalmar.com). Within spitting distance of the train station, and with internet access.

ACCOMMODATION

Kalmar has several really attractive central **hotels** with good summer discounts, though there's little to choose from in terms of price. Undoubtedly, the Baroque splendour of the main square is the location of choice.

Best Western Kalmarsund Fiskaregatan 5 ☎0480 48 03 80, ⓦkalmarsundhotel.se. A chain hotel that's a bit lacking in elegance, but with friendly, efficient service, comfortable en-suite rooms and an altogether contemporary feel. There's a sauna, hot tub and roof garden too. 1050kr/1450kr

Calmar Stadshotell Stortorget 14 ☎0480 49 69 00, ⓦprofilhotels.se. Dating from 1906, this lovely old building with a stuccoed facade in Art Nouveau style is a tasteful mix of old and new, though sadly many rooms have cheap carpets and unstylish furnishings, detracting from the elegance of the public areas. 999kr/1524kr

Clarion Collection Packhuset Skeppsbrogatan 26 ☎0480 570 00, ⓦchoicehotels.se. Housed in a former waterfront storehouse, the wooden beams of this rambling old building add to the cosiness of the compact modern rooms, many of which have views out over the harbour. A free evening buffet is included. 790kr/1390kr

Frimurarehotellet Larmtorget 2 ☎0480 152 30, ⓦfrimurarehotellet.com. Rather grand hotel, set in a castle-like building from 1878 owned by the Freemasons (hence the name: *frimurare* is Swedish for "freemason")

and offering sumptuous rooms with period furniture. 1090kr/1490kr

Slottshotellet Slottsvägen 7 ☎0480 882 60, ⓦslottshotellet.se. The prettiest and most regal – though not the priciest – of Kalmar's hotels, overlooking the castle across the bridge. The authentic interior is extremely tasteful, with a charming conservatory area and a sauna and solarium for use by guests. 1095kr/1295kr

Svanen Rappegatan 1 ☎0480 129 28, ⓦhotellsvanen .se. A combined budget hotel and youth hostel located a pleasant 15min walk north of the centre; it's well equipped, with laundry facilities and a shop for basic provisions. The youth hostel has dorm beds and simple double rooms. Dorms 195kr, hostel doubles 490kr, hotel doubles 830kr

CAMPING

Stensö Camping 3km from the centre at Stensövägen, Stensö island ☎0480 888 03, ⓦstensocamping.se; bus #401 heads out this way but it's a 1.5km walk from the closest bus stop. As well as camping, there are cabins with lake views here for rent. Open mid-April to Sept. Tents 140kr, cabins 550kr

EATING, DRINKING AND NIGHTLIFE

Athena Norra Långgatan 8 ☎0480 280 88. A bright and airy Greek restaurant with tasty traditional fare at sensible prices such as moussaka (135kr) or beef souvlaki (169kr), as well as various salads (98–109kr) and pasta dishes (98–135kr). Mon–Thurs 11am–10pm, Fri 11am–11pm, Sat noon–11pm, Sun 1–9pm.

Calmar Hamnkrog Skeppsbron 30 ☎0480 41 10 20. Built right by the water on squat stilts with great views out over the harbour, this swish but pleasantly informal place offers such delights as grilled tuna in coconut sauce (235kr), fried Baltic herring with lingonberries (149kr) and lobster soup (119kr). Mon–Thurs 11.30am–2.30pm &

6–9pm, Fri 11.30am–2.30pm & 6–10pm, Sat 11.30am–10pm, Sun 11.30pm–4pm.

★ **Hanssons krog** Norra Långgatan 1 ☎ 0480 104 21. This great restaurant, in a building dating from the late 1600s, resembles the interior of a cosy farmhouse and serves exceptionally tasty modern Swedish specialities with a touch of Provence (mains 160–275kr), such as pork tenderloin with herb sauce and artichoke pesto. Mon–Fri 11am–2pm & 5–10pm, Sat 5–10pm.

Källaren Kronan Ölandsgatan 7 ☎ 0480 41 14 00. A wonderfully atmospheric vaulted restaurant in a stone building dating from the 1660s, serving top-class Swedish food, such as angler fish with horseradish butter and venison with chanterelle sauce. The best-value option is a two-/three-course set menu for 229kr/279kr respectively. Tues–Fri 6–11pm, Sat noon–11pm, Sun 5–10pm.

Krögers Larmtorget 7 ☎ 0480 265 50. This noisy bar-restaurant with its fake stained-glass windows and model ships is one of the most popular places in town. The food isn't exactly adventurous, but neither is it too expensive: burgers for 149kr, fish and chips 156kr and steaks 209kr. There's a good choice of bottled beers too. Daily 4pm till late.

★ **Kullzénska Caféet** Kaggensgatan 26 ☎ 0480 288 82. This charming *konditori* occupying the first floor of a house dating from 1771 is easily Kalmar's best café. Its eight interconnecting rooms are awash with mahogany furnishings, Indian carpets and crumbling royal portraits. There's a wide selection of sandwiches, cakes and light lunch dishes – the coffee is particularly good. Mon–Fri 10am–6.30pm, Sat 10am–3.30pm, Sun noon–4.30pm.

Larmgatan 10 Södra Långgatan 6 ☎ 0480 865 25. A very genteel place with roped-back drapes, wall paintings and window flowers and a good range of simple home-cooked dishes like pork fillet with cognac sauce (168kr) and chicken breast with green pepper sauce (158kr). Mon–Thurs 4–11pm, Fri 4pm–midnight, Sat noon–midnight, Sun noon–10pm.

Ming Palace Fiskaregatan 7 ☎ 0480 166 86. Kalmar's premier Chinese restaurant, with a beautiful interior featuring a fish pond full of carp and goldfish. The best option is the eat-as-much-as-you-like buffet served daily until 5pm for 99kr weekdays and 140kr at weekends. Mon–Thurs 11am–10pm, Fri 11am–11pm, Sat noon–11pm, Sun noon–10pm.

Stekhuset Skeppsbron 1 ☎ 0480 42 38 58. Steaks from the farms of Småland, such as a delicious fillet steak wrapped in bacon cooked in red wine sauce, are 195–275kr. There are also a number of fish dishes on the menu, including grilled sole and sea bass. Mon–Fri 5–11pm, Sat 1–11pm, Sun 1–9pm.

Thai Silk Palace Fiskaregatan 8 ☎ 0480 281 26. Reached through the passage marked "Koppartorget" off Fiskaregatan, this ornate Thai restaurant, decorated with reclining Buddhas and lots of carved wood, has an all-day lunch buffet that's especially good value at 99kr weekdays and 109kr weekends. Mon–Fri 11am–3pm & 5–10pm, Sat noon–11pm, Sun noon–10pm.

Öland

Linked to mainland Sweden by a 6km-long bridge, the island of **Öland**, with its unspoilt beaches, mysterious forests, pretty meadows and wooden cottages, has been drawing Swedes in droves for over a century. Although it's a popular destination in summer and holiday traffic can clog the road from the bridge north to the main town **Borgholm**, this long, splinter-shaped island retains a very likeable old-fashioned holiday atmosphere. The bathing opportunities are among the best in Sweden, and the island's attractions include numerous ruined castles, Bronze and Iron Age burial cairns, runic stones and forts, all set amid rich and varied fauna and flora and striking geography. Labyrinthine **walking trails** and **bicycle routes** wend their way past more than four hundred old wooden **windmills**, which give Öland a peculiarly Dutch air. The island is perfect for **camping**, and while you can pitch tent anywhere under the rules of *Allemansrätten* (see p.33), there are plenty of official sites. Almost all are open only between May and September, and are scattered the length of the island; for more details, visit ⌨ camping-oland.com.

Brief history

A royal hunting ground from the mid-sixteenth century until 1801, Öland was ruled with scant regard for its native population. Peasants were forbidden from chopping wood, owning dogs or weapons and selling their produce on the open market. While protected wild animals did their worst to the farmers' fields, Kalmar's tradesmen exploited the restrictions on the islanders' trade to force them to sell at low prices.

6

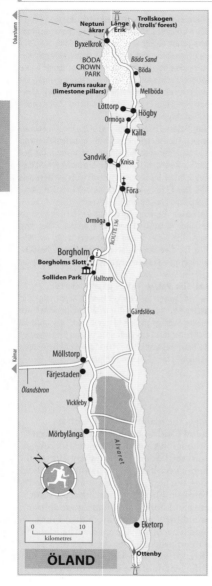

Danish attacks on Öland (and a ten-month occupation in 1612) made matters worse, with seven hundred farms being destroyed. A succession of disastrous harvests in the mid-nineteenth century was the last straw, causing a quarter of the population to pack their bags for a new life in America. In the twentieth century, mainland Sweden became the new magnet for Öland's young and, by 1970, the island's inhabitants had declined to just twenty thousand, around five thousand less than today's total.

Geology and flora

Öland's geology varies dramatically due to the crushing movement of ice during the last Ice Age, and the effects of the subsequent melting process, which took place 10,000 years ago. To the south is a massive **limestone** plain known as **alvaret**; indeed, limestone has been used here for thousands of years to build runic monuments, dry-stone walls and churches. The northern coastline is craggy and irregular, peppered with dramatic-looking **raukar** – stone stacks, weathered by the waves into jagged shapes. Among the island's **flora** are plants that are rare in the region, like the delicate rock rose and the cream-coloured wool-butter flower, both native to Southeast Asia and found in southern Öland. Further north are the twisted, misshapen pines and oaks of the romantically named **trollskogen** (trolls' forest).

Borgholm

As you walk the simple square grid of streets that makes up **Borgholm**, Öland's "capital", it becomes clear that tourism is the lifeblood of this small town. But despite being swamped by visitors each July, Borgholm is in no way the tacky resort it could be. Encircled by the flaking, turreted and verandahed villas that were the pride of the town during its first period as a holiday resort in the nineteenth century, most of the centre is a friendly, if bland, network of shops and restaurants lining the roads that lead down to the pleasant harbour.

Borgholms Slott

Sollidenvägen 5 • Daily: April & Sept 10am–4pm; May–Aug 10am–6pm • 70kr

The only real attraction in town is **Borgholms Slott**, several hundred metres southwest of the centre. A colossal stone fortification with rows of huge arches and corridors open to the skies, it's reached either through a nature reserve, signposted from the town centre, or from the first exit south off Route 136. Built in the twelfth century, the castle was fortified four hundred years later by King Johan III, and given its present shape – with a tower at each corner – in the seventeenth century. Regularly attacked, it eventually fell into disrepair, and when Borgholm was founded in 1816, the castle was already a ruin.

Solliden Park

Gardens: daily mid-May to mid-Sept 11am–6pm • 70kr

Just a few hundred metres to the south of the castle is the present royal family's summer residence, **Solliden Park**, an Italianate villa built in 1903 to a design specified by the Swedish Queen Victoria (the present king's great-grandmother); a huge, austere red-granite bust of her rises out of the trees at the entrance to the car park. Of Austrian stock, Victoria loathed Sweden, and demanded the bust face Italy, the country she most loved. The villa itself is not open to the public, but the formal **gardens** can be visited. There's a very ordered Italian Garden, a colourful Dutch Garden and a simple English-style one.

Villagatan

To see what Borgholm looked like before the likes of the *Strand Hotel* were built, head along **Villagatan**, the road to the left of the *Strand* as you face out to sea; it's lined with classic wooden villas, their porches and eaves all fancy fretwork. You can't drive along the street without authorization, though, as this is the route used by the king and queen to reach their summer home.

Blå rör

Just to the north of the town centre is Öland's largest Bronze Age cairn, **Blå rör**, a huge mound of stones excavated when a coffin was discovered in 1849. People have been turning up artefacts from time to time ever since: in the 1920s, burnt bones, indicating a cremation site, were found, along with bronze swords and tweezers – apparently common items in such tombs.

ARRIVAL AND INFORMATION
BORGHOLM

By bus The bus timetable, available from Kalmar's bus station and tourist office, is almost impossible to decipher – Ölanders mostly laugh when you refer to it. Buses #101 and #102 are safe bets, however, and run pretty well every hour from Kalmar bus station to Borgholm; timetables are online at ⓦklt.se.

Tourist office Storgatan 1 (June & Aug Mon–Fri 9am–6pm, Sat & Sun 10am–4pm; July Mon–Fri 9am–6pm, Sat 9am–5pm, Sun 10am–4pm; Sept–May Mon–Fri 9am–5pm; ☎ 0485 890 00, ⓦolandsturist.se).

ACCOMMODATION

It's imperative to book ahead if you're planning a visit to Öland during the June to August peak summer period, since the island is extremely popular with Swedish holiday-makers. Unlike elsewhere in Sweden, rooms prices go up in summer, so the lower rate is for out of season.

Borgholm Trädgårdsgatan 15–19 ☎ 0485 770 60, ⓦhotellborgholm.com. A smart central choice with interior decor by Philip Starck amongst others and some pleasant gardens, too. The beautifully appointed top-floor double rooms with their wooden floors, French balconies and stone finishes are worth splashing out on. <u>1335kr</u>

Ebbas Vandrarhem Storgatan 12 ☎ 070 990 04 06, ⓦ ebbas.se. This spacious STF hostel is right in the heart of town and boasts a delightful garden café. Accommodation is in one- to four-bed rooms and it pays to book well ahead in summer. Open May–Sept only. Dorms <u>320kr</u>, doubles <u>620kr</u>

Kapelludden Camping Sandgatan 27 ☎ 0485 56 07 70, ⓦkapelludden.se. A family-oriented campsite (under 25s not allowed unless with children) that's set on a small peninsula 5min walk from the centre. It has a number of overpriced cottages for rent. Open late April to Sept. Tents <u>140kr</u>, cottages <u>1250kr</u>

Strand Borgholm Villagatan 4 ☎ 0485 888 88, ⓦstrandborgholm.se. Straddling one side of the harbour

and blandly styled like a modern seaside hotel, its massive interior includes a small shopping mall, a disco and nightclub; this place is one of the most popular hotels in town so book early. **1290kr/890kr**
Villa Sol Slottsgatan 30 ☎ 0485 56 25 52, ⓦ villasol.nu.

A central and tranquil guesthouse located in a charming pale-yellow house with stripped wooden floors and old tiled fireplaces. The lush gardens provide fresh fruit, made into gorgeous jams for breakfast. **800kr/600kr**

EATING, DRINKING AND NIGHTLIFE

There has traditionally been a pronounced summer-holiday feel to Borgholm's **restaurants** and **bars**. Pizza places abound around Stortorget and down towards the harbour, cashing in on the summer influx of tourists; the really good places, however, are the long-standing, smart restaurants, which are rather pricey.

Glasscafé Storgatan 10. A great place for a wide range of local, island-made ice creams and sorbets from Ölandsglass, and a pleasant eating area in the back garden with a vine-covered veranda. June–Aug daily 10am–10pm.
Hotel Borgholm Trädgårdsgatan 15 ☎ 0485 770 60. This chi-chi hotel restaurant with walls covered in modern art is the best place in town for fine Swedish/pan-European food. A three-course set menu featuring a soup, pike perch and a passion-fruit dessert costs 665kr. Tues–Sat 6pm till late.
Mamma Rosa Södra Långgatan 2 ☎ 0485 129 10. Beside the harbour, a smart pizza and pasta parlour with a varied menu, including a decent selection of traditional Italian meat dishes. You should reckon on around

150–200kr per main dish. Mon–Fri 11am–11pm, Sat & Sun noon–10pm.
Pubben Storgatan 18 ☎ 0485 124 15. A cosy and extremely popular pub run by the friendliest of owners, with old radios and crystal sets for decor. As well as lager, stout and bitter, this popular bar specializes in whisky. Daily: May–Aug noon–1am; Sept–April 4pm–1am.
Robinson Crusoe Hamnvägen 1 ☎ 0485 777 58. Jutting into the harbour waters, this restaurant-cum-bar is a fine place for a drink and the Swedish home cooking on the menu is certainly tasty, though watch what you order as the prices can be a little inflated. May–Sept daily except Tues noon till late.

Northern Öland

Öland's most varied and interesting landscape is to be found towards the north, with no shortage of idyllic villages, dark woods and flowery meadows as you head up from Borgholm along the main road, **Route 136**. Though there aren't many proper hotels north of the Borgholm area, **campsites** are marked off the road every couple of kilometres; most of these high-standard sites are close to a beach. Public transport is limited to **buses** heading up Route 136 towards Böda Sand; timetables are at ⓦklt.se. The road is safe for **cycling**, too, and there are plenty of tracks that lead off the main drag.

Föra

At **Föra**, a village about 20km north of Borgholm, there's a good example of a typical Öland **church**, built in the medieval era (the font is the oldest part, dating from 1250). It doubled as a fortress, and was capable of accommodating a considerable garrison in times of war. A couple of kilometres north, a sign to **Knisa Mosse** leads to a peaceful nature reserve, centred on a shimmering lake, and to some Bronze Age burial mounds, though there's not much to see at the burial area itself.

Högby and Löttorp

Continuing north from Föra on Route 136, **Högby**, about 15km further on, has the only remaining tied church houses on the island, relics of the medieval Högby kyrka nearby; there's not a lot to see though. For a filling (though somewhat pricey) dining experience, head for the village of **Löttorp**, off Route 136, and follow the signs east for 4km down country lanes to the *Lammet & Grisen* restaurant (see opposite).

Byrums raukar and the beaches

Close to Öland's northern tip and west off Route 136, following signs for Byrums Sandvik and Raukområde, you come to **Byrums raukar**, a striking sight: solitary limestone pillars formed by the eroding action of the sea, at the edge of a sandy beach. The best **beaches** are along the east coast; starting at Böda Sand, the most popular stretch is a couple of kilometres north at **Lyckesand**, with a **nudist beach** just to the north, the start of which is marked simply by a large boulder in the sea. Small lanes run east from the main road to the beaches, and there are many campsites signposted off Route 136.

Böda Sand

From the hostel at Mellböda (see below), it's just 2km north to one of the island's best sandy beaches, **Böda Sand**. Take the narrow road heading east to reach the gently curving coastline of Böda bukten bay, which forms Öland's northeastern tip.

6

Småland

The thickly forested province of **Småland** makes up the southeastern wedge of Sweden. Although the scenery is appealing at first, the uniformity of the landscape means it's easy to become blasé about so much natural beauty. Småland is often somewhere people travel through rather than to – from Stockholm to Malmö and the south, or from Gothenburg to the Baltic coast. It does, however, have a few vital spots of interest of its own, alongside opportunities for hiking, trekking, fishing and cycling.

Historically, Småland has had it tough. The simple, rustic charm of the pretty painted cottages belies the intense misery endured by generations of local peasants: in the nineteenth century, subsistence farming failed, and the people were starving; consequently a fifth of Sweden's population left the country for America – most of them from Småland. While their plight is vividly retold at the House of Emigrants exhibition in **Växjö**, a town which makes an excellent base from which to explore the region, the province's main tourist attractions are its myriad **glass factories**. The bulk of these celebrated glassworks lie within the dense birch and pine forests that, together with a thread of lakes, make up the largely unbroken landscape between Kalmar and Växjö. Consequently, the area is dubbed **Glasriket**, or the "Glass Kingdom", with each glassworks signposted clearly from the spidery main roads.

Växjö and around

Founded by St Sigfrid in the eleventh century, **VÄXJÖ** (approximately pronounced "veck-shur"), 120km from Kalmar deep in the heart of Småland, is by far the handiest base hereabouts. Though its centre is fairly bland and quiet, Växjö, whose name derives from *väg sjö*, or "way to the lake", is within easy reach of some beautifully tranquil lake scenery. The town itself offers a couple of great **museums**, and once a year comes to life for the **Karl Oskar-dagar** (second weekend in Aug) – a long weekend of unbridled revelry in honour of the character Karl-Oskar, created by author Wilhem Moberg, who symbolized the struggles of Småland's Swedish peasants in the nineteenth century. In reality, it means Växjö's youth drink themselves silly through the nights while daytime entertainment fills the streets.

6

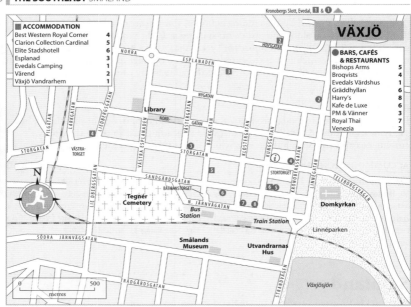

Kronobergs Slott, Evedal, **1** & **❶** ⛰

VÄXJÖ

■ **ACCOMMODATION**
Best Western Royal Corner	4
Clarion Collection Cardinal	5
Elite Stadshotell	6
Esplanad	3
Evedals Camping	1
Värend	2
Växjö Vandrarhem	1

● **BARS, CAFÉS & RESTAURANTS**
Bishops Arms	5
Broqvists	4
Evedals Värdshus	1
Gräddhyllan	6
Harry's	8
Kafe de Luxe	6
PM & Vänner	3
Royal Thai	7
Venezia	2

Smålands Museum

Södra Järnvägsgatan 2 • June–Aug Mon–Fri 10am–5pm, Sat & Sun 11am–5pm; Sept–May closed Mon • 50kr including Utvandrarnas Hus • ⓦ smalandsmuseum.se

The best place to kick off your exploration of Växjö is the **Smålands Museum**, behind the train station, which holds two permanent exhibitions: a history of Småland during the nineteenth and twentieth centuries, with a section dedicated to Växjö, and the infinitely more interesting "Six Centuries of Swedish Glass". The latter shows sixteenth-century place settings, eighteenth- and nineteenth-century etched glass and stylish Art Nouveau-inspired pieces, with subtle floral motifs. "Trees in Fog", designed in the 1950s by Kosta designer Vicke Lindstrand, illustrates just how derivative so much of the twentieth-century work actually is. Look out, in particular, for the *Absolut* vodka bottles made in nearby Limmared, which formed the basis of today's design.

Utvandrarnas Hus

House of Emigrants • May–Aug Tues–Fri 9am–5pm, Sat & Sun 11am–4pm; Sept–April Tues–Fri 9am–4pm, Sat & Sun 11am–4pm • 50kr including Smålands Museum • ☎ 0470 201 20, ⓦ utvandrarnashus.se

In a plain building directly in front of the Smålands Museum, the inspired **Utvandrarnas Hus** explores the intense hardship faced by the Småland peasant population in the mid-nineteenth century and their ensuing emigration; between 1850 and 1929, one quarter of Småland's population left to begin a new life in America.

The displays

The museum's **displays**, which include English-language translations and audio narratives, trace the lives of individual emigrants and recount the story of the industry that grew up around emigration fever. Most boats used by the emigrants left from Gothenburg and, until 1915, were British-operated sailings to Hull, from where passengers crossed the Pennines to Liverpool by train to board the transatlantic ships; conditions on board the ships were usually dire and the emigrants often shared their accommodation with oxen, pigs, calves and sheep. Exhibitions change frequently but there's generally a mock-up of a street in early 1900s Chicago, a popular destination for the emigrants, where all the stores are run by Swedes – everything from a grocer's to a photographer's shop.

Wilhelm Moberg

There's also a section on **women emigrants**, entitled "Not Just Kristina", a reference to a fictitious character in *The Emigrants*, a trilogy by one of Sweden's most celebrated writers, **Wilhelm Moberg**. Upon publication, it became the most-read Swedish history book in the country, and was made into a film starring Max von Sydow and Liv Ullman. On display here is Moberg's writing cabin, which was given to the museum after his death in 1973. Moberg would himself have emigrated, only his father sold a farrow of piglets to pay for his son to go to college in Sweden.

Research Centre

Tues–Fri 9am–4pm • 150kr/half-day, 300kr/full day

The museum's **Research Centre** charges remarkably good rates to help interested parties trace their family roots using passenger lists from ten harbours, microfilmed church records from all Swedish parishes and the archives of Swedish community associations abroad. If you want to use the centre's extensive information services during its peak season (May–Aug), it's especially worth booking ahead for an appointment with one of the staff.

Domkyrkan

Linnégatan 2 • Daily 9am–6pm

In the centre of town, the distinctive **Domkyrkan**, with its unusual twin green towers and apricot-pink facade, is certainly worth a look. The combined impact of regular restorations, the most recent in 1995, together with a catalogue of disasters, such as sixteenth-century fires and a 1775 lightning strike, have left little of note except an organ. There are, however, some brilliant glass ornaments by two of the best-known contemporary Glass Kingdom designers: Göran Wärff's wacky church font of blue glass, a stunning triptych altarpiece made entirely of glass designed by Bertil Vallien and the tree of life with Adam and Eve surrounded by glass leaves by Erik Höglund. The cathedral is set in **Linnéparken**, named after Carl von Linné (see p. 000), who was educated at the handsome school next door.

ARRIVAL AND INFORMATION VÄXJÖ

By train The train station is next to bus station in the middle of town from where it's a straightforward walk of around 10min to reach the main square.
Destinations Copenhagen via Kastrup airport (10 daily; 2hr 45min); Gothenburg (5 daily; 3hr); Jönköping (5 daily;

2hr); Kalmar (11 daily; 1hr); Malmö (10 daily; 2hr 15min).
Tourist office Stortorget (June–Aug Mon–Fri 9am–6pm, Sat 10am–2pm, also July Sun 10am–2pm; Sept to May Mon–Fri 9.30am–4.30pm; ☎0470 73 32 80, ⓦturism .vaxjo.se). Has internet access.

ACCOMMODATION

Best Western Royal Corner Liedbergsgatan 11 ☎0470 70 10 00, ⓦroyalcorner.se. Since becoming part of the Best Western chain, rooms here have been renovated and are now smart, comfortable and full of wooden panels, floors and fittings in keeping with the latest Swedish design trends. Extremely reasonable weekend and summer rates. 700kr/1350kr
Clarion Collection Cardinal Bäckgatan 10 ☎0470 72 28 00, ⓦchoicehotels.se. Complete with a free evening buffet, this winning hotel, just off the main drag, tastefully combines old and new, plus there's some decent art on the

walls. A friendly welcome, too, makes this hotel hard to beat. 690kr/1240kr
Elite Stadshotell Kungsgatan 6 ☎0470 134 00, ⓦvaxjo.elite.se. A good central location for this hotel with the usual executive-class hotchpotch of shiny marble, potted palms and terrible carpets, but with a generous buffet breakfast included in the rates and an in-house English pub, the *Bishops Arms*. 765kr/1232kr
Esplanad Norra Esplanaden 21A ☎0470 225 80, ⓦhotellesplanad.com. A reasonable family-owned

central hotel, whose compact rooms are cosy, if lacking in style, and refreshingly free of the staid chain hotel sameness. No frills, but it's appealingly inexpensive and there's always tea and coffee available. **770kr/1050kr**

Värend Kungsgatan 27 ☏0470 77 67 00, ⓦhotellvarend.se. Another standard hotel with rather plain rooms but a warm welcome from the family who own and run the place, this one also does good-value triple rooms at 200kr more than the rate for a double. The respectable prices make this exceptionally good value for money. **695kr/850kr**

Växjö Vandrarhem Evedals Brunn, 6km northeast of Växjö ☏0470 630 70, ✉vaxjo.vandrarhem@telia.com; take Linnégatan north, following signs for Evedal, or bus #1C from Växjö bus station to the end of the route (June–Aug only). This beautifully maintained STF hostel is located in an eighteenth-century house in parkland beside Helgasjön lake and boasts its own beach. Dorms **260kr**, doubles **600kr**

CAMPING

Evedals Camping Evedals Brunn ☏0470 630 34, ⓦevedalscamping.com; bus #1C comes here in summer. Located beside Växjö youth hostel at Evedals Brunn (see above). There's a decent shop for stocking up on food, and two-person cabins with cooking facilities. Tents **140kr**, cabins **700kr**

EATING AND DRINKING

Växjö is a good place to try traditional **Småland cuisine**, which shows the influence of the forests and the poverty associated with the region; look out, in particular, **foristerband**, a flavoursome, spicy sausage, and **krösamos**, mashed potato with lingonberry sauce.

Bishops Arms Kungsgatan 6 ☏0470 276 66. Like elsewhere in Sweden this fake English pub is attached to the town's *Elite* hotel and is an inordinately popular place for a drink. There are sometimes special After Work deals on beer – look out for the signs outside. Mon, Tues, Thurs & Sun 5pm–midnight, Wed 5pm–1am, Fri & Sat 5pm–2am.

Broqvists Kronobergsgatan 14 ☏0470 120 20. This café just off Stortorget may be nothing special to look at, but it's a Växjö institution nonetheless, as somewhere locals come to gossip or read the paper while enjoying a coffee and a slice of cake. Mon–Fri 8am–7pm, Sat 8am–5pm, Sun 9am–7pm.

Gräddhyllan Sandgärdsgatan 19 ☏0470 74 04 10.

IKEA

Among Swedish exports, only Volvo and ABBA spring to mind as readily as the furniture store **IKEA**, the letters standing for the name of its founder – **Ingvar Kamprad** (born 1926) – and his birthplace, Elmaryd, a farm in the Småland parish of Agunnaryd. Outside Sweden, the identity of IKEA's originator, now one of the world's richest men, is played down, and the firm is known for simple, modern design lines and prices that appeal to a mass market. Every item of furniture IKEA produces is assigned a fictional or real Swedish name; the styles of certain items are drawn from particular areas of the country, and are given a relevant name.

Founded in 1943 at Älmhult, a small town 50km southwest of Växjö, as a mail-order company, IKEA began producing furniture based on folk designs, which Kamprad had simplified. In the 1950s, Sweden's existing furniture-makers were sufficiently irritated by what they regarded as an upstart that they tried to pressure IKEA's suppliers into boycotting the company. Kamprad responded by importing furniture from abroad.

In his 1976 book, *Testament of a Furniture Dealer*, Kamprad wrote that from the outset, he wanted to promote "constructive fantasies": to change the world's view of design, rather than produce what people already believed they wanted. Having opened in Denmark in 1969, the company began expanding around the world, though it didn't enter the US market until 1985 or the UK until 1987. In 2006, IKEA opened its most northerly store in the world in Swedish Haparanda, drawing shoppers from across Lapland.

A number of biographies have been published on Kamprad, one of which (*The History of IKEA*) was authorized. They have revealed Kamprad's Nazi sympathies during World War II; in response, he blamed his former political leanings on the folly of youth.

Today, if you pass through Älmhult, you can see the original IKEA store, built in 1958; the street on which it stands is called, appropriately enough, Ikeagatan. Ironically, IKEA's headquarters are no longer in Sweden, but Leiden in the Netherlands, and Kamprad himself has lived in Switzerland since 1976.

This charming old wooden house is *the* place for fine dining in Växjö, featuring Vänern char, steak and lamb dishes; the interior is decorated in the style of an old-fashioned dining room. Set menus for 590kr and 750kr. Tues–Sat 6pm till late.

Harry's Norra Järnvägsgatan 8 ☎ 0470 123 00. The locals love this American-style bar complete with its lifesize Native American figure, half-built brick arches and faux *Dieu et mon Droit* coat of arms hanging over the bar. As a result it's a good place to meet people and get under the skin of Växjö. Mon–Thurs 4pm till late, Fri & Sat 3pm–2am.

★ **Kafe de Luxe** Sandgärdsgatan 19 ☎ 0470 74 04 09. Use the door on the left-hand side of the building to access this great retro basement café, done out in 1960s style and often belting out classic pop tunes of an evening. Mains are around the 200kr mark and include pan-fried pike-perch and moules frites. Tues–Sat 6pm till late.

★ **PM & Vänner** Storgatan 24 ☎ 0470 70 04 44. A great bar-bistro and an elegant (evening-only) fine-dining restaurant make up the two halves of this popular place.

Bistro meals such as *isterband* and potatoes go for around 200kr, whereas more sophisticated three-course affairs next door, featuring the likes of veal fillet and a blackcurrant and elderberry dessert, cost 645kr. Mon & Tues 11.30am–11pm, Wed & Thurs 11.30am–midnight, Fri & Sat 11.30am–1am.

Royal Thai Norra Järnvägsgatan 10 ☎ 0470 458 06. Ornate Thai restaurant opposite the train station with carved bamboo pillars marking the entrance. An extensive menu with Thai, Chinese and Japanese food including chicken green curry (129kr), stir-fried chicken with cashews (119kr) and a popular lunch buffet with over ten different dishes (75kr). Mon–Thurs 11am–10.30pm, Fri 11am–11.30pm, Sat noon–11.30pm.

Venezia Linnégatan 31 ☎ 0470 461 70. Serving the people of Växjö since 1974, this neighbourhood trattoria buzzes with life. It's also full of people enjoying the sensibly priced and tasty pasta dishes (85–135kr), pizzas (79–129kr) and meat mains such as pork au gratin with rosemary and tomato (150kr). Mon–Thurs 4.30–10pm, Fri 4.30–11pm, Sat noon–11pm, Sun noon–9pm.

The Glass Kingdom

Glass-making in Sweden was pioneered by King Gustav Vasa, who'd been impressed by the glass he saw on a trip to Italy in the mid-sixteenth century. He initially set up a **glassworks** in Stockholm; however, it was Småland's forests that could provide the vast amounts of fuel needed to feed the furnaces, and so a glass factory was set up in the province in 1742. Called Kosta, after its founders, Anders Koskull, Georg Bogislaus and Stael von Holstein, it is still the largest glassworks in Småland today.

Visiting the glassworks

All Mon–Fri 8.30am–3.30pm, Sat & Sun 11am–5pm • The Glassriket Pass (available at the tourist office in Växjö; 95kr) gives free entry to the glassworks (it generally costs 30kr to watch glass-blowing) and discounts on some glassware products; it can therefore be a wise investment if you're out to buy • ⊕ glasriket.se

All of the fourteen glassworks still in operation in Småland give captivating **glass-blowing** demonstrations. Several have permanent exhibitions of either contemporary glasswork or

---

GLASS-MAKING AND -BUYING IN THE GLASS KINGDOM

The **glass-making process** can be mesmerizing to watch, with a glass plug being fished out of a shimmering, molten lake (at 1200°C) and then turned and blown into a graphite or steel mould. With wine glasses, a foot is added during the few seconds when the temperature is just right – if the glass is too hot, the would-be stem will slide off or sink right through; if too cold, it won't stick. The piece is then annealed – heated and then slowly cooled – for several hours. It all looks deceptively simple and mistakes are rare, but it nevertheless takes years to become a *servitör* (glass-maker's assistant), working up through the ranks of stem-maker and bowl-gatherer.

Glassware is marketed with a vengeance in Småland – take a look at the often absurd hyperbole in the widely available *Kingdom of Crystal* magazine. If you want to buy glassware, don't feel compelled to snap up the first things you see: the same designs appear at most of the glassworks, testimony to the fact that the biggest factories by far, Kosta Boda and Orrefors, are now under the same umbrella ownership, while many of the smaller works have been swallowed up, too, even though they retain their own names.

pieces from their history, and all have a shop. **Bus** services to the glassworks, or to points within easy walking distance of them, are extremely limited, and without your own transport it is almost impossible to see more than a couple in a day (though this will satisfy most people).

Kosta Boda glassworks

Take Route 25 to Lessebo, then follow signs to Kosta, or hop on the direct bus #218 from Växjö; timetables are at ⓦ lanstrafikenkron.se • ⓦ kostaboda.se

While each glassworks has its individual design characteristics, **Kosta Boda** is the easiest to reach from Växjö, has extensive displays and gives the best picture of what's available. The Kosta Boda and Åfors glassworks are both operated by the same team. While two of Kosta's most celebrated and hyped designers, Bertil Vallien and Ulrica Hydman-Vallien, have their studios at Åfors, the bigger glassworks is at Kosta.

Outlet store

Mon–Fri 10am–5pm, Sat & Sun 11am–5pm

The **outlet store** here contains some of the most delicate fin-de-siècle glassware, designed by Karl Lindeberg; for contemporary simplicity, Anna Ehrner's bowls and vases are the most elegant. Among the most brilliantly innovative works are those by Göran Wärff – examples of his expressive work can also be found in Växjö's cathedral. Current design trends tend more towards colourful and rather graceless high kitsch; nonetheless, new designer sculptural pieces can go for astoundingly high prices: commercialized designs go for around 2500kr, although for a single, traditional *akvavit* glass you're looking at paying something like 150kr upwards.

ACCOMMODATION, EATING AND DRINKING   KOSTA

Glasbaren Stora Vägen 75 ☎ 0478 348 42. Inside the hotel is this remarkable bar; its entire decor is cobalt-blue glass – from panels on the bar to lights designed to look like icicles. Try the excellent seared marinated salmon with potatoes in a tangy mustard cream for 169kr. Mon–Fri 2pm–1am, Sat & Sun noon–1am.

Kosta Boda Art Stora Vägen 75 ☎ 0478 348 30, ⓦ kostabodaarthotel.se. No fewer than seven of Kosta's designers helped create this incredibly stylish hotel and as a result it's a glass lover's dream – even the sinks and bedside lamps are made of glass. There's also a spa complex onsite. **2590kr**

Jönköping

Perched at the southernmost tip of Lake Vättern, northwest of Växjö along Route 30, **JÖNKÖPING** (pronounced "yurn-shurping") is one of the oldest medieval trading centres in the country, having won its town charter in 1284. Today, it's famous for being the home of the **matchstick**, the nineteenth-century manufacture and worldwide distribution of which made Jönköping a wealthy place. With a plum position on the lakeshore, the town makes a pleasant place to break your journey.

Radiomuséet

Radio Museum • Tandsticksgränd 16 • Tues–Fri 10am–5pm, Sat 10am–2pm, June–Aug also Mon 10am–5pm & Sun 11am–3pm • 20kr • ⓦ radiomuseet.com

Jönköping's restored historical core is the most interesting part of town to explore. At

JÖNKÖPING FILM FESTIVAL

Each year, the town hosts a five-day **film festival** (ⓦ jonkoping-filmfestival.se). It's not pure art-house, but not mainstream Hollywood either, focusing on films from the rest of Scandinavia and across Europe, and it's undoubtedly the best time to be in town.

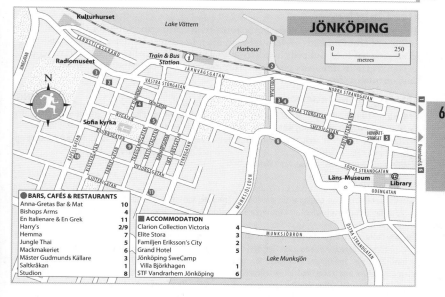

its heart is the **Radiomuséet**, dedicated to the memory of Erik Karlson from nearby Huskvarna, who built his first radio receiver in 1923 aged 14, and later opened one of Sweden's first radio stores just three months after the national broadcaster, Sveriges Radio, had taken to the air. Stuffed to the gills, the museum contains seemingly every type of radio, from early crystal sets to reel-to-reel tape recorders and mobile phones, and is a real trip down memory lane.

Jönköpings läns museum

Jönköping county museum • Dag Hammarskjöldsplats 2 • Tues–Sun 11am–5pm, Wed till 8pm • June to mid-Sept 40kr, otherwise free • Ⓦ jkpglm.se

Aside from the Radiomuséet, the only museum in town worth bothering with is **Jönköpings läns museum**, on the east side of the canal between lakes Vättern and Munksjön. A mishmash of oddities, with exhibits ranging from posters showing Swedish support for Che Guevara through garden chairs throughout the ages to samovars and doll's houses, the place is like a well-stocked junk shop. The best part is the well-lit collection of paintings and drawings by **John Bauer**, a local artist who enthralled generations of Swedes with his Tolkienesque representations of gnomes and trolls in the *Bland tomtar och troll*, a well-known series of Swedish children's books which were published around Christmas between 1907 and 1915.

Arkivhuset

Mon–Fri 9am–7pm, Sat & Sun 11am–3pm • Free

To the left of the main entrance to the museum, beyond the reference library (which is worth a stop if you want to peruse the remarkable range of foreign-language **newspapers**), you'll find an account of Jönköping's history from 1200 or so onwards in old maps, paintings and models housed in a building known as **Arkivhuset** – worth a look on a rainy day.

Free Churches

Although there's little else to see in the town centre, it is remarkable for the sheer number of **Free Churches** – over twenty in the immediate vicinity; consequently, Jönköping has been dubbed "Sweden's Jerusalem". As the traditional Church watches its congregations diminish, people are turning instead to these independent and fundamentalist churches.

ARRIVAL AND INFORMATION   JÖNKÖPING

By train The train station is part of the Resecentrum on the lake's southernmost edge, along with the bus station and the tourist office. For services to Stockholm and Malmö, change trains at Nässjö.
Destinations Nässjö (hourly; 30min); Växjö (5 daily; 2hr).

Tourist office Inside the Resecentrum (Mon–Fri 9.30am–6pm, Sat 9am–2pm, June to mid-Sept also Sun 9.30am–2pm; ☎036 10 50 50, ⓦdestinationjonkoping .se). Has free internet access.

ACCOMMODATION

There should be no problem getting accommodation in Jönköping, and especially in summer there are some good deals to be had at the central **hotels** which are keen to replace their normal business guests with tourists.

Clarion Collection Victoria F.E. Elmgrensgatan 5 ☎036 71 28 00, ⓦvictoriahome.com. The best choice in town for style, atmosphere and value for money. Afternoon coffee and cakes and an excellent buffet supper in the appealing atrium dining area are included, and the split-level sauna is the best in town. **995kr/1495kr**

Elite Stora Hotellplan ☎036 10 00 00, ⓦjonkoping .elite.se. Jönköping's most historic hotel, built 1856–60 in Italian Renaissance Baroque style. Rooms are decorated in Gustavian-style pastels, and bathrooms here have that very unusual Swedish commodity – bathtubs. Some rooms have lake views. **807kr/1317kr**

★ **Familjen Ericsson's City** Västra Storgatan 25 ☎036 71 92 80, ⓦcityhotel.nu. Just 3min walk south from the train station, this is a very comfortable choice, though plainer than many other establishments in town. Rooms in the nicer, newer, more modern section of the hotel cost a couple of 100kr more. **895kr/1395kr**

Grand Hotel Hovrättstorget ☎036 71 96 00, ⓦgrandhotel-jonkoping.se. Built in 1904, this rather elegant building is home to another of the town's family-owned hotels. Rooms are airy with wooden floors and offer exceptional value for money. The location is great, too, right on the main shopping street. **990kr/1690kr**

STF Vandrarhem Jönköping Odengatan 10, Huskvarna ☎036 14 88 70, ✉148870@hhv.com; take bus #1 from the Resecentrum and alight at the stop marked "Esplanaden". The nearest youth hostel is 6km to the east in the neighbouring town of Huskvarna; ask for a room with private facilities. Dorms **250kr**, doubles **500kr**

CAMPING

Jönköping SweCamp Villa Björkhagen Friggagatan 31, Rosenlund ☎036 12 28 63, ⓦcamping.se/f6; bus #1. Roughly halfway between the town centre and the youth hostel; if you don't come by bus, get here by walking east about 3km along the lakeside Strandpromenaden (a continuation of Norra Strandgatan). Also has cabins with cooking facilities and private bathroom. Tents **140kr**, cabins **795kr**

EATING, DRINKING AND NIGHTLIFE

Jönköping's most popular **eating** and **drinking** area is the harbour pier, though the rest of town has plenty of good, lively spots too. For a local food speciality, go for the **vätternröding** (Lake Vättern char), brought here from the unusually cold and deep Lake Vättern, which can sustain fish normally found in the Baltic Sea.

Anna-Gretas Bar & Mat Kapellgatan 19 ☎036 71 25 75. The oldest café in town and formerly the staple haunt of market traders, this popular place serves great Spanish food and an impressive range of tapas. Reckon on 25–70kr per item Mon–Thurs 11.30am–2pm & 5–11pm, Fri 11.30am–2pm & 5pm–midnight, Sat 5pm–midnight.

Bishops Arms Hotellplan ☎036 215 50 52. Attached to the *Elite Stora* hotel, this is a good choice for a drink and is a firm favourite amongst the locals. There's an impressive selection of whiskies and beers and a few bar snacks, too, such as burgers and steaks. Mon & Tues 4.30–11pm, Wed & Thurs 4.30pm–midnight, Fri 4.30pm–1am, Sat 1pm–1am, Sun 4.30–10pm.

★ **En Italienare & En Grek** Barnarpsgatan 35B ☎036 30 77 55. Well-priced, tasty Italian and Greek food (moussaka 165kr and pasta 125–150kr, pizzas from 85kr), good service and an attractive location overlooking the

ASTRID LINDGREN – CREATOR OF PIPPI LONGSTOCKING

Some 120km east of Jönköping, and reachable on Routes 31 and 33, is **Vimmerby**, near where one of Sweden's most popular children's authors, **Astrid Lindgren** (1907–2002), was born. Her most endearing character, **Pippi Longstocking** (in Swedish, Pippi Långstrump), burst upon the world in 1945. Pippi had red hair and long thin legs on which she wore non-matching stockings. Wealthy and energetic, she could do as she pleased, and her adventures appealed hugely to children everywhere.

Lindgren's face has appeared on a Swedish 6kr stamp; her eighty books have, in total, sold more than 80 million copies worldwide. Yet her writing hasn't simply been about lighthearted adventures: her cleverly conceived tale, *Bröderna Lejonhjärta* ("The Lionheart Brothers"), tries to explain the concept of death to children.

In later years, she became a Swedish Brigitte Bardot figure, campaigning on animal-rights issues, and was also involved with children's rights. Following her death in 2002 in Stockholm, she was buried in the family grave in Vimmerby cemetery, and today, Vimmerby is home to **Astrid Lindgren's Värld** (June–Aug daily 10am–6pm; 335kr, children under 13 225kr; ⓦalv .se/en), a theme park where actors take on the roles of her most famous characters. Trains to Vimmerby run from Kalmar, as does bus #325 from Jönköping.

6

turreted old tram depot in the university district. Also has outside tables in summer. Mon–Thurs 11am–10.30pm, Fri & Sat noon–midnight, Sun noon–10pm.

Harry's Brunnsgatan 13–15 ☎036 71 94 80. *Harry's* trademark half-built brick walls between the tables are well in evidence here. Inordinately popular place for a drink and a bite to eat, too. The burgers are especially tasty and juicy. Tues–Sat 5pm till late.

Hemma Smedjegatan 36 ☎036 10 01 55. The town's most popular venue for laid back live music, with very friendly service and a relaxing terrace garden. There's also a decent menu of home cooking, including salmon and various steak dishes, from 185–295kr. Mon–Thurs 11.30am–2pm & 6–10pm, Fri 11.30am–2pm & 5–11pm, Sat 6–11pm.

Jungle Thai Trädgårdsgatan 9 ☎036 13 28 28. A welcome arrival in Jönköping, though the elephant heads and plastic greenery are a bit OTT. A good choice, nonetheless, with Thai and other Asian dishes for around 128–235kr and one of the most popular places in town. Mon–Thurs 11am–3pm & 5–10pm, Fri 11am–11pm, Sat noon–11pm, Sun 11am–9pm.

Mackmakeriet Smedjegatan 26A ☎036 19 03 05. The best café in town, friendly and housed in a wonderful eighteenth-century building with an original painted ceiling portraying two young girls sitting by a lake. Delicious fresh-filled baguettes plus a drink cost 48kr to take away. Mon–Fri 9am–6.30pm, Sat 10am–4pm.

★ **Mäster Gudmunds Källare** Kapellgatan 2 ☎036 10 06 40. A fantastic old vaulted cellar restaurant from the 1600s serving good, traditional Swedish fare including reindeer, veal steak and a vegetarian option. Three-course set menus from 359kr, otherwise mains, including *vätternröding*, at 159–229kr. Mon–Fri 11.30am–2pm & 6–10pm, Sat noon–10pm, Sun noon–5pm.

Saltkråkan Hamnen (end of the pier) ☎036 12 53 53. This old boat-based restaurant appeals to many Swedes as it's featured in a long-running Swedish children's television programme, though there's also an extension on the pier itself. Serves tapas such as *gambas* in garlic and lamb cutlets in a herb sauce for 35–89kr. May–Aug Mon–Thurs 2pm–midnight, Fri 2pm–2am, Sat noon–2am, Sun noon–midnight.

Studion Södra Strandgatan 9 ☎036 71 41 19. Waterfront, chi-chi brasserie with tiled walls and floor-to-ceiling windows overlooking Munksjön lake, this is the place to come for superbly cooked local *röding* (235kr), cod (255kr), duck confit (175kr) and burgers (165kr). Mon–Fri 11am–2pm & 5–10pm, Sat 5–10pm, Sun 1–9pm.

Gränna and around

Forty kilometres north of Jönköping, the lakeside town of **GRÄNNA** is associated with the unlikely combination of pears, striped rock-candy and a gung-ho nineteenth-century Swedish balloonist (see p.216). In late spring, the hills around Gränna are a confetti of pear blossom, Per Brahe (see p.216) having encouraged the planting of pear orchards hereabouts; the Gränna pear is one of the best-known varieties in the country today. Approaching from the south, the beautiful Gränna Valley sweeps down to your left, with the hills to the right, most notably the crest of Grännaberget, which provides a majestic foil to some superb views over **Lake Vättern** and its island, Visingsö. On a hot summer's day, the trip here from Jönköping has something of the atmosphere of the French Riviera, evoked in particular by the winding roads, red-tiled roofs and the profusion of flowers in the old cottage gardens – not to mention the equal profusion of Porsche and Mercedes cars.

Brief history
Per Brahe, one of Sweden's first counts, built the town in the mid-seventeenth century, using the symmetry, regularity and spaciousness of planning that he had learnt while governor of Finland. The charming main street, **Brahegatan**, was subsequently widened and remodelled, allowing the houses fronting it to have gardens, while the other main roads were designed so Brahe could look straight down them as he stood at the windows of his now-ruined castle, **Brahehus**. The gardens along Brahegatan remain mostly intact, and until the 1920s, there were no additions to the original street layout. Even now, there's very much a village feel to the little town.

Grännaberget café
Grännaberget • May–Aug daily 10am–9pm • ☎ 0390 101 09
True, it's a bit of a climb (243 steep steps, to be precise) but there's a view from *Kaffestugan Grännaberget* which should not be missed: from the sloping main square, walk over to the church then south for 100m to the junction with Parkgränd and the wooden steps in the hillside to your left. Outside seating affords a fabulous vista over the lake. Better still, you can explore inside a range of ancient grass- and thatch-roofed buildings brought from the surrounding areas.

The Grenna Kulturgård: Andrée Expedition Polarcenter
Mid-May to Aug daily 10am–6pm; Sept to mid-May Mon–Fri 10am–4pm • 50kr • ⓦ grennamuseum.se/polarcenter
Within the Grenna Kulturgård on Brahegatan is the fascinating **Polarcenter**, dedicated to Salomon August Andrée, the Gränna-born **balloonist** who led a doomed attempt to reach the North Pole by balloon in 1897. Born at Brahegatan 37, Andrée was fired by the European obsession of the day to explore and conquer unknown areas; with no real way of directing his balloon, however, his trip was destined for disaster from the start. After a flight lasting only three days, during which time it flew more than 800km in different directions, the balloon made a forced landing on ice just 470km from its departure point. The crew of three attempted to walk to civilization, but the movement of the ice floes meant they made no progress; after six weeks' trekking, they set up camp on a floe drifting rapidly southwards. Sadly, the ice cracked and their shelter collapsed, and with it their hopes. Finally they died from the effects of cold, starvation and trichinosis, caught after they ate the raw meat of a polar bear they had managed to spear. It would be another 33 years before their frozen bodies and their equipment were discovered by a Norwegian sailing ship. They were reburied in Stockholm at a funeral attended by a crowd of forty thousand. The museum exhibition poignantly includes a diary kept by one of the crew and film taken by the team, which makes for pitiful viewing: the men are seen with the polar bear they'd hunted, and other sequences show the three hopelessly pulling their sledges across the ice sheets.

The newly renovated museum has extended its remit to cover exploration of the polar region in general, with exhibitions centring on the Arctic and Antarctic historical expeditions, using Andrée as a springboard to a wider picture.

6

ARRIVAL AND GETTING AROUND · GRÄNNA

By bus Bus #101 runs roughly every 30min from Jönköping to Gränna, though #122 is less frequent but faster.

By taxi Gränna Taxi ☎ 0390 121 00.

INFORMATION

Tourist office Grenna Kulturgård, Brahegatan 36 (daily: mid-May to Aug 10am–6pm; Sept to mid-May 10am–4pm; ☎ 0390 10 38 60, ⓦ grenna.se). Housed in the same building as the museum (see p.216) and library, with free internet access.

ACCOMMODATION

Strandterrassen ☎ 0390 418 40. Gränna's youth hostel is located down at the harbour in two separate buildings at the foot of Hamnvägen. Facilities are shared and there's a kitchen for guest use. Dorms 250kr, doubles 500kr

★ **Västanå slott** About 5km south of Gränna ☎ 0390 107 00, ⓦ vastanaslott.se; get here by taxi (see above; about 150kr). A sensational historic country manor built in 1590 by Count Sten Bielke and owned in the seventeenth century by Per Brahe. This low, white castle now belongs to the von Otters, descendants of Bielke. There are no televisions in the rooms – but the sheer majesty of the antique-strewn furnishings and the fabulous lake views from the magnificent first-floor drawing room are worth the stay alone. Open April–Dec. 1490kr

EATING

Fiket Brahegatan 43 ☎ 0390 100 57. A 1950s-themed café with a rear terrace where you can enjoy the house speciality, *madelpastej*, a rich almond tart, or their excellent Gränna *knäckebröd*, a crunchy, tasty crispbread made with linseed and sunflower and sesame seeds. Mon–Fri 8.30am–6pm, Sat 8.30am–3pm, Sun 11am–4pm.

Hamnkrogen At the harbour ☎ 0390 100 38. A very pleasing restaurant specializing in well-prepared fish and meat meals from 135kr such as gravad lax with dill potatoes or zander au gratin with feta cheese and tomato. There's outside eating in summer on the sunny terrace overlooking the lake. June–Aug daily noon–10pm; April–May & Sept–Dec shorter hours; closed Jan–March.

Vadstena

With its beautiful lakeside setting, **VADSTENA**, which once served as a royal seat and important monastic centre, is a fine place for a day or two's stay. Sixty kilometres north of Gränna, the town's main attraction is its moated **castle**, designed in the sixteenth century by Gustav Vasa as part of his defensive ring protecting the Swedish heartland around Stockholm. The cobbled, twisting streets, lined with cottages covered in climbing roses, also contain an impressive fourteenth-century abbey, whose existence is the result of the passionate work of **Birgitta**, Sweden's first female saint (see box opposite).

While Vadstena boasts numerous ancient sites and buildings, each with an information plate (in English), the two outstanding attractions here are the **castle** and the **abbey**. Vadstena is also made for romantic evening strolls, with wonderful lakeside sunsets and attractive streets of irregularly shaped houses.

Vadstena Slott

Mid-May to late May & early Sept to mid-Sept daily noon–3pm; June–Aug daily 11am–4pm, July till 6pm • Entry is 60kr; it's another 30kr for the guided tours • Tours run in English June & July daily 1.30pm, Aug daily 2pm • ⓦ vadstenadirect.se

Those who've visited the castle at Kalmar will be familiar with the antics of Gustav Vasa and his troubled family, whose saga continues at **Vadstena Slott**. With a grand moat and four round towers, each with a diameter of 7m, it was originally built as a fortification to defend against Danish attacks in 1545, but was then prettified to serve as a home to Vasa's mentally ill third son, Magnus. His elder brother, Johan III, was responsible for its lavish decorations, but fire destroyed them all just before their refurbishment was completed, and to save money they simply painted fittings and decor on the walls, including the swagged curtains that can still be seen today. The castle's last resident was Hedvig Eleanor, the widowed queen of Karl X; after she died in the 1770s the castle was regarded as hopelessly unfashionable, and so no royal would consider living there. At the end of the seventeenth century, the building fell into decay and was used as a grain store; the original hand-painted wooden ceilings were chopped up and turned into grain boxes. Today, the interior is crammed with **portraits** mainly of the Vasa family, characterized by some very unhappy and unattractive faces. It's worth joining the regular English-language **tours** to hear all the Vasa family gossip.

Klosterkyrkan

Daily April & early to mid-Sept Mon–Fri 8am–5pm, Sat & Sun 10am–4pm; May Mon–Fri 8am–5pm, Sat & Sun 10am–5pm; June–Aug 8am–7pm; July 9am–7pm; mid-Sept–March Mon–Fri 8am–3.30pm, Sat 11am–3.30pm, Sun 10am–3.30pm

St Birgitta specified that the **Klosterkyrkan**, easily reached by walking towards the lake from the castle, should be "of plain construction, humble and strong". Wide, grey and sombre, the lakeside abbey, consecrated in 1430, certainly fulfils her criteria from the outside; inside it has been embellished with a celebrated collection of medieval artwork. More memorable than the crypt containing the tombs of various royals is the statue of Birgitta, now devoid of the hands "in a state of ecstasy" – as the description puts it. To the right, the poignant "Door of Grace and Honour" was where each Birgittine nun entered the abbey after being professed – the next time they would use the door would be on the day of their funeral. Birgitta's bones are encased in a red velvet box, decorated with silver and gilt medallions, in a glass case down stone steps in the monks' choir stalls.

The **altarpiece** here is worth a glance, too: another handless Birgitta, looking rather less than ecstatic, is portrayed dictating her revelations to a band of monks, nuns and acolytes, while around her, representations of hell and purgatory depict finely sculpted faces of woe disappearing into the bloody mouth of what looks like a hippopotamus. Other than Birgitta's, a tomb to note inside the abbey is that of Gustav Vasa's mentally retarded son Magnus. His grand, raised tomb is flanked at each corner by obese, glum-faced cherubs, but the most impressive feature is the remarkably lifelike hands raised in prayer on the likeness of Magnus on the top.

The monastery and nunnery

Although now housing the *Vadstena Klosterhotel* (see p.220), the **monastery** and **nunnery** on either side of the abbey are open for tours. The most interesting part of the nunnery, housed in the thirteenth-century Bjälbo Palace, is the King's Hall, with an elegant lofty ceiling. On its conversion to a convent, Birgitta had the ceiling lowered to what she considered a more appropriate level for the nuns – it remains thus today.

ST BIRGITTA

Birgitta (1303–73) came to the village of Vadstena as a lady-in-waiting to King Magnus Eriksson and his wife, Blanche of Namur, who lived at Bjälbo Palace. Married at 13, she gave birth to eight children, and had the first of her many visions while living at the palace. Such was the force of her personality, she persuaded her royal employers (to whom she was vaguely related) to give her the palace in order to start a convent and a monastery. To obtain papal approval for the monastery, she set off for Rome in 1349, but the times were against her – the pope was in Avignon, France. She spent the next twelve years in Rome, having more visions, pressing for his return but dying before she could return to Vadstena. She was canonized in 1391, a final vision having already told her this would be the case. Her daughter, Katarina, carried on her work and brought about the building of the monastery and abbey; she too became a saint and her remains lie in the same coffin as her mother's.

6

The Hospitalsmuséet

Mental Hospital Museum • Lastköpingsgatan • Daily: June & early Aug 11am–3pm; July 11am–4pm • 55kr

Just beyond the gates of the abbey graveyard, the **Hospitalsmuséet** is based in what was Sweden's oldest mental hospital, dating from 1757 and once called Stora Dårhuset ("the big loony bin"). The display of terrifying contraptions used to control and "cure" the inmates includes a spinning chair, which difficult patients were tightly strapped to and spun until they vomited; an iron bath, in which patients were tied and then scalded; and a tub, used until 1880, in which patients were held down among electric eels. The most poignant displays on the first floor are the patients' own excellently drawn pictures, depicting the tortures inflicted on them. Also on display are moving photographs of inmates from the nineteenth century (extensive research having first been carried out to ensure that the people shown have no surviving relatives).

ARRIVAL AND DEPARTURE   VADSTENA

By public transport There are no trains to Vadstena and getting here from Gränna is circuitous. It's easiest to return to Jönköping and then take the train, via Nässjö, to Motala, from where bus #612 runs to Vadstena. Motala is also easily reached from Örebro and Norrköping. The main bus stop is in the centre of town, between the castle and the abbey; there's a twice-weekly service to Stockholm (4hr).

By car It's a straight run along the E4 and Route 50 north from Gränna.

INFORMATION

Tourist office In the castle (May & Sept Mon–Sat 10am–2pm; June & Aug Mon–Sat 10am–6pm, Sun 10am–4pm; July daily 10am–7pm; Oct–April Mon–Fri 10am–2pm; ☎ 0143 315 70, ⊛ ostergotland.info).

ACCOMMODATION

Pensionat Solgården Strågatan 3 ☎ 0143 143 50, ⊛ pensionatsolgarden.se. The best-value alternative to the pricier hotels, this beautifully maintained villa from 1905 is located in a quiet, central position, with rooms named after famous artists such as Chagall and Matisse and featuring prints of their work (300kr more for private facilities). Open May–Sept. **890kr**

STF youth hostel Skänningegatan 20 ☎ 0143 765 60, ebokning@sevadstena.se. This hostel is close to the lake and barely a 5min stroll from the centre, just up from the abbey. Advance booking is essential outside the mid-June to mid-Aug period. Dorms **250kr**, doubles **500kr**

Vadstena Klosterhotel ☎ 0143 315 30, ⊛ klosterhotel.se. Dating from 1369, this hotel is located in the nunnery next to the abbey and has suitably atmospheric public areas, though the bedrooms are rather starkly decorated in monastic style and could do with freshening up somewhat. **1650kr**

EATING AND DRINKING

Gamla Konditoriet Storgatan 18 ☎ 0143 100 35. This classic, busy bakery and *konditori* in a fine seventeenth-century house is open every day for traditional cakes and sandwiches. It's also a good choice for a spot of lunch with quiches and salads. Mon–Fri 9am–6pm, Sat 9am–4pm, Sun 10am–2pm.

På Hörnet Skänningegatan 1 ☎ 0143 131 70. An understated neighbourhood pub that serves great food, including fresh cod, oven-baked salmon and lamb steak, all around 179kr. Well worth seeking out for its home-made burgers which are especially tasty and cost just 149kr. Tues–Thurs & Sun 5.30–11pm, Fri & Sat 5.30pm–1am.

Rådhuskälleren Rådhustorget ☎ 0143 121 70. Informal restaurant set in the cosy cellars of the sixteenth-century courthouse, with main dishes like fried local char (*röding*) with fennel (195kr) or pork fillet with potato wedges (155kr). It's also a pub, particularly popular with locals on Fri and Sat. Wed 6–11pm, Thurs 6pm–midnight, Fri 6pm–2am, Sat noon–2am, Sun noon–4pm.

Vadstena Valven Storgatan 18 ☎ 0143 123 40. This is the smartest restaurant in town with a fantastic-value weekday lunch special (78kr), and on Sat and Sun there's a lunch buffet for 95kr. It specializes, though, in fine dinners such as a delicious poached Vättern char in a lobster sauce served with glazed leeks (209kr). Mon–Fri 11.30am–10pm, Sat noon–10pm, Sun noon–9pm.

Örebro

The lively and youthful town of **ÖREBRO** lies on the shores of the country's fourth largest lake, Hjälmaren, roughly two-thirds of the way between Stockholm and Karlstad and around 110km north of Vadstena. Örebro's development was dictated by its important strategic position: the main route from southwest Sweden to Stockholm, King Erik's Way, ran right through the centre, where a build-up of gravel made the river fordable (Örebro means "gravel bridge"). The heart of Örebro comes as a pleasant surprise, its much-fortified thirteenth-century **castle** forming a magnificent backdrop to the water-lily-studded **Svartån River**. Aside from the town-centre attractions, there are a couple of fun trips you can make by bike, namely to the **Naturens hus** nature centre, just east of town on the shores of Hjälmaren, and to **Tysslingen lake**, a few kilometres west; in late March, several thousand whooper swans settle here for two or three weeks to feed on their way up to northern Finland and make spectacular viewing from the lakeside (binoculars are essential).

6

Örebro Castle

Entry on tours only: mid-June to mid-Aug daily in English at 2pm • 70kr

The town's first defensive fort was built after a band of German merchants settled here in the thirteenth century, attracted by rich iron ore deposits. It was enlarged in the fourteenth century by King Magnus Eriksson, who lived here; Gustav Vasa's son Karl IX added fortifications and then, following in the footsteps of Vasa's other sons, turned

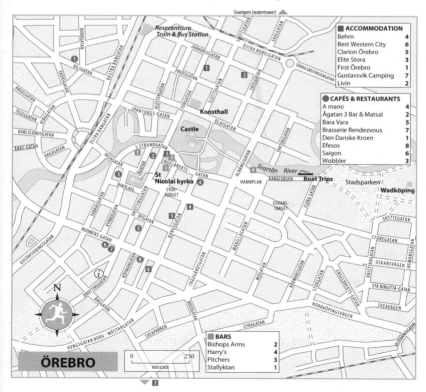

■ ACCOMMODATION	
Behrn	4
Best Western City	6
Clarion Örebro	5
Elite Stora	3
First Örebro	1
Gustavsvik Camping	7
Livin	2

● CAFÉS & RESTAURANTS	
A mano	4
Ågaten 3 Bar & Matsal	2
Bara Vara	5
Brasserie Rendezvous	7
Den Danske Kroen	1
Efesos	8
Saigon	6
Wobbler	3

■ BARS	
Bishops Arms	2
Harry's	4
Pitchers	3
Stallyktan	1

ÖREBRO

it into a splendid Renaissance castle, raising all the walls to the height of the medieval towers and plastering them in cream-coloured stucco. When the Danes were no longer a threat, the town lost its importance, and **Örebro Castle** fell into disuse and subsequently became a storehouse and a jail. In the old **prison** on the fourth floor, you can see words scratched into the walls by Russian prisoners of war. Another room was used to hold suspected witches and was well furnished by King Karl as a **torture chamber**; at the time, fear of witchcraft was reaching fever pitch, and over four hundred women lost their heads here having survived attempts to drown them in the nearby river. Naturally, the castle is said to be riddled with ghosts, ranging from that of King Magnus Eriksson's wife Blanche (also known as Blanka in Swedish and said to be in torment for having murdered her son) to Engelbrekt, who had his head lopped off two years after he stormed the castle in 1434 and led a riot on behalf of farmers oppressed by harsh taxes.

The fairytale exterior you see today is the result of renovation in the 1890s. Influenced by contemporary National Romanticism, the architects carefully restored the castle to reflect both medieval and Renaissance grandeur. The same cannot be said for the interior, where the valiant guides face a real challenge: there's no original furniture left, and many of the rooms are used for conferences, hence the emphasis on the building being a "living castle". Among the few features of interest are some fine doors and floors, dating from as recently as the 1920s, the inlays depicting historical events at Örebro; and, in the main state room, a large **family portrait** of Karl XI and his family, their eyes all popping out as a result of using arsenic to whiten their faces.

St Nicolai kyrka

Storgatan 27 • Mon–Fri 9am–8pm, Sat 10am–6pm

Just a few hundred metres south of the castle, **St Nicolai kyrka**, at the top of the very oblong Stortorget, dates from 1260. Extensive restoration in the 1860s robbed it of most of its medieval character, though recent renovations have tried to undo the damage. It was here in 1810 that the relatively unknown figure of Jean Baptiste Bernadotte, Napoleon's marshal, was elected successor to the Swedish throne. The descendants of the new King Karl Johan, who never spoke a word of Swedish, are the current royal family. Engelbrekt was also supposed to be buried here after his execution, but when his coffin was exhumed in the eighteenth century, it was empty, and his bones have never been recovered.

Konsthall

Arts Centre • Olaigatan 17B • Mon–Thurs noon–6pm, Fri noon–5pm, Sat & Sun noon–4pm • Free

Immediately behind the castle, the **Konsthall** has a surprisingly spacious series of galleries, located in a former bank, exhibiting temporary collections of contemporary international art, spread over the ground floor and in the basement in the old vaults.

OPEN ART

Between mid-June and mid-September, the city's pedestrianized centre is transformed into a huge open-air contemporary art exhibition, **Open Art**, as designers and artists display their work. Recent displays have included a gigantic upside-down teddy bear made of wood and a floating platform for model ducks and seals on the water below the castle; you name it, anything goes – the aim is to provide an urban forum for thought-provoking modern art.

Stadsparken

From the Konsthall, it's a pleasant stroll east along the waterside Olaigatan, crossing the Svartån River over Hamnbron bridge, to continue east along Kanalvägen to Örebro's stunning **Stadspark**, one of the most beautiful town parks in the country. Sunbathing locals flock here to picnic amid the park's most exceptional feature – the colour-coded border walks, each section bursting with a rainbow of flowers separated by tone.

Wadköping

May–Aug daily 11am–5pm; Sept–April Tues–Sun 11am–4pm • Free • ⊕ orebro.se/wadkoping

At the far end of the river stands an open-air museum, **Wadköping**. An entire village of centuries-old wooden cottages and shops were brought to the site in the 1950s when urban planning was threatening the historical dwellings with demolition. A local man, Bertil Waldén, campaigned to save the better ones, and relocated them here at Wadköping on the banks of the river. The extremely pretty little "high street" is flanked with low eighteenth-century buildings on one side, and on the other with taller houses from after the town fire of 1854. Some of the cottages are now lived in again and there's a very good **café**.

Naturens hus

Oljevägen 15 • Daily 11am–6pm • Free

From Wadköping, it's a pleasant cycle ride of around five to ten minutes along the banks of the Svartån River to one of Örebro's best out-of-town destinations: **Naturens hus nature centre**. The building's harmonious design and building materials (stone and glass) blend effortlessly into the natural surroundings and it's a great spot to enjoy views out over the lake, Hjälmaren. Inside you'll find information about the wildlife around the lake as well as a good café.

ARRIVAL AND GETTING AROUND   ÖREBRO

By train The train station is in the Resecentrum travel centre on Järnvägsgatan, north of the castle, along with the bus station. From Vadstena, take bus #612 north to Motala and change there for the train to Örebro.
Destinations Falun (8 daily; 2hr 50min); Gävle (7 daily; 3hr 50min); Gothenburg (7 daily; 3hr); Motala (8 daily; 1hr 10min); Stockholm (hourly; 2hr); Västerås (hourly; 50min).
By bike The town centre is easily seen on foot but if you want to get a flavour of the surrounding countryside, it's a good idea to rent a bike; you can do this at the tourist office (70kr/day).

INFORMATION

Tourist office Olof Palmestorg (Mon–Fri 10am–6pm, also June–Aug Sat & Sun 10am–4pm, Sept–May Sat & Sun noon–2pm; ☎019 21 21 21, ⊕ visitorebro.se). A 15min walk from the Resecentrum, south along Östra Bangatan and then left into Änggatan, with internet access and bike rental.

BOAT TRIPS AROUND ÖREBRO

Given Örebro's easy access to Hjälmaren just east of the town, you might want to consider taking a **boat trip** around the lake on *M/S Gustav Lagerbjelke*, which operates from late June to mid-August. There are several options available but the most popular is the five-hour **cruise** out into Hjälmaren and through the Hjälmarekanal with its many locks. Transport back to Örebro is by bus and the return ticket costs 320kr. Alternatively, shorter lunch cruises including a buffet cost a good-value 220kr. There's more information at ⊕ lagerbjelke.com.

Another option is to rent your own **canoe** or **kayak** and paddle out yourself: both are available from KFUM Örebro Kanotcenter located out of town at Hästhagsvägen (☎019 26 04 00; 40kr/hr, 160kr/day). Give them a call and they'll help with pickup and dropoff.

6

ACCOMMODATION

Behrn Stortorget 12 ☎ 019 12 00 95, ⊕ behrnhotell.se. A comfortable hotel overlooking the main square with antique furniture in an otherwise thoroughly modern structure. This hotel makes for an agreeable mix of old and new, and breakfast is served in a pleasant atrium. 1000kr/1750kr

Best Western City Kungsgatan 24 ☎ 019 601 42 00, ⊕ cityhotelorebro.se. Rooms at this business-oriented hotel, although perfectly adequate and full of the latest Scandinavian designer touches, are a little on the cramped side. Decor is typically chain-hotel: anonymous white walls, wooden floors and nondescript armchairs. 990kr/1695kr

Clarion Örebro Kungsgatan 14 ☎ 019 670 67 00, ⊕ choice.se. Well designed and stylish to a T, this place has remarkable weekend and summer discounts on its sumptuous bedrooms and wonderful bathrooms done out with black-and-white chequered tiles. On the top floor there's also a gym, sauna, jacuzzi and spa. 995kr/1470kr

★ **Elite Stora** Drottninggatan 1 ☎ 019 15 69 00, ⊕ elite.se. The oldest hotel in town – built in 1858 – with extremely attractive suites and rooms, especially on the top floor of the annexe. Said to be haunted by the ghost of a young woman who hanged herself over an arranged marriage. 935kr/1360kr

First Örebro Storgatan 24 ☎ 019 703 61, ⊕ firsthotels .se. Decked out in maritime colours and designs, this great hotel on the main drag is personally decorated in line with the owner's interests – refreshingly different for a chain hotel. Rooms are stylish and airy, making this a great choice. 1820kr

Livin Järnvägsgatan 22 ☎ 019 31 02 40, ⊕ livin.se. This newly opened hotel combines apartments with kitchenette (some have their own sauna, too), regular double rooms and simpler budget youth hostel-style accommodation, though still with private facilities. Decor is modern and features bold swirls and floral designs. 1100kr

CAMPING

Gustavsvik Camping Sommarrovägen ☎ 019 19 69 50, ⊕ gustavsvik.se. The nearest campsite is 2km south of the centre at Gustavsvik. On site there's a large open-air swimming complex as well as well-appointed cabins to rent. Open mid-April to early Nov; cabins open year-round. Tents 140kr, cabins 1035kr

EATING, DRINKING AND NIGHTLIFE

CAFÉS AND RESTAURANTS

A mano Stallbacken ☎ 019 32 33 70. Off Kungsgatan in a quiet courtyard, this style-conscious Italian place with small square tables facing a long leather bench serves classic Tuscan-inspired mains for around 280kr. Try the grilled monkfish with risotto or a three-course set dinner for 435kr. Mon–Sat 6pm till late.

Ågatan 3 Bar & Matsal Ågatan 3 ☎ 019 10 40 19. Just off Drottninggatan, a smart little restaurant with a heavy wooden interior and brown leather chairs creating a romantic atmosphere. It serves sophisticated, modern Swedish cuisine, for example, local veal or wild duck. Three courses cost 449kr. Mon–Sat 6pm till late.

★ **Bara Vara** Köpmangatan 24 ☎ 019 10 78 32. This justifiably popular place is where those in the know come for excellent cakes, muffins, ice cream, a good range of speciality coffees and a few light lunch dishes such as lasagne, quiches and salads. Mon–Fri 10am–8pm, Sat 10am–6pm, Sun noon–6pm.

★ **Brasserie Rendezvous** Drottninggatan 38 ☎ 019 10 30 80. Örebro's answer to a Parisian bistro with French posters on the walls and chi-chi red chairs, plus a menu consisting of Gallic classics such as steak frites (195kr), fillet mignon (275kr) and crème brûlée (85kr). There's a small outdoor terrace in summer. Mon–Thurs 11.30am–2pm & 5pm till late, Fri 11.30am till late, Sat noon till late.

Den Danske Kroen Kilsgatan 8 ☎ 019 611 20 69. Cosy atmosphere in an old, turreted house on the other side of the train tracks from the rest of town, this long-standing Danish restaurant serves filling Danish *smørrebrød* (open sandwiches; from 45kr), but also has a range of meat dishes, including steaks, at 229kr. Mon–Thurs 5pm till late, Fri 5pm–midnight, Sat 4pm–midnight.

Efesos Rudbecksgatan 28 ☎ 019 611 66 15. Renowned for its generous portions of tasty Greek fare, especially kebabs (129–169kr) and steaks (around 229kr). The interior here is plain and simple but that doesn't put the crowds off. Be sure to reserve a table as it's always busy. Mon–Thurs 4–11pm, Fri 4pm–midnight, Sat noon–midnight, Sun noon–10pm.

Saigon Rudbecksgatan 18 ☎ 019 10 08 75. This stylish Asian restaurant is boldly decorated in greens and oranges and the food is equally sophisticated: the tiger prawns with Thai basil, pad thai and red curry are all winners. Mains around 100kr. Daily 11am–9pm.

★ **Wobbler** Kyrkogatan 2 ☎ 019 10 07 40. Classic Swedish cooking with a modern twist at this bright and airy place with tiled floor and a separate tapas lounge. Elaborate mains (from 159kr) such as roast Hjälmaren zander with pepper and charlotte vinaigrette (229kr), and tapas plates too (175kr). Mon–Sat 11am–2.30pm & 5pm–midnight, Sun 1–10pm.

BARS

Bishops Arms Drottninggatan 1 ☎ 019 15 69 20. Hugely popular for outdoor drinking with a large summer terrace overlooking the castle, it serves a limited range of bar meals and is rightly known for an impressive selection of on-tap beers and ales. Mon & Tues 4pm–midnight, Wed & Thurs 4pm–1am, Fri 3pm–2am, Sat 1pm–2am, Sun 3–1pm.

Harry's Hamnplan 1 ☎019 10 89 89. Set in the old red-brick technical museum building on the riverside, 1min walk east of the castle, this is one of Örebro's most acclaimed bars; there's also a nightclub here on Fri and Sat evenings. Tues & Wed 5pm till late, Thurs–Sat 5pm–2am.

Pitchers Engelbrektsgatan 4 ☎019 25 30 40. A long

and narrow sportsbar with big screens showing the latest matches. Extremely busy, and popular with the town's sports followers. In summer there's also a big outdoor terrace overlooking the castle. Mon, Tues & Thurs noon–midnight, Wed noon–1am, Fri & Sat noon–2am.

Stallyktan Södra Strandgatan 3B ☎019 10 33 23. This excellent, rustic pub is a better choice for a quiet drink and dinner than most of the bigger venues. On Tues until 9pm there's a buffet for a good-value 69kr plus specials on beer. Mon 6–11pm, Tues 5–11pm, Wed & Thurs 5pm–midnight, Fri & Sat 5pm–2am.

Norrköping and around

Although ranking only as Sweden's eighth largest city, enjoyable **NORRKÖPING** punches well above its weight. It's the town's striking industrial heritage that draws people here – the old mills clustered around the Motala River, together with general youthful air, make for an appealing diversion. The last big mill closed its doors in 1992, but Norrköping retains one of Europe's best-preserved industrial landscapes, with handsome red-brick and stuccoed mills reflecting in the waters of its river. Based here, you could easily visit the **Kolmården Djurpark**, Sweden's premier zoo and safari park, as a day-trip.

Drottninggatan

Norrköping's north–south central artery, **Drottninggatan** runs ruler-straight from the train station and crosses Motala ström, the small, rushing river that attracted the Dutch industrialist **Louis De Geer** (1587–1652) to the town in the early seventeenth century. He was known as the father of Swedish industry, and his paper mill, which still operates today, became the biggest factory in town. Many of Norrköping's buildings, and the trams, are painted in De Geer's colour of choice – a tortilla-chip yellow – which has become synonymous with the town.

Just a few steps down from the station, compact **Carl Johans Park** has 25,000 cacti, formally arranged in thematic patterns and interspersed with brilliantly coloured flowers and palm trees. Glance to the right from here (with the Resecentrum behind you) across Slottsgatan, and you'll see the splendid 1906 city **theatre**, with its Art Nouveau curves and double Ionic columns. Over the river, follow the tram lines up cobbled Drottninggatan and turn right into Repslagaregatan for **Gamlatorget**, overlooked by a charismatic Carl Milles sculpture of Louis De Geer with a bale of cloth slung over his shoulder.

Konstmuseum

June–Aug Tues–Sun noon–4pm, Wed until 8pm; Sept–May Tues–Sun 11am–5pm, Tues & Thurs until 8pm • Free • ⓦ norrkoping.se/konstmuseet

At the southernmost tip of Drottninggatan, Norrköping's **Konstmuseum** holds some of the country's best-known modernist works. Founded by a local snuff manufacturer at the turn of the twentieth century, the galleries offer a fine, well-balanced progression from seventeenth-century Baroque through to twentieth-century work. As you head back north from the art museum, the bunker-like concrete building to the right at Södra Promenaden 105 is the town **library**; more user-friendly than most, it has a range of newspapers from all over the world.

DeGeerhallen

To the west of Gamlatorget lies the modern and stylish riverside **DeGeerhallen**, a concert hall surrounded by trees and providing a lovely setting for the café, *Kråkholmen* (see p.228). It's worth stepping inside for a moment, as the concert hall's apparent modernity belies the fact that this was once one of De Geer's paper factories, though little remains now of its former incarnation.

Arbetets museum

Museum of Work • Daily 11am–5pm • Free • ⓦ arbetetsmuseum.se

West along the river on your right is the exceptionally well-presented **Arbetets museum**, housed in a triangular, yellow-stuccoed factory built in 1917. Known as *Strykjärnet* ("the iron") – though its shape and colour are more reminiscent of a wedge of cheese – the building was described by Carl Milles as Europe's most beautiful factory. The museum has seven floors of exhibitions on living conditions, workers' rights and day-to-day life in the mills. The most poignant (and the only permanent exhibit) tells the story of Alva Carlsson, who worked in the building for 35 years – a fascinating insight into working-class culture and the role of Swedish women in the first half of the twentieth century.

Stadsmuseum

City Museum • Tues–Fri 11am–5pm, Sat & Sun noon–5pm • Free • ⓦ norrkoping.se/stadsmuseet

The excellent **Stadsmuseum** is set in an interconnecting (and confusing) network of old industrial properties. The most rewarding of its permanent exhibitions is a street showing various trades from the nineteenth century: there are workshops of a milliner, confectioner, chimney sweep and, in a back yard, a carriage maker. All are cleverly designed and well worth a wander.

Visualiseringscenter

Visualization Centre • Kungsgatan 54 • Tues & Wed 11am–6pm, Thurs & Fri 11am–9pm, Sat & Sun 11am–5pm • 140kr for both the exhibition and the cinema

Just to the west of Bergsbron, beyond Arbetetsmuseum, you'll find Norrköping's new pride and joy: the **Visualiseringscenter**. The centre's rather worthy aim is to explain, predominantly to younger visitors, how various visual techniques are used in science today, in areas ranging from weather forecasts to postmortems. However, it's the massive dome-shaped **cinema** which really makes a visit here worthwhile, showing a range of breathtaking 3D films.

Kolmårdens Djurpark

Kolmården wildlife park • May, June & mid-Aug to late Aug daily 10am–5pm; July to mid-Aug daily 10am–7pm; Sept Sat & Sun 10am–5pm • 379kr • Ⓦ kolmarden.com • Bus #432 from Norrköping; timetables at Ⓦ ostgotatrafiken.se

If you've only got time for one excursion from Norrköping, make it to **Kolmårdens Djurpark**, a safari park, zoo and dolphinarium that is one of Sweden's biggest attractions. Just 28km northeast of Norrköping and accessible by frequent buses, it's understandably popular with children, for whom there's a special section, and if your views on zoos are negative, it's just about possible to be convinced that this one is different. There are no cages; instead, sunken enclosures, rock barriers and moats prevent the animals from feasting on their captors as you glide silently over their heads in a cable car. Check out the dolphin shows (generally between one and four a day) and the working farm. There's a youth hostel on site, or you can camp five miles away (see p.228).

Tropicarium

Daily: May, June, Aug & Sept 10am–6pm; July 10am–8pm; Oct–April 10am–4pm • 100kr • Ⓦ tropicarium.se

The adjacent **Tropicarium** contains Sweden's largest collection of tropical plants and animals, spread out over two square kilometres. The interior really is extremely realistic, even featuring a mock-up of an alligator swamp which receives rain and thunderstorms every hour. The most popular attraction is the shark aquarium, with three different species of shark and hundreds of other tropical fish.

ARRIVAL AND DEPARTURE
NORRKÖPING AND AROUND

By train The train station is in the Resecentrum on Norra Promenaden from where it's a 10min stroll uphill towards the town centre and the museum complex.

Destinations Copenhagen via Kastrup airport (6 daily; 3hr 45min); Malmö (hourly; 3hr 15min); Nyköping (hourly; 40min); Stockholm (hourly; 1hr 15min).

INFORMATION AND TOURS

Tourist office Källvindsgatan 1 (late June to late Aug daily 10am–6pm; Oct–April Mon–Thurs 10am–5pm, Fri 10am–3pm; rest of year Mon–Fri 10am–5pm, Sat 10am–2pm; ☎011 15 50 00, Ⓦ experience.norrkoping .se). A helpful office 10min walk from the Resecentrum,

with internet connection
Tours Staff at the tourist office can explain routes and times for the 1902 vintage tram, which circles around on a sightseeing tour during summer.

ACCOMMODATION

Thanks largely to the booming local economy, Norrköping receives a lot of business trade during the week, and has a good array of **hotels** to cater for its often demanding visitors, though there are also a number of cheaper options available.

6

Best Western Princess Skomakaregatan 8 ☎011 28 58 40, ⓦprincesshotel.se. Located in a quiet street close to the museums and the main drag, this chain hotel is predictably modern, unadventurous and rather plain. Its summer and weekend prices, though, make this one exceptionally good value. <u>650kr/1100kr</u>

Centric Gamla Rådstugugatan 18–20 ☎011 12 90 30, ⓦcentrichotel.se. An inexpensive, comfortable hotel, 500m south of the train station. The reception in this stylish building from 1932 features a striking wall fresco by Gothenburg artist Lars Gillies depicting Norrköping's central areas. <u>695kr/1040kr</u>

Elite Grand Tyskatorget 2, ☎011 36 41 00, ⓦgrandhotel.elite.se. This upmarket hotel from the early twentieth century is certainly the best in town, though it doesn't come cheap. Bang in the centre, its rooms are a stylish blend of classic and modern, and its staff go the extra mile to create a home-from-home feel. <u>807kr/1317kr</u>

President Vattengränden 11 ☎011 12 95 20, ⓦprofilhotels.se. Straight out of an IKEA catalogue, the designer rooms here are well equipped, full of the latest furniture and decked out with loud, brash colours; some of the rooms also have their own private jacuzzi. Tastefully done and extremely central. <u>1095kr/1675kr</u>

Södra Södra Promenaden 142 ☎011 25 35 00, ⓦsodrahotellet.se. A calm and pleasant alternative to the chain hotels, set in a sympathetically renovated 1920s house in a residential street formerly favoured by textile-mill owners. There's also a sauna and a couple of exercise bikes for guests' use. <u>750kr/925kr</u>

Turistgården Vandrarhem Ingelstagatan 31 ☎011 10 11 60, ⓦturistgarden.se. Norrköping's comfortable and centrally located STF hostel is just a few hundred metres behind the train station. There's a choice of double rooms with private facilities as well as rooms with shared bathrooms or four-person dorms. Dorms <u>260kr</u>, doubles <u>530kr</u>

Varglyan Kolmårdens Djurpark ☎011 24 90 00. Excellent hostel within the safari park, offering five four-bed and four six-bed rooms. Mid-June to mid-Aug only. Four-bed dorms <u>940kr</u>, six-bed <u>1250kr</u>

CAMPING

First Camp Kolmården Bodaviken ☎011 39 82 50, ⓦfirstcamp.se/kolmarden. Campsite 5km from **Kolmårdens Djurpark**, with four-bed cabins and the decent *Ettans Café* next door. Tents <u>140kr</u>, cabins <u>995kr</u>

EATING AND DRINKING

There's a fair selection of **places to eat and drink** in Norrköping, some of which double as bars. Although in Swedish terms it's only a moderately sized town, the array of food on offer is unmatched for miles around. The nicest place to eat is **Knäppingsborg**, an up-and-coming area of trendy restaurants and bars.

CAFÉS AND RESTAURANTS

Bagarstugan Knäppingsborgsgatan 3 ☎011 470 20 20. The best of the new restaurants springing up in the Knäppingsborg area, this one serves delicious Italian treats such as cannelloni and unusual foccacia pizzas for around 100kr. The cheese platter at 95kr is also great value. Mon–Wed 7.30am–8pm, Thurs–Sat 7.30am–10pm.

Café Kuriosa Hörngatan 6 ☎011 10 36 70. A super, central old-fashioned café with a little garden, serving home-made cakes, savoury pies and ice cream. Quiche and salad costs 48kr. Try the fragrant Kuriosa tea, scented with apricots and vanilla. Mon–Thurs 10am–7pm, Fri 10am–6pm, Sat 10am–4pm.

Fisk Magasinet Skolgatan 1 ☎011 13 45 60. Cosy and snug fish restaurant with an entire wall decorated with pictures of tropical fish. Mains, such as poached halibut with horseradish, go for 185–320kr. The herring and crispbread plate at 120kr is good value and very tasty. Mon–Fri 11.30am–2pm & 5pm till late, Sat noon till late.

Källaren Bacchus Gamlatorget 4 ☎011 10 07 40. The oldest restaurant in town, housed in a vaulted cellar from the mid-eighteenth century, this fantastic, atmospheric restaurant serves light eats and warm grills – try the fillet of Östergötland beef in red wine sauce (225kr). The herring plate with trimmings (125kr) is another winner. Tues–Fri 5pm till late, Sat 1pm till late, Sun 1–9pm.

Kråkholmen Dalsgatan 15 ☎011 15 50 30. Outside the Concert Hall; enter through the hall, or round the back. The daily weekday 84kr lunch menu here features salads, light dishes and home-cooked meals served against the backdrop of the crashing waters of the Motala River. Mon–Fri 11.30am–1.30pm.

Sing Thai Trädgårdsgatan 15 ☎011 18 61 88. A good-value Thai restaurant right next to the town hall, open for both lunch (until 3pm) and dinner. The set lunch is 79kr, or 102kr lets you put three dishes together. Otherwise, in the evening, mains are 82kr–105kr. Mon–Thurs 11am–10pm, Fri 11am–11pm, Sat noon–11pm, Sun 1–10pm.

Trädgårn Prästgatan 1 ☎011 10 07 40. This summer bar and grill is very popular, especially on warm evenings when seemingly the entire town is squeezed in here; the entrance is beneath an iron sign marked "VIP Paraden". There are specials on food and drink 4–6pm; otherwise something and chips goes for around 150kr. Mon–Sat 4pm–1am, closed in bad weather.

BARS

Bishops Arms Drottninggatan 2 ☎ 011 36 41 20. Undoubtedly the most popular pub in Norrköping, this place has gone from strength to strength since opening in 1994 and boasts the biggest selection of beers and whiskies in town. Outdoor seating in summer. Mon–Thurs 4pm–midnight, Fri & Sat 4pm–1am, Sun 4–10pm.

Cromwell House Kungsgatan 36 ☎ 011 18 26 00. Dark, faux-English pub full of stained glass and locals in a handy location on the main street. Quite good-value grilled meat dishes cost 139–239kr. There's also a busy nightclub here at weekends. Mon 4–11pm, Tues–Thurs 4pm–midnight, Fri 4pm–3am, Sat 1pm–3am, Sun 1–10pm.

Harry's Drottninggatan 63 ☎ 011 10 80 80. One of the busier spots for a drink with the usual array of signature half-built brick walls, wooden wall panels, well-polished floors – and well-oiled locals. The whole place mutates into a nightclub on Fri & Sat which really draws the crowds. Mon–Wed 3pm till late, Thurs 3pm–1am, Fri & Sat noon–3am.

Highlander Inn St Persgatan 94 ☎ 011 16 58 90. Norrköping's answer to a real Scottish pub that's well known for its large selection of beers and whiskies and is a popular hangout with the locals. It also serves bar meals such as Wiener schnitzel and pike-perch for 149–229kr. Mon–Thurs noon–11pm, Fri & Sat noon–1am, Sun noon–10pm.

Gotland

Tales of good times on **GOTLAND** are rife. Wherever you are in Sweden, one mention of this ancient Baltic island 90km from the mainland will elicit a typical Swedish sigh, followed by an anecdote about what a great place it is. You'll hear that the short summer season is an exciting time to visit; that the place is hot, fun and lively. These claims are largely true: the island has a distinctly youthful feel, with young, mobile Stockholmers deserting the capital in summer for a boisterous time on its beaches. The flower-power era still makes its presence felt with a smattering of elderly VW camper vans lurching off the ferries, but shiny Saabs outnumber them fifty to one. During summer, the bars, restaurants and campsites are packed, the streets swarm with revellers and the sands are awash with bodies. It's not everyone's cup of tea: to avoid the hectic summer altogether, come in late May or September when, depending on your level of bravado, you might still manage to swim in the waters around the island. To experience the setting at its most frenetic, come in August during **Medieval Week** (see p.233), when people put a huge effort into dressing the part.

Brief history

Visby, Gotland's capital, has always been the scene of frenetic activity of some kind. Its temperate climate and position attracted the Vikings as early as the sixth century, and the lucrative trade routes they opened, from here through to Byzantium and western Asia, guaranteed the island its prosperity. With the ending of Viking domination, a "golden age" followed, with Gotland's inhabitants maintaining trading posts abroad and signing treaties as equals with European and Asian leaders. However by the late twelfth century, their autonomy had been undermined by the growing power of the **Hanseatic League**. Under its influence, Visby became one of the great cities of medieval Europe, as important as London or Paris, famed for its wealth and strategic power. A contemporary ballad had it that "The Gotlanders weigh their gold with twenty-pound weights. The pigs eat out of silver troughs and the women spin with golden distaffs."

Gotland today

Today, all the revelry which keeps Visby buzzing from late June to the end of August takes place against the spectacular backdrop of its medieval architecture; two hundred or so Hanseatic warehouses are dotted among stone and wooden houses, the whole lot nestled within its ancient walls.

There is a real charm to the **rest of Gotland** – rolling green countryside, forest-lined roads, fine beaches and small fishing villages. Everywhere the rural skyline is dominated by **churches**, the remnants of medieval settlements destroyed in the Danish invasion. Nowhere else in Scandinavia holds such a concentration of medieval churches, and 93

6

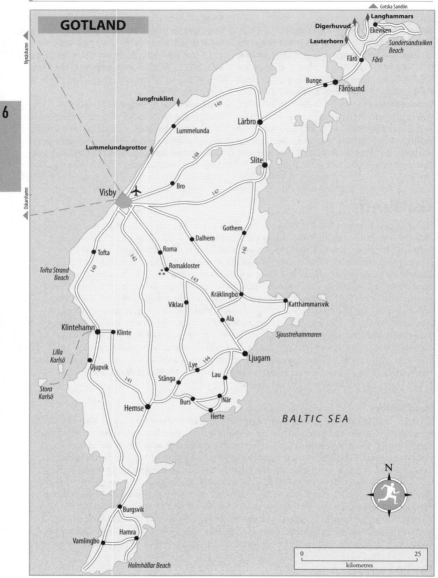

of them are still in use, displaying a unique Baltic Gothic style and providing the most permanent reminder of Gotland's ancient wealth. Churches aside, however, very few people bother to explore the island, perhaps because of Visby's magnetic pull; consequently, the main roads around Gotland are pleasingly free of traffic and minor roads positively deserted – **cycling** is a joy. As you travel, keep an eye out for the waymarkers erected in the 1780s to indicate the distance from Wisby (the old spelling of the town's name), calculated in Swedish miles – one of which is equivalent to 10km.

ARRIVAL

By plane Flights to Gotland are good value if booked early. Skyways (ⓦ skyways.se) operate from Arlanda airport in Stockholm; Gotlandsflyg (ⓦ gotlandsflyg.se) have services from Arlanda and Bromma and several provincial airports. Cheapest single tickets are 328kr.

By ferry Ferries to Gotland are numerous and, in summer, packed, so try to plan well ahead. Two mainland ports serve the island: Nynäshamn (mid-June to mid-Aug 5 daily; mid-Aug to mid-June 2 daily) and Oskarshamn (mid-June to mid-Aug 2 daily; mid-Aug to mid-June 1 daily), and crossings take about 3hr. Prices depend on season; a one-way ticket costs from 258kr. Buy tickets online at ⓦ destinationgotland.se.

GETTING AROUND

By bus It's common for there to be several hours between services so always check timetables before setting out; ⓦ gotland.se/kollektivtrafiken.

By bike For getting around the island, it's hard to resist the temptation to rent a bike, given the flat terrain and empty roads. See p.235 for rental outlets in Visby. Bikes can also easily be rented at various towns to the south of the capital, less so further north. Gotland's buses take limited numbers of bikes; the driver will hang your cycle on the back of the bus outside.

Visby

VISBY is a city made for wandering and lingering over coffees and slices of cake. Whether climbing the **ramparts** of the surrounding walls, or meandering up and down the warren of cobbled, sloping streets, there's plenty to tease the eye. Pretty **Packhusplan**, the oldest square in the city, is bisected by curving Strandgatan, which runs southwards to the fragmentary ruins of **Visborgs Slott**, overlooking the harbour. Built in the fifteenth century by Erik of Pomerania, the castle was blown up by the Danes in the seventeenth century. In the opposite direction, Strandgatan runs northwest towards the sea and the **Jungfrutornet** (Maiden's Tower), where a local goldsmith's daughter was walled up alive – reputedly for betraying the city to the Danes.

Brief history

Visby is much older than its medieval trappings suggest: its name comes from *vi*, "the sacred place", and *by*, "the settlement", a derivation that reflects its status as a Stone Age sacrificial site. After the Gotlanders had founded their trading houses in the eleventh and twelfth centuries, the Hansa or **Hanseatic League** was created, comprising a group of towns that formed a federation to assert their interests and protect their seaborne commerce. Following the foundation of Lübeck in the 1150s, German merchants began to expand into the eastern Baltic area in order to gain access to the coveted Russian market. A trading agreement between Gotlanders and the League in 1161 gave the islanders the right to trade freely throughout the whole Saxon area, while Germans were able to settle in Visby, which became the League's principal centre and the place where all lines of Baltic trade met. As Visby metamorphosed from Gotlandic village to international city, it was the Germans who led the way in form and architecture, building warehouses up to six storeys high with hoists facing the street, still apparent today.

In 1350, the **Black Death** swept through Gotland, creating ghost towns of whole parishes and leaving more than eight thousand people dead. Eleven years later, during the power struggle between Denmark and Sweden, the Danish king Valdemar III took Gotland by force and advanced on Visby. The burghers and traders of the city, well aware of the wealth here, shut the gates and sat through the slaughter which was taking place outside, only surrendering when it was over. Hostilities and piracy were the hallmarks of the following two centuries. In 1525, an army from Lübeck stormed the much-weakened Visby, torching the northern parts of the town. With the arrival of the Reformation and the weakness of the local economy, the churches could no longer be maintained, and Visby's era of greatness clanged to a close.

6

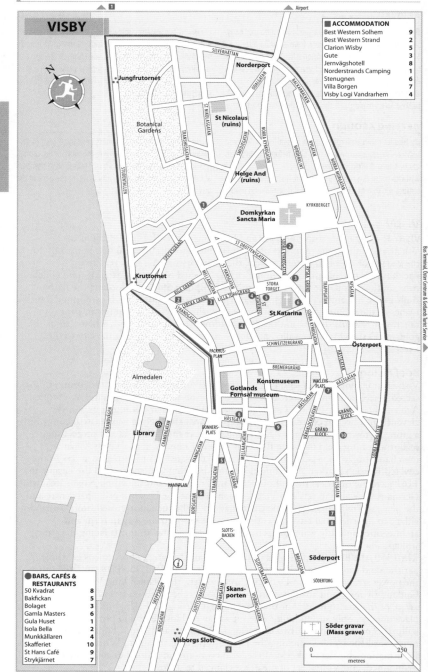

VISBY

Airport

ACCOMMODATION

Best Western Solhem	9
Best Western Strand	2
Clarion Wisby	5
Gute	3
Jernvägshotell	8
Norderstrands Camping	1
Stenugnen	6
Villa Borgen	7
Visby Logi Vandrarhem	4

SILVERHÄTTAN

Norderport

Jungfrutornet

St Nicolaus (ruins)

Botanical Gardens

KYRKBERGET

Helge And (ruins)

Domkyrkan Sancta Maria

Kruttornet

STORA TORGET

St Katarina

Österport

SCHWEITZERGRAND

BREMERGRÄND

PACKHUS-PLAN

Almedalen

Konstmuseum

Gotlands Fornsal museum

WACLERS PLATS

GRAND BLOCK

GRÄND KLOCK

HÄSTGATAN

DONNERS-PLATS

Library

@

HAMNGATAN

HAMNPLAN

SLOTTS-BACKEN

Söderport

SÖDERTORG

i

Skans-porten

Söder gravar (Mass grave)

Visborgs Slott

0   250
metres

BARS, CAFÉS & RESTAURANTS

50 Kvadrat	8
Bakfickan	5
Bolaget	3
Gamla Masters	6
Gula Huset	1
Isola Bella	2
Munkkällaren	4
Skafferiet	10
St Hans Café	9
Strykjärnet	7

Bus Terminal, Öster Centrum & Gotlands Turist Service

Ferry Terminal & Gotlandsresor (Room Booking Service)

Norra Murgatan and Studentallén

Strolling around the twisting streets and atmospheric walls is not something that palls quickly, but if you need a focus, aim for **Norra Murgatan**, above the cathedral, once one of Visby's poorest areas. The end of the street nearest Norderport enjoys the best view of the walls and city rooftops. Alternatively, head for the water's edge, where **Studentallén** is a popular late-evening haunt and the sunsets are magnificent – brilliant fiery reds, glinting mirrored waters and bobbing sailing boats in the distance.

Strandgatan and around

6

Strandgatan is the best place to view the impressive **merchants' houses** looming over the narrow streets, with storerooms above the living quarters and cellars below; most notable among these is the clearly signposted **Burmeisterska huset** in Donnerplats, which is attractive and in good condition. One of the most picturesque buildings on the street is the old pharmacy, **Gamla Apoteket**, a lofty old place with gloriously higgledy-piggledy windows; it's at the corner of Strandgatan and Lybska gränd. If you feel like something more educational, head for the fine **Fornsal museum**, which covers pretty well all there is to know about Gotland, and Visby in particular – and there's a rather good art gallery close by.

Gotlands Fornsal museum

Historical Museum of Gotland • Strandgatan 14 • June to mid-Sept daily 10am–6pm; mid-Sept to May Tues–Sun noon–4pm • 100kr • ⓦ gotlandsmuseum.se

The outstanding **Gotlands Fornsal museum** is a must-see for anyone interested in **Viking history**. Housed in a mid-eighteenth century distillery, it comprises five storeys of exhibition halls covering eight thousand years of history, plus a good café and bookstore. Among the most impressive of the displays is the **Hall of Picture Stones**. Dating mostly from the fifth to seventh centuries, these large, keyhole-shaped stones are richly ornamented. The earlier ones are covered in runic inscriptions and are more intriguing, with vivid depictions of people, animals, ships and houses. Other rooms trace the history of **medieval Visby**; look out for the original trading booth, the sort of place where the burghers of Visby and foreign merchants would have dealt in commodities – furs, lime, wax, honey and tar – brought from all over northern Europe. Gotland's ecclesiastical history is also well covered with an impressive exhibition of ornate wooden carvings of bishops, Mary Magdalene and a truly magnificent triptych dating from the early sixteenth century from Vall church on the island.

The Viking Treasury

It's the **Viking Treasury** on the first floor that really steals the show. Gotland's wealth of gold and silver objects is unique; more hoards of Viking-age treasure have been found on the island than anywhere else in the world, clearly a sign of its economic and social importance. On display are hundreds of shiny coins and trinkets – some brought to

---

MEDIEVAL WEEK

During the second week of August, Visby becomes the backdrop for a boisterous re-enactment of the conquest of the island by the Danes in 1361. **Medieval Week** (ⓦ medeltidsveckan.se) sees music in the streets, medieval food on sale in the restaurants (no potatoes – they hadn't yet been brought to Europe) and on the Sunday a procession re-enacting Valdemar's triumphant entry through Söderport to Storatorget. Here, people in the role of burghers are stripped of their wealth, and the procession then moves on to the Maiden's Tower. Locals and visitors alike really get into the spirit of this festival, with a good fifty percent of people dressed up and on the streets. There are weekly **jousting tournaments** throughout July and early August.

Gotland from as far afield as Samarkand, Persia and Afghanistan, others from England. In a room off the treasury, the world's largest find of Viking-age silver, the **Spillings Hoard**, is proudly exhibited in a vast glass cabinet. Discovered in a farmer's field in the north of Gotland in 1999, the hoard, which lay buried for 1130 years, is truly breathtaking. It comprises 87kg of silver and bronze, including over 14,000 coins (the earliest dating from 539AD), neck rings, armbands and spiral rings. Elsewhere in the museum, look out for the two skeletons displayed in glass cases. The occupant of one, a 40-year-old man buried in foetal position with two pieces of antler and flint arrows, is, at roughly 8000 years old, one of the oldest in Sweden.

Gotlands Konstmuseum

St Hansgatan 21 • Mid-June to mid-Aug daily 11am–5pm; mid-Aug to mid-June Tues–Sun noon–4pm • 50kr • ⓦ gotlandsmuseum.se

A couple of streets up from the Fornsal museum, Gotland's **Konstmuseum** has some innovative temporary exhibitions of contemporary painting and sculpture, and installations which tease the eye. Though for the most part much less exciting, the permanent collection on the top floor is given over to twentieth-century Gotlandic art; among the few notable classics is Axel Lindman's 1917 oil of Visby from the beach, showing brilliant dabs of sun before a storm. The eye is also drawn to a stunning picture by William Blair Bruce of his wife, the sculptor Carolina. The painting, from 1891, shows her at work, and the lifelike qualities of the style are remarkable.

The town wall

The oldest of the towers in Visby's **town wall** is the dark, atmospheric **Kruttornet** (Gunpowder Tower) by Almedalen, built in the eleventh century to protect the old harbour and offering some grand views of Visby. The **wall** itself, a 3km circuit enclosing the entire settlement, was built around the end of the thirteenth century for a rather different purpose: it was actually aimed at isolating the city's foreign traders from the locals.

Söder gravar

Just outside the wall to the east of Söderport (South Gate), **Söder gravar** is a mass grave, excavated in the twentieth century, of two thousand people; more than half were women, children and invalids who were slaughtered when Danish king Valdemar attacked the town in 1361. There's a cross here, erected by the survivors of the carnage; the inscription reads: "In 1361 on the third day after St James, the Goths fell into the hands of the Danes. Here they lie. Pray for them."

Valdemar's Breach

A section of the wall near Söderport was broken down to allow Valdemar to ride through as conqueror. **Valdemar's Breach** is recognizable by its thirteen crenellations representing, so the story goes, the thirteen knights who rode through with the Danish king. Valdemar soon left, in possession of booty and trade agreements, and Visby continued to prosper while the countryside around it stagnated, its people and wealth destroyed.

Domkyrkan Sancta Maria

Daily: mid-June to mid-Aug daily 9am–9pm; mid-Aug to mid-June 9am–5pm

At the height of its power, Visby maintained more **churches** than any other town in Sweden – sixteen in all, most of which are dramatic ruins today. However, one, the **Domkyrkan Sancta Maria**, is still in use. Constructed between 1190 and 1225, it was built for visiting Germans, becoming the German parish church when they settled in the city. In 1300, a large Gothic chapel was built to the south, the eastern tower was elevated and the nave was raised to create storage space; this was where the burghers kept their money, papers and records. It's been heavily restored, and about the only original fixture left is the thirteenth-century sandstone font inside. Most striking are its **towers**, a square one at the western front end and two slimmer eastern ones, standing sentry over the surrounding buildings. Originally each had spires, but following an eighteenth-century fire, they were crowned with fancy Baroque cupolas, giving them the appearance of inverted ice-cream cones. Inside, have a look beneath the pulpit, decorated with a fringe of unusually ugly angels' faces.

St Nicolaus

Seventeenth- and eighteenth-century builders and decorators found the smaller churches in the city to be an excellent source of free limestone, tiles and fittings – which accounts for the fact that most are ruins today. Considering the number of tourists clambering about them, it's surprising that the smaller church ruins manage to retain a proud yet abandoned look. Best of what's left is the great **St Nicolaus** ruin, just down the road from the Domkyrkan. Destroyed in 1525, its part-Gothic, part-Romanesque shell hosts a week-long **chamber music festival** (Ⓦ gotlandchamber.se), starting at the end of July; tickets cost around 200kr for most events and are available from the tourist office.

St Katarina

One of the loveliest ruins to view at night is **St Katarina** in Storatorget; its Gothic interior is one of the finest in Visby, having belonged to one of the town's first Franciscan monasteries, founded in 1233. This church was built in 1250; at night its glorious arches, lit creamy yellow, frame the blue-black sky.

ARRIVAL AND GETTING AROUND   VISBY

By plane Visby airport is 3km north of town and a 5min ride by taxi into the centre (not more than 135kr).
By ferry Ferries serving Visby dock at the same terminal, just outside the city walls; for the centre, turn left out of the terminal and keep walking for 5min.

By bike You can rent bikes just outside the ferry terminal from Gotlands Cykeluthyrning, Skeppsbron 2 (from 85kr/day; Ⓦ gotlandscykeluthyrning.com) and from Visby Hyrcykel at Östervägen 1 near Österport (85kr/day; Ⓦ visbyhyrcykel.se).

INFORMATION

Tourist office Skeppsbron 4–6 (May to mid-June & mid-to end Aug Mon–Fri 8am–5pm, Sat & Sun 10am–4pm; mid-June to mid-Aug daily 8am–7pm; Sept Mon–Fri 8am–5pm, Sat & Sun 11am–2pm; Oct–April Mon–Fri 8am–noon & 12.30–4pm; ☎ 0498 20 17 00, Ⓦ gotland .info). Visby's main tourist office is conveniently en route between the ferries and the old town, has plentiful maps and information brochures and the informative English-language guide, *The Key to all of Gotland's Churches*, which

lists the key features of all the island's churches in alphabetical order.
Tours The tourist office runs several tours, one of which, the walking tour of the town (mid-June to mid-Aug 2–3 times a week; 100kr), is worth considering, especially if time is short.
Internet There are no internet cafés in Visby, but the library (Mon–Fri 10am–7pm, Sat & Sun noon–3pm) at Cramergatan 5, by Almedalen, has free access.

ACCOMMODATION

Finding accommodation in Visby should seldom be a problem. There are plenty of **hotels** (though few are particularly cheap), several **campsites** with cabins and a couple of good **hostels**. Unlike most other places in Sweden, prices in Gotland are higher in summer; the lower price we give is for out of season and non-summer weekends.

Best Western Solhem Solhemsgatan 3 ☎ 0498 25 90 90, Ⓦ hotellsolhem.se. Just outside the city walls at Skansporten, this large, comfortable chain hotel has a basement sauna and is quieter than the more central

options. Rooms are modern, if uninspiring, though do vary in size so ask to see one before you accept. **1194kr/841kr**
Best Western Strand Strandgatan 34 ☎ 0498 25 88 00, Ⓦ strandhotel.net. A rather glamorous place in a

6

quiet cobbled street in the heart of town, with a sauna, steam bath, indoor pool and a stylish atmosphere. Altogether more luxurious, and expensive, than its sister hotel, the Solhem. **1504kr/1062kr**

★ **Clarion Wisby** Strandgatan 6 ☎ 0498 25 75 00, ⊕ wisbyhotell.se. Splendid, central hotel in a building dating back to the Middle Ages when it was used as a merchant's storehouse. Rooms are beautifully decorated with wooden panelling, soft lighting and period furniture, and there's a sumptuous pool, too. **1970kr/1770kr**

Gute Mellangatan 29 ☎ 0498 20 22 60, ⊕ hotellgute .se. Very central and reasonably comfortable hotel housed in a building dating from 1887 which once served as Visby's cinema. All rooms are individually decorated though some are overly flowery and fussy. **1195kr/995kr**

Jernvägshotell Adelsgatan 9 ☎ 0498 20 33 00, ⊕ gtsab.se. Although train services on Gotland ceased in 1960, this former railway hotel, now a youth hostel, is still in operation with modern, comfortable rooms, though with no dorms. In summer guests must be aged over 25 years old. Doubles **300kr**

Stenugnen Korsgatan 4–6 ☎ 0498 21 02 11, ⊕ stenugnen.nu. Bright and airy rooms abound at this cosy hotel where the decor has a subtle maritime feel. The staff are friendly and personable and breakfast is served in a sunny glass atrium at the rear. **799kr/499kr**

Villa Borgen Adelsgatan 11 ☎ 0498 20 33 00, ⊕ www .gtsab.se. Attractive family hotel in the middle of the action, yet with lovely, peaceful gardens. Tastefully decorated en-suite, though rather small, rooms. There's a sauna and solarium too. **1695kr/895kr**

★ **Visby Logi** Vandrarhem St Hansgatan 31 ☎ 070 752 20 55, ⊕ visbylogi.se. Five cosy double rooms decorated in tasteful whites and greys make up this youth hostel in an atmospheric old house dating from the 1600s. Rooms are up to 550kr cheaper outside the peak June–Aug period. **950kr**

CAMPING

Norderstrands Camping Österväg 3A ☎ 0498 21 21 57, ⊕ www.gtsab.se. Barely 800m outside the city walls – follow the cycle path that runs through the Botanical Gardens along the seafront. It's imperative to book early to ensure a place here as this campsite is extremely popular. Has cabins for rent. Open June–Aug only. Tents **160kr**, cabins **750kr**

EATING, DRINKING AND NIGHTLIFE

Adelsgatan is lined with **cafés** and **snack bars**. At lunchtime, the eating places at Wallérsplats, the square at Adelsgatan's northern end, and Hästgatan, the street leading off the square to the southwest, are particularly busy; Strandgatan is the focus of Visby dining in the evening, though Hästgatan also boasts a number of places for dinner. For inexpensive eating at night, lively **Donnersplats** has lots of stalls selling takeaway food during summer. Youthful **nightlife** is mainly down at the harbour.

CAFÉS

★ **Gula Huset** Tranhusgatan 2 ☎ 0498 24 96 90. Close to the Botanical Gardens and a favourite amongst locals who flock here on sunny weekends: a cosy garden café outside a vine-covered cottage, deservedly well known for delicious port-wine cake with cream and fruit (48kr). Sat & Sun noon–5pm.

Skafferiet Adelsgatan 38 ☎ 0498 21 45 97. Appealing, characterful café in a lovely eighteenth-century house with coarsely hewn timber walls, chequered curtains and a lush garden at the back. Baked potatoes, great cakes and vast, generously filled baguettes which suffice for a full meal. Tues–Fri 11am–5pm, Sat 11am–4.30pm.

St Hans Café St Hansplan 2 ☎ 0498 21 07 72. Between May and Sept this café has outdoor seating in the rear garden amid a series of atmospheric medieval church ruins – for atmosphere it's hard to beat. Terrific cakes, muffins and pies as well as light lunches. Mon–Fri 10am–6pm.

RESTAURANTS

50 Kvadrat St Hansplan ☎ 0498 27 83 80. Not only Gotland's but one of Sweden's finest restaurants, whose frequently changing menu features Swedish cuisine expertly blended with influences from across the world. The result is simply irresistible, if expensive: starters are around 220kr, mains around 350kr. Mon–Fri 6–10pm, Sat 6–11pm.

Bakfickan Storatorget 1 ☎ 0498 27 18 07. A quiet, relaxed little restaurant with a tiled interior that specializes in some of the best seafood in town. The fried Baltic herring with mashed potato (134kr) is superb, so, too, fish soup with aioli (149kr). Starters from 73kr. Mon–Fri 11am–11pm, Sat & Sun noon–11pm.

Bolaget Storatorget 6 ☎ 0498 21 50 80. A delightful, though extremely small French bistro right on the main square with a good range of French classics: confit de canard (199kr), bouillabaisse (189kr) and a delicious warm goat's cheese starter (99kr) are all good bets. Tues–Fri 11.30am till late, Sat & Sun 1pm till late.

★ **Gamla Masters** Stora Kyrkogatan 10 ☎ 0498 21 66 55. A justifiably popular bistro decked out with mosaic tiles serves everything from solid Swedish home cooking (meatballs 175kr, whitefish roe 190kr) to more upmarket, sophisticated meat and fish dishes (175–275kr). A great place, too, for an after-dinner drink. Daily 6pm–2am.

Isola Bella Södra Kyrkogatan 20 ☎0498 21 87 87. Great Italian trattoria, with a superb vaulted cellar restaurant to the rear. Pasta, for example tortelloni stuffed with asparagus and ricotta, from 145kr, pizzas from 123kr as well as great meat dishes, such as chicken schnitzel with spinach risotto, from 205kr. Mon–Sat 6pm till late, Sun 5pm till late.

Munkkälleren Lilla Torggränd 2 ☎0498 27 14 00. This vast place in one corner of the main square is massively fashionable, and consequently crowded. There's an extensive array of grilled meats and fish, for example salmon and lamb, from 195kr. They also serve bar snacks including burgers. Mon–Thurs 6pm–2am & Sat, Fri 5pm–2am.

★ **Strykjärnet** Wallersplats 3 ☎0498 28 46 22. This fantastic low-ceilinged crêperie is squeezed into the narrowest of triangular buildings at the corner of Adelgatan and Hästgatan (it's named "the iron" for its shape). A wide range of savoury gallettes (including vegetarian options) from 95kr; sweet crêpes from 39kr. Daily 11am till late.

Roma

Just 15km southeast of Visby on Route 143, the small settlement of **ROMA** (bus #11 from Visby; timetable available from the tourist office) actually has nothing to do with Rome, but instead takes its name from "room" or "open space" – this was the original location of ancient Gotland's courthouse. The place looks something of a ghost town as its century-old sugar-beet factory, to the right of the main road as you approach from Visby, has recently closed, and the early twentieth-century cottages fronting Route 143 are also deserted (they can't be demolished, though, as they're protected for their rarity value). The church here, dating from 1215, is large and pretty; the three-aisled nave gives it a surprisingly Romanesque appearance, and because of this the church is known as the False Basilica.

Romakloster

Café: May & Sept Sat & Sun 10am–6pm; June & mid- to end Aug daily 10am–6pm; July to mid-Aug daily 10am–9pm

Just 1km further down the road from Roma, the Cistercian cloister ruins of **Romakloster**, in the hamlet of the same name, are the real draw of the area; follow the sign left down a long avenue of beech trees. The crumbling Roma monastery, dating from 1164, lacks both apse and tower, being Romanesque in design; it would once have comprised a church with three wings built around a rectangular cloister. What is left is sturdy stuff – big arches of grey stone blocks so regular they could be breeze blocks. The multitude of spotlights set in the ground here make it very dramatic as a backdrop for night-time **theatre** (Shakespeare performances are staged each summer), though they detract from the site's timeless character by day. The ruin is not the isolated site one might expect, as it's behind the cream-stucco **manor house**, Kungsgården, built in the 1730s for the county governor. Part of the monastery was in fact destroyed by the Danish crown during the Reformation of the early sixteenth century, and it was further ruined when the governor used materials from it in the building of the house. Temporary art exhibitions are held within the manor house (20kr), and there's a **café**, *Drängstugan*, serving delicious sweet pies and sandwiches.

EATING   ROMA

KonstnärsGården Ala, 15km southeast of Roma just off Route 143 ☎0498 550 55. This is a complex of art galleries, though the main reason to come here is to eat at the appealing and popular restaurant round the back, serving filling meals including excellent fish and meat dishes for around 150kr. There's also a café, offering the usual baguettes and cakes. Open mid-May to late Aug daily noon–9pm.

Hemse and around

The so-called "capital" of the south, **HEMSE**, around 50km from Visby along Route 142 (buses #10, #11 and #12), is little more than a main street. You can rent **bikes** from Endrells, Ronevägen 4, which is the cheapest place in town (☎0498 48 03 33).

6

Taking Route 144 east from Hemse, signposted for Burs, you'll find the countryside is a glorious mix of meadows, ancient farms and dark, mysterious forest. One of the most charming villages just a couple of kilometres further on, **Burs** has a gorgeous thirteenth-century saddle church, so-called because of its low nave and high tower and chancel. There's a fabulously decorated ceiling, medieval stained-glass windows and ornately painted pews. A couple of kilometres further, the sandy **beach** at **Herte** is one of the best on the island.

EATING
HEMSE AND AROUND

Jonassons Bageri & Konditori Storgatan 54, Hemse ☎0498 48 00 07. A good local café and bakery serving delicious fresh bread and a limited range of sandwiches and cakes. Mon–Fri 10am–6pm, Sat 10am–3pm.

Ljugarn

For Gotland's best beach (see box below), and the nearest thing it has to a resort, the lively and charming town of **LJUGARN** makes a good base. You can get here from Roma by heading straight down Route 143 for around 30km. Though full of restaurants and obviously aimed at tourists, Ljugarn no longer has a tourist office. It's famous for its *raukar* – tall limestone stacks rising up from the sea. From the main street, it's only 100m to the town **beach**. A delightful cycle or stroll down Strandvägen follows the coastline through woods and clearings carpeted in *blåelden* (viper's bugloss), the electric-blue flowers for which the area is known. The *raukar* along the route stand like ancient hunched men, their feet lapped by the waves.

ACCOMMODATION
LJUGARN

STF youth hostel Storgatan 1 ☎0498 49 31 84, eljugarn@gotlandsturist.se. Ljugarn's hostel is located in an atmospheric former customs house from the 1850s right in the centre of the village. There's a kitchen on site for self-catering. This place fills up quickly so it's essential to book well in advance to secure a bed. Open mid-May to Aug. Dorms 180kr, doubles 400kr

EATING

Espegards Konditori & Bagels Storvägen 58 ☎0498 49 30 40. For a splendid café, this is a must, serving some of the best cakes around – try the almond and blueberry tart. Their famously good breads, in particular *ljugarslimpa*, a dark, slightly chewy loaf, have been made here and shipped to the mainland since the 1930s. The place is very popular, so expect a queue in summer. Tues–Sun 10am–5pm.

Ljugarns Strandcafé & Restaurang Strandvägen 6 ☎0498 49 33 78. Located on the beach itself, this is the

---

GOTLAND'S BEST BEACHES

Gotland is renowned throughout Sweden for its fine sandy beaches, The coast between **Sjaustrehammaren** and **Ljugarn** on the east coast, backed by pine forest, is the best beach on the entire island, a vast, unsullied stretch of golden sand; the southern section in front of Mullvalds strandskog forest is popular with **naturists**. Get here on bus #41 to Gammelgarn from where it's a fifteen-minute cycle ride along the road to Ljugarn and then follow one of the narrow forest tracks which lead down off left to the shore.

The best of the rest are detailed below; all are marked on the map on p.230.

Snäck is a 5km cycle ride north of Visby and popular with families who appreciate the gently sloping sands which make paddling particularly easy and safe for kids.

Tofta strand (take bus #10 south from Visby) is also suited to families with children, since the water is relatively shallow and warm.

Sundersandsviken on Fårö (take bus #20 from Visby to the ferry at Fårösund, then a taxi to the beach itself; book on ☎0498 20 20 00) is a perfectly formed sandy bay.

Holmhällar in the south is surrounded by wild, unspoilt countryside and limestone *raukar*; bus #11 will take you here.

INGMAR BERGMAN

From the mid-1960s until his death in 2007, Sweden's best-known film director and screenwriter, **Ingmar Bergman** lived for much of the time on the island of Fårö, off northernmost Gotland. He was born in Uppsala in 1918, the son of a Lutheran pastor. The combination of his harsh upbringing, his interest in the religious art of old churches and the works of August Strindberg inspired Bergman to constantly consider the spiritual and psychological conflicts of life in his films. The results – he made forty feature films between 1946 and 1983 – are certainly dark, and for many, deeply distressing and/or depressing. He made his first breakthrough at the Cannes Film Festival in 1944, winning the Grand Prix for his film *Hets (Persecution)*, based on his school life. Among his best-known movies are *The Seventh Seal* (1957), starring Max von Sydow, and *Wild Strawberries* (also 1957). The two most prevalent themes in his films were marriage and the motives for marital infidelity, and the divide between sanity and madness. One of his finest films, *Fanny and Alexander* (1982), portrays bourgeois life in Scandinavia at the turn of the twentieth century; it's actually based on the lives of his own maternal grandparents and is the last major film he made. Bergman married five times, divorcing all but the last of his wives, who died in 1995.

6

loveliest place in town, serving delicious, top-notch Swedish specialities, such as pan-fried salmon with potato salad and wild garlic crème; its large, open-air terrace is beautifully placed for a drink right on the sand. Mid-June to mid-Aug daily 10am–midnight.

Lummelundagrottor and Jungfruklint

Thirteen kilometres north of Visby on Route 149, or by bus #61, are the **Lummelundagrottor**: limestone caves, stalagmites and stalactites that are disappointingly dull and damp despite being marketed as Gotland's most visited tourist attraction. The cave adventures here are of interest if you enjoy clambering around in the damp, and are not recommended if you suffer from claustrophobia (minimum age 15).

There's a more interesting natural phenomenon 10km to the north, where you'll see the highest of Gotland's coastal *raukar* (see p.204). The remnants of reefs formed over four hundred million years ago, the fact that the stacks are now well above the tide line is proof that sea levels were once much higher. This particular stack, 11.5m high and known as **Jungfruklint**, is said to look like the Virgin and Child – something you'll need a fair bit of imagination to discern.

Bro

Instead of taking the coastal road from Visby, you could head around 10km inland along Route 148 towards the village of **BRO**, which has one of the island's most beautiful **churches**. Several different stages of construction are evident from the Romanesque and Gothic windows in its tower. The most unusual aspect is the south wall, with its flat-relief picture stones, carved mostly with animals, which were incorporated from a previous church that once stood on the site. On the whole, though, it's better to press on further into the eminently picturesque north, where many of the secluded cottages are summer-holiday homes for urban Swedes.

The Bothnian coast

GAMMELSTAD, LULEÅ

The Bothnian coast

Sweden's east coast, bordering the Gulf of Bothnia (Bottenhavet), forms a corridor of land that is quite unlike the rest of the north of the country; the forest, so apparent in other parts of the north, has been felled here to make room for settlements. Although the entire coastline is dotted with towns and villages that reveal a faded history – some, like Gävle and Hudiksvall, still have their share of old wooden houses, though sadly much was lost during the Russian incursions of the eighteenth century – it is cities like Sundsvall, Umeå and Luleå that are more typical of the region: modern, bright and airy metropolises that rank as some of northern Sweden's liveliest and most likeable destinations.

7

All along the coast you'll find traces of the religious fervour that swept the north in centuries past; **Skellefteå** and particularly **Luleå** (included on the UNESCO World Heritage List) both boast excellently preserved **kyrkstäder** or church towns – clusters of old wooden cottages dating from the early eighteenth century, where villagers from outlying districts would spend the night after making the lengthy journey to church in the nearest town. Working your way up the coast, perhaps on the long train ride to Swedish Lapland, it's worth breaking your trip at one or two of these places.

The highlight of the Bothnian coast is undoubtedly the stretch known as the **Höga Kusten**, or the High Coast (see p.259), north of Härnösand: for peace and quiet, this is easily the most idyllic part of the Swedish east coast. Its indented coastline is best seen from the sea, with shimmering fjords that reach deep inland, tall cliffs and a string of pine-clad islands that make it possible to island-hop up this section of coast. The weather here may not be as reliable as further south, but you're guaranteed clean beaches (which you'll often have to yourself), crystal-clear waters and some of the finest countryside for walking.

GETTING AROUND THE BOTHNIAN COAST

Unlike southern Sweden, travel anywhere in the north of the country requires careful planning. Many **trains** only operate once or twice daily and **bus** services to destinations off the beaten track can be skeletal – particularly between mid-June and mid-August when, arguably, the need for transport is greatest. Before setting off, make sure you check all travel details thoroughly: two good places to start are the SJ and Resrobot websites, ⓦ sj.se and ⓦ resrobot.se.

By train Following the completion of a new section of track north of Härnösand (the Botniabanan railway), the train route to northern Sweden now hugs the coast from Gävle all the way up to Umeå; it's thought services could start running here in late 2013 though the opening date has already slipped by several years. Until the new track opens fully, services operate via Gävle, Ånge and Örnsköldsvik on their way to and from Umeå. From Sundsvall trains run inland to Östersund via Ånge where you can connect with services operating on the Inlandsbanan through central and northern parts of the country.

By bus From Sundsvall bus services run north to major towns along the coast, bound for all points north to Haparanda. There are also several bus services running inland from Umeå and Skellefteå, which can whisk you up

ELK BULL, BJURHOLM

Highlights

❶ **Stone architecture, Sundsvall** Admire the grand avenues of this vibrant northern city, lined with elegant turn-of-the-twentieth-century stone buildings. **See p.252**

❷ **Högbonden, High Coast** A night in the former lighthouse on this unspoilt island, complete with shore-side sauna, is unbeatable. **See p.260**

❸ **Elk farm, Bjurholm** Come face to face with the elusive "King of the Forest" at this fascinating farm outside Umeå. **See p.268**

❹ **Pite Havsbad, Piteå** Northern Sweden's premier beach resort is renowned for long hours of sunshine and warm waters. **See p.271**

❺ **Gammelstad, Luleå** Four hundred and fifty gnarled wooden cottages make up Sweden's most extensive church town, offering an insight into the country's religious past. **See p.275**

❻ **Luleå archipelago** Take a boat trip to one of the dozens of pine-clad islands at the very top of the Gulf of Bothnia. **See p.276**

HIGHLIGHTS ARE MARKED ON THE MAP ON P.244

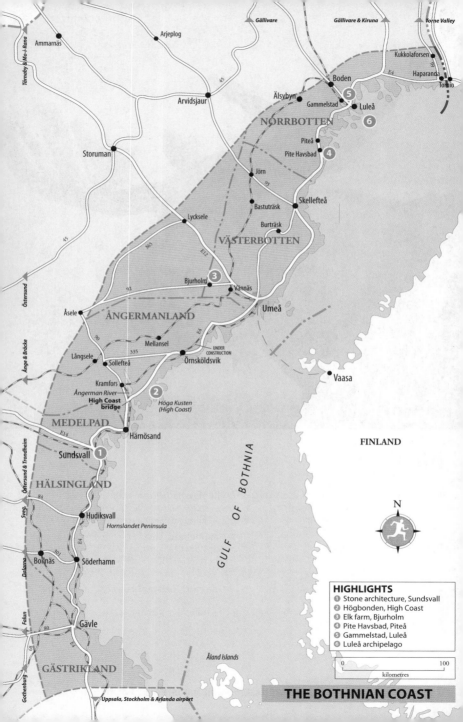

THE BOTHNIAN COAST

HIGHLIGHTS
1. Stone architecture, Sundsvall
2. Högbonden, High Coast
3. Elk farm, Bjurholm
4. Pite Havsbad, Piteå
5. Gammelstad, Luleå
6. Luleå archipelago

0   100
kilometres

into the mountains of Swedish Lapland, should you wish to head inland from further up the Bothnian coast.

By ferry Along the High Coast, island-hopping north of Härnösand via Högbonden, Ulvön and Trysunda (see p.260) is a wonderful way to make your way north and to take in one of northern Sweden's most beautiful regions at the same time. Ferry tickets here are good value; see p.262 for details. Once again, though, you'll need to carefully check departure times to make sure you're not left stranded either on the islands or the mainland; the general pattern of services is given in the text.

Gävle and around

It's only ninety minutes north by train from Stockholm to **GÄVLE** (pronounced "yerv-luh", and confusingly similar to a much-used Swedish swear word), capital of the province of Gästrikland. Gävle is also the southernmost city of **Norrland**, the region – comprising almost two-thirds of Sweden – which represents wilderness territory in the minds of most Swedes. To all intents and purposes, Norrland, Sweden's main reservoir of natural resources with vast forests and large ore deposits, means everything north of Uppsala; crossing into here from Svealand (which together with Götland makes up the southern third of the country) is – as far as the Swedish psyche is concerned – like leaving civilization behind.

Although Gävle is one of the bigger towns in Norrland, you can comfortably see everything in a day. Your first point of call should be **Gamla Gefle**, the old town district, where you'll also find the town's two museums, **Joe Hill-Gården** and **Länsmuséet Gävleborg**. Nearby, the **Heliga Trefaldighets kyrka** is a riot of seventeenth-century woodcarving and makes a pleasant stop en route to Gävle's city park, **Boulognerskogen**, a vast expanse of forested parkland ideal for a picnic or a leisurely stroll.

Brief history

Gävle's town charter was granted as long ago as 1446, a fact that's at variance with the modernity of the centre's large squares, broad avenues and proud monumental buildings. The city was almost completely rebuilt after a devastating fire in 1869 and its docks and warehouses reflect the heady success of its late nineteenth-century industry, when Gävle was one of Sweden's main ports for the export of locally produced iron ore and timber. Today, the city is more famous as the home of **Gevalia coffee** ("Gevalia" being the old Latinized name for the town), which you'll no doubt taste during your time in Sweden and certainly smell in the air in Gävle.

Gamla Gefle

It's only a ten-minute walk from the train station, across the Gavleån River, to the district of **Gamla Gefle**, which escaped much of the fire damage and today passes itself off as the authentic old town. Unfortunately, though it's the most interesting part of the city, it doesn't amount to much. The few remaining narrow cobbled streets – notably Övre Bergsgatan, Bergsgränd and Nedre Bergsgränd – boast pastel-coloured wooden cottages, window boxes overflowing with flowers in summer and old black lanterns. It's all very attractive and quaint and the jumbled lanes now house the odd craft shop and a café or two.

Joe Hill-Gården

Nedre Bergsgatan 28 • June–Aug daily 10am–3pm; other times by arrangement • Free • ☎ 026 65 26 41, ⓦ joehill.se

For a glimpse of social conditions a century ago, visit the **Joe Hill-Gården**, the birthplace of one Johan Emanuel Hägglund in 1879. He emigrated to the United States in 1902, changed his name to Joe Hill and became a working-class hero – his songs and speeches became rallying cries to comrades in the International Workers of the World, a Utah-based syndicalist organization, which runs the museum today. Its

7

GÄVLE

BARS, CAFÉS & RESTAURANTS
Bishops Arms	8
Brända Bocken	4
Brasserie Absint	3
Church Street Saloon	7
Helt Enkelt	6
Kungshallen	1
Österns Pärla	2
Trattoria Cinque	9
Wayne's Coffee	5

ACCOMMODATION
Annexet & Järnvägshotellet	2/3
Aveny	8
Boulogne	5
Clarion Winn	4
Furuviks Camping	6
Gamla Gefle Vandrarhem	7
Scandic CH	1

collection of pictures and belongings is given piquancy by the inclusion of the telegram announcing his execution in 1915 – he was framed for murder in Salt Lake City – and his last will and testament.

Länsmuséet Gävleborg

Södra Strandgatan 20 • Mid-June to mid-Aug Mon–Fri 11am–5pm, Sat & Sun noon–4pm; mid-Aug to mid-June Tues–Fri 10am–4pm, Wed until 9pm, Sat & Sun noon–4pm • Free • ⓦ lansmuseetgavleborg.se

On the northern edge of Gamla Gefle on the riverside, the county museum, **Länsmuséet Gävleborg**, has displays of artwork by some of the great Swedish artists from the seventeenth century to the present day, including Gunnar Cyrén, Nils Kreuger and Carl Larsson. Also on display is the work of a local artist, Johan-Erik Olsson (popularly known as "Lim-Johan"), whose vivid imagination and naive technique produced some strange childlike paintings.

Central Gävle

The modern city lies north of the river, its broad streets and avenues designed to prevent fires from spreading. A slice through the middle of the centre is comprised of parks, tree-lined spaces and fountains, running north from the spire-like **Rådhus** to the beautiful nineteenth-century **theatre** designed by Axel Nyström. All the main banks, shops and stores are in the grid of streets on either side of Norra Kungsgatan and Norra Rådmansgatan; the **Resecentrum** is about 700m to the east.

Gävle Slott

Follow the river west from the **Länsmuséet Gävleborg** to the double bridges of Rådmansbron and Kungsbron and you'll come to **Gävle Slott**, the seventeenth-century residence of the county governor, which lost its ramparts and towers years ago and now lurks behind a row of trees like some minor country house. However, it's not open to the public.

The warehouses

From the train station, look across the tracks and you'll see the beginnings of an industrial area. Home to three parallel streets of old dock-side **warehouses**, off Norra Skeppsbron just by the river, it's a reminder of the days when ships unloaded coffee and spices in the centre of Gävle. To get to the warehouses, use the subway to head under the railway tracks, and walk east to the riverside. Today, with company names emblazoned on the red, wooden fronts of the empty buildings, the area feels more like a Hollywood movie set than a Swedish town. Continue to the far eastern end of the warehouses and the heady smell of roasting coffee becomes ever stronger: Gevalia has its production centre here right next to the harbour at Nyhamn, north off Norra Skeppsbron.

Sveriges Järnvägsmuseum

Rälsgatan 1 • June–Aug daily 10am–4pm; Sept–May Tues–Sun 10am–4pm • 40kr • ⓦ jarnvagsmuseum.se

On a rainy day (or even a fine one) you may find yourself contemplating the **Sveriges Järnvägsmuseum** or Swedish Railway museum. Located in what used to be Gävle's engine shed, it's a train enthusiast's paradise, stuffed to the gills with really old locomotives and information on SJ's pride and joy, the X2000. The highlight is the hunting coach dating from 1859; one of the world's oldest railway carriages, it once belonged to King Karl XV.

Boulognerskogen park

West of the city centre and a twenty-minute stroll down picturesque Kungsbäcksvägen, a narrow street lined with brightly painted wooden houses beginning at Heliga Trefaldighets kyrka, you'll come to the rambling nineteenth-century park, **Boulognerskogen**. It's a good place for a picnic and a spot of sunbathing or a visit to the music pavilions, open-air **café** or the sculpture, by Carl Milles, of five angels playing musical instruments.

Heliga Trefaldighets kyrka

Kaplansgatan • Mon–Fri 11am–3pm

From **Gävle Slott**, a short walk west following the river leads to a wooden bridge, across which is Kaplansgatan and the **Heliga Trefaldighets kyrka**, the Church of the Holy Trinity, a seventeenth-century masterpiece of **woodcarved** decoration: check out the pulpit, towering altarpiece and screen, each the superb work of the German craftsman, Ewardt Friis.

Furuvik amusement park

Daily: late May to mid-June & mid- to late Aug 10am–5pm; mid-June to mid-Aug 10am–7pm • Entry is 195kr plus a further 195kr for an åkband ticket covering unlimited rides on the attractions • ⓦ furuvik.se • Trains run every 2hr; get off at the stop called "Furuvik"

The most popular attraction outside Gävle is the **Furuvik amusement park**, handily located just a seven-minute train ride away. The place boasts a zoo with chimpanzees and orangutans, fairground, parks and playgrounds.

Beaches

Northeast of Gävle, the beaches at **Engeltofta** or **Engesberg** are also within easy striking distance without your own transport; catch bus #95 from the Rådhus. From Engesberg, the bus continues to **Bönan**, where an old lighthouse marks a good spot for swimming. Other enjoyable beaches are on the island of **Limön**, connected by a summer ferry, **MS Drottning Silvia** (up to 3 daily; 40min; 40kr; ⓦgavle.se/limobaten), from Södra Skeppsbron, behind the Resecentrum, calling at Engeltofta on the way, if required.

ARRIVAL AND DEPARTURE   GÄVLE

By train Travel by train to and from Gävle is much more convenient than by bus, as services are not only more frequent but also faster. The train station shares space with the bus station in the Resecentrum on Centralplan.
Destinations Falun (2 hourly; 1hr); Hudiksvall (hourly; 1hr

15min); Kiruna (1 daily; 15hr); Luleå (2 daily; 14hr); Örebro (2 hourly; 4hr); Östersund (5 daily; 4hr 30min); Stockholm (hourly; 1hr 30min); Sundsvall (hourly; 2hr); Umeå (1 daily; 9hr 30min); Uppsala (hourly; 45min).

INFORMATION

Tourist office Inside the Gallerian Nian shopping centre, Drottninggatan 922 (Mon–Fri 9am–7pm, Sat 10am–4pm, Sun noon–4pm; ☎026 17 71 17, ⓦgastrikland.com). A

10min walk from the Resecentrum.
Internet There are terminals at the tourist office, and at Sidewalk Express in the Resecentrum.

ACCOMMODATION

Aveny Södra Kungsgatan 31 ☎026 61 55 90, ⓦaveny .nu. A small and comfortable family-run hotel south of the river, whose thirty-odd brightly painted rooms are hung with wall paintings and have nice wooden floors. There's a small buffet provided free to guests Mon–Thurs. **696kr/950kr**
Boulogne Byggmästargatan 1 ☎026 12 63 52, ⓦhotellboulogne.com. Cosy, basic hotel, with just seven plainly decorated rooms with breakfast brought to your room on a tray; room prices here are among the lowest in town. Freshly brewed coffee available every evening. Close to Boulognerskogen park. **620kr/650kr**
Clarion Winn Norra Slottsgatan 9 ☎026 64 70 00, ⓦclarionwinngavle.se. A large, smart hotel with 200 rooms, its own pool, sauna and sunbeds. Rooms are tasteful, if rather dark, with neutral decor and wooden floors. The extensive breakfast buffet is one of the best in northern Sweden. **810kr/1410kr**
Gamla Gefle Vandrarhem Södra Rådmansgatan 1 ☎026 62 17 45, ⓔstf.vandrarhem@telia.com. Rooms at this STF establishment, beautifully located in the cobbled old town, are a little on the small side but the location is great. It's worth timing your arrival carefully as reception is not staffed from 10am–5pm. Dorms **235kr**, doubles **580kr**

Järnvägshotellet & Annexet Centralplan 3 and Norra Skeppsbron 3C ☎026 12 09 90, ⓦjarnvagshotellet.nu. Nineteen individually decorated rooms sharing facilities opposite the train station make up *Järnvägshotellet*, whilst there are eight smarter rooms with private facilites, decked out in maritime colours, overlooking the river in the *Annexet* section, which cost around 250kr more. **620kr/695kr**
Scandic CH Nygatan 45 ☎026 495 84 00, ⓦscandichotels.se. One of the smartest hotels in town, with old-fashioned en-suite rooms decorated in different colours on different floors. The "red floor" rooms with their bold wallpaper designs in reds and pinks are particularly attractive. **940kr/1490kr**

CAMPING

Furuviks Camping Södra Kungsvägen, Furuvik ☎026 17 73 00, ⓦcamping.se/x12; reached on bus #501 (roughly every 30min). Gävle's campsite, complete with open-air swimming pool, is located by the amusement park, off Östnäsvägen, out at Furuvik (see p.247), Also has cabins for rent. Open late May to late Aug. Tents **140kr**, cabins **500kr**

EATING AND DRINKING

Bishops Arms Södra Kungsgatan 7 ☎026 65 25 75. This pseudo-English pub comes complete with heavy floral wallpaper and even brass coal scuttles and chamber pots

hanging from the ceiling. With outdoor seating in summer, it's *the* place to do your boozing. Mon & Tues 4–11pm, Wed, Thurs & Sun 4–10pm, Sat 1pm–1am, Sun 4–10pm.

Brända Bocken Stortorget ☎ 026 12 45 45. Young and fashionable, with outdoor seating in summer, plus an upstairs terrace. Inventive, modern menu featuring mango and chilli roast beef (192kr) as well as snacks such as bagels (72kr) and a tasty salmon sandwich (89kr). Mon–Thurs 11am–11pm, Fri 11am–1am, Sat noon–1am.

Brasserie Absint Norra Slottsgatan 9 ☎ 026 64 70 00. A delightful French brasserie with lots of mirrors and black tiling, attached to the *Clarion Winn* hotel. A wide range of dishes ranging from the house pasta (130kr) to Norwegian turbot with vegetable risotto and a salmon sauce (230kr). Mon & Tues 4pm–midnight, Wed–Sat 4pm–1am.

★ **Church Street Saloon** Kyrkogatan 11 ☎ 026 12 62 11. A fun American saloon diner complete with riding boots, bridles and saddles and an American flag in the window. Plenty of Wild West grills on the plates and can-can dancing on the tables at weekends. Meaty mains from around 250kr. Mon–Thurs 5pm–midnight, Fri 5pm–1am, Sat 11.45am–1am.

Helt Enkelt Norra Kungsgatan 3 ☎ 026 12 06 04. Modern Swedish mains with a hint of the Mediterranean dominate the menu at this stylish restaurant: salmon stuffed with cream cheese (149kr), seafood linguini (139kr) and the house burgers (129kr) are all worth trying. Mon–Thurs 4pm–midnight, Fri 4pm–1am, Sat noon–1am, Sun 3–10pm.

Kungshallen Norra Kungsgatan 17 ☎ 026 12 03 01. A smart and friendly pizzeria serving mammoth pizzas from 55kr, steaks from 119kr and salads from 74kr, as well as a selection of excellent-value chicken dishes for 99kr with potato wedges and salad. Mon–Fri 11am–10pm, Sat & Sun noon–11pm.

Österns Pärla Ruddammsgatan 23 ☎ 026 51 39 68. A stylish Asian restaurant with brushed metal interior walls decorated with bamboo poles. A good selection of Thai, Chinese, Japanese and vegetarian options, such as chicken with almonds (118kr). Three set Chinese dishes with dessert for 105kr. Mon–Thurs 11am–10pm, Fri 11am–11pm, Sat 12.30–11pm, Sun 1–10pm.

Trattoria Cinque Södermalmstorget 1 ☎ 026 61 07 70. The best Italian in town with a delightful year-round veranda. Accomplished mains such as zander with potato salad or veal schnitzel with gnocchi and tapenade go for around 175kr, starters hover around 85kr. Mon–Sat 4–11pm, Sun 2–10pm.

Wayne's Coffee Drottninggatan 16 ☎ 026 66 08 66. As always with this chain, excellent coffees and cakes make this the best and busiest café in Gävle, centrally located in the main square. It's on the first floor where there's also access to outdoor seating at the rear. Mon–Fri 9.30am–10pm, Sat 10am–10pm, Sun 11am–10pm.

Hudiksvall and around

On the first leg of the coastal journey further into Norrland, train services are frequent. Along this stretch of coast, **HUDIKSVALL** makes for a leisurely stop en route to the bigger towns and tourist centres further north. Its wood-panelled architecture and convenience for visiting the natural beauty of the nearby **Hornslandet peninsula**, jutting out into the Gulf of Bothnia, are the main draws.

Brief history

Granted town status in 1582 by King Johan III and accordingly the second oldest town in Norrland, **Hudiksvall** has seen its fair share of excitement over the years. Though the original settlement was built around what had been the bay of Lillfjärden, at the mouth of the Hornån River, the harbour began to silt up, and so it was decided in the early 1640s to move the town to its current location: the old bay is now a lake, connected to the sea by a small canal.

The town has suffered no fewer than ten **fires**, the worst occurring in 1721 when Russian forces swept down the entire length of the Bothnian coast, burning and looting as they went. Then an important commercial and shipping centre, the town bore the brunt of the onslaught. A further blaze, east of Rådhustorget, in 1792 led to a rethink of the town's layout, and so the street plan which exists today was conceived.

St Jakobs kyrka

Mon–Thurs: June–Aug 10am–4pm; Sept–May 11am–3pm

Still pockmarked with cannonball holes today, the town's church, **St Jakobs kyrka**, was the only building to remain standing after the harrying events of 1721 during the Great

Northern War between Sweden and Russia. Although the white stone exterior topped with a green onion dome is elegant enough, it's the interior that really impresses; unusually ornate for the Swedish Orthodox church, nineteenth-century renovators opted for brown marble hand-painted wall decoration, delicately lit by ornate candle-bearing chandeliers. The incongruous cannonball by the steps to the pulpit is a replica of the original fired by the Russians at the church.

Möljen

Turn right out of the train station and cross the narrow canal, Strömmingssundet ("Herring Sound"), and you'll soon see the small old **harbour** on the right; this area is known as **Möljen**. Here the wharfside is flanked by a line of red wooden fishermen's cottages and storehouses, all leaning into the water; it's a popular place for locals to while away a couple of hours in the summer sunshine, dangling their feet into the water. The back of the warehouses hides a run of handicraft studios.

Fiskarstan

More impressive and much larger than Möljen, **Fiskarstan** (Fishermen's Town), beyond the *First Hotel Statt* down Storgatan, contains neat examples of the so-called "Imperial" wood-panel architecture of the late eighteenth and nineteenth centuries. It was in these tightly knit blocks of streets, lined with beautiful wooden houses and fenced-in plots of land, that the fishermen used to live during the winter. Take a peek inside some of the little courtyards – all window boxes, flowers and cobblestones.

Hälsinglands Museum

Storgatan 31 • Mon & Sat noon–4pm, Tues–Fri 10am–4pm • Free • ⓦ halsinglandsmuseum.se

The history of the buildings in Fiskarstan is put into context in the excellent **Hälsinglands Museum**, which traces the development of Hudiksvall as a harbour town since its foundation. The museum's real showstoppers, however, are the ornately decorated **Malsta rune stone**, from around 1000 AD, ornately engraved with the letter-less Helsinge runic script – ask at the museum reception for a translation of the inscription – the expertly executed Post-Impressionist works by local artist, John Sten (see box below) – and the quite breathtaking collection of **medieval church art** kept in a dimly lit room, just behind the café on the ground floor. From altar screens to intricately carved wooden figures of Sweden's saints, this astounding array of outstanding craftsmanship is sure to impress; the centrepiece is the early sixteenth-century figure of the Madonna and Child by renowned local artist Haaken Gulleson, from the village of Fläcka in Hälsingland; his style is easy to spot – heavy eyelids, ruddy cheeks and a benign expression.

ARRIVAL AND DEPARTURE	HUDIKSVALL
By train The train station is opposite the bus station on Stationsgatan, from where it's a 2min walk to the town centre.	Destinations Gävle (hourly; 1hr 15min); Stockholm (hourly; 2hr 30min); Sundsvall (hourly; 50min); Uppsala (hourly; 1hr 50min).

HÄLSINGLAND'S GAUGUIN: JOHN STEN

If you're visiting the Hälsinglands Museum, be sure also to see the paintings by **John Sten** (1879–1922) on the first floor: born near Hudiksvall, he moved to Paris at the age of 30, where he was greatly influenced by Post-Impressionist master, Paul Gauguin. Tragically, Sten died of dysentery at the age of 42 in Bali; like many artists of his day he travelled extensively in Southeast Asia collecting impressions and designs, and became one of the first to work with Cubism, from which his work extends towards a more decorative, fanciful style.

MUSIK VID DELLEN

Undoubtedly the best time to visit Hudiksvall is during the beginning of July, when the town hosts the **Musik vid Dellen**, a multifarious cultural ten-day festival, including folk music and other traditional events (for more information, contact the tourist office or see ⓦ musikviddellen.se), held in churches and farms in the surrounding countryside.

INFORMATION

Tourist office Storgatan 33 (mid-May to mid-June & mid-Aug to mid-Sept Mon–Fri 10am–5pm; mid-June to mid-Aug Mon–Fri 10am–6pm, also July Sat & Sun 10am–3pm; mid-Sept to mid-May Mon–Fri 10am–4pm; ☎ 0650 191 00, ⓦ hudiksvall.se/turism). Has maps of the town and free internet access.

ACCOMMODATION

First Statt Storgatan 36 ☎ 0650 150 60, ⓦ firsthotels .se. The swishest hotel in town, dating from 1878 and still retaining many of the original features and flourishes. It was here that the barons of the timber industry made merry, coining the phrase "Glada Hudik" ("Happy Hudiksvall"), after its lively social life. 998kr/1625kr
Malnbadens camping and youth hostel | Out at Malnbaden, 3km from town ☎ 0650 132 60, ⓦ malnbadenscamping.com; bus #5 runs hourly in summer (10am–6pm); at other times you'll have to get here by taxi. In addition to the campsite there are STF youth hostel rooms and cottages for rent for 640kr for two people. Open all year. Dorms 260kr, doubles 520kr, tents 140kr
Temperance Håstagatan 16 ☎ 0650 311 07, ⓦ hotelltemperance.se. For atmospheric hotel accommodation in a grand old building dating from 1904, this place has just six doubles with private facilities plus hostel dorm beds; dorm bed prices include bedding and breakfast. Dorms 400kr, doubles 1020kr

EATING AND DRINKING

Dackås Konditori Storgatan 34 ☎ 0650 123 29. For a snack, try this Hudiksvall institution that's been here since the 1950s, now decked out as a modern lounge-style café, offering a range of baked potatoes, quiche and pancakes in addition to coffee and cakes. Mon–Fri 7am–6pm, Sat 8am–3pm.
★ **Hot Chili** Hamngatan 5 ☎ 0650 757 50. Try this superb option near the bus and train stations for authentically spicy Asian stirfries, rustled up before your eyes by chefs in the open kitchen for just 89kr (also takeaway); it's arguably the best and most popular place in town for lunch. Mon & Tues 11am–8pm, Wed–Fri 11am–10pm, Sat noon–10pm, Sun noon–8pm.
Pub Tre Bockar Bankgränd 1 ☎ 0650 999 94. Hudiksvall's one and only bar is opposite the fishermen's warehouses at Möljen, with occasional live music. Each Wed there's a deal known as the "29-er" – a selection of sandwiches, wraps and *pytt i panna* for just 29kr each. Wed 6pm–2am, Fri & Sat 8pm–2am.
Texas Bar-B-Q Saloon Hamngatan 5 ☎ 0650 121 50. With cacti and lifesize models of cowboys and Indians, the Wild West has truly arrived in Hudiksvall at this fun restaurant serving juicy steaks (from 219kr) and burgers (from 129kr); bison steaks are generally available, too (349kr). Mon–Fri 5pm–1am, Sat 1pm–1am, Sun 2–10pm.

The Hornslandet peninsula

For a day-trip from Hudiksvall, head southeast out to the beautiful and unspoilt **Hornslandet peninsula**, renowned for its quaint fishing villages of red wooden cottages and sandy **beaches**. This egg-shaped chunk of land is the geological result of continuous land rise since the last Ice Age; as recently as the Viking era, the Arnösund sound, which once separated Hornslandet from the mainland, was easily navigable and remained an important channel for seafarers until the tenth century. Today, though, the sound has silted up and the peninsula is effectively an extension of the Bothnian coast. This whole area is rich in flora and fauna, as well as being ideal for swimming, fishing and walking; there are two villages to head for in particular: **Hölick** and **Kuggörarna**.

Hölick

Located at the southern tip of the peninsula, **HÖLICK**, the larger of the two villages, traces its history back to the sixteenth century when a small fishing community became established here. Although there are no sights to speak of, the main purpose for coming here is to enjoy the plentiful peace and tranquillity on the very edge of the Gulf of Bothnia; a set of wooden steps leads up from the pilot boat station (*lotsstation*) in the centre of the village onto the rocks from where there are unsurpassed **views** out over the sea. A 7km circular **walking path** (allow around 2hr) will take you through the surrounding nature reserve to some of the peninsula's finest **beaches**: from the village the path leads southeast out to the Hornslandsudden promontory – there are sandy stretches of coast all the way to the furthest point of the promontory – from where it cuts inland, heading over a series of low hills, back towards Hölick. Heading in the opposite direction and following the road out of Hölick back towards Arnöviken and Hudiksvall, you'll come to another popular beach (near Arnöviken), frequented by **naturists** (details at ⓦnaturistnet.org).

Kuggörarna

Tiny **KUGGÖRARNA**, actually located on a small island, is joined to the rest of the peninsula by a narrow bridge across the dividing sound. Once again, it's for solitude and great sea vistas that most visitors come here, although the hamlet does have a couple of things worth seeking out: the eighteenth-century **chapel** up on the hill above the houses is worth a quick look (you'll find the key hanging by the door), and, just to the north of the cluster of houses, is a well-preserved stone **labyrinth**, a collection of winding walkways delineated by large stones on the ground, used in centuries past by superstitious fishermen to ensure a good catch. There's neither accommodation nor anywhere to eat here.

ARRIVAL   HORNSLANDET PENINSULA

By public transport Getting to the Hornslandet peninsula by public transport is only possible in summer: take bus #37 (mid-June to mid-Aug, 2 daily; ⓦxtrafik.se) which runs from the bus station via Hölick (40min) to Kuggörarna (1hr); otherwise, with your own transport, Route 778 leads to Kuggörarna from Hällby, just north of Hudiksvall.

ACCOMMODATION AND EATING

Hölick Havsresort Arnöviken, Hölick 84 (look out for the signs where the road into the village ends) ☎0650 56 50 32, ⓦholick.se. Accommodation in Hölick is restricted to this gem of a resort which has superb new cabins decorated in maritime whites and blues for rent. Open May–Sept. Cabins **1050kr**

Sjöboa Hölick 10 ☎0650 56 50 02. Hölick boasts one restaurant, whose fish buffet for 229kr is truly superb, though it also has a smoked whitefish platter (178kr) as well as a couple of meat dishes such as schnitzel (155kr) and pork fillet (198kr). Mid-June to Aug daily noon–9pm.

Sundsvall

The capital of the tiny province of Medelpad, **SUNDSVALL** is often referred to as "Stone City", for the simple reason that most of its buildings are made of stone – a fact that distinguishes it immediately from other coastal towns here. Having gawped at Sundsvall's imposing architecture, most visitors then make for the city's other main attraction: **Kulturmagasinet**, a superb museum complex located right in the city centre housing the paintings and sculptures of local artist Carl Frisendahl, amongst others. In summer, **Gaffelbyn**, Sundsvall's outdoor craft village, is definitely worth a look, too – try your hand here at baking the northern Swedish flatbread, **tunnbröd**.

Brief history

Once home to a rapidly expanding timber industry, the whole city burned to the ground the day after Midsummer in June 1888. A spark from the wood-burning steamboat *Selånger* (promptly dubbed "The Arsonist") set fire to a nearby brewery, and the rest, as they say, is history – so much so that the remark "that hasn't happened since

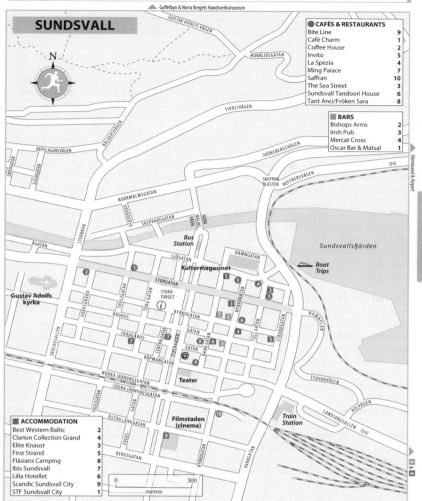

SUNDSVALL

Gaffelbyn & Norra Bergets Handsverksmuseum

GUSTAV ADOLFS VÄGEN

N

CAFÉS & RESTAURANTS
Bite Line	9
Café Charm	1
Coffee House	2
Invito	5
La Spezia	4
Ming Palace	7
Saffran	10
The Sea Street	3
Sundsvall Tandoori House	6
Tant Anci/Fröken Sara	8

BARS
Bishops Arms	2
Irish Pub	3
Mercat Cross	4
Oscar Bar & Matsal	1

Härnösand & Airport

7

Sundsvallsfjärden

Boat Trips

ACCOMMODATION
Best Western Baltic	2
Clarion Collection Grand	4
Elite Knaust	3
First Strand	5
Fläsians Camping	8
Ibis Sundsvall	7
Lilla Hotellet	6
Scandic Sundsvall City	9
STF Sundsvall City	1

the town burned down" is now an established Sundsvall saying. Nine thousand people lost their homes in the resulting blaze. The work of rebuilding the city began at once, and within ten years a new centre had been constructed, entirely of **stone**. The result is a living document of turn-of-the-twentieth-century urban architecture, designed and crafted by architects who were involved in rebuilding Stockholm's residential areas at the same time. Wide streets and esplanades that would serve as firebreaks in the event of another fire formed the backbone of their work. These thoroughfares are home to 573 residential buildings, all of which went up in four years; the centrepiece is the house that dominates the main square, Storatorget.

The reconstruction, however, was achieved at a price: the workers who had laboured on the city's refurbishment became the victims of their own success. They were shifted from their old homes in the centre and moved out south to a run-down suburb – the glaring contrast between the wealth of the new centre and the poverty of the surrounding districts was only too obvious. When **Nils Holgersson**, a character created by the children's author Selma Lagerlöf (see p.142), looked down from the back of his flying goose (see the picture on 20kr notes), he remarked: "There was something funny about it when you saw it from above, because in the middle there was a group of high stone houses, so impressive that they hardly had their equal in Stockholm. Around the stone houses was an empty space, and then there was a circle of wooden houses, which were pleasantly scattered in little gardens, but which seemed to carry an awareness of being of lesser value than the stone houses and therefore dared not come too close."

Storatorget

As you walk in from the train station, the sheer scale of the rebuilding here after the 1888 fire is clear to see. **Esplanaden**, the wide central avenue, cuts the grid of streets in two; towards its northern end it's crossed by **Storgatan**, the widest road in town. **Storatorget**, the central square, is a delightfully roomy shopping and commercial centre, home to the city hall and various impromptu exhibitions and displays, as well as a fresh fruit and veg market (May to early Sept Mon–Sat 9am-4pm). The limestone and brick buildings are four- and five-storey palatial structures. As you stroll the streets, you can't help but be amazed by the tremendous amount of open space that surrounds you, even in the heart of the city; Sundsvall is unique among Swedish cities in this respect, yet it's the most densely populated metropolis in northern Sweden.

Kulturmagasinet

Packhusgatan 4 • Mon–Thurs 10am–7pm, Fri 10am–6pm, Sat & Sun 11am–4pm • Free • ⓦ sundsvall.se/kulturmagasinet

Several of the buildings in the centre are worth a second look, not least the sturdy **Kulturmagasinet**, housed within two blocks of late nineteenth-century warehouses, spanned by a glass roof, at, down by the harbour. The buildings stood empty for twenty years before a decision was taken to turn them into what's now the **Kulturmagasinet**, comprising museum, library and café. The museum is actually built over an old street, Magasinsgatan, once boasting train tracks running between the warehouses to carry loads of coffee and rice. Deserving of a quick look, the first floor of the museum does its best to depict the history of Sundsvall, including the great fire of 1888, and the province of Medelpad. Up on the second and third floors, the art exhibition warrants a few minutes of your time: the works of twentieth-century Swedish artists are on show here, in particular, those of the local artist and sculptor Carl Frisendahl (1886–1948) whose early style is heavily influenced by Rodin. At the age of 20, Frisendahl studied in Paris where he met his wife, Marie Barbaud. Forsaking his native Sweden for a studio in Montparnasse, he began painting in the 1920s; his works, which often depict animals and mythological figures in combat, clearly show inspiration from Delacroix and Orthon Friesz.

Gustav Adolfs kyrka

Rådhusgatan 36 • June–Aug daily 11am–4pm; Sept–May Mon–Sat noon–3pm

At the western end of the main pedestrian street, Storgatan, you'll come across a soaring red-brick structure from 1894, **Gustav Adolfs kyrka**, which marks the western end of the new town. The church's interior looks like a large Lego set, its pillars, vaults and window frames all constructed from smooth bricks, making an eye-pleasing picture of order.

Norra Berget and Gaffelbyn

Beyond the city's design, the most attractive diversion is the tiring 3km climb to the heights of **Gaffelbyn** on **Norra Berget**, the hill that overlooks the city to the north;

walk up Storgatan, cross over the main bridge and follow the sign to the youth hostel. If you'd prefer to spare your legs, any bus for Norra Berget will take you up there. The view on a clear day is fantastic, giving a fresh perspective on the city's planned structure and the restrictive nature of its location, hemmed in on three sides by hills and the sea. From here you can see straight across to Södra Berget, the southern hill, with its winter ski slopes.

The viewing tower

The best views can be had from the top of the **viewing tower** which has stood on this spot since 1897. Originally made entirely from wood, the tower fell victim over the years to the Swedish winter. By the 1930s it was in such poor condition that during one particularly severe autumn storm, the entire thing blew down; the present concrete replacement, 22m high, dates from 1954.

Norra Bergets Hantverksmuseum

Norra Bergets Handicrafts Museum · Norra Berget · Daily 11am–5pm · 20kr

The **Norra Bergets Hantverksmuseum** is an open-air handicrafts museum with the usual selection of twee wooden huts and assorted activities, though you can often try your hand at baking some *tunnbröd*, the thin bread that's typical of northern Sweden. The idea is to roll out your dough extra thin, brush off as much flour as you can, slip the bread into the oven on a big, wooden pizza-type paddle, and count slowly to five.

ARRIVAL AND DEPARTURE SUNDSVALL

By plane The airport, 24km north of town on the way to Härnösand, is linked to Sundsvall by an airport bus (41kr), timed to coincide with flights to and from Stockholm; alternatively, a taxi will cost around 230kr.

By train From the train station, it's a 5min walk to the city centre; turn left as you come out of the station, cross the car park then take the underpass beneath Parkgatan.

Destinations Gävle (hourly; 2hr); Hudiksvall (hourly; 45min); Östersund (8 daily; 2hr); Stockholm (hourly; 3hr 30min).

By bus The bus station is close by at the bottom of Esplanaden, though if you want information or advance tickets for the daily express bus south to Stockholm, north

to Umeå, or inland to Östersund, visit Y-Bussen at Sjögatan 7 (Mon–Fri 8.30am–5pm; ☎060 17 19 60, ⊕ybuss.se). For the twice-weekly Lapplandspilen express bus to Vilhelmina, Storuman and destinations to Klippen contact ☎0940 150 30, ⊕lapplandspilen.se. Reliable services run several times daily between Sundsvall and Umeå, generally connecting with trains to and from Sundsvall; change buses in Umeå to continue further north towards Haparanda and across to Tornio in Finland. Other bus services run from the coast into central northern Sweden, often linking up with the Inlandsbanan.

Destinations Docksta (7 daily; 1hr 45min); Härnösand (twice hourly; 50min); Umeå (7 daily; 4hr).

INFORMATION

Tourist office Stadshuset, Storatorget (June to mid-Aug Mon–Fri 10am–6pm; mid-Aug to May Mon–Fri 10am–5pm; ☎060 61 04 50, ⊕visitsundsvall.se).

Internet Try the tourist office or Pressbyrån, at Esplanaden 2, where you'll find a couple of Sidewalk Express terminals.

ACCOMMODATION

Rooms in Sundsvall, even in summer, are plentiful, and so finding somewhere to stay is unlikely to be a problem. The majority of the city's hotels are centrally located, and throw up some incredibly good bargains.

BOAT TRIPS FROM SUNDSVALL

Sailing from the eastern end of Hamngatan between May and September, *M/S Medvind* makes an enjoyable tour around the nearby island of Alnö, which lies due east of Sundsvall. The boat generally does two trips a day: one at lunchtime and one early evening; both are three hours and thirty minutes and a buffet lunch or dinner is included in the price (315kr/395kr respectively). You'll find detailed departure times and more information at ⊕msmedvind.com.

7

Best Western Baltic Sjögatan 5 ☎060 14 04 40, ⓦbaltichotell.com. Centrally located, near the Kulturmagasinet and the harbour, with tastefully decorated rooms with carpets and chandeliers in a compact building dating from the 1880s. The smaller economy rooms off reception are excellent value. 772kr/1665kr

Clarion Collection Grand Nybrogatan 13 ☎060 64 65 60, ⓦchoicehotels.se. The sauna and jacuzzi suite and gym are excellent and included in the room rate; the rooms, however, are on the small side, though nicely decorated in classic, modern Swedish style with wooden floors and smart furnishings. 850kr/1250kr

Elite Knaust Storgatan 13 ☎060 608 00 00, ⓦelitehotels.se. Dominated by a magnificent marble staircase in the entrance hall, this is the most luxurious option in town. The accomplished mix of old-world opulence and Scandinavian designer chic is a winning combination. The sumptuous loft suites here all feature the original beamed roofs. 1100kr/1550kr

First Strand Strandgatan 10 ☎060 64 65 60, ⓦfirsthotels.se. Handily located close to the train station, rooms are modern and feature either pleasant maritime decor or more contemporary, bolder colours and stripes. Furnishings are modern Nordic and the beds are especially comfortable. 911kr/1271kr

Ibis Sundsvall Trädgårdsgatan 31–33 ☎060 64 17 50, ⓦibishotel.se. Quite a sizeable pile with over 140 rooms – all are en suite and some even have baths. Worth trying, especially if the cheaper hotels are full, though breakfast is an extra 85kr. 570kr/895kr

Lilla Hotellet Rådhusgatan 15 ☎06061 35 87, ⓦlilla-hotellet.se. Built one year after the great fire, this fine old hotel has lots of charm: high ceilings, period furniture and ornate chandeliers. One of the most reasonably priced hotels in town with just eight rooms, all en suite. Smaller budget singles cost 250kr less and are a great bargain. 750kr/850kr

Scandic Sundsvall City Esplanaden 29 ☎060 785 6200, ⓦscandichotels.se. Expertly renovated and stylish to a T, with gorgeous nature prints covering entire walls of the rooms. This chain hotel boasts saunas, sunbeds and a good breakfast, too, with reasonable prices to match the opulence. 880kr/1410kr

STF Sundsvall City Sjögatan 11 ☎060 12 60 90, ⓦsundsvallcityhostel.se. Sundsvall now finally has a good-quality central youth hostel: this new venture has a mix of doubles with regular beds as well as bunks, plus dorms where facilities are in the room itself rather than down the corridor. Dorms 220kr, doubles 500kr

CAMPING

Fläsians Camping Norrstigen 15 ☎060 55 44 75, ⓦcamping.se/y26. Sundsvall's campsite is 4km south of town, close to the E4; the tourist office can help with directions. Also has cabins: either fully equipped two-bed ones or smaller, simpler affairs. Open mid-May to Aug. Tents 140kr, small cabins 375kr, two-bed cabins 650kr

EATING AND DRINKING

Restaurants have mushroomed in Sundsvall over the last couple of years, and there's a good choice of places to eat and cuisines to choose from, including unusual options such as Vietnamese, Spanish and Indian – something you may want to make the most of if you're heading further north, where culinary options are limited.

CAFÉS

Café Charm Storgatan 34. Very much of the old school, this café is bedecked with chandeliers and has a quiet and refined seating area at the rear. A good choice for coffee and cake, sandwiches, pastries and naughty-but-nice cream concoctions. Mon–Fri 9am–7pm, Sat 9.30am–5pm, Sun 11am–4pm.

Coffee House Storgatan 31. At the far end of Sundsvall's main street, a small and agreeable modern café with window stools and a couple of tables serving various coffees, teas and sandwiches, with Swedish newspapers for perusal. Mon–Fri 10am–9pm, Sat & Sun 11am–6pm.

Tant Anci/Fröken Sara Bankgatan 15 ☎060 785 52 00. A mother-and-daughter team have opened this acclaimed café/restaurant/takeaway serving locally sourced, organic treats such as a Norrland platter of cheeses, smoked reindeer and cloudberry jam (149kr). The pasta with pesto and grilled lamb fillet are also delicious.

Mon–Thurs 10am–10pm, Fri 10am–8pm, Sat 11am–5pm.

RESTAURANTS

★ **Bite Line** Köpmangatan 20 ☎060 61 00 29. Fun American pizza joint serving genuine deep-pan pizzas from 110kr for a two-person number. Also has salad options for 89kr. Football matches are shown live on the big screen here. There's an eat-as-much-as-you-can taco buffet every evening until 9pm. Mon & Tues 11am–10pm, Wed–Fri 11am–11pm, Sat noon–11pm, Sun 1–10pm.

Invito Storgatan 6–8 ☎060 15 39 00. Wonderful modern Italian cuisine is served up in this smart and elegant brasserie: fish and meat mains, such as grilled veal with olive tapenade and ruccola crème, go for 199–298kr. Also home-made pasta dishes from 159kr. Mon–Thurs 11am–2pm & 5–11pm, Fri 11am–2pm & 5pm–1am, Sat 5pm–2am.

La Spezia Sjögatan 6 ☎ 060 61 12 23. If money's tight, look no further than this long-established pizzeria serving a wide range of decent bargain-basement pizzas from 55kr; the interior may be nothing special but it has a handy takeaway service. Mon–Fri 11am–8pm, Sat & Sun noon–10pm.

Ming Palace Esplanaden 10 ☎ 060 61 53 00. The best Chinese restaurant in Sundsvall which has been successfully feeding the masses for years with an impressive range of dishes, including beef with bean sprouts, from 95kr, to eat in, or take away. Tues–Thurs 11am–10pm, Fri 11am–10.30pm, Sat 1–10.30pm, Sun 1–11pm.

Saffran Nybrogatan 25 ☎ 060 17 11 07. An authentic and much-praised Spanish restaurant whose menu allows you to choose a meat dish (around 210kr) and then add your own sauce such as chimichurri or mojo, a delicious pepper sauce from the Canary Islands. Mon–Sat 5pm till late.

The Sea Street Sjögatan 9 ☎ 060 17 30 31. Genuine Japanese sushi restaurant which has taken Sundsvall by storm and is exceptional value for money. Mix and match: nine pieces for 75kr, eleven for 99kr and fifteen for 145kr. Mon–Fri 11am–8pm, Sat noon–8pm, Sun 1–6pm.

★ **Sundsvall Tandoori House** Kyrkogatan 12 ☎ 060 17 59 59. One of the country's best Indian restaurants – and the only one boasting an open-air roof terrace – this place serves up first-class meals, including lots of tandoori specialities, from 135kr per main course. Note, the restaurant is on the first floor. Mon–Thurs 11am–2pm & 4–10pm, Fri 11am–2pm & 4pm–1am, Sat noon–1am, Sun 1–9pm.

BARS

Bishops Arms Storgatan 13 ☎ 060 608 00 11. Yet another Swedish attempt to create a traditional British wood-panelled pub in Norrland. The result is not bad though, and it's a fine place to sample a wide selection of British ales and beers. Mon–Thurs 4pm till late, Fri 4pm–2am, Sat 1pm–2am, Sun 4–11pm.

Irish Pub Nybrogatan 16 ☎ 060 12 50 22. This Irish pub not only brews its own beer in the basement, but also has a broad selection of traditional ales, beers and stouts, plus bar meals, music and darts. Tues–Sat 5pm–2am.

Mercat Cross Esplanaden 29 ☎ 060 19 88 33. Attached to the *Scandic Sundsvall City* at the southern end of Esplanaden, this Scottish theme pub complete with heavy wood panelling serves just about every variety of whisky you can think of. Mon & Tues 4–11pm, Wed–Sat 4pm–midnight.

Oscar Bar & Matsal Bankgatan 11 ☎ 060 12 98 11. A good, lively Euro-lounge bar with retro floral wallpaper and leather chairs and sofas. It's one of Sundsvall's most popular places for a drink and is packed to the rafters on Fri and Sat nights. Mon & Tues 5–11pm, Wed & Thurs 5pm–midnight, Fri & Sat 5pm–3am.

7

Härnösand

An hour's trip along the coast from Sundsvall and full of architectural delights, including a number of old wooden cottages dating from the 1730s, **HÄRNÖSAND** is definitely worth a stop on the way north. The town's highlights are the architectural treasures around the harmonious main square, **Storatorget**, and winding **Östanbäcksgatan** with its eighteenth-century wooden houses painted in gentle pastel shades. A short walk from the town centre, the extensive open-air museum at **Murberget** showcases vernacular architecture from around the country. Härnösand also marks the beginning of the stunningly beautiful region of **Ångermanland** – one of the few areas in Sweden where the indented, soaring coastline resembles the fjordlands of neighbouring Norway.

Brief history

A pleasant little place at the mouth of the Ångerman River, **Härnösand** was founded in 1585 by King Johan III. In 1647, the town was selected as the capital of the second most northerly diocese in Sweden and, accordingly, the new bishop decreed that the old stone church, which already stood in the town, be enlarged into a cathedral. The town has since had more than its fair share of disasters: in 1710, flames tore through it after drunken churchgoers accidentally set fire to a boathouse; just four years later, Härnösand fell victim to a second great fire, started by a group of school students. Newly rebuilt, the town was razed by a third blaze in 1721, during the Great Northern War, when invading Russian forces burnt every house to the ground, bar one (see p.258).

Storatorget

For a provincial place, Härnösand reeks of grandeur and self-importance, each of its proud civic buildings a marker of the confidence the town exudes. The main square, **Storatorget**, was once declared by local worthies as the most beautiful in Sweden and it's easy to see why: its western edge is proudly given over to the governor's residence, built in Neoclassical style by the court architect, Olof Tempelman, using local brick.

Konsthall

Arts Centre • Storatorget 2 • June–Aug Mon–Fri 9.30am–6pm, Sat & Sun 10am–3pm; Sept–May Mon–Fri 8am–5pm • Free

Inside the Neo-Renaissance former provincial government building, on the southwestern edge of Storatorget, you'll find both the town's tourist office (see opposite) and the **Konsthall**, whose small collection of contemporary Swedish art is worth a quick glance on your way in and out of the tourist office.

Domkyrkan

Franzéngatan 14 • Daily 10am–4pm

From Storatorget take a stroll up Västra Kyrkogatan to the heights of the Neoclassical **Domkyrkan**, the smallest cathedral in the country. Dating from the 1840s, it incorporates elements from earlier churches on the site; the Baroque altar is from the eighteenth century, as are the VIP boxes in the nave.

Östanbäcksgatan

From the Domkyrkan, turn right and follow the road round and back down the hill until you come to the narrow old street of **Östanbäcksgatan**, with its pretty painted wooden houses from the 1730s. This is one of the oldest parts of town, Östanbäcken, where the houses were among the first to be built after the Russian incursions.

Rådhuset

For a taste of the town's architectural splendour, take a walk up the hilly main street, **Nybrogatan**, to its junction with Storgatan: the Neoclassical pastel orange **Rådhuset** here, complete with white semicircular portico, originally served as a school and home to the diocesan governors. While further up the hill, at the corner of Brunnshusgatan, the headquarters of the regional administration is particularly beautiful, housed in a Neo-Baroque and Art Nouveau building with a yellow ochre facade. From the top of Nybrogatan, there are good **views** back over the town and the water.

Murberget

Late June to early Aug Tues–Sun 11am–4pm • Free • ⓦ murberget.se • It's a 30min walk up here from the town centre, or, alternatively, buses #2 and #52 run from Nybrogatan in front of the Rådhuset

Whilst in town it's worth retracing your steps back down Nybrogatan to the train station, from where Stationsgatan (turning into Varvsallén) turns right, passing through the docks on its way to the impressive **open-air museum** at **Murberget**, the second biggest in Sweden after Skansen (see p.58).

The first building to take up its location here was a bell tower, which was moved from the village of Ullånger on the High Coast to its current position in 1913. There are around eighty other buildings, most notably traditional Ångermanland farmhouses and the old Murberget church, once a popular venue for local weddings. Look out for the **Rysstugan**, the one and only wooden building to escape the devastating fire caused by the

Russians in 1721. The nineteenth-century **Spjute Inn** here is still home to a restaurant, and also contains a skittle alley dating from 1910, where you can have a game.

ARRIVAL AND INFORMATION   HÄRNÖSAND

By public transport Buses and trains operate from the new Resecentrum on Järnvägsgatan, a 5min walk from the centre.

Tourist office Storatorget 2 (June–Aug Mon–Fri 9.30am–6pm, Sat & Sun 10am–3pm; Sept–May Mon–Fri 8am–5pm; ☎0611 881 40, ⓦharnosand.se/turism). This central office has free maps, bus times and free internet access.

ACCOMMODATION

First Stadt Härnösand Skeppsbron 9 ☎0611 55 44 40, ⓦfirsthotels.se. The biggest and plushest of the town's hotels with a perfect waterside location and well-appointed, if rather staid, rooms decked out in predicatable chain-hotel Scandinavian style. There is, however, a decent buffet breakfast available. **811kr/1075kr**

★ **Östanbäcken Logi** Östanbäcksgatan 14, ☎0611 155 60 00, ⓦostanbackenlogi.com. These cute red-and-white wooden cottages hidden in a charming garden off Östanbäcksgatan are a real find. Pine interiors, en-suite bathrooms and a fully fitted kitchen make them the number one place to stay. Bed linen is an extra 50kr. **790kr**

Royal Strandgatan 12 ☎0611 204 55, ⓦhotelroyal.se. Perfectly located for the Resecentrum, this nineteenth-century pile with just 24 rooms has wonderful high ceilings and generously proportioned windows. It is also the cheapest hotel in Härnösand, though rooms are perfectly comfortable. **730kr/990kr**

Sälstens Camping Sälsten ☎0611 181 50, ⓦcamping.se/y21. This waterfront campsite also has a small selection of four-bed cabins. It's around 2km northeast of the town centre, next to a string of pebble beaches; to get there, take Storgatan off Nybrogatan and follow the road as it swings eastwards along the coast. Open mid-May to Aug. Tents **140kr**, cabins **400kr**

STF Vandrarhem Härnösand Köpmangatan 7 & Franzéngatan 14 ☎0611 243 00, ⓔmitti@telia.com. Located in two central buildings, one beside the cathedral in a charming building from 1844, the other by the quayside, the town's youth hostel is modern, clean and a great money saver; all rooms have private facilities. Open year-round. Dorms **275kr**, doubles **550kr**

EATING AND DRINKING

Make no mistake, Härnösand may be an architectural feast, but its culinary prowess most certainly isn't. Eating places are thin on the ground and, sadly, rather uninspiring, bar one outstanding exception.

New China Restaurant Storgatan 34 ☎0611 136 06. A run-of-the-mill Asian restaurant with a decent range of predictable Chinese mains (from 88kr) as well as better Indonesian ones (from 125kr). It's one of the most popular places in town for lunch. Mon–Thurs 11am–9pm, Fri 11am–10pm, Sat 1–10pm, Sun 1–9pm.

Östanbäckens Pizzeria Östanbäcksgatan 1 ☎0611 50 05 52. This neighbourhood pizzeria and grill restaurant is a good bet for tasty pizzas from 60kr as well as pasta dishes (65–70kr), salmon fillet (85kr) and pork steak (90kr). It also has a choice of burgers from 60kr. Mon–Sat 11am–10pm, Sun 11am–9pm.

Ruom Thai Storgatan 34 ☎0611 55 60 42. Next door to *New China*, this rather cavernous and dingy Thai restaurant serves up mains such as green chicken curry for 89–119kr;

the quality of the food isn't bad but it's not overly authentic. There's takeaway service, too. Mon–Thurs 11am–9pm, Fri 11am–10pm, Sat noon–9pm.

Rutiga Dukan Västra Kyrkogatan 1. A snug and cosy café below the cathedral that's a great place for a cup of coffee and good home-baked pastries. Also has good-value weekday lunch specials which are worth seeking out. Mon–Fri 6.30am–6pm, Sat 10am–4pm.

Vägg i Vägg Brunnshusgatan 1 ☎0611 164 40. Head and shoulders above any other restaurant in Härnösand, this elegant place is beautifully located in a timber lodge built in 1871. It serves well-prepared mains such as venison fillet, local Arctic char and Wallenbergare for 150kr–255kr. Mon–Sat 6pm–midnight.

Höga Kusten – the High Coast

Designated a UNESCO World Heritage Site in late 2000, **HÖGA KUSTEN** (ⓦhighcoast.net), or the High Coast, is the highlight of any trip up the Bothnian coast. This stretch of striking coastline north of Härnösand is elementally beautiful: rolling mountains and verdant valleys plunge precipitously into the Gulf of Bothnia, and the rugged shoreline of sheer cliffs and craggy outcrops gives way to gently undulating pebble coves. The dramatic landscape of Höga Kusten is the result of the isostatic uplift that has occurred since the last Ice Age; as the ice melted, the land, no longer weighed down by ice up to 3km thick, rose by 286m. There's nowhere in the world where the uplift has been so great as in this part of Sweden, and, in fact, it is still rising at a rate of 8mm every year.

Off Höga Kusten are dozens of islands, some no more than a few metres square in size, others much larger and covered with dense pine forest. It was on these islands that the tradition of preparing the foul-smelling **surströmming** is thought to have begun (see p.263). A trip here is a must for anyone travelling up or down the Bothnian coast; from out at sea, you'll get the best view possible of the coastal cliffs which (as the very name High Coast suggests) are the tallest in the country. The islands themselves are havens of peace and tranquillity, offering the chance to get away from it all. Among the most beautiful in the chain are, from south to north: **Högbonden**, **Ulvön** and **Trysunda**. Each of these islands can be visited using a combination of buses and boats; before setting off, make sure you've understood the boat timetables (available at tourist offices), which are in Swedish only and can be confusing.

GETTING AROUND THE HIGH COAST

By boat The boats that serve the islands here operate only in summer, except for the *M/S Ulvön*, which sails for Ulvön all year round. For the latest bus and ferry times, check out ⓦ dintur.se or ⓦ ornskoldsvikshamn.se. All boats accept bicycles but not cars.

By car Travelling between Härnösand and Örnsköldsvik along the E4 will involve crossing over the Ångerman River via the stunning High Coast bridge (no tolls). One of the longest suspension bridges in the world, with a span of 1210m, it has dramatically shortened the journey by cutting out a lengthy detour upriver to the old bridge between Lunde and Klockestrand. Reaching a height of 180m above the water, the bridge is only 70m shorter than San Francisco's Golden Gate Bridge, which it closely resembles.

Högbonden

After a mere ten-minute boat ride from Bönhamn on the mainland, the steep sides of the tiny island of **HÖGBONDEN** rise up in front of you. Although the island can feel a little overcrowded with day-trippers in peak season (July to mid-Aug), at its best it's a wonderfully deserted, peaceful haven. There are no shops – so bring any provisions you'll need with you – and no hotels on the island; in fact the only building here is a former lighthouse, now converted into a **youth hostel** (see p.262). It's situated on a rocky plateau at the island's highest point, where the pine and spruce trees, so prominent elsewhere on the island, have been unable to get a foothold; Högbonden's flora also includes rowan, sallow, aspen and birch trees, as well as various mosses that compete for space with wild bilberries.

You'll only get to know the special charm of Högbonden if you stay a couple of nights and take time to explore: a narrow gorge runs north–south across the island, and there are also forested hillsides and a shoreline where eider ducks glide by with their young. The **views** out across the Gulf of Bothnia are stunning; on a sunny day you could easily imagine you're in the middle of the Mediterranean.

Wood-burning sauna

At any time, you can head for the traditional **wood-burning sauna** down by the sea, two minutes' walk from the jetty (it's signposted "bastu" off the island's one and only path); you'll need to book your slot with the youth hostel staff, who keep the sauna's key. Afterwards, you can take a quick skinny-dip in the cool waters of the Gulf of Bothnia. The sunsets, seen from the boardwalk in front of the sauna, are truly idyllic.

CLOCKWISE FROM TOP HOUSE IN THE LULEÅ ARCHIPELAGO (P.276); A TIN OF *SURSTRÖMMING* (P.263); LIGHTHOUSE AT HÖGBONDEN (P.260) >

ARRIVAL

HÖGBONDEN

By boat Sailing from the mainland village of Bönhamn, *M/S Högbonden* makes the 10min trip out to Högbonden (May to early Oct up to 4 daily; 150kr return; ☜ hkship.se).
By bus To get to Bönhamn on public transport from Härnösand, take the 11.20am bus to Ullånger, where you

change for a connection to Nordingrå and once there, change again for Bönhamn (check times at ☜ dintur.se).
By car To reach Bönhamn by car, turn off the E4 at Gallsäter onto the minor road leading there via Nordingrå.

ACCOMMODATION

★ **Youth hostel** In the former lighthouse ☎ 0613 230 05, ☜ hogbonden.se. The hostel's main building houses a kitchen, two bathrooms and several small dorms (with creaking floorboards) located over three floors. Two more rooms are in the building in the garden. To add to the

novelty of sleeping in a converted lighthouse, the building's clifftop vantage point affords sweeping sea views from the kitchen and the dorms. Breakfast costs 90kr. Open May– Oct. Dorms <u>**300kr**</u>

7

Ulvön

ULVÖN, 20km northeast of Högbonden and 12km southwest of Trysunda, is really two islands, Norra and Södra Ulvön, their combined area making it the largest in the High Coast archipelago. The southern island is uninhabited, separated from its northern neighbour by a narrow channel, Ulvösund, which provides a well-protected harbour. During the seventeenth and eighteenth centuries, Ulvön became home to the High Coast's biggest fishing community, as fishermen from Gävle came here to exploit the rich fishing grounds off the island; in subsequent centuries, though, many islanders moved to the mainland, especially after World War II, when the industry started to decline. Today, there are only around fifty permanent residents.

Ulvön is famous for its production of **surströmming**, fermented Baltic herring (see box opposite); two of the firms involved, Söderbergs Fisk and Ruben Madsen, are based in the main village of Ulvöhamn (see below) and it's possible to buy the locally produced stuff in the island's shop.

Ulvöhamn

All boats to the island dock at the main village, **ULVÖHAMN**, a picturesque one-street affair with red-and-white cottages and tiny boathouses on stilts snuggling up eave to eave. Walking along the waterfront, you'll pass the pretty **fishermen's chapel**, dating from 1622 and now the oldest wooden building in Ångermanland (mid-June to mid–Aug daily noon–3pm; free); inside, its walls are covered with flamboyant eighteenth-century murals. The chapel was established by Gävle fishermen, who began summer fishing forays up the Baltic coast in the sixteenth century. Its detached bell tower was once used to signal that it was time to assemble for the daily fishing trip. To get to the **beaches**, follow the sign marked "Strandpromenad Söder" from the tourist office (see opposite); it's about twenty minutes on foot past small sandy coves to the harbour entrance and a promontory of red rocks, Rödharen, beyond which lie several pebbly stretches. The unusual red rock here is a granite known by its Finnish name, **rappakivi**.

ARRIVAL

ULVÖN

From Härnösand To reach Ulvön from Härnösand, take the 8.55am bus to the village of Docksta (50min) and alight at the jetty, from where the *M/S Kusttrafik* leaves at 10.15am (June–Aug daily; ☎ 0613 105 50, ☜ hkship.se; 140kr one-way, 195kr day return), arriving in Ulvöhamn, on Ulvön, at 11.30am, heading back to the mainland at 3pm.

From Köpmanholmen Ulvön is easily reached from the north, too. From Köpmanholmen on the mainland (just south of Örnsköldsvik) there are sailings to Ulvöhamn, which sometimes go via Trysunda. Timetables change according to the time of year but can be found at ☜ ornskoldsvikshamn.se.

SURSTRÖMMING

Mention the word *surströmming* to most Swedes and they'll turn up their noses in disgust. It's best translated as "fermented Baltic herring" – though to the non-connoisseur, the description "rotten" would seem more appropriate. The tradition of eating the foul-smelling stuff began on Ulvön sometime during the sixteenth century when salt was very expensive; as a result just a little was used in preserving the fish, a decision which inadvertently allowed it to ferment.

The number of **salthouses** producing the herring has dwindled from several hundred early in the twentieth century to around twenty to thirty manufacturers now. Today, *surströmming* is made in flat tins containing a weak salt solution. Over the course of the four- to ten-week fermentation process, the tins blow up into the shape of a soccer ball under the pressure of the odious gases produced inside. Restaurants refuse to open the tins on the premises because of the lingering stink that's exuded, not unlike an open sewer; the unpleasant job has to be done outside in the fresh air.

The **season** for eating *surströmming* begins on the third Thursday in August, ending around two to three weeks later, when supplies run out. The fish can be accompanied with the yellow, almond-shaped variety of northern Swedish potatoes and washed down with beer or *akvavit*; alternatively it's put into a sandwich, perhaps with onion or tomato, all rolled up in a piece of *tunnbröd*, the thin unleavened bread traditional in this part of the country. More information at ⓦ surstromming.se.

INFORMATION

Tourist office In a tiny wooden hut beside the fishermen's chapel (mid-June to mid-Aug daily 11am–5pm; ☎ 0660 22 40 93; ⓦ ulvon.info). You can rent bikes here and pick up information about the Ulvöregatta, an annual gathering for ostentatious yachting types that takes place in mid-July.

ACCOMMODATION

Färjeläget Just by the village shop ☎ 0660 22 41 57, ⓦ ulvon.com. Four four-bed pine cabins with cooking facilities and fantastic views out over the harbour, with ten other log cabins located a 10min walk up the hill behind the harbour. Pine cabins <u>925kr</u>, Fri or Sat <u>975kr</u>; log cabins <u>850kr</u>, Fri or Sat <u>950kr</u>

Ulvö Skärgårdshotell Hamngatan 1 ☎ 0660 22 40 09, ⓦ ulvohotell.se. Just to the right of the quay as you come off the boat, the island's only hotel has cosy, modern rooms decorated in stylish floral swirls and bold colours with good views of the sea (those in the annexe cost 100kr less). Open May–Sept. <u>2048kr</u>

EATING AND DRINKING

If you are self-catering, the village **shop**, at the southern end of Ulvöhamn's main street, has a decent array of provisions. Out of season, you'll have no choice but to cook for yourself since all eating places close down for the winter. There's a pleasant **pub** and café below the hotel that buzzes in summer.

Almagränd Near the tourist office ☎ 0660 22 41 32. The place to come for burgers, pizzas and other grilled mains costing in the range of 150kr. The menu may be less than stimulating but it's a fine location to dine and enjoy fantastic views over the harbour from this waterfront location. Mid-June to mid-Aug daily 11am–1am.

Café Måsen Near the tourist office. A charming garden café where you can sit outside among the wild flowers and herbs and enjoy home-baked bread, sublime cakes, salads, sandwiches and pasta. Run by the gregarious Ruben Madsen (he of *surströmming* fame, see opposite) who sometimes appears as a clown. June–Aug daily 10am–6pm.

Ulvö Skärgårdshotell Hamngatan 1 ☎ 0660 22 40 09, ⓦ ulvohotell.se. This excellent hotel restaurant offers adventurous main courses (175–345kr) such as duck leg confit and Merguez lamb sausages as well as a mouthwatering fish and seafood buffet for 215kr which includes cold and warm smoked salmon, whitefish, eel, prawns – plus a dessert. Mon–Fri 11am–2pm & 6–9.30pm, Sat & Sun 6–9.30pm.

Trysunda

The charming fishing village of **TRYSUNDA**, on the tiny island of the same name, is the best preserved in Ångermanland, hemmed in around a narrow U-shaped harbour, with forty or so red-and-white houses right on the waterfront. The village's wooden **chapel**, which is usually unlocked, is one of the oldest on the Bothnian coast, dating from around 1655. Like the church on neighbouring Ulvön, the interior is decorated with colourful murals.

Trysunda is crisscrossed with walking paths, leading through the forests of dwarf pine that cover the island – many of which have become gnarled and twisted under the force of the wind. The island's gently sloping rocks make it ideal for bathing, and you'll find plenty of secluded spots where you can do so. There's a **sandy beach** at **Björnviken**, a bay on the eastern part of the island, and some smooth rocks on the north coast, just to the east of **Bockviken**. An easily walked path from the village will take you to both beaches and round the entire island in an hour or two. To continue east from Björnviken, don't be tempted to strike off round the headland, as the rocks there are impassable; instead, stay on the path, which cuts inland, and follow the signs for Storviken.

Skrubban

As you approach or leave the island, you might be lucky enough to catch a glimpse of elk on the neighbouring island, the volcanic and uninhabited **Skrubban**. Although the island has been a nature reserve since 1940, every year some hunting is allowed to control the animal population and prevent unnecessary suffering from starvation, a practice followed elsewhere in Sweden too.

ARRIVAL AND INFORMATION   TRYSUNDA

By boat Heading here in summer (mid-June to mid-Aug) from Ulvön, you'll first need to get the boat to Köpmanholmen, from where you can catch the twice-daily ferry to Trysunda. Outside the summer season, there's a direct boat (daily except Sat) from Ulvön to Trysunda,

avoiding the need to travel via Köpmanholmen. Boat times are at ⓦ ornskoldsvikshamn.se.
Map There's a free map of the island available at the village shop.

ACCOMMODATION AND EATING

Trysunda Gästhamn ☎ 0660 430 38, ⓦ trysunda.com. There are 23 beds in rather cramped double rooms sharing facilities located right by the harbour inside the red building which functions as the service centre for the marina. There are also a kitchen, dining room, sauna and

washing machine on site, available to guests. May–Sept. Doubles **500kr**
Village shop Stocks the bare necessities, including fresh and smoked fish, and the dreaded *surströmming*.

Umeå and around

UMEÅ is the biggest city in the north of Sweden, with a current population of 114,000 people, which means that an astonishing one in ten of the residents of Norrland live here. Demographically speaking, it's probably Sweden's youngest city, a notion borne

---

CITY OF BIRCH TREES

Umeå is sometimes referred to as the "City of Birch Trees", after the trees that were planted along every street following a devastating fire in 1888. Most of the city was burnt to the ground in the blaze, and two-thirds of the town's three thousand inhabitants lost their homes. In the rebuilding which soon began apace, two wide esplanades, one of which is Rådhusesplanaden, were constructed to act as fire breaks and help prevent such a disaster happening again. A decree was then handed down stating that the birch was the most suitable tree to add life to the town's newly reconstructed streets; even today, the city council places ads for free trees in the local papers and provides free birch saplings every spring to anyone who wants them.

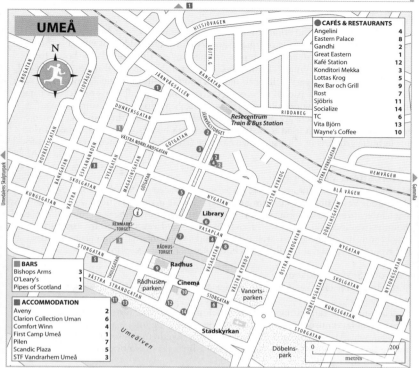

UMEÅ

N

Resecentrum
Train & Bus Station

Library

Rådhus

Cinema

Stadskyrkan

Umeälven

Döbelns-
park

out by taking a stroll round the airy modern centre: you'll form the impression that anyone who's not in a pushchair is pushing one, and that the cafés and city parks are full of teenagers. Indeed one in five people are in their twenties, figures that are partly due to the presence of Norrland University. Its youthfulness may well be responsible for the fact that Umeå is the one of the few towns or cities in northern Sweden where there's an air of dynamism: new restaurants and bars are opening all the time, there's a thriving cultural scene and by late 2012, the **Botniabanan** high-speed rail link to Stockholm should be completed, making it possible to reach the capital in just five and a half hours; a new combined rail and bus station is being constructed in anticipation.

The sound of the **rapids** along the Ume River gives the city its name: **uma** means "roar". With its fast-flowing river – a feature few other Swedish coastal cities enjoy – and wide, stylish boulevards, Umeå is an appealing metropolis. It would be no bad idea to spend a couple of days here, sampling some of its bars and restaurants – the variety of which you won't find anywhere else in Norrland.

Gammlia

Gammliavägen • Late June to late Aug daily 10am–5pm • Free • ⓦ vbm.se • Local bus #2 or #7, or a 20min walk from the train or bus stations

Most visitors to Umeå want to see **Gammlia**, the city's excellent museum complex which is home to a terrific collection of exhibitions on everything from *Sámi* life to skiing and merits a good half-day's exploration. In summer, the open-air section even has people dressed in period costume going about their daily tasks much as their predecessors did several centuries ago.

Friluftsmuseum

Gammlia grew out of the **Friluftsmuseum**, an open-air cluster of twenty regional buildings, including a couple of squat *Sámi* structures, the oldest of which is the seventeenth-century gatehouse you pass on the way in. The grounds are home to the customary farmyard animals – cows, pigs, geese and the like – and the guides dressed in period costume are very willing to tell you about life in their mock town. The *Sámi* section also has the occasional reindeer tethered close by. It all helps to create a rural ambience including a windmill, church, two threshing floors and a smokehouse for pork. At the bakery there are demonstrations of how to make the thin unleavened bread, *tunnbröd*, which used to be baked in people's homes. You can also take a ride through the grounds in a horse-drawn carriage (free), an experience that's bound to entertain kids.

Västerbottens Museum

Mid-June to mid-Aug daily 10am–5pm; mid-Aug to mid-June Tues–Fri 10am–4pm, Sat noon–4pm, Sun noon–5pm • Free

The indoor **Västerbottens Museum** houses Gammlia's main collection: three exhibitions that canter through the county's past, from prehistoric times (the section on this period contains the oldest ski in the world, over five thousand years old) to the Industrial Revolution. It's all good stuff, well laid out and complemented by an array of videos and recordings; a useful English guidebook is available at reception.

Fiske och Sjöfartsmuseum

Fishing and Maritime Museum • Late June to late Aug daily noon–5pm; late Aug to late June Tues–Sat noon–4pm, Sun noon–5pm • Free

Back outside, you can resume your exploration of provincial history in the separate **Fiske och Sjöfartsmuseum**, which tries its best to be a regional maritime museum: the tug, *Egil*, which once operated in the Ume River together with several fishing and rowing boats are squeezed into the small hall which also has a brief display about seal hunting in the region.

Bildmuséet

Mid-June to mid-Aug Wed–Sun noon–5pm; mid-Aug to mid-June Tues–Sat noon–4pm, Sun noon–5pm • Free • ⓦ bildmuseet.umu.se

Destined for the new Kulturens Hus being constructed on Västra Strandgatan back in town, the **Bildmuséet**, which is Umeå university's art museum, will house thought-provoking displays of contemporary Swedish and international art, photojournalism and visual design.

Umedalens Skulpturpark

2km west of the centre • Always open • Free • ⓦ umedalenskulptur.se • Take bus #1 or #61 here from Vasaplan in town and get off at the stop called "Löftets gränd"

Occupying the grounds of Umeå's former mental hospital out at Umedalen, a couple of kilometres west of the centre, this acclaimed **sculpture park** is a riot of modern form in all shapes and sizes. As well as work from visiting international sculptors, the permanent alfresco exhibition contains pieces from, amongst others, Miroslaw Balka, Tony Cragg and Antony Gormley.

ARRIVAL AND DEPARTURE

By plane Umeå's busy airport is 6km south of the city, with direct domestic flights to and from Stockholm (Bromma and Arlanda), Gothenburg, Kiruna, Luleå and Östersund as well as international flights to Vaasa in Finland and Riga in Latvia; it's linked with the centre by airport buses (40kr) and taxis (145kr).

By train Trains calling at Umeå pull in at the northern end of the city centre on Järnvägsallén. Note that train times to Stockholm will reduce to around 5hr 30min once the Botniabanan is complete – possibly from late 2012 onwards.

Destinations Gävle (1 daily; 7hr 40min); Luleå (4 daily; 3hr 30min); Narvik (1 daily; 13hr 30min); Stockholm (1 daily; 9hr 40min); Uppsala (1 daily; 9hr).

By bus The bus station shares premises with the train station. Destinations Haparanda/Tornio, Finland (2 daily; 6hr 30min); Luleå (4 daily; 4hr); Mo-i-Rana, Norway (1 daily; 8hr); Östersund (2 daily; 6hr 30min); Skellefteå (4 daily;

2hr); Storuman and Tärnaby/Hemavan (Mon–Sat 3 daily, Sun 1 daily; 3hr 40min to Storuman, 6hr to Tärnaby/Hemavan); Sundsvall (7 daily; 4hr).

By ferry RG Line ferries to and from Vaasa in Finland dock at Holmsund, 20km south of Umeå but there is no connecting bus to the port. There's a return service to Vaasa (1 daily; 4hr; ⍟ rgline.com).

INFORMATION

Tourist office Renmarkstorget (May to mid-June & mid-Aug to Sept Mon–Fri 10am–6pm, Sat 10am–2pm; mid-June to mid-Aug Mon–Fri 9am–7pm, Sat 10am–4pm, Sun 11am–3pm; Oct–April Mon–Fri

10am–5pm; ☎ 090 16 16 16, ⍟ visitumea.se).
Internet Sidewalk Express is in McDonalds at Västra Rådhusgatan 7, whilst the tourist office also has a couple of terminals.

ACCOMMODATION

Aveny Rådhusesplanaden 14 ☎ 090 13 41 00, ⍟ profilhotels.se/hotelaveny. The city's new outstanding design hotel deserves a stay in its own right: an orgy of marine blues, organic greens and golden hues at every turn. The beds are sumptuous beyond belief – in short, come here for serious pampering. **990kr/1795kr**

Clarion Collection Uman Storgatan 52 ☎ 090 12 72 20, ⍟ choicehotels.se. Located in the grand former home of the city's chief medical officer, this cosy place, decked out with a medical theme, really is a home from home, an evening buffet for all guests included in the price. **1190kr/1790kr**

Comfort Winn Skolgatan 64 ☎ 090 71 11 00, ⍟ choicehotels.se. Smart and comfortable, though lacking character and with rather cramped rooms. The bizarre purple colour scheme may be a little sombre but thankfully a good breakfast is served in a glass atrium flooded with natural light. **670kr/1570kr**

Pilen Pilgatan 5 ☎ 090 14 14 60, ⍟ hotellpilen.se. One of the smaller, cheaper hotels with just twenty-odd, smartly renovated rooms, whose cosy interiors have been redesigned to reflect the style of the building which dates

from the turn of the last century. **775kr/975kr**

Scandic Plaza Storgatan 40 ☎ 090 205 63 00, ⍟ scandichotels.se/plazaumea. For a treat, head for this very smart place which is popular with business travellers, with rooms decorated in the latest Scandinavian designs. There are superb views from the fourteenth-floor sauna suite, which is worth a stay here in itself. **930kr/1680kr**

STF Vandrarhem Umeå Västra Esplanaden 10 ☎ 090 77 16 50, ⍟ umeavandrarhem.com. With bright and airy en-suite rooms, this centrally located hostel with 28 rooms and good catering facilities, just 450m from the stations, is one of Sweden's best. Dorms **210kr**, doubles **420kr**

CAMPING

First Camp Umeå Nydalasjön 2, Nydala ☎ 090 70 26 00, ⍟ firstcamp.se/umea; take buses #2, #6, #7 or #9, get off at Nydala and walk for around 5min towards Nydalabadet, which is signposted. Umeå's campsite is located 5km from town on the shore of a lake, and has a whole variety of cabins. Open year-round. Tents **140kr**, cabins **690kr**

EATING, DRINKING AND ENTERTAINMENT

Eating and drinking opportunities are varied and generally of a high standard in Umeå, partly because of the size of the city and partly due to the large student population. Many of the popular places, though, are closed on Sun.

CAFÉS

Kafé Station Östra Rådhusgatan 2L ☎ 090 14 19 90. Handily located next to the Filmstaden cinema. Rough brick walls, tiled floors and a wide selection of sandwiches as well as great coffee and cheesecake. A firm favourite with all Umeåites. Mon–Thurs 11am–9pm, Fri & Sat 11am–midnight.

Konditori Mekka Rådhusesplanaden 15 ☎ 090 77 44 04. Close to the train station, this long-established café is known for its delicious baked goods, especially its mouthwatering blueberry, carrot and squidgy *kladdkaka* cakes. Also has a good array of sandwiches, handy for last-minute purchases before boarding the train. Mon–Thurs

7am–9pm, Fri 7am–7pm, Sat & Sun 11am–7pm.
Wayne's Coffee Storgatan 50 ☎ 090 70 17 00. With stylish 1960s retro chic decor, this branch of *Wayne's* is one of the best in Sweden, with a fantastic range of excellent coffee as well as sandwiches and muffins. It's a popular student hangout, too, and a good place to strike up a conversation. Mon–Thurs 10am–10pm, Fri & Sat 11am–midnight, Sun 11am–10pm.

RESTAURANTS

★ **Angelini** Rådhusesplanaden 14 ☎ 090 13 41 00. Style is high on the agenda at this Italian-American restaurant with mosaic walls and wooden floors. The menu is equally tasty: burgers (165kr), ribeye steak (285kr) and linguini with prawns (159kr) are all good bets. Daily 5–11pm.

Eastern Palace Vasagatan 12 ✆090 13 88 39. This place serves really good Japanese and Thai food; teriyaki salmon for 145kr or Thai mains 95–148kr. The weekday lunch buffet is excellent value at 85kr. Mon–Thurs 11am–10pm, Fri 11am–11pm, Sat noon–11pm, Sun noon–10pm.

Gandhi Rådhusesplanaden 17B ✆090 17 50 75. Perfect location opposite the train station for authentically tasty Indian food, including tandoori specialities, at sensible prices, 135kr–155kr. Mon–Thurs 11am–10pm, Fri 11am–11pm, Sat noon–11pm, Sun 3–9pm.

Great Eastern Magasinsgatan 17 ✆090 13 88 38. The best Chinese restaurant in Norrland. Very popular lunch buffet as well as evening chicken and beef dishes from 98kr as well as a Mongolian barbecue for 159kr. Also has a few Thai mains from 92kr and Japanese options from 70kr. Mon–Fri 11am–2pm & 4–9pm, Sat noon–10pm, Sun 1–9pm.

Lottas Krog Nygatan 22 ✆090 12 95 51. Upmarket pub food served in one of the town's most popular eating places. The extensive menu is a mix of Swedish and World food: Mexican fajitas (159kr), steak and chips (220kr) and pasta carbonara (129kr). Also has some twenty different beers on tap, including Boddingtons. Mon 3–11pm, Tues 3pm–midnight, Wed & Thurs 3pm–1am, Fri 11am–2am, Sat noon–2am.

★ **Rex Bar och Grill** Rådhustorget ✆090 12 60 50. Umeå's very own Swedish-French bistro serving Swedish classics given a French twist such as reindeer fillet (290kr), pan-fried scallops (285kr) and turbot with horseradish (280kr); three courses cost 570kr. Mon & Tues 11am–2pm & 5–11pm, Wed & Thurs 11am–2pm & 5pm–midnight, Sat noon–2am.

Rost Skolgatan 62 ✆090 13 58 00. A superb and justifiably popular vegetarian restaurant where the food is freshly prepared and they even produce their own cheeses: hummus sandwich is 75kr, apple salad 85kr and a cheese platter with lentils and bulgur wheat is a good-value 77kr. Mon & Sat 11am–4pm, Tues 11am–7pm, Wed & Thurs 11am–8pm, Fri 11am–9pm.

Sjöbris Kajen 10 ✆090 77 71 23. An excellent fish restaurant on board an elegant old white steamer built in 1915. Well-prepared fish dishes such as Baltic herring from 119kr, grilled meats from 219kr and different themed buffets each evening for 189kr. There's a quayside terrace, too. Open May–Sept: daily 11am–late.

Socialize Vasagatan 1 ✆090 77 79 09. Housed within a sturdy stone basement, this new, arty restaurant has everything from birch trees as interior decor to a retro 1960s lounge bar. The menu is inventive modern Swedish, for example, elk carpaccio with rhubarb and lingonberries or Jerusalem artichoke gratin. Mains are around 150kr. Tues–Thurs 4–10pm, Fri 4–11pm, Sat 4pm–2am.

TC Vasaplan ✆090 15 63 21. Short for Teatercafé, this is a firm favourite among all age groups. It's the best place in town for top-quality northern Swedish specialities such as grilled salmon (185kr), locally sourced steak fillet (245kr) and pan-fried Arctic char (240kr). There's outdoor seating in summer. Mon–Thurs 11am–1.30pm & 3.30–11pm, Fri 11.30am–1.30pm & 3pm–2am, Sat 4pm–2am.

Vita Björn Kajen 12 ✆090 12 00 12. This elegant wooden boat from 1899 is a favourite summertime haunt for its salmon, Baltic herring and prawn concoctions; reckon on around 189kr for a main dish. Quayside terrace, too. Open May–Sept daily 10.30am–late.

BARS

Umeå buzzes at night, with plenty of stylish and friendly **bars** to choose from, most of them British-style pubs or brasseries. The city centre is most lively during termtime when students are around.

Bishops Arms Renmarkstorget 8 ✆090 10 09 90. Umeå's attempt at an English-style pub and consequently one of the most popular places to be seen and to do the seeing in – always packed. There's outdoor seating in summer, and for those chilly evenings, blankets and free-standing gas heaters. Mon 4pm–midnight, Tues–Thurs 4pm–1am, Fri 3pm–2am, Sat noon–2am, Sun noon–10pm.

O'Leary's Västra Norrlandsgatan 5 ✆090 13 58 30. A popular pub spilling over two floors with large video screens showing various sports, and live entertainment on Fri and Sat nights. Happy hour 10–11.30pm on Wed, Fri & Sat nights when it's standing room only. Mon 4–10pm, Tues & Wed 4pm–2am, Thurs 4–11pm, Fri 3pm–2am, Sat 2pm–2am, Sun 2–10pm.

Pipes of Scotland Rådhusesplanaden 14 ✆090 13 41 00. Umeå's very own Scottish theme pub really pulls the crowds with its After Work weekday buffet of nibbles for just 39kr until 7pm. It's a fun place for a drink, though, at any time and a good place to meet the city's student population. Tues 5–11pm, Wed, Fri & Sat 5pm–2am, Thurs 5pm–1am.

Around Umeå: Älgens hus elk farm

Västra Nyliden 23, Bjurholm • Mid-June to mid-Aug Tues–Sun noon–6pm; mid-Aug to mid-June by advance booking on ✆0932 500 00 • 120kr • 🌐 algenshus.se • You can reach Bjurholm by bus (daily: every 1–2hr; 1hr; 🌐 resrobot.se) from Umeå

Umeå is ideally placed for a jaunt to the Älgens hus **elk farm** in **Bjurholm**, a small village 65km west of the city. Driving around Sweden you may well have caught the briefest glimpse of the "King of the Forest", Europe's largest land animal, as tall as a horse but with antlers. The farm, though, provides an excellent opportunity to come face to face with these cumbersome-looking beasts and to learn all about their behaviour from the knowledgeable staff, who also make cheese from elk milk – a rare and inordinately expensive delicacy. Incidentally, elk love bananas, so you may wish to pack a few for your visit.

Skellefteå

There used to be a religious fervour about the town **SKELLEFTEÅ**, 140km northeast of Umeå. In 1324, an edict in the name of King Magnus Eriksson invited "all those who believed in Jesus Christ or wanted to turn to him" to settle between the Skellefte and Ume rivers. Many heeded the call, and parishes mushroomed on the banks of the Skellefte River. By the end of the eighteenth century, a devout township was centred around the town's monumental church, which stood out in stark contrast to the surrounding plains and wide river. Nowadays, though, more material occupations, including computer and electronics industries, and the mining of gold and silver, support the town. Since there's little to see in the town centre you would fare better concentrating on nearby **Bonnstan**, comprising an engaging collection of battered log cottages gathered together to form the **kyrkstad** (church town), plus the proud Neoclassical **church**, which houses one of Norrland's proudest exhibits – the **medieval carving** of the Virgin of Skellefteå.

Nearby, the rickety **Lejonströmsbron** is Sweden's oldest wooden bridge, offering elevated views of the Skellefte River. Skellefteå is also well placed for jaunts into the Swedish inland with good bus connections to Arvidsjaur and Arjeplog.

Bonnstan

Skellefteå's church and **church town**, known as **Bonnstan**, are within easy striking distance of the centre: walk west along Nygatan and keep going for about fifteen minutes. An evocative sight, the **kyrkstad** (see box below) here comprises five long rows of weather-beaten log houses, with battered wooden shutters. The houses are protected by law: any renovations, including the installation of electricity, are forbidden, making this the most genuine example of all Sweden's church towns. You

---

SWEDEN'S CHURCH TOWNS

After the break with the Catholic Church in 1527, the Swedish clergy were determined to teach their parishioners the Lutheran fundamentals, with the result that, by 1681, church services had become compulsory. There was one problem with this requirement, though – the population in the north was spread over considerable distances, making weekly attendance impossible. The clergy and the parishes agreed a compromise: it was decreed that those living within 10km of the church should attend every Sunday; those between 10km and 20km away, every fortnight; and those 20–30km away, every three weeks. The scheme worked, and within a decade, **church towns** (kyrkstäder) had appeared throughout the region to provide the travelling faithful with somewhere to spend the night after a day of praying and listening to powerful sermons.

Of the 71 church towns Sweden originally had, only eighteen are left today, predominantly in the provinces of **Västerbotten** and **Norrbotten**. Each kyrkstad consists of rows of simple wooden houses grouped tightly around the church. The biggest and most impressive, at **Gammelstad** near Luleå (see p.275), is included on the UNESCO World Heritage List. Today, they are no longer used in the traditional way, though people still live in the old houses, especially in summer, and sometimes even rent them out to tourists.

can take a peek inside, but bear in mind that these are privately owned summer houses today.

Landskyrka

Kyrkvägen, Nordanå • Daily 10am–4pm

Next to the cottages is the **landskyrka**, a proud white Neoclassical church which so enthused Leopold von Buch, a traveller who visited here in the nineteenth century, that he was moved to describe it as "the largest and most beautiful building in the entire north of Sweden, rising like a Palmyra's temple out of the desert". Its domed roof is supported by four mighty pillars along each of the walls; inside, there's an outstanding series of medieval sculptures. Look out too for the 800-year-old **Virgin of Skellefteå**, a walnut **woodcarving** immediately behind the altar on the right – it's one of the few remaining Romanesque images of the Virgin in the world. Nearby, on the Skellefte River, the islet of **Kyrkholmen**, reached by a small wooden bridge, is a pretty place to sit and while away an hour or two. It's home to an outdoor **café** that specializes in waffles with cloudberry jam (mid-June to mid-Aug).

7

Lejonströmsbron

From the church you have two walking routes back to the centre: either take Strandpromenaden along the river's edge, interrupted by barbecue sites and grassy stretches; or cross **Lejonströmsbron**, one of the oldest and longest wooden bridges in Sweden, beneath the hill where the church stands. Dating from 1737, the bridge was the scene of mass slaughter when Russian and Swedish forces clashed there during the marvellously named War of the Hats, which started in 1741. Once on the south side of the river, you can stroll back to Parksbron, past the occasional boat and silent fisherman.

ARRIVAL AND INFORMATION   SKELLEFTEÅ

By bus The bus station is at the top of the central modern paved square, Torget.
Destinations Arjeplog (2 daily; 3hr 15min), Arvidsjaur (2 daily; 2hr); Bodø, Norway (Mon–Fri & Sun 1 daily; 9hr); Luleå (9 daily; 2hr 45min); Umeå (10 daily; 2hr).

Tourist office Trädgårdsgatan 7 (end June to early Aug Mon–Fri 10am–6pm, Sat 10am–3pm, Sun noon–3pm; early Aug to end June Mon–Fri 10am–5pm, Sat 10am–2pm; ☎0910 45 25 00, ⓦdestinationskelleftea.se). There are internet terminals here.

ACCOMMODATION

Best Western Malmia Torget 2 ☎0910 73 25 00, ⓦmalmia.se. A good central location in the main square for this modern hotel offering everything you'd expect from a chain hotel – creature comforts but with few flourishes; rooms are sadly rather plain and uninspiring. <u>722kr/1270kr</u>
Skellefteå Camping About 1.5km north of the centre on Mossgatan, just off the E4 ☎091073 55 00, wskecamp.mammon.se. As well as camping, you can rent two-bed cabins here. The site also has a heated outdoor swimming pool, wave machine and jacuzzi. Tents <u>140kr</u>, cabins <u>450kr</u>
Stadshotell Stationsgatan 8–10 ☎0910 71 10 60, ⓦskellefteastadshotell.se. Skellefteå's new pride and joy, a full-service modern business-oriented hotel with smart Nordic-style rooms and a superlative gym and sauna

department. Streets ahead of any other establishment in town. <u>790kr/1295kr</u>
Victoria Trädgårdsgatan 8 ☎0910 174 70, ⓦhotelvictoria.se. Of the central hotels, this is the cheapest, a family-run establishment on the top floor of one of the buildings on the south side of the main square. Rooms are adequate if rather unexceptional. <u>699kr/1299kr</u>
Youth hostel Brännavägen 25 ☎0910 72 57 00, ⓦstiftsgardenskelleftea.com. A 30min walk from the centre, this rustic, red, two-storey building by the banks of the Skellefte River is well worth seeking out though it only takes advance bookings. Head west along Nygatan (which later becomes Brännavägen) until the junction with Kyrkvägen, where the hostel is on the corner. No dorm beds. Doubles <u>480kr</u>

EATING AND DRINKING

For all its contemporary go-ahead industry, modern Skellefteå is quiet and retiring; however, its restaurants and bars come as a pleasant surprise since they are among the best in Norrland.

Lilla Mari Köpmangatan 13J ☎ 0910 391 92. For a café, try this popular place set in an old-fashioned low-ceilinged wooden cottage in a small courtyard next to Nygatan 33K; for atmosphere it's unbeatable, feeling not unlike a grandmother's parlour. Outdoor seating in summer. Mon–Sat 9am–4pm.

Nygatan 57 Nygatan 57 ☎ 0910 134 44. A new and welcome departure for Skellefteå at this first-floor restaurant with smart floral wallpaper and white tablecloths, serving locally sourced specialities such as Arctic char and zander as well as dependables like spinach and ricotta tortellini: mains are 149–259kr. Mon–Fri 11am–1.30pm & 5pm till late, Sat 5pm till late.

Old Williams Pub Trädgårdsgatan 13–15 ☎ 0910 73 91 61. Drinking is best done at this faux-English pub in the main square which is located on the first floor and entered via *Tattung* Chinese restaurant. Mon–Thurs 5pm–midnight, Fri 4pm–2am, Sat 3pm–2am, Sun 3pm–midnight.

Stekhus Kriti Kanalgatan 51 ☎ 0910 77 95 35. This long-established and popular place is an excellent choice for Greek food with steaks from 245kr, moussaka platter with beans, calamari and Greek salad at 220kr and lamb cutlets for 250kr; there's also a decent bar here. Mon–Thurs 4–10pm, Fri 4–11pm, Sat 1–11pm, Sun 1–10pm.

Pite Havsbad

From Skellefteå it's 70km north along the E4 highway to the superb sandy **beaches** and swimming complex of **Pite Havsbad**, northern Sweden's main beach resort. Renowned for its long hours of summer sunshine, relatively warm water temperatures and sweeping strands of golden sand, it's a great place to unwind. There's even an official **nudist beach:** turn left along the beach and look out for a large rock marked "Naturist Bad".

Äventyrsbadet

Swimming complex: Late June to late Aug daily 10am–8pm; late Aug to late June Mon–Thurs 4–8pm, Fri 2–-8pm, Sat & Sun 10am–6pm • Summer 140kr, otherwise Mon–Fri & Sun 80kr, Sat 120kr • ☎ 0911 327 31

In the swimming complex, you'll find open-air pools with water slides, and the indoor Äventyrsbadet, with fun pool, jacuzzis, saunas, steam room and yet more water slides.

Icebreaker tours

Mid-Jan to late March/early April: Sat 11am • 995kr per person; minimum 10 people required for tour to operate • Advance booking essential on ☎ 0911 327 20

In winter don't miss the fabulous **icebreaker tours** onboard the *Arctic Explorer*, which was built in Finland in 1963. After retiring from official service, the boat now sails from Piteå out into the frozen expanses of the Gulf of Bothnia. There's also the unmissable opportunity to don a survival suit and float off the stern of the ship amid the ice blocks the ship has just broken.

ARRIVAL
PITE HAVSBAD

By bus Buses between Umeå and Luleå call in at Pite Havsbad. For timetables, consult ⓦ resrobot.se.

ACCOMMODATION

Hotell Pite Havsbad ☎ 0911 327 00, ⓦ pite-havsbad .se. A choice of superbly appointed, modern rooms within the hotel complex, many with sweeping sea views or, next door, right on the beach, there are four-bed cabins. Doubles **15980kr**, cabins **1990kr**

Luleå

When **LULEÅ**, 65km from Pite Havsbad up the E4, was founded in 1621 it had at its centre a church town (see p.269) and medieval church. Numerous trading ships would load and unload their goods at its tiny harbour, reflecting the importance of trade with Stockholm even in those days.

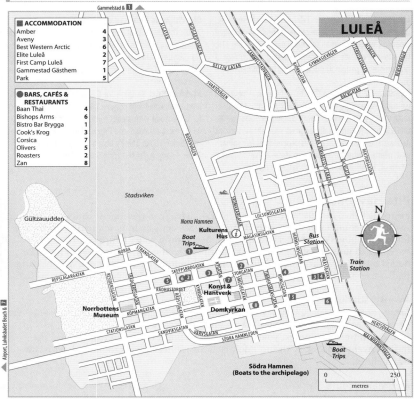

LULEÅ

■ ACCOMMODATION
Amber	4
Aveny	3
Best Western Arctic	6
Elite Luleå	2
First Camp Luleå	7
Gammestad Gästhem	1
Park	5

● BARS, CAFÉS & RESTAURANTS
Baan Thai	4
Bishops Arms	6
Bistro Bar Brygga	1
Cook's Krog	3
Corsica	7
Olivers	5
Roasters	2
Zan	8

7

Airport, Luleåbadet Beach & 7

Although shipping is still important today, in recent years Luleå has become the hi-tech centre of the north, specializing in metallurgy; it also has an important **university**. The town's wide streets and lively, friendly atmosphere make it immediately likeable, and if you're heading north for the wilds of the Torne valley, Gällivare and Kiruna, or to the sparsely populated regions of Swedish Lapland, Luleå represents your last chance to enjoy a decent range of restaurants and bars. Be mindful of the weather, though: Luleå is built on a peninsula which takes the full brunt of the northerly winds. If you're here in summer, taking a boat out into the **archipelago** (see p.277), makes a wonderful day-trip – departures are daily and there's a whole array of islands in the Gulf of Bothnia to choose from: beaches, walking trails and plenty of peace and solitude are the main draws.

Brief history

The harbour soon proved too small, thanks to the growth in business, and so, by royal command, the settlement was moved to its present site in 1649; only the church and church town, today part of Luleå's **Gammelstad** (Old Town), remained in situ. Up until the end of the eighteenth century, Luleå was still little more than a handful of houses and storage huts; indeed Linnaeus, Sweden's famous botanist, who passed through here in 1732 on his journey to Swedish Lapland, described Luleå as a village. Though the town had started to become something of a shipbuilding centre in the nineteenth century, it wasn't until the construction in 1888 of the Malmbanan, the railway built to transport iron ore from the Gulf of Bothnia for wintertime export at the ice-free Norwegian port of Narvik, that Luleå's fortunes really started to flourish. Luleå was at one end of the line, and its port was vital for lucrative iron exports (the main ironfields were – and are – around Kiruna and Gällivare).

Domkyrkan

Rådhustorget · Late June to mid-Aug Mon–Fri 10am–6pm; mid-Aug to late June Mon–Fri 10am–3pm · Free

Just to the south of **Storgatan**, the main street, lies Luleå's main square, **Rådhustorget**, with the **Domkyrkan** in the corner. The medieval incarnation of the cathedral disappeared centuries ago and the present one, built in 1893 on the same spot as its predecessor, is a modern barrage of copper chandeliers hanging like Christmas decorations. Unusually for northern Sweden, it's built of brick, in late-Gothic style to the design of the architect Adolf Emil Melander. The interior was completely renewed in 1938 when the original wooden walls and fittings were removed, revealing the brickwork underneath which was then painted white.

Kulturens Hus

House of Culture · Skeppsbrogatan 17 · Mon–Fri 10am–6pm, Sat noon–4pm · Free

Northeast of the Domkyrkan, **Kulturens Hus** is not only home to the tourist office and the city library but also the **Konsthall art exhibition hall** which is sometimes worth a look, with interesting displays of changing work from modern Swedish artists and sculptors.

Konst & Hantverk

Smedjegatan 13 · Mon–Fri 10am–6pm, Sat 10am–2pm

There's local art and **handicrafts** on sale at Konst & Hantverk, a treasure trove of a store that sells everything from handmade coat hooks in the shape of rams' horns to the seemingly obligatory "Välkommen" sign which no Swedish summer cottage is complete without. It's all produced by local artists, and this is a great place to pick up a souvenir or two without paying over the odds.

Norrbottens Museum

Storgatan 2 · Mon–Fri 10am–4pm, Sat & Sun noon–4pm; closed Mon in winter · Free · ⓦ norrbottensmuseum.se

From the main square, walk 300m west along Köpmangatan, and you'll come to the **Norrbottens Museum**. Although most of the collection is an informative if rather dull resumé of county history and the effects of the 1809 war with Russia when northern Sweden's borders were redrawn following the loss of Finland, the museum is worth a look mainly for the **films** which are available for viewing in the small cinema upstairs. In particular try to see the superb hour-long *Herdswoman* (in Swedish with English subtitles), about three generations of *Sámi* women from Nordmaling near Umeå and their ground-breaking court case in 2006 to establish traditional indigenous grazing rights for their reindeer herds; ask for the film at reception. The museum also has a pleasant **café**.

The beaches

When the weather's good, it's worth heading to the oddly named **Gültzauudden**, a wooded promontory that has a great **beach**; it was named after the German shipbuilder, Christian Gültzau, who helped to make Luleå a shipbuilding centre. It's easily reachable on foot from the centre: head north from the cathedral along Rådstugatan, which later changes its name to Norra Strandgatan and veers northwest past the Norrbotten theatre to the junction with Fagerlindsvägen. Turn right and follow the road down to the beach. Another good bet on a warm day is the long sandy beach at **Lulviksbadet**, just south of the airport, which also has a naturist section. To get here take the airport bus all the way to the airport and then walk south for a further fifteen minutes, following the main road, until you come to the beach on your left-hand side.

ARRIVAL AND DEPARTURE
LULEÅ

By plane The busy airport lies 10km west of the city, with buses (50kr) and taxis (180kr) linking it with Luleå; there are flights to and from Gothenburg, Pajala, Östersund, Sundsvall and Stockholm Arlanda.
By train Train services from the station on Prästgatan are few and far between so it pays to check timetables thoroughly in advance rather than just turn up hoping to jump on a train.
Destinations Gällivare (5 daily; 2hr 30min); Gävle (2 daily; 14hr); Gothenburg (1 daily; 18hr 30min); Kiruna (5 daily;

3hr 20); Narvik (2 daily; 7hr); Stockholm (2 daily; 14hr); Umeå (4 daily; 3hr 30min); Uppsala (2 daily; 13hr 15min).
By bus The bus station is located at the eastern end of Storgatan. Buses from here provide the most direct way of accessing villages in Swedish Lapland from Luleå. Destinations Arvidsjaur (Mon–Fri & Sun 2 daily, Sat 1 daily; 3hr); Jokkmokk (Mon–Fri & Sun 2 daily, Sat 1 daily; 3hr); Pajala (Mon–Fri & Sun 2 daily, Sat 1 daily; 3hr 30min).

INFORMATION

Tourist office Kulturens Hus, Skeppsbrogatan 17 (mid-June to mid-Aug Mon–Fri 9am–7pm, Sat & Sun 10am–4pm; mid-Aug to mid-June Mon–Fri 10am–5pm;

☎ 0920 45 70 00, ⊛ visitlulea.se).
Internet Sidewalk Express at Pressbyrån, Storgatan 67.

ACCOMMODATION

Amber Stationsgatan 67 ☎ 0920 102 00, ⊛ amber-hotell.se. A small and cosy family-run place in an old timber building close to the train station. Each of the sixteen rooms is individually decorated in a modern style: all are airy with high ceilings and large windows. **790kr/980kr**
★ **Aveny** Hermelinsgatan 10 ☎ 0920 22 18 20, ⊛ hotellaveny.com. Great emphasis is placed on creating a home-from-home atmosphere at this cosy hotel whose corridors are decorated to resemble old-fashioned shopping streets and small alleyways – unusual, but it works. Rooms are pleasantly, though simply, furnished. **690kr/970kr**
Best Western Arctic Sandviksgatan 80 ☎ 0920 109 80, ⊛ arctichotel.se. This smart little hotel, very handy for the train station, has cosy rooms with wooden floors and chic Nordic decor in bold reds and greens. Contemporary in feel, though still rather homely. **632kr/1112kr**
Elite Luleå Storgatan 15 ☎ 0920 27 40 00, ⊛ lulea.elite.se. Over a hundred years old, this grand old place is the most elegant of all the city's hotels, with old-fashioned rooms, kitted out with curtains and large armchairs, and a huge breakfast buffet. **765kr/1317kr**

Gammelstads Gästhem Lustigbacken 20, Gammelstad ☎ 070 50 67 00 ⊛ gammelstadsgasthem.se. There's still an institutionalized feel to Luleå's new STF hostel out in Gammelstad, located in a former old people's home. However, all rooms have private bathrooms (some share showers) and there are good self-catering facilities. Dorms **200kr**, doubles **700kr**
Park Kungsgatan 10 ☎ 0920 21 11 49, ⊛ parkhotell.se. With just fourteen smartly renovated rooms, all with private facilities, this homely little place is the cheapest of Luleå's hotels; there's also access to a fully fitted kitchen for self-catering. **650kr/890kr**

CAMPING

First Camp Luleå Arcusvägen 110, Karlsvik ☎ 0920 603 00, ⊛ firstcamp.se/lulea; bus #6 from Smedjegatan in the city centre (every 1–2hr; 20min). Boasts a superb waterside location with views back towards Luleå, though remember the place is right next to E4 and can be noisy at night. Also has cabins for rent. Tents **140kr**, cabins **550kr**

EATING AND DRINKING

While the city often has a busy feel in summer, Luleå is much livelier when the university is in session. **Drinking** is generally done at the main restaurants listed below; the most interesting **places to eat** are all found along Storgatan.

Baan Thai Kungsgatan 22 ☎ 0920 23 18 18. Less than authentic Thai menu with chicken, beef and pork dishes for 119kr and rice and noodle mains from 105kr, served in a

kitsch pink interior with hideous mosaic pillars; still a rare find, though, in the north. Mon–Thurs 10.30am–10pm, Fri 10.30am–11pm, Sat noon–11pm, Sun 1–9pm.

Bishops Arms Storgatan 15 ☎0920 27 40 30. Attached to the *Elite Stadshotellet*, this pseudo-English pub with its bookshelves of battered old novels is undoubtedly the most popular place for a drink in town and is always busy with hotel guests and locals alike. Daily 4pm till late.

Bistro Bar Brygga Skeppsbrogatan ☎0920 22 00 00. Known colloquially as *BBB*, this floating pontoon and boat comprise Luleå's most enjoyable outdoor restaurant, offering lots of summer grill dishes such as burger and fries (178kr) and Cajun beef with roast tomatoes (219kr) as well as bouillebaisse (209kr). Mid-May to early Sept Mon–Sat 5pm–3am; closed when sister establishment Olivers (see below) is open.

Cook's Krog Storgatan 17 ☎0920 20 10 25. Intimate and cosy, this is the best place in Luleå for steak and reindeer cooked over a charcoal grill, for 192–319kr. The five-course set Northern Swedish speciality menu at 695kr, which includes reindeer and whitefish roe, is definitely worth considering. Mon–Sat 6pm till late.

Corsica Nygatan 14 ☎0920 158 40. A none-too-authentic French bistro, though with some good-value items on the menu: pasta dishes are just 99kr, salads go for 89kr, whilst a choice of steaks can be had for 199kr.

Arguably though, pasta with reindeer is the safest bet. Mon–Fri 11am–11pm, Sat & Sun noon–11pm.

Olivers Storgatan 11 ☎0920 22 72 72. At last, a decent Mediterranean-style restaurant has made it to northern Sweden: the butter-fried cod with chorizo and couscous compote (235kr) is delicious, or, alternatively, there are a couple of local dishes such as reindeer fillet (299kr) and Arctic char (245kr). Mon–Thurs 11am–1.30pm, Fri 11am–1.30pm & 4pm–3am, Sat 6pm–3am; closed when BBB (see above) is open.

Roasters Storgatan 43. Perfectly located on the main drag, this is one of the best cafés in Luleå with magnificent espressos, cappuccinos and lattes. Also has a good selection of sandwiches, light snacks, quiches and salads. Very popular outdoor seating area in summer. Mon–Sat 10am–midnight, Sun noon–8pm.

★ **Zan** Smedjegatan 10 ☎0920 104 41. A great Persian restaurant with a Gladys Knight-style figure painted across the rear wall (*zan* is Persian for woman) and a tasty menu featuring a selection of meze for 140kr, marinated chicken with tzatziki for 180kr and an aubergine platter with mince and rice for 105kr; mains are 105–280kr. Mon–Thurs 11am–8pm, Fri 11am–10pm, Sat noon–10pm, Sun 2–7pm.

Gammelstad church town

One of the most significant places of historical interest north of Uppsala, **GAMMELSTAD** (ⓦlulea.se/gammelstad), the original settlement of Luleå and 11km northwest of the present city, is included on UNESCO's World Heritage List. When Luleå moved to the coast, a handful of the more religious among the townsfolk stayed behind to tend the church, and the attached **church town**, the largest in Sweden, remained in use. It comprises over four hundred timber **cottages**, which can only be occupied by people born in Gammelstad (even people from Luleå must marry a local to gain the right to live here).

Visningsstugan

Show cottage • Framlänningsvägen close to the junction of Skolgränd • Early May to mid-June Sat & Sun noon-4pm; mid-June to mid-Aug Mon–Fri 9am–3pm, Sat & Sun noon–4pm • Free

Although Gammelstad's cottages are privately owned and therefore not open to the public, it is possible to enter one of them, no. 253/254, below the church, and known as the "**visningsstugan**" or "show cottage". Inside you'll see a narrow box bed which is typical of the cramped sleeping conditions in the church town.

Nederluleå kyrka

Sockenvägen • Mid-June to mid-Aug daily 9am–6pm; mid-Aug to mid-June Mon–Fri 10am–2pm • Free

The **Nederluleå kyrka** here was completed at the end of the fifteenth century; originally intended to be a cathedral, it's one of the largest churches in Norrland, and among the most impressive in the whole of Sweden. On the outside are decorative brick and plaster gables and there's an opening above the south door through which boiling oil was poured over unwelcome visitors. The high altar, made in Antwerp, is adorned with finely carved biblical scenes; the decorated choir stalls and ornate triptych are other medieval originals. Have a close look at the sumptuous 1712 pulpit, too, a splendid example of Baroque extravagance, its details trimmed with gilt cherubs and red-and-gold bunches of grapes, made by local craftsman Nils Fluur.

Friluftsmuséet Hägnan

Hägnan Open Air Museum • Gamla Hamngatan 21 • Mid-June to mid-Aug daily 11am–5pm • Free • ⓦ lulea.se/hagnan

Down the hill from the church and the cottages is **Friluftsmuséet Hägnan** an open-air heritage park, whose main exhibits are several old farmstead buildings from the eighteenth century, including a bakery, smithy and stables. During summer, it plays host to displays of rural skills, such as sheep-rearing, making traditional wooden roof slates and baking of northern Sweden's unleavened bread, *tunnbröd*. There's also a **café** serving light snacks, beautifully located beside an ancient pine tree.

ARRIVAL AND INFORMATION	GAMMELSTAD
By bus Gammelstad, 11km northwest of the modern city centre, is readily reached by bus from Luleå: bus #9 runs every 1–2hr leaving from Smedjegatan in the town centre. **Tourist office** Right by Nederluleå kyrka at Kyrktorget 1 (June–Aug daily 9am–6pm; Sept–May Tues–Thurs	10am–noon & 1–4pm; ☎0920 45 70 10, ⓦlulea.se/gammelstad). The staff organize guided walks (Jun–Aug daily at 10am, 11am, 1pm & 3pm; 65kr) around the village and have brochures telling you all about the historical significance of the place.

EATING

Kyrkbyns kök Lulevägen 1 • ☎0920 25 14 14. There's a range of pizzas (75kr), pasta dishes (89kr) and unusual Afghan specialities (from 129kr) such as fried aubergine	with mint and garlic at this cheerful grill restaurant, close to the old church. Daily 11am–9pm.

The Luleå archipelago

Luleå's **archipelago** is the only one in the world surrounded by brackish water (the Atlantic Ocean off the Norwegian port of Narvik contains ten times more salt than this part of the Gulf of Bothnia). Made up of over 1700 islands and skerries, most of which are uninhabited and unexploited, it's well worth a visit; the islands are renowned for rich bird-life and a profusion of wild berries: lingonberries, blueberries and raspberries are very common, with Arctic raspberries, cloudberries, wild strawberries and seabuckthorn also found in large numbers.

The **islands** mentioned below are among the most **popular** destinations in the archipelago; being served by once-daily passenger boats from Luleå, they're also the most accessible. With a few notable exceptions, the islands are relatively small – no more than a couple of square kilometres in size – and are therefore ideal for short **walks**. Few are inhabited year-round and hence there are barely any facilities – you should take all provisions with you and shouldn't count on being able to buy anything once you leave the boat. Although it's perfectly feasible to take a tent and camp on the islands, other **accommodation** is severely limited (we have listed where cabins exist) and most visitors to the islands are day-trippers.

Brändöskär

The wildest and most beautiful of all the islands, **Brändöskär**, is located far out in the Gulf of Bothnia and is consequently exposed to the weather and can often be very windy. Its best features are some terrific upland scenery with plentiful mosses and areas of heathland interspersed with smooth rocks along the coast, ideal for sunbathing. At the island's southern point there's a wooden **fishermen's chapel** dating from 1774 whose altarpiece depicts an impressive fishing catch; ask locally for the key if the chapel is locked.

Hindersön

People have lived and worked on **Hindersön**, one of the bigger islands here, since the sixteenth century. Then, fishing, farming and catching seals were the main occupations; today, this is the only island north of Arholma in the Stockholm archipelago which is still farmed. Much of the island is covered with spruce forest, though, if you look carefully, you may also find wild strawberries, Arctic raspberries, the rare Siberian primrose and ghost orchid; ospreys (*fiskgjuse* in Swedish) also nest on the island.

Kluntarna

Kluntarna has a little of everything – small fishing villages, dense pine forest and thousands of seabirds such as black guillemots and cormorants as well as waders like the greater ringed plover – and is a good choice, especially if you've only time to visit one island. Visitors are requested to show special respect for the delicate environment since the entire island is a protected nature reserve.

Rödkallen

Far out in the outer archipelago, south of Luleå, is **Rödkallen**. Site of an important lighthouse which once guarded the difficult southern approaches to Luleå, this tiny island offers fantastic sea and sky views; parts of it have been declared a nature reserve and the barren, rocky landscape is characteristic of its exposure to the elements.

Sandön

Klubbviken, a bay on the island of **Sandön**, is the place to come for good sandy beaches, and has the added advantage of regular boat connections to Luleå. Walking paths crisscross the island, taking in some terrific pine moorland scenery.

ARRIVAL AND INFORMATION

THE LULEÅ ARCHIPELAGO

By boat Boats leave Södra Hamnen for the various islands in the archipelago from late June to mid-Aug, with a reduced service running from mid-Aug to mid-Sept; routes and times vary from year to year but the latest timetable can be found at ⓦlulea.se/skargard or by contacting the tourist office in Luleå (see p.274). A single ticket to Klubbviken is 50kr, 100kr to any of the other islands.
Website There's English-language information on ⓦbatlivlulea.nu/english.

ACCOMMODATION

BRÄNDÖSKÄR

Löjan There's just one simple four-bed cottage for rent on Brandöskär, without water and electricity, located on the island's southeast coast at Persögrundet beside the main jetty. There's also a sauna close by which is available to guests. Book via the Luleå tourist office. **690kr**

HINDERSÖN

Jopikgården ☎0920 600 12, ⓦjopikgarden.se. Choose between individually decorated doubles, decked out in rustic colours, with private facilities in a beautifully restored farmhouse, or, in a separate building across the yard simpler hostel-style rooms with shared bathrooms. **650kr**

KLUBBVIKEN

Klubbviken Havsbad ☎0920 25 86 05, ⓦklubbviken .se. The choice of four two-berth cabins perched on a hillock overlooking the sea, or, better, ten snug two-berth cabins with smart white interiors, right by the water's edge (sharing facilities). **850kr** and **450kr** respectively

KLUNTARNA

Tärnan/Måsen/Truten Located in the main bay, Storviken, three very simple cottages for rent which can be reserved though Luleå tourist office. None has water or electricity; *Tärnan* and *Måsen* sleep four, *Truten* can sleep ten. There's a sauna here for your use as well. Tärnan/Måsen **690kr**, Truten **1090kr**

Haparanda and around

Right by the Finnish border, at the very northern end of the Gulf of Bothnia, **HAPARANDA** is hard to like. The signpost near the bus station reinforces the fact that the town is a very long way from anywhere: Stockholm, 1100km away; the North Cape in Norway, 800km; and Timbuktu 8386km. Viewed from the south, Haparanda is at the end of a very long road to nowhere. However, turn the map upside down, look a little wider and it's easy to see why IKEA took a strategic risk in late 2006 and opened its most northerly store in the world in Haparanda – a town of barely 10,000 people. The gamble paid off and shoppers from the whole of northern Scandinavia, even from as far afield as Murmansk in Russia, now travel here to get their hands on those famous flat-packs. Other companies have followed the retailer's lead and set up business here giving the local economy a long overdue kickstart.

Brief history

The key to Haparanda's late coming of age is the neighbouring Finnish town of **Tornio**. Finland was part of Sweden from 1105 until 1809, with Tornio an important trading centre, serving markets across northern Scandinavia. Things began to unravel when Russia attacked and occupied Finland in 1807; the Treaty of Hamina followed, forcing Sweden to cede Finland to Russia in 1809 – thereby losing Tornio. It was decided that Tornio had to be replaced, and so in 1821, the trading centre of Haparanda was founded on the Swedish side of the new border, which ran along the Torne River. However, the new town was never more than a minor upstart compared to its neighbour across the water. With both Sweden and Finland now members of the European Union, Haparanda and Tornio have declared themselves a **Eurocity** – one city made up of two towns from different countries. The inhabitants of Haparanda and Tornio are bilingual and use both the euro and the Swedish *krona*; roughly half of the children in Haparanda have either a Finnish mother or father. Services are also shared between the two: everything from central heating to post delivery is centrally coordinated. If a fire breaks out in Tornio, for example, Swedish fire crews from Haparanda will cross the border to help put out the flames.

The train station

Other than the IKEA store, there are only two real sights in town. The **train station**, a grand-looking structure built in 1918, was the result of the town's aspirations to be a major trading centre after World War I and still dominates the suburban streets of southern Haparanda from its location at the junction of Stationsgatan and Järnvägsgatan. Constructed from red brick and complete with stone tower and lantern, it provided Sweden's only rail link to Finland until 1992 when it became another victim of SJ closures. From the platforms, you'll be able to discern two widths of track – Finnish trains run on the wider, Russian, gauge. The track between Haparanda and Luleå has now been upgraded and electrified which, in theory at least, will make it possible to once again operate trains via this route to Tornio in Finland, though it's likely to be some time yet before services resume. Until then, the empty sidings, overgrown with weeds and bushes, give the place a strangely forlorn air.

Haparanda kyrka

Smedjegatan 5 • Mid-June to mid-Aug daily 7am–7pm

After the train station, the only other place worthy of some attention is the copper-coloured **Haparanda kyrka**, a monstrous construction that looks like a cross between an aircraft hangar and an apartment building. When the church was finished in 1963, its design caused a public outcry: it won the prize for being the ugliest church in Sweden.

ARRIVAL AND DEPARTURE

HAPARANDA

By bus Haparanda is the terminus for the services that run up the Bothnian coast from Umeå. Arriving by bus, you'll be dropped at the station at the northern end of Haparanda's main street, Stationsgatan, which runs parallel to the Torne River (the buildings you can see here across the river are in Finland). From here it's a 5min walk south along Storgatan to the main square, Torget.

Destinations Pajala (Mon–Fri 2–3 daily, Sat & Sun 1 daily; 3hr 30min); Tornio, Finland (hourly; 5min).

INFORMATION

Tourist office In Tornio, Finland, in the Green Line Welcome Center (Swedish time: June to early Aug Mon–Fri 8am–6pm, Sat & Sun 10am–5pm; early Aug to May Mon–Fri 8am–5pm; ☎0922 120 10, ⓦ haparandatornio.com).

ACCOMMODATION

Cape East Sundholmen 1 ☎0922 80 07 90 ⓦ capeeast .se. Pamper yourself at this new spa hotel just 1.5km south of the centre on the banks of the Torne River. Rooms are ultra-modern and Nordic in design and the place boasts the world's biggest sauna, too. **1990kr**

Haparanda Stadshotel Torget 7 ☎0922 614 90, ⓦ haparandastadshotell.se. Perfectly located in the main square, this is an elegant and sumptuous hotel dating from 1900 with wooden floors and opulent chandeliers. Rooms are well appointed with period furniture and some rooms even have their own private sauna. **1090kr/1610kr**

STF youth hostel Strandgatan 26 ☎0922 611 71, ⓦ haparandavandrarhem.se. The cheapest beds in town are at this smart two-storey riverside place, affording good views to Finland. Rooms have private facilities and bed linen costs an extra 50kr should you require it. There's a good kitchen, too, for self-catering. Dorms **200kr**, doubles **480kr**

EATING

As far as eating, drinking and nightlife go, you're better off in Tornio in every respect. Friday nights there are wild, the streets full of people trying to negotiate the return leg over the bridge; meanwhile, Haparanda sleeps undisturbed. It used to be the case that Tornio was much cheaper than Haparanda, but prices are now roughly the same, although drinking is still a little less expensive in Finland.

Hasans Pizzeria Storgatan 88 ☎0922 104 40. For eating without trekking over to Finland, this place has a range of pizzas for around 50kr; true the interior is nothing to write home about but the low prices keep the locals happy. Tues–Fri 10.30am–8pm, Sat & Sun noon–8pm.

IKEA Norrskensvägen 5 ☎0775 70 05 00. Though the thought of eating inside a flat-pack furniture store may not immediately appeal, it's clear that the price and quality of what's on offer in the in-store restaurant are streets ahead of any other option in town; eight meatballs and mash costs just 19kr Mon–Fri. Daily 10am–7pm.

Leilani Köpmansgatan 15 ☎0922 107 17. Long-established Asian restaurant serving a selection of Thai dishes such as curries and stirfries (from 128kr) as well as dependable Chinese mains (from 92kr) and rather uninspiring pizzas. Mon 10am–9pm, Tues–Fri 10am–10pm, Sat noon–10pm, Sun noon–9pm.

Umpitunneli Hallituskatu 15 ☎358 40 126 02 00. Across in Tornio, your best bet is this riverside restaurant, bar and nightclub all rolled into one, and serving Arctic char and grilled chicken for around €15 and a half-litre of beer for €4; it's always packed but don't expect people to speak much English. Finnish time: Mon–Fri 3–9.30pm, Sat 1–9.30pm, Sun 1–8pm.

TWO COUNTRIES: ONE TOWN

Given that Haparanda and Tornio are so closely related, it seems only right that they should share a **tourist office**. Not only does it hold information about both places but it can also help with general queries about Finland. Indeed, there are two phone lines in the office, one for calls from Sweden, the other with enquiries from Finland; staff switch effortlessly from one language to another depending on which line is ringing. To get here from the bus station head towards the "Finland" signs on the nearby bridge; there are no border formalities, and so you can simply walk over the bridge to Finland and wander back whenever you like. It's worth remembering that **Finnish time** is one hour ahead of Swedish time and that Haparanda and Tornio have different names in Swedish (Haparanda and Torneå) and Finnish (Haaparanta and Tornio).

Central
Sweden

HIKING IN THE HÄRJEDALEN MOUNTAINS

Central Sweden

In many ways, the long wedge of land that comprises central Sweden – the sparsely populated provinces of Dalarna, Härjedalen and Jämtland – encompasses all that is most typical of the country. This vast area of land is really one great forest, broken only by the odd village or town. Rural and underpopulated, it epitomizes the image most people have of Sweden: lakes, log cabins, pine forests and wide, open skies. Until just one or two generations ago, Swedes across the country lived in this sort of setting, taking their cue from the people of these central lands and forest, who were the first to rise against the Danes in the sixteenth century.

Dalarna, centred around **Lake Siljan**, is an intensely picturesque – and touristy – region, its inhabitants maintaining a cultural heritage (echoed in contemporary handicrafts and traditions) that goes back to the Middle Ages. You won't need to brave the crowds of visitors for too long, as even a quick tour around one or two of the more accessible places here gives an impression of the whole: red cottages with a white door and window frames, sweeping green countryside, water that's bluer than blue and a riot of summer festivals. Dalarna is *the* place to spend midsummer, particularly **Midsummer's Eve**, when the whole region erupts in a frenzy of celebration.

The privately owned **Inlandsbanan**, the great Inland Railway, cuts right through central Sweden and links many of the towns and villages covered in this chapter. Running from **Mora** in Dalarna to Gällivare, above the Arctic Circle, it ranks with the best of European train journeys, covering an enthralling 1067km in two days; the second half of the journey, north of Östersund (where you have to change trains), is covered in the Swedish Lapland chapter; see p.310. Buses connect the rail line with the mountain villages that lie alongside the Norwegian border, where the surrounding Swedish *fjäll*, or mountains, offer some spectacular and compelling hiking, notably around **Ljungdalen** in the remote province of **Härjedalen**. Marking the halfway point of the line, **Östersund**, the only town of any size along it and the capital of the province of **Jämtland**, is situated by the side of Storsjön, the great lake that's reputed to be home to the country's own Loch Ness monster, Storsjöodjuret. From here trains head in all directions: west into Norway through Sweden's premier **ski** resort, **Åre**, south to Dalarna and Stockholm, east to Sundsvall on the Bothnian coast and north into the wild terrain of Swedish Lapland.

Dalarna

A sizeable province, **DALARNA** takes in not only the area around **Lake Siljan** but also the ski resorts of **Sälen** and **Idre**, close to the Norwegian border. The area holds a special misty-eyed place in the Swedish psyche and should certainly be seen, although not to

THE INLANDSBANAN

Highlights

❶ **Boat trip, Lake Siljan** Take a trip on the
serene waters of Lake Siljan and enjoy
unparalleled views of the rolling Dalarna
countryside. **See p.288**

❷ **Riding the Inlandsbanan** A chance to see
Sweden's vast forests and fast-flowing rivers
close up without leaving the comfort of your
train seat. **See p.291**

❸ **Orsa Grönklitt björnpark, Dalarna**
Northern Europe's largest bear park offers a
unique chance to see these shy animals at close
quarters. **See p.292**

❹ **Hiking in the Härjedalen mountains** Get
back to nature and experience the wild side of
central Sweden in this remote mountainous
province. **See p.296**

❺ **Årets Näck, Hackås** This fun riverside
competition featuring naked male fiddle players
has its roots in Swedish folklore. **See p.302**

❻ **Monster spotting, Östersund** Go hunting
for Sweden's version of the Loch Ness monster
in this appealing lakeside town. **See p.305**

HIGHLIGHTS ARE MARKED ON THE MAP ON P.284

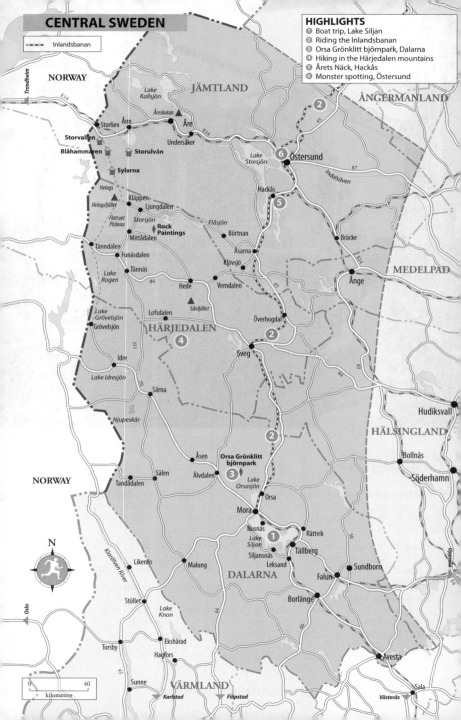

CENTRAL SWEDEN

Inlandsbanan

HIGHLIGHTS
1. Boat trip, Lake Siljan
2. Riding the Inlandsbanan
3. Orsa Grönklitt björnpark, Dalarna
4. Hiking in the Härjedalen mountains
5. Årets Näck, Hackås
6. Monster spotting, Östersund

NORWAY

Trondheim

JÄMTLAND

ÅNGERMANLAND

Lake Kallsjön

Storlien   Ånn
Åreskutan   Åre
Storvallen   Undersåker

Blåhammaren

Lake Storsjön   Östersund

Sylarna   Indalsälven

Helags   Hackås

Helagsfjället   Kläppen   Ljungdalen

Flatruet Plateau   Storsjön   Rock Paintings   Flåsjön

Mittådalen   Börtnan   Bräcke

Tänndalen   Funäsdalen   Åsarna   MEDELPAD

Lake Rogen   Tännäs   Klövsjö

Hede   Vemdalen   Ånge

Lake Grövelsjön   Lofsdalen   Sånfjället

Grövelsjön   Överhogdal

HÄRJEDALEN   HÄLSINGLAND

Idre   Sveg   Hudiksvall

Lake Idresjön

Särna   Bollnäs

Njupeskär   Söderhamn

Åsen   Orsa Grönklitt björnpark

Sälen   Älvdalen   Lake Orsasjön

Tandådalen   Orsa

Mora   Rättvik

Nusnäs   Lake Siljan   Tällberg

Likenäs   Siljansnäs   Sundborn

Kläralven River   Malung   Leksand   Falun

DALARNA   Borlänge   Avesta

Stöllet   Lake Knon

Oslo   Uppsala

Torsby   Ekshärad

Hagfors   Sala

Sunne   VÄRMLAND   Västerås

Karlstad   Filipstad

0   40
kilometres

N

the exclusion of places further north. Tiny countryside villages and rolling meadows sweet with the smell of summer flowers make up most of Dalarna, a rural idyll given a handsome backdrop by the land to the northwest of Lake Siljan, which rises slowly to meet the chain of mountains that forms the border with Norway. One small lakeside town can look pretty much like another, so if time is short, restrict yourself to visiting just one or two: **Leksand** and **Mora** are the best options, and the latter is also the starting point for Sweden's most beautiful train journey, along the **Inlandsbanan** to the Arctic Circle.

North of Mora, the province becomes more mountainous and less populous, the only place of note here being **Orsa**, with its fascinating **bear park**. There's no need to worry about **accommodation** in the province: you'll find numerous hotels, hostels and campsites around.

Falun and around

About 220km northwest of Stockholm and 90km west of Gävle, **FALUN** is essentially an industrial town – a pleasant one at that – known for copper mining, which began here in the eleventh century; today, the mines, which closed as recently as 1992, can be visited on hour-long guided tours. Falun is also handily placed for a jaunt to nearby **Sundborn**, the former home of well-known artist, Carl Larsson, whose back-to-basics paintings have had more than a passing influence on IKEA's designs over the years.

The mines

Guided tours: May–Sept daily 9.30am–4.30pm; Oct–April daily noon–4pm • 190kr including museum; 50kr for museum only • English commentary available • ⓦ falugruva.se • From the centre walk around 1km along Bergshauptmansgatan right to the far end

8

Falun grew in importance during the seventeenth and eighteenth centuries, when its **copper mines** produced two-thirds of the world's copper ore. Commensurate with its status as what was then the second largest town in Sweden, Falun acquired grand buildings and an air of prosperity. The few old, wooden houses that survive (in 1761, two fires wiped out virtually all of central Falun) are worth seeking out to gain an idea of the cramped conditions mine workers had to live in; you'll find these buildings in the districts of **Elsborg** (southwest of the centre), Gamla Herrgården and Östanfors (both north of the centre).

By far the most interesting attraction in Falun is its **mines**. Mandatory **guided tours**, lasting around an hour, are organized on the site, beginning with an elevator ride 55m down to a network of old mine roads and drifts. The temperature down below is only 5°C, so make sure you bring warm clothing; try also to wear old shoes, as your footwear is likely to come out tinged red.

Museum

The site has a worthy **museum**, recounting the history of Falun's copper production. Conditions below ground in the mines were appalling, said by the botanist Carl von Linné to be as dreadful as hell itself. One of the most dangerous aspects of eighteenth-century copper mining was the presence everywhere in the mines of **vitriol** gases, which

---

SWEDEN'S RED HOUSES

As you travel around Sweden, you can't help but notice that virtually every timber structure is painted deep red. Many outsiders mistakenly see this lack of individuality and expression as stifling social democractic conformity. It is actually more a question of practicalities. In a climate as severe as Sweden's, wood needs special protection from the elements and the red paint used on structures across the country, produced in Falun, contains a natural copper preservative. Known as **Falu rödfärg**, this paint is Sweden's aesthetically more pleasing answer to pebbledash.

are strong preservatives. It's recorded that the body of a young man known as *Fet Mats* (Fat Mats) was found in the mines in 1719; though he'd died 49 years previously in an accident, his corpse was so well preserved when discovered that his erstwhile fiancée, by then an old woman, recognized him immediately.

Be sure not to miss peering into the **Great Pit** (Stora Stöten), just nearby, which is 100m deep and 300–400m wide. It suddenly appeared on Midsummer Day in 1687, when the entire pit caved in – the result of extensive mining and the unsystematic driving of galleries and shafts.

Dalarnas Museum

Stigaregatan 2–4 • Tues–Fri 10am–5pm, Sat & Sun noon–5pm; Sept–May also Wed until 9pm • Free • ⓦ dalarnasmuseum.se

Back in Falun's centre, the riverside **Dalarnas Museum** makes for a worthwhile visit. Containing sections on the province's folk art, the Dala horse, dresses and music, it includes a reconstruction, on the ground floor, of the dark, heavily wood-panelled study where the author Selma Lagerlöf (see p.142) worked when she moved to Villavägen 34 in Falun in 1897, as well as a number of black-and-white photographs of her and her home; a copy of Lagerlöf's books, including her most famous work *Nils Holgerssons underbara resa genom Sverige* ("The Wonderful Adventures of Nils"), are displayed on the bookshelves. Look out, too, for the curious black-and-white photographs of the bin Laden family, who visited Falun in 1971 on a family holiday to Sweden when Osama was a teenager.

Carl Larssongården

May–Sept daily 10am–5pm; Oct–April Mon–Fri guided tours at 11am • 120kr • ⓦ carllarsson.se • Take the hourly #64 from Östra Hamngatan

"It was here I experienced the unspeakably delightful feeling of seclusion from all the world's noise and din".

Carl Larsson's words on living in Sundborn

Ideally placed for an easy day trip from Falun, the village of **SUNDBORN**, just 13km to the northeast, was once home to artist Carl Larsson. One of Sweden's most visited tourist attractions, the delightful **Carl Larssongården** was at first the summer dwelling of Carl and his wife Karin, later becoming their permanent home. The artist's own murals and portraits of his children form part of the decor, as do the embroidery and tapestries of his wife. At the start of the twentieth century, when the Larssons had done the place up, the house represented an entirely new decorative style for Sweden, its bright, warm interior quite unlike the dark and sober colours used until that time. The artist is buried in the churchyard just outside.

ARRIVAL AND DEPARTURE
FALUN

By train Falun is easily reached by train from Stockholm, Arlanda airport and Uppsala, and there are also useful through services from Gävle and Örebro. The train station is to the east of the centre.
Destinations Gävle (2 hourly; 1hr); Stockholm (2 hourly; 2hr 45min); Örebro (2 hourly; 2hr 45min); Uppsala (2 hourly; 2hr).

By bus The bus station is east of the centre. For the #64 bus to Sundborn, head to the stop on Östra Hamngatan.

INFORMATION

Tourist office Opposite the *First Grand* hotel at Trotzgatan 10–12 (mid-June to mid-Aug Mon–Fri 10am–6pm, Sat 10am–2pm, Sun 11am–2pm; mid-Aug to mid-June closed Sun; ☏ 023 830 50, ⓦ visitfalunborlange.se). Has free internet access.

ACCOMMODATION

Clarion Collection Bergmästaren Bergskolegränd 7 ☏ 023 70 17 00, ⓦ choicehotels.se. For a homely feel with rooms decorated in soft pastel shades of green and yellow, try this place near the train station, which has a superb sauna suite complete with jacuzzi and sunbeds. 870kr/1270kr

Falun Trotzgatan 16 ☏ 023 291 80, ⓦ hotelfalun.nu. Falun's budget hotel has a good central location and offers double rooms both with and without private facilities. Rooms are plainly decorated but at their good-value weekday prices leave little room for complaint. **750kr/950kr**

First Grand Falun Trotzgatan 9–11 ☎ 023 79 48 80, ⓦ firsthotels.se. The swankiest hotel in town is the central *First Grand*, whose rooms are sumptuous to say the least. However, it's the generously sized pool, spa and gym which really make a stay here worth the money. **998kr/1299kr**

Lugnets Camping Lugnetvägen 5 ☎ 023 654 00, ⓦ lugnetscamping.se. The nearest campsite is up at Lugnet by the National Ski Stadium, 1.5km from the town centre. There's also a choice of cabins with full self-catering facilities or much smaller, simpler ones. Tents **140kr**, small cabins **355kr**, self-catering cabins **975kr**

Youth hostel Vandrarvägen 3 ☎ 023 105 60, ⓦ stffalun.se; take bus #701 from the centre to Hosjö, and get off at the stop called "Koppartorget". The nearest hostel, this is located 4km from the centre in the Haraldsbo part of town. Rooms are located in three separate single-storey brick buildings which each have a guest kitchen. Dorms **220kr**, doubles **480kr**

EATING AND DRINKING

★ **Banken** Åsgatan 41 ☎ 023 71 19 11. A trendy bistro with a grand stuccoed ceiling which takes its name from the former bank that once stood here. Changing modern Swedish dishes make up the menu here (around 230kr), although there are always burgers and pasta dishes available (145kr). Mon–Thurs 11.30am–11pm, Fri 11.30am–midnight, Sat 1pm–midnight.

Bishops Arms Östra Hamngatan 12 ☎ 023 123 90. One of *the* places to be seen, this fake-English pub has wooden beams and lots of brass ornaments and serves a range of bar meals such as burgers and steaks as well as a good selection of beer on tap. Mon & Tues 4–11pm, Wed & Thurs 4pm–midnight, Fri & Sat 4pm–2am, Sun 4–10pm.

Falu Stekhus Stora torget 1 ☎ 023 254 00. Located under the Rådhus, this is an atmospheric place to indulge in succulent grilled steaks for around 250kr per main course. On Fri there's a special deal on the salad buffet including a beer for 99kr. Wed & Thurs 5pm–midnight, Fri & Sat 5pm–2am.

Hammars Pizza & Pasta Åsgatan 28 ☎ 023 390 39. A chi-chi new brasserie serving good-quality Italian antipasti as well as juicy steaks, local fish, pasta and pizza. Look out for its lunchtime pizza and pasta buffet served weekdays until 2pm. Tues & Sun 3–10pm, Wed–Sat 3pm–midnight.

The Kings Arms Falugatan 3 ☎ 023 71 13 44. A cosy and popular bistro pub with a heavy wooden interior and models of rigged sailing ships in the windows. Light bar meals such as burgers (125kr) and fish and chips (135kr) are available as well as heftier steak and fish meals (from 155kr). Mon–Thurs 11am–2pm & 4pm–1am, Fri 11am–2pm, Sat noon–2am, Sun 4pm–1am.

Around Lake Siljan

Things have changed since Baedeker, writing in 1889, observed that "Lake Siljan owes much of its interest to the inhabitants of its banks, who have preserved many of their primitive characteristics. In their idea of cleanliness they are somewhat behind the age." Today it's not the people who draw your attention but the setting. **Lake Siljan**, created millions of years ago when a meteorite crashed into the earth, is what many people come to Sweden for, its gently rolling surroundings, traditions and local handicrafts weaving a subtle spell on the visitor. There's a lush feel to much of the region, the charm of the forest heightened by its proximity to the lake, all of which adds a pleasing dimension to the low-profile towns and villages that interrupt the rural scenery. Only **Mora** stands out as being bigger and busier, with the hustle and bustle of holiday-makers and countless caravans crowding the place in summer.

Leksand

Perhaps the most traditional of the Dalarna villages, **LEKSAND**, about 50km northwest of Falun, is certainly worth making the effort to reach at midsummer, when it stages festivals recalling age-old dances performed around the **maypole** (Sweden's maypoles are erected in June – in May the trees here are still bare and the ground can be covered with snow). The celebrations culminate in the **church boat (kyrkbåtar) races**, a waterborne procession of sleek wooden longboats, which the locals once rowed to church on Sundays. Starting on Midsummer's Day in nearby **Siljansnäs** – take the roughly hourly bus #84 from Leksand – and continuing for ten days at different locations around the lake, the races hit Leksand on the first Saturday in July. Leksand's tourist office will have details of the arrangements for each summer's races.

> ## MUSIK VID SILJAN
>
> Should you be around during the first week or so of July, don't miss **Musik vid Siljan**, nine days of musical performances in lakeside churches, the stunning former limestone quarry, Dalhalla, and at various locations out in the surrounding forest. The range of music covered is exceptionally wide, including chamber music, jazz, traditional folk songs and dance-band music, with proceedings starting in the early morning and carrying on until late evening every day. Full details at ⓦ musikvidsiljan.se.

Leksands kyrka

Kyrkallén 27 • Daily 9.30am–3.30pm

There's little to do in Leksand other than take it easy. A relaxing stroll along the riverside brings you to **Leksands kyrka**, one of Sweden's biggest village churches; it has existed in its present form since 1715, although the oldest parts of the building date back to the thirteenth century. The church enjoys one of the most stunning locations of any in the land, its peaceful churchyard lined with whispering spruce trees and looking out over the lake to the distant shore.

Hembygdsgård

Homestead Museum • Kyrkallén 3 • No set hours • Free

Next door to the church is the region's best open-air **Hembygdsgård** – about a dozen old timber buildings grouped around a maypole, ranging from simple square huts used to store hay during the long winter months to a magnificent *parstuga*, which forms the centrepiece of the collection. Built in 1793, this two-storey dwelling, constructed of thick circular logs, is notable because buildings of the period were rarely more than one storey in height, since timber was expensive. From directly behind the museum a narrow track leads down to the lake, where there's a reconstruction of a church boathouse used to house the *kyrkbåtar* for which Dalarna is known throughout Sweden.

Lake cruises

Timetables vary • Check sailing times at ⓦ wasanet.nu

Whilst in Leksand, it's worth taking one of the **cruises** on Lake Siljan aboard the lovely old steamship *M/S Gustaf Wasa*, built in Stockholm in 1876, which depart between May and September from the quay near the homestead museum; take the track down to the reconstructed boathouse (see above) and turn left following the lakeside to the bridge and the quay. The excursions include a round-trip to Mora and back (150kr), or a two-hour cruise round a bit of the lake (100kr).

ARRIVAL AND INFORMATION   LEKSAND

By train There are frequent trains between Mora and Stockholm in both directions, all of which stop at Leksand.
Tourist office Kyrkallén 8 (mid-June to mid-Aug Mon–Fri 10am–7pm, Sat & Sun 10am–5pm; mid-Aug to mid-June

Mon–Fri 10am–5pm; ☎ 0247 79 61 30, ⓦ siljan.se). A 10min walk from the train station up Villagatan towards the centre of town, then left along Sparbanksgatan and right into Norsgatan which becomes Kyrkallén.

ACCOMMODATION

★ **Korstäppens Herrgård** Hjortnäsvägen 33 ☎ 0247 123 10, ⓦ korstappan.se. This wonderful old manor house is tastefully decked out in traditional Dalarna colours. Its sitting and dining rooms look out over the lake, whose lapping waters can be reached by a path behind the hotel. **910kr/1100kr**
Leksand Strand Siljansvägen 61 ☎ 0247 138 00, ⓦ leksandstrand.se. This lovely lakeside campsite, a

20min walk from the tourist office along Tällbergsvägen, has a sandy beach along Lake Siljan as well as its own swimming pool. There are also cabins for rent. Tents **140kr**, cabins **1290kr**
Moskogen Insjövägen 50 ☎ 0247 146 00, ⓦ moskogen .com. Instead of traditional hotel rooms, this place offers accommodation in comfortable rooms inside log cabins which come fully equipped with running water, private

bathroom, kitchenette and fridge. A buffet breakfast is included in the price. **1120kr**
Youth hostel Parkgattu 6 ☎0247 152 50, ⓦvandrarhemleksand.se; bus #58. Leksand's cosy STF

hostel is one of the oldest in Sweden, located around 2.5km from the train station, over the river. Accommodation is in small wooden cabins as well as regular rooms in the main building. Closed Jan. Dorms **230kr**, doubles **560kr**

EATING AND DRINKING

Bosporen Torget 1 ☎0247 132 80. Feeding the folk of Leksand for over thirty years, this is the village's main restaurant, located in the tiny pedestrianized main square, serving pizzas from 77kr as well as meat and fish dishes such as pork schnitzel or plaice from 98kr. Mon–Thurs 4–10pm, Fri 4pm–midnight, Sat noon–midnight, Sun noon–10pm.
Legends Torget 7 ☎0247 100 80. Fulfilling a long need for a proper pub in Leksand, this newly opened sports bar and restaurant looks set to really draw the crowds. The menu is

heavy on pub grub such as fish and chips and burgers (around 159kr), whilst the pub downstairs is the place to watch football on big screens. Mon 11.30am–11pm, Tues 11.30am–8pm, Wed & Thurs 11.30am–10pm, Fri 11.30am–1am, Sat noon–1am, Sun 3–8pm.
Siljans Konditori Torget. The summer terrace is a wonderful place from which to watch the world go by while sipping a cup of coffee. They serve up sandwiches with fantastic home-made bread, and salads and quiches. Mon–Fri 8.30am–7pm, Sat 9am–5pm, Sun 11am–5pm.

Tällberg

If you believe the tourist blurb, then **TÄLLBERG**, all lakeside log cabins amid rolling hills, *is* Dalarna. Situated on a promontory in the lake 10km north of Leksand, this folksy hillside village, whose wooden cottages are draped with flowers in summer, first became famous in 1850 when the Danish writer Hans Christian Andersen paid it a visit; on his return to Copenhagen, he wrote that everyone should experience Tällberg's peace and tranquillity, and marvel at its wonderful lake views. Ever since, hordes of tourists have flooded into the tiny village to see what all the fuss was about – prepare yourself for the crowds that unfortunately take the shine off what is otherwise quite a pretty little place. Tällberg today is also a prime destination for wealthy middle-aged Swedes, who come to enjoy the good life for a few days, savour the delicious food dished up by the village's hotels, and admire the fantastic views out over Lake Siljan. To escape the crowds, walk down the steep hill of Sjögattu, past the campsite, to the calm lapping water of the lake and a small sandy beach; keep going through the trees to find a couple of more secluded spots.

8

ARRIVAL   TÄLLBERG

By train Tällberg is on the main train line round Lake Siljan; the station is a 10–15min walk from the village.

ACCOMMODATION

★ **Siljansgården** Sjögattu 36 ☎0247 500 40, ⓦsiljansgarden.com. For accommodation, avoid the expensive hotels and walk down Sjögattu to this wonderful old wooden farm building with a cobbled courtyard and a fountain, and rooms that are comparable to those in hostels. **600kr**

Tällbergs Camping Sjögattu 38 t0247 503 01, ⓦtallbergscamping.se. A little further along from *Siljansgården* – head down to the lakeshore and turn left – and you'll find this delightful lakeside campsite; note there are no cabins here and facilities are basic but clean. Tents **140kr**

Mora and around

At the northwestern corner of the lake, 60km from Leksand, **MORA** is the best place to head for hereabouts, handy for onward trains on the Inlandsbanan (see p.291) and for moving on to the ski resorts of Idre (see p.294) and Sälen (see p.293). An appealing, laidback town, its main draws are two excellent museums, one dedicated to the painter Anders Zorn, and the other to the Vasaloppet ski race.

Zornmuséet

Vasagatan 36 • Mid-May to mid-Sept Mon–Sat 9am–5pm, Sun 11am–5pm; mid-Sept to mid-May daily noon–4pm • 60kr or 140kr with Zorngården • ⓦzorn.se

The main attraction in Mora is the outstanding **Zornmuséet**, showcasing the work of Sweden's best-known painter, **Anders Zorn** (1860–1920), who moved here in 1896. Most successful as a portrait painter, he worked in both oil and watercolour and spent periods living in both St Ives in Britain and Paris. Zorn even went to the United States to paint American presidents Cleveland, Theodore Roosevelt and Taft. At the museum, look out for his larger-than-life self-portrait dressed in wolfskin from 1915 and the especially pleasing *Midnatt* (Midnight) from 1891, which depicts a woman rowing on Lake Siljan, her hands blue from the cold night air. The artist's remarkable silver collection, containing four hundred pieces ranging from tankards to teaspoons, is also on display.

Zorngården

Vasagatan 36 • Mid-May to mid-Sept Mon–Sat 10am–4pm, Sun 11am–4pm; mid-Sept to mid-May daily, hourly guided tours at noon–3pm • 90kr or 140kr with the museum

Across the museum lawn is Anders Zorn's home, **Zorngården**, where the artist and his wife Emma lived during the early twentieth century. What really makes the place unusual is its cavernous 10m-high hall with a steeply V-shaped roof, entirely constructed from wood and decked out in traditional Dalarna designs and patterns, where the couple lived out their roles as darlings of local society.

Vasaloppsmuséet

Ski Museum • Vasaloppets Hus, Vasagatan • Mid-June to mid-Aug Mon–Wed & Fri–Sun 10am–5pm, Thurs 10am–3pm; mid-Aug to mid-June Mon–Wed 10am–4.30pm, Thurs 10am–3pm, Fri 10am–noon • 40kr • ⓦ vasaloppet.se

The other museum in town worth considering is the **Vasaloppsmuséet**; it's east of the Zorn Museum, on the other side of Vasagatan, and covers the history of the ski race, Vasaloppet, held on the first Sunday in March. The event commemorates King Gustav Vasa's return to Mora after he escaped from the Danes on skis; two men from Mora caught up with him and persuaded him to come back to their town, where they gave him refuge. The longest cross-country ski race in the world, the competition was the idea of a local newspaper editor, who organized the first event in 1922; it was won by a 22-year-old from Västerbotten who took seven and a half hours to complete the course. Today, professionals take barely four hours to cover the 90km. Although the Vasaloppet enjoys royal patronage (the current Swedish king has skied it), it does have a somewhat chequered past, since women were forbidden from taking part until 1981. Whilst here, make sure you watch the half-hour **film** (with English subtitles) about the race – the impressive aerial shots really help to portray the massive scale of the competition.

Grannas A. Olssons Hemslöjd

Mid-June to mid-Aug Mon–Fri 9am–6pm, Sat & Sun 9am–4pm; rest of year Mon–Fri 9am–4pm, Sat 10am–1pm • Free • ⓦ grannas.com • You can get to Nusnäs from Mora on bus #108 (Mon–Fri 3 daily; 20min)

Whilst in Mora you might want to consider a visit to **Nusnäs**, just east of town on the lakeside, where you'll find **Grannas A. Olssons Hemslöjd**, the **workshop** of the Olson

---

THE DALA HORSE

No matter where you travel in Sweden, you'll come across small wooden figurines known as **Dala horses** (*dalahästar*). Their bright red colour, stumpy legs and garish floral decorations are, for many foreigners, high kitsch and rather ugly; the Swedes, however, adore bright colours (the redder the better) and love the little horses – it's virtually an unwritten rule that every household in the country should have a couple on display. Two brothers from the town of **Nusnäs**, **Nils** and **Jannes Olsson**, began carving the horses in the family baking shed in 1928, when they were just teenagers. Though they were simply interested in selling their work to help their cash-strapped parents make ends meet, somehow the wooden horses started catching on – Swedes are at a loss to explain why – and soon were appearing across the country as a symbol of rural life.

brothers, creators of Sweden's much-loved **Dala horses** (see box opposite). Skilled craftsmen carve the horses out of wood from the pine forests around Lake Siljan and then hand-paint and varnish them.

ARRIVAL AND DEPARTURE   MORA

By train For the centre of town, you should leave the train at Mora Strand station (which consists of little more than a platform), one stop after the main Mora station on trains coming from the south; the Inlandsbanan (see box below) begins at Mora Strand before calling at Mora station.
Destinations Leksand (2 hourly; 40min); Östersund (June & Aug 1 daily; July 2 daily; 6hr); Stockholm (2 hourly; 3hr

50min); Sveg (June & Aug 1 daily; July 2 daily; 2hr 45min); Uppsala (2 hourly; 3hr).
By bus The bus station is at Moragatan, close to Mora Strand and just off the main Strandgatan.
Destinations Idre (2 daily; 2hr 30min); Orsa (hourly; 25min); Östersund (2 daily; 5hr 15min); Sälen (1 daily; 2hr) Sveg (2 daily; 2hr).

INFORMATION

Tourist office Opposite Mora Strand station at Strandgatan 14 (mid-June to mid-Aug Mon–Fri 9am–6pm, Sat & Sun 10am–5pm; mid-Aug to mid-June Mon–Fri 10am–5pm, Sat

10am–2pm; ☎0250 59 20 20, ⊚siljan.se). Has all the usual literature, including a map of the Vasaloppsleden hiking route, which you can follow north from Mora to Sälen (see p.293).

ACCOMMODATION

Although Mora sees a sizeable influx of tourists for the Vasaloppet race and during the summer season, there's a surprising lack of choice in terms of places to **stay**. Hence, it pays to book ahead from mid-June to mid-August in particular.

Best Western Mora Strandgatan 12 ☎0250 59 26 50, ⊚www.morahotell.se. Mora's biggest and best hotel, opposite Mora Strand station, with both modern and old-fashioned rooms hung with Zorn pictures. There's also a first-class sauna suite and gym with pool and jacuzzi. Prices are rather steep for such a provincial location. 1128kr/1598kr
Kristineberg Kristinebergsgatan 1 ☎0250 150 70, ⊚kunggosta.se. An annexe of the *Kung Gösta*, this is a plain and simple B&B-style alternative with dorm beds as well as rather cramped en-suite double rooms; guests

make their own beds with linen provided. There's a kitchen for self-catering. Dorms 180kr, doubles 795kr
Kung Gösta Kristinebergsgatan 1 ☎0250 150 70, ⊚kunggosta.se. Close to the main train station, this is a modern hotel with identikit rooms cheaply decorated with tacky pictures of cherubs here and there. However, there's a choice between bathrooms with tubs or showers, and an excellent swimming pool, too. 1095kr
Målkullan Fredsgatan 6 ☎0250 381 96, ⊚malkullan.se. A comfortable STF hostel in the heart of Mora at the finishing

8

THE INLANDSBANAN

Stretching over 1000km from Mora to Gällivare, north of the Arctic Circle, the privately operated **Inlandsbanan**, the Inland Railway, is a great way of travelling off the beaten track through central and northern Sweden; onboard guides provide commentaries and information about places along the route to ensure you get the most out of the journey. State-owned until 1992, it's now run as a private venture, supported by the fifteen municipalities that the route passes through.

INLANDSBANAN INFORMATION

Trains run on the Inlandsbanan between June and August; the latest timings and prices (Mora–Östersund, for example, is 414kr) are at ⊛grandnordic.se and InterRail cards are valid. **Timetables** are only approximate, and the train will stop whenever the driver feels like it – perhaps for a spot of wild-strawberry picking or to watch a beaver damming a stream. Generally in June & August, there's one daily train north from Mora at around 2.35pm, supplemented by a northbound morning departure around 8am in July. Done in one go, the journey from Mora to Gällivare lasts two days, with an overnight stop in Östersund. It's much better idea, though, to take it at a more relaxed pace, with a couple of stops along the route (you can break your journey as many times as you like on one ticket).

If you're planning using the Inlandsbanan a lot, consider investing in the **Inland Railway Card** (Inlandsbanekort; 1595kr), which gives unlimited travel for two weeks.

line for the Vasaloppet race, with double rooms as well as dorm beds located in two separate buildings; there are some rooms with private facilities. Dorms 230k, doubles 300kr **Mora Parken** Parkvägen 1 ☎0250 276 00, ⓦmoraparken.se. A comfortable modern hotel catering for families with children; there's a playground nearby as well as a lake for swimming. It also has a selection of cottages for rent. It's a 10min walk from the centre along Hantverkaregatan, which begins near the bus station. Doubles 995kr/1295kr, cottages from 330kr

EATING AND DRINKING

China House Strandgatan 6 ☎0250 152 40. The food here isn't overly authentic but this is the only Chinese restaurant for miles around. There are both Chinese and Thai dishes on the menu, with mains starting at 140kr (three-course set menu 245kr). Alternatively there are steaks, from 150kr. Mon–Fri 11am–10pm, Sat & Sun noon–10.30pm.
Pizzeria Prima Fridhemsplan 2D ☎0250 120 11. The interior may be plain and simple, but the pizzas here are tasty and the range on offer impressive. It's perfectly placed for a last-minute dash to the bus station. Reckon on around 75kr per pizza. Daily 11am–10pm.
★ **Vasagatan 32** Vasagatan 32 ☎0250 102 27. With walls decorated with local art and photographs, this bright new brasserie is a breath of fresh air: well-prepared classic dishes such as pan-fried salmon and fried plaice go for 125–199kr. Lunch is in buffet form with a choice of meat or fish. Mon–Wed 11am–2pm, Thurs & Fri 11am–2pm & 4–10pm, Sat & Sun noon–10pm.
Wasastugan Tingnäsvägen 6 ☎0250 177 92. Set within a huge log building between the main train station and the Vasaloppsmuséet and serving up Cajun dishes such as blackened salmon (199kr), tuna fishcake (79kr) and a massive barbecue-burger (145kr) that really hits the spot. Daily 11am–10pm.

Orsa and the bear park

An uneventful little place barely 20km from Mora, sitting beside Lake Orsasjön, a northerly adjunct of Lake Siljan, **ORSA**'s draw is its location – right in the heart of Sweden's bear country – and its fascinating bear park. It's reckoned that there are a good few hundred **brown bears** roaming the dense forests around town, though few sightings are made in the wild.

Orsa Grönklitt björnpark

Bear Park • Daily: mid-June to mid-Aug 10am–6pm; mid-Aug to mid-June 10am–3pm • 210kr • ⓦorsabjornpark.se • The bear park is located 16km from Orsa, and can be reached by taking bus #118 (Mon–Fri 2 daily, Sun 1 daily) from Orsa bus station; from Mora, take #104 to Orsa and then change

The **Orsa Grönklitt björnpark** is the biggest **bear park** in Europe. The bears here aren't tamed or caged, but wander around the 277 thousand square metres of the forested park at will, much as they would in the wild. It's the human visitors who are confined, having to clamber up viewing platforms and along covered walkways.

The bears are fascinating to watch: their behaviour is amusing, and they're gentle and vegetarian for the most part (though occasionally they're fed the odd dead reindeer or elk that's been killed on the roads). Trying hard not to be upstaged by the bears are a few lynx, wolves and wolverines, the other three Swedish predators – although you'll be lucky to spot the wolves in particular; in fact, it's a good idea to bring along a pair of binoculars to help you pick out any rustlings in the undergrowth. In addition, the park has a couple of Siberian tigers, two truly enormous Kamchatka bears from eastern Russia (the male weighs a whopping 900kg) and a pair of Eurasian eagle owls, the largest owl in the world, and found throughout Sweden's forests.

Ever-expanding, the park now features a new **Polar World** section, where you'll find a couple of polar bears, and a leopard centre where you can observe several different species including a snow leopard.

ARRIVAL AND INFORMATION   BEAR PARK

By public transport Orsa's train station for Inlandsbanan arrivals and departures is right in the centre of town on Järnvägsgatan, opposite the bus station. The bear park is easily reached on the #118 bus from Orsa bus station.
Tourist office Dalagatan 1, Orsa (mid-June to mid-Aug Mon–Fri 9am–6pm, Sat & Sun 10am–5pm; mid-Aug to mid-June Mon–Fri 10am–5pm, Sat 10am–2pm; ☎0250 55 25 50, ⓦsiljan.se). Near the train and bus stations, this office can help with local accommodation.

ACCOMMODATION

Orsa Järnvägsgatan 4 ☎0250 409 40, ⊛orsahotell.se. Built in 1894 to serve the new-fangled railway and located right in the centre by the station, this atmospheric old place is now a budget hotel with modern rooms. **500kr**
Orsa Grönklitt ☎0250 462 00, ⊛orsagronklitt.se. Should you want to stay up at the bear park itself there's a well-equipped hostel with double rooms and also a

number of cabins for rent. **490kr**
Orsa hostel Gillevägen 3 ☎0250 421 70, ⊛orsavandrarhem.se. A beautifully located hostel, 1km west of the centre by the side of Orsasjön lake; some rooms have private facilities and some also have showers. There are two fully fitted kitchens for guest use, and in summer breakfast is also available. Dorms **390kr**, doubles **600kr**

EATING

Ugglan & Björnen Next door to the hostel at Grönklitt ☎0250 462 31. There are filling Swedish meals available on site here; pork ribs or grilled trout with salad is just

110kr, and there are also themed buffet evenings including tacos, deep-pan pizzas and game. Tues–Sat 7–9pm.

Northwestern Dalarna

The area to the northwest of Mora offers travellers approaching from the south a first taste of what northern Sweden is really all about. The villages in this remote part of Dalarna lie few and far between, separated by great swathes of coniferous forest which thrive on the poor sandy soils of the hills and mountains which predominate here. On its way to the Norwegian border, **Route 70**, the main artery through this part of the province, slowly climbs up the eastern side of the Österdalälven River valley. After the tiny village of Åsen, the road leaves the river behind and strikes further inland towards the mountains which mark the border between Sweden and Norway. Buses to Särna, Idre and Grövelsjön follow this route, whereas services to Sälen only travel as far as Älvdalen before heading west towards Route 297.

It is predominantly to ski (in winter) or to hike (in summer) that most visitors come to this part of Dalarna. Indeed, **Sälen** and **Idre** are two of Sweden's most popular **ski resorts** and, in season, the slopes and cross-country trails here are busy with Swedes from further south, where snowfall is less certain. In summer, though, **Grövelsjön** makes a better destination than its sleepy neighbours, thanks to some superb hiking trails through the mountains which begin here.

Sälen

Considered as one entity, **SÄLEN** and the surrounding resorts of Lindvallen, Högfjället, Tandådalen, Hundfjället, Rörbäcksnäs and Stöten constitute the biggest **ski centre** in the Nordic area, with over a hundred pistes and guaranteed snow from November to May. It isn't unreasonable to lump all these places together, as each of the minor resorts, despite having its own ski slope, is dependent on Sälen for shops (not least its Systembolaget) and services. Novice skiers can take advantage of Sälen's special lifts,

HIKING AROUND SÄLEN

The route taken by skiers on the first Sunday in March during the annual Vasaloppet race, the **Vasaloppsleden** from Sälen to **Mora** (90km) is equally rewarding to explore on foot. The path starts just outside Sälen, in **Berga**, and first runs uphill to Smågan, then downhill all the way to Mora via Mångsbodarna, Risberg, Evertsberg, Oxberg, Hökberg and Eldris. For **accommodation**, there are eight **cabins** along the route, each equipped with a stove and unmade beds.

Another hike to consider is the little-known **southern Kungsleden** (which starts at the *Högfjällshotellet* on **Högfjället**, and leads to **Drevdagen**, a 30min drive west of Idre off Route 70 (bus #128 runs once daily Mon–Fri between Idre and Drevdagen), where it continues to Grövelsjön and all the way north to **Storlien**. There's no accommodation on the Högfjället–Drevdagen stretch.

8

nursery slopes and qualified tuition; there are also plenty of intermediate runs through the densely forested hillsides and, for advanced skiers, twenty testing runs as well as an off-piste area. To get the best value for money, it's really worth buying a package rather than trying to book individual nights at local hotels; prices are high and in season they're packed to capacity. During the **summer**, Sälen specializes in assorted **outdoor activities** – fishing, canoeing and beaver safaris are all available, and the hills, lakes and rivers around the town will keep you busy for several days. There's also some fantastic hiking to be had in the immediate vicinity (see box, p.293).

ARRIVAL AND INFORMATION   SÄLEN

By public transport Bus #95 heads from Mora to Sälen (see ⓦ dalatrafik.se for times). Coming here from further south, first take the train to Borlänge, where you change to a train to Malung, from where bus #157 takes an hour to reach Sälen. The bus calls at each resort in turn, terminating at Stöten.

Tourist office On the straggly main street that runs through the village (late April to late June & mid-Aug to Nov Mon–Thurs 9am–6pm, Fri 10am–6pm, Sat 10am–2pm; rest of year closed Sat & Sun; ☎ 0280 187 00, ⓦ salen.se), inside the Centrumhuset building.

ACCOMMODATION

Gräsheden hostel Gräsheden, near Stöten ☎ 0280 820 40, ⓦ salensvandrarhem.se. With undisturbed mountain views, this great hostel is really out in the wilds; the bus from Sälen to Stöten will drop you close by, though you need to reserve ahead before heading out. Breakfast can be ordered in advance and there's a kitchen, laundry room and sauna. Dorms <u>200kr</u>, doubles <u>400kr</u>

Högfjällshotellet Högfjället ☎ 0280 870 00, ⓦ hogis .se; reached by 3–4 buses daily from Sälen. A wonderfully situated place just inside the tree line; it has a restaurant and a bar with fantastic panoramic views, though is only open during the ski season. There's also a superb sauna suite in the basement, and a swimming pool with whirlpool and jet streams. <u>1195kr</u>

Idre and around

IDRE is one of Sweden's main **ski resorts** and home to the country's southernmost community of reindeer-herding *Sámi*. However, if you're expecting wooden huts and reindeer herders dressed in traditional dress, you'll be disappointed – the remaining six herding families live in conventional houses in the area around Idre, and dress like everyone else. Idre is a tiny one-street affair; if you come in summer, it's where you should stay, rather than up the hill at Idrefjäll, which will be completely void of life. The main street, where the bus drops you, is where you'll find everything of any significance, including a supermarket and bank.

The continental climate here – Idre is located at one of the wider points of the Scandinavian peninsula, and thus isn't prone to the warming influence of the Atlantic – means that the summers are relatively dry; consequently Idre, like its fellow ski resort, Sälen (see p.293), offers plenty of seasonal **outdoor activities**. Its tourist office can help arrange fishing trips, horseriding, mountain biking, tennis, climbing and golf. There are some good sandy beaches along the western shore of **Idresjön**, a lake that's a kilometre east of town; to go canoeing, you can rent a boat through the tourist office, where staff can also advise on local hiking routes, many of the best of which are in nearby Grövelsjön (see box opposite).

Continuing up the mountain (two daily buses; 20min), you'll come to Idre's ski slopes up at **IDREFJÄLL**, one of the most reliable places for snow in the entire country, with particularly cold winters. Although not quite on the scale of Sälen, Idre's ski resort manages to be Sweden's third largest and one of the most important in the Nordic area. In winter the place is buzzing – not only with skiers but also with reindeer, who wander down the main street hoping to lick the salt off the roads.

With your own transport, it's an easy day-trip from Idrefjäll to see the stunning waterfall, **Njupeskär**, near the village of Särna. Alternatively, you can continue by bus to **Grövelsjön**, where there's some of the best hiking anywhere in central Sweden waiting right outside the comfortable fell station accommodation.

ARRIVAL AND INFORMATION

IDRE

By bus Bus #170 from Mora follows the densely forested valley of the Österdalälven on its 2hr 30min journey here; timetables are at ⓦdalatrafik.se.

Tourist office Framgårdsvägen 1 (mid-June to mid-Aug daily 10am–7pm; mid-Aug to mid-June Mon–Fri 9am–5pm; ☎0253 59 82 00, ⓦvisitidre.se). Near the entrance to the village when approaching from Mora, in a turf-roofed building off the main Byvägen.

ACCOMMODATION

Idregården Byvägen 2, Idre ☎0253 201 50, ⓦidregarden.se. This small and comfortable hotel is located by the entrance to the village and first opened for business in 1935. Its rather basic rooms are clean and small and come with and without private facilities. **595kr**

Pernilla Wiberg Idrefjäll ☎0253 59 30 00, ⓦpernillawiberghotel.com. Idrefjäll's main hotel is named after one of Sweden's most successful downhill skiers. In addition to the surrounding ski slopes and lifts, the hotel also boasts a state-of-the-art sauna suite and modern, well-appointed rooms. **1680kr**

EATING AND DRINKING

Idregården Byvägen 2 ☎0253 201 50. A homely hotel restaurant known for its traditional Swedish home cooking such as meatballs and salmon, with mains going for around 170kr. Daily noon–9pm.

Restaurang Lodjuret Framgårdsvägen 1 ☎0253 200 12. This place next to the tourist office has a range of tasty home-cooking specials as well as pizzas and pasta dishes for around 150kr. Mon–Fri & Sun noon–10pm, Sat noon–11pm.

Around Idre: Njupeskär waterfall

From Idre, it's well worth a trip to **Särna**, 30km away, to see the impressive **Njupeskär waterfall**, Sweden's highest, with a drop of 125m. In winter it's particularly popular with **ice climbers**, as the waterfall freezes completely. An easy, circular **walking route** is clearly signposted from the car park to the waterfall and back, making for a good two-hour hike. There's no public transport from Idre; by **car**, take the main road to Särna, then turn right following signs for Mörkret and later for Njupeskärsvattenfall.

Grövelsjön

Surrounded by nature reserves and national parks, **GRÖVELSJÖN**, 45km northwest of Idre and reachable by bus #170 from Mora via Idre, is where the road ends and the mountains and wilderness really start. The area is renowned throughout Sweden for its stark, beautiful mountain scenery; in summer, the pasture around here is home to hundreds of grazing reindeer.

DAY-HIKES FROM GRÖVELSJÖN

The *fjällstation* (see p.296) makes an ideal base for **hikes** (summer only) out into the surrounding countryside, with a variety of routes available, some lasting a day, others several days.

Among the established **day-hikes** is the clearly marked route (16km round-trip) from the *fjällstation* up to Storvätteshågnen (1183m), with fantastic views over the surrounding peaks and across the border into Norway. Another worthwhile hike starts with a short walk from the *fjällstation* to Sjöstugan on Lake Grövelsjön (roughly 1500m away), from where you take the morning boat to the northern (Norwegian) end of the lake. You can now return along the lake shore to the *fjällstation* (9km) by way of the Linné path, following in the footsteps of the famous botanist who walked this route in 1734. It's possible to do the whole route in the opposite direction, heading out along the Linné path in the morning and returning by boat in the late afternoon; ask at the *fjällstation* for details of boat departure times. A third option is to strike out along the path leading northwest from Sjöstugan, heading for the Norwegian border and Salsfjellet (1281m) on the other side of it (16km round trip). There's no need to take your passport as the border is all but invisible; people wander back and forth across it quite freely.

8

ACCOMMODATION GRÖVELSJÖN

STF Grövelsjön fjällstation ☎0253 59 68 80, ⓦstfgrovelsjon.com. This is virtually the only building here, with a variety of rooms with private facilities and prices depending on the season; it boasts a restaurant, kitchen, sauna, massage room and solarium. Closed May to mid-June & Oct to Christmas, but open New Year. Doubles **690kr**

Härjedalen

From Mora and Orsa, the Inlandsbanan trundles through the northern reaches of Dalarna before crossing the provincial border into **Härjedalen**, a sparsely populated fell region stretching north and west to the Norwegian border, and containing some of the best scenery anywhere in Sweden. Indeed, the region belonged to Norway until 1645, and the influence of the Norwegian language is still evident today in the local dialect. Härjedalen got its name from the unfortunate Härjulf Hornbreaker, a servant to the Norwegian king, who mistakenly killed two of the king's men and was banished from the court. He fled to Uppsala, where he sought protection from King Amund, but after falling in love with Amund's cousin, Helga, and arousing the king's fury he was forced to make another hasty exit. It was then he came across a desolate valley in which he settled and which he named after himself: Härjulf's dale, or Härjedalen, as it's known today.

From the comfort of the Inlandsbanan, you'll be treated to a succession of breathtaking vistas of vast forested hill and mountainsides (Härjedalen boasts more than thirty mountains of over 1000m) – these are some of the emptiest tracts of land in the whole country, also home to the country's largest population of bears. Although the sleepy provincial capital, **Sveg**, holds little of appeal, it's from here that **buses** head northwest to the remote mountain villages of **Funäsdalen** and **Tänndalen**, both with easy access to excellent and little-frequented **hiking trails** through austere terrain which features a handful of shaggy musk oxen that have wandered over the border from Norway. Nearby, across the lonely **Flatruet plateau**, with its ancient rock paintings, tiny **Ljungdalen** is the starting point for treks to Sweden's southernmost glacier, **Helags**, on the icy slopes of Helagsfjället (1797m).

Sveg and around

Around three hours and 140km north of Mora by the Inlandsbanan, **SVEG** is the first place of any significance after Lake Siljan. With a tiny population of just 2600, the town is far and away the biggest in Härjedalen – though that's not saying much. Even on a Friday night in the height of summer you'll be hard pushed to find anyone on the streets. But though there's not an awful lot to do or see, Sveg's a pretty enough place: the wide streets are lined with grand old wooden houses, and the beautiful Ljusnan River runs through the centre of town.

Train station

There are a couple of diversions worthy of attention, the first of which is ideally located for arrivals by both train and bus: on permanent display inside the **train station** building on Järnvägsgatan (which is also used as the bus station) is a free **exhibition** of the life and times of the Inlandsbanan, in old photos and maps. Unfortunately the text and captions are only in Swedish but it's pretty evident that without the railway Sveg probably wouldn't be here at all. The town's lifeblood since 1909, when the line to Orsa was opened by King Gustaf V and Queen Viktoria, the Inlandsbanan not only brings visitors to the region during the short summer months, but also provides a means of transporting timber and peat pellets (see p.298) to southern Sweden.

CLOCKWISE FROM TOP LEFT BEARS IN ORSA GRÖNKLITT BJÖRNPARK (P.292); CROSS-COUNTRY SKIERS SEEN AT THE START OF THE ANNUAL VASALOPPET SKI RACE (P.290); CROSS-HATCHED WOODEN FENCE, DALARNA COUNTRYSIDE (P.282) >

Svegs kyrka

From the station, your next port of call should be the parish church, **Svegs kyrka**, on Vallarvägen. A church has stood on this spot since the latter part of the eleventh century when Sveg was also the site of an ancient Viking *ting*, or parliament. In 1273 a border treaty between Sweden and Norway was hammered out here, when the church was part of the bishopric of Trondheim. Sadly, though, the glory days are long gone. The present building dates only from 1847 and contains few of the fittings which once made its predecessors so grand; it's predominantly the woven textiles inside that catch the eye today.

The wooden bear

In front of the church, beside the main crossroads in town, looms the world's largest **wooden bear**, a mammoth and weirdly ominous structure reaching 13m in height; it's meant as a reminder to passers-by that this is bear country – it's thought there are around 1200 animals in Härjedalen and neighbouring Jämtland.

Kulturcentrum Mankell

Ljusnegatan 1 • Mon–Fri 9am–3.30pm • 40kr

Sveg's final attraction is the **Kulturcentrum Mankell**, opposite the bear inside the Folkets Hus. Here you'll find a simple museum dedicated to Sveg's most famous son, Henning Mankell, who's one of Sweden's best-known novelists, particularly for his *Wallander* crime novels (see p.183). Translated into everything from Faroese to Chinese, a collection of Mankell's books is available inside for persual.

The outskirts of Sveg

At the western end of Fjällvägen, a pleasant **walk** of twenty to thirty minutes takes you across the road and train bridge on Brogatan to the riverbank, ideal for a picnic and a bit of skinny-dipping. Once over the bridge, just beyond the point where the railway line veers left and leaves the road, head right over a little stream into the forest, all the time walking back towards the river's edge. Hidden from the road by the trees is a wonderful sweet-smelling open flower meadow, but don't forget your mosquito repellent – the countryside around Sveg is made up of vast tracts of uninhabited marshland and countless small lakes, ideal breeding grounds for the insect. However, Sveg has the surrounding swamps to thank for its livelihood; Härjedalen's biggest factory, on the outskirts of town, turns the peat into heating pellets which are then transported down the Inlandsbanan to Uppsala.

ARRIVAL AND INFORMATION   SVEG

By public transport The train and bus stations are on Järnvägsgatan.

Tourist office In the Folkets Hus building, Ljusnegatan 1 (Mon–Fri 8am–4.30pm; ☎0680 107 75,

ⓦherjedalsporten.se). Has leaflets about local hiking routes, useful for their maps even if you don't understand Swedish; to get here from the train station, walk east along Gränsgatan for around 10min.

SWEDEN'S BROWN BEARS

It's estimated there are currently over three thousand **brown bears** in Sweden, the highest number since the 1800s, roaming across an area stretching from the far north as far south as northern Värmland. Since the early 1940s it's been legal in Sweden to **hunt** bears every autumn to keep the population in check and each year around 250 animals are culled. Although it's rare to spot a bear in the wild, should you be hiking in an area where bears are present, you're advised to whistle or talk loudly to alert the bear to your presence, particularly in autumn when they are present in the forests gorging on wild berries ahead of hibernation.

ACCOMMODATION

Härjedalen Vallarvägen 11 ☏0680 103 38, ⓦhotellharjedalen.se. A 10–15min walk from the station located near the main square, this rambling old place from the late 1800s has comfortable and spacious rooms and has been run for the past fifty-odd years by the same family. 850kr/1150kr

Mysoxen Fjällvägen 12 ☏0680 170 00, ⓦmysoxen.se. Just the other side of the main square, this austere place lacks charm and is rather unwelcoming, but in Sveg choices

are limited and you may well find yourself here. Smile and hope for the best. It also doubles as the town's hostel. Dorms 285kr, hostel doubles 570kr, hotel doubles 920kr/1265kr

Svegs Camping Kyrkogränd 1 ☏0680 130 25, ⓦcaping.se/z32. Enjoying a wonderful riverside location, the campsite is just a stone's throw from the tourist office and also has amazing-value two-berth cabins. Open mid-June to mid-Aug only. Tents 140kr, cabins 375kr

EATING

Knuten Berggatan 4 ☏0680 130 15. A rather dreary pizzeria off the main square, serving standard pizzas (70kr) and salads (80kr) 70kr, plus a range of steaks for 115kr, fried plaice and schnitzel (both 75kr). Mon–Thurs & Sun 11am–9pm, Fri & Sat 11am–10pm.

Mysoxen Fjällvägen 12 ☏0680 170 00. The often empty restaurant inside the hotel churns out fish dishes from 130kr and steaks for 175kr without much enthusiasm. The

food is tasty but it's a strange experience sitting alone in a relatively large restaurant. Mon–Thurs 11am–1.30pm & 6–10pm, Fri 6–10pm.

Thai Take Away Älvgatan 8 ☏0680 102 84. The authentic Thai cuisine expertly prepared here by native chefs is genuinely delicious (125kr for a main course) and comes as a real treat in unadventurous little Sveg – meals are available to take away and eat in. Tues–Fri 11am–7pm.

Tännäs

Although Sveg may be shy, retiring and void of major attractions, what it does have is some blockbuster scenery right on its doorstep. It's worth leaving the Inlandsbanan at Sveg to travel into the far reaches of Härjedalen and explore one of Sweden's least visited and most rewarding landscapes, where compelling views of the vast, uninhabited forest unfold at every turn. The remote outpost of **TÄNNÄS**, at the junction of Routes 311 and 84, is remarkable for its **church town**, a handful of gnarled wooden cottages clinging to the south-facing valley-side where, quite unbelievably for such a high altitude and latitude location, corn was once grown.

ARRIVAL   TÄNNÄS

By bus From Sveg, bus #633 (ⓦlanstrafiken-z.se) winds its way northwest towards the tiny village of Lofsdalen,

from where a connecting service continues to Tännäs.

ACCOMMODATION

Tännäs youth hostel Bygatan 51 ☏0684 240 67, ⓦtannasgarden. This well-equipped hillside hostel lies just to the west of the main road junction and enjoys

tremendous views; it's open all year, though advance booking is required in May to mid-June & Oct–Dec. It also serves food. Dorms 250kr, doubles 500kr

Funäsdalen

From Tännäs the bus heads a further 15km west to reach the pretty mountain resort of **FUNÄSDALEN**, which is surrounded by kilometres of superb hiking trails. Curling gracefully around the eastern shore of Funäsdalssjön lake, this appealing little village, barely 30km from the Norwegian border, enjoys some fantastic views of the surrounding mountains. It's best seen from the top of the sheer Funäsdalsberget mountain (977m), which bears down over the village and is reached by **chairlift** – you can get to the base-station by walking ten minutes along the road signed to Ljungdalen at the eastern end of the village.

Härjedalens Fjällmuseum

Rörosvägen 30 • Mid-June to Sept daily 10am–6pm; Sept to mid-June Mon–Fri 10am–5pm • 100kr • ⓦfjallmuseet.se

The main thing to do in Funäsdalen is visit **Härjedalens Fjällmuseum**, the province's mountain museum, which has a short slide-show about the province as well as informative explanations of how the mountain farmers of these parts managed to survive in such a remote location; transhumance (the practice of moving animals to higher ground during summer to fatten them on the fresh lush pasture) is given particular prominence. The adjacent outdoor **Fornminnesparken** homestead museum (unrestricted access; free), the oldest in Sweden and established in 1894 by a local trader, contains the usual collection of old timber buildings, plus a former customs house from the early nineteenth century used to regulate cross-border trade with Norway.

ARRIVAL AND INFORMATION   FUNÄSDALEN

By bus There is no bus station in Funäsdalen. Instead buses to and from Östersund (Mon–Sat 2 daily, Sun 1 daily; 3hr 30min) pull up outside the Fjällmuseum on the main road.
Tourist office Rörosvägen 30 (mid-June to Sept daily

10am–6pm; Sept to mid-June Mon–Fri 10am–5pm; ☎0684 155 80, ⒲funasfjallen.se). The best place for advice on the dozens of local hiking trails; also has useful information about canoe rental.

ACCOMMODATION AND EATING

Funäsdalen ☎0684 214 30, ⒲hotell-funasdalen.se. The top place to stay in the village is this huge red building with the green roof down by the lakeside on Strandvägen. The comfortable modern rooms have unsurpassed views out over the lake; in the winter high season, when prices shoot up, bookings are only accepted for long weekends or one week. **545kr/1845kr**
Norrbyns Stugby Vallarvägen 25 ☎0684 212 05, ⒲norrbyns-stugby.nu. Two-person cabins are available

at this place with terrific views out over Anåfjället mountain; in winter bookings are by the week only. **575kr**
Veras Stekhus & Pub Rörosvägen 23 ☎0684 215 30. Located opposite the tourist office on the main road, this is the best place to eat, not only for its delicious Arctic char and grilled meats, including reindeer (around 200kr), but also its wonderful views of the lake. Wed & Thurs 5–9pm, Sat & Sun 5–10pm.

The Flatruet plateau and around

From Funäsdalen, an unnumbered road, actually the highest in the country, heads north for the bumpy ascent to the hamlet of Mittådalen and beyond to the **Flatruet plateau** (975m), a bare stretch of desolate, rocky land, punctuated only by electricity poles and herds of grazing reindeer. The plateau is renowned for its 4000-year-old Stone Age **rock paintings** (*hällmålningar* in Swedish) at the foot of the Ruändan mountain at the eastern edge of this extensive upland area; get here by turning right in Mittådalen for another hamlet, Messlingen, where you should leave your vehicle. East of the settlement, a track off to the left leads towards Byggevallen and Ruvallen; from the latter a footpath then leads to the paintings – from the road it's a walk of 5–6km. Fashioned from a mix of iron ochre and animal fat and etched into slabs of rock, the twenty or so figures show, in remarkable clarity, elk, reindeer and even bears. Bus #620 makes this journey once daily on weekdays; timetables are at ⒲lanstrafiken-z.se.

Ljungdalen

Once over the plateau, the road descends steeply towards the charming village of **LJUNGDALEN**, hemmed in on three sides by high mountains, occupying an area of flat grassland near the head of the Ljungan River.

Helags glacier

Though the fifty or so wooden houses are pleasant enough, it's as a base from which to reach the **Helags glacier** that Ljungdalen really comes into its own. From the ICA supermarket in the centre of the village, take the road signed for "Helags/Kläppen" which leads to a car park after 6km, from where the hiking trail starts. Before the car park though, the road passes a small settlement, Kläppen, where you should take Kläppenvägen uphill, following the signs. Once at the car park it's 12km to the STF mountain cabin at Helags.

INFORMATION

Tourist office (late June to early Aug Mon–Fri 11am–6pm, Sat 11am–4pm, Sun noon–4pm; ☎0687 200 79, ⓦljungdalen.com). Ljungdalen's tourist office occupies a red-painted wooden house in the centre of the village and has good advice about hiking to Helags and about onward travel possibilities; there's no bus over the plateau to Funäsdalen, though it is possible to hike there.

ACCOMMODATION AND EATING

Dunsjögården hostel On the main street ☎0687 202 85. This hostel with its thirteen rooms also has a swimming pool and sauna nearby for relaxing those aching muscles after hiking, and you can cook here. Dorms 175kr, doubles 450kr
Restaurang Fjällsippan In the centre of the village ☎0687 200 24. The best eating alternative in the village, serving good pizzas (75kr) and Swedish dishes (around 150kr) as well as home-made cakes; it's also fully licensed. Tues & Thurs–Sat noon–10pm, Mon, Wed & Sun noon–8pm.

Route 535: the road to Åsarna

From Ljungdalen, one of the most beautiful journeys anywhere in northern Sweden unfolds. Although the 110km trip to Åsarna certainly requires stamina, it offers a real taste of wild Sweden. The switchback road cuts through some of the most spectacular mountain and lakeside landscapes you'll witness in the north, threading its way around serpentine bends and across narrow isthmuses between the extensive areas of swampland and spruce forest that characterize this forgotten corner of the country.

Curiously for such a remote route, it is served by **bus**: the #613 runs from Ljungdalen to Åsarna (bus times at ⓦlanstrafiken-z.se) providing a rare insight for anyone without their own transport into life in backwoods Sweden – as the bus trundles through the tiny villages, you'll notice how the lumberjack culture is alive and well in these parts. Indeed, the stretch of road between the Härjedalen/Jämtland border and the village of **Börtnan** (1hr 10min from Ljungdalen) runs through one of the region's most important forestry areas; mountains of timber line the roadside awaiting transport to the nearest railhead.

Jämtland

Stretching from just north of Sveg to the border with Lapland, a distance of around 250km, the province of **JÄMTLAND** is centred round one of Sweden's greatest lakes, **Storsjön**, and its associated watercourses. Altogether more pastoral than its wilder and more mountainous neighbour to the south, Härjedalen, it was the plentiful supply of fish from the lake coupled with successful cultivation of the rich lands around its shores that enabled the region's first settlers to eke out an existence so far north – Stockholm, for example, is 550km to the south. Although the province can trace its history back to the early Iron Age, Jämtland has only been Swedish since 1645, before which it was part of Norway. The people here have a strong sense of regional identity and, in recent years, have even called (albeit rather half-heartedly) for independence from Sweden. Spend any length of time here and you'll soon encounter the tremendous pride the locals have in their villages, forests and lakes.

Approaching from the south, it's the cross-country skiing centre of **Åsarna** that you'll reach first. Just beyond here, **Hackås** is the location for the wildly entertaining *Årets Näck* competition, which sees a group of naked male fiddle-players compete for the prestigious title. The most enjoyable town in the province is the provincial capital of **Östersund**, situated on Storsjön lake, whose murky waters reputedly hide Sweden's own version of the Loch Ness monster. West of Östersund, **Åre** is Sweden's most popular ski destination for foreign tourists, whilst nearby **Storlien** has some great summer hiking right on its doorstep.

Åsarna and around

From Sveg, the Inlandsbanan veers eastwards in order to skirt the vast area of marshland north and east of the town. The train line finally swings west at Överhogdal, where the Viking Age tapestries now on display in Östersund were discovered (see opposite), before crossing the provincial border into Jämtland and continuing north to **ÅSARNA**. Blink and you'll miss the place, a tiny one-street affair 109km north of Sveg that serves as a diminutive service centre for the southern part of Jämtland. Other than the train station, a filling station and a hotel, all lined up along the nameless main road, there's nothing to recommend an overnight stay here. For a stroll or an afternoon picnic in summer, wander past the campsite cabins behind the Skicenter (see below) and down to the river; turn right here and follow the age-old Kärleksstigen ("Lover's Lane") along the water's edge – you can cross the river over an old stone bridge, further upstream by the rapids, and return on the opposite bank along a minor road. The smooth, low rocks by the bridge make an ideal spot to fish or catch a few rays of sunshine.

Skicenter

Olstavägen 45 • Daily: June–Aug 8am–10pm; Sept–May 8am–8pm • Free entry to museum • ☎ 0687 302 30, ⓦ asarnaskicenter.se

The Inlandbanan makes a stop of forty minutes in both directions in Åsarna, allowing time enough to check out the **Skicenter** and its **museum**, which has worthy displays of the Åsarna ski club's Olympic and World Championship medals and equipment, as well as photographs of famous Swedish skiers and a couple of video exhibits. Established by four of the region's many skiing champions – Tomas Wassberg, Torgny Mogren, Jan Ottosson and Hans Persson – the centre also organizes cross-country skiing in winter and provides advice on hiking in summer.

ARRIVAL AND DEPARTURE

ÅSARNA

By train Åsarna train station lies beside the one and only main road, Olstavägen, which runs through the village. Destinations Mora (1–2 daily; 4hr); Östersund (1–2 daily; 1hr 15min); Sveg (1–2 daily; 1hr 30min).

By bus Buses pull up at the Skicenter.
Destinations Ljungdalen (1 daily; 1hr 45min); Östersund (6 daily; 1hr 20min); Sveg (2 daily; 1hr 30min).

INFORMATION

Tourist information Åsarna's Skicenter (daily: June–Aug 8am–10pm; Sept–May 8am–8pm; ☎ 0687 302 30, ⓦ asarnaskicenter.se) has limited amounts of tourist information.

ACCOMMODATION AND EATING

Åsarna hostel Olstavägen 45, ☎ 0687 302 30, ⓦ asarnaskicenter.se. Down by the river's edge, accommodation here is spread across several timber buildings behind the Skicenter and there's also a small bathing pool and a sauna. Dorms 200kr, doubles 400kr

Skicenter The restaurant here is hard to beat for cheap meals, with breakfast, *dagens rätt* until 6pm and evening meals for 95kr. Daily until 8pm, June–Aug 10pm.

NUDE MALE FIDDLERS: ÅRETS NÄCK

One of the most intriguing and quintessentially Swedish events you'll witness takes place in **Hackås**, just 35km north of Åsarna, on the second Thursday in July. The **Årets Näck** competition (ⓦ näck.nu) features a succession of naked male fiddle players, who compete for the prestigious title by sitting in the unflatteringly chilly waters of the local river to play their instruments. The roots of this eye-opening spectacle of public nudity are to be found in the mists of Swedish folklore where the *näck*, a long-haired, bearded, naked water sprite, would sit by a river rapid or waterfall and play his fiddle so hauntingly that women and children from miles around would be lured to him, only to drown in his watery home. The event begins around 9pm on the island of Gaveriholmen near Strömbacka mill; Hackås is on the Inlandsbanan and is served by buses to and from Östersund.

8

Vemdalen

The road from Åsarna to Funäsdalen is especially worth travelling, crossing the provincial border back into Härjedalen and following the ancient track used by the region's merchant farmers through the **Vemdalsskalet pass**. Bound for **VEMDALEN**, the road descends sharply and offers clear views of another of Härjedalen's mighty peaks: the impressive sugarloaf-shaped **Sånfjället** mountain (1278m) to the southwest. Back in the 1900s the forest and fell terrain around the mountain was declared a national park in an attempt to maintain its delicate ecosystem – with great success, since the park is now a favourite habitat for Härjedalen's bear population.

The church

Once through the pass and down into Vemdalen, you'll find a stunning octagonal **wooden church** right by the roadside in the centre of the village. Built in Rococo style in 1763, eight years after its separate onion-domed bell tower, the church supports a deep two-stage roof and a central onion turret. Inside, the work of a couple of local craftsmen is proudly displayed: the pulpit, with its bowing cherrywood panels, was made in Ljungdalen, whilst the altar was carved by a carpenter from Klövsjö.

Östersund

Sitting gracefully on the eastern shore of the mighty **Storsjön** (Great Lake) about halfway up Sweden, **ÖSTERSUND** is the only large town along the Inlandsbanan (until Gällivare inside the Arctic Circle, another 750km further north), and is well worth a stop. Östersund's **lakeside** position lends it a seaside-holiday atmosphere, unusual this far inland, and it's an instantly likeable place. In addition to the youthful buzz about town, there's an air of commercialism here, too (lacking in most other inland towns), since Östersund is also a centre for the engineering and electronics industries, as well as the Swedish armed forces, who maintain two regiments here. However, it's for its lake **monster**, the Storsjöodjuret, that Östersund is perhaps best known.

Brief history

King Gustav III gave the town its charter two hundred years ago with one thing in mind: to put an end to the lucrative trade that the region's merchant farmers carried out with neighbouring Norway. Travelling over the mountains, they bartered and sold their goods in Trondheim before returning back to the Storsjön region. Although rival markets in Östersund gradually stemmed the trade, it took another century for the town's growth to really begin, heralded by the arrival of the railway from Sundsvall in 1879.

Jamtli open-air museum

Museiplan; a 15min walk north from the centre along Kyrkogatan • Late June to late Aug daily 11am–5pm; late Aug to late June closed Mon • 240kr for a two-day visit • ⓦ jamtli.com

Most visitors head straight for Östersund's top attraction, **Jamtli**, home to the beautiful **Överhogdal Viking tapestries** and an **open-air museum** which expertly – and enjoyably – brings to life Östersund from years past. It's full of people milling around in nineteenth-century costume, farming and milking much as their ancestors did. Everyone else is encouraged to join in – baking, tree felling, grass cutting and so on. The place is ideal for children, and adults would have to be pretty hard-bitten not to enjoy the enthusiastic atmosphere. Intensive work has been done on getting the settings right: the restored and working interiors are authentically gloomy and dirty, and the local store, Lanthandel, among the wooden buildings around the square near the entrance, is suitably old-fashioned. In the woodman's cottage (presided over by a bearded lumberjack, who makes pancakes for the visitors), shoeless and scruffy youngsters snooze contentedly in the wooden cots. Beyond the first cluster of houses is

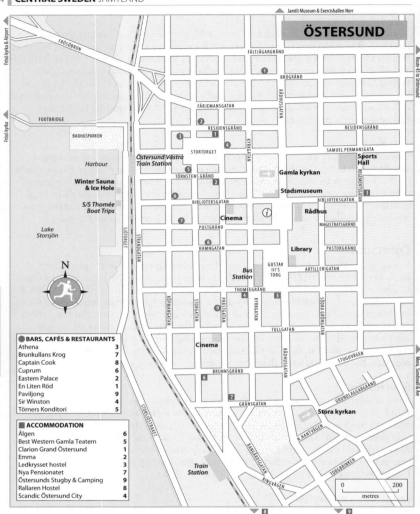

Jamtli Museum & Exercishallen Norr

ÖSTERSUND

Frösö kyrka & Airport

FRÖSÖBRON

Route 45 to Strömsund

Frösö kyrka

FOOTBRIDGE

BADHUSPARKEN

FÄLTJÄGARGRÄND

BROGRÄND

RÅDHUSGATAN

FÄRJEMANSGATAN

RESIDENSGRÄND

RESIDENSGRÄND

SAMUEL PERMANSGATAN

STORTORGET

KYRKGATAN

Harbour

Östersund Västra
Train Station

Winter Sauna
& Ice Hole

TÖRNSTENS GRÄND

Gamla kyrkan

Sports
Hall

REGEMENTSGATAN

S/S Thomée
Boat Trips

Stadsmuseum

BIBLIOTEKSGATAN

BIBLIOTEKSGATAN

Rådhus

Lake
Storsjön

Cinema

MAGISTRATSGRÄND

POSTGRÄND

Library

PASTORGRÄND

HAMNGATAN

SJÖTORGET

STRANDGATAN

GUSTAV
III'S
TORG

ARTILLERIGATAN

Bus
Station

THOMÉEGRÄND

KYRKGATAN

N

TULLGATAN

KÖPMANGATAN

STORGATAN

PRÄSTGATAN

SÖDRA GRÖNGATAN

Mora, Sundsvall & Åre

Cinema

RÅDHUSGATAN

STUGUVÄGEN

BRUNNSGRÄND

GRUNDLAGGARGRÄND

GRÄNSGATAN

Stora kyrkan

N. HANTVÄGEN

Train
Station

BANGÅRDSGATAN

SÖDRA ÖSTRAKEJ

RINGVÄGEN

TORGBRINNEN

0   200
metres

● **BARS, CAFÉS & RESTAURANTS**

Athena	3
Brunkullans Krog	7
Captain Cook	8
Cuprum	6
Eastern Palace	2
En Liten Röd	1
Paviljong	9
Sir Winston	4
Törners Konditori	5

■ **ACCOMMODATION**

Älgen	6
Best Western Gamla Teatern	5
Clarion Grand Östersund	1
Emma	2
Ledkrysset hostel	3
Nya Pensionatet	7
Östersunds Stugby & Camping	9
Rallaren Hostel	8
Scandic Östersund City	4

8

a reconstructed farm, **Lillhärdal**, where life goes on pretty much as it did in 1785, when the land was ploughed using horses, and crops were sown and harvested by hand – even the roaming cattle and the crop varieties are appropriate to the period.

The indoor museum

The **indoor museum** on the same site is the place to get to grips with Östersund's **monster**. Ask to see the fascinating film (with English subtitles) about the creature, which contains a series of telling interviews with local people who claim to have seen it; one very Swedish thing leaps out at you – having witnessed something unusual out on the lake, many people took several months, even years, to talk about their experience for fear of ridicule. Having seen the film, head downstairs for a further display of monster-catching gear, alongside what's claimed to be a pickled embryo of a similar

STORSJÖODJURET – THE "GREAT LAKE MONSTER"

The people of Östersund are in no doubt: **Storsjöodjuret** is out there, in their lake. Eyewitness accounts – there are hundreds of people who claim to have seen it – speak of a creature with a head like a dog, long pointed ears and bulging eyes, that sweeps gracefully through the water, sometimes making a hissing or clucking sound, often several hundred metres away from the shore; each summer sees new reports of sightings. Although several explanations have been given that dispel the myth – a floating tree trunk, a row of swimming elk, the wake from a passing boat, a series of rising water bubbles – the monster's existence is taken so seriously that a protection order has now been slapped on it, using the provisions of paragraph fourteen of Sweden's Nature Conservation Act. For most people, though, the monster will be at its most tangible not in the lake, but on the web (🅦 storsjoodjuret.com).

In 1894, the hunt for this sinister presence began in earnest, when King Oscar II founded a special organization to try to catch it. Norwegian whalers were hired to do so, but the rather unorthodox methods they chose proved unsuccessful: a dead pig gripped in a metal clasp was dangled into the water as bait, and large, specially manufactured pincers were on hand to grip the creature and pull it ashore. Their tackle is on display at Jamtli, together with photographs that claim to be of the creature.

If you fancy a bit of monster-spotting, consider taking a **steamboat cruise** on the lake on board *S/S Thomée*, a creaking 1875 wooden steamship. Routes and timetables vary, but in general the boat does a two-hour trip (100kr) round the lake leaving from the harbour in town. Also available are trips out to the island of **Verkön**, where there's a nineteenth-century castle (5hr 30min; 130kr).

monster found in the lake in 1895; this quite grotesque thing is kept in a small glass jar on a shelf next to the foot of the stairs.

Överhogdal tapestries

The museum's prize exhibits are the awe-inspiring Viking **Överhogdal tapestries**, crowded with brightly coloured pictures of horses, reindeer, elk and dogs, and different types of dwellings. Dating from the ninth and tenth centuries and woven from flax, most of the tapestries were discovered by accident in an outhouse in 1910. One piece was rescued after being used as a doll's blanket – rumour has it the child had to be pacified with a 2kr reward to hand it over – and another was being used as a cleaning rag in the local church. Be sure, too, to watch the informative ten-minute slideshow explaining the tapestries' history and their likely significance.

Exercishallen Norr

Infanterigatan 30 • Thurs–Sun noon–4pm • Free

Close to Jamtli, **Exercishallen Norr** is an excellent modern art museum with constantly changing and thought-provoking exhibitions. Housed in a former military building, the spacious exhibition hall can easily be visited on the way to Jamtli.

Badhusparken

Sauna: Mid-Jan to mid-March Tues & Thurs 6–8pm • 130kr • ☎ 063 10 05 20, 🅦 vinterparken.se

Whilst the lakeside **Badhusparken**, is an extremely popular sunbathing spot in summer, in winter it is the place for a quick dip in the invigorating waters of Lake Storsjön – a hole in the ice is kept open here for this purpose (mid-Jan to late March). Once you're out of the water, head straight for the nearby **sauna** or you'll be covered in frost faster than you can say "Storsjöodjuret". This is also the place to rent skates to go long-distance **skating** on the lake (150kr/day), which freezes over each winter.

Frösön

Take the footbridge across the lake from Badhusparken, or the road bridge a little further north, and you'll come to the island of **Frösön**. People have lived here since prehistoric times; the name comes from the original Viking settlement, which was associated with the pagan god of fertility, Frö. There's plenty of good walking on the island, as well as a couple of historical sights. Just over the bridges, in front of the red-brick offices, look for the eleventh-century **rune stone** telling of Austmaður ("East Man"), son of Guðfast, the first Christian missionary to the area. From here, you can clamber up the nearby hill of Öneberget to the fourth-century settlement of **Mjälleborgen**, where a pleasant walking trail of around 4km leads through the area.

Frösö kyrka

Five kilometres west of the bridges, along the island's main road and up the main hill, is the beautiful **Frösö kyrka**, an eleventh-century church with a detached bell tower. In 1984, archeologists digging under the altar came across a bit of old birch stump surrounded by animal bones – bears, pigs, deer and squirrels – evidence of the cult of ancient gods, who were known as *æsir*. Today, the church is one of the most popular in Sweden for weddings – to tie the knot here at midsummer, you have to book years in advance. Bus #3 from the centre comes here.

ARRIVAL AND DEPARTURE   ÖSTERSUND

Östersund is a major transport hub: the E14 runs through on its way to the Norwegian border; the Inlandsbanan stops here and other trains run west to Åre, Storlien and Trondheim in Norway, east to Sundsvall (a very beautiful run which hugs lakeshore and riverbank the entire way) and south to both Stockholm and Gothenburg, through some of Sweden's most stunning primeval forest. Coming from Swedish Lapland, train connections can be made for Östersund in nearby Bräcke.

By plane The town's airport, with flights from Stockholm Arlanda, Gothenburg, Luleå and Umeå, is on Frösön, an island 11km west of town, from where buses (connecting with flights; 70kr) and taxis (365kr) run to the centre.
By train From the train station on Strandgatan, it's a 5min walk north to the town centre
Destinations Åre (3 daily; 1hr 45min); Arvidsjaur by Inlandsbanan (summer 1 daily; 9hr); Gällivare by Inlandsbanan (summer 1 daily; 15hr); Gothenburg (1 daily;

12hr); Mora by Inlandsbanan (summer 1–2 daily; 6hr); Stockholm (3 daily; 5hr 30min); Storlien (3 daily; 2hr); Sundsvall (8 daily; 2hr 15min); Sveg by Inlandsbanan (summer 1–2 daily; 3hr 30min); Trondheim (2 daily; 4hr).
By bus The bus station is in the centre of town in Gustav IIIs torg.
Destinations Åsarna (6 daily; 1hr 15min); Funäsdalen (2 daily; 3hr 30min); Mora (2 daily; 5hr 30min); Sveg (3 daily; 2hr 50min); Umeå (2 daily; 6hr).

INFORMATION

Tourist office Rådhusgatan 44 (early June & Aug Mon–Fri 9am–5pm, Sat & Sun 10am–3pm; late June & July Mon–Sat 9am–7pm, Sun 10am–5pm; Sept–May Mon–Fri

9am–5pm; ☎06314 40 01, ⓦ visitostersund.se). A couple of blocks north of the bus station, opposite the minaret-topped Rådhus.

ACCOMMODATION

Älgen Storgatan 61 ☎063 51 75 25, ⓦ hotelalgen.se. Handy for the train station, this small, central hotel has plain and comfortable en-suite rooms with rather uninspiring modern furnishings. Special emphasis is placed on providing guests with a full breakfast with plentiful fresh fruit and freshly baked bread. <u>895kr/1065kr</u>
Best Western Gamla Teatern Thoméegränd 20 ☎063 51 16 00, ⓦ gamlateatern.se. The most atmospheric hotel in town, housed in a turn-of-the-twentieth-century theatre with sweeping wooden staircases. The Art Nouveau rooms are snug and cosy, and many have delightful pieces of period furniture. Choose carefully, though, because some are rather small. <u>1104kr/1486kr</u>
★ **Clarion Grand Östersund** Prästgatan 16 ☎063 55 60 00, ⓦ choicehotels.se. This business-oriented hotel is

Östersund's finest – the very best rooms have their own marbled hallway, sitting room and sumptuous double beds. The cheaper rooms are less glamorous but still worth the splurge. <u>1070kr/1370kr</u>
Emma Prästgatan 31 ☎063 51 78 40, ⓦ hotelemma .com. Eighteen tastefully decorated rooms with high ceilings, wooden floors, old tiled corner stoves and lots of chequers and bold colours, all en suite, in a perfect location on the main drag; reception is not 24hr so be prepared to ring if closed. <u>850kr/1090kr</u>
Ledkrysset hostel Biblioteksgatan 25 ☎063 10 33 10, ⓦ ostersundledkrysset.se. Östersund finally has a smart, central STF hostel, housed in a soaring brick building. Interior design, featuring lots of natural woods, has been chosen to reflect the natural surroundings of the Swedish

8

mountains. Rooms have private facilities or share with just one other. Dorms 210kr, doubles 500kr

Nya Pensionatet Prästgatan 65 ☎063 10 20 05, ⓦnyapensionatet.se. The cheapest place in town, this tastefully decorated guesthouse dating from around 1900 has just six rooms; all bar one have washbasins, but the bathrooms are shared. There's access to a microwave, fridge and kettle, too. 650kr

Rallaren Hostel Bangårdsgatan 6 ☎063 13 22 32, ⓦrallarens.se. Accessed from the platform at the train station, this hostel has dorm beds in rooms sleeping 2–6. Bear in mind that the noise from passing goods trains in the night may disturb your sleep. Dorms 160kr

Scandic Östersund City Kyrkgatan 70 ☎063 57 57 00, ⓦscandichotels.se. A massive modern hotel with 126 newly renovated rooms; high on Scandinavian design and quality – with wooden floors and leather armchairs. The location, too, is unbeatable, right in the heart of the city. 850kr/1340kr

CAMPING

Östersunds Stugby & Camping Krondikesvägen 95C ☎063 14 46 15, ⓦcamping.se/z11. Located a couple of kilometres south of the town centre and perfect for the fantastic indoor swimming complex, Storsjöbadet. There are also cottages here. Tents 140kr, cottages 690kr

EATING AND DRINKING

Athena Stortorget 3 ☎063 51 63 44. Tucked away in one corner of Stortorget, this rather dingy place serves tasty, authentic pizzas from 75kr, as well as steaks from 255kr. The house speciality is lamb chops marinated in rosemary served with fried mushrooms and Greek salad for 228kr. Mon–Wed 2–9.30pm, Thurs & Fri 2pm–10pm, Sat noon–10pm, Sun 1–9pm.

Brunkullans Krog Postgränd 5 ☎063 10 14 54. This old-fashioned, home-from-home restaurant, with polished lanterns and a heavy wooden interior dating from the 1880s, offers modern Swedish dishes, such as oven-baked salmon and marinated chicken breast for 199kr. Tues–Sat 5pm till late.

Captain Cook Hamngatan 9 ☎063 12 60 90. This moderately priced place has a selection of delicious Australian-style specials that really draw in the crowds – try the Bushman sandwich with bacon and coleslaw (109kr) or an Aussie burger (139kr). Another favourite is the grilled salmon with whitefish roe (195kr). Tues 5–10pm, Wed & Thurs 5pm–midnight, Fri 4pm–2am, Sat 5pm–2am.

Cuprum Biblioteksgatan 5 ☎063 10 64 64. A newly opened lounge bar and restaurant serving winning dishes such as venison steak (253kr), Arctic char (224kr) and cannelloni unusually, though tastily, stuffed with ricotta and cauliflower (176kr). Mon–Thurs & Sun 4pm–2am, Fri & Sat 3pm–2am.

Eastern Palace Storgatan 15 ☎063 51 00 15. The town's best Chinese restaurant with an enormous central aquarium and giant Ming vases, with the usual dishes from 115kr. They also have a number of Szechuan mains for 115–170kr and an evening Mongolian barbecue and Korean buffet at 135kr. Mon–Thurs 11am–10pm, Fri 11am–11pm, Sat 1–11pm, Sun 2.30–9pm.

En Liten Röd Brogränd 19 ☎063 12 63 26. A cosy neighbourhood restaurant with a good choice of meat dishes from 235kr and a selection of fondues: chocolate fondue for two people (145kr), cheese fondue for two (235kr) and a delicious seafood fondue for four people (565kr). All fondues, except the meat one, should be ordered one day in advance. Mon–Sat 5–10.30pm.

★ **Paviljong** Prästgatan 50B ☎063 13 00 99. The modest interior decor may suggest otherwise, but this is the best Indonesian/Thai restaurant in central Sweden – make the most of it, and try the excellent massamam chicken curry or chicken with garlic chilli and Thai basil (both 129kr). Mon–Thurs & Sun 1–9pm, Fri & Sat 1–10pm.

Sir Winston Prästgatan 19 ☎06310 68 00. An English-style pub with carpets, wooden wall panels and chandeliers overlooking the main square with locally sourced mains like elk entrecôte marinated in juniper (245kr), Arctic char with crayfish tails (195kr) and burgers with smoked ham from Jämtland (135kr). Mon–Fri & Sun 4pm–midnight, Sat 4pm–1am.

8

GO WEST: PILGRIMS AND VIKINGS

Heading west from Östersund, the **E14** and the **train** line follow the course trudged by medieval **pilgrims** on their way to Nidaros (now Trondheim in Norway) over the border, a twisting route that threads its way through sharp-edged mountains rising high above a bevy of fast-flowing streams and deep, cold lakes. Time and again, the eastern **Vikings** assembled their armies beside the holy Storsjön lake to begin the long march west, most famously in 1030, when King Olaf of Norway collected his mercenaries for the campaign that led to his death at the Battle of Stiklestad.

Today, although the scenery is splendid, the only real attractions en route are the winter skiing and summer walking centres of **Åre** (see p.308) and **Storlien** (see p.309).

★ **Törners Konditori** Storgatan 24. A modern Euro-café rather than a traditional Swedish *konditori* with a good selection of cakes, pastries, sandwiches and quiches; this is the best and largest café in town, perfect for people-watching. Mon–Fri 7.30am–7pm, Sat 9am–5pm, Sun 11am–5pm.

Åre

The alpine village of **Åre**, 100km west of Östersund, is Sweden's most prestigious ski resort, with over forty lifts, 110 ski slopes and guaranteed snow between December and May. In summer, the village is a quiet, likeable haven for ramblers, sandwiched as it is between the Åresjön lake and a range of craggy hills that's overshadowed by Sweden's seventh highest peak, the mighty **Åreskutan** mountain (1420m).

Kabinbanan

A cable car, the **Kabinbanan** (125kr return), whisks you from just behind Storlien's main square to the viewing platform (1274m) and *Stormköket* restaurant (mid-Feb to late April & late June to late Sept daily 10am–4.30pm), some way up Åreskutan. The ride takes just seven minutes, and it'll take you a further thirty minutes to clamber to the summit. Wear sensible shoes and warm clothes, as the low temperatures are intensified by the wind, and it can be decidedly nippy even in summer. From the top the view is stunning – on a clear day you can see over to the border with Norway and a good way back to Östersund. There's a tiny wooden **café**, *Toppstugan*, at the summit, serving coffee and extortionately priced sandwiches. Even the shortest route back down to Åre (2hr) requires stamina; other, longer, paths lead more circuitously back down to the village. One word of warning: there are phenomenal numbers of **mosquitoes** and other insects up here in July and August, so make sure you are protected by repellent.

Åre Gamla kyrka

In the centre of town, **Åre Gamla kyrka** (use the key hanging on a hook outside the door to get in), just above the campsite, is a marvellous thirteenth-century stone building: inside, the simple blue decoration and the smell of burning candles create a peaceful ambience.

ARRIVAL AND DEPARTURE   ÅRE

By train Åre train station is known as Station Åre and is located at St Olafsväg 35.
Destinations Gothenburg (1 daily; 14hr); Östersund (3 daily; 1hr 45min); Stockholm (1 daily; 10hr); Trondheim (2 daily; 2hr 30min)
By bus Though buses pull up right outside the train station, the only service you're likely to want to take is the twice-daily one to Östersund (1hr 30min).

INFORMATION

Tourist office Station Åre, St Olavsväg 35 (May to mid-June & early Sept to mid-Dec Mon–Fri 10am–6pm, Sat & Sun 10am–3pm; rest of year daily 9am–6pm; ☎ 0647 177 20, ⊚ are360.com). Station Åre also contains a supermarket, cash machines and the library, which is where you'll find internet access.
Ski rental Ski equipment isn't that expensive to rent: downhill and cross-country gear starts at 290kr/day from *Skistar Shop* (☎ 0771 84 00 00) and *Hanson* (☎ 0647 520 00), both in the main square.

ACCOMMODATION

During the **ski season**, rooms here are like gold dust and prices sky high: book accommodation for this period well in advance through the tourist office or, better still, take a package trip. In summer, however, most places are either closed or only take groups, but it's worth asking the tourist office about fixing up a **private room** (from around 250kr per person), almost all of which will have a kitchen, shower and TV.

Åre torg Hotell In the park below the square ☎ 0647 515 90, ⊕ info@hotellaretorg.se. The cheapest place to stay is this unofficial youth hostel, with bright, airy dorms sleeping 4–5 people. Dorms **190kr/240kr**

Holiday Club Åre Strand ☎ 0647 120 00, ⊚ holidayclub .se. This lakeside hotel is a whole resort in itself, comprising top-notch Scandinavian-design rooms and apartments as well as a swimming pool, spa and bowling alley. **1730kr**

HIKING AND BIKING AROUND ÅRE

A network of tracks crisscrosses the hills around Åre; ask the tourist office for the excellent *Hikebike.se and Sommarguiden* booklets, which will tell you all you need to know. A popular hiking route south of nearby Storlien is the **Jämttriangle**, from Sylarna STF *fjällstation* mountain lodge (☎0647 722 00, ⓦstfsylarna.com; dorms 250kr, doubles 800kr) via the one at Blåhammaren (☎0647 722 00, ⓦ.stfblahammaren.com; dorms 375kr, doubles 1000kr) to Storulvån (☎0647 722 00, ⓦstfstorulvan.com; dorms 260kr, doubles 1200kr), which takes in fantastic wilderness scenery close to the Norwegian border and involves overnight stays in the mountain lodges. The mountains around Åre are also as good a place as any to go **mountain biking**; the tourist office can help sort out a bike for you and has information about a series of trails, known collectively as Åre Bike Park.

EATING AND DRINKING

Broken Årevägen 80 ☎0647 506 33. A small and snug yet incredibly popular American bar and grill restaurant, open all year, with fajitas for 125kr, burgers from 105kr and a range of fresh salads, including a good tuna nicoise, from 110kr. Mon–Thurs 4pm till late, Fri–Sun noon till late.

Dahlbom på Torget Årevägen 78 ☎0647 508 20. A smart brasserie offering mushroom pasta, Asian salad with chilli-and-lime-baked salmon and other international fare such as steak in bearnaise sauce; mains are 159–265kr. Mon–Sat 5pm–late.

★ **Villa Tottebo** Parkvägen 1 ☎0647 506 20. The best food in town can be sampled at a former wood-panelled hunting lodge from 1897 opposite the train station. It cooks up gourmet meat and fish dishes, including game meatballs, ox cheek with haricot verts and roast beef for 160–280kr. Ski season only daily 6–11pm.

Weréns Årevägen 101 ☎0647 66 55 60. With its walls of white tiles, this stylish brasserie is extremely popular and even allows you to fry your own meat at table during the winter. During the summer months, it's a pizza place – 95kr will buy one. Mon–Fri & Sun 5pm till late, Sat noon till late.

Storlien

Just 6km from the Norwegian border and linked to Åre by infrequent train, **tiny STORLIEN** is an excellent place to stop if you're into hiking, surrounded as it is by rugged, scenic terrain. The **southern stretch of the Kungsleden** (see p.343) starts here and winds its way south via Sweden's southernmost glacier on the slopes of Helagsfjället, continuing on to Tänndalen and Grövelsjön, terminating on the hills above Sälen. Storlien is also prime berry-picking territory (the rare cloudberry grows here); mushrooms can also be found in great numbers hereabouts, in particular the delicious chanterelle. Storlien is little more than a couple of streets and a supermarket amid open countryside.

ACCOMMODATION AND EATING

Storvallens fjällgård Vackerlidsvägen 9 ☎0647 700 58; a 4km walk across the tracks from the train station to the E14 and then left down the main road. A pleasant mountain lodge with a total of 46 beds in rooms sleeping up to four people and self-catering kitchens. Dorms <u>250kr</u>, doubles <u>500kr</u>

Le Ski Vintergatan 25 ☎0647 701 51. The best bet for a bite to eat is this restaurant and bar at the station, which has cheapish eats for lunch and dinner; the sliced reindeer with mashed potato for just 125kr is a winner every time, while there are more substantial steaks for 169kr. Daily 11am–9pm.

8

Swedish Lapland

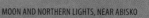

MOON AND NORTHERN LIGHTS, NEAR ABISKO

9

Swedish Lapland

Swedish Lapland, the heartland of the indigenous *Sámi* people, is Europe's last wilderness, characterized by seemingly endless forests of pine and spruce, thundering rivers that drain the snow-covered fells and peaceful lakeside villages high amongst the hills. The irresistible allure of this vast and sparsely populated region is the opportunity to experience raw nature at first hand. This unsullied corner of the country is a very long way away for many Swedes; in terms of distance, Gothenburg, for example, is closer to Venice than it is to Kiruna. The reputation of the local people for speaking their mind or, alternatively, not speaking at all, has confirmed the region's image within Sweden: remote, austere yet still rather fascinating.

One constant reminder of how far north you've come is the omnipresent **reindeer** that are still fundamental to the livelihood of many families here, but the enduring *Sámi* culture, which once defined much of this land, is now under threat. Centuries of mistrust between the *Sámi* and the Swedish population have led to today's often tense standoff; *Sámi* accusing Swede of stealing their land, Swede accusing *Sámi* of scrounging off the state. Back in 1986, the Chernobyl nuclear accident led to a fundamental change in *Sámi* living patterns: the fallout affected grazing lands, and even today the lichen (the reindeer's favourite food) in certain parts of the north is unfit for consumption, a fact which the *Sámi*, perhaps understandably, are keen to play down. The escalating problems posed by tourism – principally the erosion of grazing land under the pounding feet of hikers – have also made the *Sámi*'s traditional existence increasingly uncertain.

The best way to discover more about *Sámi* culture is to drive the 360km-long **Wilderness Way** (Vildmarksvägen) from **Strömsund**, a notable canoeing centre, over the barren Stekenjokk plateau to isolated **Fatmomakke**, a church town of dozens of traditional wooden *kåtor* (huts) beside the steely waters of Kultsjön lake. The road terminates at **Vilhelmina**, another tiny church town which makes an interesting diversion on the way north. **Storuman** and neighbouring **Sorsele** have handy train and bus connections that are useful access points for a small handful of charming mountain villages close to the Norwegian border, where hiking is the main draw. More accessible **Arvidsjaur**, reached by the Inlandsbanan offers a fascinating insight into indigenous culture at its *lappstad*, a diverting collection of religious dwellings and storehuts.

However, it's **Jokkmokk**, just north of the **Arctic Circle**, that is the real centre of *Sámi* life – not least during its Winter Market when thousands of people brave the chill to buy and sell everything from reindeer hides to wellington boots. Moving further north,

TENT PITCHED ON THE ROUTE OF THE KUNGSLEDEN HIKING TRAIL

Highlights

❶ Vildmarksvägen By bus or your own car, the Wilderness Way really lives up to its name offering a taste of nature in the raw and some great *Sámi* sites, too. **See p.316**

❷ Lappstaden, Arvidsjaur The square timber huts and cabins at this *Sámi* church town offer an insight into the life of Sweden's indigenous people. **See p.325**

❸ The Arctic Circle, Jokkmokk Crossing the magic line gives real sense of achievement and here's undoubtedly the best place to see the midnight sun. **See p.329**

❹ Icehotel, Jukkasjärvi Spend a night in a thermal sleeping bag in this awe-inspiring hotel constructed from snow and ice, where the interior temperature hovers at a chilly -5ºC. **See p.341**

❺ Kungsleden trail Don your hiking boots and discover Sweden's longest trail which winds its way through some of the most haunting scenery the north has to offer. **See p.343**

❻ Northern lights, Abisko Witness one of the most breathtaking sights in the world in the far north of Swedish Lapland. **See p.345**

HIGHLIGHTS ARE MARKED ON THE MAP ON P.314

9 the iron-ore mining centres of **Gällivare** (where the Inlandsbanan ends) and **Kiruna** share a rugged charm, though it's undoubtedly the world-famous **Icehotel** in nearby **Jukkasjärvi** that is the real winter draw. Beyond, the rugged **national parks** offer a chance to hike and commune with nature like nowhere else: the **Kungsleden trail** runs for 500km from the tiny village of **Abisko** – oddly, yet reassuringly for hikers, the driest place in all of Sweden – to **Hemavan**, northwest of Storuman, through some of the most gorgeous stretches anywhere in the Swedish mountains.

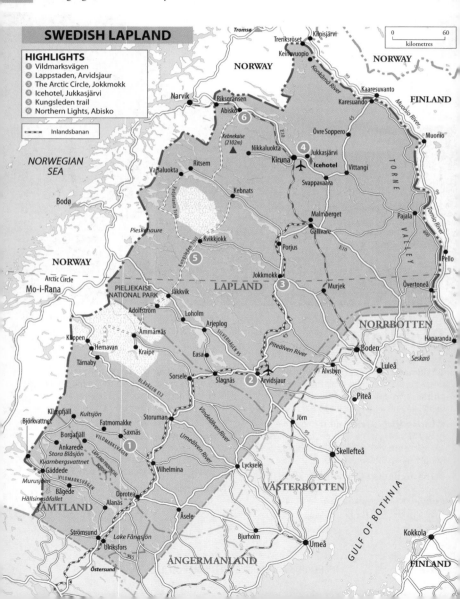

SWEDISH LAPLAND

HIGHLIGHTS
1. Vildmarksvägen
2. Lappstaden, Arvidsjaur
3. The Arctic Circle, Jokkmokk
4. Icehotel, Jukkasjärvi
5. Kungsleden trail
6. Northern Lights, Abisko

▭▭▭ Inlandsbanan

0   60
kilometres

LAPLAND, LAPPLAND OR SÁPMI

Whilst Lapland's strong cultural identity is evident in every town and village across the north, it's a much trickier task to try to pin down the region geographically. The word **Lapland** means different things to different people. Mention it to a Swede (the Swedish spelling is **Lappland**) and they'll immediately think of the northern Swedish province of the same name which begins just south of Dorotea, runs up to the Norwegian and Finnish borders in the north, and stretches east towards (but doesn't include) the Bothnian coast. For the original inhabitants of the north, the *Sámi*, the area they call **Sápmi** (the indigenous name for Lapland) extends from Norway through Sweden and Finland to the Russian Kola peninsula, an area where they've traditionally lived a semi-nomadic life, following their reindeer from valley bottom to fell top. Most foreigners have a hazy idea of where Lapland is; for the sake of this guide, we've assumed Swedish Lapland (the English spelling) to be located within the borders of the administrative province of Lappland but have included all of Route 342 – The Wilderness Way, or Vildmarksvägen – beginning in Strömsund (see below), which crosses into Lappland, as well as the Torne Valley, which also lies partly within the province.

Strömsund and routes north

Around 7.15am every morning between June and August (exact times at ⓦgrandnordic.se), the Inlandsbanan sets out from Östersund (see p.303) on its fifteen-hour journey to Gällivare, north of the Arctic Circle. Just outside Östersund, the train crosses the Indalsälven River, one of Sweden's greatest natural sources of power, the first sure sign that civilization is slowly being left behind and only the wilds of nature lie ahead. Indeed, it's a good hour and a half before the train makes the first stop of any significance: Ulriksfors, the wayside halt for the small waterside town of **Strömsund**, which is the starting point for Route 342, the **Wilderness Way** (*Vildmarksvägen*), a circular road looping out towards the Norwegian border. The route passes through stunning scenery more than worthy of its name, rejoining the main Inlandsvägen in Vilhelmina which, in turn, is directly linked to Strömsund via the appealing little town of **Dorotea**.

Strömsund and around

Built on a narrow isthmus of land between Russfjärden lake and the extensive **Ströms Vattudal** network of **waterways** that stretches to the northwest, **STRÖMSUND** is a shy and retiring sort of place. It consists of no more than a couple of parallel streets sporting the odd shop or two, and is of interest mainly as a centre for **canoeing** (around 200kr/day) and also provide information – walking routes, details of places to stay and maps – on the road known as the **Wilderness Way** (see p.316), which starts here.

Stone age rock paintings

Strömsund's other claim to fame is its proximity to the impressive **Stone Age rock paintings** (*hällmålningar* in Swedish) at **Fångsjön**, around 10km southeast along Route 345. The paintings, created by hunter-gatherers around 2500BC, were a plea to their gods for plentiful game.

ARRIVAL AND INFORMATION **STRÖMSUND**

By public transport and taxi Although there's no actual train station in Strömsund, you can get off at nearby Ulriksfors and walk the 4km into town or take a taxi (pre-booking essential on ☎020 45 00 45; 100kr). The Inlandsexpressen bus #45 stops in the town itself.

Tourist office Storgatan 6 (late June to mid-Aug Mon–Fri 10am–6pm, Sat 10am–3pm; mid-Aug to late June Mon–Fri 9am–noon & 1–4pm; ☎0670 164 00, ⓦstromsund.se). The office is in the centre of town, and rents bikes for around 150kr/day.

9

GETTING AROUND SWEDISH LAPLAND

Covering a whopping 110,000 square kilometres – an area only fractionally smaller than the whole of England – Swedish Lapland is inevitably going to make getting from one place to another take up a lot of time. During the short summer months, the **Inlandsbanan** provides the easiest and most enjoyable form of transport. Slowly snaking its way across the northern hinterland, the train often has to stop so that elk and reindeer – and occasionally bears – can be cleared from the tracks, and it often stops at least once for a bite to eat or a cup of coffee in a wayside café. At the **Arctic Circle** it stops again, so that everyone can jump off and take some photos. The train terminates in Gällivare, 100km north of the Arctic Circle, where there are mainline train connections linking most of the major centres and attractions.

Route 45 – the **Inlandsvägen** – is the best **road** north through Swedish Lapland; from Östersund, it sticks close to the train line on its way to Gällivare. It's easy to drive and well surfaced for the most part, although watch out for reindeer with a death wish – once they spot a car hurtling towards them they seem to do their utmost to throw themselves in front of it. You could drive from Östersund to Gällivare in a day if you left very early and put your foot down, but you're better off taking it in stages. Bus #45 (ⓦlanstrafiken-z.se), the daily **bus** service that runs from Östersund to Gällivare, follows Route 45; it's not as much fun as the train, but is faster and very comfortable.

ACCOMMODATION

Grand Bredgårdsvägen 4 ☎0670 61 10 00, ⓦhotel nordica.se/grand. Dominating Strömsund since 1909, this venerable old place right in the centre of town has smart, bright rooms with high ceilings and generously proportioned windows. Guests also have free use of the sauna. 995kr/1395kr

Strömsunds Camping Strömsvägen 38 ☎0670 164

10, ⓦstromsundscamping.com. On the outskirts of town – about 1km out – on the way to Östersund, this peaceful campsite has three heated outdoor pools, and reasonably priced cabins to rent. Open all year round, though outside the June–Aug period check-in is at the tourist office. Tents 140kr, cabins 350kr

EATING

Annexet Grill Huset Lövbergavägen 1 ☎0670 61 40 00. No-nonsense burgers, kebabs and Mexican burritos (all around 75kr) are dished up here in a small restaurant on

the main road through town. Elegant it certainly isn't but in Strömsund you can't afford to be too choosy. Mon–Sat 10am–10pm, Sun 11am–10pm.

Vildmarksvägen: the Wilderness Way

From Strömsund, **Route 342**, the 360km-long **Wilderness Way** (*Vildmarksvägen*), strikes out northwest towards the mountains at Gäddede, before hugging the Norwegian border and crossing the barren Stekenjokk plateau (876m; only open from early June to mid-Oct). It then swings inland again, joining Route 45 at Vilhelmina. The route ranks as one of the most beautiful and dramatic in Sweden, passing through great swathes of **virgin forest**, tiny forgotten villages and true wilderness. It's also the part of Sweden with the densest population of **bears**. If you're driving, stop wherever you can, turn off the engine and listen to the deep silence, broken only by the calls of the birds and the whisper of the forest.

There are plenty of **lakes** along the way ideal for nude bathing – you can choose whichever one you want to make your own as there'll be nobody else there. One of the most beautiful stretches of rocky beach is just south of the tiny village of Alanäs on the beautiful Flåsjön lake, before you get to Gäddede.

Hällsingsåfallet

If you have your own transport, you should turn left at **Bågede** and follow the minor, very rocky road along the southern shore of **Fågelsjön lake** to reach **Hällsingsåfallet**, an impressive **waterfall**. Sweden's answer to Niagara Falls, it has an 800m-long canyon,

TRAVELLING THE WILDERNESS WAY BY BUS

The #425 **bus** runs from **Strömsund** to **Gäddede**. There's one daily service and two buses on Fridays (W lanstrafiken-z.se). Travelling on a Friday is best since you can take the first bus, get off wherever you like (just tell the driver to stop), and spend the late afternoon and early evening walking or chilling out by the side of a lake and then continue on to Gäddede. On weekdays the bus connects in Gäddede with the #472 to Stora Blåsjön and Anakarde, beside the pretty Stora Blåsjön lake.

GETTING OVER THE STEKENJOKK PLATEAU

There's no bus connection from Stora Blåsjön over the Stekenjokk plateau to **Klimpfjäll**, from where bus #420 runs down to Saxnäs and Vilhelmina (Mon–Fri 2 daily, Sat & Sun 1 daily; W tabussen.nu). However, there are three options to cross into Lappland: take a **taxi** from Stora Blåsjön (T 0672 201 53); **hitch** between the two places – there are a lot of German and Dutch camper vans on this stretch of the road who may be able to help out with a lift over the plateau; or **hike** from Ankarede towards Raukasjön lake before heading north up over the Norra Borgafjällen mountains for Slipsiken lake and down into Klimpfjäll – a distance of approximately 40km, best covered over two days.

into which the falls plummet 43m; the canyon's that's getting longer every year due to continuing erosion.

Gäddede and Murusjöen lake

The only town along the route is **Gäddede**, whose name means "the spot where the northern pike can no longer go upstream". The name may be cute but the place certainly isn't; give it a miss and instead turn off the main road and follow the road signed "Nordli" for a few kilometres to the long and empty sandy beaches of **Murusjöen lake**, right on the border with Norway (the beach is in Sweden, the water in Norway). You'll be hard pushed to find a more idyllic spot: the silence is total, the deep blue water still and calm, and the mountains in the distance dark and brooding.

Stora Blåsjön and Ankarede

Stora Blåsjön, a lake 50km to the north of Gäddede, is surrounded by blue mountains; the village of Stora Blåsjon is where the road starts to climb above the tree line to cross the desolate, boulder-strewn **Stekenjokk plateau** into the province of Lappland. Just outside Stora Blåsjön, look out for the minor road leading to **Ankarede**, an age-old meeting place for the local *Sámi*; even today, families from Sweden and Norway get together here at midsummer and again in the autumn. Its old wooden **church** dates from 1896 and is located by the lake, between the two rivers. In addition there are around twenty circular *Sámi* wooden huts – *kåtor* – close by. The Stekenjokk plateau is the temporary summer home of several *Sámi* families, who tend their reindeer on the surrounding slopes, including those of the magnificent peak of **Gervenåkko** (1141m) to the east of the road.

Fatmomakke

After dropping into the minuscule village of **Klimpfjäll**, the Way continues east. Taking the first turn to the left, after about 12km and then following the signs, you'll reach **Fatmomakke**, a fascinating *Sámi* **church town** made up of eighty *kåtor* and twenty cottages, gathered neatly around the church, and twenty log cabins lined up by the side of Kultsjön lake. The first church on the site was built in 1790, but the *Sámi* met together here long before that for special religious celebrations including marriages, christenings and funerals, travelling vast distances on skis, horseback or by boat to reach here. The huts are made out of birch wood, with a hole in the roof to let the smoke out, and birch twigs on the floor to sit on. Everything inside is orderly, the fireplace in the middle, the cooking area at the back; there's a strict code of behaviour

9

as well – you must first wait in the entrance before being invited to enter. Look out for the signposted *visningskåta*, the "show hut" to the right of the church up on the hill, and have a peek inside.

Saxnäs

About 20km further east of Fatmomakke, the lakeside hamlet of **SAXNÄS** is as good a place as any to break your journey and enjoy some of the magnificent scenery hereabouts. It's also a good spot for adventure activities, or some pampering at the spa resort (see below). If you're keen to get out exploring, the resort also rents out mountain bikes, canoes, fishing tackle and motor boats and in winter, arranges dog-sledding trips and snow-mobile rental.

ACCOMMODATION

Kultsjögården Kultsjögården ☎0940 700 44, ⓦkultsjogarden.se. A nicely located STF hostel with views of the Marsfjällen mountains. Guests have access to a fully fitted kitchen for self-catering or can opt for half board. Dorms 200kr, doubles 400kr

Saxnäsgården ☎0940 377 00, ⓦsaxnas.se. A health complex and spa resort combined, this wilderness hotel also has lakeside cabins for rent, with open fireplaces and a sauna. There's a divine 34°C swimming pool, herbal health baths, massage facilities, saunas, a fitness centre and sports hall, too. Also rents out a whole heap of outdoor equipment (see above). Cabins 950kr, doubles 1100kr

North to Dorotea

Avoiding the Wilderness Way detour, it's possible to head directly north from Strömsund both along the Inlandsbanan and the Inlandsvägen to tiny **DOROTEA**, 71km north, a journey of around an hour by rail or road. A textbook example of a linear village, its houses and shops strung out in a long line either side of the main road, Dorotea has a few attractions which merit a stop on the long journey north. For one thing, it has the biggest **bear** population in Sweden; bears regularly wander into town during the night to rummage through rubbish bins for scraps of food.

Jakt och Fiskmuseum

Hunting and Fishing Museum • Storgatan 42 • Mon–Fri 10am–noon & 1–4pm • 40kr

At the top of the village, in the same building as the tourist office, the **Jakt och Fiskemuseum** is a taxidermist's dream: inside, there's a varied collection of stuffed local wildlife, everything from a bear to a wolverine, as well as a tired exhibition of glass boxes containing a motley group of butterflies, grasshoppers and beetles. More interesting, however, is the adjacent **aquarium** where there are live specimens of the bream, perch, pike, trout and Arctic char found in vast numbers in the surrounding lakes.

Last Supper sculpture

Whilst in Dorotea, make sure to see the powerful Björn Martinius group **sculpture** of the Last Supper. Housed in a small chapel in the church graveyard on a low hill just off the main road, the life-size wooden figures sit around three long trestle tables – the very size of the sculpture, filling an entire room, the striking bright colours used to paint the figures, as well as the intense expressions, create a sense of life and motion that's enough to send a shiver down the spine of the most ardent agnostic.

INFORMATION

DOROTEA

Tourist office Storgatan 42 (Mon–Fri 10am–noon & 1–4pm; ☎0942 140 63, ⓦturismlappland.se). Located at the top of the village, a 10min walk along the main road from the train station, and with good advice on local hiking routes and fishing trips.

Internet At the tourist office or the library on Storgatan opposite *Görans Konditori*.

9

ACCOMMODATION

Doro Camping Lappland ☎ 0942 102 38, ⓦ dorocamp .com. Beautifully situated beside the Bergvattenån River, this campsite has two- and four-bed cabins, as well as a number of simple hostel-style double rooms with access to showers and a sauna in the nearby service building. Tents 140kr, cabins 550kr, doubles 450kr

Nordica Bergsvägen 2 ☎ 0942 477 80, ⓦ hotelnordica .se/dorotea. Rooms in Dorotea's one and only hotel are bright and clean though a little lacking in style. There is, however, a decent sauna suite available for guests. 895kr/1195kr

EATING

Ankis Bar & Pizzeria Storgatan 37 ☎ 0942 100 68. Substantial meaty meals for around 100kr, including pizzas and a daily *dagens rätt*. The interior is a little plain and the quality of the food is not great but that doesn't seem to deter the locals. Mon–Fri 10am–8pm, Sat & Sun 10am–9pm.

Görans Konditori Parkvägen 2. A popular café serving the locals for over thirty years and a favourite place for swapping gossip. There's a weekday set lunch as well as a number of open sandwiches and cakes — everything is baked on the premises. Mon–Fri 7am–6pm, Sat 9am–4pm, Sun 11am–4pm.

Vilhelmina

The Inlandsvägen and the Wilderness Way meet up again in the pretty town of **VILHELMINA**, 54km north of Dorotea. Once an important forestry centre, now a quiet, unassuming little place with just one main street, it is named after the wife of King Gustav IV Adolf, Fredrika Dorotea Vilhelmina (as is its southerly neighbour, Dorotea).

Church town

The principal attraction is the **church town**, nestling between Storgatan and Ljusminnesgatan, whose thirty-odd wooden cottages date back to 1792 when the first church was consecrated. It's since been restored, and the cottages can be rented out via the tourist office (see below).

Museum

Storgatan 7 • Daily: June & Aug 10.30am–3pm; July 10.30am–6pm • 30kr

The **museum** here contains a mind-numbingly dull display of local history from prehistoric times to the present day, featuring the likes of an old sledge, a mockup of a former school classroom and a portrait of Queen Fredrika Dorotea V; give it a miss and instead have a look inside the *Sámi* **handicraft store**, Risfjells Sameslöjd, opposite at Storgatan 8 (Mon–Fri 10am–5.30pm, Sat & Sun 10am–4pm).

ARRIVAL AND INFORMATION

By public transport The town's train station on Järnvägsgatan also serves as the bus arrival and departure point.

Tourist office Tingsgatan 1 (mid-June to mid-Sept daily 8am–7pm; mid-Sept to mid-June Mon–Fri 10am÷4pm; ☎ 0940 398 86, ⓦ sodralappland.se). A 10min walk from the train station: head up Postgatan towards the town centre and then turn left into the main street, Volgsjövägen.

ACCOMMODATION

Lilla Granvägen 1 ☎ 0940 150 59, ⓦ lillahotellet. vilhelmina.com. Wonderfully friendly staff are on hand to welcome you to this winning little hotel whose rooms are decorated in cosy, home-from-home style. The new spa in the basement is great for whiling away an hour or two and there's even an osteopath on hand. 850kr/1095kr

Saiva Camping Baksjön ☎ 0940 107 60, ⓦ saiva.se.

The campsite has two- to six-berth cabins for rent and a great sandy beach; to get there walk down the main Volgsjövägen from the centre and take a left turn after about 10min, just before the Volvo garage. Tents 140kr, cabins 290–690kr

Vilhelmina hostel Storgatan ☎ 0940 398 86, ⓔ tuby @vilhelmina.se. Idyllically located in several of Vilhelmina's

9

snug church town cottages, the youth hostel is by far the most atmospheric place to stay, replete with creaking floorboards and low ceilings. Some cottages have their own bathrooms and kitchens. Dorms 240kr, doubles 480kr
Wilhelmina Volgsjövägen 16 ☎0940 554 20,

ⓦ hotellwilhelmina.se. Showy though rather rambling hotel where each room (and the sauna) has stunning views out over Volgsjön lake and the distant mountains. In summer, breakfast is served on the open-air terrace, high above the lake. 850kr/1200kr

EATING AND DRINKING

Krogen Torget 3 ☎0940 108 88. Has simple dishes such as pasta carbonara and meatballs for 65kr, and is also a popular place for a drink or two. There's also a summer beer garden at the rear surrounded by a small hedge. Mon–Sat 10am–9pm, Sun 11am–9pm.
Martin Bergmans fisk Junction of Vildmarksvägen and Route 45 ☎0940 250 90. Accomplished smokehouse and deli serving top-notch smoked salmon and other seafood; plans are afoot to open a restaurant, too. This place can be easily reached on foot from town by walking around 3km along the lakeside path, Strandpromenaden. Mon–Fri 9am–5.30pm, Sat 10am–5pm.
Stenmans Konditori Volgsjövägen 21B ☎0940 128

28. Long-standing and much-acclaimed *konditori* which now has a nice and airy upstairs lounge, as well as outdoor seating in summer. A good choice of panini, salads and home-made quiches as well as coffee and cakes. Mon–Fri 7am–6pm, Sat 9am–5pm, Sun 11am–4pm.
Wilhelmina Volgsjövägen 16 ☎0940 554 20. For something more upmarket, try this hotel's traditional northern Swedish dishes such as Arctic char (165kr). However, the house speciality is pork schnitzel stuffed with Västerbotten cheese and Dijon mustard (155kr). Mains cost 145–275kr. Mon–Fri 10.30am–9pm, Sat 11.30am–8pm, Sun 11.30am–7pm.

The E12: Blå vägen

The one defining factor that unites the small settlement of **Storuman** with its northwesterly neighbours, **Tärnaby** and **Hemavan**, is the **Blå vägen** (Blue Way) or E12, as it is less poetically known, running through all three villages. This major artery, one of northern Sweden's better roads, is so named because it follows the course of the great Ume River that flows down from the mountains of southern Lappland to Umeå on the Bothnian coast. Water is omnipresent hereabouts, not only in Storuman, a sleepy little town which sits on the banks of the eponymous lake, best used as an access point to the mountains, but also all the way up to Tärnaby, a small-time skiing centre, and Hemavan, the start of Sweden's longest and best hiking trail, the Kungsleden, leading 500km north to Abisko.

Storuman

In 1741, the first settler arrived in what was to become **STORUMAN**, 68km north of Vilhelmina. His first neighbours didn't appear until forty years later and even by World War I, Storuman, then called Luspen (the *Sámi* name for a river which emerges from a lake) numbered barely forty inhabitants working just eight farms. Things changed, though, with the arrival of the railway in the 1920s; today Storuman is an important centre for the generation of hydroelectric power. That said, there's not much to the town: the centre consists of one tiny street that supports a couple of shops and banks. Whilst in Storuman check out the town's emblem, **Wildman**, a giant-sized red figure who stands near *Hotell Toppen* (see opposite) madly brandishing a club, a traditional symbol for Lapland encapsulating strength, riches and determination.

Old railway hotel

Arriving at the train-cum-bus station on Järnvägsgatan, you can't fail to spot the wonderful **old railway hotel**, on the opposite side of the street. Built in association with the Inlandsbanan in 1924, the wide-planked, tarred exterior in National Romantic style hides an ornate interior, complete with wrought-iron chandeliers and decorative wall painting (similar to folk art styles found in Dalarna), that's well worth a peek. It now houses the local **library** (Mon & Wed 11am–4pm, Tues & Thurs 11am–7pm, Fri 11am–3pm).

Utsikten tower

If you find yourself at a loose end whilst waiting for buses or trains, one diversion is the worthwhile short walk signed "Utsikten" from the main square, which leads up to a wooden **tower** from where there are fantastic views out over the surrounding lakes and forest towards the mountains which mark the border with Norway; it's around a 2km uphill walk to the platform from the town centre.

ARRIVAL AND DEPARTURE   STORUMAN

Just over an hour by the Inlandsbanan from Vilhelmina, Storuman is a **transport hub** for this part of southern Lapland. From here, **buses** run northwest up the E12, skirting the Tärnafjällen mountains to Tärnaby and Hemavan, before wriggling through to Mo-i-Rana in Norway; in the opposite direction, the road leads down to Umeå via Lycksele, from where there are also train connections to Umeå.

By train The train station is on Järnvägsgatan, along with the bus station.
Destinations Arvidsjaur (summer 1 daily; 3hr); Gällivare (summer 1 daily; 9hr); Jokkmokk (summer 1 daily; 6hr 30min); Östersund (summer 1–2 daily; 5hr); Vilhelmina (summer 1–2 daily; 1hr 30min).
By bus Services from Vilhelmina (⚲tabussen.nu) stop

behind the train station building. A direct bus, Lapplandspilen (⚲lapplandspilen.se), links Storuman with Stockholm.
Destinations Gällivare (1 daily; 6hr); Mo-i-Rana, Norway (2 daily; 4hr 15min); Stockholm (2 weekly; 12hr); Tärnaby (5 daily; 1hr 45min); Östersund (2 daily; 4hr 45min); Umeå (6 daily; 3hr 30min); Vilhelmina (4 daily; 1hr).

ACCOMMODATION

Luspen Järnvägsgatan 13 ☎0951 333 70, ⚲hotelluspen.se. Housed in SJ's former railway offices, this pleasant hotel beside the rail tracks has individually decorated rooms with private facilities. Guests also have access to a kitchen including microwave, cooker and fridge. Also has youth hostel doubles for 400kr. 750kr/850kr
Storumans Bad & Camping Lokgränd 3 ☎0951 143 00, ✉storumanscamping@storuman.se. Lakeside campsite with on-site saunas for guest use, as well as a church built in the style of a *kåta*, a traditional *Sámi* hut;

there are also cabins here for rent. Open mid-June to mid-Aug. Tents 140kr, cabins 680kr
Toppen Blå Vägen 238 ☎0951 777 00, ⚲hotelltoppen .se. With pine and birchwood rooms, this hotel is altogether more luxurious and correspondingly expensive than anything else Storuman has to offer. Cheaper simpler rooms with shared facilities (300kr) and kitchens are in the annexe next door. To get here, walk up Stationsgatan from the station. 850kr/1295kr

EATING AND DRINKING

Café Akkan Skolgatan 23 ☎070 536 62 77. Attached to the library, this is a good place for coffee, cakes and sandwiches and also serves light lunches including quiches and salads. Mon 10am–4pm, Tues–Fri 9am–4pm, Sat 11am–4pm.
Kita's Krog Järnvägsgatan 20C ☎0951 260 30. Opposite the train station, this welcome Thai restaurant, run by a Swedish man and his Thai wife, has a wide range of southeast Asian mains, such as a tasty red chicken curry, for

around 124kr. Mon–Thurs & Sun 11am–8pm, Fri & Sat 11am–10pm.
Toppen Blå Vägen 238 ☎0951 777 00, whotelltoppen .se. Serving locally sourced produce and with a good range of traditional fare such as reindeer and elk, the hotel restaurant here serves the finest food in Storuman. There's also a good lunch menu on weekdays. Mon–Thurs 11am–8.30pm, Fri 11am–7.30pm, Sat noon–6.30pm, Sun noon–5.30pm.

Tärnaby and around

TÄRNABY, 125km northwest of Storuman along the E12, is the birthplace of Sweden's greatest skier, **Ingemar Stenmark**. A double Olympic gold medallist, he occasionally spiced up his training here with a spot of tightrope walking and monocycling. It's a pretty place: yellow flower-decked meadows run to the edge of

9

the mountain forests, the trees felled to leave great empty swathes that accommodate World Cup ski slopes. Since there's not much to do in Tärnaby itself, it's a much better idea to explore the surrounding countryside: a popular **walk** leads across the nearby mountain, **Laxfjället**, which affords fantastic views down over the village – it can be reached by chair lift from either of the two hotels listed (see below). Another good walk for a sunny day leads to the beach at **Lake Laisan**, though the water is rarely warm enough to swim even in the height of summer; to get there, take the footpath that branches off right from the main Sandviksvägen past the campsite or ask the tourist office for precise directions.

ARRIVAL AND INFORMATION   TÄRNABY

By bus The bus station in Tärnaby is at the junction of the main road, the E12, and Granäsvägen. Services from Storuman (1hr 55min) pull in here, in addition to through services to Mo-i-Rana in Norway and Umeå on the Bothnian coast.

Tourist office Västra Strandvägen 1 (mid-June to mid-Aug Mon–Fri 9am–7pm, Sat & Sun 10am–6pm; mid-Aug to mid-June Mon–Fri 9am–5pm; ☎0954 104 50, ⍟hemavantarnaby.se). This office, on the main road, can supply advice about the excellent local fishing.

ACCOMMODATION

Åkerlundska gården Östra Strandvägen 16 ☎0954 104 20, ⍟tarnabyfjallhotell.com. With just a dozen rooms which book up fast, this popular youth hostel is 2km east of the village, located up above the *Fjällhotell*. It has self-catering facilities, too. Open all year round. Dorms 245kr, doubles 570kr

Tärnaby Camping Sandviksvägen 4 ☎0954 100 09, ⍟tarnabycamping.se. A riverside campsite which also has dorm beds and cabins. There's even a sauna for rent,

located beside river rapids for a refreshing dip afterwards. Tents 140kr, dorms 125kr, cabins 550kr

Tärnaby Fjällhotell Östra Strandvägen 16 ☎0954 104 21, ⍟tarnabyfjallhotell.com. Located below the youth hostel, this smart hotel has been providing weary skiers with comfortable, snug accommodation since the mid-1960s. The sauna has amazing 360-degree views out over the surrounding fells. 940kr/1700kr

EATING AND DRINKING

Backfickan Östra Strandvägen 16 ☎0954 104 21. The hotel restaurant is the best place to find some good Swedish home cooking such as *falukorv* sausages with

Västerbotten cheese and local Arctic char for around 150kr; there's also a tolerable pub here. Daily 11am–1.30pm & 6–8pm.

Hemavan

Buses continue from Tärnaby to **HEMAVAN**, 18km northwest, which marks the beginning and the end of the 500km **Kungsleden** trail (see p.343). This tiny, nondescript village, straddling the main road, is totally devoid of attractions. It's purely and simply a service centre which provides accommodation and eating opportunities to hikers starting and ending the trail here. Hemavan can be busy during the peak summer season (mid-June to mid-Aug) and at this time it's therefore wise to book a bed in advance to be sure of somewhere to stay.

ARRIVAL   HEMAVAN

By plane The village is reachable from Stockholm on direct flights (☎0951 305 30, ⍟hemavansflygplats.nu; journey time 1hr 45min).

By bus Bus #31 (⍟tabussen.nu) makes the 2hr drive northwest from Storuman.

ACCOMMODATION AND EATING

Hemavan hostel Renstigen 1 ☎0954 300 02, ⍟hemavansfjallcenter.se. The STF youth hostel here is always busy with hikers, so it's essential to book ahead all year. You'll find a swimming pool, sauna, steam room, jacuzzi and even a climbing wall on site. The in-house restaurant serves a respectable lunch buffet on

weekdays throughout the year and is also open in the evenings for dinner during the ski season. The bar upstairs also serves pub meals and snacks. Mon–Fri 11am–2pm, during winter also Sat & Sun noon–3pm. Dorms 225kr, doubles 530kr

Sorsele and around

The next major stop on the Inlandsbanan north of Storuman (also served by bus from Storuman) is **SORSELE**, 76km away – a pint-sized, quiet little town on the **Vindelälven River**. The town became a *cause célèbre* among conservationists in Sweden when activists forced the government to abandon its plans to build a hydroelectric power station, which would have regulated the river's flow. Consequently, the Vindelälven remains in its natural state today – seething with rapids – and is one of only four rivers in the country that hasn't been tampered with in some way or other.

The big event here is the **Vindelälvsdraget**, a 400km, four-day dog-sled race from Ammarnäs to Vännäsby held in the third week of March. Sorsele is an ideal base for **fly-fishing**: the Vindelälven and the other local river, Laisälven, are teeming with grayling and brown trout, and there are a number of local lakes stocked with char. Ask at the tourist offices for details.

Inland Railway museum

June–Aug Mon–Fri 9am–6pm, Sat & Sun 10am–5pm; Sept–May Mon–Fri 9am–noon & 1–3pm • 20kr

Aside from the river, Sorsele's only other attraction is the Inland Railway **museum**, in the same building as the tourist office, detailing the life and times of the Inlandsbanan; the labelling here is in Swedish only, though there is an English-language factsheet available, which will help make sense of the evocative black-and-white photographs of German troops travelling up and down the line during World War II; during the height of the conflict, the so-called "horseshoe traffic" (named after the shape of the route) saw 12,000 German soldiers and significant amounts of war material transported every week between Narvik and Trondheim in occupied Norway, travelling via Gällivare, Arvidsjaur and Östersund along the Inlandsbanan in supposedly neutral Sweden.

ARRIVAL AND INFORMATION   SORSELE

By train The train station is beside the main road, Stationsgatan.

Destinations Arvidsjaur (summer 1 daily; 1hr 30min); Gällivare (summer 1 daily; 7hr); Jokkmokk (summer 1 daily; 5hr); Storuman (summer 1 daily; 1hr); Östersund (1 daily; 6hr).

By bus Buses stop outside the train station on Stationsgatan.

Destinations Ammarnäs (2 daily; 1hr 15min); Gällivare

(1 daily; 5hr 15min); Östersund (2 daily; 6hr); Storuman (2 daily; 1hr).

Tourist office Stationsgatan 19 (June–Aug Mon–Fri 9am–6pm, Sat & Sun 10am–5pm; Sept–May Mon–Fri 9am–noon & 1–3pm; ☎ 0952 40 90, ⍟ sorsele.se). At the train station, with information about local activities such as fishing and canoe rental.

Internet Free access is available at the village library at Storgatan 11.

ACCOMMODATION

Sorsele Camping Torggatan 3 ☎ 0952 101 24, ⍟ lapplandskatan.nu. A riverside campsite with four-bed cabins. The campsite is also the location for the small STF **youth hostel** whose rooms all have bunk beds but no private facilities; there's a kitchen for self-catering. Tents **100kr**, dorms **225kr**, doubles **470kr**, cabins **595kr**

Sorsele River Hotellgatan 2 ☎ 0952 121 50, ⍟ sorseleriverhotel.se. The only hotel in town is a smart place featuring tasteful rooms with wooden floors and modern furnishings as well as a superb sauna and jacuzzi suite; from the train station, turn left into Stationsgatan, right into Södra Esplanaden, left again into Vindelvägen and finally right into Hotellgatan. **910kr/1075kr**

EATING

Bicaut Café Stationsgatan 16. Inside the Folkets hus community centre, this simple but cheerily painted café, full of bright greens and whites, is a real find. They do a

decent daily set lunch as well as an impressive range of home-made cakes. Mon–Thurs 10am–3pm, Fri 10am–2pm.

9

Sorsele River Hotellgatan 2 ☎0952 121 50. At lunchtime, head for the *Sorsele River* hotel, which has a buffet of tasty local fare (until 2pm); its gourmet restaurant is also open in the evenings for northern Swedish delicacies at around 100–200kr per dish. Mon–Fri 11am–7pm, Sun 2–6pm.

Ammarnäs

The tiny mountain village of **AMMARNÄS**, with a population of just 250, lies ninety minutes' bus ride northwest of Sorsele; the road only reached this remote corner of Sweden in 1939. Set in a wide river valley by the side of the **Gautsträsk lake** and at the foot of the towering **Ammarfjället mountains**, the village offers peace and tranquillity of the first order. This is **reindeer** country (one-third of the villagers here are reindeer herders), and for hundreds of years the local *Sámi* are known to have migrated with their animals from the coast to the surrounding fells for summer pasture.

Brief history

The first settlement began here in 1821 when two *Sámi* brothers, Måns and Abraham Sjulsson, were granted permission to set up home at Övre Gautsträsk. When they failed to keep the terms of their agreement, a new tenant, Nils Johansson, took over. He eked out an existence by cultivating the land and is responsible for *Potatisbacken* or Potato Hill, adjacent to the church at the eastern end of the village at the junction of Kyrkvägen and Nolsivägen (get here by following Nolsivägen from opposite the *Ammarnäsgården* hotel, signed "Norra Ammarnäs"), where the northern Swedish potato (a sweet, yellow variety), is grown – unusual for a location so far north. With the founding of a postal station in 1895, the village changed its name from Gautsträsk (*gaut* is a *Sámi* word meaning "bowl" – an accurate description of its valley-bottom location) to Ammarnäs – the foreland between the Tjulån and Vindelälven rivers. A stone plinth now stands in Nils Johansson's memory across from the church on Strandvägen.

Sámi church town and Samegården

The **Sámi church town**, near the potato hill on Nolsivägen, was built in 1850, and was moved to its present site in 1911. The dozen or so square wooden huts, which are perched on horizontal logs to help keep them dry, are still used today. Three times a year *Sámi* families gather here, much as they have done for centuries, to celebrate important **festivals**: the *Sámi* festival (Sun before midsummer), Vårböndagshelgen (spring intercession day, on the first Sun in July) and Höstböndagshelgen (autumn intercession day, on the last Sun in Sept). The nearby **Samegården** (*Sámi* museum; ring for opening times on ☎0952 602 39) on Strandvägen has a simple display of *Sámi* history and traditions.

Naturum Vindelfjällen

Nature Centre • Tjulträskvägen • Mid-June to mid-Sept daily 9am–5pm • Free

The **Naturum Vindelfjällen** has information about the local geology, flora and fauna, and an unflattering selection of stuffed animals, including bear, lynx and wolverine. It also shows a 1940s film of bears in the woods along the Vindelälven – just ask them to put it on. Look out also for the model of the surrounding peaks, which will give you an idea of just how isolated Ammarnäs is, locked in on three sides by mountains.

ARRIVAL AND INFORMATION   AMMARNÄS

By bus Buses from Sorsele will drop you along the main road, Tjulträskvägen.

Tourist office Ammarnäsgården (mid-June to mid-Sept daily 9am–5pm; ☎0952 600 00, ⓦammarnas.nu). Has plenty of maps and brochures on the surrounding countryside, and useful information on hiking, and can also help with the renting of dog sleds and snowmobiles in winter, and rides on Icelandic ponies.

ACCOMMODATION AND EATING

Ammarnäs Fjällhotell Tjulträskvägen 1 ☎0952 600 03, ⍟ammarnasfjall.se. The only hotel in the village, with rather simple en-suite rooms aimed at hikers walking the Kungsleden; its decent sauna and pool complex in the basement makes up for the lack of creature comforts in the rooms. There are also basic youth hostel dorms in a separate building. The hotel's bar and restaurant are your only eating and drinking options in town. No fixed opening times. Dorms 180kr, doubles 990kr

Ammarnäs youth hostel Nolsivägen 6 ☎0952 602 00, ✉ammarnas.fiskecentrum@telia.com. Virtually opposite the tourist office, the village youth hostel is open all year round and has accommodation in cabins as well as the main building. There's a sauna and a guest kitchen on site, too. Dorms 230kr

Arvidsjaur

An hour and a half by Inlandsbanan and 89km north of Sorsele, **ARVIDSJAUR** was for centuries where the region's **Sámi** gathered to trade and debate. Their presence was of interest to Protestant missionaries, who established the first church here in 1606. The success of this Swedish settlement was secured when silver was discovered in the nearby mountains, and the town flourished as a staging point and supply depot. While these developments unfolded, the *Sámi* continued to assemble on market days and during religious festivals. At the end of the eighteenth century, they built their own church town of simple wooden huts. Today, out of a total population of five thousand, there are still twenty *Sámi* families in Arvisdjaur who make their living from reindeer husbandry, and the town is a good place to get a real hands-on experience of *Sámi* life.

Arvidsjaur is not one of Sweden's more attractive towns – its streets of drab houses strung out either side of the main drag lined with a dozen or so shops make a pretty depressing impression on any first-time visitor. However, although the modern town is decidedly unappealing, it hides one of northern Sweden's top attractions in the traditional *Sámi* village of **Lappstaden**.

Lappstaden

Reached by walking west along Storgatan and turning right into Lappstadsgatan • Always open • Free • Daily tours mid-June to mid-Aug at 6pm, 50kr

A good way to find out more about the *Sámi* culture (which manifests itself more and more as you travel north from here) is to visit **Lappstaden**. Although you probably won't meet any *Sámi* here, you will at least be able to see how they used to live in traditional huts, or *kåtor*. About eighty of these huts in the eighteenth-century *Sámi* **church town** have survived, and are clumped unceremoniously next to a yellow, modern apartment building. The design of these square wooden buildings supporting a pyramid-shaped roof is typical of the Forest *Sámi* who lived in the surrounding forests, constructing their homes of indigenous timber. Local *Sámi* schoolteacher, Karin Stenberg, made it her life's work to preserve Lappstaden and, the huts are still used today during the last weekend in August as a venue for a special **festival**, Storstämningshelgen.

ARRIVAL AND DEPARTURE   .   ARVIDSJAUR

By plane Flights from Stockholm's Arlanda airport land at the modern airport terminal, 15km east of town, which has been designed to resemble a *Sámi* wooden *kåta*; you can get from here to the centre by taxi (☎0960 104 00; 100kr).

By train The train station is at the junction of Järnvägsgatan and Stationsgatan.

Destinations Gällivare (summer 1 daily; 6hr); Jokkmokk

(summer 1 daily; 3hr 30min); Östersund (summer 1 daily; 8hr).

By bus The bus station is in the centre of town at Västlundavägen, just behind the Konsum supermarket.

Destinations Arjeplog (3 daily; 1hr); Bodø, Norway (1 daily; 7hr); Gällivare (1 daily; 4hr); Jokkmokk (1 daily; 2hr 15min); Luleå (2 daily; 2hr 40min); Östersund (2 daily; 7hr).

9

INFORMATION

Tourist office Östra Skolgatan 18C, just off Storgatan (mid-June to mid-Aug Mon–Fri 9.30am–6pm, Sat & Sun noon–4.30pm; mid-Aug to mid-June Mon–Fri 8.30am–noon & 1–4.30pm; ☎0960 175 00, ⓦpolcirkeln.nu). A 5min walk from the train station, up Stationsgatan.

Internet For access, head for the tourist office or the library in Medborgarhuset, Storgatan 12.

Steam train trips Available from Arvidsjaur between mid-July and mid-Aug, featuring vintage coaches from the 1930s. The train runs from Arvidsjaur along the Inlandsbanan west to Slagnäs on Fri and Sat (5.45pm; 200kr), stopping at Storavan beach for swimming and a barbecue. Buy tickets on the train.

River rafting In July and Aug river-rafting trips (☎070 253 0583, ⓦoutdoorlapland.com; 445kr) are possible on the Piteälven River, 45km north of Arvidsjaur. The starting point (reachable by bus) is the Burmabron bridge where Route 45 crosses the river. Tours start at 450kr and vary in difficulty; safety helmets and life jackets are provided.

ACCOMMODATION

If you're planning to visit Arvidsjaur during the winter (when the higher price code applies), it's imperative to book well in advance to secure a room, especially in February and March.

Camp Gielas Järnvägsgatan 111 ☎0960 556 00, ⓦgielas.se. This campsite also has waterside cabins for with TV, shower and running water. It sits beside one of the town's dozen or so lakes, Tvättjärn, with its bathing beaches; there's a sports hall here, too, as well as a gym, sauna, tennis courts and mini-golf. Tents 140kr, cabins 540kr

Lapland Lodge Östra Kyrkogatan 18 ☎0960 137 20, ⓦlaplandlodge.eu. A comfortable bed and breakfast place near the church with brightly decorated rooms in a former manor house. Toilet facilities are shared but all rooms have either a shower or a washbasin. 700kr/850kr

★ **Laponia** Storgatan 45 ☎0960 555 00, ⓦhotell-laponia.se. The sole hotel in town, with 200 comfortable, modern en-suite rooms and a swimming pool; popular with test drivers from Europe's leading car companies between Jan and April when on-demand prices apply. 890kr/1270kr

Silvercross 45 Villavägen 56 ☎070 644 2862, ⓦsilvercross45.se. For inexpensive accommodation this private youth hostel has double rooms with private facilities but no dorm beds. 400kr

EATING AND DRINKING

Afrodite Storgatan 10 ☎0960 173 00. You can sit down here to an Arvidsjaur interpretation of Mediterranean food with pizzas from 70kr, meat and fish mains from 99kr and a few Greek dishes for around 159–199kr. Mon–Thurs 10.30am–9pm, Fri 10.30am–10pm, Sat 11am–10pm, Sun 11am–9pm.

Greya Knut Stationsgatan 20. A nice touch to this welcome café is an interior designed to resemble a wooden cabin; serves snacks, coffee, fresh pastries and bread, and also has cheap lunches, sandwiches (often filled with reindeer meat) and salads; there's outdoor seating here in summer. Mon–Thurs 9am–8pm, Fri 9am–6pm, Sat 11am–4pm.

Around Arvidsjaur: Båtsuoj Sámi Center

Hedgatan 40 • Short visit 220kr; half-day trip 600kr, plus optional overnight stay for an extra 350kr per person • ☎0960 130 14 or ☎070 642 31 66, ⓦbåtsuoj.se • From Arvidsjaur, head west on Route 45 until the village of Slagnäs, from where you take the unnumbered minor road 19km north towards Arjeplog. You can reach Slagnäs by Inlandsbanan, from where Båtsuoj staff will collect you if you book in advance

Seventy kilometres west of Arvidsjaur, in the village of **GASA**, the **Båtsuoj Sámi Center** is a good place to get to grips with the everyday life of the *Sámi*. Here, you'll not only come face to face with **reindeer** (*båtsuoj* in *Sámi*) but also meet real reindeer herders, who'll teach you about their religion and way of life, including the way to milk a reindeer and the tricks of baking their traditional bread; frozen reindeer meat is also available for purchase.

A short visit to Båtsuoj of around an hour or so includes a chance to taste dried reindeer meat sitting around the fire in a *kåta*; a longer half-day trip includes dinner of reindeer cooked over an open fire as well as information about the *Sámi* way of life; you can stay overnight for an extra 350kr per person. The centre also arranges all-day **cloudberry-picking** and medicinal herb-gathering expeditions (Aug; 700kr); the rare cloudberries grow in the most inaccessible of northern Sweden's marshlands – hence the hefty price.

Arjeplog

Stretching northwest of Arvidsjaur out towards the Norwegian border, the
municipality of **Arjeplog**, roughly the size of Belgium, supports a population of just
three thousand – two-thirds of whom live in the eponymous lakeside town, 85km
from Arvidsjaur. It's one of the most beautiful parts of Sweden, with nearly nine
thousand lakes and vast expanses of mountains and virgin forests. The air is clear
and crisp, the rivers clean and deep and the winters mighty cold – in 1989 a
temperature of -52°C was recorded here. January and February, in particular, are
bitter, dark and silent months, but it's during winter that Arjeplog is at its busiest:
hundreds of test drivers from across the world descend on the town to put cars
through their paces in the freezing conditions, with brakes and road-holding being
given a thorough examination on the frozen lakes; the ABS braking system, for
example, was developed here. In summer, Arjeplog is a likeable little place away
from the main inland road and rail routes, where **hiking**, **canoeing** and **fishing** are
all popular activities, each offering the chance of blissful isolation, be it by the side
of a secluded mountain tarn or in a clearing deep in the pine forest. In late July you
can go **cloudberry picking** in the surrounding marshland, and in the autumn you
can hunt for lingonberries, blueberries and wild mushrooms.

Silvermuséet

Silver Museum • Mon–Fri 10am–4pm, Sat 10am–2pm • 60kr • ⓦ silvermuseet.arjeplog.se

Arjeplog town itself is a tiny, unassuming sort of place, barely one main street leading
to what passes as a main square, but is really only a car park between the tourist office
and the **Silvermuséet**, the only sight in town. Housed in a yellow wooden building
opposite the tourist office, it's home to fascinating collections of over 700 pieces of
Sámi silver, including several ornate silver collars that were handed down from mother
to daughter; if a mother had several daughters she would divide her chain amongst
them. Whilst in the museum, make sure to visit the Scinema in the basement, where
you can see a **slide show** about the surrounding countryside and nature and how people
in this remote part of Sweden learnt to adapt to the harsh climate.

Galtispuoda mountain

15km north of Arjeplog; take Route 95 towards Arvidsjaur then turn left where Galtispuoda is signposted

If you're in Arjeplog with your own transport, it's worth making every effort to see
the jaw-dropping panoramic vistas from the top of **Galtispuoda mountain** (808m),
which lies 15km north of the village. On a clear day from the peak, you can see over
130km in all directions across the surrounding marshland and forest with views
extending even into Norway. From this amazing vantage point, you start to realize
just how sparsely populated this remote part of Sweden is: if Stockholm, for
example, had the same population density as Arjeplog it would have just fifty
inhabitants.

ARRIVAL AND INFORMATION   ARJEPLOG

By bus There are daily buses to Arjeplog from Arvidsjaur.
They arrive and depart from the bus station on
Storgatan.
Tourist office In the main square (mid-June to mid-Aug

Mon–Fri 8am–7pm, Sat 10am–5pm, Sun noon–5pm;
mid-Aug to mid-June Mon–Fri 8am–5pm; ☎ 0961 145 20,
ⓦ polcirkeln.nu). Can help with local hiking trails, fishing
and bike rental.

ACCOMMODATION

Bear in mind that in winter (Dec–May), accommodation hereabouts is often booked months in advance by the major car
manufacturers and on-demand prices apply.

9

Hornavan Västra Skeppsholmen 3 ☎ 0961 77 71 00, ⓦ hornavanhotell.se. With gorgeous views out over Sweden's deepest lake, Hornavan, this new hotel, perched atop a small hillock, is a great find: rooms are decorated in modern flat-pack style but quite comfortable. **700kr/950kr**

Kraja A 10min walk along Silvervägen ☎ 0961 315 00. This lakeside campsite has snug and well-appointed cabins as well as a number of double rooms; there's also an outdoor swimming pool which is open to non-residents (free). Tents **140kr**, cabins **795kr**, doubles **995kr**

Lyktan Lugnetvägen 4 ☎ 0961 612 10, ⓦ hotellyktan -arjeplog.se. This central hotel offers comfortable modern rooms of the highest standard, and also incorporates the palatial youth hostel, itself the best-value accommodation in town; every room in the hostel sleeps a maximum of four and has en-suite facilities. Hostel only open May–Oct. Hotel **850kr/1040kr**; hostel dorms **270kr**, doubles **540kr**

EATING AND DRINKING

Harry's Drottninggatan 2 ☎ 0961 101 06. Yes, *Harry's* has even made it to little Arjeplog with yet more signature half-built brick walls and chandeliers in a squat new build opposite the museum. It's steaks and pasta dishes here, mostly for around 150–250kr. A popular place to drink, too. Mon, Tues & Thurs 10am–11pm, Wed 10am–1am, Fri 10am–2am, Sat noon–2am, Sun noon–11pm.

Hornavan Västra Skeppsholmen 3 ☎ 0961 77 71 00. This hotel restaurant is the place to look for expertly prepared Lapland delicacies such as reindeer in its various guises, bear salami and elk heart. More conventional fare, too, such as chicken breast and Arctic char; two courses for around 295kr. Thurs–Sat 5–10pm.

Kraja Värdshus At the campsite ☎ 0961 315 00. For gourmet food where you can tuck into fillet of elk or saddle of reindeer; reckon around 200kr for a main course. From mid-June to mid-Aug food is served in a *Sámi kåta* in the middle of the campsite. Mon–Thurs & Sun 5–11pm, Fri & Sat 5pm–1am.

Mathörnan Drottninggatan 4 ☎ 0961 614 44. Although this place is rather basic to look at, locals swear the quality of the food is good. Serves up moderately priced reindeer, Arctic char and traditional Swedish home cooking at around 150kr per main dish. Mon–Fri 11am–8pm, Sat noon–8pm, Sun 1–7pm.

Jokkmokk and around

During his journey in Lapland, the botanist Carl von Linné said, "If not for the mosquitoes, this would be earth's paradise." His comments were made after journeying along the river valley of the Lilla Luleälven during the short summer weeks, when the mosquitoes are at their most active. Along this valley is the town of **JOKKMOKK**, its name deriving from one particular bend (*mokk* in *Sámi*) in the river (*jokk*). The densely forested municipality through which the river runs is the size of Wales and has a tiny population: just three thousand.

The town is a welcome oasis, although not an immediately appealing one; the prettiest part is around Stationsgatan, which links the train station with the main street, Storgatan, where the wooden houses and shops are oddly reminiscent of small-town America. At one time winter quarters for the *Sámi*, by the beginning of the seventeenth century the site had a market and church, which heralded the start of a permanent settlement. Today, as well as being a well-known handicraft centre, Jokkmokk functions as the capital of the *Sámi* and is home to **Samernas Folkhögskola**, the only further education college in Sweden using the *Sámi* language, teaching handicraft-making, reindeer husbandry and ecology.

Ájtte museum

Kyrkogatan 3 · Mid-June to mid-Aug daily 9am–6pm; mid-Aug to mid-June Tues–Fri 10am–4pm, Sat 10am–2pm · 60kr · ⓦ ajtte.com

Jokkmokk's fascinating **Ájtte museum** (*ájtte* means storage hut in *Sámi*) is the place to really mug up on the *Sámi*; it's a brief walk east of the centre, off the main street, Storgatan. The displays and exhibitions recount the tough existence of northern Scandinavia's original settlers, and show how things have slowly improved over time – today the modern *Sámi* are more dependent on snow scooters and helicopters to herd

9

THE ARCTIC CIRCLE AND THE MIDNIGHT SUN

Just 7km south of Jokkmokk, the Inlandsbanan finally crosses the **Arctic Circle**, the imaginary line drawn around the earth at roughly 66°N, which links the northernmost points along which the sun can be seen on the shortest day of the year. Crossing into the Arctic is occasion enough for a bout of whistle-blowing by the train, as it pulls up to allow everyone to take photos. However, the painted white rocks that curve away over the hilly ground here, a crude delineation of the Circle, are completely inaccurate. Due to the earth's uneven orbit, the line is creeping northwards at a rate of 14–15m every year; the real Arctic Circle is now around 1km further north than this line. It won't be for another ten to twenty thousand years that the northward movement will stop – by which time the Circle will have reached 68°N – and then start moving slowly south again.

Thanks to the refraction of sunlight in the atmosphere, the **midnight sun** can also be seen south of the Arctic Circle – Arvidsjaur marks the southernmost point in Sweden where this happens – for a few days each year. The further north you travel, the longer the period when the phenomenon is visible, and conversely the longer the polar winter. True midnight sun occurs when the entire sun is above the horizon at midnight. The following is a list of the main towns and the dates when the midnight sun can be seen; remember, though, that even outside these periods, there is still 24-hour daylight in the north of Sweden in summer, since only part of the sun ever dips below the horizon.

Arvidsjaur and Haparanda	June 20/21
Arjeplog	June 12/13 to July 28/29
Jokkmokk	June 8/9 to July 2/3
Gällivare	June 4/5 to July 6/7
Kiruna	May 28/29 to July 11/12
Karesuando	May 26/27 to July 15/16
Treriksröset	May 22/23 to July 17/18

---

their reindeer than on the age-old methods employed by their ancestors. The collection of traditional costumes and silver spoons, which gave the owner prestige and were a symbol of social status, is particularly engaging. The museum also has an impressive collection of stuffed eagles and owls; the enormous golden eagle is truly impressive.

Fjällträdgård

Alpine Garden • Lappstavägen • Early June to mid-Aug Mon–Fri 11am–5pm; July to mid-Aug also Sat & Sun noon–5pm • 30kr, 60kr including Ájtte

Close to the Ájtte museum on Lappstavägen, the **Fjällträdgård** is home to moor-king, mountain avens, glacier crowfoot and other vegetation that's found on the fells around Jokkmokk. There's also a small section of edible plants which the *Sámi* have traditionally used for medicinal purposes.

Sámi Duodji

Porjusvägen 4 • Mid-Aug to June Mon–Fri 10am–3pm; July to mid-Aug daily 10am–5.30pm

While you're in town, it's worth popping into **Sámi Duodji**; this *Sámi* handicrafts shops sells a selection of locally produced knives, drinking bowls, leatherware and jewellery and is a good place to pick up a few knick-knacks.

Gamla kyrka

Junction of Hantverkargatan and Köpmangatan • Daily 8am–4pm, until 6pm early June to early Aug

The **Gamla kyrka**, off Stortorget, is a recent copy of the 1753 church on the same site (the original burnt down in 1972). The octagonal design, curiously shaped tower and colours inside the church represent *Sámi* styles; outside, notice the space in between

A BRIEF LOOK AT THE SÁMI

Among the oldest people in Europe, the **Sámi** – erroneously known to many as "Lapps" – are probably descended from the original prehistoric inhabitants of much of Scandinavia and northern Russia. Today there are around 58,000 *Sámi*, stretched across the whole of the northernmost regions of Norway, Sweden, Finland and Russia; traces of their nomadic culture have even been discovered as far south as Poland. In Sweden itself – though the population is declining – they number around 17,000 (ten percent of the population of northern Sweden), their domain extending over half the country, stretching up from the northern parts of Dalarna.

The *Sámi* **language** is a rich one, strongly influenced by their harmonious natural existence. There are no words for certain alien concepts (like "war"), but there are ninety different terms to express variations in snow conditions. One of the Finno-Ugric group of languages, which also contains Finnish and Hungarian, the *Sámi* language is divided into three dialects which are not mutually comprehensible. In Sweden you'll come across two words for *Sámi*: the politically correct *Sámi* (as used by the *Sámi* themselves), and, more commonly, the Swedish corruption *Same* (plural *Samer*).

Reindeer, of which there are estimated to be 250,000 in Sweden (the maximum allowed by law is 280,000), have been at the centre of *Sámi* life and culture for thousands of years, with generations of families following the seasonal movements of the animals. Accordingly, the *Sámi* year is divided into eight separate seasons, ranging from early spring, when they traditionally bring the reindeer cows up to the calving areas in the hills, through to winter, when they return to the forests and the pastures.

The *Sámi* were dealt a grievous blow by the **Chernobyl** nuclear disaster of 1986, which contaminated not only the lichen that their reindeer feed on in winter, but also the game, fish, berries and fungi that supplement their own diet. Contamination of reindeer meat meant the collapse of exports of the product to southern Scandinavia, Germany, America and the Far East; promises of government compensation came late in the day and failed to address the fact that this disaster wasn't just on an economic level for the *Sámi*, their traditional culture being inseparably tied to reindeer herding. However, perhaps as a consequence of Chernobyl, there has been an expansion in other areas of *Sámi* culture. Traditional **arts and crafts** have become popular and are widely available in craft shops, and *Sámi* **music** (characterized by the rhythmic sounds of **joik**, a form of throat-singing) is being given a hearing by fans of world music. On balance, it would appear that the *Sámi* are largely managing to retain their culture and identity in modern Sweden. For more on the *Sámi* in Sweden, visit ⓦ sametinget.se.

the coarsely hewn timbers which was used to store coffins during winter, waiting for the thaw in May when the *Sámi* could go out and dig graves again (temperatures in this part of Sweden regularly plunge to -30°C and below).

The Winter Market

Known simply in Swedish as *Jokkmokks marknad*, the town's 400-year-old **Great Winter Market** (ⓦ jokkmokksmarknad.se) traces its origins back to 1602, when King Karl IX decreed that a series of market sites should be set up in the north to help extend Swedish territory and increase taxes to fund his many wars. A chapel, a parsonage and a row of market sheds were built in Jokkmokk, and the rest is history. Today the market is held on the first Thursday to Sunday of each February, when thirty thousand people force their way into town – ten times the normal population. It's the best (and coldest) time of year to be here; with lots of drunken stallholders trying to flog reindeer hides and other unwanted knick-knacks to even more drunken passers-by, there's a Wild West feeling in the air at this time. Held on the frozen Talvatissjön lake behind *Hotell Jokkmokk* (see p.332), the **reindeer races** run during

CLOCKWISE FROM TOP LEFT INSIDE THE ICEHOTEL (P.341); REINDEER PULLING SLEDS, JOKKMOKK (P.328); LAPPSTADEN, ARVIDSJAUR (P.325) >

9

the market can be a real spectacle, as man and beast battle it out on a specially marked-out ice track. The reindeer, however, often have other ideas and every now and then veer off with great alacrity into the crowd, sending spectators fleeing for cover. A smaller, historical market is held on the proceeding Monday to Wednesday, when people dress in traditional costume and put on various theatrical performances.

ARRIVAL   JOKKMOKK

By public transport From Arvidsjaur, 161km away, it's a 3hr 30min journey to Jokkmokk on the Inlandsbanan, or just over 2hr on the Inlandsexpressen bus. If you're arriving here for the Winter Market, take the train to Murjek (between Boden and Gällivare), from where bus #43 runs west to Jokkmokk.

INFORMATION

Tourist office Stortorget 4 (mid-June to mid-Aug daily 9.30am–6.30pm, Sat & Sun 10am–5pm; mid-Aug to mid-June Mon–Fri 8.30am–noon & 1–4pm; during the Winter Market Thurs–Sat 9am–6pm, Sun noon–4pm; ☎ 0971 222 50, ⦿ turism.jokkmokk.se). The tourist office has internet access and all sorts of literature useful for planning a hike in the region.

Fishing During the summer, Talvatissjön, the lake behind *Hotel Jokkmokk* (see below), is the preferred spot for catching Arctic char and rainbow trout. To fish here you'll need a permit (*fiskekort*), available from the tourist office. There's a barbecue on the lakeside behind the hotel, should you catch anything.

Canoeing It's possible to go canoeing on the unspoilt surrounding lakes and rivers as well as hiking in the nearby national parks. For more information and bookings, contact Jokkmokkguiderna (☎ 0971 122 20, ⦿ jokkmokkguiderna .com), based in the village of Skabram, 3km west of Jokkmokk. They'll collect you from Jokkmokk once you've made a firm booking.

ACCOMMODATION

Since accommodation options in Jokkmokk are rather limited, it's a good idea to book ahead, particularly during the summer months when the Inlandsbanan is running, as well as during the Winter Market, when a reservation is required at least two years in advance (if Jokkmokk is full, try looking for rooms in Arvidsjaur and Gällivare). That said, the tourist office arranges simple dormitory accommodation in the local school for around 250kr per person, and puts together a list of **private rooms** at 500kr per person.

Gästis Herrevägen 1 ☎ 0971 100 12, ⦿ hotell-gastis .com. Handily situated in the town centre, close to the train station, the simple, brightly decorated en-suite rooms here are clean and tidy if lacking in character. There's an attractive sauna suite and a very good restaurant on site. **995kr/1195kr**

Jokkmokk Solgatan 45 ☎ 0971 777 00, ⦿ hoteljokkmokk.se. In a pretty lakeside location, rooms here (ask for one with a lake view) are modern and comfortable. The sauna suite of red-and-white tiles in the basement is one of the best in northern Sweden. **1025kr/1595kr**

Jokkmokk Camping Center Notudden ☎ 0971 123 70, ⦿ jokkmokkcampingcenter.com. Located by the Lule River, 3km southeast of town off Route 97 towards Luleå, this pleasant campsite also has cabins. The best way to get here is to rent a bike from the youth hostel. Tents **140kr**, cabins **695kr**

Jokkmokk youth hostel Åsgatan 20 ☎ 0971 559 77, ⦿ jokkmokkhostel.com. This wonderful old house, surrounded by a pretty garden, has a great central location and cosy double rooms as well as dorms. However, it fills fast so it's wise to book well in advance. Dorms **180kr**, doubles **470kr**

EATING AND DRINKING

Ájtte museum Kyrkogatan 3 ☎ 0971 170 70. For traditional northern Swedish and *Sámi* home cooking, head for the restaurant inside the museum, where lunch deals go for 75kr; there are also a couple of reindeer dishes on the menu. Mon–Fri 9am–4pm.

City Konditoriet Storgatan 28 ☎ 0971 106 50. For pastries and a cup of coffee, try this place on Jokkmokk's main street which also serves up good sandwiches and other light snacks such as quiches and cakes. Mon–Fri 6am–5pm, Sat 9am–2pm.

Gästis Herrevägen 1 ☎ 0971 100 12. You'll find some of the best food in the whole of Swedish Lapland served up here: reindeer steak, Arctic char and other local delicacies are usually on the changing menu but the house speciality is a juicy *plankstek* (planked steak) with accompaniments. Reckon on 200kr per main course. Mon–Fri 10.30am–2pm & daily 6–10pm.

Kowloon Föreningsgatan 3 ☎ 0971 100 85. At this cheap and cheerful restaurant, lunch is 65kr and Chinese meals start at 99kr at other times. Curiously for a Chinese restaurant, it also serves pizzas – albeit none too authentic ones. Tues–Fri 11am–9pm, Sat 1–9pm, Sun 1–8pm.

Opera Storgatan 36 ☎0971 105 05. This is the cheapest place in town for reindeer meat, which is usually available at lunchtime, though there are also pizzas, salads and a range of à la carte meat dishes such as schnitzel and *pytt i*

panna. Mon–Thurs 10am–10pm, Fri & Sat 10am–1am, Sun 10am–11pm.

Thai Muang Isaan Porjusvägen 4 ☎0971 104 00. Very welcome, new Thai place just off the main road serving a range of southeast Asian dishes for around 150kr. There's a weekday lunch buffet until 2pm. Mon–-Fri 11am–8pm, Sat noon–8pm.

Gällivare and around

Seven hundred and fifty kilometres north of Östersund, the Inlandsbanan finally reaches its last stop, **GÄLLIVARE**, two and a quarter hours up the line from Jokkmokk. Although the town is not immediately appealing, it is one of the few relatively sizeable ones in this part of northern Sweden, and it's a good idea to spend a day or two here enjoying the relative civilization before striking out in the wilds beyond – Gällivare is a good starting point for walking in the national parks, which fill most of the northwestern corner of the country (see p.335). The town is also one of the most important areas for iron ore in Europe – if you have any interest in seeing a working mine, don't wait until Kiruna's tame "tourist tour" (see p.339); instead, take a trip down the more evocative mines here.

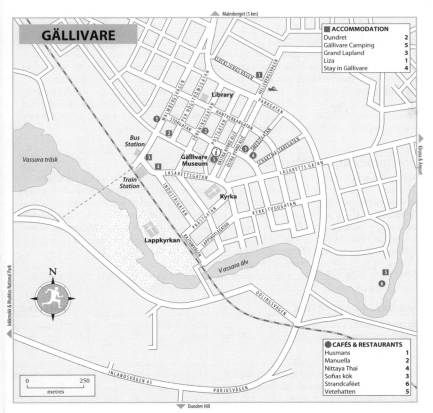

9

Located just north of the 67th parallel, Gällivare has a pretty severe **climate**: as you stroll around the open centre, have a look at the double-glazed windows here, all heavily insulated to protect against the biting Arctic cold.

The site the town occupies was once that of a *Sámi* village, and one theory has it that the name Gällivare comes from the *Sámi* for "a crack or gorge (*djelli*) in the mountain (*vare*)". You may also come across the alternative spelling, Gellivare; pronunciation, though, is the same – "yell-i-vaar-eh".

Lappkyrkan

Lasarettsgatan 10 • June–Aug daily 10am–3pm

The *Sámi* church, **Lappkyrkan**, down by the river near the train station, is a mid-eighteenth-century construction; it's known as the *Ettöreskyrkan* ("1 öre" church) after the sum Swedes were asked to contribute to the subscription drive that paid for its construction.

Gällivare Museum

Storgatan 16 • Mon–Fri 11am–3.30pm; late June to early Aug also Sat & Sun noon–2pm • Free

In the town centre, in the same building as the *Vetehatten* café (see opposite), there's a simple **museum** dealing with *Sámi* history and forestry. Keep an eye out, too, for the curious exhibition about a local man, Martin Stenström, who lived his entire life alone in a cabin deep in the forest.

Midnight sun tours

June to mid-July daily 11pm; mid-July to early Aug daily 10pm • 160kr return • Tickets available from the tourist office

Though there's precious little else to see or do in the town centre, do try to take a tour to the top of **Dundret** hill, one of the two peaks dominating Gällivare, to see the **midnight sun**. Special taxis run from the train station to the end of the winding road which leads up to the top of the hill. Remember that the sky needs to be free of cloud for you to see the midnight sun properly; whatever the weather, though, there are free waffles and ice cream available before the return down to Gällivare.

The mines at Malmberget

Iron-ore mine tours Mid-June to mid-Aug daily 9.30am • 280kr • **Copper mine tours** Mid-June to mid-Aug Mon, Wed & Fri 2pm • 280kr

Tucked away at **Malmberget**, the other hill that overlooks the town, the modern mines and works are distant, dark blots down which the tourist office ferries relays of tourists in summer. There are two separate tours, both running from mid-June to mid-August: one of the underground *LKAB* **iron-ore mine**, the other to the open-cast **copper mine** known as *Aitik*, the largest of its kind in Europe (and also Sweden's biggest gold mine – the metal is recovered from the slag produced during the extraction of the copper). The ear-splitting noise produced from the mammoth-sized trucks (they're five times the height of a human being) in the iron-ore mine can be quite disconcerting in the confined darkness.

ARRIVAL AND DEPARTURE	GÄLLIVARE
By train The train station is on Lasarettsgatan. Destinations Kiruna (5 daily; 1hr); Luleå (5 daily; 2hr	20min); Narvik (2 daily; 4hr); Stockholm (1 daily; 15hr 30min).

INFORMATION	
Tourist office Storgatan 16 (mid-June to mid-Aug daily 9am–7pm; mid-Aug to mid-June Mon–Fri 9am–5pm; ☎ 0970 166 60, ⊚ gellivarelapland.se). A 5min walk from	the train station, with good free maps, hiking information and internet access.

ACCOMMODATION

Advance **bookings** for places to stay in Gällivare are a good idea from mid-June to mid-August, when, thanks to its strategic location at the junction of two major rail routes, the town receives trainloads of backpackers.

Dundret Per Högströmsgatan 1 ☎0970 550 40, ⓦhotelldundret.se. A small, friendly guesthouse with just eight comfortable rooms and shared facilities. There are also larger apartments sleeping up to four people for rent in the adjacent building. Doubles 800kr, apartments 900kr

Gällivare Camping Malmbergsvägen 2 ☎0970 100 10, ⓦgellivarecamping.com. Following recent investments, this campsite is now a pleasant place to stay and enjoys an enviable location close to the centre and right by the river, off Porjusvägen (Route 45 to Jokkmokk). There are also simple cabins with cooking and toilet facilities and youth hostel dorm beds. Open all year. Tents 140kr, cabins 550kr, dorms 200kr

Grand Lapland Lasarettsgatan 1 ☎0970 77 22 90, ⓦghl.se. The best of the bunch in the town centre, with smart, tastefully decorated rooms and a good restaurant; sit in the sauna and enjoy views of the station and the main street below. 1077kr/1775kr

Liza Klockljungsvägen 2 ☎0970 162 00, ⓦlizahotell .se. A new modern hotel with sixty smart, Scandinavian-style doubles in a modern block of red brick resembling a school, close to the swimming pool. There's also a decent sauna on site and free coffee and nibbles available. 1095kr/1495kr

Stay in Gellivare Lasarettsgatan 3 ☎070 216 6965, ⓦgellivarelapland.se. A welcome new venture for Gällivare; offering bright and airy hostel-standard rooms, sharing facilities, but with kitchen and sauna access, handy for the train station. Dorms 300kr

EATING AND DRINKING

Husmans Malmbergsvägen 1 ☎0970 170 30. A simple cafeteria-style place with various Swedish home-style dishes on the menu, plus a variety of burgers, sausages, lasagne and schnitzel: oddly, lunch here is served all day. Mains from around 75kr. Mon–Fri 9am–9pm, Sat & Sun 11am–8pm.

Manuella Storgatan 9 ☎0970/123 80. Another of Gällivare's fast-food outlets, though this one tries hard to be an Italian restaurant, serving a range of pizzas (75kr), including deep-pan varieties, as well as a couple of steaks around 150kr. Mon–Thurs 10.30am–8pm, Fri 10.30am–9pm, Sat noon–9pm, Sun noon–8pm.

Nittaya Thai Storgatan 21B ☎0970 176 85. If you're longing for Thai or Indonesian food, make a beeline to this newly opened restaurant which is delighting the people of Gällivare with the likes of nasi goreng and green chicken curry; mains around 110kr. Mon 10am–2pm, Tues–Thurs 10am–9pm, Fri 10am–10pm, Sat 1–10pm, Sun 1–8pm.

Sofias Kök Storgatan 19 ☎0970 554 50. *The* place in Gällivare for traditional home cooking, such as pea soup with pancakes, pork loin with mushrooms and pan-fried saithe with prawns, that really pulls in the punters. Now a popular place for a beer, too. Mon–Fri 7.30am–1am, Sat & Sun 10.30am–3am.

Strandcaféet Malmbergsvägen 2. Beautifully located campsite café right by the graceful Vassara River with a small range of open sandwiches, cakes and light lunches of quiches, baked potatoes and salads. June–Aug daily 10am–10pm.

Vetehatten Storgatan 16 ☎0970 666 30. A Gällivare institution, right in the town centre and serving up a selection of sandwiches and gooey cakes. There's also the possibility to sit outside here on Gällivare's main shopping street during the summer months. Mon–Fri 6.30am–5pm, Sat 10am–3pm.

Swedish Lapland's national parks

It's not a good idea to go **hiking in the national parks** of northern Sweden on a whim. Even for experienced walkers, the going can be tough and uncomfortable in parts, downright treacherous in others. The best **time to go** hiking is from late June to September: during May and early June the ground is still very wet and boggy as a result of the rapid snow melt. Once the snow has gone, wild flowers burst into bloom, making the most of the short summer months. The weather is very changeable – one moment it can be hot and sunny, the next cold and rainy – and snow showers are not uncommon in summer.

Mosquitoes are a real problem: it's difficult to describe the utter misery of being covered in a blanket of insects, your eyes, ears and nose full of the creatures. Yet the beautiful landscape here is one of the last wilderness areas left in Europe – it's one vast

9

THE LAPONIA WORLD HERITAGE AREA

"It is one of the last and unquestionably largest and best preserved examples of an area of transhumance, involving summer grazing by large reindeer herds", said the UNESCO World Heritage Committee when they established **Laponia** as a **heritage area** in 1996. Covering a vast area of 9400 square kilometres, including the Padjelanta, Sarek and Stora Sjöfallet **national parks**, Laponia is the home and workplace of Forest and Mountain **Sámi** families from seven different villages, who still tend their reindeer here much as their ancestors did in prehistoric times. The Forest *Sámi* move with their herds within the forests and the Mountain *Sámi* follow their animals from the lichen-rich forests, where they spend the winter, up to the tree line by the time spring comes, then on into the mountains for summer; in August they start making their way down. Come September, many animals will be slaughtered either at the **corrals** in Ruokto, on the road between Porjus and Kebnats, or at highland corrals between Ritsem and Sitasjaure.

expanse of forest and mountains, where roads and human habitation are the exception rather than the norm. **Reindeer** are a common sight, as the parks are their breeding grounds and summer pasture, and **Sámi** settlements are dotted throughout the region – notably at **Ritsem** and **Vaisaluokta**.

The hiking trails in the five **national parks** (ⓦ fjallen.nu) here range in difficulty from moderately challenging to a positive assault course. Four of the parks lie about 120km northwest of Gällivare in the tract of Swedish wilderness edging Norway, whereas easy **Muddus** national park lies between Gällivare and Jokkmokk. The low fells, large lakes and moors of **Padjelanta**, **Stora Sjöfallet** and **Abisko** (see p.347) parks act as the eyebrows to the sheer face of the mountainous and inhospitable **Sarek** park. For coverage of the Kungsleden hiking trail, see p.343.

Muddus national park

Recommended for novice hikers, **Muddus national park** is a 500-square-kilometre pine-forested and marshland park between Jokkmokk and Gällivare, hemmed in by the Inlandsbanan on one side and the train line from Luleå to Gällivare on the other. Muddus is home to bears, lynx, martens, weasels, hares, elk and (in summer), also reindeer; among birds, the whooper swan is one of the most common sights. The terrain here is gently undulating, consisting of bog and forest, though there are clefts and gorges in the southern stretches. The park's western edges are skirted by Route 45; the easiest approach is to leave the highway at **Liggadammen** (there are also buses here from Gällivare) and then follow the small road to **Skaite**, where an easy hiking **trail** begins; two suggested routes are Skaite–Muddusfallet–Måskoskårså–Skaite (24km) or Skaite–Muddueluobbal–Manson–Skaite (44km). There are cabins along the trail (April–Sept; at other times the keys can be obtained from Jokkmokk and Gällivare tourist offices), and a campsite at Muddus Falls. There are no outlets for buying food or provisions en route.

Padjelanta

Padjelanta is the largest of Sweden's national parks; its name comes from *Sámi* and means "the higher country", an apt description for this plateau that lies almost exclusively above the tree line. The **Padjelanta trail** (150km) runs from **Vaisaluokta** through the **Laponia World Heritage Area** (see box above) south to **Kvikkjokk**, and is suited to inexperienced walkers – allow at least a week to finish it.

Stora Sjöfallet

You can get to Vaisaluokta by taking a **bus** from Gällivare to Ritsem, which will take you through the beautiful **Stora Sjöfallet** national park with its luxuriant forests and sweeping vistas, from where a boat takes you across Akkajaure lake to Vaisaluokta (details at ⓦstfturist.se/ritsem).

ARRIVAL AND GETTING AROUND

By bus To get to Kvikkjokk, hop on a bus in Jokkmokk. Buses also operate to Ritsem from Gällivare; all bus times are at ⓦltnbd.se.

By helicopter There's a helicopter service, operated by

NATIONAL PARKS

Lapplandsflyg, between Kvikkjokk, Staloluokta and Ritsem (late June to early Sept daily; 1710kr per person over whole route, 950kr over part of route; ☎0971 210 40, ⓦlapplandsflyg.se).

ACCOMMODATION

In addition to the two accommodation options listed below, simpler **cabins** can be found elsewhere along the route and wardens have information about the nearest **food** stores.

Kvikkjokk mountain lodge Kvikkjokk ☎0971 210 22, ⓦkvikkjokkfjallstation.se. Perched on a rocky outcrop above an impressive set of rapids, this STF mountain lodge enjoys a perfect position – mosquitoes notwithstanding. All rooms have a washbasin but other facilities are shared. Self-catering is possible but there's also an on-site restaurant. Open Feb to mid-Oct. Dorms **375kr**, doubles **875kr**

Ritsem hostel Ritsem 4 ☎0973 420 30, ⓦstfturistse/ritsem. Simple, single-storey STF hostel with eighty-odd beds divided into 26 rooms, sharing facilities and a kitchen. The hostel looks out over Akkajaure lake and is perfectly located for accessing the Padjelanta national park. Open mid-Feb to early May & mid-June to late Sept. Dorms **355kr**, doubles **650kr**

Kiruna and around

One hundred and twenty-three kilometres northwest of Gällivare, **KIRUNA** (the town's name comes from the *Sámi* word "Giron", meaning "ptarmigan") was the hub of the battle for the control of the iron-ore supply during World War II; ore was transported north from here by train to the great harbour at Narvik, over the border in Norway. Much German firepower was expended in an attempt to interrupt the supply to the Allies and wrest control for the Axis. In the process, Narvik suffered grievously, whilst Kiruna – benefiting from supposed Swedish neutrality – made a packet selling to both sides. Today the train ride to Kiruna, 200km north of the Arctic Circle, rattles through sidings, slag heaps and ore works, a bitter contrast to the surrounding wilderness.

Partly due to its proximity to the world-famous **Icehotel** in the nearby village of **Jukkasjärvi**, and partly because it's the most northerly town in Sweden, Kiruna has become *the* destination in Swedish Lapland, the place that everyone wants to visit. However, don't come here expecting monumental architectural delights, tree-lined avenues and big-city sophistication – it has none of that, at least not for the time being. All that, however, could change when the town ups sticks and moves location for, indeed, that is what is set to happen over the next decade (see box below). Ahead of the move, the present town still retains a strangely likeable down-to-earth feel. Although there are a few sights, it's mainly attractive as a base from which to visit this corner of northern Lapland, with rail connections northwest to the start of the Kungsleden trail

THAT SINKING FEELING

Due to severe **subsidence** caused by the mines over 1km below the town, Kiruna is sinking. Though it has been decided to move the entire city, the exact location still has to be determined; a favourite choice is to the southeast, near the airport. First to relocate will be the train station and the E10 highway, followed by individual houses, which will be loaded onto trailers for transportation. Oddly, local people seem unperturbed by the enormity of the task ahead, perhaps because they are painfully aware that without the iron-ore mines on which Kiruna is dependent, the place would cease to exist.

9

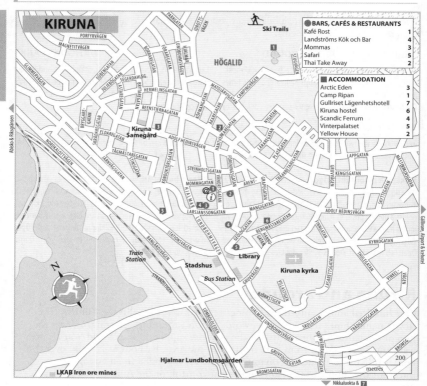

(see p.343) and Riksgränsen, as well as bus connections into the Torne Valley (see p.348). Sweden's highest mountain, **Kebnekaise** (2102m), is also within easy reach of Kiruna. It's accessed from the tiny village of **Nikkaluokta**, the departure point for ambitious ascents of the peak.

Brief history
When Swedish pioneers first arrived in what is now Kiruna in the early 1600s, they found the *Sámi* already in place here. Completely ignoring the indigenous population, the Swedes opened their first mine in 1647 at nearby Masugnsbyn ("Blast Furnace Village"), but it wasn't until the beginning of the following century that the **iron-ore** deposits in Kiruna itself were finally discovered. Exploratory drilling began in the 1880s, which nicely coincided with the building of the **Malmbanan**, the iron-ore railway between Luleå and Narvik in Norway, and the first train laden with iron ore trundled out from Malmberget in Gällivare in March 1888. In 1900, the settlers braved their first winter in Kiruna, a year which is now regarded as the town's birthday. Built on a hill to try to keep the temperature up (warm air rises), Kiruna was planned to withstand the coldest snaps of winter – even the streets are curved as protection against the biting polar wind. Sadly, though, much of the wooden architecture of Kiruna's early days, gloriously painted in reds, greens and yellows, was ripped down to make way for today's unprepossessing concrete structures; the town even won an award in the 1960s for its out-with-the-old-in-with-the-new policy.

SUNRISE AND SUNSET IN STOCKHOLM AND KIRUNA

	Stockholm		Kiruna	
	Sunrise	Sunset	Sunrise	Sunset
January	8.47am	2.55pm	24hr darkness	
February	8.01am	4.01pm	8.59am	2.45pm
March	6.48am	5.12pm	7.02am	4.41am
April	6.17am	7.26pm	5.52am	7.33pm
May	4.52am	8.37pm	3.43am	9.29pm
June	3.47am	9.44pm	24hr daylight	
July	3.40am	10.02pm	24hr daylight	
August	4.35am	9.13pm	3.02am	10.29pm
September	5.46am	7.50pm	5.08am	8.10pm
October	5.54am	5.21pm	5.53am	5.04pm
November	7.08am	3.54pm	7.50am	2.55pm
December	8.19am	2.54pm	10.14am	12.41pm

Stadshuset

Hjalmar Lundbohmsvägen 31 • Mon–Fri 8am–5pm

Not surprisingly, most sights are firmly wedded to iron in one way or another. The tower of the **Stadshus** is a strident metal pillar, designed by Bror Marklund and harbouring an intricate latticework clock face and 23 sundry bells that chime raucously; incomprehensibly, the Stadshus won an award in 1964 for being the most beautiful Swedish public building. Inside, there's a tolerable art collection and, in summer, occasional displays of *Sámi* handicrafts.

The mines

Tours: mid-June to mid-Aug 4 daily; early June & late Aug 2 daily • 295kr

The **mines**, ugly brooding reminders of Kiruna's prosperity, still dominate the town, much more depressingly so than in Gällivare; despite its new central buildings and open parks, Kiruna retains a grubby industrial feel. The tourist office arranges **guided tours** around the mines, on which visitors are bussed down into the *InfoMine*, a closed-off section of the rabbit warren of tunnels comprising a working mine. Inside you'll see facilities such as petrol stations and a workers' canteen, and mining paraphernalia, including trains for transporting ore and equipment, and mills for crushing the ore-bearing rock.

Kiruna kyrka

Gruvvägen 2 • Daily 11am–4.45pm

Standing proud in the centre of town, **Kiruna kyrka** causes a few raised eyebrows when people see it for the first time: built in the style of a *Sámi* hut and the size of a small aircraft hangar, it's an origami-like creation of oak beams and rafters. LKAB, the iron-ore company (and the town's main employer) which paid for its construction, was also responsible for the Hjalmar Lundbohmsgården.

Hjalmar Lundbohmsgården

Ingenjörsgatan 1 • Mon–Fri 10am–4pm • 30kr • ⓦ hjalmarsgard.se

The displays in this country house, once used by the former managing director of LKAB, who was the town's "founder", consist mostly of early twentieth-century photographs featuring the man himself and his personal study, much as he left it. Try to visit the house in order to get a perspective on the town's history before going down the mine; you'll be

9

all the more aware afterwards how, without the mine, Kiruna would be a one-reindeer town instead of the thriving place it is today – quite a feat when you consider its location on the map (don't be surprised to see snow on the slag heaps in the middle of June).

Kiruna Samegård

Brytaregatan 14 • Mon–Fri 7am–noon & 1–4pm • 20kr

For the most rewarding exhibition of *Sámi* culture in town, head for the handicraft centre, **Kiruna Samegård**. The handicrafts you'll see here may well be familiar by now; what probably won't be is its small but impressive display of *Sámi* art featuring scenes from everyday life in the north. It also has a souvenir shop, where you can pick up a piece of antler bone or reindeer skin.

ARRIVAL AND DEPARTURE   KIRUNA

By plane Kiruna is served by flights from London Heathrow (winter only), Stockholm and Luleå. The airport, 10km away to the east, is linked to town by a bus (late June to mid-Sept only; 40kr; ⊛ ltnbd.se) that then continues to Narvik via Abisko; taxis (250kr) run all year round.
By train The train station is at Bangårdsvägen. From

here it's a 10min walk uphill to the tourist office in the main square.
Destinations Luleå (5 daily; 3hr 20min); Narvik (5 daily; 3hr); Stockholm (1 daily; 16hr 30min).
By bus The bus station is at the corner of Biblioteksgatan and Hjalmar Lundbohmsvägen.

INFORMATION

Tourist office In Folkets Hus, on the central square at Lars Janssongatan 17 (late June to mid-Aug Mon–Fri 8.30am–8pm, Sat & Sun 8.30am–5pm; mid-Aug to late June Mon–Fri 8.30am–5pm, Sat 8.30am–2pm; ☎ 0980

188 80, ⊛ kirunalappland.se). From the train station, it's a brisk 10min walk up the steep road, Konduktörsgatan, to the tourist office, where there's also internet access.

ACCOMMODATION

Arctic Eden Föraregatan 18 ☎ 0980 611 86, ⊛ hotelarcticeden.se. A nice combination of wooden floors and brick walls with *Sámi* art and design, this new hotel is one of the best places to stay in Kiruna. There's a small pool and sauna suite available for guest use. 1195kr/2000kr
Gullriset Lägenhetshotell Bromsgatan 12 ☎ 0980 109 37, ⊛ www.fabmf.se. A good choice of bright and breezy modern apartments for one to four people, perfect for self-catering. All have private bathrooms and fully fitted kitchens. There's also a sauna on site for guest use. Two-person apartment 595kr
Kiruna hostel Bergmästaregatan 7 ☎ 0980 171 95, ⊛ kirunahostel.com. Dorm beds (in rooms sleeping up to ten people) are the best option at this centrally located youth hostel though there are also double rooms. Boasting its own sauna, it fills quickly and reservations are necessary at any time of year. Dorms 200kr, doubles 500kr
Scandic Ferrum Lars Janssongatan 15 ☎ 0980 39 86 00, ⊛ scandichotels.se/ferrum. By far the most anonymous place in town, with characterless chain-hotel rooms and indifferent staff, but the palatial sauna suite on

the top floor is a wonderful place to relax and watch the midnight sun. 1200kr/1570kr
Vinterpalatset Järnvägsgatan 18 ☎ 0980 677 70, ⊛ vinterpalatset.se. A listed building with wooden floors, large double beds and rooms decorated with antique furniture. There's also a superb sauna and jacuzzi suite on the top floor. You'll find four cheaper, more basic rooms in the annexe. 990kr/1530kr
Yellow House Hantverkaregatan 25 ☎ 0980 137 50, ⊛ yellowhouse.nu. Budget hotel-cum-youth hostel with dorm beds and double rooms sharing facilities. Linen is not included in the room rate but is available for 60kr extra per stay. Guests also have access to the kitchen and sauna. Dorms 170kr, doubles 440kr

CAMPING

Camp Ripan Campingvägen 5 ☎ 0980 630 00, ⊛ ripan .se. A 20min walk from the centre, this is much more than a campsite. There are ninety well-appointed cabins, imaginatively decorated in Nordic colours and designs, plus, in winter (Dec–April), ice igloos for just 300kr more per person. Tents 140kr, cabins 1195kr

EATING AND DRINKING

Kafé Rost Lars Janssonsgatan 17 ☎ 0980 166 05. This open-plan first-floor café serves up decent sandwiches,

including various reindeer concoctions, as well as quiches, salads and ciabattas. It's also a good place from which to take in Kiruna's goings-on, with an outside terrace in summer. Mon–Fri 11am–6pm, Sat 11am–4pm.

Landströms Kök & Bar Föreningsgatan 11 ☎0980 133 55. A good place to look for some traditional northern home-cooking dishes such as topside of elk, stewed reindeer with mushrooms, smoked whitefish with capers and cured grilled salmon – reckon on 150–225kr per main course. Mon, Tues & Thurs 6–11pm, Wed 6pm–midnight, Fri & Sat 6pm–1am.

Mommas Lars Janssonsgatan 15 ☎0980 39 86 07. Inside the *Scandic Ferrum* hotel, this American-style steakhouse with wooden booths, serves up good burgers (150kr), steaks (220kr) and sautéed reindeer with mash

and lingonberries (155kr). Mon–Thurs 6pm–midnight, Fri & Sat 6pm–2am, Sun 6–11pm.

Safari Geologgatan 4 ☎0980 174 60. A charming café with elegant wallpaper and wooden floors that's easily the best choice in town for tea, coffee, sandwiches, salads and baked potatoes, with outdoor seating in summer and a curiously continental feel. Mon–Fri 9am–6pm, Sat 10am–4pm.

Thai Take Away Föreningsgatan 17 ☎0980 608 44. Sourcing fresh ingredients inside the Arctic Circle is not easy, but this Thai eat-in restaurant manages to serve up some decent dishes, albeit lacking the fire of the original. A good selection of vegetarian (95kr) and meat mains, such as green pork curry, from 125kr, though the lunch buffet is arguably the best deal. Daily 11am–10pm.

Jukkasjärvi village

An obvious destination for any tourist travelling around Kiruna in winter is the tiny village of **JUKKASJÄRVI** (known locally simply as "Jukkas"), 17km east of Kiruna and 200km north of the Arctic Circle, and the location for Swedish Lapland's blockbuster attraction: **Icehotel**. What's effectively the world's largest igloo, *Icehotel* is built every year by the side of the Torneälven River in late October, from when it stands proudly until temperatures rise definitively above zero in May, and it finally melts away back into the river.

Although *Icehotel* totally dominates tiny Jukkasjärvi from its position at the entrance to the village, it's worth taking a stroll down the main (and only) road, Marknadsvägen, passing a handful of simple dwellings owned by locals – not all of whom are in favour of the changes that the hotel has brought to their village.

Icehotel

Marknadsvägen 63 • ☎0980 668 00, ⊕icehotel.com

The brains behind **Icehotel** belong to Yngve Bergqvist, a southern Swede who moved to Lapland in the 1980s. In 1989, he built an igloo – barely sixty square metres in size – as an art gallery to showcase local *Sámi* crafts and design. Visitors asked to sleep in the igloo, and the concept was born. Today, covering a colossal 5000 square metres, *Icehotel* is constructed of thirty thousand tonnes of snow and four thousand tonnes of ice (cut from the Torne River); its exact shape and design changes from year to year, though there's always a chapel, in which couples can marry. From the entrance hall there's usually one main walkway filled with ice **sculptures**, from which smaller corridors lead off to the bedrooms and suites (all with electric lights, and beds made out of blocks of compact snow covered with reindeer hides) that make up the bulk of the hotel.

Staying in the hotel

There are two reception areas – one for cold accommodation (*Icehotel* itself) and another for warm accommodation (double rooms and cabins); simply follow the direction signs. Staff in the cold reception will dish out warm clothing and general information about how to survive a night in sub-zero temperatures. When it's time to go to bed, you should leave your valuables and most of your clothes in lockers provided close to reception (where there are also heated bathrooms with showers and a sauna) and then make a run for it from here to your room (wearing as little as possible; see p.342) and dive into your sleeping bag as quickly as you can – the temperature inside the hotel is −5°C, outside it's generally around −20 or −30°C. Guests are provided with specially made, tried-and-tested **sleeping bags** of a type used by the Swedish army, who have used the hotel for Arctic survival training; the

9

bags are supposed to keep you warm in temperatures down to -35°C. However, as they enclose your entire body and head (bar a small area for your eyes and nose) they are rather claustrophobic. You should take off all the clothes you're still wearing and sleep naked to prevent sweating; stuff your clothes into the bottom of the sleeping bag to keep them warm and place your shoes on the bed with you to stop them freezing. Don't expect to sleep – you won't – it's simply too cold and uncomfortable. In the morning, you can refresh yourself with a sauna and have a hearty breakfast at the restaurant across the road, though you'll soon notice from people's faces that nobody else has slept a wink either.

Activities

There are seemingly countless organized **activities** from the *Icehotel* and the range varies from year to year; full details are online at ⓦicehotel.com. Generally, though, they include a dog-sledding trip through the neighbouring forests with a short stop for coffee and cake (1390kr); an accompanied daytime drive on snow scooters down the Torne River and into the wintry forests (895kr); or a night-time snowmobile spin to see the northern lights (1750kr). In **summer** there are generally organized fishing and hunting tours as well as canoeing, though exact details change once again from year to year and prices are available on the website.

The church

Marknadsvägen 3 • Daily: June–Aug 8am–10pm; Sept–May 8am–8pm

A traditional sight awaits at the end of the dead-end Marknadsvägen: an old wooden *Sámi* **church**, parts of which date from 1608, making it the oldest surviving church in Lapland. Check out the richly decorated altarpiece by Uppsala artist Bror Hjorth, depicting the revivalist preacher, **Lars Levi Laestadius** (see p.349), alongside the woman who inspired him to rid Lapland of alcohol, Maria of Åsele. The triptych was given to the church in 1958 by the mining company, LKAB, then celebrating its 350th anniversary.

Under the floor are the mummified remains of villagers who died here in the eighteenth century (not on display). The sandy ground and frost are thought to have been responsible for keeping the bodies, including that of a woman dressed in a white wedding dress and high-heeled shoes, so remarkably well preserved. The organ above the door is made from reindeer horn and birch wood; the artwork in the centre of the organ, suspended over the pipes, symbolizes the sun rising over the Lapporten (see p. 000), the two U-shaped mountain-tops near Abisko which are one of Lapland's most enduring images.

Nutti Sámi Siida

Sámi Homestead Museum • Marknadsvägen 84 • Daily 11am–5pm • 100kr

Across the road from the church, the wooden houses of the rather pedestrian **Nutti Sámi Siida** contain the usual suspects: a stuffed reindeer, an old sleigh, a rickety spinning wheel and other equally dull paraphernalia.

ARRIVAL AND DEPARTURE   JUKKASJÄRVI

By bus To get to and from Jukkasjärvi take bus #501 which links the village with Kiruna (20min; ⓦltnbd.se).

By dog sledge Undoubtedly the best way to arrive is by dog sledge from Kiruna airport; for a hefty 5900kr (price includes up to four people) you can be met at your plane and pulled all the way to your room; you can arrange this via *Icehotel* (see below).

ACCOMMODATION

Icehotel Marknadsvägen 63 ☏0980 668 00, ⓦicehotel.com. Warm and cold accommodation can be booked through the website and you should book well in advance. *Icehotel* is open from early Dec until it thaws, and the dubious pleasure of spending a night in the freezer doesn't come cheap – we've given the high-season Thurs–Sun prices (less expensive rates Mon–Wed), which apply from Dec to March; the low-season rate is applicable for just two weeks in early to mid-April. Special prices apply at New Year and over Valentine's Day. The simplest double rooms are known as "snow rooms"; the more stylish "ice rooms" are decorated with furniture made of ice and adorned with ice carvings and ornaments; then there are similar, though larger "ice suites"; and finally a top-of-the-range deluxe suite with more sculptures than you can shake an ice pick at. As for warm accommodation, prices are less for a regular double room, known as *kaamos* (Finnish for twilight or polar night) and beautifully designed in modern Scandinavian style, or a more homely cabin complete with kitchen. Between May and Sept the *Icehotel* site serves as the location for an STF hostel (same contact details as the *Icehotel*); accommodation is in double rooms with private facilities which also have access to a communal kitchen and washing facilities. Hostel **800kr**, *kaamos* **2290kr**, cabin **3390kr**, snow room **3800kr**, ice room **4900kr**, ice suite **5800kr**, deluxe suite **7000kr**

EATING AND DRINKING

Absolut Icebar Inside the Icehotel. The *Icebar* is just that: a bar made of transparent blocks of ice with seating in the form of designer chairs and stools made of snow and ice; dress accordingly. It pays to like vodka because that's all they serve, in glasses made of ice. Winter only; daily 1pm–1am.

Icehotel restaurant Marknadsvägen ☎ 0980 668 84. You can eat a buffet lunch and à la carte dinner here, with a good selection of tasty northern Swedish specialities in the range of 275–395kr. The set Ice Menu (835kr) consists of four courses of local delicacies and comes served on an ice platter. Winter only; daily 11am–2pm & 6–10pm.

Old Homestead Marknadsvägen ☎ 0980 668 84. Housed in the former village school from 1768, this solid timber structure is a great place for hearty meals such as steaks and chicken breast; mains around 225kr. The outdoor terrace, open in summer, has good views of the Torne River. Daily 6–9pm.

Nikkaluokta and Kebnekaise

NIKKALUOKTA, 66km west of Kiruna and reached on the twice-daily bus, is the starting point for treks towards and up Sweden's highest mountain, **Kebnekaise** (2102m). The mountain was first conquered in 1883 by a Frenchman, Charles Robot; today it can be reached in eight to nine hours by anyone in decent physical condition. Two paths lead to the peak: the eastern route goes over Björling glacier, includes some climbing and is only recommended for experts; the western route is much longer and is the one most people opt for.

ACCOMMODATION   KEBNESKAISE

Fjällstation mountain lodge Kebnekaise ☎ 0980 550 00, ⊛ stfkebnekaise.com. Known colloquially as simply "Keb", this STF place at the foot of the mountain is not accessible by road; instead from nearby Nikkaluokta a 19km trail leads here. There are self-catering facilities as well as a sauna, though is also a restaurant, too. Open mid-Feb to early May & mid-June to mid-Sept. Dorms **550kr**, doubles **1550kr**

The Kungsleden

The **Kungsleden** (literally "King's Trail") is the most famous and popular hiking route in Sweden. A well-signposted, 500km-long path from **Abisko** in the north to **Hemavan**, near Tärnaby (see p.321), it takes in Sweden's highest mountain, **Kebnekaise**, en route. If you're looking for splendid isolation, this isn't the trail for you; it's the busiest in the country, though it's the section from Abisko to Kebnekaise that sees most hikers (one of the least busy sections is between Jäkkvik and Adolfström).

Abisko and around

Leaving Kiruna, it's 98km northwest along the E10 to **ABISKO**. Although accessible by both rail and road, it's by **train** that most people arrive at the start of the Kungsleden trail. The train line from Luleå, via Kiruna, to Narvik, known as the **Malmbanan**, is Europe's northernmost line, and would never have been built had it not been for the rich deposits of iron ore around Gällivare and Malmberget.

9

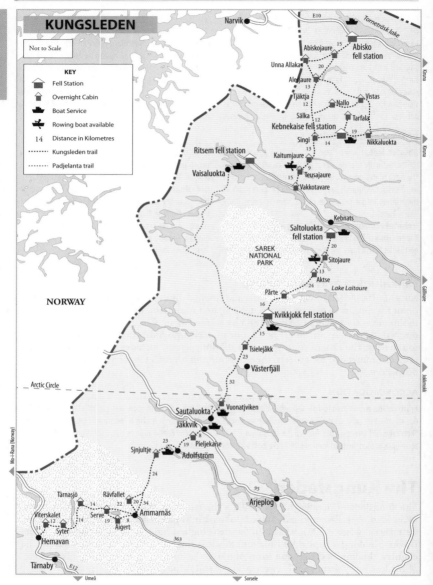

Brief history

The idea to construct the Malmbanan, which connects the Bothnian coast with the Atlantic coast (170km), passing through some of the remotest and most inhospitable parts of Europe, was talked about on and off throughout the nineteenth century, when the only means of transporting the ore was by reindeer and sleigh. Finally, in 1884, an English company was awarded the contract to build it; by 1888, the line had reached

9

REACHING THE KUNGSLEDEN BY PUBLIC TRANSPORT

You can get to **Abisko** pretty easily by **train**; it's just before the Norwegian border on the Kiruna–Narvik run. The **Inlandsbanan** will get you to Jokkmokk, from where you can get a bus to Kvikkjokk, another point on the trail.

There are also several useful **bus** routes that you can take to link up with the trail, listed below; most of these services are run by Länstrafiken Norrbotten and Länstrafiken Västerbotten (ⓦ ltnbd.se and ⓦ tabussen.nu). The buses operate a *bussgods* service, which allows you to send your pack ahead to your destination or, alternatively, back to your starting point, sparing you the effort of lugging your stuff around; ask about this service at bus stations or on the bus.

#31 Hemavan to Umeå
#47 Jokkmokk to Kvikkjokk
#92 Kiruna to Nikkaluokta (19km from Kebnekaise fell station)
#93 Gällivare to Ritsem (passes through Vakkotavare and Kebnats for the boat to Saltoluokta)
#200 Arjeplog to Jäkkvik
#341 Ammarnäs to Sorsele

Gällivare from the Bothnian coast and the company was bankrupt. Ten years passed before the state took over the project; in July 1902, the navvies – who'd been subject to temperatures of -30°C and lower and incredibly harsh conditions – finally shovelled their way through deep snow at Riksgränsen to cross the Norwegian border. A year later the line was officially opened by King Oscar II.

The chairlift

Even if you don't intend to walk the Kungsleden, there are a couple of attractions right on Abisko's doorstep. Departing from directly opposite the *Turiststation*, you can take a **chairlift** (195kr return) 500m up Nuolja mountain (1169m), from where there are fantastic views of the surrounding wilderness, including the 70km-long Torneträsk Lake, the spectacular U-shaped mountain-tops of **Lapporten**, which have come to represent the gateway to Lapland and are used as landmarks by the *Sámi* for guiding their reindeer between their summer and winter grazing land, and the vast wooded land.

Aurora Sky Station

Tours: Dec–March Tues–Sat 8pm–midnight • 690kr • ⓦ auroraskystation.se

Tucked away in one corner of the **café** at the end of the chairlift, the **Aurora Sky Station** is the best place for miles around to observe the **northern lights**; Abisko lies in a rain shadow and the sky is consequently often free of cloud. Containing all kinds of equipment to measure and hear the lights (they often emit a series of hisses and clicks), it's a perfect introduction for the non-initiated into this most complicated of scientific phenomena, since experts are on hand to explain what you're seeing and hearing. For 2950kr it's possible to spend the night on a camp bed up at the Sky Station and be woken by your guide once the aurora is visible; the price includes transport on the chairlift and breakfast the next morning.

Rallarvägen

Nuolja is the starting point for an easy walking path (7km; 2–3hr) leading downhill to nearby **Björkliden**, 9km away by road, comprising nothing more than a few houses gathered around the train station. From here, the **Rallarvägen** (**Navvy Road**) leads to Rombaksbotn, near Narvik, in Norway; the road was built alongside the Malmbanan, then under construction, in order to transport materials needed for the line. Today it provides a walking or mountain-biking route between Abisko and Narvik – though it can be fairly narrow and rough going in parts.

9

ARRIVAL AND DEPARTURE   ABISKO

By train Arriving by train from Kiruna, get off at Abisko Turiststation (not the first stop, Abisko Ö).

Destinations Gällivare (5 daily; 2hr 20min); Kiruna 5 daily; 1hr 20min); Narvik (2 daily; 1hr 30min); Riksgränsen (2 daily; 40min); Stockholm (1 daily; 18hr).

ACCOMMODATION

Abisko Turiststation ☎ 0980 402 00, ⌨ abisko.nu. A superbly located STF lodge beside the vast Torneträsk Lake. There are 300 beds in both private rooms and two-berth cabins, a great basement sauna suite, and a restaurant and bar with views over the lake. Dorms 360kr, doubles 890kr

Riksgränsen

From Abisko and Björkliden, the train line and the E10 continue on to **RIKSGRÄNSEN**, 34km from Abisko, a self-contained mountain ski and spa resort 400km north of the Arctic Circle in the shadow of the Norwegian border. The proud claim of Riksgränsen is that plentiful precipitation means there's never any need for artificial snow; you can ski and snowboard until midsummer. Although the minuscule settlement consists of barely a couple of houses supplemented by a top-notch **hotel** it's the chance to explore the only high alpine area in Sweden – sixty peaks over 1350m – that brings trainloads of people here, predominantly during the winter season (mid-Feb to late June). During the summer months, there's some great **fishing** and **hiking** to be had in these parts; the youth hostel (see below) can supply detailed information as well as rent **mountain bikes** (350kr) for cycling along the Rallarvägen (see p.345) or **canoes** for use on the lake here (350kr). Bear in mind, though, that Riksgränsen is one of the wettest places in the entire country in summer, subject to frequent heavy downpours due to its proximity to the mountains that form the border with Norway.

ARRIVAL AND DEPARTURE   RIKSGRÄNSEN

By train The train station lies immediately to the south of the E10, beside the minor road, Riksgränsvägen, which leads down into the village itself.

Destinations Abisko (2 daily; 40min); Gällivare (2 daily; 3hr); Kiruna (2 daily; 2hr); Narvik (2 daily; 1hr); Stockholm (1 daily; 19hr).

ACCOMMODATION

Riksgränsen Riksgränsvägen 15 ☎ 0980 400 80, ⌨ riksgransen.nu. This luxury hotel certainly buzzes in season: it's one of the Swedes' favourite ski destinations. The hotel also boasts a well-appointed spa centre complete with five massage rooms, gym, jacuzzi and outside hot tubs from where there are breathtaking views over Vassijaure Lake. 2000kr

Riksgränsen hostel Riksgränsvägen 4 ☎ 0980 430 88. Open all year, there's quality accommodation here in nicely appointed double rooms with private facilities as well as access to no fewer than three kitchens for self-catering. A good place, too, for hiking advice. Dorms 350kr, doubles 700kr

Along the Kungsleden trail

As Sweden's premier hiking trail, there is no doubt that the **Kungsleden**, particularly its northern stretches, can be busy with trekkers. However, it's not difficult to get away from the crowds. Most people start the trail at Abisko, but it's equally feasible to begin further south – see box, p.345.

The ground is easy to walk, with bridges where it's necessary to ford streams; marshy ground has had wooden planks laid down to ease the going, and there are either boat services or row-boats with which to get across several large lakes. The route, which passes through the national parks (see p.335), is traditionally split into the five stages described below. For the distances between the places mentioned on each segment, see the map on p.344; the best map to have of the entire area is Lantmäteriet Kartförlaget's *Norra Norrland* (scale 1:400,000).

9

Stage 1: Abisko to Kebnekaise (6 days; 105km)

From its starting point at Abisko Turiststation, the Kungsleden winds through the elongated **Abisko National Park**, which contains some of the most lush and dense vegetation of the trail, including beech forest lining the valley bottom. From the Alesjaure cabins, perched on a mountain ridge 35km from the start, you'll get a fantastic view over the open countryside below; there's a sauna here, too. The highest point on this segment is the Tjäktja pass (1105m), 50km from the start, from where there are also wonderful views.

Stage 2: Kebnekaise to Saltoluokta (3 days; 51km)

One of the quietest sections of the trail, this segment takes in beech forest, open fells and deep valleys. First of all you backtrack 14km to **Singi**, before heading south again with an unobstructed view of the hills and glaciers of Sarek National Park. You then paddle across the river at **Teusajaure** and climb over a plateau, from where you drop steeply through more beech forest to **Vakkotavare**.

Stage 3: Saltoluokta to Kvikkjokk (4 days; 73km)

This segment involves crossing two lakes and also passes through a bare landscape edged by pine and beech forests. A long uphill climb of around five to six hours leads first to **Sitojaure**, on a bare high fell. The shallow lake here, which you have to cross, is choppy in the strong wind; take the boat service operated by the cabin caretaker. You then cross the wetlands on the other side of the lake, making use of the wooden planks laid down here, to **Aktse**, where there's a vast field of yellow buttercups in summer. Using the row-boats provided, row across **Lake Laitaure** for Kvikkjokk; as you approach you'll see pine forest.

Stage 4: Kvikkjokk to Ammarnäs (8 days; 166km)

Not recommended for novices, this is one of the most difficult stretches of the trail (distances between cabins can be long, and there are four lakes to cross); it is, however, one of the quietest. From **Kvikkjokk** you take the boat over Saggat Lake and walk to the first cabin at **Tsielejåkk**. It's 55km to the next cabin at **Vuonatjviken**. You then take the boat across Riebnesjaure and walk to Hornavan for another boat across to the village of **Jäkkvik**. It's a short hike of 8km to the next cabin, then on to the village of **Adolfström**. Then you get another boat over Iraft Lake and on to the cabins at **Sjnjultje**. From there there's a choice of routes: 34km direct to Ammarnäs, or 24km to Rävfallet and then another 20km into Ammarnäs.

Stage 5: Ammarnäs to Hemavan (4 days; 78km)

This is the easiest part of the trail: you'll pass over low fells and heather-covered moors and through beech forests and wetlands, the horizon lined with impressive fell peaks. The only steep climb is 8km long between **Ammarnäs** and **Aigert**, where there's an imposing waterfall and a traditional steam sauna in the cabin. On the way to the Syter cabin, 48km from Aigert, you'll pass a network of bridges, which cross the various lakes in what is called the Tärnasjö archipelago.

ACCOMMODATION   **ALONG THE KUNGSLEDEN TRAIL**

There are basic **cabins** (all open late Feb to April & late June to mid-Sept; advance bookings not possible) along the entire route, and from Abisko to Saltoluokta, north of the Arctic Circle, and in the south between Ammarnäs and Hemavan, and also better-equipped STF *fjällstationer*, or **mountain lodges**.

Stage 1 There are cabins en route at Abiskojaure, Alesjaure, Tjäktja (before the pass), Sälka and Singi. At the end of this section of cabins lies Kebnekaise *fjällstation* mountain lodge (see p.343), from where it's possible to leave the main trail and head to Nikkaluokta (see p.343), 19km away (served by buses to Kiruna).

Stage 2 From Vakkotavore a bus runs to the quay at Kebnats, and then a short boat trip brings you to Saltoluokta *fjällstation* mountain lodge (☎ 0973 410 10, ⊛ stfsaltoluokta.com; late Feb early May & mid-June to mid-Sept; dorms 395kr, doubles 1090kr) and the start of the next section. There are cabins en route at Singi, Kaitumjaure, Teusajaure and Vakkotavare.

9

Stage 3 There are cabins en route at Sitojaure, Aktse, and Pårte; at Kvikkjokk there's a *fjällstation* mountain lodge. **Stage 4** Accommodation en route is at Tsielejåkk, Vuonatjviken, Jäkkvik village, Pieljekaise, Adolfström village, Sjnjultje, Rävfallet and Ammarnäs. The only bookable cabins are at Jäkkvik (*Kyrkans Fjällgård*; ☎ 0961 210 39, ⓦ kyrkansfjallgardjakkvik.com) and Adolfström (*Adolfströms Handelsbod & Stugby*; ☎ 0961 230 41, ⓦ adolfstrom.com).

Stage 5 There are no fell stations on this stretch of the trail; cabins en route are at Aigert, Serve, Tärnasjö, Syter, Viterskalet and Hemavan.

The Torne Valley

Along the border with Finland, the lush, gentle slopes of the **TORNE VALLEY** (*Tornedalen* in Swedish) are among the most welcoming sights in northern Sweden. Stretching over 500km from the mouth of the Gulf of Bothnia to Sweden's remote northern tip, the three rivers, Torne, Muonio and Könkämä, mark out the long border between Sweden and Finland. The valley is home to Swedes, Finns and *Sámi*, who speak an archaic Finnish **dialect** known as *tornedalsfinska* (Torne Valley Finnish, an official minority language), though Swedish is widely understood and is the language of choice for the youth. Refreshingly different from the coast and the heavily wooded inland regions, the area is dotted with small villages, bordered by flower meadows. To either side of Route 400, the main road along the valley, lie open fields providing much-needed grazing land for the farmers' livestock.

Arriving from Gällivare or Kiruna, you can enter the valley by **bus** at its midway point, **Pajala**. From the south, buses also run daily from Haparanda (see p.278).

Pajala

Over time we understood that Pajala didn't actually belong to Sweden… we'd made it by chance. A northerly appendage, desolate swampland where a few people just happened to live, who only partly managed to be Swedish … no roe deer, hedgehogs or nightingales. Just interminable amounts of mosquitoes, Torne Valley Finnish swearwords and Communists.

Popular Music, Mikael Niemi, on growing up in Pajala during the 1960s and 1970s

The valley's main village is pretty **PAJALA**, a place that has earned itself a reputation and a half throughout Sweden on two counts: first, the inordinately successful book, and now film, *Popular Music*, is set here (see p.374), and second, the locals' need of women (see box below). In order to appreciate the former claim to fame, you really need to have read the book (one in eight Swedes owns a copy) or seen the film, which played to sell-out audiences in cinemas across the country. Based around the life of Matti, a

---

BRIDES OF THE ARCTIC CIRCLE

The predominance of heavy labouring jobs in the north of Sweden has produced a gender imbalance here – around three men to every woman (a fact which also explains the ridiculously macho behaviour that seems to prevail in these parts). So, to celebrate the village's four-hundredth anniversary in 1987, the local council placed advertisements in the national papers inviting women from the south of the country up to Lapland to take part in the birthday festivities. Journalists outside Sweden soon heard of the ads, and articles about the unusual invitation began to appear in newspapers across Europe. Before long, busloads of women from all over the continent were heading for the village. The anniversary festivities proved to be a drunken, debauched bash that tiny Pajala wouldn't forget in a long time, but they did help to redress the gender problem: dozens of East European women lost their hearts to gruff Swedish lumberjacks, and began new lives north of the Arctic Circle. Naturally a succession of winters spent in darkness and in temperatures of -25°C takes its toll and some women have already left; to date, though, about thirty have stayed the course.

teenage boy who dreams of becoming a rock star, the book offers a rare insight into the psyche of the northern Swede and life in the remote Torne Valley. Dotted across town, striking yellow signposts proudly point the way to some of the most infamous locations to feature in the dramatization: Vittulajänkkä, Paskajänkkä and slightly more sedate Strandvägen, all plotted on the free map available from the tourist office.

Having dealt with Pajala the film location, there's little else to do in this unprepossessing town other than rest up for a day or so – take a walk along the riverside, or head off in search of the great grey **owl** (*strix nebulosa*) that sweeps through the nearby forests. The huge wooden **model** of the bird in the bus station will give you an idea of its appearance: lichen grey, with long, slender tail feathers and a white crescent between its black and yellow eyes. Close by, on Torggatan, is the largest **sundial** in the world, a circular affair with a diameter of 38m which tells the real solar time – always 18–25min different to that of a regular watch or clock.

Laestadiuspörtet

Laestadius Museum • Laestadiusvägen 36 • Early June to mid-June & mid-Aug to late Aug Mon–Fri 10am–5pm; mid-June to mid-Aug daily 10am–6pm • 40kr

The solid timber structure known in Swedish as **Laestadiuspörtet** is where Lars Levi Laestadius lived whilst rector in Pajala and is now a museum dedicated to his life. The spartan interior, including the bedroom where he died in 1861, has been left as it was when he lived here. The guided tour will help make sense of the man and his teachings and throw some light onto his rantings about alcohol and his relationship with the *Sámi*. Laestadius strove throughout his life to rid Lapland of alcohol abuse though he was rarely popular hereabouts since many workers were paid for their toils in hard liquor. His **grave** is located in the middle section of the old graveyard next to Pajala kyrka on Kyrkallén.

ARRIVAL AND INFORMATION — PAJALA

By bus The bus station is right in the centre of town.

Tourist office In the bus station (mid-June to mid–Aug Mon–Fri 9am–7pm, Sat & Sun 11am–5pm; mid-Aug to mid-June Mon–Fri 8am–4pm; Ⓣ 0978 100 15, Ⓦ heatoflapland.com).

ACCOMMODATION

★ **Aurora Retreat** Prästgården, Junosuando Ⓣ 0978 300 61, Ⓦ auroraretreat.se; take bus #53 towards Kiruna. The best place to stay is out of town in the quiet village of Junosuando (57km northwest): *Aurora* is an eco-friendly haven of stripped pine and potted plants in the former vicarage dating from 1928. Rooms here are airy and spacious and the emphasis is on minimal environmental impact. **Full board 1590kr**

Smedjan Fridhemsvägen 1 Ⓣ 0978 108 15, Ⓦ hotellsmedjan.se. A rather functional place featuring modern en-suite rooms; it's a 10min walk from the centre, east along Tornedalsvägen and then right into Kengisgatan.

LAESTADIUS AND THE DEMON DRINK

No other man has made a greater impression on northern Scandinavia than **Lars Levi Laestadius** (1800–61), the Swedish revivalist preacher who dedicated his life to saving people in three countries from the perils of **alcoholism**. Born in Jäkkvik in 1800 and educated in Kvikkjokk, the young Laestadius soon developed a close relationship with the indigenous *Sámi*, many of whom had turned to drink to escape the harsh reality of their daily lives. It was while the priest was working in Karesuando (1826–49) that he met **Mary of Åsele**, the *Sámi* woman who inspired him to steer people towards a life of total purity. Following Laestadius's death in Pajala in 1861, the movement continued under the leadership of Juhani Raattamaa before splitting into two opposing branches: a conservative western group in Sweden and Norway, and a more liberal eastern one in Finland. Today tens of thousands of teetotal Swedes, Finns, Norwegians and *Sámi* across the Arctic area of Scandinavia still follow Laestadius's teachings; as well as not drinking, they're not allowed to have flowers or curtains in their homes, nor are they permitted to wear a tie, listen to the radio or watch TV.

9

RÖMPÄVIIKO AND THE PAJALA MARKET

Taking place in the last week in September, the **Römpäviiko** ("romp week") cultural festival, featuring live music and street stalls selling food and handicrafts, is undoubtedly the liveliest time to be in the village. However, the second weekend after midsummer is another good time to visit, when up to forty thousand people flood into town for the Pajala **market**, one of the biggest in northern Sweden, selling everything from chorizos to reindeer antlers.

Its saving grace is that there's a free sauna on site, too. **890kr/1090kr**

Snickarbacken Snickargatan 9 ☎0978 100 70, ⊛snickarbacken.se. Well-sized apartments with decent kitchens are available for rent at this new venture on the edge of town, opposite the hospital. There's also a handful of hostel-style rooms, too, and a sauna for guest use. Apartments **690kr**, dorms **195kr**

EATING AND DRINKING

Café Nova Tornedalsvägen 2 ☎0978 100 95. A friendly retro-style café in the town centre with loads of 1960s furniture for authenticity. It's a good choice for sandwiches, salads and light lunches and there's internet access, too. Mon–Fri 10am–5pm, Sat 11am–2pm.

Thai Dan Sai Medborgarvägen 3 ☎0978 70 05 70. This new Thai place serves standards such as green chicken curry and spring rolls to a grateful local clientele. Prices are low too, with mains around 90kr. Mon–Thurs 11am–9pm, Fri 11am–2am, Sat noon–2am.

Tre Kronor Tornedalsvägen 11B ☎0978 107 70. This long-standing pizzeria and fast-food place serves pizzas (from 65kr), burgers (65kr) and steaks (from 79kr). It's not exactly fine dining but at prices like these there are few complaints. Mon–Thurs 10.30am–7pm, Fri 10.30am–8pm, Sat & Sun 10.30am–1.30pm.

Karesuando and around

Sweden's northernmost village, **KARESUANDO**, 180km north of Pajala, is a surprisingly likeable little place that you can reach from Pajala by bus by changing in nearby **Vittangi**, where, incidentally, there's a great **elk park** (June–Aug daily 10am–6pm; call ahead at other times on ☎070 247 69 06, ⊛moosefarm.se; 120kr). This far corner of Sweden is as good a spot as any to take stock of just where you've reached: the North Cape is barely 500km away, you're as far north as the northern tip of Alaska, and the tree line slices through the edge of the village. **Winters** up here can be particularly severe; the first snow falls at the end of September or early October and stays on the ground until late May, when the Muonioälven, the river which curls around the village, also melts. Just a few centimetres beneath the surface, the ground is in the grip of **permafrost** all year round. Summer here is short and sweet – but the region becomes a mosquito paradise in the warmer and lighter months. Karesuando is right in the midst of *Sámi* heartland; reindeer husbandry, particularly in the nearby villages of Övre, Nedre Soppero and Idivuoma, where many herders live, is of primary importance.

With your own transport, it's well worth the short drive south along Route 400 for fantastic **views**: some five or ten minutes after leaving the village, take the right turn marked "Kaarevaara" and continue past a small lake, whereupon the road begins to climb up past a TV mast and ends in a small car park. On a clear day you can see for miles across the Swedish and Finnish tundra. The vast tract of land stretching away to the northwest contains **Treriksröset**, the point where Sweden, Finland and Norway meet (see box opposite).

Lars Levi Laestadius museum

Laestadiusvägen • No set hours • Free

The only sight to speak of in Karesuando is beyond the tourist office: the wooden cabin here was once the rectory of **Lars Levi Laestadius**, the village's most famous son (see box, p.349). Complete with simple wooden pews, it was used as a meeting place while Laestadius was rector in Karesuando, and is now a simple **museum** of his life.

TRERIKSRÖSET

Heading north for **Treriksröset** – the **three-nation marker post** where Sweden, Norway and Finland meet – walk over the bridge to Kaaresuvanto in Finland, from where a daily bus leaves at 2.35pm (Finland is an hour ahead of Sweden) for **Kilpisjärvi** (journey time 1hr 40min). From June to mid-September a second daily bus leaves at 4.25pm for Tromsø in Norway, travelling via Kilpisjärvi. From Kilpisjärvi, there are two ways to get to Treriksröset. One of these is a hike of 11km down a track which passes through an area of dwarf woodland before running around a small lake to reach Sweden's northernmost point; don't forget your camera and mosquito repellent. The path then continues (14km) towards the **northernmost peak** in Sweden, **Pältsan** (1445m); the going here is rocky in parts.

The STF **cabins** (no advance booking; mid-March to April & mid-July to mid-Sept; dorm beds 370kr) at the foot of the mountain, boast thirty beds and a sauna. There's an easy hike (40km) from the cabins back to **Keinovuopio**, then cross the river to the village of Peera, on the main E8 road in Finland, where you can catch the bus back to Karesuando (daily; approximately 1.45pm, also June to mid-Sept daily at 11.25am; check Finnish bus times at ⓦmatkahuolto.fi).

Alternatively, you can reach Treriksröset from Kilpisjärvi by getting a **boat ride** across the lake on *M/S Malla*, which shortens the hike to just 3km. The boat requires at least four passengers to sail (late June to early Aug 10am, 2pm & 6pm Finnish time; 45min; €25 return).

Vita Huset

Village Museum • Laestadiusvägen 113 • Mon–Fri 8am–11am & noon–3pm • 20kr

Along the road to the campsite and worth a quick look is the village **museum**, known as **Vita Huset**, containing a few atmospheric black-and-white photographs from 1944, when Karesuando was inundated by Finns fleeing the approaching German forces – with their cattle. Look for the picture of Olga Raattamaa, known locally as Empress Olga, who once lived in nearby Kummavuopio, and single-handedly saved the lives of dozens of Finns by rowing them across the Könkämä River to safety in neutral Sweden.

INFORMATION

Tourist office In the customs house on the bridge across to Finland (June–Sept daily 9am–6pm; Oct–May Mon–Fri 9am–3pm; ☏0981 202 05, ⓦkaresuando.se). This tourist office seems to pick and choose when it opens.

KARESUANDO

ACCOMMODATION

Karesuando Laestadiusvägen 153 ☏0981 203 30, ⓦkaresuando.se. It seems that this hotel is continually under new ownership. If it's operating when you're in town, you'll find modern rooms in *Sámi* colours. All rooms have a toilet and most have a shower, too. 950kr

Karesuando Camping Laestadiusvägen 185 ☏0981 201 39 or ☏070 605 1124, ⓦkaresuandocamping.blogspot.com. A 2km walk past the church on the Pajala road, this riverside campsite has regular cabins and a few *Sámi*-style *kåtor*. There's a separate toilet and shower block. Open June to Aug. Tents 140kr, cabins and *kåtor* 500kr

Youth hostel Laestadiusvägen opposite the Karesuando ☏0981 203 30, ⓦarcticstarhotel.com. Run by the hotel opposite, this hostel enjoys a fantastic waterside location and is the best place to stay. In theory, it's open April to mid-Sept but check ahead of arrival. Dorms 190kr, doubles 480kr

EATING AND DRINKING

Arctic Livs ☏0980 203 70. Located between the filling stations, a fast-food place serving burgers and reindeer fry-ups as well as Asian dishes such as lemon chicken rice. A main dish costs around 120kr. Daily 11am–6pm.

GETTING TO THE NORTH CAPE

From Karesuando it's a drive of 510km to the North Cape in Norway, routing via Enontekiö in Finland and then Kautokeino and Alta in Norway; it will take at least six hours with your own car. By public transport, the easiest option is to walk across to Karesuvanto in Finland and pick up the bus for Tromsø which operates from June to mid-September. Change buses in Skibotn on Norway's E6 highway and then head east towards Alta for connections to the North Cape. Finnish bus timetables are at ⓦeskelisen-lapinlinjat.com, Norwegian ones at ⓦboreal.no.

THE GOLDEN HALL, STADSHUSET, STOCKHOLM

Contexts

History

Sweden has one of Europe's longest documented **histories**, but for all the upheavals of the Viking times and the warring of the Middle Ages, the country has, in modern times, seemed to delight in taking a historical back seat. For a brief period in 1986, when Prime Minister Olof Palme was shot dead, Sweden was thrust into the limelight. Since then, the country has regained some of its equilibrium, though political infighting and domestic disharmony often threatens the one thing that Swedes have always been proud of, and that other countries aspire to: the politics of *consensus*, the potential passing of which is arguably of far greater importance than even the assassination of their prime minister.

Early civilizations

It was not until around 6000 BC that the **first settlers** roamed north and east into Sweden, living as nomadic reindeer hunters and herders. By 3000 BC people had settled in the south of the country and were established as farmers; from 2000 BC there are indications of a development in burial practices, with **dolmens** and **passage graves** found throughout the southern Swedish provinces. Traces also remain of the **Boat Axe People**, named after their characteristic tool and weapon, shaped like a boat. The earliest horse riders in Scandinavia, they quickly held sway over the whole of southern Sweden.

During the **Bronze Age** (1500–500 BC) the Boat Axe People traded furs and amber for southern European copper and tin – large finds of finished ornaments and weapons show a comparatively rich culture. This was emphasized by elaborate burial rites, the dead laid in single graves under mounds of earth and stone.

The deterioration of the Scandinavian climate in the last millennium before Christ coincided with the advance across Europe of the Celts, which halted the flourishing trade of the Swedish settlers. With the new millennium, Sweden made its first mark upon the Classical world. In the *Historia Naturalis*, Pliny the Elder (23–79 AD) mentioned the "island of Scatinavia" far to the north. Tacitus was more specific: in 98 AD he mentioned a powerful people who were strong in men, weapons and ships, the *Suinoes* – a reference to the **Svear**, who were to form the nucleus of an emergent Swedish kingdom by the sixth century.

The Svear settled in the rich land around Lake Mälaren and became rulers of most of the territory comprising modern Sweden, except the south. They gave Sweden its modern name: *Sverige* in Swedish or *Svear rik*, the kingdom of the Svear. More importantly, their first dynastic leaders had a taste for expansion, trading with Gotland and holding suzerainty over the Åland Islands.

6000BC	98AD	First century AD	Ninth century AD
First settlers arrive	Tacitus refers to northern tribes as Suinoes	Svear tribe become rulers of land now Sweden	Swedish Vikings travel to Black and Caspian seas

> **VIKING NAMES**
> The Vikings were settlers as well as traders and exploiters, and their long-term influence was marked. Embattled Slavs to the east gave them the name **Rus**, and their creeping colonization gave one area in which the Vikings settled its modern name, Russia. Russian names today – Oleg, Igor, Vladimir – can be derived from the Swedish – Helgi, Ingvar, Valdemar.

The Viking period

The Vikings – raiders and warriors who dominated the political and economic life of Europe and beyond from the ninth to the eleventh centuries – came from all parts of southern Scandinavia. But there is evidence that the **Swedish Vikings** were among the first to leave home, the impetus being rapid population growth, domestic unrest and a desire for new lands. Sweden being located on the eastern part of the Scandinavian peninsula, the raiders largely turned their attention further eastwards, in the knowledge that the Svear had already reached the Baltic. By the ninth century, the trade routes were well established, with Swedes reaching the Black and Caspian seas and making valuable trading contact with the **Byzantine Empire**. Although more commercially inclined than their Danish and Norwegian counterparts, Swedish Vikings were quick to use force if profits were slow to materialize. From 860 onwards Greek and Muslim records relate a series of raids across the Black Sea against Byzantium, and across the Caspian into northeast Iran.

Domestically, **paganism** was at its height; dynastic leaders would claim descent from Freyr, "God of the World". It was a bloody time: nine **human sacrifices** were offered at the celebrations held every nine years at Uppsala. Adam of Bremen recorded that the great shrine there was adjoined by a sacred grove where "every tree is believed divine because of the death and putrefaction of the victims hanging there".

Viking **law** was based on the **Thing**, an assembly of free men to which the king's power was subject. Each largely autonomous province had its own assembly and its own leaders: where several provinces united, the approval of every *Thing* was needed for any choice of leader. For centuries in Sweden, each newly elected king had to make a formal tour to receive the homage of the individual provinces.

The arrival of Christianity and the early Middle Ages

Christianity was slow to take root in Sweden. Whereas Denmark and Norway had accepted the faith by the turn of the eleventh century, the Swedes remained largely heathen. Missionaries met with limited success: no Swedish king was converted until 1008, when **Olof Skötkonung** was baptized. He was the first known king of both Swedes and Goths (that is, ruler of the two major provinces of Västergötland and Östergötland), and his successors were all Christians. Nevertheless, paganism retained a grip on Swedish affairs, and as late as the 1080s the Svear banished the then king, Inge, when he refused to take part in the pagan celebrations at Uppsala. By the end of the eleventh century, though, the temple at Uppsala had gone and a Christian church was built on its site. In the 1130s, Sigtuna – the original centre of the Swedish Christian faith – was replaced by Uppsala as the main episcopal seat, and in 1164 Stephen, an English monk, was made the first archbishop.

1008	1157	1229	1323
Baptism of first Swedish king to be converted to Christianity	Swedes lead crusade against heathen Finland	Birger Jarl assumes power in Stockholm	Sweden's eastern frontiers formalized with Russia

The whole of the early Middle Ages in Sweden was characterized by a succession of struggles for control of a growing central power: two families, the Sverkers and the Eriks, waged battle against each other throughout the twelfth century. **King Erik** was the first Sverker king to make his mark: in 1157 he led a crusade to heathen Finland, but was killed in 1160 at Uppsala by a Danish pretender to his throne. Within 100 years he was to be recognized as patron saint of Sweden, and his remains interred in the new Uppsala cathedral.

Erik was succeeded by his son **Knut**, whose stable reign lasted until 1196, a period marked by commercial treaties and strengthened defences. Following his death, virtual civil war weakened royal power. As a result, the king's chief ministers, or **jarls**, assumed much of the executive responsibility for running the country, so much so that when Erik Eriksson (last of the Eriks) was deposed in 1229, his administrator **Birger Jarl** assumed power. With papal support for his crusading policies, he confirmed the Swedish grip on the southwest of Finland. He was succeeded by his son, Valdemar, who proved a weak ruler and didn't survive the family feuding after Birger Jarl's death.

In 1275, Valdemar's brother, **Magnus Ladulås**, assumed power. He earned his nickname "Ladulås" ("Barn-lock") from his having prevented the nobility from claiming maintenance at the expense of the peasantry, who travelled from estate to estate. Magnus's reign represented a peak of Swedish royal might that wasn't to be repeated for 300 years. While he was king, his enemies dissipated; he forbade the nobility to meet without his consent, and began to issue his own authoritative decrees. He also began to reap the benefits of conversion: the clergy became an educated class upon whom the monarch could rely for diplomatic and administrative duties. By the thirteenth century, there were ambitious Swedish clerics in Paris and Bologna, and the first stone churches were appearing in Sweden, the most monumental of which is the early Gothic **cathedral** built at Uppsala.

Meanwhile, the nobility had come to constitute a military class, exempt from taxation on the understanding that they would defend the Crown. In the country, the standard of living was still low, although an increasing population stimulated new cultivation. The forests of Norrland were pushed back, more southern heathland was turned into pasture, and crop rotation was introduced. Noticeable, too, was the increasing **German influence** within Sweden as the Hansa traders spread. Their first merchants settled in Visby and, by the mid-thirteenth century, in Stockholm.

The fourteenth century – towards unity

Magnus died in 1290, power shifting to a cabal of magnates led by **Torgil Knutsson**. As marshal of Sweden, he pursued an energetic foreign policy, conquering western Karelia to gain control of the Gulf of Finland and building the fortress at Viborg, only lost with the collapse of the Swedish Empire in the eighteenth century.

Magnus's son Birger came of age in 1302 and soon quarrelled with his brothers Erik and Valdemar, who had Torgil Knutsson executed. They then rounded on Birger, who was forced to divide up Sweden among the three of them. An unhappy arrangement, it lasted until 1317 when Birger had his brothers arrested and starved to death in prison – an act that prompted a shocked nobility to rise against Birger and force his exile to Denmark. The Swedish nobles restored the principle of elective monarchy by calling on

1323	1350s	1397	1477
Finland becomes part of Sweden	Black Death kills one third of population	Kalmar Union established with Denmark and Norway	Uppsala university founded

the 3-year-old **Magnus** (son of a Swedish duke, and already declared Norwegian king) to take the Swedish crown. During his minority, a treaty was concluded in 1323 with Novgorod in Russia to define the frontiers in eastern and northern Finland. This left virtually the whole of the Scandinavian peninsula (except the Danish provinces in the south) under one ruler.

Yet Sweden was still anything but prosperous. The **Black Death** reached the country in 1350, wiping out whole parishes and killing around a third of the population. Subsequent labour shortages and troubled estates meant that the nobility found it difficult to maintain their positions. German merchants had driven the Swedes from their most lucrative trade routes: even the copper and iron-ore **mining** that began around this time in Bergslagen and Dalarna relied on German capital.

Magnus soon ran into trouble, and was threatened further by the accession of Valdemar Atterdag to the Danish throne in 1340. Squabbles concerning sovereignty over the Danish provinces of Skåne and Blekinge led to Danish incursions into Sweden; in 1361, Valdemar landed on Gotland and sacked **Visby**. The Gotlanders were refused refuge by the Hansa merchants, and massacred outside the city walls.

Magnus was forced to negotiate, and his son **Håkon** – now king of Norway – was married to Valdemar's daughter Margaret. When Magnus was later deposed, power fell into the hands of the magnates who shared out the country. Chief of the ruling nobles was the Steward **Bo Jonsson Grip**, who controlled all Finland and central and southeast Sweden. Yet on his death, the nobility turned to Håkon's wife **Margaret**, already regent in Norway (for her son Olof) and in Denmark since the death of her father, Valdemar. The nobles were anxious for union across Scandinavia, to safeguard those who owned frontier estates and strengthen the Crown against any further German influence. In 1388 she was proclaimed "First Lady" of Sweden and, in return, confirmed all the privileges of the Swedish nobility. Called upon to choose a male king, Margaret nominated her nephew, **Erik of Pomerania**, who was duly elected king of Sweden in 1396. As he had already been elected to the Danish and Norwegian thrones, Scandinavian unity seemed assured.

The Kalmar Union

Erik was crowned king of Denmark, Norway and Sweden in 1397 at a ceremony in **Kalmar**. Nominally, the three kingdoms were now in union but, despite Erik's kingship, real power remained in the hands of Margaret until her death in 1412.

Erik was at war with the Hanseatic League throughout his reign. He was vilified in popular Swedish history as an evil and grasping ruler, and the taxes he raised went on a war that was never fought on Swedish soil. He spent his time instead directing operations in Denmark, leaving his queen Philippa (sister to Henry V of England) behind. Erik was deposed in 1439 and the nobility turned to **Christopher of Bavaria**, whose early death in 1448 led to the first major breach in the union.

No one candidate could fill the three kingships satisfactorily, and separate elections in Denmark and Sweden signalled a renewal of the infighting that had plagued the previous century. Within Sweden, unionists and nationalists skirmished, the powerful unionist **Oxenstierna** family opposing the claims of the nationalist **Sture** family, until 1470 when **Sten Sture** (the Elder) became "Guardian of the Realm". His victory over the unionists at the **Battle of Brunkeberg** (1471) – in the centre of what's now modern

1483	1520	1520	1542
Sweden's first printing press appears	Danes invade, killing nobility and clergy in Stockholm Bloodbath	King Gustav Vasa flees on skis to Norway	First edition of the Bible in the vernacular appears

Stockholm – was complete, gaining symbolic artistic expression in the **statue of St George and the Dragon** that still adorns Storkyrkan in Stockholm.

Sten Sture's primacy fostered a new cultural atmosphere. The first **university** in Scandinavia was founded in Uppsala in 1477, with Sweden's first printing press appearing six years later. Artistically, German and Dutch influences were predominantly, traits seen in the decorative art of the great Swedish medieval churches. Only remote **Dalarna** kept a native folk art tradition alive.

Belief in the union still existed though, particularly outside Sweden, and successive kings had to fend off almost constant attacks and blockades emanating from Denmark. With the accession of **Christian II** to the Danish throne in 1513, the unionist movement found a leader capable of turning the tide. Under the guise of a crusade to free Sweden's imprisoned archbishop Gustav Trolle, Christian attacked Sweden and killed Sture. After Christian's coronation, Trolle urged the prosecution of his Swedish adversaries (who had been gathered together under the pretext of an amnesty) and they were found guilty of heresy. Eighty-two nobles and burghers of Stockholm were executed, their bodies burned in what became known as the **Stockholm Bloodbath**. A vicious persecution of Sture's followers throughout Sweden ensued, a move that led to widespread reaction and, ultimately, the downfall of the union.

Gustav Vasa and his sons

Opposition to Christian II was vague and disorganized until the appearance of the young **Gustav Vasa**. Initially unable to stir the locals of the Dalecarlia region into open revolt, he was on his way to Norway, and exile, when he was chased on skis and recalled, the people having had a change of heart. The chase is celebrated still in the **Vasaloppet** race, run each year by thousands of Swedish skiers.

Gustav Vasa's army grew rapidly. In 1521, he was elected regent, and subsequently, with the capture of Stockholm in 1523, king. Christian had been deposed in Denmark and the new Danish king, Frederick I, recognized Sweden's de facto withdrawal from the union. Short of cash, Gustav found it prudent to support the movement for religious reform propagated by Swedish Lutherans. More of a political than a religious **Reformation**, the result was a handover of Church lands to the Crown and the subordination of Church to state. It's a relationship that is still largely in force today, the clergy being civil servants paid by the state.

In 1541, the first edition of the Bible in the vernacular appeared. Suppressing revolt at home, Gustav Vasa strengthened his hand with a centralization of trade and government. On his death in 1560, Sweden was united, prosperous and independent.

Gustav Vasa's heir, his eldest son **Erik**, faced a difficult time, not least because the Vasa lands and wealth had been divided among him and his brothers Johan, Magnus and Karl (an uncharacteristically imprudent action of Gustav before his death). The Danes, too, pressed hard, reasserting their claim to the Swedish throne in the inconclusive **Northern Seven Years' War**, which began in 1563. Erik was deposed in 1569 by his brother, who became **Johan III**, his first act being to end the war by the **Peace of Stettin** treaty. At home, Johan ruled more or less with the goodwill of the nobility, but matters were upset by his Catholic sympathies: he introduced a new Catholic liturgy, familiarly known from its binding as the *Red*

1563	1607	1611	1618
Northern Seven Year's War begins	Gothenburg founded to trade with west	Gustav II Adolf becomes king	Thirty Years' War breaks out

Book, which the clergy accepted only under protest. On Johan's death in 1592, his son and heir, Sigismund (who was Catholic king of Poland) agreed to rule Sweden in accordance with Lutheran practice, but failed to do so. When Sigismund returned to Poland, the way was clear for Duke Karl (Johan's brother) to assume the regency, a role he filled until declared King **Karl IX** in 1603.

Karl, the last of Vasa's sons, had ambitions eastwards but was routed by the Poles and staved off by the Russians. He suffered a stroke in 1610 and died the year after. His heir was the 17-year-old Gustav II, better known as **Gustav II Adolf**.

Gustav II Adolf and the rise of the Swedish empire

Sweden became a European power during the reign of **Gustav II Adolf**. Though still in his youth he was considered able enough to rule, and proved so by concluding peace treaties with Denmark (1613) and Russia (1617), the latter pact isolating Russia from the Baltic and allowing the Swedes control of the eastern trade routes into Europe.

In 1618, the **Thirty Years' War** broke out. It was vital for Gustav that Germany should not become Catholic, given the Polish king's continuing pretensions to the Swedish crown and the possible threat Germany could pose to Sweden's growing influence in the Baltic. In 1629, the Altmark treaty with a defeated Poland gave Gustav control of Livonia and four Prussian seaports, and the income this generated financed his entry into the war in 1630 on the Protestant side. After several convincing victories, Gustav pushed on through Germany, delaying an assault upon undefended Vienna. The decision cost him his life: Gustav was killed at the **Battle of Lützen** in 1632, his body stripped and battered by the enemy's soldiers. The war dragged on until the **Peace of Westphalia** in 1648.

With Gustav away at war for much of his reign, Sweden ran smoothly under the guidance of his friend and chancellor, **Axel Oxenstierna**. Together they founded a new Supreme Court in Stockholm (and did the same for Finland and the conquered Baltic provinces); reorganized the national assembly into four Estates of nobility, clergy, burghers and peasantry (1626); extended the university at Uppsala (and founded one at Åbo – modern Turku in Finland); and fostered the mining and other industries that provided much of the country's wealth. Gustav had many other accomplishments, too: he spoke five languages and designed a new light cannon which assisted in his routs of the enemy.

The Caroleans

The Swedish empire reached its territorial peak under the **Caroleans**. Yet the reign of the last of them was to see Sweden crumble. Following Gustav II Adolf's death and the later

1632	1658	1662	1741
Gustav II Adolf killed at the Battle of Lützen	Treaty of Roskilde secures southern provinces for Sweden	Work begins on Drottningholm palace	Carl von Linné becomes a professor at Uppsala university

abdication of his daughter Kristina, **Karl X** succeeded to the throne. War against Poland (1655) led to some early successes and, with Denmark espousing the Polish cause, gave Karl the opportunity to march into Jutland (1657). From there his armies marched across the frozen sea to threaten Copenhagen; the subsequent **Treaty of Roskilde** (1658) broke Denmark and gave the Swedish empire its widest territorial extent.

However, the long regency of his son and heir, **Karl XI**, did little to safeguard Sweden's vulnerable position, so extensive were its borders. On assuming power in 1672, Karl was almost immediately dragged into war: beaten by a smaller Prussian army at Brandenberg in 1675, Sweden was suddenly faced with war against both the Danes and the Dutch. Karl rallied, though, to drive out the Danish invaders, and the war ended in 1679 with the reconquest of Skåne and the restoration of most of Sweden's German provinces.

In 1682, Karl XI became **absolute monarch** and was given full control over legislation and *reduktion* – the resumption of estates previously alienated by the Crown to the nobility. The armed forces were reorganized too: by 1700, the Swedish army had 25,000 soldiers and twelve regiments of cavalry; the naval fleet had expanded to 38 ships and a new base had been built at **Karlskrona** (which was nearer to the likely trouble spots than Stockholm).

Culturally, Sweden began to benefit from the innovations of Gustav II Adolf. *Gymnasia* (grammar schools) continued to expand, and a second university was established at **Lund** in 1668. A national **literature** emerged, helped by the efforts of **George Stiernhielm**, father of modern Swedish poetry. **Olof Rudbeck** (1630–1702) was a Nordic polymath whose scientific reputation lasted longer than his attempt to identify the ancient Goth settlement at Uppsala as Atlantis. Architecturally, this was the age of **Tessin**, both father and son. Tessin the Elder was responsible for the glorious palace at **Drottningholm**, work on which began in 1662, as well as the cathedral at **Kalmar**. His son, Tessin the Younger, succeeded him as royal architect and was to create the new royal palace at Stockholm.

In 1697, the 15-year-old **Karl XII** succeeded to the throne; under him, the empire collapsed. Faced with a defensive alliance of Saxony, Denmark and Russia, there was little the king could have done to avoid eventual defeat. However, he remains a revered figure for his valiant (often suicidal) efforts to take on the rest of Europe. Initial victories against Peter the Great and Saxony led him to march on Russia, where he was defeated and the bulk of his army destroyed. Escaping to Turkey, where he remained as guest and then prisoner for four years, Karl watched the empire disintegrate. With Poland reconquered by Augustus of Saxony, and Finland by Peter the Great, he returned to Sweden only to have England declare war on him.

Eventually, splits in the enemy alliance led Swedish diplomats to attempt peace talks with Russia. Karl, though, was keen to exploit these differences in a more direct fashion. Wanting to strike at Denmark, but lacking a fleet, he besieged Fredrikshald in Norway (then united with Denmark) in 1718 – and was killed by a sniper's bullet. In the power vacuum thus created, Russia became the leading Baltic force, receiving Livonia, Estonia, Ingria and most of Karelia from Sweden.

The Age of Freedom

The eighteenth century saw absolutism discredited in Sweden. A new constitution vested power in the Estates, who reduced the new king **Frederick I**'s role to that of

1741	1744	1778	1809
Sweden declares war on Russia	Anders Celsius dies	Death of Carl von Linné	Sweden loses Finland to Russia

nominal head of state. The chancellor wielded the real power, and under **Arvid Horn** the country found a period of stability. His party, nicknamed the "Caps", was opposed by the hawkish "Hats". The latter forced war with Russia in 1741, a disaster in which Sweden lost all of Finland and had its whole east coast burned and bombed. Most of Finland was returned with the agreement that **Adolphus Frederick** (a relation of the crown prince of Russia) would be elected to the Swedish throne on Frederick I's death. This duly occurred in 1751.

During his reign, Adolphus repeatedly tried to reassert royal power, but found that the constitution had been strengthened against him. The Estates' power was such that when Adolphus refused to sign any bills, they simply utilized a stamp bearing his name. The resurrected "Hats" forced entry into the **Seven Years' War** in 1757 on the French side, another disastrous venture, as the Prussians were able to repel every Swedish attack.

The aristocratic parties were in a state of constant flux. Although elections of sorts were held to provide delegates for the *Riksdag* (parliament), foreign sympathies, bribery and bickering were hardly conducive to democratic administration. Cabals continued to rule Sweden, the economy was stagnant, and reform delayed. It was, however, an age of **intellectual and scientific advance**, surprising in a country that had lost much of its cultural impetus. **Carl von Linné**, the botanist whose classification of plants is still used, was professor at Uppsala from 1741 to 1778; **Anders Celsius** initiated the use of the centigrade temperature scale; **Carl Scheele** discovered chlorine. A royal decree of 1748 organized Europe's first full-scale **census**, a five-yearly event by 1775. Other fields flourished, too. The mystical works of **Emmanuel Swedenborg**, the philosopher who died in 1772, encouraged new theological sects; and the period encompassed the life of **Carl Michael Bellman** (1740–95), the celebrated Swedish poet whose work did much to identify and foster a popular nationalism.

With the accession of **Gustav III** in 1771, the Crown began to regain the ascendancy. A new constitution was forced upon a divided *Riksdag* and proved a watershed between earlier absolutism and the later aristocratic squabbles. A popular king, Gustav founded hospitals, granted freedom of worship and removed many of the state controls over the economy. His determination to conduct a successful foreign policy led to further conflict with Russia (1788–90) in which, to everyone's surprise, he managed to more than hold his own. But with the French Revolution polarizing opposition throughout Europe, the Swedish nobility began to entertain thoughts of conspiracy against a king whose growing powers they now saw as those of a tyrant. In 1792, at a masked ball in Stockholm Opera House, the king was shot by an assassin hired by the disaffected aristocracy. Gustav died two weeks later and was succeeded by his son **Gustav IV**, with the country being led by a regency during his minority.

The wars waged by revolutionary France were at first studiously avoided in Sweden but, pulled into the conflict by the British, Gustav IV entered the **Napoleonic Wars** in 1805. However, Napoleon's victory at Austerlitz two years later broke the coalition, and Sweden found itself isolated. Attacked by Russia the following year, Gustav was later arrested and deposed, and his uncle was elected king.

A constitution of 1809 established a liberal monarchy in Sweden, responsible to the elected *Riksdag*. Under this constitution **Karl XIII** was a mere caretaker, his heir a Danish prince who would bring Norway back to Sweden – some compensation for finally losing Finland and the Åland Islands to Russia (1809) after five hundred years of Swedish rule.

1814	**1860**	**1867**	**1896**
Norway becomes Swedish	Emigration begins to America	Famine hits Sweden	Death of Alfred Nobel

On the prince's sudden death, however, Marshal Bernadotte (one of Napoleon's generals) was invited to become heir. Taking the name of **Karl Johan**, he took his chance in 1812 and joined Britain and Russia to fight Napoleon. Following Napoleon's first defeat at the Battle of Leipzig in 1813, Sweden compelled Denmark (France's ally) to exchange Norway for Swedish Pomerania.

By 1814 Sweden and Norway had formed an uneasy union. Norway retained its own government and certain autonomous measures. Sweden decided foreign policy, appointed a viceroy and retained a suspensive (but not absolute) veto over the Norwegian parliament's legislation.

The nineteenth century

Union under Karl Johan, or **Karl XIV** as he became in 1818, could have been disastrous. He spoke no Swedish and just a few years previously had never visited either kingdom. However, under Karl and his successor **Oscar I**, prosperity ensued. Construction of the **Göta Canal** (1832) helped commercially, and liberal measures by both monarchs helped politically. In 1845, daughters were given an equal right of inheritance. A Poor Law was introduced in 1847, restrictive craft guilds reformed, and an Education Act passed.

The 1848 revolutions throughout Europe cooled Oscar's reforming ardour, and his attention turned to reviving **Scandinavianism**. It was still a hope, in certain quarters, that closer cooperation between Denmark and Sweden–Norway could lead to some sort of revived Kalmar Union. Expectations were raised with the **Crimean War** of 1854: Russia as a future threat could be neutralized. But peace was declared too quickly (at least for Sweden) and there was still no real guarantee that Sweden would be sufficiently protected from Russia in the future. With Oscar's death, talk of political union faded.

His son **Karl XV** presided over a reform of the *Riksdag* that put an end to the Swedish system of personal monarchy. The Four Estates were replaced by a representative **two-house parliament** along European lines. This, together with the end of political Scandinavianism (following the Prussian attack on Denmark in 1864 in which Sweden stood by), marked Sweden's entry into modern Europe.

Industrialization was slow to take root in Sweden. No real industrial revolution occurred, and development – mechanization, introduction of railways, etc – was piecemeal. One result was widespread **emigration** amongst the rural poor, who had been hard hit by famine in 1867 and 1868. Between 1860 and 1910 over one million people left for America (in 1860 the Swedish population was only four million). Given huge farms to settle, the emigrants headed for land similar to that they had left behind – to the Midwest, Kansas and Nebraska.

At home, Swedish **trade unionism** emerged to campaign for better conditions. Dealt with severely, the unions formed a confederation (1898) but largely failed to make headway. Even peaceful picketing carried a two-year prison sentence. Hand in hand with the fight for workers' rights went the **temperance movement**. The level of alcohol consumption was alarming, and various abstinence programmes attempted to educate the drinkers and, if necessary, eradicate the stills. Some towns made the selling of spirits a municipal monopoly – not a big step from the state monopoly that exists today.

With the accession of **Oscar II** in 1872, Sweden continued on an even, if uneventful, keel. Keeping out of further European conflict (the Austro-Prussian War,

1905	1930s	1940
Norway gains independence from Sweden	Welfare state established	Sweden surrounded by Nazi Germany

Franco-Prussian War and various Balkan crises), the country's only worry was growing dissatisfaction in Norway with the union. Demanding a separate consular service, and objecting to the Swedish king's veto on constitutional matters, the Norwegians brought things to a head, and in 1905 declared the union invalid. The Karlstad Convention confirmed the break, and Norway became independent for the first time since 1380.

The late nineteenth century was a happier time for Swedish culture. **August Strindberg** enjoyed great critical success, and artists like **Anders Zorn** and **Prince Eugene** made their mark abroad. The historian **Artur Hazelius** founded the Nordic and Skansen museums in Stockholm; and the chemist, industrialist and dynamite inventor **Alfred Nobel** left his fortune to finance the Nobel Prizes. It's an instructive tale: Nobel hoped that the knowledge of his invention would help eradicate war, optimistically believing that humankind would never dare unleash the destructive forces of dynamite.

The two world wars

Sweden declared strict neutrality on the outbreak of **World War I**, influenced by much sympathy within the country for Germany that stemmed from long-standing cultural, trade and linguistic links. It was a policy agreed with the other Scandinavian monarchs, but a difficult one to pursue. Faced with British demands to enforce a blockade of Germany and with the blacklisting and eventual seizure of Swedish goods at sea, the economy suffered grievously; rationing and inflation mushroomed. The **Russian Revolution** in 1917 brought further problems for Sweden. The Finns immediately declared independence, waging civil war against the Bolsheviks, and Swedish volunteers enlisted in the White Army. But a conflict of interest arose when the Swedish-speaking Åland Islands wanted a return to Swedish rule rather than stay under the victorious Finns. The League of Nations overturned this claim, granting the islands to Finland.

After the war, a liberal–socialist coalition remained in power until 1920, when **Branting** became the first socialist prime minister. By the time of his death in 1924, franchise had been extended to all men and women over 23, and the state-controlled alcohol system (Systembolaget) set up. Following the Depression of the late 1920s and early 1930s, conditions began to improve after a Social Democratic government took office for the fourth time in 1932. A **welfare state** was rapidly established, offering unemployment benefit, higher old-age pensions, family allowances and paid holidays. The **Saltsjöbaden Agreement** of 1938 drew up a contract between trade unions and employers to help eliminate strikes and lockouts. With war again looming, all parties agreed that Sweden should remain neutral in any struggle, and so the country's rearmament was negligible, despite Hitler's apparent intentions.

World War II was slow to affect Sweden. Unlike in 1914, there was little sympathy in the country for Germany, but Sweden again declared neutrality. The Russian invasion of Finland in 1939 brought Sweden into the picture, with the Swedes providing weapons, volunteers and refuge for the Finns. Regular Swedish troops were refused, though, the Swedes fearing intervention from either the Germans (then Russia's ally) or the Allies. Economically, the country remained sound – less dependent on imports than in World War I and with no serious shortages. The position became stickier in 1940 when the Nazis marched into Denmark and Norway, isolating Sweden. Concessions were made – German troop transit allowed, iron-ore exports continued

1943	1943	1953	1967
Sweden takes in Jews from across Europe	IKEA founded by 17-year-old Ingvar Kamprad	Sweden's Dag Hammarskjöld becomes UN Secretary-General	Sweden changes from left- to right-hand traffic

– until 1943–44, when Allied pressure had become more convincing than the failing German war machine.

Sweden became the recipient of countless refugees from the rest of Scandinavia and the Baltic. Instrumental in this process was **Raoul Wallenberg**, who rescued Hungarian Jews from the SS and persuaded the Swedish government to give him diplomatic status in 1944. Anything up to 35,000 Jews in Hungary were sheltered in "neutral houses" (flying the Swedish flag), and fed and clothed by Wallenberg. But when Soviet troops liberated Budapest in 1945, Wallenberg was arrested as a suspected spy and disappeared; he was later reported to have died in prison in Moscow in 1947. However, unconfirmed accounts had him alive in a Soviet prison as late as 1975; in 1989 some of his surviving relatives flew to Moscow in an unsuccessful attempt to discover the truth about his fate.

The end of the war was to engender a serious crisis of conscience in the country. Though physically unscathed, Sweden was now vulnerable to **Cold War** politics. The Finns had agreed to let Soviet troops march unhindered through Finland, and in 1949 this led neighbouring Sweden to refuse to follow the other Scandinavian countries into **NATO**. The country did, however, much to conservative disquiet, return into Stalin's hands most of the Baltic and German refugees who had fought against Russia during the war – their fate is not difficult to guess.

Postwar politics

The wartime coalition quickly gave way to a purely Social Democratic government committed to welfare provision and increased defence expenditure – now non-participation in military alliances did not mean a throwing-down of weapons.

Tax increases and a trade slump lost the Social Democrats seats in the 1948 general election, and by 1951 they needed to enter into a **coalition** with the Agrarian (later the Centre) Party to survive. This coalition lasted until 1957, when disputes over the form of a proposed extension to the pension system brought it down. An inconclusive referendum and the withdrawal of the Centre Party from government forced an election. Although the Centre gained seats and the Conservatives replaced the Liberals as the main opposition party, the Social Democrats retained a (slim) majority.

Sweden regained much of its international moral respect (lost directly after World War II) through the election of **Dag Hammarskjöld** as Secretary-General of the United Nations in 1953. His strong leadership greatly enhanced the prestige (and effectiveness) of the organization, which under his guidance participated in the solution of the 1956 Suez crisis and the 1958 Lebanon–Jordan affair. He was killed in an air crash in 1961, towards the end of his second five-year term.

Domestic reform continued unabated throughout the 1950s and 1960s. It was during these years that the country laid the foundations of its much-vaunted social security system, although at the time it didn't always bear close scrutiny. A **National Health Service** gave free hospital treatment, but only allowed for small refunds on doctor's fees and the costs of medicines and dental treatment – hardly as far-reaching as the British system introduced immediately after the war.

The Social Democrats stayed in power until 1976, when a **non-Social Democrat coalition** (Centre–Liberal–Moderate) finally unseated them. In the 44 years since 1932, the socialists had been an integral part of government in Sweden, their role tempered

1974	1976	1976	1986
ABBA win Eurovision Song Contest in Brighton, England	Social Democrats lose power after forty years	Swedish king, Carl Gustav, marries German commoner	Olof Palme assassinated

only during periods of war and coalition. It was a remarkable record, made more so by the fact that modern politics in Sweden has never been about ideology so much as detail. Socialists and non-socialists alike share a broad consensus on foreign policy and defence matters, even on the need for the social welfare system. The argument in Sweden has instead been about economics, a manifestation of which is the issue of **nuclear power**. A second non-Socialist coalition, formed in 1979, presided over a referendum on nuclear power (1980); the pro-nuclear lobby secured victory, the result being an immediate expansion of nuclear power generation.

Olof Palme

The Social Democrats regained power in 1982, subsequently devaluing the *krona*, introducing a freeze on prices and cutting back on public expenditure. They lost their majority in 1985, having to rely on Communist support to get their bills through. Presiding over the party since 1969, and prime minister for nearly as long, was **Olof Palme**. He was assassinated in February 1986 (see p.55), and his death threw Sweden into modern European politics like no other event. Proud of their open society (Palme had been returning home unguarded from the cinema), Swedes were shocked by the gunning down of a respected politician, diplomat and pacifist. The country's social system was placed in the spotlight, and shock turned to anger and then ridicule as the months passed without his killer being caught. Police bungling was criticized and despite the theories – Kurdish extremists, right-wing terror groups – no one was charged with the murder.

Then the police came up with **Christer Pettersson**, who – despite having no apparent motive – was identified by Palme's wife as the man who had fired the shot that night. Despite pleading his innocence, claiming he was elsewhere at the time of the murder, Pettersson was convicted of Palme's murder and jailed. There was great disquiet about the verdict, however, both at home and abroad. Pettersson was eventually acquitted on appeal; it was believed that Palme's wife couldn't possibly be sure that the man who fired the shot was Pettersson, given that she had only seen the murderer once, on the dark night in question, and then only very briefly. The police appear to believe they had the right man all along, but in recent years some convincing evidence of the involvement of the South African secret services has come to light (Palme having been an outspoken critic of apartheid).

Carlsson and Bildt

Ingvar Carlsson was elected prime minister after Palme's murder, a position confirmed by the **1988 General Election** when the Social Democrats – for the first time in years – scored more seats than the three non-socialist parties combined. However, Carlsson's was a minority government, and with a background of rising inflation and slow economic growth, the government announced an **austerity package** in January 1990. This included a two-year ban on strike action, and a wage, price and rent freeze – strong measures which astounded most Swedes, used to living in a liberal, consensus-style society.

The **General Election of 1991** merely confirmed that the consensus model had finally broken down. A four-party centre-right coalition came to power, led by **Carl Bildt**, which promised tax cuts and economic regeneration, but the recession

1992	1994	1995
Unemployment hits post-war record of fourteen percent	*Estonia* ferry sinks with loss of 852 lives	Sweden joins European Union

sweeping western Europe did not pass Sweden by. Unemployment hit a postwar record and in autumn 1992 – as the British pound and Italian lira collapsed on the international money markets – the *krona* came under severe pressure. In an attempt to steady nerves, Prime Minister Bildt and Carlsson, leader of the Social Democratic opposition, made the astonishing announcement that they would ignore party lines and work together for the good of Sweden – and then proceeded with drastic **public expenditure cuts**.

The fat was trimmed off the welfare state – benefits were cut, health care was opened up to private competition, and education was given a painful shake-up. But it was too little, too late. Sweden was gripped by its worst **recession** since the 1930s and unemployment had reached record levels of fourteen percent – the days of a jobless rate of one or two percent were well and truly gone. Poor economic growth coupled with generous welfare benefits, runaway speculation by Swedish firms on foreign real estate and the world recession all contributed to Sweden's economic woes.

The return of the Social Democrats

A feeling of nostalgia for the good old days of Social Democracy swept through the country in September 1994, and Carl Bildt's minority Conservative government was booted out. Swedes voted in massive numbers to return the country's biggest party to power, headed by **Ingvar Carlsson**. He formed a government of whom half the ministers were women.

During 1994, negotiations on Sweden's planned **membership of the European Union** were completed and the issue was put to a referendum, which succeeded in splitting Swedish public opinion right down the middle. The *Ja till EU* lobby argued that little Sweden would have a bigger voice in Europe and would be able to influence pan-European decisions if it joined. *Nej till EU* warned that Sweden would be forced to lower its standards to those of other EU countries, unemployment would rise, drug trafficking would increase, and democracy would be watered down. But in November of that year, the Swedes followed the Austrians and the Finns in voting for membership from 1 January 1995 – by the narrowest of margins, just five percent.

Following membership the *krona* fell to new lows as money-market fears grew that the minority government wouldn't be able to persuade parliament to approve cuts in state spending. However, the cuts were duly introduced – the welfare state was trimmed back further and new taxes were announced to try to rein in the spiralling debt. Unemployment benefit was cut to 75 percent of previous earnings, benefits for sick leave were reduced, and lower state pension payments also came into force; a new tax was also slapped on newspapers. To try to keep public support on his side, Finance Minister **Göran Persson** reduced the tax on food from a staggering 21 percent to just 12 percent.

Just when everything appeared under control, Carlsson resigned to be replaced by the bossy Persson, known to friends and enemies alike as HSB – short for *han som bestämmer*, he who decides. As the new millennium approached, the Swedish government concentrated its efforts on turning the economy round and experts argue this quiet period was necessary to muster strength to face the challenges to come.

2002	2003	2003
Sámi officially recognized as minority language	Foreign Minister Anna Lindh murdered	Referendum vote rejects membership of the euro

POLITICAL ASSASSINATION

In September 2003, as Swedes prepared to hold a public referendum on adopting the **euro**, the nation was thrown into shock by the **murder** of the former foreign minister, **Anna Lindh**, one of Sweden's most popular politicians, who was tipped to become the country's first female prime minister. Lindh was stabbed repeatedly by a man with a history of psychiatric problems whilst she was out shopping; she later died of massive internal bleeding. **Mijailo Mijailovic**, born in Sweden to Serbian parents, is now serving a life sentence for her murder.

Sweden today

Sweden's export-led **economy** has rendered the country extremely susceptible to changes in world finances. As globalization has gathered momentum since the turn of the millennium, Sweden has faced a number of difficult choices which would have been unthinkable during the heady days of Social Democracy. Privatizations, mergers and general cost-cutting measures within the much-cherished welfare state have brought Sweden more into line with countries that went through equally painful economic change decades ago. Some economists argue it is this enforced shaking up of the business environment from outside, rather than any direct government measures, that is responsible for Sweden's improved economic fortunes since 1998 – although **unemployment** remains stubbornly above government targets.

The perceived bungling of aid to Swedes caught up in the Indian Ocean **tsunami disaster** in December 2004 cost Persson dear in September 2006 when he lost the general election to the Conservative Fredrik Reinfeldt, who slashed the welfare state even further over the next few years in an attempt to stimulate the economy and create jobs. More recently, Sweden has found itself at the centre of the scandal surrounding **Julian Assange**, the founder of the media website, Wikileaks. Wanted for questioning by Swedish police over sexual assault charges, a court ruling in 2011 cleared the way for Assange's extradition to Sweden. The case has brought the Swedish legal system to the world's attention amid claims that Sweden's rape laws would not hold water in an international court of law.

2006	2009	2011
Deep cuts to Sweden's extensive welfare state to boost economy	Sale of Volvo to Chinese confirmed	Wikileaks' Julian Assange to be extradited to Sweden

Swedish architecture

The all-encompassing Swedish preoccupation with **design** and the importance attached to the way buildings interact with their wider environment have provided Sweden with a remarkable wealth of buildings, both domestic and commercial, during the past century. Despite this, planning for a perceived shortage of affordable housing has also meant that almost every town of any size is blighted with a plethora of faceless postwar apartment blocks which can look more Soviet than Scandinavian. To get the most out of Sweden's hugely rich architectural history, it's invariably worth seeking out the historic heart of a settlement – from small country towns to larger commercial cities.

There are rich pickings in terms of **Romanesque** and **Gothic** buildings, particularly ecclesiastical and royal ones, and the number of **Renaissance** and **Baroque** buildings is quite remarkable. But Sweden's architectural heritage is not always so grand; the more vernacular constructions – from rural cottages to fishermen's homes – provide a fascinating insight into how Swedes have lived and worked for centuries.

Prehistoric buildings

Discussion of **prehistoric** building in Sweden is mostly a matter of conjecture, for the only structures to have survived from before 1100 are ruined or fragmentary. The most impressive structures of **Bronze Age** Sweden are the numerous grassy burial barrows and the coastal burial sites (particularly apparent on the island of Gotland) that feature huge boulders cut into the shapes of a prow and stern. One of the best known of the latter type is at **Ales Stennar** on the South Skåne coast – a Swedish Stonehenge set above windy cliffs.

More substantial are the **Iron Age** dwellings from the **Celtic** period (c. 500 BC to 800 AD). The best example of a fortification from this era is at **Ismantorp** on the Baltic island of Öland. Dating from the fifth century AD, this remarkable site has limestone walls up to fifteen feet high and some eighty foundations arranged into quarters, with streets radiating like spokes of a wheel.

From the remnants of pre-Christian-era houses, a number of dwelling types can be identified. The open-hearth hall, for example, was a square house with an opening in the roof ridge by which light entered and smoke exited. The two-storey gallery house had an open upper loft reached via an exterior stair, while the post larder was a house on stilts allowing for ventilation and protection from vermin.

Romanesque to Gothic

The Christianization of Sweden is dated from 1008, the year St Sigfrid is said to have baptized King Olof. In the eleventh and twelfth centuries the Church and the monastic orders were the driving force behind the most significant building projects, with the most splendid example of Romanesque architecture being **Lund cathedral**. Consecrated in 1145, when Lund was the largest town in Scandinavia and the archiepiscopal see, this monumental building was designed as a basilica with twin western towers, and boasts some tremendously rich carvings in the apsidal choir and vast crypt. The chief centre of Romanesque church building, however, was the royal town of **Sigtuna** to the northwest of Stockholm. Apart from boasting Sweden's oldest street, Sigtuna has the ruins of three eleventh-century churches – one of which, St Peter's, features the country's oldest groin vault.

Round arches, a distinctive feature of Romanesque architecture, flourished wherever limestone and sandstone were found – principally in regions of southern and central Sweden, such as Västergötland, Östergötland and Närke, as well as Skåne. An easy supply of both types of stone was to be found on the Baltic island of Gotland, from where numerous baptismal fonts and richly carved sandstone decorations were exported to the mainland both to the west (Sweden proper) and the east (Swedish-controlled Finland).

Of the great monastic ruins from this period, the finest is the **Alvastra monastery** (1143), just south of Vadstena near the eastern shores of Lake Vättern. A portion of the huge barrel-vaults can still be seen, though much of the graceful structure was carted off by Vasa to build his castle at Vadstena.

Gothic architecture emerged in the thirteenth century, one of the finest early examples being the **Maria church** in Sigtuna (1237), which with its red-brick step gables is markedly unlike the austere grey-stone churches of a century earlier. The cathedral at **Strängnäs**, due east of Stockholm, is another superb piece of Gothic brick architecture, while in Malmö, the German-inspired **St Peter's church** survives as a fine example of brick Gothic, a style often known as the Hanseatic Style. The cathedral at Uppsala (the largest in Scandinavia) is another intriguing specimen, designed to a French High Gothic plan by Parisian builders as a limestone structure, but eventually built in brick in a simpler, **Baltic Gothic** form. A good example of late Gothic is **Vadstena convent church**; begun in 1384, this austere limestone and brick hall was built exactly as decreed by St Birgitta, the founder of the church.

Few examples of the castles and fortifications of this period exist today. One of the best examples, **Varberg's fortress** in Halland, just south of Gothenburg, was built by the Danes, while the best Swedish-built medieval fortifications are in Finland, a Swedish province until the early nineteenth century. One stark and beautifully unmolested example of a fortification in Danish-controlled Skåne is the castle of Glimmingehus; dating from around 1500, it was built by Adam van Duren, who also supervised the completion of the cathedral of Lund.

Renaissance and Baroque architecture

Gustav Vasa (ruled 1523–60) could not have had a more pronounced effect on Swedish architecture. In 1527, with his reformation of the Church, Catholic properties were confiscated, and in many instances the fabric of monasteries and churches was used to build and convert castles into resplendent palaces. Wonderful examples of such Renaissance palaces are **Kalmar castle**, in the south of Småland, and **Vadstena's castle** – though, unlike Kalmar, the latter's interior has been stripped of its original furnishings. Another magnificent Vasa palace, a glorious ruin since a nineteenth-century fire, is **Borgholm castle** on the Baltic island of Öland.

While few churches built in this period enjoyed much prominence, one of outstanding elegance is the **Trefaldighetskyrkan** (Trinity church) in Kristianstad, Danish king Christian IV's model Renaissance city in Skåne. With its tall windows, slender granite pillars and square bays, it is the epitome of sophistication and simplicity.

GOTLAND GOTHIC

The most rewarding place to explore Sweden's Gothic architecture is **Gotland** – the countryside is peppered with almost one hundred richly sculpted medieval churches, while the island's capital, the magnificently preserved Hanseatic seat of **Visby**, is replete with excellent domestic as well as ecclesiastical Gothic.

BAROQUE BEAUTY

The most glorious of palatial buildings from the Baroque era is **Drottningholm** outside Stockholm, a masterpiece created by Tessin for Dowager Queen Hedvig Eleonora. Tessin's other great creation was **Kalmar cathedral**, the finest church of the era and a truly beautiful vision of Italian Baroque. Nicodemus Tessin the Younger followed his father as court architect and continued his style. He designed the new **Royal Palace at Stockholm** following the city's great fire of 1697 and the two contrasting **Karlskrona** churches: the domed rotunda of the Trefaldighetskyrkan (Trinity church) and the barrel-vaulted basilica of the Fredrikskyrkan (Fredrik's church). Karlskrona, like **Gothenburg**, is a fine example of regulated town planning, a discipline that came into being during this era.

By the time Gustav II Adolf ascended the throne in 1611, a greater opulence was becoming prevalent in domestic architecture. This tendency became even more marked in the **Baroque** area, which in Sweden commenced with the reign of Queen Kristina, the art-loving and extravagant daughter of Gustav II Adolf. The first wave of Baroque was largely introduced by the German Nicodemus Tessin the Elder, who had spent much time in Italy.

The eighteenth century

In the eighteenth century **Rococo** emerged as the style favoured by the increasingly affluent Swedish middle class, who looked to France for their models. This lightening of architectural style paved the way for the Neoclassical elegance which would follow with the reign of Gustav III, who was greatly impressed by the architecture of Classical antiquity. Good examples of this clear Neoclassical mode are the **Inventariekammaren** (Inventory Chambers) at Karlskrona, and the **King's Pavilion at Haga**, designed for Gustav III by Olof Temelman, complete with Pompeiian interiors by the painter Louis Masreliez.

Another, and quite distinct aspect of late eighteenth-century taste, was the fascination with **chinoiserie**, due in large measure to the power and influence of the Gothenburg-based Swedish East India Company, founded in 1731. The culmination of this trend was the **Kina Slott** (Chinese Pavilion) at Drottningholm, a tiny Palladian villa built in 1763 and now beautifully restored.

The nineteenth century

Two vast projects dominated the Swedish architectural scene at the beginning of the nineteenth century: the remarkable **Göta Canal**, a 190-kilometre waterway linking the great lakes of Vänern and Vättern, Gothenburg and the Baltic; and the **Karlsborg fortress** on the western shores of Vättern, designed to be an inland retreat for the royal family and the gold stocks, but abandoned ninety years later in 1909.

By the mid-nineteenth century, a new style was emerging, based on Neoclassicism but flavoured by the French-born king's taste. This **Empire Style** (sometimes referred to as the Karl Johan Style) is most closely associated with the architect **Fredrik Blom** of Karlskrona, whose most famous building is the elegant pleasure palace **Rosendal** on Djurgården, Stockholm.

During the reign of Oscar I (1844–59), while the buildings of Britain's manufacturing centres provided models for Sweden's industrial towns, the styles of the past couple of centuries began to reappear, particularly Renaissance and Gothic. One of the most glamorous examples of late nineteenth-century neo-Gothic splendour is **Helsingborg town hall**, built around 1890 as a riot of fairy-tale red-brick detail. The names which crop up most often in this era include Fredrik Scholander, who designed the elaborate **Stockholm synagogue** in 1861, and Helgo Zetterwall, whose churches of the 1870s and 1880s bear a resemblance to neo-Gothic buildings in Britain and Germany.

The twentieth century to the present

Some of the most gorgeous buildings in Sweden's cities are the result of a movement which germinated in the final, resurgent years of the nineteenth century – **National Romanticism**, which set out to simplify architecture and use local materials to create a distinctive Swedish style. Its finest example, which was much influenced by the Arts and Crafts movement in Britain, is Stockholm's **Stadshuset**, built in 1923 from plain brick, dressed stone and rustic timber. Another luscious example is Lars Israel Wahlmann's **Tjolöholm castle**, just south of Gothenburg – a city in which some of the finest apartment buildings are those produced in the associated Art Nouveau style, known in Sweden as **Jugendstil**. One beautifully renovated building in full *Jugendstil* form is the theatre in Tivoli Park in **Kristianstad**, a town otherwise known for its Renaissance buildings. Stockholm's 1910-built *Hotel Esplanade* is a fine example, though the cities of Gothenburg, Malmö and Lund amongst others are rich in the heritage. The small town of Hjö on the western shores of Lake Vättern has a fine clutch of *Jugendstil* houses.

In the second quarter of the century a new movement – **Functionalism** – burst onto the scene, making great use of "industrial" materials such as stainless steel and concrete. The leading architect of his generation was **Gunnar Asplund**, famed for Stockholm City Library (mid-1920s) and his contribution to many other buildings – his interior of the law courts in **Gothenburg's Rådhus** is a favourite among architecture students and enthusiasts today.

The creation of the welfare state went hand in hand with the ascendancy of a functionalist approach to architecture, which rejected many of the individualistic features of traditional Swedish design. By the 1960s, the faceless **International Style** had gained dominance in Sweden, as town planning gave way to insensitive clearance of old houses and their replacement with bland high-rises.

The late 1980s and early 1990s saw restoration becoming the order of the day with areas that had been left to decay – such as the old working-class neighbourhood of **Haga** in Gothenburg – gently gentrified and preserved. More recently the emphasis has shifted towards environmentally sympathetic architecture. Intrinsically Nordic in their tone, these new buildings are often low-level structures constructed from locally sourced wood, with vast areas of glass capitalizing on natural light.

A little further south, in Gothenburg, the natural science museum, **Universeum** is a splendidly organic building – all rough-hewn wood, glass and concrete reflecting in the pools of water outside. One of the highest-profile projects of the last decade is the **Moderna Muséet** and **Arkitekturmuséet** (Modern Museum and Museum of Architecture) on the island of Skeppsholm, in Stockholm harbour. Designed by the Spaniard **Rafael Moneo**, the building eloquently complements the diverse structures of the city's waterfront without trying to overshadow them.

Geography

Sweden is known above all else for its forests and lakes, yet the sheer diversity of its terrain is less familiar. While there are indeed a vast number of lakes, the largest – Vättern and Vänern – home to a wide variety of fish, and swathes of forest blanket vast tracts of the country, the southern shores are fringed with sandy beaches, and the east and west coasts are a myriad of rocky islands forming archipelagos. The Baltic islands of Gotland and Öland provide an entirely different habitat to anywhere on mainland Sweden, with limestone plateaus, dramatic sea-stacks and a variety of flora found nowhere else in Scandinavia.

The appearance of Sweden's terrain owes most to the last **Ice Age**, which chafed the landscape for 80,000 years before finally melting away 9000 years ago. Grinding ice masses polished the mountains to their present form, a process particularly evident in scooped-out U-shaped mountain valleys such as **Lapporten** near Abisko, in the extreme north of the country. Subsequent to the thaw, the landmass rose, so that former coastlines are now many kilometres inland, manifested in the form of huge plains of rubble, while the plains of Sweden were created by the deposition of vast quantities of silt by the meltwater.

The northwest of the country is dominated by **mountains**, which rise well above the timber line. Deciduous trees are most prevalent, except in the most southerly regions, where coniferous forest predominates.

Sweden also boasts some of Europe's most impressive **archipelagos**, such as the dramatically rugged Bohuslän coast on the west, and Stockholm's own archipelago of 24,000 islands, many covered in meadows and forest, on the east.

The country is also known for its **lakes**, which number more than 100,000. These support rich aquatic life, mostly salmon and salmon trout, although the coastlines are where most of the country's fishing takes place.

The north

Sweden's mountainous north is home to many of the country's national parks. The mountains here are part of the **Caledonian range**, the remains of which are also to be found further south in Europe, notably in Scotland and Ireland. Formed around 400 million years ago, the range is at its highest at **Kebnekaise** and **Sarek**, both above 2000m, in the extreme northwest of Sweden. Ancient spruce, pine and birch forest extends continuously along most of the 1000km range, providing an unspoilt habitat for birds such as the golden eagle. The treeline here lies at around 800m above sea level; higher up are great expanses of bare rockface and heathland, the latter often covered in wild orchids.

Central Sweden

The most extensive of Sweden's plains is in the **central Swedish lowlands**, a broad belt spanning from the Bohuslän coast in the west to Uppland and Södermanland in the east. Divided by steep ridges of rock, this former seabed was transformed by volcanic eruptions that created rocky plateaus such as Ålleberg and **Kinnekulle** (Flowering Mountain) to the west of Lidköping. The latter is Sweden's most varied natural site, comprising deciduous and evergreen woodland, meadows and pastures, and treeless limestone flats. Particularly notable among the flora here are cowslips, lady's-slipper orchids, wild cherry trees and, in early summer, the unusual and intensely fragrant bear-garlic.

Stretching some 160km north from Gothenburg up to the Norwegian border, the rough and windswept **Bohuslän coast** possesses a considerable **archipelago** of around three thousand islands. Most of these are devoid of trees – any which existed were cut down to make into boats and houses during the great fishing era of the eighteenth century. This low coastal landscape is peppered with deeply indented bays and fjords, interspersed with islands and peninsulas. To the north of the region, the waves have weathered the pink and reddish granite, and the resulting large, smooth stone slabs with their distinctive cracks are characteristic of the province. Inland from this stretch of coast are steep hills and plateaus which are separated from one another by deep valleys, the inland continuations of the fjords. Long, narrow lakes have developed here, the Bullaren lakes being the largest.

One of the region's most splendid areas of virgin forest is **Tiveden National Park**, around 50km northeast of Karlsborg and just to the northwest of **Lake Vättern**, one of the two enormous lakes in this part of Sweden, the other being **Vänern**. Fishing being a major sport in Sweden, Vänern and Vättern attract thousands each year who wish to try their luck. Around 1300 tonnes of fish are taken from Vänern alone each year, with commercial fisheries accounting for around eighty percent of the catch. The lake's waters were once the most productive for salmon in Sweden, but the construction of hydroelectric dams ruined the spawning grounds, and by the 1970s salmon was almost extinct here. In an effort to complement natural reproduction, salmon and brown trout have been raised in hatcheries and released into the lake with considerable success.

The south

The southernmost third of Sweden, the country's most highly populated and industrialized region, is a mixture of highlands (in the north), forests, lakes and cultivated plains. In southeastern Sweden, the forests of **Småland** have kept the furnaces of the province's glass factories alight since the seventeenth century. In the south, where the highlands give way to a gently undulating landscape, the combination of pastures and fields of rape and poppy makes for some glorious summertime scenery in **Skåne**. Though this province has a reputation for being monotonous and agricultural (true of much of its southwest), it also boasts tracts of conifers, a spectacular coastline and lush forests of beech, best seen in the first weeks of May. The province also boasts dramatic natural rock formations at **Hovs Hallar**, a stunning castellation of red-rock sea-stacks on the northern coast of the Bjäre peninsula.

To the east of Skåne, the **Stenshuvud National Park** has rocky coastal hills surrounded by woods of hornbeam and alder and moorlands full of juniper. Animals untypical of Sweden live here, such as tree frogs, sand lizards and dormice.

Öland and Gotland

Sweden's two largest islands, **Gotland** and **Öland**, lying in the Baltic Sea to the east of the mainland, have excited botanists and geologists for centuries. When Carl von Linné first arrived in Öland in the mid-eighteenth century, he noted that the terrain was "of an entirely different countenance" from the rest of the country, and indeed the island's limestone plateaus – known as **alvar** – are unique in Sweden. In southern Öland, **Stora Alvaret** (Great Limestone Plain) is a thin-soiled heathland with vividly colourful flora in spring and summer.

Gotland is the more dramatic of the two great islands, thanks to its tall sea-stacks (*raukar*), the remains of old coral reefs which loom like craggy ghosts along the island's shoreline. Like Öland, Gotland sustains rich floral life, including at least 35 species of orchid.

Books

English-language books on Sweden are remarkably scant. Although Swedish publishing houses are producing quality titles – particularly fiction – remarkably few find their way into English. Books marked ★ are particularly recommended.

HISTORY AND POLITICS

Sheri Berman *The Social Democrat Movement*. A comparison between the Swedish and German social democratic systems between World War I and World War II. Whilst Sweden placed itself at the forefront of the drive for democratization after the Great Depression, Germany lacked direction and opted for Hitler.

H.R. Ellis Davidson *The Gods and Myths of Northern Europe*. This "Who's Who" of Norse mythology, which includes some useful profiles of the more obscure gods, displaces the classical deities and their world as the most relevant mythological framework for northern and western European culture.

Eric Elstob *Sweden: A Traveller's History*. An introduction to Swedish history from the year dot to the twentieth century, with useful chapters on art, architecture and cultural life.

Bridget Morris *St Birgitta of Sweden*. A comprehensive and intelligently researched book offering a rounded perspective on Sweden's first female saint and her extraordinary life. Accessible and educational without being over-academic in approach.

Lee Miles *Sweden and European Integration*. A political history of Sweden comparing the period 1950–66 with the accession to the European Union in 1995.

Michael Roberts *The Early Vasas: A History of Sweden 1523–1611*. A clear account of the period. Complements the same author's *Gustavus Adolphus and the Rise of Sweden* and *The Age of Liberty: Sweden 1719–1772*, which, more briefly and enthusiastically, covers the period from 1612 to Gustav's death in 1632.

Franklin Daniel Scott *Sweden, The Nation's History*. A good all-round account of Sweden's history from a poor, backward warrior nation to the prosperous modern one of today.

Jan-Öjvind Swahn *Maypole, Crayfish and Lucia – Swedish Holidays and Traditions*. This little edition is superbly written and informative about how and why Swedish traditions have evolved. In contrast to the pictures, the prose is historically accurate and both entertaining and frank about what makes Sweden tick.

ART, ARCHITECTURE AND DESIGN

★ **Henrik O. Andersson and Fredric Bedoire** *Swedish Architecture 1640–1970*. With superb colour plates, this is the definitive survey of the subject, with parallel English/Swedish text.

Katrin Cargill *Creating the Look: Swedish Style*. A great book to help you create cheerful Swedish peasant interiors. Includes lots of evocative photographs by Christopher Drake and a long list of stockists of the materials you'll need. A practical guide, the book includes some background information to place the designs in context.

Görel Cavalli-Björkman and Bo Lindwall *The World of Carl Larsson*. A charming and brilliantly illustrated volume, charting the life and work of one of Sweden's most admired painters.

Barbro Klein and Mats Widbom *Swedish Folk Art*. A lavishly illustrated and richly documented history of its subject, relating ancient crafts to modern-day design ideas.

Mereth Lindgren, Louise Lyberg, Birgitta Sandström and Anna Greta Wahlberg *A History of Swedish Art*. A fine overview of Swedish painting, sculpture

and, to a lesser extent, architecture, from the Stone Age to the present. Clear text and good, mostly monochrome, illustrations.

★ **Nils-Olof Olsson** *Skåne Through The Artist's Eye*. A likeable, cleverly balanced illustrated book encompassing everything from the prehistoric to the present day in its coverage of the country's southernmost province. Steering clear of the usual demarcations in art history, it shows how much contemporary artwork can help with our understanding of history.

★ **Håkan Sandbring & Martin Borg** *Skåne – Wide Horizons*. A glorious visual study of Skåne – the ultimate coffee-table tome for anyone who loves the sort of beauty at which Sweden excels. From country scenes to urban visions and all the quirks of Swedish life in between, these brilliantly hued photographs will keep you absorbed for hours.

Lars Sjöberg and Ursula Sjöberg *The Swedish Room*. An exceptionally well-documented journey through developments in the design of Swedish homes, covering the period from 1640 through to the nineteenth century (stopping short of National Romanticism, Art Nouveau and

Functionalism). The book sets design patterns in their historical and political context, and includes beautiful photographs by Ingalill Snitt. There's also a section on achieving classic Swedish decor effects, and a good list of suppliers of decorative materials, though without exception all are in America.

LITERATURE

★ **Hugh Beach** *A Year in Lapland*. As a young man, Beach went to live with the *Sámi* reindeer herders of Jokkmokk. In later life he returns to the Arctic Circle to chart the fascinating changes that have occurred to northern Sweden and its traditionally nomadic inhabitants.

Frans G. Bengtsson *The Long Ships: A Saga of the Viking Age*. A real gem of historical fiction, bringing the Viking world vividly alive with solid background on arcane Norse traditions such as "trollcraft", "gold-luck" and "the Ale-death". This marvellously pacy adventure story is literally laugh-out-loud funny.

★ **Andrew Brown** *Fishing in Utopia: Sweden and the future that disappeared*. After living in Sweden in his 20s, the author returns to the country in later life to explore his relationship with it in general and social democracy in particular.

Marikka Cobbold *Frozen Music*. Cobbold – who is herself Swedish, though lives in England – paints a very true-to-life picture of Swedish mannerisms and way of life. This novel about the relationship between a Swedish architect and an English woman is set on a very well-drawn Swedish island.

Stig Dagerman *A Burnt Child*. One of the author's best works, this intense short narrative concerns the reactions of a Stockholm family to the death of the mother. A prolific young writer, Dagerman had written short stories, travel sketches, four novels and four plays by the time he was 26; he committed suicide in 1954 at the age of 31.

★ **Kerstin Ekman** *Blackwater*. A tightly written thriller by one of Sweden's most highly rated novelists. Set in the forests of northern Sweden, the plot concerns a woman whose lover is murdered; years later, she sees her daughter in the arms of the suspect.

★ **Kerstin Ekman** *Under the Snow*. In a remote Lapland village, a police constable investigates the death of a teacher following a drunken brawl. The dark deeds of winter finally come to light under the relentless summer sun.

Robert Fulton *Preparations for Flight*. Eight Swedish short stories from the last 25 years, including two rare prose outings by the poet Niklas Rådström.

Pers Christian Jersild *A Living Soul*. The work of one of Sweden's best novelists, this is a social satire based around the "experiences" of an artificially produced, bodyless human brain floating in liquid. Entertaining, provocative reading.

Selma Lagerlöf *The Wonderful Adventures of Nils*. Lagerlöf is Sweden's best-loved children's writer. The tales of Nils Holgren, a little boy who flies all over the country on the back of a magic goose, are continued in *The Further Adventures of Nils*.

Stieg Larsson *The Girl with the Dragon Tattoo*. The gripping international bestseller which charts the efforts by Lisbet Salander and Michael Blomkvist to discover why Harriet Vanger disappeared over forty years earlier.

Sara Lidman *Naboth's Stone*. A novel set in 1880s Västerbotten, in Sweden's far north, charting the lives of settlers and farmers as the industrial age – and the railway – approaches.

Torgney Lindgren *Merab's Beauty*. Short stories capturing the distinctive flavour of family life in northern Sweden.

Ivar Lo-Johansson & Rochelle Wright *Peddling My Wares*. An intriguing exploration of life for a young, self-educated Swede. This autobiographical tale is written by the last surviving member of the "Thirties Generation" and is as popular today in Sweden as when it appeared in 1953.

★ **Vilhelm Moberg** *The Emigrants*. From one of Sweden's greatest twentieth-century writers, this is one of four novels depicting Karl Oskar and Christina Nilsson as they struggle their way from Småland to Minnesota. It's a highly poignant story dealing with the emigration of Swedes to the US.

★ **Michael Niemi** *Popular Music*. The enchanting tale of two boys, Matti and Niila, growing up in Pajala in northern Sweden in the 1960s and 1970s. Dreaming of an unknown world beyond the Torne Valley, they use their fantasy to help take them there. Winner of the August Prize for Sweden's best novel in 2000.

Agneta Pleijel *The Dog Star*. By one of Sweden's leading writers, *The Dog Star* is the powerful tale of a young girl's approach to puberty. Pleijel's finest novel yet, full of fantasy and emotion.

Clive Sinclair *Augustus Rex*. August Strindberg dies in 1912 – and is then brought back to life by the Devil in 1960s Stockholm. Bawdy, imaginative and very funny treatment of Strindberg's well-documented neuroses.

August Strindberg *Plays: One (including The Father, Miss Julie and The Ghost Sonata); Plays: Two (The Dance of Death, A Dream Play and The Stronger)*. The major plays by the country's most provocative and influential playwright, analysing the roles of the sexes both in and out of marriage. Only a fraction of Strindberg's huge output has been translated into English.

Hjalmar Söderberg *Short Stories*. Twenty-six short stories from the stylish pen of Söderberg (1869–1941). Brief, ironic and eminently suited to dipping into.

Swedish language

For most foreigners, Swedish is nothing more than an obscure, if somewhat exotic, language spoken by a few million people on the fringe of Europe, and whose most famous speaker is the Swedish chef from *The Muppets*. Many travellers take their flirtation with the odd hurdy-gurdy sounds of the language no further than that, since there is no need whatsoever to speak Swedish to enjoy a visit to Sweden – recent surveys have shown that 95 percent of Swedes speak English to some degree. However, Swedish deserves closer inspection, and if you master even a couple of phrases you'll meet with nothing but words of encouragement.

Despite what you might think, Swedish is one of the easiest languages for English-speakers to pick up; its grammar has developed along similar lines to that of English and therefore has no case system to speak of (unlike German). Many everyday words are common to both English and Swedish, having been brought over to Britain by the Vikings, and anyone with a knowledge of northern English or lowland Scottish dialects will already be familiar with a good number of Swedish words and phrases. Your biggest problem is likely to be perfecting the "tones", different rising and falling accents which Swedish uses (the hurdy-gurdy sounds you're no doubt already familiar with).

Swedish is a Germanic language and, as such, related to English in much the same way as French is related to Italian. However, its closest cousins are fellow members of the North Germanic group of tongues: Danish, Faroese, Icelandic, Norwegian. Within that subgroup, Swedish is most closely linked to Danish and Norwegian, and the languages are mutually intelligible to quite an extent. A knowledge of Swedish will therefore open up the rest of Scandinavia to you; in fact Swedish is the second official language of Finland. Unlike Danish, for example, Swedish spelling closely resembles pronunciation, which means you stand a sporting chance of being able to read words and make yourself understood.

Basics

Swedish **nouns** can have one of two **genders**: common or neuter. The good news is that three out of four nouns have the common gender. The **indefinite article** precedes the noun, and is *en* for common nouns, and *ett* for neuter nouns. The **definite** article, as in all the other Scandinavian languages, is suffixed to the noun, for example, *en katt*, a cat, but *katten*, the cat; *ett hus*, a house, but *huset*, the house. The same principle applies in the plural: *katter*, cats, but *katterna*, the cats; *hus*, houses, but *husen*, the houses. The plural definite article suffix is therefore *-na* for common nouns and *-en* for neuter nouns (and confusingly identical with the definite article suffix for common nouns).

Forming **plurals** is possibly the most complicated feature of Swedish. Regular plurals take one of the following endings: *-or*, *-ar*, *-er*, *-r*, *-n*, or no ending at all. Issues like the gender of a word, whether its final letter is a vowel or a consonant, and stress can all affect which plural ending is used. You should learn each noun with its plural, but to be honest, the chances are you'll forget the plural ending and get it wrong. Swedes have no apparent difficulty in forming plurals and can't understand why you find it so hard. Show them the plurals section in any grammar and savour their reaction.

Adjectives cause few problems. They generally precede the noun they qualify and agree in gender and number with it; *en ung flicka*, a young girl (ie no ending on the adjective); *ett stort hus*, a big house; *fina böcker*, fine books. The *-a* ending is also used

rticle, irrespective of number, *det stora huset*, the big house, *de fina*
books; and also after a possessive, once again irrespective of number,
my big garden, or *stadens vackra gator*, the town's beautiful streets.
ing of a mixed blessing. There is only one form for all persons,
, in all tenses, which means there are no irksome endings to
I am, *du är* – you (singular) are, *ni är* – you (plural) are, *han/vi är*
......, – uiey are. All verbs take the auxiliary *att ha* (to have) in the perfect and
pluperfect tenses (eg *jag har gått* – I have gone, *jag har talat* – I have spoken; *jag hade*
gått – I had gone, *jag hade talat* – I had spoken). The price for this simplicity is
unfortunately four different conjugations which are distinguished by the way they form
their past tense. Verbs are always found as the second idea in any Swedish sentence, as
in German, which can often lead to the inversion of verb and subject. However, in
Swedish, there are no "verb scarers" which are responsible for the suicidal pile-up of
verbs which often occurs at the end of German sentences.

Pronunciation

Rest assured – you're never going to sound Swedish, for not only can **pronunciation**
be difficult, but the sing-song **melody** of the language is beyond the reach of most
outsiders. Swedish uses two quite different **tones** on words of two or more syllables
– one rises throughout the entire word, while the other falls in the middle before
peaking at the end of the word. It's this second down-then-up accent which gives
Swedish its distinctive melody. Unfortunately, identical words can have two different
meanings depending on which tone is used. For example, *fem ton* with a rising accent
throughout each word means "five tons", whereas *femton* where the accent dips during
the *fem-* and rises throughout the *-ton* means "fifteen". Equally, *komma* with a rising
tone throughout means "comma", whereas *komma* with a falling tone followed by a
rising tone is the verb "to come". In short, try your best, but don't worry if you get it
wrong. Swedes are used to foreigners saying one word but meaning another and will
generally understand what you're trying to say.

Vowels can be either long (when followed by one consonant or at the end of a word)
or short (when followed by two consonants). Unfamiliar or unusually spelt vowels are
as follows:

ej as in m**a**te	**ä** as in g**e**t
y as in **ew**e	**ö** as in f**u**r
å when short, as in h**o**t; when long, sort of as in r**a**w	

Consonants are pronounced approximately as in English except:

g before e, i, y, ä or ö as in **y**et; before a, o, u, å as in **g**ate; sometimes silent	**s** as in **s**o (never as English z)
j, **dj**, **gj**, **lj** as in **y**et	**sj**, **skj**, **stj** approximately as in **sh**ut (different from soft k sound and more like a sh-sound made through the teeth but with rounded lips – this sound takes much practice; see below)
k before e, i, y, ä or ö approximately as in **sh**ut and similar to German **ch** in "ich", otherwise hard	
qu as in **kv**	**tj** approximately as in **sh**ut and with same value as a soft **k**
rs as in **sh**ut (also when one word ends in r and the next begins with s, for example *för stor*, pronounced "fur shtoor")	**z** as in **s**o (never as in **z**oo)

The soft sound produced by **sj**, **skj** and **stj** is known as the **sj-sound** and is a
peculiarity of Swedish. Unfortunately it appears widely and its pronunciation varies
with dialect and individual speakers. To confuse matters further there are two variants,
a back sj-sound formed by raising the back of the tongue and a front sj-sound formed
by raising the middle or front of the tongue. Gain instant respect by mastering this

Swedish tongue twister: *sjuttiosju sjuksköterskor skötte sju sjösjuka sjömän på skeppet till Shangai*, meaning "seventy-seven nurses nursed seven seasick sailors on the ship to Shanghai".

Books

Swedes are always keen to practise their English, so if you're intent on learning Swedish, perseverance is the name of the game. The excellent *Colloquial Swedish* by Philip Holmes and Gunilla Serin (published by Routledge) is the best **textbook** around and should be your starting point.

Of the handful of **grammars** available, by far the most useful is the six-hundred-page *Swedish: A Comprehensive Grammar* by Philip Holmes and Ian Hinchliffe (Routledge), which is head and shoulders above anything else on the market. Good bookshops can supply the *Collins Gem Swedish Dictionary*, perfect for checking basic words whilst travelling around. It's also available in Sweden under the title *Norstedts engelska fickordbok*. Of the **phrasebooks**, the most useful is *Swedish Phrase Book and Dictionary* (Berlitz).

USEFUL WORDS AND PHRASES

BASIC PHRASES

yes/no	ja/nej	**American**	amerikan
hello	hej/tjänare	**Canadian**	kanadensare
good morning	god morgon	**Australian**	australier
good afternoon	god middag	**a New Zealander**	nyzeeländare
good night	god natt	**what's your name?**	vad heter du?
today/tomorrow	idag/imorgon	**what's this called in**	vad heter det här
please	tack/var så god	**Swedish?**	på svenska?
here you are/	var så god	**do you speak English?**	talar du engelska?
you're welcome		**I don't understand**	jag förstår inte
thank you (very much)	tack (så mycket)	**you're speaking**	du talar för
where?/when?	var?/när/hur dags?	**too fast**	snabbt
what?/why?	vad?/varför?	**how much is it?**	hur mycket kostar det?
how (much)?	hur (mycket)?		
I don't know	jag vet inte	**GETTING AROUND**	
do you know? (a fact)	vet du...?	**how do I get to...?**	hur kommer jag till...?
could you...?	skulle du kunna...?	**left/right**	till vänster/till höger
sorry/excuse me	förlåt/ursäkta	**straight ahead**	rakt fram
here/there	här/där	**where is the**	var ligger
near/far	nära/avlägsen	**bus station?**	busstationen?
this/that	det här/det där	**the bus stop for...**	busshållplatsen till...
now/later	nu/senare	**train station**	järnvägsstationen/
more/less	mera/mindre		centralen
big/little	stor/liten	**where does the bus**	varifrån går bussen
open/closed	öppet/stängt	**to... leave from?**	till...?
women/men	kvinnor/män	**is this the train for**	åker detta tåg till
toilet	toalett	**Gothenburg?**	Göteborg?
bank/change	bank/växel	**what time does**	hur dags går det?
post office	posten	**it leave?**	
stamp(s)	frimärke(n)	**what time does it**	hur dags är det
where are you from?	varifrån kommer du?	**arrive in...?**	framme i...?
I'm English	jag är engelsman/engelska	**which is the road**	vilken är vägen
Scottish	skotte	**to...?**	till...?
Welsh	walesare	**where are you**	vart går du?
Irish	irländare	**going?**	

I'm going to...	jag går till...
that's great, thanks a lot	jättebra, tack så mycket
stop here please	stanna här, tack
ticket to...	biljett till...
return ticket	tur och retur

ACCOMMODATION

where's the youth hostel?	var ligger vandrarhemmet?
is there a hotel round here?	finns det något hotell i närheten?
I'd like a single/ double room	jag skulle vilja ha ett enkelrum/dubbelrum
can I see it?	får jag se det?
how much is it a night?	hur mycket kostar det per natt?
I'll take it	jag tar det
it's too expensive, I don't want it now	det är för mycket, jag tar det inte
can I/we leave the bags here until...?	kan jag/vi få lämna väskorna här till... ?
have you got anything cheaper?	har du något billigare?
with a shower?	med dusch?
can I/we camp here?	får jag/vi tälta här?

DAYS AND MONTHS

Monday	måndag
Tuesday	tisdag
Wednesday	onsdag
Thursday	torsdag
Friday	fredag
Saturday	lördag
Sunday	söndag
January	januari
February	februari
March	mars
April	april
May	maj
June	juni
July	juli
August	augusti
September	september
October	oktober
November	november
December	december

THE TIME

what time is it?	vad är klockan?
it's...	den/hon är...
at what time...?	hur dags...?
at...	klockan...
midnight	midnatt
one in the morning	klockan ett på - natten
ten past one	tio över ett
one fifteen	kvart över ett
one twenty-five	fem i halv två
one thirty	halv två
one thirty-five	fem över halv två
one forty	tjugo i två
one forty-five	kvart i två
one fifty-five	fem i två
two o'clock	klockan två
noon	klockan tolv
in the morning	på morgonen
in the afternoon	på eftermiddagen
in the evening	på kvällen
in ten minutes	om tio minuter
ten minutes ago	för tio minuter sedan

NUMBERS

1	ett
2	två
3	tre
4	fyra
5	fem
6	sex
7	sjö
8	åtta
9	nio
10	tio
11	elva
12	tolv
13	tretton
14	fjorton
15	femton
16	sexton
17	sjutton
18	arton
19	nitton
20	tjugo
21	tjugoett
22	tjugotvå
30	trettio
40	fyrtio
50	femtio
60	sextio
70	sjuttio
80	åttio
90	nittio
100	hundra
101	hundraett
200	två hundra
500	fem hundra
1000	tusen
10,000	tio tusen

FOOD AND DRINK TERMS

BASICS AND SNACKS

ägg	egg	kaviar	caviar
bröd	bread	krabba	crab
bulle	bun	kräftor	freshwater crayfish
glass	ice cream	lax	salmon
grädde	cream	makrill	mackerel
gräddfil	sour cream	räkor	shrimps/prawns
gröt	porridge	röding	arctic char
kaka	cake	rödspätta	plaice
keks	biscuits	sardiner	sardines
knäckebröd	crispbread	sik	whitefish
olja	oil	sill	herring
omelett	omelette	sjötunga	sole
ost	cheese	strömming	Baltic herring
pastej	paté	torsk	cod
peppar	pepper		
pommes	fries		

VEGETABLES (GRÖNSAKER)

ris	rice
salt	salt
senap	mustard
småkakor	biscuits
smör	butter
smörgås	sandwich
socker	sugar
sylt	jam
tårta	cake
vinäger	vinegar
våffla	waffle

ärtor	peas
blomkål	cauliflower
brysselkål	Brussels sprouts
bönor	beans
gurka	cucumber
lök	onion
morötter	carrots
potatis	potatoes
rödkål	red cabbage
sallad	lettuce/salad
spenat	spinach
svamp	mushrooms
tomater	tomatoes
vitkål	white cabbage
vitlök	garlic

MEAT (KÖTT)

älg	elk
biff	beef
fläsk	pork
hjort	venison
kalvkött	veal
korv	sausage
kotlett	cutlet/chop
köttbullar	meatballs
kyckling	chicken
lammkött	lamb
lever	liver
oxstek	roast beef
renstek	roast reindeer
rådjursstek	roast venison
skinka	ham

FRUIT (FRUKT)

ananas	pineapple
apelsin	orange
äpple	apple
aprikos	apricot
banan	banana
citron	lemon
hallon	raspberry
hjortron	cloudberry
jordgubbar	strawberries
lingon	lingonberry/red whortleberry
päron	pear
persika	peach
vindruvor	grapes

FISH (FISK)

ål	eel
ansjovis	anchovies
blåmusslor	mussels
fiskbullar	fishballs
forell	trout
hummer	lobster

CULINARY TERMS

ångkokt	steamed
blodig	rare
filé	fillet

friterad	deep fried
genomstekt	well done
gravad	cured
grillat/halstrat	grilled
kall	cold
kokt	boiled
lagom	medium
pocherad	poached
rökt	smoked
stekt	fried
ungstekt	roasted/ baked
varm	hot

DRINKS

apelsinjuice	orange juice
chocklad	hot chocolate
citron	lemon
fruktjuice	fruit juice
grädde	cream
kaffe	coffee
lättöl	light beer
mellanöl	medium-strong beer
mineralvatten	mineral water
mjölk	milk
öl	beer
rödvin	red wine
saft	juice
skål	cheers!
starköl	strong beer
storstark	large strong beer
te	tea
vatten	water
vin	wine
vitt vin	white wine

SWEDISH SPECIALITIES

ål	eel, smoked and served with creamed potatoes or scrambled eggs (äggröra)
ärtsoppa	yellow pea soup with pork, spiced with thyme and marjoram; a winter dish traditionally eaten on Thursdays
biff Rydberg	sautéed chucks of beef served with fried potatoes, onions and mustard
filmjölk	soured milk
fisksoppa	fish soup usually including several sorts of fish, prawns and dill
getost	goat's cheese
glögg	mulled wine, usually fortified with spirits to keep out the cold, and drunk at Christmas
gravad lax	salmon marinated in dill, sugar and seasoning; served with mustard sauce and lemon
hjortron	a wild, orange-coloured berry (the cloudberry), served with fresh cream and/or ice cream. Also made into jam
Janssons frestelse	potato and anchovy
köttbullar	meatballs served with a brown creamy sauce and lingonberries
kräftor	crayfish
lingon	lingonberry (sometimes known as red whortle-berries), a red berry made into a kind of jam and served with meat dishes as well as on pancakes and in puddings, eaten at Christmas
långfil	a special type of soured milk from northern Sweden
lövbiff	sliced, fried beef with onions
matjessill	sweet-pickled herring
pepparkakor	thin, spiced gingerbread biscuits popular at Christmas
plättar	thin pancakes, often served with pea soup
potatissallad	potato salad, often flavoured with dill or chives
pytt i panna	cubes of meat and fried potatoes with a fried egg and beetroot
semla	sweet bun with almond paste and whipped cream; associated with Lent
sillbricka	various cured and marinated herring dishes; often appears as a first course in restaurants at lunchtime

sjömansbiff	sailors' beef casserole: thin slices of beef baked in the oven with potatoes and onions, topped with parsley
smultron	wild strawberries, known for their concentrated taste
strömming	Baltic herring
surströmming	Baltic herring fermented for months until it's rotten and the tin it's in buckles – very smelly and eaten in very, very small quantities. Not for the faint-hearted!
Wallenbergare	burgers made of minced veal mixed with cream and egg yolks

Glossary

älg elk
ångbåt steamboat
ankommande arriving
ankomst arrival
avgående departing
avgång departure
bad swimming (pool)
bastu sauna
berg mountain
biljett ticket
bio cinema
björn bear
bokhandel bookshop
bro bridge
brygga jetty/pier
båt boat/ferry
cyckelstig cycle path
dagens rätt dish of the day
domkyrka cathedral
drottning queen
ej inträde no entrance
extrapris special offer
färja ferry
gamla old
gamla stan old town
gata (g.) street
gränd alley
hamn harbour
hantverk handicrafts
hembygdsgård homestead museum
hiss lift
järnvägsstation train station
kapell chapel
kåta traditional Sámi hut
klockan (kl.) o'clock
kyrka church

lilla little
loppis flea market
muséet museum
nakenbad naturist beach
öppet open
öppettider opening hours
pressbyrå newsagent
rabatt discount
rea sale
ren reindeer
restaurang restaurant
rådhuset town hall
rökning förbjuden no smoking
simhall swimming pool
sjö lake
skog forest
slott palace/castle
storstark strong beer
smörgåsbord spread of different dishes
sovvagn sleeping car
spår track
stadshus city hall
stora big
strand beach
stuga cottage
systembolaget alcohol store
stängt closed
torg square/market place
tunnelbana underground (metro)
turistbyrå tourist office
tåg train
tältplats campsite
universitet university
vandrarhem hostel
väg (v.) road

Small print and index

A ROUGH GUIDE TO ROUGH GUIDES

Published in 1982, the first Rough Guide – to Greece – was a student scheme that became a publishing phenomenon. Mark Ellingham, a recent graduate in English from Bristol University, had been travelling in Greece the previous summer and couldn't find the right guidebook. With a small group of friends he wrote his own guide, combining a highly contemporary, journalistic style with a thoroughly practical approach to travellers' needs.

The immediate success of the book spawned a series that rapidly covered dozens of destinations. And, in addition to impecunious backpackers, Rough Guides soon acquired a much broader readership that relished the guides' wit and inquisitiveness as much as their enthusiastic, critical approach and value-for-money ethos.

These days, Rough Guides include recommendations from budget to luxury and cover more than 200 destinations around the globe, as well as producing an ever-growing range of eBooks and apps.

Visit **roughguides.com** to see our latest publications.

Rough Guide credits

Editor: Ann-Marie Shaw
Layout: Umesh Aggarwal and Anita Singh
Cartography: Animesh Pathak
Picture editor: Natascha Sturny
Proofreader: Jennifer Speake
Managing editor: Keith Drew
Assistant editor: Jalpreen Kaur Chhatwal
Production: Rebecca Short, Gemma Sharpe
Cover design: Nicole Newman, Dan May, Umesh Aggarwal
Editorial assistant: Eleanor Aldridge

Senior pre-press designer: Dan May
Design director: Scott Stickland
Travel publisher: Joanna Kirby
Digital travel publisher: Peter Buckley
Reference director: Andrew Lockett
Operations coordinator: Becky Doyle
Publishing director (Travel): Clare Currie
Commercial manager: Gino Magnotta
Managing director: John Duhigg

Publishing information

This sixth edition published September 2012 by
Rough Guides Ltd,
80 Strand, London WC2R 0RL
11, Community Centre, Panchsheel Park,
New Delhi 110017, India
Distributed by the Penguin Group
Penguin Books Ltd,
80 Strand, London WC2R 0RL
Penguin Group (USA)
375 Hudson Street, NY 10014, USA
Penguin Group (Australia)
250 Camberwell Road, Camberwell,
Victoria 3124, Australia
Penguin Group (NZ)
67 Apollo Drive, Mairangi Bay, Auckland 1310,
New Zealand
Penguin Group (South Africa)
Block D, Rosebank Office Park, 181 Jan Smuts Avenue,
Parktown North, Gauteng, South Africa 2193
Rough Guides is represented in Canada by Tourmaline
Editions Inc. 662 King Street West, Suite 304, Toronto,
Ontario M5V 1M7
Printed in Singapore by Toppan Security Printing Pte. Ltd.

392pp includes index
A catalogue record for this book is available from the
British Library
ISBN: 978-1-40538-966-2
The publishers and authors have done their best to
ensure the accuracy and currency of all the information in
The Rough Guide to Sweden, however, they can accept
no responsibility for any loss, injury, or inconvenience
sustained by any traveller as a result of information or
advice contained in the guide.
1 3 5 7 9 8 6 4 2

MIX
Paper from
responsible sources
FSC™ C018179
www.fsc.org

Help us update

We've gone to a lot of effort to ensure that the sixth
edition of **The Rough Guide to Sweden** is accurate and
up-to-date. However, things change – places get "discovered", opening hours are notoriously fickle, restaurants
and rooms raise prices or lower standards. If you feel we've
got it wrong or left something out, we'd like to know, and
if you can remember the address, the price, the hours, the
phone number, so much the better.

Please send your comments with the subject line
"**Rough Guide Sweden Update**" to ✉ mail@uk
.roughguides.com. We'll credit all contributions and send a
copy of the next edition (or any other Rough Guide if you
prefer) for the very best emails.

Find more travel information, connect with fellow
travellers and book your trip on ⊕ roughguides.com

Acknowledgements

James Proctor: After two months on the road updating
this new edition, I encountered many people who went
out of their way to help me with my countless queries
and questions. In Sweden, for all their help and advice, I
am especially grateful to: Jan at SJ, Sylvie in Stockholm,
Lena in Gothenburg, Gunn-Viol in Örebro, Sara in Varberg,
Kerstin in Växjö, Viveca in Norrköping, Cecilia in Sundsvall

and Sara in Helsingborg. Thanks, too, to Annie in Cheshire
whose sound editorial judgement steered this edition to
fruition under tight time constraints.

However, I owe my greatest thanks to Elin Lindén at
Visit Sweden in London, who, with seemingly effortless
efficiency, made the whole thing possible.

ABOUT THE AUTHORS

James Proctor has been with Rough Guides since 1995 and is the company's original Nanook of the North. Co-author of the Rough Guides to Sweden, Iceland and Finland, James has also written the only English-language guides to the Faroe Islands and Lapland. One of his more obscure talents is speaking fluent Swedish – something which never fails to impress and bemuse most Swedes (and most other people) he meets. Having lived and worked in Stockholm during the mid-1990s as the BBC's Scandinavia correspondent, James now returns to Sweden at frequent intervals to commune with nature at his log cabin deep in the forest.

Neil Roland is a law graduate, co-author of several Rough Guides since 1996 and now works as a photographic artist exhibiting in Manchester, London and across the globe. His first novel, *Taken For A Ride*, was published in 2003, reprinted in 2007.

Photo credits

The publisher would like to thank the following for their kind permission to reproduce their photographs. All other photos © Rough Guides.

(Key: t-top; c-centre; b-bottom; l-left; r-right)

p.1 Alamy: Arctic Images (t)
p.2 SuperStock: Travel Library Limited.
p.4 Imagebank.sweden.se: Ola Ericson (t)
p.7 Getty Images: Anders Blomqvist/Photographer's Choice (t) SuperStock: Imagebroker.net (b)
p.8 Corbis: Zhang Xiaowei/Xinhua Press (b)
p.9 Alamy: tbkmedia.de (b); Imagebank.sweden.se: Conny Fridh (c); Rodrigo Rivas Ruiz (t)
p.10 Alamy: Nordicphotos.
p.11 Alamy: Arco Images GmbH (b); Getty Images: BERTHIER Emmanuel/hemis.fr (t)
p.12 Imagebank.sweden.se: Peter Grant (b)
p.13 Alamy: Imagebroker (cl); Corbis: Arctic-Images (tl); Getty Images: Konrad Wothe/Look (b)
p.14 Alamy: Simon Pentelow (cr); Getty Images: Johner Images (cl); Imagebank.sweden.se: Per-Erik Berglund (b); Tomas Utsi (t)
p.15 Alamy: Travel Pictures (b); SuperStock: Age fotostock (tl)
p.16 Alamy: Peter de Clercq (b); Getty Images: Johner Images (br)
p.17 Alamy: Colouria Media (b); Getty Images: BOISVIEUX Christophe/Hemis (tl, tr); Jeppe Wikstram (c)
p.18 Alamy: Howard Davies (b); Imagebank.sweden.se: Ola Ericson (t);
p.19 Imagebank.sweden.se: Andreas Nordström (b); Miriam Preis (tl)
p.20 Alamy: Ingemar Edfalk (t); Peter Adams Photography Ltd (b)
p.21 Alamy: Nigel Hicks (t); Imagebank.sweden.se: Helena Wahlman (b). SuperStock: Eye Ubiquitous (c)
p.22 Corbis: Jonn/Johnér Images (tl); Getty Images: Lars Dahlstrom/Nordic Photos (tr)
p.24 Imagebank.sweden.se: Ola Ericson (t)
p.40 Corbis: Jon Hicks
p.43 Alamy: Johan Furusjo (t)
p.59 Corbis: Keren Su (t) Getty Images: Michele Falzone (b); www.stockholmfoto.se: Ola Ericson/imagebank.sweden. se (c);
p.76 Imagebank.sweden.se: Ola Ericson.
p.79 Corbis: Christophe Boisvieux (t)

p.91 Alamy: Frank Chmura (tr); Howard Davies (tl); picturesbyrob (br); Corbis: Mario Cipriani (bl)
p.105 Imagebank.sweden.se: Göran Assner
p.107 Imagebank.sweden.se: Joachim Brink (t)
p.117 Alamy: Iain Masterton (tr); Travel Pictures (tl, bl); Rohan Van Twest (br)
p.127 SuperStock: imagebroker.net
p.129 Corbis: Arctic-Images (t)
p.137 Alamy: Caro (tl); INTERFOTO (tr); Imagebroker (bl); Keith Shuttlewood (br)
p.144 Alamy: Anders Sellin
p.147 SuperStock: Photononstop (t)
p.167 Robert Harding Picture Library: Arcaid (tl); Alamy: Anders Ryman (tr); Corbis: BJORN LARSSON ROSVALL/ SCANPIX/epa (bl); SuperStock: Imagebroker.net (br)
p.190 Alamy : Arndt Sven-Erik/Arterra Picture Library
p.193 Corbis: Alfredo Dagli Orti/The Art Archive (t)
p.217 Alamy : Arterra Picture Library (tr); Getty Images: Pierre Rosberg/ Nordic Photos (tl); Imagebank.sweden.se: Jan Simonsson (b);
p.240 SuperStock: JTB Photo;
p.243 Alamy: LOOK Die Bildagentur der Fotografen GmbH (t)
p.261 Alamy: Hemis (t); Alamy: LOOK Die Bildagentur der Fotografen GmbH (bl); neil setchfield yuckfood.com (br)
p.280 Corbis: Roger Borgelid/Naturbild.
p.283 Alamy: Colouria Media (t)
p.297 Alamy: Bjorn Svensson (tl); Corbis: ULF PALM/epa (tr); Getty Images: Jorgen Larsson/Nordic Photos (b)
p.310 SuperStock: JTB Photo
p.313 SuperStock: Imagebroker.net (t)
p.331 Alamy: Arco Images GmbH (b); Getty Images: Arctic-Images (tl); SuperStock: Nordic Photos (tr)
p.352 Getty Images: BOISVIEUX Christophe (t)

Front cover Snow-covered trees © Nordic Photos/AWL
Back cover Dala horse © Imagebank.sweden.se: Cecilia Larsson (cl); Beach huts in Skanör © Imagebank.sweden. se: John Sander (cr); Sightseeing boat and sunbathers on Långholmen, Stockholm © SuperStock: Nordic Photos (tt)

Index

Maps are marked in grey

Map symbols

The symbols below are used on maps throughout the book

✈	Airport	♦	Place of interest	◡	Bridge	▭	Building
★	Bus/taxi	⁞	Ruin	≈	Swimming pool/area	⊡	Church
Ⓣ	T-bana station	🎇	Waterfall	▲	Mountain peak	▢	Beach
@	Internet café/access	⊙	Statue	🏠	Lodge	▨	Park
ⓘ	Information office	⊥	Church (regional maps)	🎿	Ski trail	—	Wall
P	Parking	⊤	Gardens	⚶	Viewpoint	▰▰▰	Pedestrian street
✚	Hospital	🗼	Lighthouse	⛴	Boat	⁝⁝⁝	Unpaved road
🏛	Stately home	♨	Castle				

Listings key

■ Accommodation
● Restaurant/café/bar
■ Bar/club/live-music venue